No. 1414. HLD. BON BON. SQUARE
Pond Lily
No. 410 - 11" VASE
Rustic
No. 1416 - 8"
GRAPE DISH.
Leaf Chain
No. 1406
9½ IN. CAKE PLATE.
Orange Tree

Fenton Art Glass

1907 – 1939

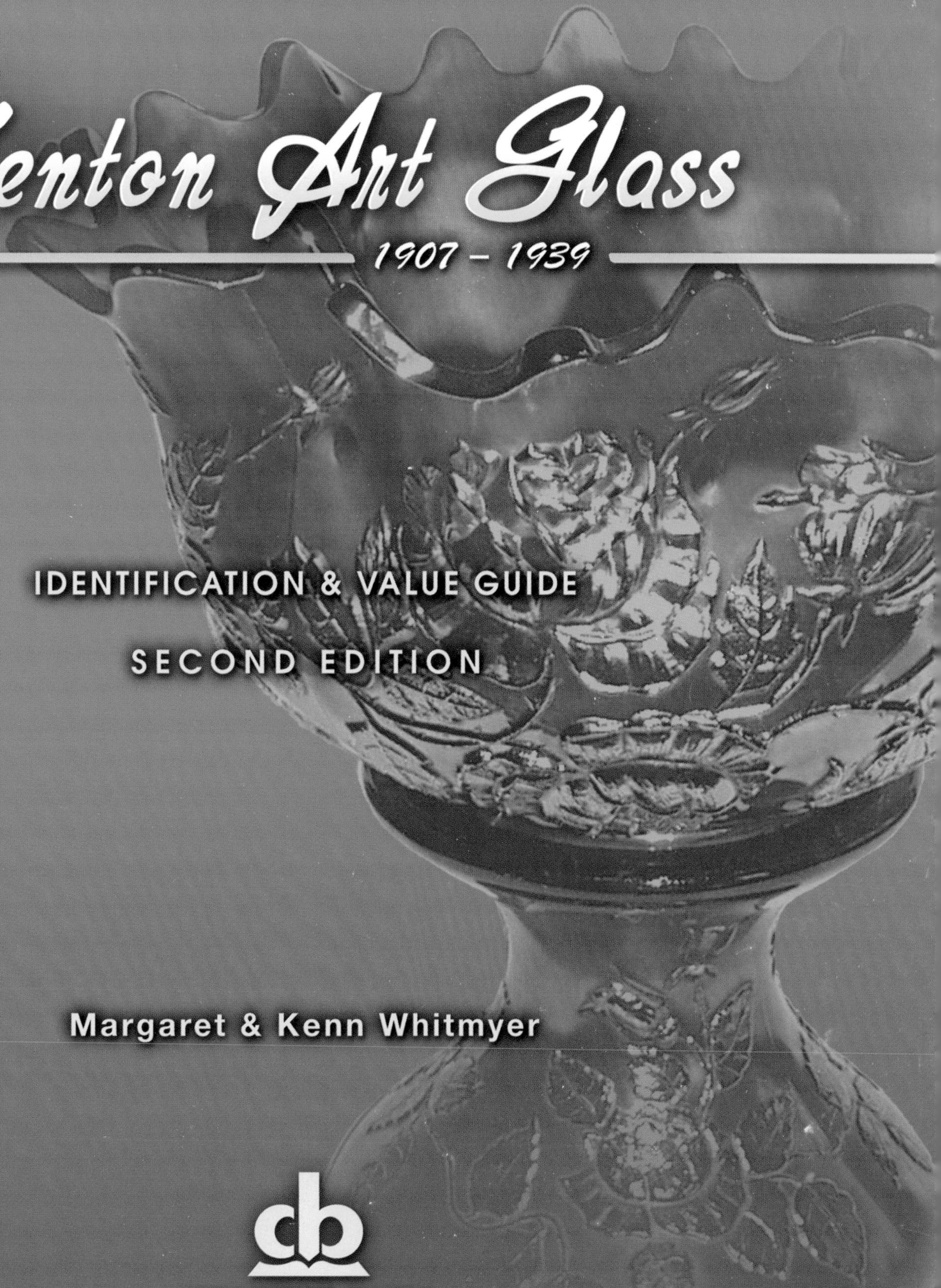

IDENTIFICATION & VALUE GUIDE

SECOND EDITION

Margaret & Kenn Whitmyer

COLLECTOR BOOKS

A Division of Schroeder Publishing Co., Inc.

On the Cover: Top left, lilac 6½" macaroon jar; top right, blue opalescent dolphin-handled 7" comport; bottom left, Celeste blue with ebony base 8½" candlestick; bottom center, Chinese yellow cologne with moonstone stopper; bottom right, jade green and moonstone "Elizabeth" vanity set; background, carnival Wreath of Roses punch bowl.

Back Cover: Top right, Chinese yellow 1-lb. candy jar; top left, ruby Dancing Ladies 12" covered urn; bottom right, jade green Dancing Ladies 18" urn lamp; bottom left, Mosaic 7½" vase.

Cover design: Beth Summers
Book design: Mary Ann Hudson

COLLECTOR BOOKS
P.O. Box 3009
Paducah, Kentucky 42002–3009
www.collectorbooks.com

Margaret & Kenn Whitmyer
P.O. Box 30806
Columbus, OH 43230

SEARCHING FOR A PUBLISHER?

We are always looking for people knowledgeable within their fields. If you feel that there is a real need for a book on your collectible subject and have a large comprehensive collection, contact Collector Books.

The current values in this book should be used only as a guide. They are not intended to set prices, which vary from one section of the country to another. Auction prices as well as dealer prices vary greatly and are affected by condition as well as demand. Neither the authors nor the publisher assumes responsibility for any losses that might be incurred as a result of consulting this guide.

DEDICATION

This book is dedicated to the Fenton families who produced this beautiful glassware. Without their endeavors a terrific void would exist in the lives of many.

CONTENTS

PREFACE

The purpose of this book is to acquaint the reader with the multitude of items produced by The Fenton Art Glass Company from the period 1907 to 1939. Categories included are early Pattern and Opalescent Glassware, Carnival Glass, Stretch Glass, Non-Iridescent Opaque and Transparent Glass of the 1920s and 1930s, and Tableware Patterns and Satin Glass patterns of the 1930s. Intentional omissions include in-depth coverage of plain crystal and crystal cut glassware, and opalescent glassware produced in the late 1930s. A listing of some of the crystal cut items has been compiled from inventory records and is included in the Crystal Wheel Cut Designs section, pg. 20. Opalescent glassware produced in the late 1930s is included in *Fenton Art Glass Patterns, 1939 – 1980.*

This book originally started as a book about opalescent and collectible Fenton glassware of the post-World War II era. It's just a little strange that very little of that type of glassware found its way into these pages. Oddly enough, we had almost finished photographing for the original format before Frank L. Fenton managed to persuade us that we should really discover the secrets of carnival and stretch glass. Thus, we did an abrupt about-face and decided to write a comprehensive book on Fenton glassware from 1907 to 1970.

The wealth of information soon became so overwhelming that we discovered one book could not handle the volume. Therefore, we decided to divide the book into two parts. The first section, which is now in your hands, covers the types of glass produced from 1907 to 1939. The convenient arrangement of this book includes an order which should allow most readers to find desired items. Items of similar nature are arranged together in the same section. Catalog reprints have been used in conjunction with photographs to render a more comprehensive understanding of the shapes and decorations.

Computer composition and enhancement have been used in an effort to produce sharp clear photographs. Hopefully, this method has also resulted in an arrangement which is easy to use. Our overworked computer sure is relieved that this project is finally finished. It did survive but found itself replaced by a more powerful and "smarter" machine. Hopefully pictures for the second book will be processed in a more efficient manner.

Working on this book has been a real learning experience. We appreciated the opportunity to work and conduct our research at the Fenton Art Glass Museum. The treasures there are certainly worth a visit by anyone interested in glassware. Also, there is the gift shop to experience afterward, or maybe before and after.

FENTON CLUBS AND NEWSLETTERS

The Fenton Art Glass company publishes a quarterly newsletter to keep collectors abreast of company events. To subscribe, send $12.00 to *Glass Messenger*, The Fenton Art Glass Company, Williamstown, WV 26187.

The following national clubs have been organized to promote the collection of Fenton Art Glass:

The Fenton Art Glass Collectors Club of America
Membership: $20.00 per year
Dues to: FAGCA • P.O. Box 384 • Williamstown, WV 26187

The National Fenton Glass Society
Membership: $20.00 per year
Dues to: NFGS • P.O. Box 4008 • Marietta, OH 45750

The Pacific Northwest Fenton Association
Membership: $23.00 per year
Dues to: PNWFA • 8225 Kilchis River Rd. • Tillamook, OR 97141

ACKNOWLEDGMENTS

It is probably hard for the casual reader to appreciate the fact that producing a volume of this magnitude involves the energies of a virtual army of dedicated people — not just the authors. It is very difficult to give these hard workers the recognition they deserve, but without their efforts this book would not have been possible. Many of these names will be familiar to readers as serious collectors of Fenton glassware, and others are close friends and associates who have helped us on previous works. We would like to thank all of them for their patience and cooperation.

Foremost on the list is Frank M. Fenton. Without his knowledge, assistance, and encouragement, this book would not exist. He provided us with historical information and granted us complete freedom to copy company records and catalogs. He also allowed us to photograph items at will in the Fenton Art Glass Museum. He graciously assisted by answering our questions and providing everything we needed for our photography and research.

Nancy Fenton, Frank's daughter-in-law, who succeeded in capturing Frank and Bill Fenton and the younger generation on film.

Several Fenton employees also deserve special acknowledgment. Among them are Anne Martha, Frank's secretary, who is knowledgeable enough to know all his hiding places. Jennifer Maston, the sweet girl who is mistress (and a very gracious hostess) of The Fenton Art Glass Museum. Tamara Armstrong, an information specialist who has actually performed the miracle of cataloging Fenton's archives. And "Muscle" Charley who graciously removed many of the heavy covers from the cases in the museum so we could proceed with our photography.

Berry Wiggins, a noted author and researcher of early glassware was often at the Fenton plant to offer help and lend support. We appreciate his guidance in some areas in which we had little experience. His knowledge was invaluable.

Skipping to the West Coast, we thank Carrie Domitz used to think photography was fun. She won't be that naive next time. Carrie, an avid collector and enthusiastic Fenton supporter, shared her vast knowledge and was always there to answer our questions and provide the help we needed. We would like to extend a special thanks to Gerry Domitz for providing us with transportation and helping with photography.

The Pacific NW. Fenton Association was extremely hospitable. Their convention was a great learning experience. Members provided us with valuable information and allowed their treasures to be photographed.

Russell and Kitty Umbraco, authors and researchers in the field of stretch glass, contributed greatly in the area of their expertise.

Ed and Shirley Lehew of the Williamstown Antique Mall (that's back in West Virginia) provided information, glass to photograph, and support.

Kevin Kiley became a collector and expert on off-hand glassware just when we needed one.

Bill Crowl, obsessed collector of Fenton glassware, owns more unusual Fenton than anyone can imagine. Thank you for taking the time to share some with us.

Others who contributed in a large way are:

Randy and Debbie Coe
Jackie Shirley
Lynette and Greg Galusha
Connie Rich
Jacque Metcalfe
Fred McMorrow
Liz Paldanius
Janice Estrada
Bill Harmon
Debbie Lane
Jerry and Connee Hack
Jeanne Word
Kelvin Russell and Debra Jennings
Henke and Anne van Bemmelen
Max and Lou Wenger
Luane French
Gordon and Darlene Cochran
Nancy Maben
Caroline Kriner
Sam and Becky Collins
Rick and Ruth Teets
Eddie and Neil Unger
Lynn Welker
Barbara Ryley
Irwin Gratz

PRICING

The prices in this book represent average retail prices for mint condition pieces. Pieces that are chipped, cracked, or excessively worn should only bring a fraction of the listed price. Also, collectors should be aware that certain currently rare items that are now valued at a high dollar amount may prove hard-to-sell if a large quantity of these items is discovered. A few items that have been found listed in the company catalogs, but are not known to be available, may not be priced in the listings.

A price range is included to allow for some regional differences. This book is intended to be only a guide, and it is not the intention of the authors to set or establish prices.

Prices are for each piece unless a set is indicated in the description. Candlesticks are priced each. The prices listed are those we have seen collectors pay and prices collectors have told us they would be willing to pay.

HISTORY

Brothers Frank L. and John W. Fenton opened the Fenton Art Glass Company as a cutting and decorating shop in July 1905, in Martins Ferry, Ohio. The business began as a decorating shop that used blanks supplied by various glass manufacturing companies. Not long afterward, brother Charles H. gained employment with the firm.

As the firm prospered, it became evident to the Fentons that their suppliers either could not or would not meet their increasing demands for more glassware. Therefore, it was an almost inevitable decision that to survive and prosper, they would have to produce their own glass. A decision was made to purchase a site and build a plant in Williamstown, West Virginia. The first glass from the new Fenton Art Glass plant was produced on January 2, 1907.

In late 1907, the officers of the company included John as president and Frank as general manager. Charles was still with the company as head of the decorating department, and brother James E. joined the force as maintenance supervisor in late 1908. John left the Williamstown operation in 1909, and went to Millersburg, Ohio, to found a glass plant there. In 1910, older brother Robert C. was brought in to assist Frank L. who had assumed the presidency vacated by John. At this time Frank L. also retained the positions of treasurer and general manager.

The first plant manager was Jacob Rosenthal, a seasoned veteran of the glassmaking business. He had learned his skills in over 25 years of working at the various glasshouses around the country. He brought with him many secret formulas, and his knowledge of color was soon tested by the fledgling Fenton operation. Colored glassware in opalescents, Persian blue, and chocolate was soon pouring from the plant. Upon Jacob's retirement, his son Paul became plant manager, and glassware continued to be produced using the same unique formulas.

Early glassware also included pressed glass pieces in green, crystal, topaz opalescent, blue opalescent, ruby, and amethyst. Iridescent glassware soon became the rage, and the Fenton plant produced vast amounts of carnival glass. Patterns were numerous, production expanded, and the company prospered. In 1912, the company was back into the decorating business. By 1918, the volume in the cutting shop peaked and then gradually declined until Fenton finally phased out the cutting operation in the early 1930s.

The general appeal of pressed pattern carnival glass began to recede during the early 1920s. Thus, Fenton countered with another type of iridescent glass — stretch glass. Also another line of new colors was introduced about this time. These were solid opaque colors called jades in green, yellow, blue, and moonstone. Sales of the new types of glass reached lofty heights.

In 1925, Frank L. Fenton tried a different approach in the production of handmade glassware when he hired a group of highly skilled European workers to create off-hand art glass. They produced beautiful and highly artistic pieces, but this endeavor failed when the public refused to pay the necessary price for these creations. A year later Fenton was no longer producing off-hand art glass, but it was still trying to market much of what had been produced.

The economy of the Great Depression forced Fenton to produce "necessary" products. Tableware lines such as Lincoln Inn and Georgian were born, and more production focused on producing essentials such as lamps, mixing bowls, and reamers. With the end of Prohibition, Fenton welcomed the thirsty public by providing decanter and beverage sets to all who needed them.

As unreal as it may sound, a small Hobnail cologne bottle was responsible for rescuing Fenton from the doldrums following the Great Depression. In 1938, Fenton's Chicago representative, Martin M. Simpson, used his contacts with a perfume company to have a market test of a Hobnail cologne bottle that was produced by Fenton. The test results were phenomenal, and Fenton's romance with Hobnail was born. A continuation of Fenton's history during the Hobnail and opalescent era is included in *Fenton Art Glass Patterns 1939 – 1980.*

Photo shown right:
Second generation Fentons
Left: Wilmer C. "Bill" Fenton, past president; current chairman of the board.
Right: Frank M. Fenton, past president and chairman of the board; current historian.

Photo shown below:
Third generation Fentons
Front: Michael D. Fenton, purchasing manager & safety director; George W. Fenton, president; Thomas K. Fenton, vice president of manufacturing.
Rear: Randall R. Fenton, treasurer of the Fenton gift shop; Shelley A. Fenton-Ash, graphics manager & key accounts; Nancy G. Fenton, director of design; Christine L. Fenton, data processor, Fenton gift shop; and Don A. Fenton, vice president of sales.

ENAMELED WATER SETS

Early catalogs confirm crystal and colored water and lemonade sets with enameled decorations were produced starting about 1907. Some of these same shapes were also produced with carnival colors. Notice the Drapery pattern of the ruby set.

Color	Item	Value	Item	Value
Crystal	Pitcher, #628	$70.00 – 75.00	Tumbler, #628	$12.00 – 15.00
Green	Pitcher, #628	$100.00 – 120.00	Tumbler, #628	$18.00 – 20.00
Crystal	Pitcher, #629	$70.00 – 75.00	Tumbler, #629	$12.00 – 15.00
Green	Pitcher, #629	$100.00 – 120.00	Tumbler, #629	$18.00 – 20.00
	Pitcher, #820	$75.00 – 95.00	Tumbler, #820	$12.00 – 15.00
	Pitcher, #821	$125.00 – 175.00	Tumbler, #821	$12.00 – 20.00
Crystal	Tankard, #626	$75.00 – 80.00	Tumbler, #626	$12.00 – 15.00
Green	Tankard, #626	$120.00 – 130.00	Tumbler, #626	$18.00 – 20.00
	Tankard, #822	$75.00 – 80.00	Tumbler, #822	$12.00 – 15.00
Photo below				
Green	Pitcher, #821	$120.00 – 130.00	Tumbler, #821	$18.00 – 20.00
Amethyst	Pitcher, #821	$140.00 – 160.00	Tumbler, #821	$18.00 – 20.00
Ruby	Pitcher, #821	$180.00 – 200.00	Tumbler, #821	$40.00 – 45.00
Crystal	Pitcher, #821	$95.00 – 120.00	Tumbler, #821	$12.00 – 15.00

#821 Water Set

#821 Water Set

#821 Water Set

#821 Jug

626 GREEN
629 CRYSTAL
626 CRYSTAL
628 GREEN
629 GREEN
628 CRYSTAL

Colored Enameled Water Set Reprints Circa 1907 to 1910 Courtesy Of: The Fenton Art Glass Museum

821
822
820

PATTERN GLASS

In the last half of the nineteenth century and during the early 1900s, many glass companies were producing pressed pattern glassware. Fenton was no exception, as early catalogs from 1908 to 1910 record production of several pattern glass lines that are pictured here. Most sizes of bowls will be found in a variety of shapes — flared, cupped, crimped, and regular. Pieces of the Beaded Stars, Northern Star, Honeycomb and Clover, and Waterlily and Cattails patterns may also be found in carnival and opalescent colors. Some items may be found with cuttings, gold decorations, or flashed finishes. Beaded Stars pieces may frequently be found with advertising replacing the star in the bottom of the item. The #410 vase, with a smooth top, will also be found in chocolate glass. Items in the Beaded Stars pattern may be found with a swag design. These variant pieces are called Beaded Stars with Swag; prices are the same as Beaded Stars.

*Beaded Stars	Crystal
Bonbon, 5" cupped	$8.00 – 10.00
Bowl, 7" ftd.	$15.00 – 18.00
Plate, 11"	$12.00 – 15.00

*Beaded Stars	Green
Bowl, 6" crimped	$18.00 – 22.00
Plate, 11"	$20.00 – 22.00

*with gold decoration or advertising add 20%

#100 Honeycomb and Clover	Crystal	Green with Gold
Bowl, 4 ½"	$4.00 – 5.00	$7.00 – 9.00
Bowl, 7"	$10.00 – 12.00	$25.00 – 27.00
Butter	$35.00 – 45.00	$90.00 – 100.00
Creamer	$10.00 – 12.00	$25.00 – 28.00
Pitcher	$35.00 – 45.00	$75.00 – 90.00
Spooner	$10.00 – 12.00	$35.00 – 45.00
Sugar and lid	$12.00 – 15.00	$28.00 – 35.00
Tumbler	$5.00 – 6.00	$12.00 – 15.00

Beaded Stars

7" Cupped Bowl with Advertising

6" Crimped Bowl with Advertising

5" Cupped Bonbon

Honeycomb & Clover

Creamer

Spooner

Butter

Sugar

Northern Star

#65-8 1/2" Flared Nappy

#65-9" Shallow Nappy

#65-7 1/2" Regular Nappy

NO. 250 AND NO. 580 ASSORTMENT

Catalog records show Fenton produced a vertical ribbed pattern glass tableware assortment in 1916. The undecorated version was sold as the No. 250 Assortment and the decorated assortment was No. 580.

	No. 250	No. 580
Butter & cover	$35.00 – 45.00	$45.00 – 55.00
Creamer	$8.00 – 10.00	$12.00 – 15.00
Jug, ½ gallon	$30.00 – 35.00	$45.00 – 55.00
Nappy, 4½"	$3.00 – 4.00	$4.00 – 6.00
Nappy, 8"	$7.00 – 9.00	$10.00 – 12.00
Spooner	$9.00 – 11.00	$12.00 – 15.00
Sugar & cover	$12.00 – 14.00	$18.00 – 22.00
Tumbler	$6.00 – 7.00	$9.00 – 11.00

Catalog Reprint Circa 1916
Courtesy Of:
The Fenton Art Glass Museum
580 Spoon.
580 Butter + Cover.
580 Sugar + Cover.
580 Cream
580 Tumbler
580 8" Nappy
580 4½" Nappy.
580 ½ Gal. Jug.

Production of crystal and crystal satin pieces of Waterlily and Cattails started in 1907. Known pieces include a complete table set, berry set, and water set along with a few plates, a comport, and various sizes of bowls. The 2-handled footed comports and the orange bowls are not easily found.

Fenton's Waterlily and Cattails was a very popular pattern and was made for many years in various colors. For additional colors, see the Early Opalescent Pattern Glass (p. 19) and Carnival Glass (p. 100) sections of this book.

#8 Waterlily and Cattails	Crystal/ Crystal Frosted	#8 Waterlily and Cattails	Crystal/ Crystal Frosted
Bowl, 4½"	$9.00 – 11.00	Creamer	$25.00 – 30.00
Bowl, 7"	$18.00 – 22.00	Pitcher	$65.00 – 75.00
Bowl, 8" (regular, flared, cupped)	$25.00 – 30.00	Plate, 6"	$6.00 – 8.00
Bowl, oval	$40.00 – 50.00	Plate, 10"	$15.00 – 18.00
Bowl, orange	$125.00 – 150.00	Sugar and lid	$40.00 – 45.00
Butter	$50.00 – 60.00	Spooner	$30.00 – 35.00
Comport, 2-H ftd.	$100.00 – 120.00	Tumbler	$22.00 – 25.00

Crystal & Crystal Frosted Waterlily & Cattails

Oval Bowl

Sugar & Lid

Creamer

2-Handled Comport

Pitcher

Sugar & Lid

#400 Crystal "Sunburst" Assortment	Crystal	#400 Crystal "Sunburst" Assortment	Crystal
Bonbon, #405 – 6" flared	$6.00 – 9.00	Vase, #411 – 6½"	$14.00 – 16.00
Bonbon, #406 – 5½" handled	$6.00 – 9.00	Vase, #412 – 6½" crimped	$14.00 – 16.00
Bonbon, #407 – 6" handled	$6.00 – 9.00		
Bowl, #400 – 6½"	$7.00 – 10.00	**#65 Northern Star**	**Crystal**
Bowl, #400 – 7" belled	$7.00 – 10.00	Nappy, 4½"	$6.00 – 8.00
Bowl, #402 – 7" oval	$7.00 – 10.00	Nappy, 7½" regular	$10.00 – 12.00
Bowl, #403 – 7" square	$7.00 – 10.00	Nappy, 8" flared	$12.00 – 14.00
Bowl, #404 – 7" crimped	$7.00 – 10.00	Nappy, 9" shallow	$12.00 – 14.00
Plate, #401 – 7½"	$6.00 – 9.00	Nappy, 10" scalloped	$14.00 – 16.00
Vase, #410 – 6½"	$14.00 – 16.00	Plate, 11"	$10.00 – 12.00

NO. 400 CRYSTAL ASSORTMENT

Contains 1 dozen each of the 12 items shown on this page

412—6½ in. Vase Crimped

401--7 1/2 in. Plate

403--7 in. Nappy Square

411--6 1/2 in. Vase

406—5½ in. Handled Bon Bon

402--7 in Oval

400--6 1/2 in. Nappy

404--7 in Nappy Crimped

410--6 1/2 in. Vase

400--7 in. Nappy Belled

407 6 in. Handled Bon Bon Triangle

405--6 in. Nappy Flared

Northern Star

8 IN. REGULAR
4 DOZ. IN BBL. BBLS. 50C,
PER DOZ 80C.

10 IN SCALLOPED.
4 DOZ. IN BBL. BBLS. 50C,
PER DOZ 80C.

11 IN. FLAT PLATE.
4 DOZ. IN BBL. BBLS. 50C
PER DOZ 90C

EARLY OPALESCENT PATTERN GLASS

Some early Fenton pattern glass pieces produced during the years 1908 to 1912 were made in opalescent colors. Colors include amethyst opalescent, blue opalescent, crystal opalescent, and green opalescent. Crystal opalescent became known as "French Opalescent" in the 1930s.

Patterns found in opalescent colors are Basketweave with Open Edge, Beaded Stars, Blackberry Spray, Buttons and Braids, Coin Spot, Fenton's Drapery, Honeycomb and Clover, Stag and Holly, and Waterlily and Cattails.

Early Basketweave pattern pieces were bowls in various sizes. In the early 1930s, pieces of this pattern were again made in opalescent colors. Opalescent Beaded Star pieces include 8" bowls, 6½" bonbons, and an 11" plate. The opalescent Blackberry Spray items are a hat-shaped novelty vase and a 6½" nappy. We have seen the hat-shaped item in crystal, amethyst, and blue opalescent colors. Variations of the pattern include 2 or 4 sprigs of blackberries. Water sets were made in Buttons and Braids and Coin Spot patterns. They were made in blue, green, and crystal opalescent colors. A water set was also made in Fenton's Drapery pattern in the same colors. Additional pieces made in this pattern include a hat novelty vase, a plate, a spittoon whimsy, and several sizes of tall vases. Colors include amethyst, blue, green, and crystal opalescent. The Honeycomb and Clover pattern was made in blue, green, and crystal opalescent. Pieces made include a berry set, a table set, and a water set. Numerous pieces were made in the Waterlily and Cattails pattern. Various sizes of bowls, a large plate, a table set, and a water set may be found in amethyst, green, crystal, and blue opalescent. A gravy boat whimsy pulled from a creamer has been found.

In addition, many of the pieces found in these patterns may also be found in carnival colors. Some pieces will be found in plain non-opalescent colors. Some pieces of Waterlily and Cattails were also made in chocolate. The three #350 series water sets were made intermittently through the 1920s and 1930s in opalescent colors.

The Waterlily and Cattails pattern was also made by Northwood, and pieces of Buttons and Braids were made by the Jefferson Glass Company.

(Computer Colorized) *Courtesy Of:*

Early Opalescent Fenton Catalog Reprint Circa 1910 ***The Fenton Art Glass Museum***

OPALESCENT WATER SET ASSORTMENT

Made in Blue, Green and Crystal Opalescent. One dozen assorted sets to package.

Basketweave with Open Edge

Shallow Flared Bowl

Blackberry Spray

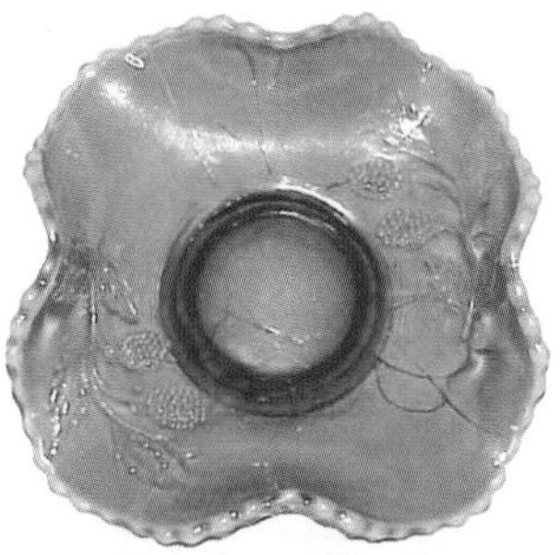

Hat-shaped Bonbon

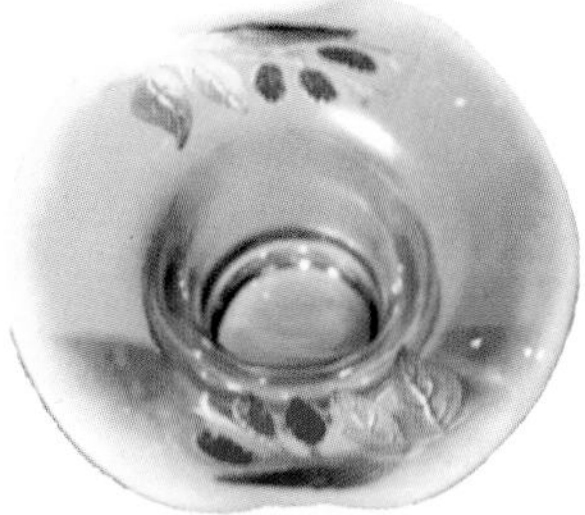

Hat-shaped Bonbon

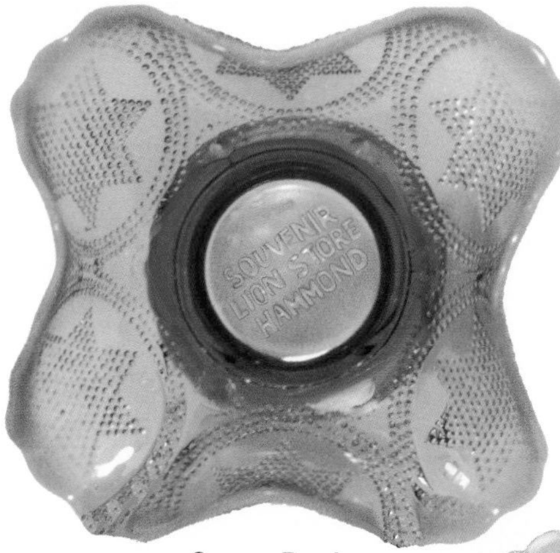

Square Bowl

Bonbon

Beaded Stars

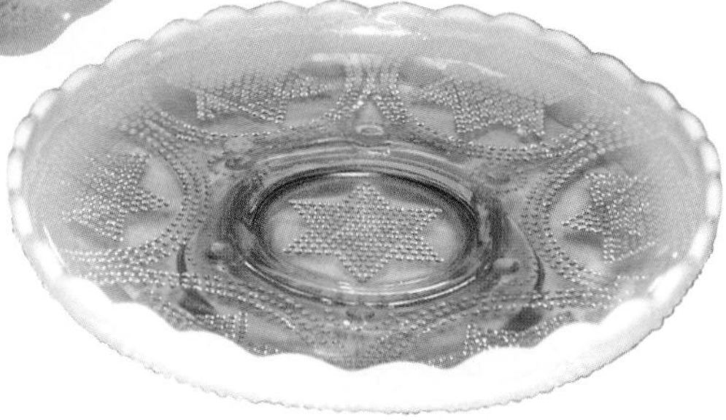

Shallow Flared Bowl

Buttons & Braids

Pitcher

Item	Pattern	French/Green Opalescent	Blue Opalescent	Amethyst Opalescent
Bowl, 7" flared	Basketweave, open edge	$25.00 – 27.00	$32.00 – 37.00	
*Bonbon, 5"	Beaded Stars	$18.00 – 20.00	$25.00 – 30.00	
*Nappy, 6" crimped	Beaded Stars	$15.00 – 20.00	$20.00 – 25.00	
*Bowl, 8"	Beaded Stars	$20.00 – 25.00	$27.00 – 35.00	
Plate, 11"	Beaded Stars	$20.00 – 25.00		
Bonbon, 5½" square	Blackberry Spray	$15.00 – 20.00	$25.00 – 30.00	$35.00 – 40.00
Vase, hat-shape	Blackberry Spray	$15.00 – 20.00	$25.00 – 30.00	$35.00 – 40.00
Pitcher	Buttons & Braids	$125.00 – 165.00	$350.00 – 400.00	
Tumbler	Buttons & Braids	$10.00 – 12.00	$25.00 – 30.00	
Pitcher	Coinspot	$125.00 – 165.00	$220.00 – 250.00	$400.00 – 450.00
Tumbler	Coinspot	$20.00 – 22.00	$25.00 – 30.00	
*with advertising add 20%				

Fenton's Drapery

Plate

Tulip-shape Hat Novelty

Spittoon

Pitcher

Honeycomb & Clover

Pitcher

Creamer

Spooner

Master Berry

Individual Berry

Pitcher

Item	French/Green Pattern	Blue Opalescent	Amethyst Opalescent	Opalescent
Bowl, 9" crimped	Fenton's Drapery	\$22.00 – 25.00	\$32.00 – 35.00	\$35.00 – 45.00
Pitcher	Fenton's Drapery	\$100.00 – 250.00	\$245.00 – 325.00	
Plate	Fenton's Drapery	\$18.00 – 25.00	\$25.00 – 30.00	\$60.00 – 65.00
Spittoon	Fenton's Drapery	\$75.00 – 85.00		
Tumbler	Fenton's Drapery	\$15.00 – 20.00	\$25.00 – 30.00	
Vase, hat-shape	Fenton's Drapery	\$70.00 – 80.00		
Bowl, individual berry	Honeycomb & Clover	\$14.00 – 16.00	\$18.00 – 20.00	
Bowl, master berry	Honeycomb & Clover	\$40.00 – 45.00	\$60.00 – 65.00	
Butter	Honeycomb & Clover	\$60.00 – 75.00	\$90.00 – 110.00	
Creamer	Honeycomb & Clover	\$22.00 – 27.00	\$32.00 – 37.00	
Pitcher	Honeycomb & Clover	\$80.00 – 95.00	\$120.00 – 155.00	
Spooner	Honeycomb & Clover	\$22.00 – 27.00	\$32.00 – 37.00	
Sugar and lid	Honeycomb & Clover	\$40.00 – 45.00	\$50.00 – 55.00	
Tumbler	Honeycomb & Clover	\$15.00 – 18.00	\$40.00 – 45.00	

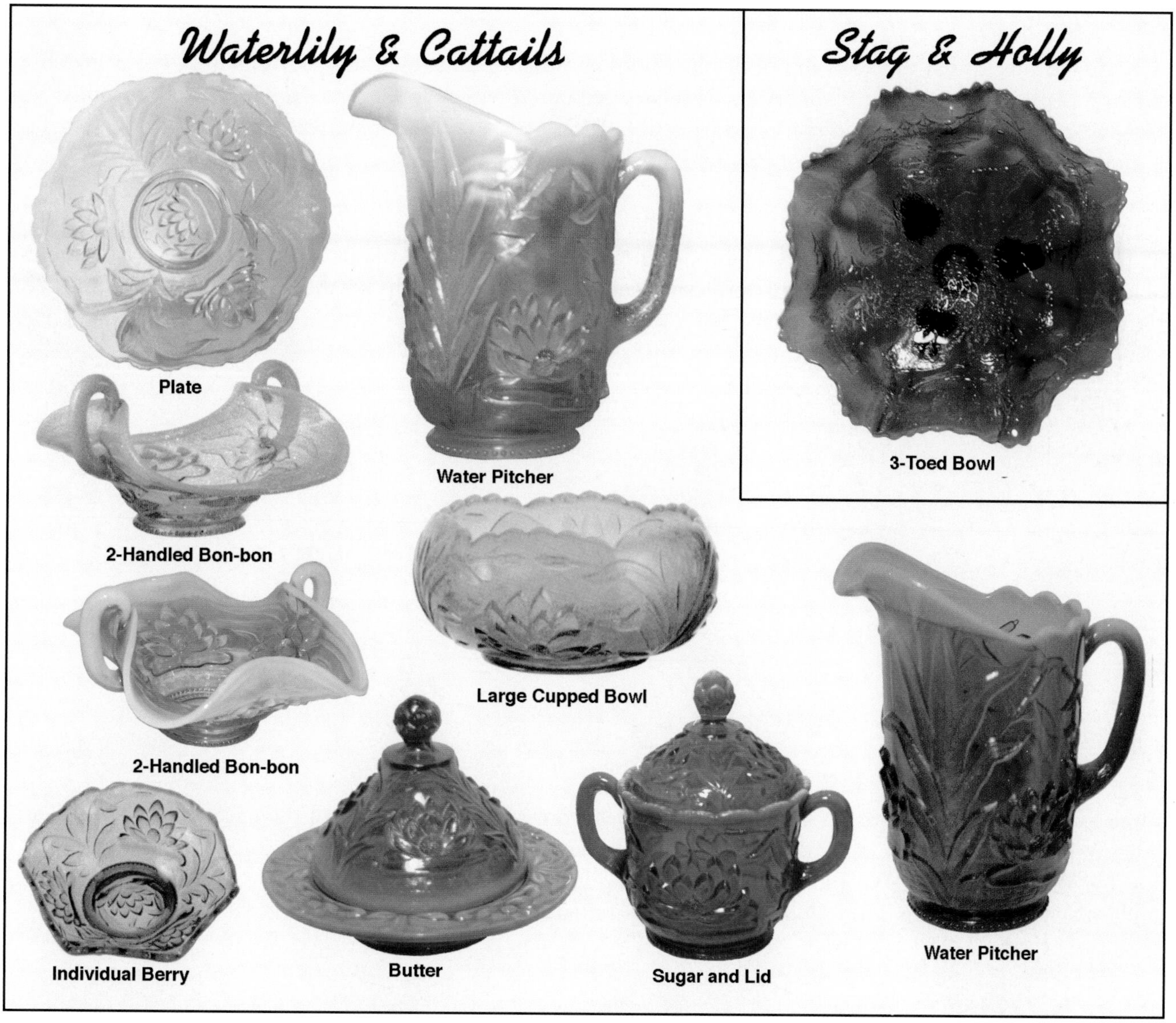

Plate; Water Pitcher; 3-Toed Bowl; 2-Handled Bon-bon; Large Cupped Bowl; 2-Handled Bon-bon; Water Pitcher; Individual Berry; Butter; Sugar and Lid

Item	Pattern	French/Green Opalescent	Blue Opalescent	Amethyst Opalescent
Bowl, 11" 3 ftd.	Stag & Holly	$100.00 – 125.00		$250.00 – 300.00
Gravy boat	Waterlily & Cattails	$22.00 – 25.00	$45.00 – 50.00	$70.00 – 75.00
Bonbon, 2-handled	Waterlily & Cattails	$18.00 – 20.00	$22.00 – 25.00	$37.00 – 40.00
Bowl, 5" individual berry	Waterlily & Cattails	$10.00 – 12.00	$14.00 – 16.00	$18.00 – 22.00
Bowl, 7" all shapes	Waterlily & Cattails	$27.00 – 30.00	$37.00 – 40.00	$60.00 – 70.00
Bowl, 9" master berry	Waterlily & Cattails	$30.00 – 35.00	$40.00 – 45.00	$70.00 – 80.00
Creamer	Waterlily & Cattails	$18.00 – 20.00	$22.00 – 27.00	$40.00 – 45.00
Pitcher	Waterlily & Cattails	$115.00 – 150.00	$180.00 – 220.00	$250.00 – 300.00
Plate, 6"	Waterlily & Cattails	$7.00 – 9.00	$10.00 – 12.00	$12.00 – 14.00
Plate, 10"	Waterlily & Cattails	$18.00 – 20.00	$20.00 – 25.00	$32.00 – 37.00
Spooner	Waterlily & Cattails	$18.00 – 20.00	$22.00 – 27.00	$40.00 – 45.00
Sugar and lid	Waterlily & Cattails	$30.00 – 35.00	$37.00 – 42.00	$57.00 – 65.00
Tumbler	Waterlily & Cattails	$18.00 – 22.00	$22.00 – 25.00	$40.00 – 45.00

Also, the following pattern is not pictured but is listed in opalescent colors on inventory records. For examples of this pattern, see the Pattern Glass section, page 12.

Item	Pattern	French/Green Opalescent	Blue Opalescent	Amethyst Opalescent
Nappy, 4½"	Northern Star	$8.00 – 10.00		
Nappy, 7"	Northern Star	$20.00 – 25.00		
Plate, 11"	Northern Star	$14.00 – 16.00		$20.00 – 25.00

CRYSTAL WHEEL CUT DESIGNS

Continued success led to expansion of product lines and the establishment of a cutting and decorating shop at the Fenton plant in about 1912. Plain crystal ware was decorated with floral, grape, star, and other cuttings. Much of this glassware was produced and marketed from about 1914 to 1917. Labor shortages during World War I seriously limited production of this type of product. The cutting operation never regained momentum after the war, and all cutting ended by the mid 1930s.

Cut decorations were also used on Grecian Gold pieces. For examples, see the Grecian Gold section in this book, pages 134 and 135. Colored patterns produced with cuttings during the late 1920s include Diamond Optic and Dolphin. For illustrations of these patterns with cuttings, see the sections on these patterns in Part VI: Fenton Patterns.

Item	Date	Design	Value
Vase, #97	1914	Floral cut	$8.00 – 10.00
Vase, #98	1914	Floral cut	$8.00 – 10.00
Vase, #99	1914	Floral cut	$8.00 – 10.00
Vase, #100	1914	Floral cut	$8.00 – 10.00
Vase, #165½	1914	Floral cut	$8.00 – 10.00
Vase, #209½	1914	Grape cut	$8.00 – 10.00
Vase, #299	1914	Floral cut	$8.00 – 10.00
Vase, #721	1914	Floral cut	$8.00 – 10.00

The following is a listing of crystal items and shapes from inventory records of the cutting shop. These items may be found with wheel cut designs. Values of most pieces are generally reasonable. Sugar and creamer sets are selling for about $8.00 – 10.00. Pitchers, tumblers, and vases are priced about the same as the ones on page 23. Small bowls are usually found for about $3.00 – 5.00, and large bowls are valued around $8.00 – 10.00.

Item	Shape No.	Color	Item	Shape No.	Color	Item	Shape No.	Color
Bonbon	743	Crystal	Creamer	187	Crystal	Jug	167	Crystal
Candy jar	100	Crystal	Creamer	209	Crystal	Jug	168	Crystal
Cheese dish		Crystal	Creamer	211	Crystal	Jug	170	Crystal
Claret jug	216	Crystal	Creamer	295	Crystal	Jug	210	Crystal
Claret tumbler	3600	Crystal	Creamer	299	Crystal	Jug	397	Crystal
Creamer	5	Crystal	Creamer	721	Crystal	Jug	600	Crystal
Creamer	145	Crystal	Creamer	1000	Crystal	Jug	1101	Crystal
Creamer	146	Crystal	Creamer	3500	Crystal	Nappy	299	Crystal
Creamer	147	Crystal	Custard	165	Crystal	Nappy, 4"	106	Crystal
Creamer	165	Crystal	Custard	165	Crystal	Nappy, 4"	106	Crystal
Creamer	165	Crystal	Custard	177	Crystal	Nappy, 4"	116	Crystal
Creamer	167	Crystal	Custard	178	Crystal	Nappy, 4"	126	Crystal
Creamer	174	Crystal	Custard	265	Crystal	Nappy, 4"	136	Crystal
Creamer	177	Crystal	Custard	277	Crystal	Nappy, 4"	3500	Crystal
Creamer	178	Crystal	Custard	300	Crystal	Nappy, 6"	126	Crystal
Creamer	178	Crystal	Jug	81	Crystal	Nappy, 8"	126	Crystal
Creamer	179	Crystal	Jug	165	Crystal	Nappy, 8"	3500	Crystal
Creamer	180	Crystal	Jug	165	Crystal	Night bottle	1202	Crystal

Item	Shape No.	Color	Item	Shape No.	Color	Item	Shape No.	Color
Night bottle	3500	Crystal	Sugar	300	Crystal	Tumbler, belled	721	Crystal
Sherbet	165	Crystal	Sugar	1000	Crystal	Tumbler, Elite	171	Crystal
Sherbet	177	Crystal	Sugar	3500	Crystal	Tumbler, ice tea	1201	Crystal
Sherbet	178	Crystal	Tumbler	165	Crystal	Tumbler, ice tea	1201	Crystal
Sugar	146	Crystal	Tumbler	165	Crystal	Tumbler, ice tea	209½	Crystal
Sugar	165	Crystal	Tumbler	167	Crystal	Tumbler, straight	295	Crystal
Sugar	167	Crystal	Tumbler	168	Crystal	Tumbler, wine	299	Crystal
Sugar	167	Crystal	Tumbler	170	Crystal	Vase	215	Crystal
Sugar	174	Crystal	Tumbler	185	Crystal	Vase	216	Crystal
Sugar	177	Crystal	Tumbler	209	Crystal	Vase	217	Crystal
Sugar	178	Crystal	Tumbler	209	Crystal	Vase, 10"	3600	Crystal
Sugar	180	Crystal	Tumbler	600	Crystal	Vase, 8"	209	Crystal
Sugar	187	Crystal	Tumbler	3600	Crystal	Vase, 8"	3600	Crystal
Sugar	209	Crystal	Tumbler, belled	295	Crystal	Vase, bud	209	Crystal
Sugar	295	Crystal	Tumbler, belled	296	Crystal	Water bottle	299	Crystal
Sugar	299	Crystal	Tumbler, belled	299	Crystal			

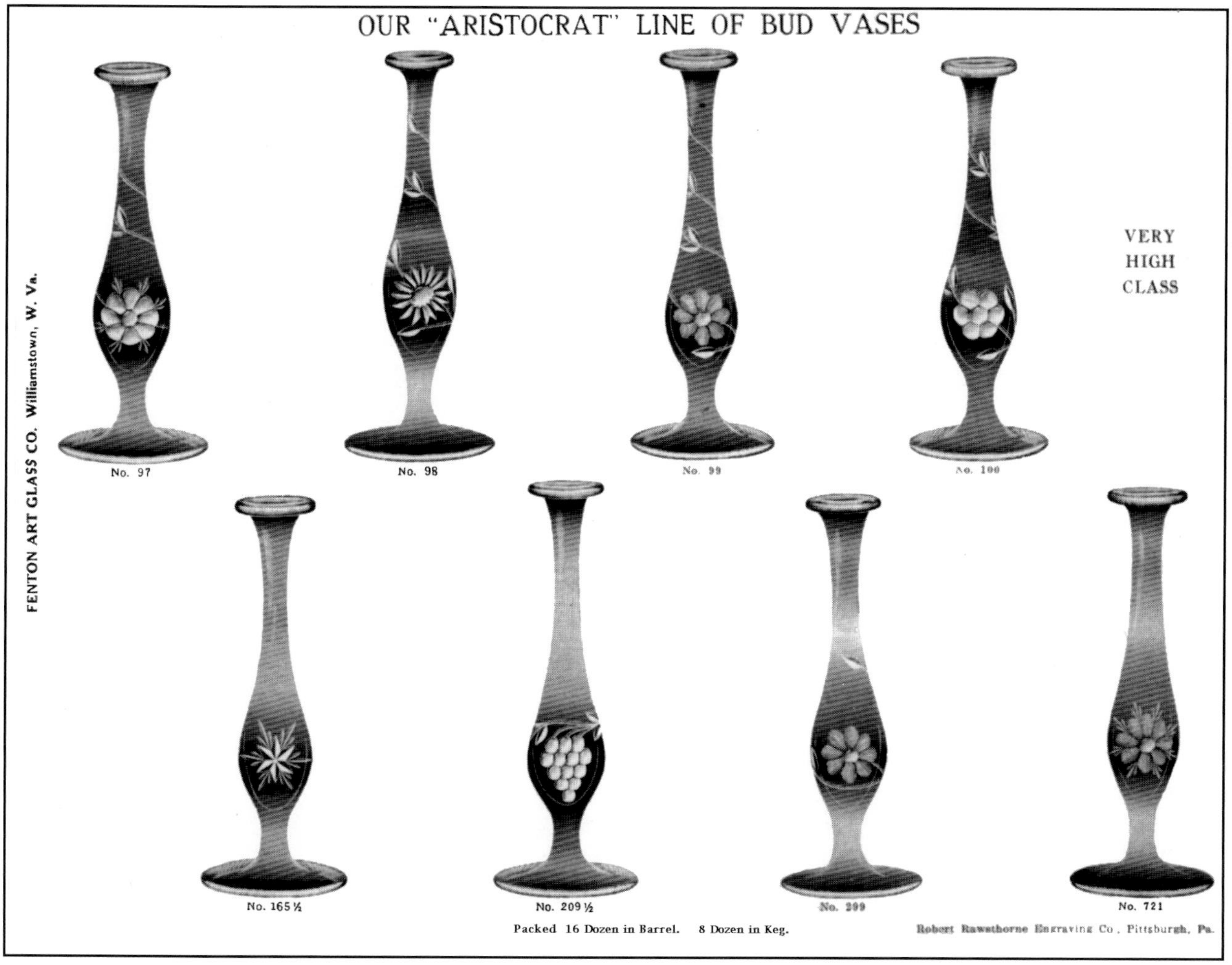

No. 208. Cut Water Set Packs 1 dozen sets to barrel.

No. 209. Cut Water Set Packs 1 dozen sets to barrel.

No. 211. Cut Water Set Packs 1 dozen sets to barrel.

No. 210. Cut Water Set Packs 1 dozen sets to barrel.

Cut Water Set Catalog Reprints Circa 1914-1917 Courtesy Of: **The Fenton Art Glass Museum**

FENTON ART GLASS CO., WILLIAMSTOWN, W. VA.

No. 125 Cut Water Set

Grape Design

made from mould no7

Robert Rawsthorne Eng. Co., Pittsburgh, Pa.

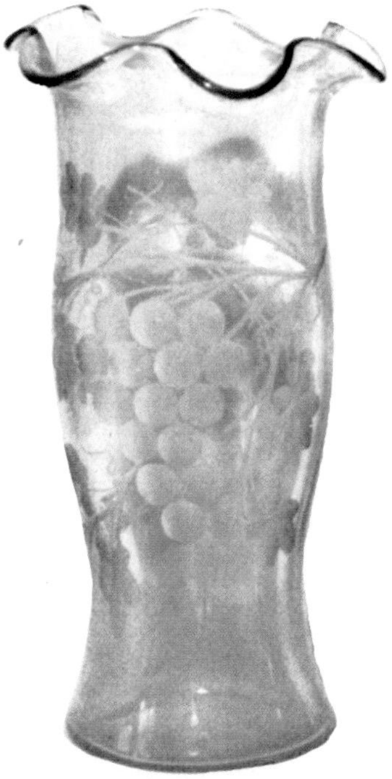

9" Ruffled Vase w/ Grape Cutting

10" Vase w/ Floral Cutting

3-Piece Nappy Set With Floral Cutting

4 7/8" Nappy

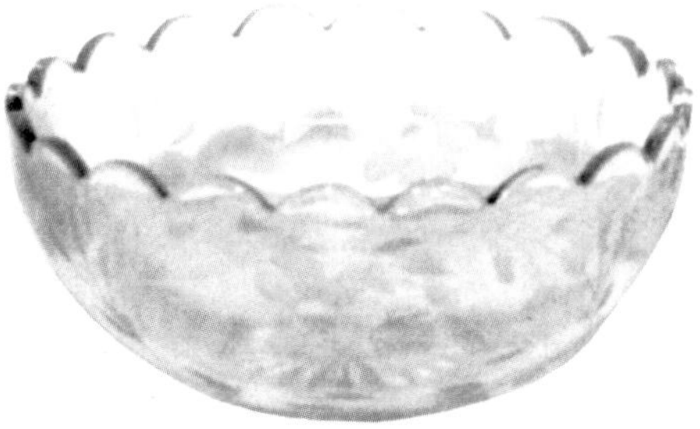

6 1/4" Nappy

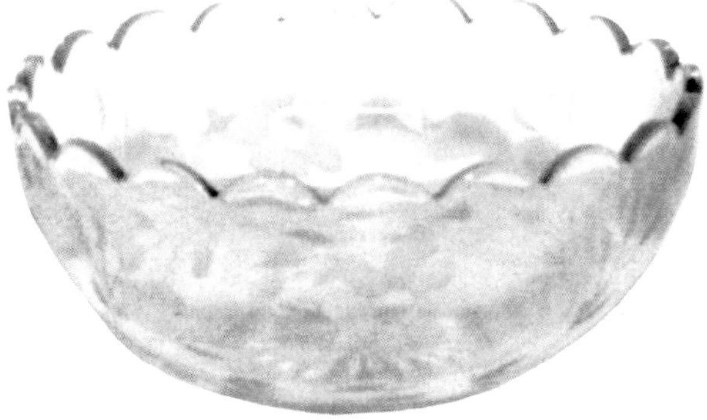

8 1/2" Nappy

Item	Date	Design	Value
Water set, #125	1917	Grape cut	
Pitcher			\$25.00 – 35.00
Tumbler			\$4.50 – 6.00
Water set, #208	1914	Floral cut	
Pitcher			\$25.00 – 30.00
Tumbler			\$4.00 – 5.00
Water set, #209	1914	Grape cut	
Pitcher			\$32.00 – 40.00
Tumbler			\$5.00 – 6.00
Water set, #210	1914	Floral cut	
Pitcher			\$25.00 – 32.00
Tumbler			\$4.00 – 5.00
Water set, #211	1914	Floral cut	
Pitcher			\$25.00 – 32.00
Tumbler			\$4.00 – 5.00

Item	Value
Nappy, 4⅞"	\$5.00 – 6.00
Nappy, 6¼"	\$6.00 – 7.00
Nappy, 8½"	\$10.00 – 14.00
Vase, 9" ruffled	\$12.00 – 15.00
Vase, 10"	\$18.00 – 20.00

CUSTARD GLASS

Custard glass is an opaque cream color. Fenton inventory records listed this color as ivory, and the color of the pieces will vary from a very pale off-white to a deep rich cream color. Most collectors prefer the darker color. Much of Fenton's early production of this color occurred about 1915, and the only pattern produced with a significant number of pieces was Cherry and Scale. This is the same pattern that carnival glass collectors call Fentonia Fruit. Collectors are able to find a water set, a full table set, and a berry set in this pattern. Pieces are often found with a reddish brown decoration that is called nutmeg by some. Early Fenton catalogs referred to this treatment as "Peach Blo."

Other occasional pressed pattern glass pieces of Fenton custard glass may be found. These are listed in the price guide below. Many of these custard pieces will be found decorated with either a nutmeg or green stain. Most of these shapes and patterns will also be found in carnival colors.

Another custard glass assortment produced by Fenton accents the patterns with multicolor hand-painted decorations. These colorful items are featured in the reprint shown at the top of page 27. Note the various shapes decorated with the colorful hand-painted Prayer Rug decoration.

Newer custard glass was produced by Fenton in 1976, and will be marked with the Fenton logo. Two pieces of Hobnail, the #3872 candle bowl, and the #3958–8" crimped vase were made in satin custard. In addition, twelve pieces of the Old Virginia line were produced in shiny custard.

Items from the Old Virginia line are as follows:

#1995 slipper	#1970 candleholder
#1921 oval bowl	#2807 student lamp
#9102 fairy light	#9120 compote
#9122 footed bowl	#9127 – 7" bowl
#9137 basket	#9157 – 4" footed vase
#9158 swung vase	#9180 candy box

Other newer custard glass items, produced since 1972 may be found with a satin finish. Satin custard is a base color for many hand-painted decorations. Undecorated custard pieces with a shiny finish that are not part of the Old Virginia line were sold as seconds through the Fenton Gift Shop.

Cherry and Scale	Value
Bowl, #1134 – 10" 3-ftd.	$120.00 – 150.00
Bowl, #1134 – 6" 3-ftd.	$50.00 – 65.00
Butter, #1134	$185.00 – 225.00
Creamer, #1134	$65.00 – 75.00
Pitcher, #1134	$240.00 – 260.00
Spooner, #1134	$65.00 – 75.00
Sugar and lid, #1134	$85.00 – 100.00
Tumbler, #1134	$40.00 – 45.00

Cherry & Scale

Spooner

Butter and Cover

Sugar and Lid

Cherry & Scale Catalog Reprint
Courtesy of:
The Fenton Art Glass Museum

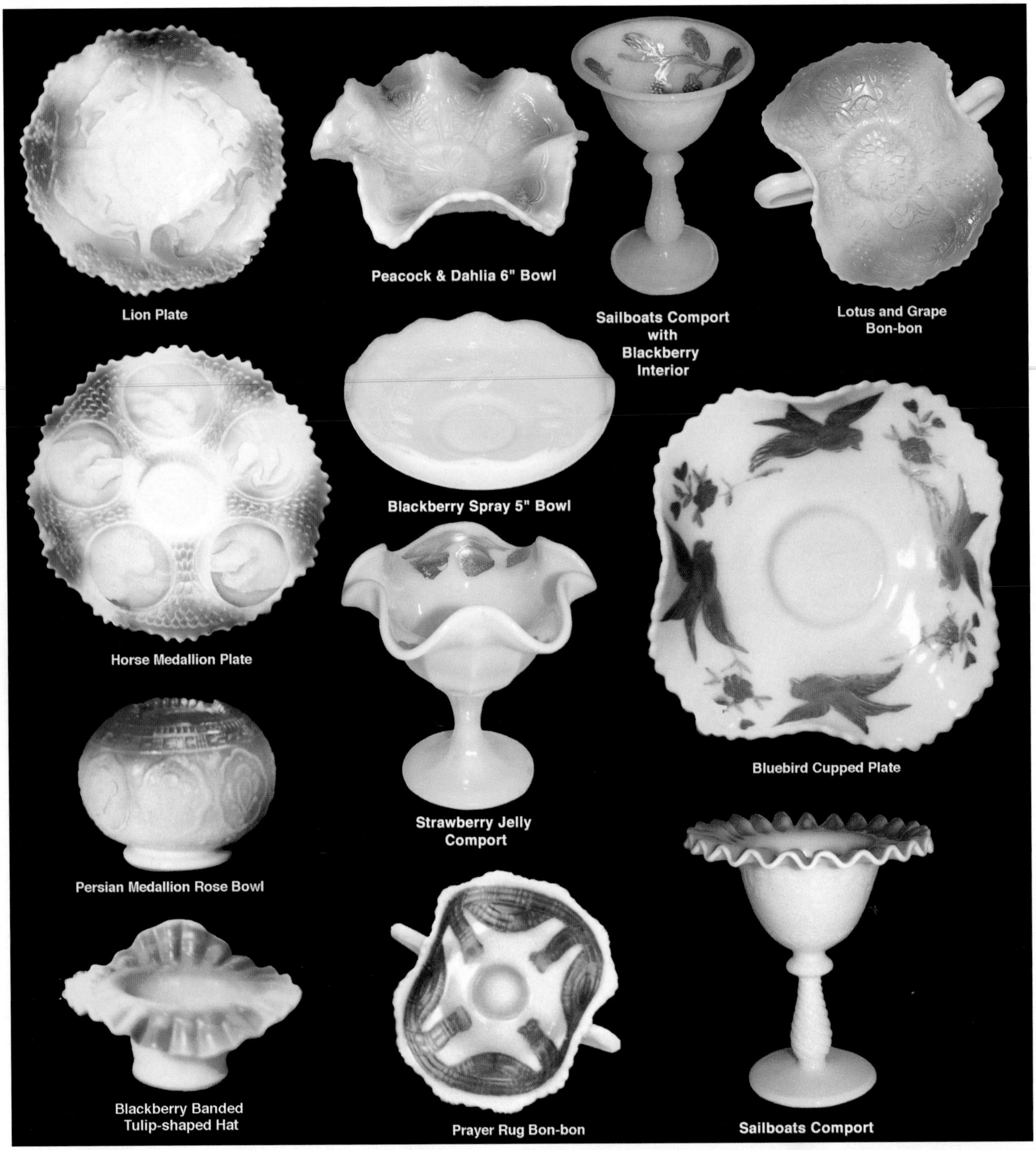

Lion Plate

Peacock & Dahlia 6" Bowl

Sailboats Comport with Blackberry Interior

Lotus and Grape Bon-bon

Horse Medallion Plate

Blackberry Spray 5" Bowl

Bluebird Cupped Plate

Persian Medallion Rose Bowl

Strawberry Jelly Comport

Blackberry Banded Tulip-shaped Hat

Prayer Rug Bon-bon

Sailboats Comport

Item	Pattern	*Value	Item	Pattern	*Value
Bonbon, 2-handled	Prayer Rug	$25.00 – 30.00	Mug, #2 handled	Rose	$27.00 – 32.00
Bonbon, #1745 – 2-hdld.	Lotus and Grape	$25.00 – 30.00	Plate, 7"	Horse Medallion	$30.00 – 35.00
Bonbon, #1414 – 2-hdld.	Pond Lily	$22.00 – 25.00	Plate, 7½"	Blackberry Spray	$25.00 – 28.00
Bonbon, tulip-shape hat	Blackberry Banded	$25.00 – 30.00	Plate, 7"	Lion	$28.00 – 32.00
Bowl, #1645 – 6" shallow	Peacock & Dahlia	$30.00 – 35.00	Plate, #1645 – 7½"	Peacock & Dahlia	$30.00 – 35.00
Bowl, 7" shallow	Horse Medallion	$50.00 – 55.00	Plate, #928 – 7½"	Prayer Rug	$25.00 – 30.00
Bowl, 7"	Lion	$55.00 – 60.00	Plate, 8" cupped	Bluebird	$45.00 – 55.00
Bowl, #927 – 5"	Blackberry Spray	$22.00 – 27.00	Rose bowl	Persian Medallion	$30.00 – 35.00
Bowl, #928 – 5"	Prayer Rug	$25.00 – 30.00	Vase	Blackberry Spray	$32.00 – 35.00
Comport, #7 (nut dish)	Sailboats	$30.00 – 35.00	Vase, 8"	Butterfly & Berry	$45.00 – 50.00
Goblet	Sailboats	$25.00 – 30.00	Vase, #8 bud	Prayer Rug	$25.00 – 30.00
Jelly comport, #526	Strawberry	$25.00 – 30.00			

*with excellent color stain add 10%

No. 927 Fruit Nappy.
No. 2 Hand. Mug.
No. 5 Sq. Bon Bon.
No. 6 Tulip Vase
No 1 Oval Rose Basket.
928-7½" Plate.
No. 8 Bud Vase.
No 4. Oval Bon Bon
No. 3 Violet Vase.
928-Flared Nappy.
No 7. Nut Dish
No 526 Jelly.

Catalog Reprints Circa 1915 Courtesy Of: The Fenton Art Glass Museum

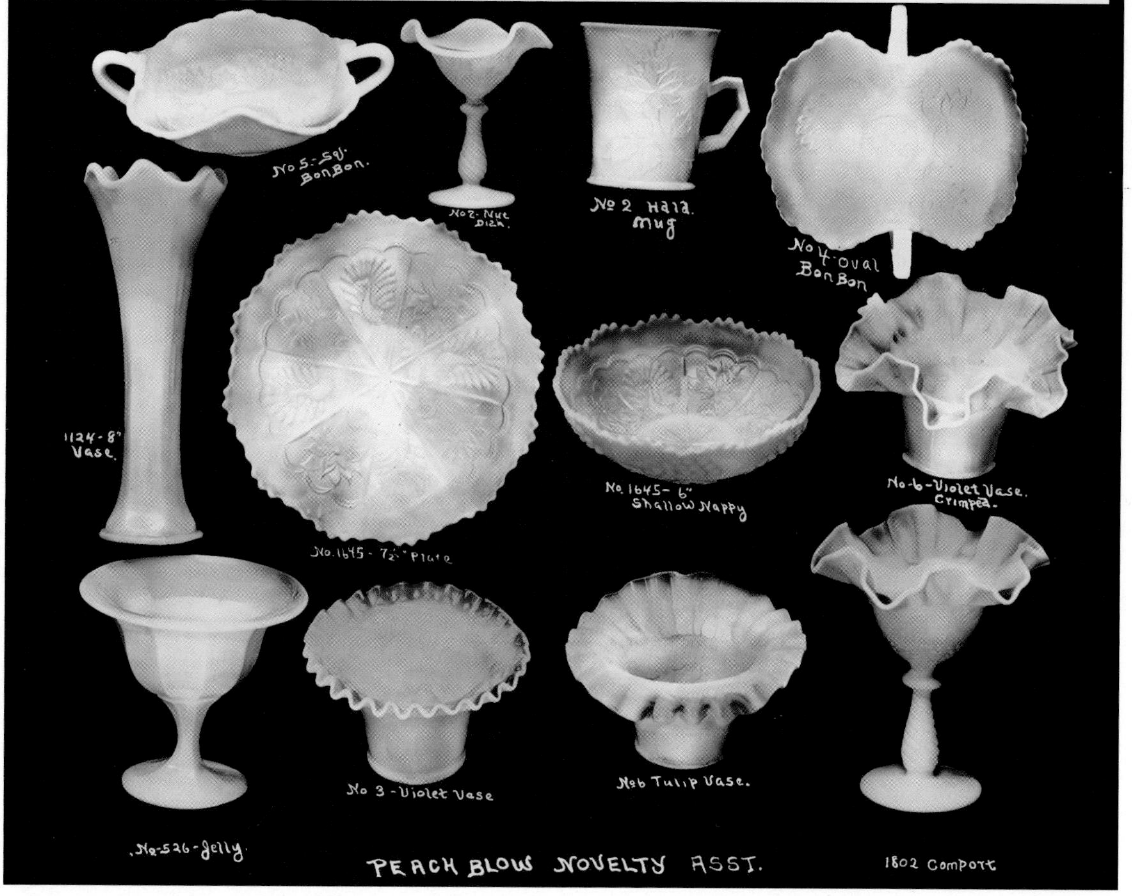
No 5.-Sq. BonBon.
No 2- Nut Dish.
No 2 Hand. Mug
No 4 Oval Bon Bon
1124-8" Vase.
No. 1645- 6" Shallow Nappy
No-6-Violet Vase. Crimped.
No.1645 - 7½" Plate
No 3 - Violet Vase
No 6 Tulip Vase.
No-526-Jelly.
PEACH BLOW NOVELTY ASST.
1802 Compote

CHOCOLATE GLASS

Chocolate glass is an opaque caramel color that is sometimes referred to as "caramel slag" because many pieces will also have swirls of a deep brown color. Some pieces may have a slight iridescent appearance, and others will have a deep red coloration around the edges. The formula for this color glass was developed by Jacob Rosenthal at Greentown, Indiana, while he was working for the Indiana Tumbler and Goblet Company. Fenton used this color from about 1907 to 1910 on some of their early pattern glass shapes. The #410 vase, shown with the crystal pattern glass vase on page 15, was produced in chocolate, but this colored piece differs from its crystal counterpart in that it has a smooth top.

The following pieces of chocolate color glass appear in the inventory records during 1925: a #607 salver, a #600 salver, a #600 salad bowl, and a #549 candlestick. Although we have not seen or heard of these pieces in this color, they may eventually be found.

Later, in 1976, Fenton utilized the talents of chemist Subodh Gupta to reproduce the chocolate color for a special issue of seven American Bicentennial pieces. Some items, primarily in the Cactus pattern, were also made for LeVay from about 1975 to 1985.

#8 Waterlily & Cattails	Value
Bowl, 4"	$60.00 – 65.00
Butter	$280.00 – 320.00
Creamer	$140.00 – 160.00
Pitcher	$630.00 – 680.00
Spooner	$150.00 – 170.00
Sugar and lid	$275.00 – 300.00
Tumbler	$300.00 – 350.00

Item	Pattern	Value
Bowl, 9½" 3-ftd.	Panther	$600.00 – 650.00
Fern dish	Vintage	$160.00 – 185.00
Hatpin holder	Orange Tree	$600.00 – 700.00
Puff box	Orange Tree	$300.00 – 350.00
Vase	#410 Sunburst	$400.00 – 450.00
Vase, 6"	Waterlily & Cattail w/Butterfly	$650.00 – 700.00

Water Lily and Cattail with Butterfly
6" Vase

#8 Water Lily and Cattails
Water Pitcher

Orange Tree
#1410 Hatpin Holder

Water Lily and Cattails Sugar and Creamer

Water Lily and Cattails Butter

Water Lily and Cattails Spooner

#922 Vintage Fern Dish

Water Lily and Cattails 4" Berry

PERSIAN BLUE

Persian blue is a translucent turquoise color which Fenton introduced about 1915. Typical pattern glass sets — berry, table, and water — were offered in the Banded Laurel pattern. The pattern consists of a single band of white enamel or gold color leaves over a plain Persian blue body. In addition a puff box and an 8" vase can be found in this pattern.

Also, a few other pattern glass pieces are found in this color. Many of these will be accented with white enamel decorations.

#599 Banded Laurel	Value
Bowl, 4½"	$9.00 – 11.00
Bowl, 8"	$30.00 – 35.00
Butter	$120.00 – 145.00
Creamer	$35.00 – 45.00
Jug	$145.00 – 170.00
Puff box	$70.00 – 80.00
Sherbet, 4" cupped	$10.00 – 12.00
Spooner	$35.00 – 45.00
Sugar and lid	$60.00 – 75.00
Tumbler	$27.00 – 32.00
Vase, 8"	$35.00 – 40.00

Item	Pattern	Value
Bonbon, #597 (oval, square)	Pond Lily	$30.00 – 32.00
Creamer, #596	Enameled Floral	$22.00 – 27.00
Sugar, #596	Enameled Floral	$22.00 – 27.00
Mug, #595	Orange Tree	$45.00 – 65.00
Pin tray, #594	Blackberry	$25.00 – 30.00
Rose bowl, #598	Persian Medallion	$45.00 – 55.00
Vase, #592 tulip	Holly	$25.00 – 28.00
Vase, #593 violet	Holly	$25.00 – 28.00

#595-9 oz. Mug

#597 Oval Bon-bon

#599 Puff Box

#594 Pin Tray

#599-8" Nappy

#599-4 1/2" Nappy

Photo Below: Courtesy Of:

Persian Blue Catalog Reprint *Circa 1915* **The Fenton Art Glass Museum**

No. 69 PERSIAN NOVELTY ASSORTMENT
596-Sugar
596-Cream.
595-Mug.
592-Tulip Vase.
597-Oval Bon Bon.
594-Pin Tray.
593-Violet Vase.
599-8" Vase.
599·4½" Nappy.
598-Rose Bowl.
599·Puff Box.
597 Square Bon Bon.

THE FENTON ART GLASS CO.
General Offices and Factory WILLIAMSTOWN, W. VA., U. S. A.
A WORLD PRODUCT
FOR HOME DECORATION
BRANCH OFFICES AND SAMPLE ROOMS
HORACE C. GRAY CO.
Fifth Ave. Building
New York City
DOHRMANN COMMERCIAL CO.
135 Stockton St.
San Francisco, Cal.
W. T. OWEN & CO.
16 Park Ave.
Baltimore, Md.
LEWIS H. SIMPSON & CO.
17 No. Wabash Ave.
Chicago, Ill.
NATIONAL GLASS CO.
1, Charterhouse St.
Holborn Circus
London, England
GEO. B. HALL
473 Broadway
New York, N. Y.
South American Agency
H. P. & H. F. HUNT CO.
41 Pearl St.
Boston, Mass.
RICHARDSON, ORR & CO.
Australia and New Zealand Agency
215 Clarence St.
Sidney, Australia
131 Featherston St.
Wellington, New Zealand
A. S. LASCELLES & CO., Inc.
Maritime Building
8-10 Bridge St.
New York
South African Agency
U. S. CROCKERY & GLASS EXCHANGE
922 Chestnut Street
Philadelphia, Pa.
C. C. MAYER
614 Granite Bldg.
St. Louis, Mo.
IRWIN, HARRISONS & CROSFIELD, Inc.
127-129 Water Street
New York
Dutch East Indies
Republic of China
Federated Malay States
British North Borneo
Straits Settlements

Carnival Glass Advertising Plates

Furniture & Clothing
UNION AVE. & EAST BURNSIDE ST.

Glendive, Mont.

Eat Paradise Sodas

CARNIVAL GLASS

INTRODUCTION

The carnival glass of interest to most collectors is an iridized pressed pattern glass that was produced from shortly after the turn of the century into the late 1920s. Iridescence is achieved by spraying a coating composed of a mixture of metallic salts over the hot glass and then firing the finished product to produce a permanent finish. Starting in 1907, the Fenton Art Glass Company became the first company to produce this type of glass. Intense production continued throughout this period, and the Fenton Art Glass Company became one of the leading makers of carnival glass. This mass-produced iridescent glassware was affordable to the average American, and over 150 patterns and numerous colors were made by Fenton. Determining the exact date of production of all the patterns is not yet possible as the original catalog information is incomplete. Also, since information is scarce, production of patterns usually will not be limited to only the year(s) found in the price guide. Whenever a single date is noted, it will indicate the earliest possible confirmed date of production. Ranges of years will indicate a pattern was found listed for that time period, but not all pieces of a pattern may have been produced for the entire time.

The carnival glass section of this book is arranged alphabetically by pattern. Although it is not possible to picture every item, we have attempted to list all the known iridescent pieces of each pattern in the price guide. In addition, the description of the pattern contains a listing of many of the other confirmed colors which are not actually carnival colors but are of interest to other collectors of Fenton glassware. Many of these pieces will be listed and priced again in other appropriate areas of the book for the convenience of other collectors. The order of listing for color is the brilliant colors followed by the pastels, special treatments, and variations of the primary colors.

NAMING CARNIVAL GLASS

Pattern names of carnival glass generally have been contributed by researchers. Over the years this has led to duplicate names for numerous patterns. Usage of some names has become more common, while other names have been relegated to the background. We have placed the more commonly found names first in the following listings. The more obscure, but sometimes used, names may be found in parentheses following the more common name. Generally accepted authors whose names have been used in this book include Marion Hartung, Rose M. Presnick, Sherman Hand, and William Heacock. For further information on works by these authors, see the bibliography at the end of this book.

CARNIVAL GLASS COLORS

Fenton's primary brilliant carnival colors were golden (marigold) over crystal, royal blue, violet (amethyst), green, and red. Some of the more commonly found iridized pastel colors include amber, aqua, white, ice blue, ice green, smoke, clambroth, and topaz. In order to determine the base color, look through the iridescence to determine the actual color of the glass. The addition of the hot metallic spray to the hot glass initially produces a silvery appearance. Successive sprayings produce gold, red, green, and finally blue iridescence. An excessive amount of spray will produce a silvery look, and the value for items with a silvery appearance will be less than for a piece with brilliant iridescence. Special treatments include the application of iridescence over opaque colors and the addition of opalescence to a color.

Many of the color names found in this guide have been designated by collectors to differentiate the variations in the basic colors. Some of the color differences are a result of variations in the quality of the raw materials which produced lighter or darker than normal products. For further examples and a clearer understanding about Fenton colors, see the sections on stretch glass and non-iridescent colors of the late 1920s and early 1930s.

BRILLIANT COLORS

GOLDEN (marigold) is an orange-yellow color applied over a crystal base. Fenton used the term "golden" in early catalogs, but collectors usually refer to this color as "marigold."

ROYAL BLUE (cobalt) is the Fenton name for a deep blue which approaches cobalt.

GREEN is normally a deep emerald color but may sometimes be laced with traces of yellow.

VIOLET (amethyst) is an early Fenton name for the deep purple color which is now usually called amethyst by collectors.

RED is a deep rich transparent color which does not blend to yellow or bleed to black. Maintaining a true red color was a difficult task during this era.

PASTEL COLORS AND SPECIAL TREATMENTS

AMBER or AMBER IRIDESCENT is a honey-colored glass with a sprayed-on iridized finish.

AMBER OPALESCENT is a honey-colored glass accented with milky areas. The same formula was used for Cameo opalescent glass produced during the 1920s.

AMBERINA is a transparent red color which tends to run toward yellow, especially around the edges.

AQUA or AQUA IRIDESCENT is a light blue-green color base glass with an iridized finish.

AQUA OPALESCENT is a blue-green color with a milky white appearance, especially around the edges.

BLACK AMETHYST is ebony glass which exhibits a purple color when held to a strong light.

BLUE OPALESCENT is a light transparent blue glass accented with milky white.

BRICK RED (Venetian red) is an opaque red which may vary in color from almost bright red to a deep burgundy.

CELESTE BLUE or FLORENTINE BLUE is a transparent deep sapphire blue-colored glass with an iridized satin finish.

CLAMBROTH is a lightly iridized crystal glassware producing a light champagne color.

CRYSTAL or CRYSTAL IRIDESCENT is clear glass with an iridescent overspray.

CUSTARD is off-white or beige opaque glass.

GOLDEN IRIDESCENCE over CUSTARD GLASS is a beige-colored base glass with a sprayed-over golden iridescent finish.

GOLDEN IRIDESCENCE over MILK GLASS is an opaque white glass with a sprayed-on golden iridized finish.

ICE BLUE (azure blue) is a pale transparent blue color with an iridescent finish.

ICE GREEN (Florentine green) is a pale transparent green color usually with a golden iridescent finish.

ICE GREEN OPALESCENT is a pale green opal-colored glass with a sprayed-over iridescent finish.

IRIDIZED MOONSTONE is an opaque white translucent colored glass with a sprayed-on iridescence.

LAVENDER is a light amethyst color which may often have traces of blue.

LIME GREEN is a soft yellow-green color.

LIME GREEN OPALESCENT is a soft yellow-green-colored glass with a milky white opal color.

MILK GLASS is a white opaque colored glass.

MOONSTONE is a white translucent colored glass.

PEACH OPALESCENT is an iridescent glassware with a pinkish-beige transparent center. This color flows outward toward a milky opalescent edge.

PERSIAN BLUE is a translucent light turquoise color. Some pieces in this color will be found with iridescence.

PINK is a transparent rose-colored glass.

PURPLE is a name which collectors call a color which is lighter than amethyst.

RED (RUBY) OPALESCENT is transparent red glass with a milky white trim.

RUBY is a transparent red color.

TEAL is a blue-green color.

TOPAZ is a yellow color which is sometimes blended with tinges of green to approach a color which many of today's collectors call vaseline. Pieces in this color glow when placed under a black light.

TOPAZ OPALESCENT is a yellow-colored glass accented with opaque yellow areas.

SMOKE is a gray color.

VIOLET OPALESCENT is a light colored amethyst with a milky opal color.

WHITE (WHITE CARNIVAL) is called Persian Pearl later in the stretch glass era. This is a satin crystal glass with a satin iridescent coating.

PRICING CARNIVAL GLASS

Condition, quality of iridescence, collector desirability, and the ease with which an item may be found are all important factors in determining value. Prices in this guide are for items with good iridescence and without chips or cracks. Generally, bubbles and straw marks are acceptable as long as they are not disfiguring.

RARITY INDICATOR

All items in the price guide have been evaluated for their degree of difficulty to find in the marketplace. The rating is as follows:

5. **Common** — easily found.
4. **Scarce** — difficult to find, but will be obtained with moderate searching.
3. **Rare** — will require diligence and a little luck to obtain.
2. **Very Rare** — finding this will require luck and a bucket of money.
1. **Extremely Rare** — only a few examples have been found.

REPRODUCTIONS AND REISSUES

In the decades after 1930, some carnival glass molds have been used by the Fenton Art Glass Company to produce both iridized and non-iridized glassware. New iridescent glass has been made since 1970 as limited edition specials and will have the Fenton logo in an oval on the bottom of the piece. This identification emblem enables new collectors to differentiate between new and old iridescent glass and also helps to protect the value of the original glassware. Veteran collectors should be able to tell new iridescent glass from old without any difficulty. "Original Formula Carnival" was reintroduced into the line in 1970 on glassware with a dark amethyst base color. None of the original ten items were from old Fenton carnival glass molds. In the ensuing years, new pieces were added, and some of the original pieces were discontinued, until the color was dropped in 1983. Orange carnival, similar to the old golden color, was offered in 1972 to 1973, and cobalt carnival, called Independence blue, was made in 1975 to 1976. Some pieces were also made in red carnival during 1976 and 1977. This color was used again in 1995 to commemorate Fenton's 90th anniversary. Pieces which have been re-issued will be identified in the introduction to each pattern, and the new colors will be listed along with the date of re-issue.

ACORN #835 (GRAPE LEAVES AND ACORNS) Circa 1924

Three clusters of acorns and oak leaves are arranged in a circular pattern. This pattern should not be confused with Fenton's similar Autumn Acorns pattern. The Autumn Acorns pattern has a leaf in the center of each piece. This center leaf is lacking in the Acorn pattern. A comport with a similar acorn pattern was made by Millersburg. Fenton did not make a comport in the Acorn pattern. The 8½" round deep bowl is more scarce than the shallow bowl. Plates have only been found in violet and royal blue, and there are not many of these in collections. The shallow 7" bowl is one of the more common Fenton carnival pieces and was produced in about every imaginable color. This shallow bowl may be found flared and crimped or with a scalloped, cupped edge.

	Bowl, 7"	Rarity	Bowl, 8½"	Rarity	Plate, 8¾"	Rarity
Golden	$55.00 – 62.00	(5)				
Green	$70.00 – 82.00	(5)				
Red	$750.00 – 800.00	(4)	$800.00 – 850.00	(2)		
Royal Blue	$50.00 – 60.00	(5)			$600.00 – 650.00	(3)
Violet	$125.00 – 150.00	(5)			$625.00 – 675.00	(3)
Topaz	$150.00 – 170.00	(2)	$225.00 – 250.00	(2)		
Amber	$160.00 – 180.00	(2)				
Amber Opalescent	$200.00 – 270.00	(2)				
Amberina	$325.00 – 350.00	(4)	$600.00 – 650.00	(2)		
Aqua	$100.00 – 135.00	(5)	$100.00 – 125.00	(3)		
Aqua Opalescent	$700.00 – 800.00	(3)				
Brick Red	$485.00 – 560.00	(3)				
Celeste Blue	$850.00 – 950.00	(2)				
Golden Irid. over WMG	$600.00 – 650.00	(2)				
Ice Blue	$750.00 – 850.00	(3)				
Lime	$80.00 – 100.00	(3)				
Moonstone	$160.00 – 190.00	(4)				
Peach Opalescent	$250.00 – 300.00	(2)				

APPLE TREE #1561 Circa 1912 – 1925

The #1561 water set is the only production item in this pattern. Sets were listed in Fenton catalogs from 1912 and also may be found in later Butler Brothers' catalogs from 1925. In 1925, Butler Brothers sold sets of a pitcher and six tumblers for $15.00 per dozen. A few vases, made from the pitcher mold without the applied handle, have been found in golden and royal blue. Vases have shown up with both crimped and flared tops. These vases have sold for around $2,000.00 at several auctions and are too scarce to have been a regular production item. White carnival water sets are scarce. A Golden iridescent over milk tumbler has been found. Both the pitcher and tumblers were produced in red carnival for Fenton's 90th anniversary in 1995. The large bulbous vase was produced in the 1930s in a number of opaque, transparent and opalescent colors. Lamps were also fashioned from drilled vases in some of the later colors.

Pitcher	Value	Rarity	Tumbler	Value	Rarity
Golden	$220.00 – 300.00	(5)	Golden	$30.00 – 40.00	(5)
Royal Blue	$500.00 – 600.00	(3)	Royal Blue	$65.00 – 75.00	(3)
White	$750.00 – 800.00	(2)	White	$180.00 – 220.00	(2)

APRIL SHOWERS #412 Circa 1911

This pattern is found on swung vases ranging in size from 5" to slightly taller than 15". The pattern is similar to Fenton's Rustic and Northwood's Tree Trunk. However, April Showers vases have a variegated hobnail pattern, while the hobs on Rustic are more evenly spaced. The Tree Trunk design features hobs within oval lines. The Peacock Tail pattern is sometimes found as an interior design on April Showers vases.

	Vase, 5" squat	Rarity
Golden	$45.00 – 55.00	(5)
Green	$100.00 – 120.00	(4)
Royal Blue	$90.00 – 110.00	(4)
Violet	$60.00 – 85.00	(4)
White	$165.00 – 225.00	(2)
	Vase, 10"-15"	
Golden	$35.00 – 40.00	(5)
Green	$70.00 – 80.00	(5)
Red	$1800.00+	(1)
Royal Blue	$50.00 – 65.00	(5)
Violet	$60.00 – 70.00	(5)
White	$250.00 – 275.00	(3)
Topaz	$250.00 – 350.00	(2)

AUTUMN ACORNS — Circa 1910

This pattern features acorns accompanied by Vintage pattern grape leaves. This pattern can be distinguished from Fenton's Acorn pattern by the presence of a leaf in the center of the piece. Plates have only been found in green, violet, and royal blue.

	Bowl, 7½"	Rarity	Plate	Rarity
Golden	$55.00 – 60.00	(5)		
Green	$80.00 – 85.00	(5)	$1400.00 – 1700.00	(2)
Red	$4000.00 – 5000.00	(1)		
Royal Blue	$80.00 – 85.00	(5)	$1100.00 – 1300.00	(3)
Violet	$120.00 – 145.00	(5)	$1000.00 – 1200.00	(2)
Topaz	$200.00 – 225.00	(3)		
Lime Opal	$160.00 – 180.00	(4)		

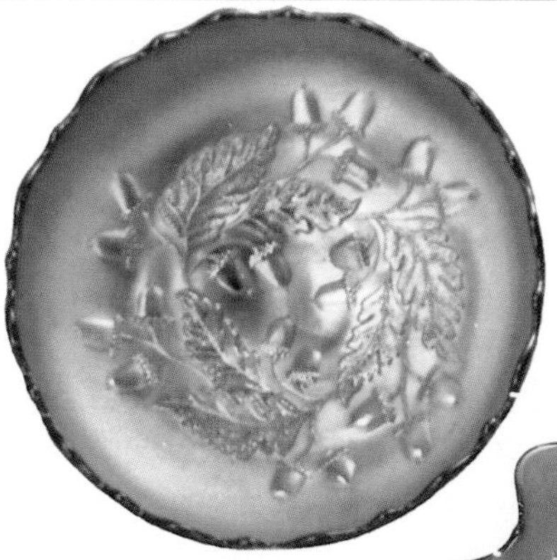

ACORN
Green

APPLE TREE
Royal Blue

APPLE TREE
Royal Blue

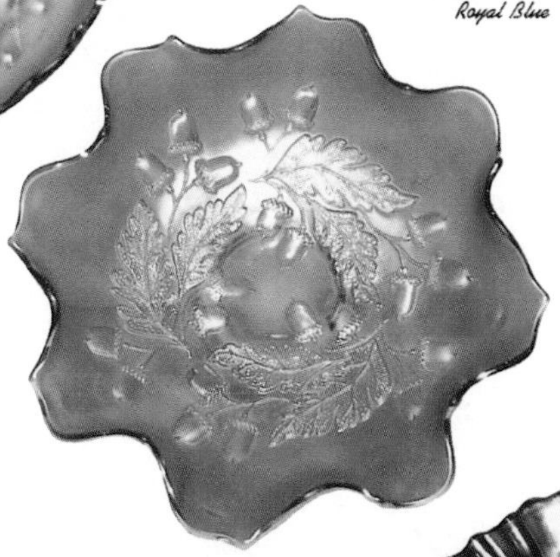

ACORN
Golden

AUTUMN ACORNS
Violet

AUTUMN ACORNS
Green

APRIL SHOWERS
Golden

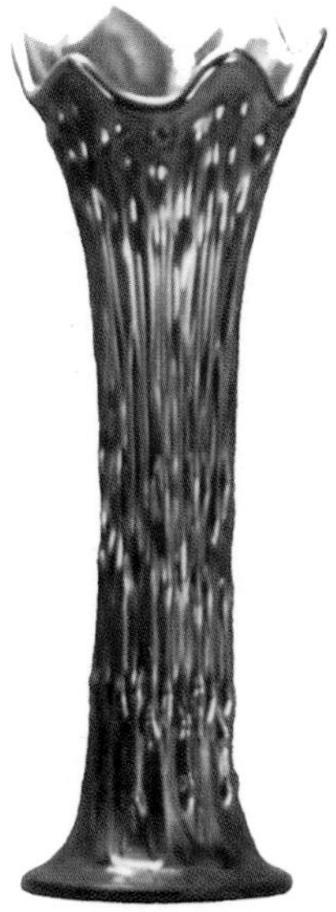

APRIL SHOWERS
Violet

BANDED DRAPE #1016 (RIBBON AND DRAPE, IRIS AND RIBBON) Circa 1912

Water sets with an enameled floral decoration were produced. Hand-painted decorations shown in the catalog reprint on the next page include Forget-Me-Not and Iris. The Banded Drape name is derived from the embossed rib which forms a sash-like decoration. The matching enameled tumbler found with this set is from the Prism Band line.

	Pitcher	Rarity	Tumbler	Rarity		Pitcher	Rarity	Tumbler	Rarity
Golden	$175.00 – 225.00	(5)	$40.00 – 45.00	(5)	Violet	$500.00 – 550.00	(2)	$75.00 – 85.00	(2)
Green	$525.00 – 575.00	(3)	$70.00 – 80.00	(5)	White	$700.00 – 800.00	(3)	$90.00 – 110.00	(3)
Royal Blue	$400.00 – 450.00	(3)	$50.00 – 60.00	(3)					

BASKETWEAVE WITH OPEN EDGE #1092 (FENTON'S BASKET) Circa 1911 – 1925

Fenton produced numerous small novelty open edge plates and bowls with a basketweave pattern. This pattern is sometimes called Fenton's Basket. Pieces may be found with either two or three rows of open lace. The small deep bowl on the top right on page 39 is called a deep nut. It has a Blackberry pattern on the inside, and the color is Golden iridescence over an aqua base. Shapes of the deep nut include two sides up, four sides up, tulip, square, or flared. Some items will also be found with advertising embossed on the bottom. Northwood also made a pattern called Basket, but these pieces do not have open edges. Non-iridized opalescent color pieces were produced from about 1910 until the early 1930s and Basket style pieces were made in pastel stretch colors from the early 1920s until the early 1930s. The 6½" open edge deep bowl was reintroduced in August, 1970, in amethyst carnival. A basket was also made from this bowl by applying a handle. Both the bowl and basket were produced in 1976 in Ruby Carnival, Independence Blue, and Rosalene. The bowl was made in a crystal satin color called Crystal Velvet in 1977. Later in 1987, both pieces were produced in Provincial blue opal, and Provincial blue. New colors that year also included Peaches and Cream, Minted Cream, and Blue Carnival. In 1988 and 1989 the bowl was made in Teal Marigold. In 1990, the deep bowl was made in black for QVC and in Red Carnival for the Canadian Carnival Collector's Association.

	Bonbon, tulip crimp	Rarity	Bowl, 5 – 6½" deep nut	Rarity	Plate	Rarity
Golden	$40.00 – 50.00*	(5)	$35.00 – 45.00	(5)		
Green	$225.00 – 250.00*	(3)	$50.00 – 60.00	(4)	$1500.00+	(1)
Red	$450.00 – 500.00	(4)	$350.00 – 400.00	(4)		
Royal Blue	$75.00 – 90.00	(5)	$45.00 – 50.00	(5)	$1800.00+	(1)
Violet	$180.00 – 220.00	(3)	$50.00 – 60.00	(5)		
Amber	$150.00 – 190.00	(2)				
Amberina	$450.00 – 500.00	(3)				
Aqua	$145.00 – 200.00	(4)				
Black Amethyst	$150.00 – 175.00	(4)				
Celeste Blue	$250.00 – 300.00	(2)	$275.00 – 325.00	(4)		
Ice Blue	$375.00 – 425.00	(3)	$500.00 – 600.00	(3)	$2000.00+	(1)
Ice Green	$195.00 – 225.00	(2)	$200.00 – 250.00	(4)		
Lime Green	$110.00 – 125.00	(3)				
Smoke	$500.00 – 550.00	(3)				
Topaz	$125.00 – 150.00	(3)				
White	$200.00 – 225.00	(3)	$175.00 – 225.00	(4)		

*With advertising add 10 – 20%.

	Bowl, 8"-10"	Rarity	Rose Bowl	Rarity
Golden	$100.00 – 125.00	(1)	$1000.00 – 1500.00	(2)
Royal Blue	$140.00 – 160.00	(1)	$1500.00 – 2000.00	(2)
Violet	$120.00 – 140.00	(1)		
Celeste Blue	$800.00 – 900.00	(3)		
Ice Green	$275.00 – 325.00	(4)		
White	$100.00 – 150.00	(3)		

BANDED DRAPE
Royal Blue

BASKETWEAVE, OPEN EDGE
Golden

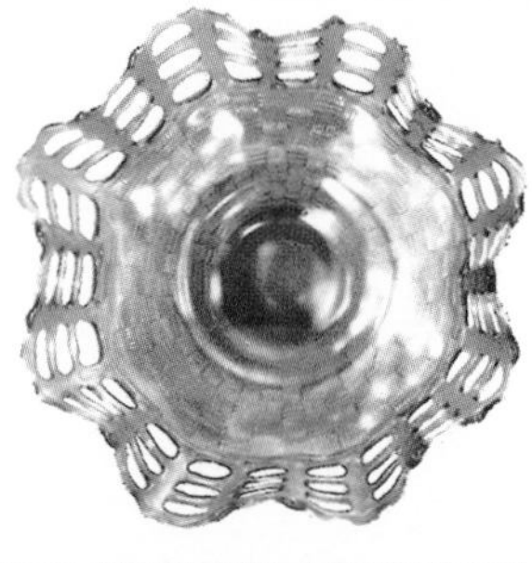

BASKETWEAVE, OPEN EDGE
Aqua

BASKETWEAVE, OPEN EDGE
BLACKBERRY INTERIOR
Violet

VENETIAN LEMONADE
SET ASSORTMENT
1014
1014
1016
1016

Catalog Reprint
Circa 1912

Courtesy Of: **The Fenton Art Glass Museum**

BEADED STARS

Circa 1908

The small 5" footed bowl is the most frequently found piece of Beaded Stars. It may be found with either a crimped or scalloped edge. Both plates and bowls will also be found in non-iridescent and opalescent colors. See the Early Opalescent Pattern Glass (pg. 16) and Pattern Glass (pg. 12) sections for other pricing.

	Bowl	Rarity	Bowl, banana	Rarity	Plate, 9"	Rarity	Rose bowl	Rarity
Golden	$27.00 – 32.00	(5)	$90.00 – 100.00	(4)	$100.00 – 120.00	(4)	$45.00 – 55.00	(5)

BEARDED BERRY (BERRY AND LEAF CIRCLES)

Circa 1911

Six bunches of berries and leaves are joined together by a thin vine which encircles the bowls. Fenton used this only as an exterior pattern on some items. Prices for pieces with this exterior are determined by using the name of the interior pattern

BIRDS AND CHERRIES #1075

Circa 1911

This pattern is more commonly found on bonbons and small comports. Berry sets (large berry and individual berries) and plates also exist, although they are scarce.

	Bonbon, 2-H	Rarity	Bowl, 5"	Rarity	Bowl, 9" crimped	Rarity	Comport	Rarity	Plate, 10	Rarity
Golden	$45.00 – 55.00	(4)	$65.00 – 75.00	(3)	$185.00 – 210.00	(3)	$45.00 – 50.00	(4)	$1400.00 – 1600.00	(1)
Green	$65.00 – 75.00	(5)					$65.00 – 75.00	(5)	$2000.00 – 2400.00	(2)
Royal Blue	$57.00 – 67.00	(5)			$400.00 – 475.00	(2)	$60.00 – 85.00	(5)	$2500+	(2)
Violet	$70.00 – 90.00	(4)	$90.00 – 100.00	(3)	$385.00 – 420.00	(2)	$60.00 – 65.00	(4)		
Topaz	$140.00 – 160.00	(4)					$140.00 – 160.00	(3)		

BIRMINGHAM AGE HERALD

Circa 1911

These plates and bowls were a gift from paper boys to customers of the *Birmingham Age Herald* and are scarce today. They have only been found in violet, and the exterior pattern is Wide Panel.

	Bowl, 9¼" shallow	Rarity	Bowl, deep	Rarity	Plate, 10"	Rarity
Violet	$1800.00 – 2000.00	(2)	$1500.00 – 1800.00	(2)	$2500.00 – 3200.00	(2)

BLACKBERRY WITH OPEN EDGE

Circa 1911

The Blackberry design is often found on the inside of Fenton's Basket Weave novelties. The plate has an open edge and a bottom design of the Basketweave pattern. The basket novelty is a hat-shaped deep bowl with various edge shapes which include two sides up, four sides up, tulip, square, or flared. The 8¼" vase has an exterior Basket Weave pattern and is an extremely scarce whimsy. A Blackberry pattern was also made by Northwood. See the Basket Weave pattern on page 39, top right, for another color of a Basket novelty with a Blackberry interior.

	Basket (Hat)	Rarity	Plate, 7½"	Rarity	Vase, 8¼"	Rarity	Spittoon	Rarity
Golden	$30.00 – 40.00	(5)	$850.00 – 950.00	(2)	$675.00 – 750.00	(3)	$3500.00 – 4000.00	(1)
Green	$100.00 – 120.00	(5)						
Red	$500.00 – 575.00	(4)						
Royal Blue	$45.00 – 60.00	(5)	$3500.00 – 4000.00	(1)	$1300.00 – 1600.00	(3)	$4000.00 – 5000.00	(1)
Violet	$50.00 – 65.00	(5)						
Amber	$50.00 – 60.00	(4)						
Aqua	$90.00 – 120.00	(3)						
Topaz	$120.00 – 140.00	(4)						
White	$$80.00 – 95.00	(3)						

BIRMINGHAM AGE HERALD
Violet

BIRDS & CHERRIES
Green

BEARDED BERRY
Royal Blue

BEADED STARS
Golden

BIRDS & CHERRIES
Green

BEADED STARS
Golden

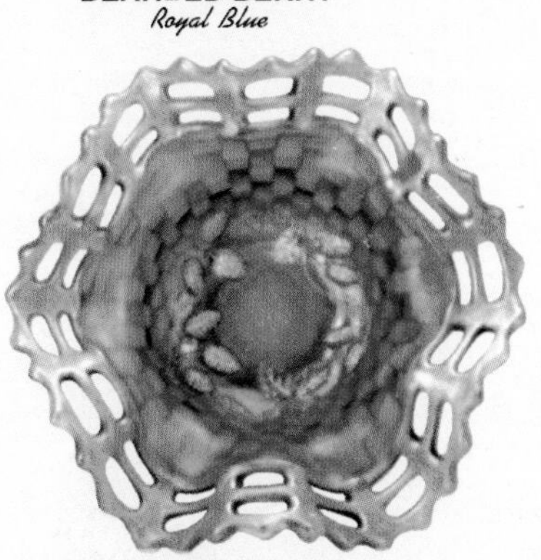

BLACKBERRY
Violet

Composite From Original Catalog Reprint Circa 1916 **Courtesy Of:** **The Fenton Art Glass Museum**

1607 -10" Shallow
Golden.
(Little Fishes)

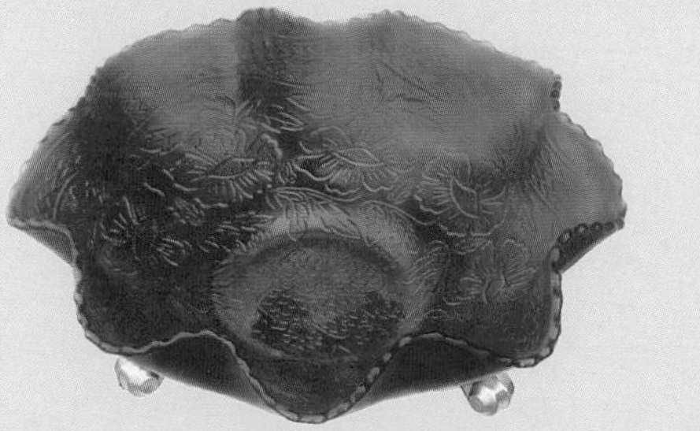

1707 -10" Crimp.
Royal Blue.
(Two Flowers)

1807 -10" Shallow
Golden.
(Water Lily)

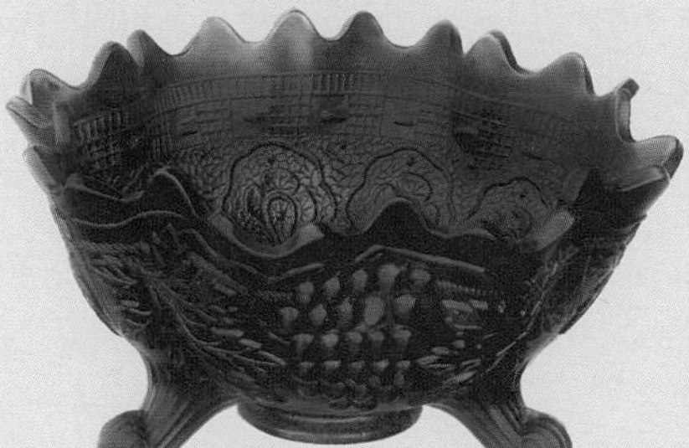

920 Crimp
Royal Blue.
(Grape and Cable with Persian Medallion interior)

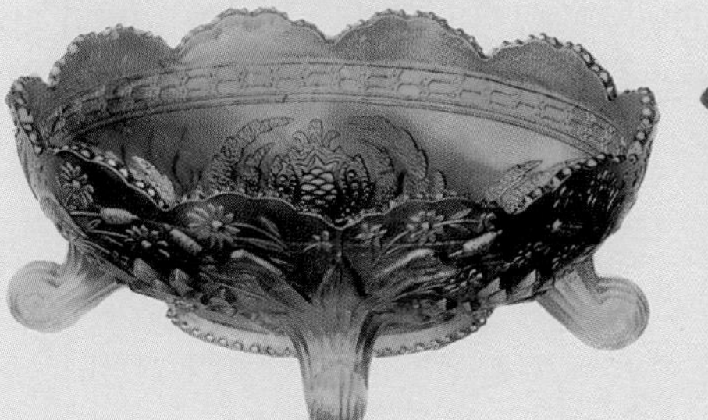

1120. Oval.
Golden.
(Thistle Banana Boat)

921. Crimp
Royal Blue.
(Orange Tree)

BLACKBERRY BANDED

Circa 1912

A hat-shaped bonbon is the only piece which has been found with this pattern. The most commonly found colors are golden and royal blue. This pattern may be easily differentiated from the Blackberry Spray pattern by looking for the presence of a band of short vertical lines around the middle of the interior of the bonbon. Custard glass examples of this bonbon may also be found. Pieces in the custard color were produced in about 1915.

	Bonbon (Hat)	Rarity		Bonbon (Hat)	Rarity
Golden	$30.00 – 35.00	(5)	White	$120.00 – 140.00	(3)
Green	$50.00 – 55.00	(5)	Moonstone	$75.00 – 100.00	(4)
Royal Blue	$45.00 – 50.00	(5)	Golden Irid. over Moonstone	$120.00 – 140.00	(3)

BLACKBERRY BLOCK

Circa 1911

Water sets with a tankard-style jug were the only pieces made in this pattern. It is a block-like pattern interwoven with vines and berries.

	Tankard	Rarity	Tumbler	Rarity
Golden	$320.00 – 360.00	(5)	$45.00 – 55.00	(5)
Green	$1300.00 – 1600.00	(4)	$90.00 – 110.00	(4)
Royal Blue	$950.00 – 1100.00	(3)	$70.00 – 80.00	(4)
Violet	$1100.00 – 1300.00	(3)	$95.00 – 115.00	(4)
White	$5000.00 – 5500.00	(1)	$250.00 – 300.00	(1)
Topaz	$6000.00+	(1)	$350.00 – 400.00	(1)

BLACKBERRY BRAMBLE #303

Circa 1910

This commonly found pattern resembles the Blackberry design of the Open Edge pieces but is larger and fuller, with much more foliage. The only piece in this pattern is a footed comport.

	Comport	Rarity
Golden	$30.00 – 35.00	(5)
Green	$45.00 – 50.00	(5)
Royal Blue	$40.00 – 45.00	(3)
Violet	$40.00 – 45.00	(5)

BLACKBERRY MINIATURE

A small 4½" diameter comport found in several colors and crimped in various styles is the only available piece in this pattern. It is scarce in any color and might be considered rare in white or violet. A footed plate-shaped variation has turned up in royal blue. It is uncommon and is usually found priced in the $300.00 range.

	Comport, 4½"	Rarity
Golden	$90.00 – 110.00	(5)
Violet	$225.00 – 250.00	(3)
Green	$200.00 – 225.00	(4)
White	$600.00 – 650.00	(2)
Royal Blue	$60.00 – 80.00	(4)

BLACKBERRY SPRAY #1216 — Circa 1911

This pattern has four separate blackberry branches arranged in a circular pattern. One mold was used to fashion bonbons which differ in appearance — hat, tulip, square, and flared crimped. Variations of this pattern will sometimes only have two sprigs of blackberries. Non-iridescent colored opalescent bonbons and nappies first appeared about 1908. Pieces were made in custard glass about 1915. The custard glass pieces were sometimes decorated with hand-painted colors accenting the pattern or with green or nutmeg trim.

	Bonbon	Rarity		Bonbon	Rarity
Golden	$35.00 – 40.00	(5)	Aqua Opalescent	$500.00 – 600.00	(2)
Green	$85.00 – 115.00	(4)	Blue Opalescent	$275.00 – 325.00	(2)
Red	$375.00 – 425.00	(4)	Brick Red	$200.00 – 300.00	(4)
Royal Blue	$45.00 – 50.00	(5)	Lime Green	$100.00 – 125.00	(3)
Violet	$45.00 – 50.00	(5)	Red Opalescent	$700.00 – 900.00	(3)
Amberina	$340.00 – 370.00	(3)	Rev Amberina Opal	$700.00 – 850.00	(3)
Aqua	$85.00 – 95.00	(5)	Topaz	$85.00 – 95.00	(3)
French Opalescent	$150.00 – 200.00	(3)	Violet Opalescent	$200.00 – 250.00	(4)

BLACKBERRY MINIATURE
Royal Blue

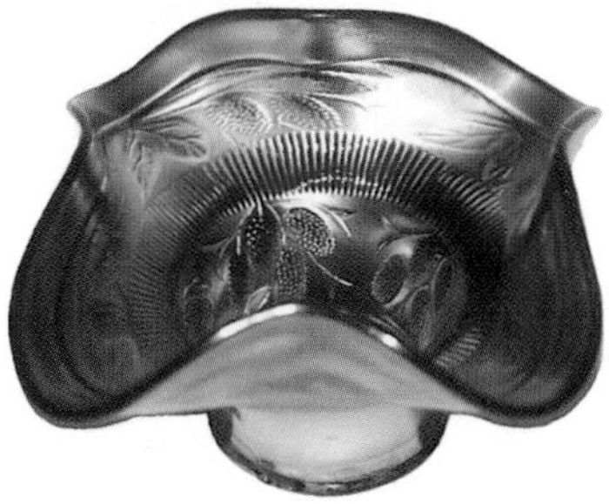

BLACKBERRY BANDED
Royal Blue

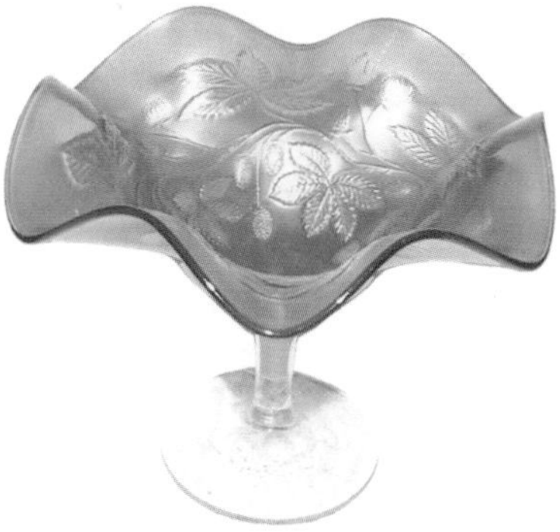

BLACKBERRY BRAMBLE
Green

BLACKBERRY BLOCK
Golden

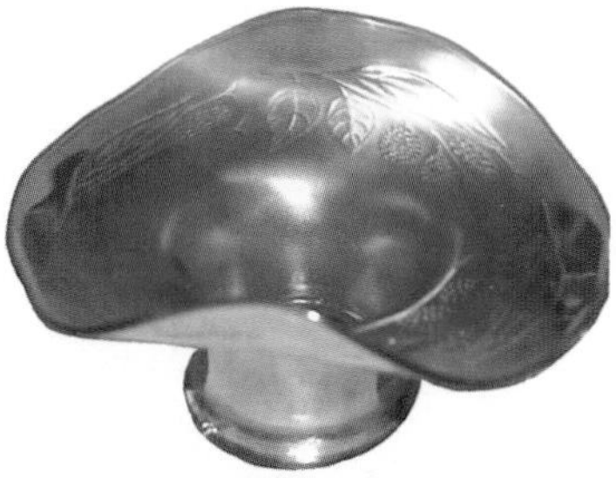

BLACKBERRY SPRAY
Golden

Composite from Original Catalog Reprint — Courtesy Of: The Fenton Art Glass Museum

Basket Weave with Open Edge Assortment Circa 1912

1092 · Flared
Pearl.
1091 Oval
Pearl.
1093 · Tulip ·
Pearl.
1093 Shallow
Pearl.

BLUEBERRY #1562 — Circa 1912

This early Fenton carnival water set features a large pitcher with a fancy scalloped top. Seven-piece water sets were advertised in 1914 at 55 cents per set. Pitchers are scarce and have only been found in golden and royal blue colors, but tumblers also exist in green and white carnival.

	Pitcher	Rarity	Tumbler	Rarity
Golden	$450.00 – 550.00	(4)	$45.00 – 55.00	(4)
Green			$90.00 – 110.00	(2)
Royal Blue	$850.00 – 950.00	(3)	$75.00 – 90.00	(3)
White			$110.00 – 120.00	(2)

BOGGY BAYOU (FENTON'S DRAPERY, REVERSE DRAPE AND FLORAL) — Circa 1910

This pattern was named "Fenton's Drapery" by William Heacock, but carnival glass collectors prefer to call it "Boggy Bayou." The carnival glass pieces are comprised of vases that range in size from 6" to about 15." Numerous vases exist in both iridized and opalescent colors. Opalescent plates, vases, and hat-shaped bonbons were also made by Fenton in this pattern. See examples of these items as "Fenton's Drapery" in the Early Opalescent Pattern Glass section, page 18. Fenton also claims a water set in this pattern (see the Enameled Water Sets section for shapes) that has also been called Reverse Drape and Floral. Other items such as a tall, narrow vase, rose bowl, and candy in a pattern also called Drapery are attributed to Northwood. Fenton vases have a series of eight arches. A similar vase called Pulled Loop was made by Dugan, but this vase has only five arches.

	Vase, 5"	Rarity	Vase, swung	Rarity
Golden	$50.00 – 70.00	(5)	$35.00 – 50.00	(5)
Green	$60.00 – 80.00	(3)	$120.00 – 145.00	(3)
Royal Blue	$100.00 – 120.00	(4)	$125.00 – 150.00	(4)
Violet	$95.00 – 110.00	(4)	$90.00 – 115.00	(4)

BLUEBERRY
Golden

BOGGY BAYOU
Golden

BOUQUET
Royal Blue

BUTTERFLIES
Green

BOUQUET
Royal Blue

BOUQUET (SPRING FLOWERS)

Bouquet water sets are found in golden and royal blue. The pitcher is bulbous with a crimped top. The embossing is typically strong, and the usual combination of brilliant iridescence produces a striking set.

	Pitcher	Rarity	Tumbler	Rarity
Golden	$250.00 – 280.00	(5)	$32.00 – 37.00	(5)
Royal Blue	$500.00 – 550.00	(3)	$45.00 – 50.00	(3)

BUTTERFLIES

Circa 1910

In the Butterflies pattern, eight butterflies form a circle around a single central butterfly. Bonbons have been found in various shapes (including a flat card tray-style), and some examples have Horlacher advertising around their base. This bonbon was produced in custard glass about 1915. Later in 1972 – 1973, it was produced in amethyst carnival. It made an appearance in orange carnival in 1973 and was made in red carnival in 1992. The bonbon was made in non-iridized colors such as Rosalene, Lime Sherbet, Blue Satin, and Custard in the mid-1970s. These later issues may be identified by the presence of the Fenton logo.

	Bonbon, 2-hdld.	Rarity	Bonbon w/advertising	Rarity
Golden	$45.00– 50.00	(5)	$100.00 – 120.00	(4)
Green	$60.00 – 70.00	(5)	$90.00 – 100.00	(3)
Royal Blue	$60.00 – 70.00	(4)		
Violet	$75.00 – 85.00	(5)	$110.00 – 125.00	(4)

BUTTERFLY AND BERRY #1124 (BUTTERFLY AND GRAPE) Circa 1911 – 1925

Butterfly and Berry was a large carnival line produced by Fenton in the early 1900s. Pieces may be found listed in catalogs as early as 1911 and as late as 1925. Included in the offering were a table set, a water set, and numerous accessory items. Rarely found colors include red, white, and amber. There are two sizes of the footed master berry. The larger 10" one is sometimes found with a Grape Wreath interior pattern, and the 8½" size will sometimes be decorated with a Fantail pattern on the inside. The 5½" berry is found both plain and with the Panther interior. The elongated vases were stretched from the tumbler mold. Most of the resulting heights were between 9" and 12". A ruffled top cuspidor was fashioned from the sugar bowl. The 9" vase was produced in custard glass about 1915. Some of these vases may be found with colored trim. A small 3-footed vase with a rolled top edge was made in ebony about 1919. The 8½" deep 3-footed bowl with the Fantail interior was re-issued in transparent pink in 1930. It appeared again in the line in 1974 in amethyst carnival. It was made in Cobalt Marigold Carnival in 1975, in Independence Blue in 1976, and in ruby iridescent from 1976 through 1977. Later in 1988, it was sold as a Fantail pattern bowl in topaz opalescent. The tumbler reappeared briefly in 1972 – 1974 in amethyst carnival. A handled Cobalt Marigold Carnival 5" basket was made from the tumbler in 1986. A top hat was produced from the tumbler mold in 1988 in topaz opalescent. A handle was also added to this hat to produce a basket. Colors made included topaz opalescent, Peaches and Cream, Minted Cream, Country Garden, Crystal Velvet, and Burmese. The large 3-footed bowl with the berry interior is currently being made for an importing company. New colors include cobalt, red, and a milky white clambroth-style color. This piece is not being made by Fenton and appears very crude in comparison to Fenton's glassware.

	Golden	Rarity	Green	Rarity	Red	Rarity	Royal Blue	Rarity
Bowl, 5½"	$30.00 – 35.00	(5)	$60.00 – 70.00	(5)	$800.00 – 1000.00	(2)	$50.00 – 60.00	(5)
Bowl, 10" 3-ftd	$90.00 – 100.00	(5)	$200.00 – 240.00	(4)	$150.00 – 175.00	(5)		
Bowl, 8½" 3-ftd.	$70.00 – 80.00	(5)			$100.00 – 125.00	(5)		
Butter	$130.00 – 150.00	(5)	$250.00 – 300.00	(3)	$170.00 – 200.00	(4)		
Creamer	$55.00 – 65.00	(5)	$120.00 – 150.00	(3)	$85.00 – 95.00	(5)		
Cuspidor							$2000.00+	(2)
Fernery	$750.00 – 850.00	(3)			$1000.00 – 1200.00	(2)		
Hatpin holder	$1100.00 – 1400.00	(1)			$1600.00 – 1800.00	(1)		
Pitcher, ½ gal.	$200.00 – 250.00	(4)	$800.00 – 900.00	(3)	$500.00 – 550.00	(4)		
Spooner	$60.00 – 75.00	(5)	$150.00 – 170.00	(3)	$80.00 – 90.00	(5)		
Sugar and lid	$80.00 – 95.00	(5)	$145.00 – 160.00	(3)	$120.00 – 140.00	(5)		
Tumbler, 8 oz.	$30.00 – 35.00	(5)	$90.00 – 110.00	(3)	$45.00 – 55.00	(5)		
Vase, 9"-10"	$40.00 – 50.00	(5)	$160.00 – 180.00	(4)	$2000.00 – 2200.00	(2)	$70.00 – 90.00	(5)

	Brick Red	Rarity	Purple	Rarity	Violet	Rarity	White	Rarity
Bowl, 5½"	$600.00 – 800.00	(4)			50.00 – 55.00	(5)	$90.00 – 110.00	(4)
Bowl, 10" 3-ftd			$140.00 – 160.00	(5)	$150.00 – 170.00	(4)	$275.00 – 350.00	(2)
Bowl, 8½" 3-ftd.					$100.00 – 120.00	(4)		
Butter					$210.00 – 230.00	(3)		
Creamer					$95.00 – 115.00	(4)		
Cuspidor					$2000.00+	(2)		
Fernery					$900.00 – 1100.00	(2)		
Pitcher, ½ gal.					$500.00 – 600.00	(3)	$1000.00 – 1200.00	(1)
Spooner					$100.00 – 115.00	(4)		
Sugar and lid					$135.00 – 150.00	(3)		
Tumbler, 8 oz.					$70.00 – 80.00	(3)	$90.00 – 110.00	(4)
Vase, 9"-10"	$800.00 – 900.00	(3)			$75.00 – 95.00	(3)		

	Amber		Sapphire		Topaz	
Vase, 9"-10"	$750.00 – 800.00	(3)	$230.00 – 250.00	(4)	$170.00 – 190.00	(4)

Butterfly & Berry

Royal Blue

Golden

Golden

Golden

Red

Royal Blue

Golden

Green

Green

Green

Green

Catalog Reprint Composite
Courtesy Of:
The Fenton Art Glass Museum

#1124 Butterfly & Berry

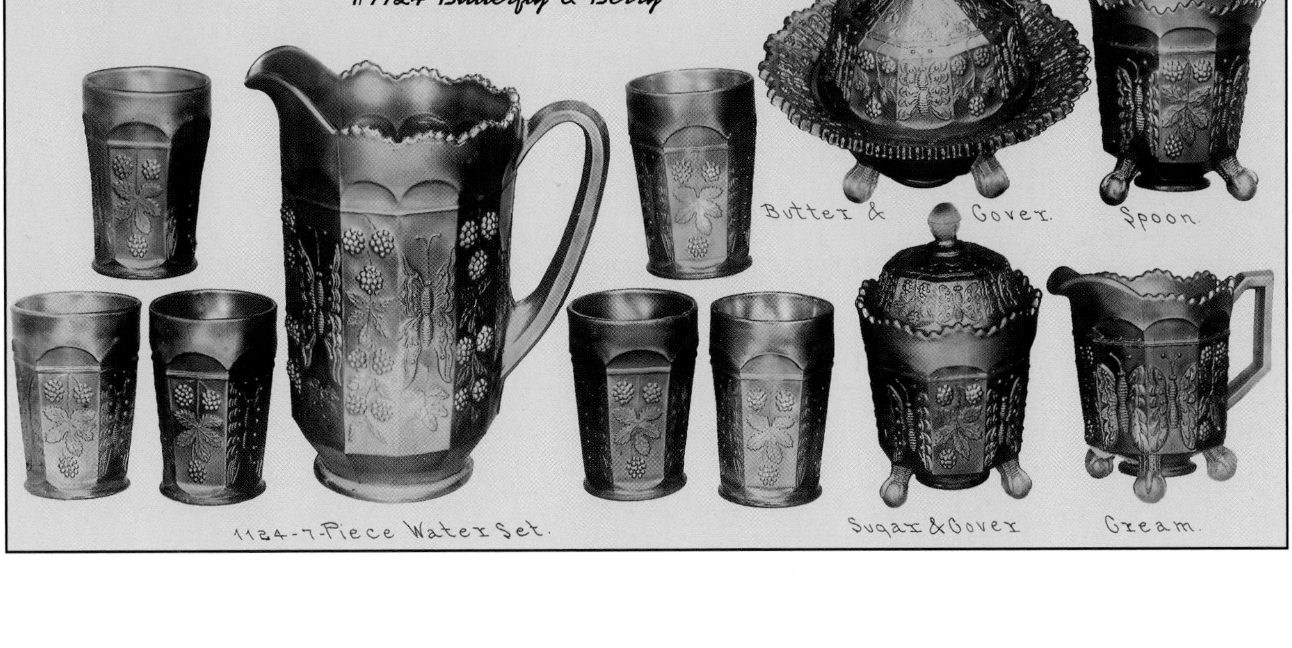
Butter & Cover.
Spoon.
1124-7-Piece Water Set.
Sugar & Cover
Cream.

BUTTERFLY & FERN #910

Water sets were the only items produced in this pattern. A few pitchers are known without the fern pattern.

	Pitcher	Rarity	Tumbler	Rarity
Golden	$220.00 – 260.00	(5)	$42.00 – 47.00	(4)
Green	$635.00 – 680.00	(2)	$75.00 – 85.00	(3)
Royal Blue	$600.00 – 675.00	(4)	$55.00 – 60.00	(5)
Violet	$400.00 – 450.00	(3)	$50.00 – 60.00	(4)

BUTTERFLY MINIATURE ORNAMENT — Circa 1918

This small ornament is listed in inventory records for 1917 and 1918. According to the accounts of those who remember the time, this was an item some florists included with the purchase of a plant. Old ornaments measure 3" across the wings and are scarce. New butterfly ornaments (which are much larger than the old ornaments) have been made in various colors for Fenton Art Glass of America, a club for collectors of Fenton glass.

	Ornament	Rarity		Ornament	Rarity
Golden	$900.00 – 1100.00	(2)	Aqua	$1800.00+	(1)
Green	$1200.00 – 1300.00	(2)	Ice Blue	$1500.00+	(1)
Royal Blue	$1100.00 – 1200.00	(2)	Topaz	$1400.00 – 1600.00	(2)
Violet	$1000.00 – 1200.00	(2)	White	$1800.00+	(1)

CANNON BALL VARIANT (Not illustrated)

This is an enameled water set with a white floral design. The matching tumblers are straight sided and have wide vertical panels. For an illustration, see the catalog reprint on page 10 that shows various enameled water sets. Some of these usual crystal sets were sometimes iridized and are now collected as carnival by some collectors.

	Pitcher	Rarity	Tumbler	Rarity
Golden	$200.00 – 245.00	(5)	$35.00 – 45.00	(5)
Royal Blue	$250.00 – 300.00	(4)	$65.00 – 75.00	(4)
White	$500.00 – 600.00	(2)	$135.00 – 175.00	(2)

CAPTIVE ROSE

Inspired by old fashioned lace work, this pattern consists of fancy embroidery circles and lace designs which conspire to decorate assorted sizes of bowls, comports, and plates.

	Bonbon	Rarity	Bowl, 8-10"	Rarity	Comport	Rarity
Golden	$60.00 – 70.00	(4)	$65.00 – 75.00	(4)	$50.00 – 60.00	(4)
Green	$90.00 – 120.00	(3)	$100.00 – 110.00	(5)	$90.00 – 100.00	(5)
Violet	$60.00 – 70.00	(5)	$85.00 – 95.00	(5)	$60.00 – 70.00	(5)
Amber	$90.00 – 110.00	(3)				
White	$220.00 – 240.00	(3)				

	Plate, 7"	Rarity	Plate, 9"	Rarity
Golden	$130.00 – 150.00	(4)	$300.00 – 350.00	(3)
Green	$170.00 – 190.00	(4)	$700.00 – 850.00	(3)
Royal Blue	$180.00 – 200.00	(4)	$475.00 – 550.00	(4)
Violet	$180.00 – 200.00	(4)	$600.00 – 700.00	(3)
White	$320.00 – 370.00	(3)		

CHERRIES AND BLOSSOMS (Cannon ball shape) — Circa 1910

This pattern consists of a water set with a bulbous pitcher and tumbler with a white enameled decoration.

	Pitcher	Rarity	Tumbler	Rarity
Royal Blue	$130.00 – 160.00	(5)	$20.00 – 25.00	(5)

BUTTERFLY ORNAMENT
Green

BUTTERFLY & FERN
Green

CAPTIVE ROSE
Golden

CHERRIES & BLOSSOMS
Royal Blue

SPECIAL SUNSET
IRIDESCENT LEMONADE
SET ASSORTMENT

Catalog Reprint
Courtesy Of:
The Fenton Art Glass Museum

No. 1109 _ VIOLET

No. 910 - GREEN

No. 1012 - ROYAL

CHERRY

Circa 1912

Cherry is the exterior pattern of the Mikado comport, and the pattern has also been found on an elusive banana boat shape bowl in golden and royal blue.

	Bowl, banana boat	Rarity	Comport	Rarity
Golden	$975.00 – 1200.00		$225.00 – 250.00	(5)
Green			$2200.00 – 2400.00	(2)
Red			$7000.00+	(1)
Royal Blue	$1000.00 – 1250.00	(4)	$400.00 – 450.00	(5)
Violet			$900.00 – 1000.00	(3)
White			$2500.00+	(1)

CHERRY CHAIN

Circa 1914

The Cherry Chain pattern may be found on various sizes of bowls, and plates. The design consists of an all-over pattern of small branches of cherries connected with a fancy ornamental cable. The exterior pattern is Orange Tree. Several new pieces have been made in recent years in both iridized and non-iridized colors. New pieces have an Orange Tree exterior. A 7½" bowl was made in Burmese and carnival in 1986, and a 10" crimped bowl was made in Teal Marigold in 1989. A handled 10" basket was made in Red Carnival in 1992.

	Bonbon	Rarity	Bowl, 6"	Rarity	Bowl, 9"	Rarity
Golden	$35.00 – 40.00	(5)	$35.00 – 40.00	(5)	$55.00 – 65.00	(5)
Green	$55.00 – 60.00	(5)			$95.00 – 120.00	(4)
Royal Blue	$50.00 – 60.00	(5)	$50.00 – 60.00	(5)	$80.00 – 95.00	(5)
Violet	$55.00 – 60.00	(5)	$55.00 – 60.00	(5)	$75.00 – 95.00	(5)
White	$120.00 – 140.00	(4)	$115.00 – 125.00	(4)	$125.00 – 150.00	(4)

	Plate, 6" – 7"	Rarity	Plate, 11"	Rarity
Golden	$95.00 – 115.00	(5)	$1500.00 – 1800.00	(1)
Green	$700.00 – 800.00	(1)		
Royal Blue	$120.00 – 140.00	(5)		
Violet	$600.00 – 700.00	(1)		
White	$180.00 – 200.00	(3)	$600.00 – 800.00	(2)
Clambroth			$250.00 – 300.00	(3)

CHERRY CIRCLES #1426 (CHERRIES AND HOLLY WREATH)

Circa 1921

Cherry Circles may be distinguished from Cherry Chain by examining the interconnecting cable between the bunches of cherries; the Cherry Circles pattern lacks the fancy curls contained in the Cherry Chain pieces. A card tray shape variation of this bonbon will be found.

	Bonbon, 2-hdld.	Rarity		Bonbon 2-H	Rarity
Golden	$45.00 – 55.00	(5)	Royal Blue	$65.00 – 75.00	(5)
Green	$90.00 – 110.00	(4)	Violet	$55.00 – 65.00	(5)
Red	$5000.00+	(2)	Aqua	$300.00 – 350.00	(2)

CHRYSANTHEMUM (WINDMILL AND MUMS)

Circa 1914 – 1924

Fenton made large 9" and 11" bowls in this pattern. A large Chrysanthemum chop plate with a Greek Key border was produced by Imperial. The Imperial plate will sometimes be signed "NU-ART."

	Bowl, 9"	Rarity	Bowl, 11" 3-ftd.	Rarity
Golden	$80.00 – 90.00	(5)	$75.00 – 95.00	(5)
Green	$135.00 – 155.00	(5)	$200.00 – 250.00	(4)
Red	$5000.00 – 5500.00	(2)		
Royal Blue	$110.00 – 135.00	(5)	$150.00 – 175.00	(5)
Violet	$110.00 – 130.00	(5)	$145.00 – 160.00	(5)
Black Amethyst			$550.00 – 650.00	(3)
Topaz			$225.00 – 250.00	(4)

CHERRY
Royal Blue

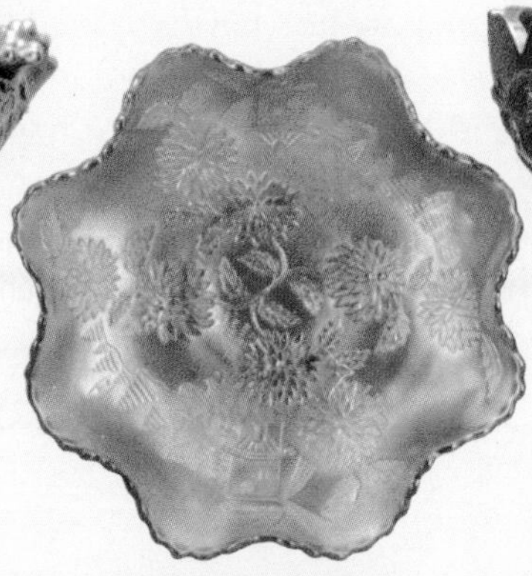

CHRYSANTHEMUM
Red

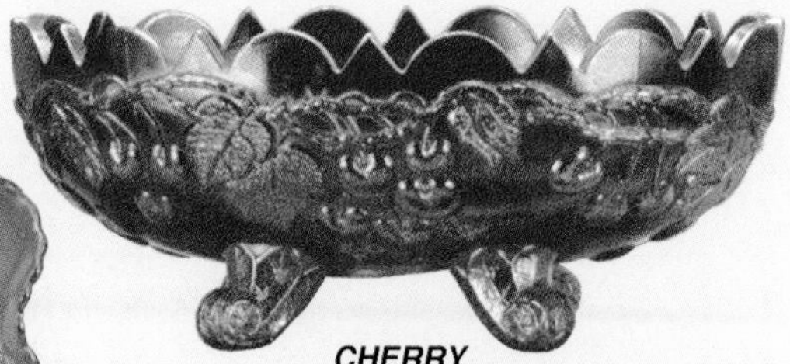

CHERRY
Royal Blue

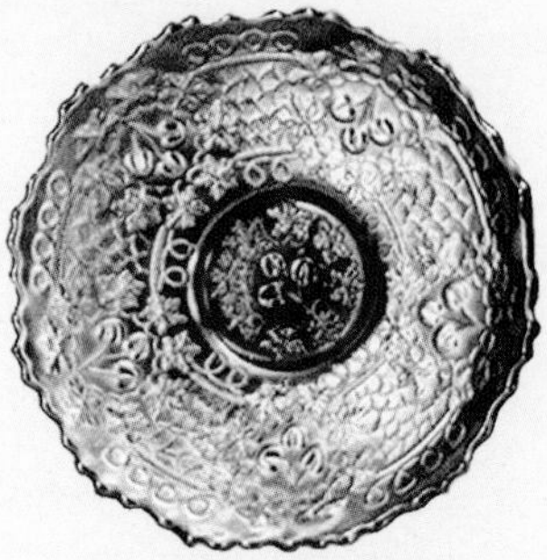

CHERRY CHAIN
Royal Blue

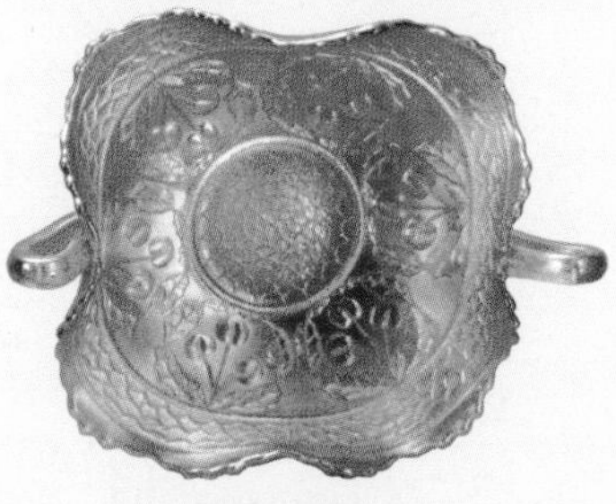

CHERRY CIRCLES
Golden

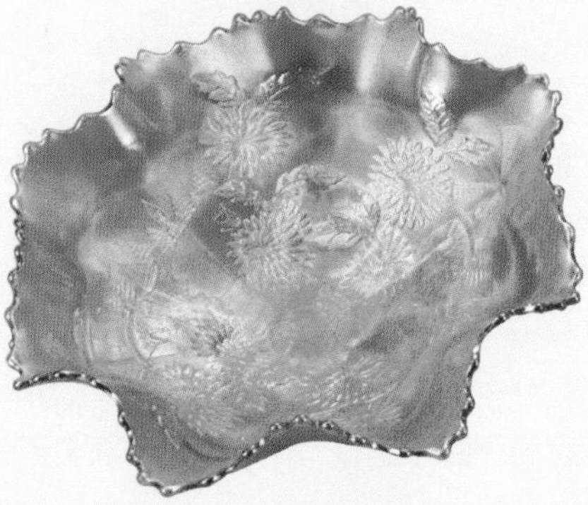

CHRYSANTHEMUM
Golden

CHERRY CIRCLES
Golden

Computer Colorized Catalog Reprint Courtesy Of: **The Fenton Art Glass Museum**

919-FLARED

919-CRIMPED

919-SHALLOW

HIGH FOOTED ORANGE BOWL ASSORTMENT
Golden and Royal Blue. Diameter 10″. Height 7″.

COIN DOT

This pattern is very similar to a Coin Dot pattern produced by Westmoreland. However, the dots in Fenton pieces are stippled, and the Westmoreland items do not have stippled dots. Many of the blue opalescent pieces were probably made by Westmoreland. Both sizes of bowls may be found with a crimped or smooth edge. There are two sizes of rose bowls. The smaller one measures about 5" in diameter and has been selling for about 10% more than the larger rose bowl.

	Bowl, 6"	Rarity	Bowl, 9½"	Rarity	Pitcher	Rarity
Golden	$25.00 – 30.00	(5)	$35.00 – 40.00	(5)	$350.00 – 400.00	(3)
Green	$40.00 – 50.00	(5)	$40.00 – 50.00	(5)	$525.00 – 575.00	(3)
Red	$1100.00 – 1200.00	(2)	$1100.00 – 1300.00	(5)		
Royal Blue	$45.00 – 50.00	(5)	$35.00 – 40.00	(5)	$500.00 – 550.00	(3)
Violet	$40.00 – 50.00	(5)	$40.00 – 50.00	(5)	$500.00 – 550.00	(3)

	Plate, 8"	Rarity	Rose Bowl	Rarity	Tumbler	Rarity
Golden	$240.00 – 270.00	(3)	$65.00 – 75.00	(5)	$200.00 – 225.00	(3)
Green	$325.00 – 375.00	(3)	$120.00 – 140.00	(4)	$300.00 – 325.00	(3)
Red			$1800.00 – 2000.00	(2)		
Royal Blue	$325.00 – 375.00	(3)			$250.00 – 300.00	(3)
Violet	$300.00 – 350.00	(3)	$90.00 – 110.00	(5)	$250.00 – 300.00	(3)
Topaz			$90.00 – 100.00	(4)		

CONCORD #1036 (LATTICED GRAPE; CONCORD GRAPE) — Circa 1911

The Concord pattern consists of large bowls and plates which are elusive. The design features grapes against a fine lattice background.

	Bowl, 9"	Rarity	Plate, 10"	Rarity
Golden	$300.00 – 350.00	(3)	$1700.00 – 2000.00	(3)
Green	$450.00 – 500.00	(3)	$3000.00 – 4000.00	(2)
Royal Blue	$240.00 – 280.00	(3)		
Violet	$255.00 – 285.00	(3)	$2800.00 – 3500.00	(2)
Amber	$350.00 – 400.00	(3)	$2000.00 – 2500.00	(1)

CORAL

The Coral pattern background is similar to Little Fishes and Peter Rabbit. This probably was not a very popular pattern since pieces are scarce.

	Bowl, 9"	Rarity	Comport	Rarity	Plate, 9½"	Rarity
Golden	$160.00 – 180.00	(5)	$400.00 – 500.00	(1)	$1000.00 – 1200.00	(2)
Green	$260.00 – 290.00	(2)				
Royal Blue	$345.00 – 380.00	(2)				

COSMOS VARIANT (COSMOS)

In this pattern, large bowls are found more frequently than the somewhat elusive 10" plates. This pattern has been attributed to Fenton by researchers, but there is no catalog proof to document this assignment.

	Bowl, 9"	Rarity	Plate, 10"	Rarity
Golden	$35.00 – 40.00	(5)	$140.00 – 160.00	(3)
Royal Blue	$70.00 – 75.00	(5)		
Violet	$60.00 – 65.00	(5)	$200.00 – 220.00	(2)

DAISY CUT BELL (NEAR-CUT BELL) — Circa 1912

The 6" tall Daisy Cut Bell is golden with a clear handle. It was listed as a "tea bell" in old trade catalogs.

	Bell	Rarity
Golden	$400.00 – 500.00	(3)

DIAMOND AND RIB #504 (DIAMOND AND THUMBPRINT) — Circa 1911

The Diamond and Rib pattern consists of a large diameter jardiniere and swung vases of assorted sizes. The large diameter funeral vase is hard to find and very expensive. Smaller diameter tall vases are not commanding extremely high prices.

	Jardiniere, 6"	Rarity	Vase, 8"–12"	Rarity	Funeral Vase, 18"–21"	Rarity
Golden	$1100.00 – 1400.00	(3)	$35.00 – 40.00	(5)	$700.00 – 900.00	(3)
Green	$1200.00 – 1400.00	(1)	$55.00 – 60.00	(5)	$1300.00 – 1500.00	(3)
Royal Blue			$60.00 – 75.00	(5)	$1200.00 – 1400.00	(3)
Violet	$1400.00+	(2)	$50.00 – 60.00	(5)	$1000.00 – 1200.00	(3)
White			$95.00 – 115.00	(4)	$1200.00 – 1400.00	(3)

DIAMOND POINT COLUMNS

This Fenton pattern features vases that have alternating vertical columns of ribs and diamond points. The diameter at the base is about 3½", and the smaller sizes start at about 5" in height. Larger vases may be swung to about 12" high. A swung carnival version of this vase was made in 1973. Vases from this later issue will have the Fenton logo on the bottom.

	Vase, 6"	Rarity	Vase, 7"–12"	Rarity
Golden	$35.00 – 45.00	(5)	$40.00 – 50.00	(5)
Green	$55.00 – 60.00	(5)	$55.00 – 70.00	(5)
Royal Blue	$85.00 – 95.00	(4)	$80.00 – 95.00	(4)
Violet	$40.00 – 50.00	(5)	$50.00 – 60.00	(5)
Lime Green	$70.00 – 85.00	(4)		

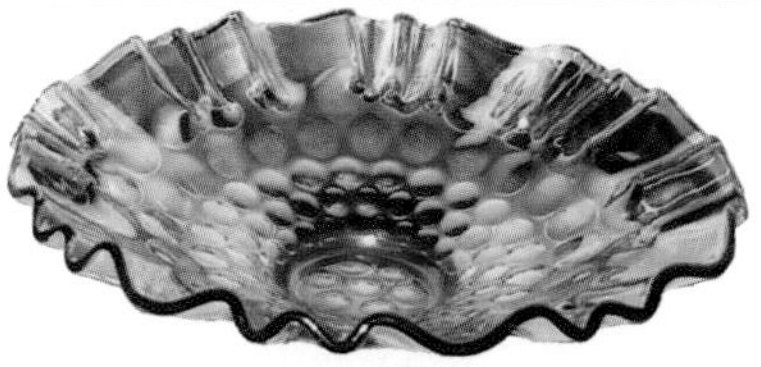
COIN DOT
Green

COSMOS VARIANT
Green

CONCORD
Green

DAISY CUT BELL
Golden

CORAL
Golden

DIAMOND POINT COLUMNS
Golden

DIAMOND AND RIB
Violet

DIAMOND AND RIB
Green

DRAGON AND LOTUS #1656

Circa 1920

Dragon and Lotus is a popular Fenton pattern. Bowls are not very difficult to find in various colors, but all plates are scarce. The 9" bowl may be found in either footed or flat variations — flared, crimped, or cupped styles.

	Bowl, 9"	Rarity	Plate, 9½"	Rarity
Golden	$60.00 – 70.00	(5)	$2200.00 – 2500.00	(2)
Green	$180.00 – 220.00	(5)		
Red	$3500.00 – 4000.00	(4)	$8000.00 – 9000.00	(1)
Royal Blue	$100.00 – 120.00	(5)	$1800.00 – 2000.00	(2)
Violet	$110.00 – 125.00	(5)	$1500.00 – 1800.00	(1)
Amber	$150.00 – 175.00	(4)		
Amberina	$900.00 – 1200.00	(2)		
Aqua Opalescent	$2000.00 – 2200.00	(3)		
Gold Irid. over WMG	$1300.00 – 1500.00	(3)		
Lime Green	$225.00 – 270.00	(4)		
Lime Green Opalescent	$300.00 – 400.00	(4)		
Moonstone	$650.00 – 750.00	(3)		
Peach Opalescent	$300.00 – 350.00	(4)	$900.00 – 1100.00+	(1)
Topaz	$190.00 – 225.00	(5)		
Red Opalescent	$2500.00 – 3000.00	(2)		
Violet Opalescent	$1000.00 – 1200.00	(2)		

DRAGON AND STRAWBERRY (DRAGON AND BERRY)

Most pieces of Dragon and Strawberry are elusive. The pattern has been found on footed and flat bowls. The pattern of a dragon and a cluster of three strawberries alternates around the pieces.

	Bowl, 9" flat	Rarity	Bowl, 9½" footed	Rarity
Golden	$350.00 – 425.00	(5)	$350.00 – 395.00	(5)
Green	$800.00 – 900.00	(3)	$1600.00 – 1850.00	(2)
Royal Blue	$650.00 – 750.00	(4)	$600.00 – 650.00	(4)
Violet	$1800.00 – 2200.00	(1)	$1800.00 – 2200.00	(1)
Aqua Opal	$2400.00 – 2600.00	(2)		

DRAGON'S TONGUE

Circa 1914

An 11" footed bowl may be found infrequently in the golden color. Light shades have been found with golden iridescence over WMG and in a few pastel colors.

	Bowl, 11" ftd.	Rarity	Shade	Rarity
Golden	$800.00 – 950.00	(2)		
Gold Irid. over WMG			$95.00 – 110.00	(4)
Moonstone			$100.00 – 150.00	(4)
Peach Opalescent			$100.00 – 120.00	(3)

ELK, ATLANTIC CITY

Circa 1911

Elk commemorative items were made available to members at their conventions. There are three Atlantic City Elk pieces — a bell, a 7" bowl, and a plate.

	Bell	Rarity	Bowl	Rarity	Plate	Rarity
Green					$2500.00 – 2700.00	(1)
Royal Blue	$2000.00 – 2300.00	(1)	$980.00 – 1200.00	(2)	$1500.00 – 1800.00	(1)

ELK, DETROIT — Circa 1910

	Bowl	Rarity
Golden	$1400.00 – 1600.00	(2)
Green	$800.00 – 850.00	(3)
Royal Blue	$600.00 – 800.00	(3)
Violet	$800.00 – 1000.00	(2)
Purple	$600.00 – 700.00	(3)

ELK, PARKERSBURG — Circa 1914

	Bell	Rarity	Plate	Rarity
Green			$1700.00 – 1900.00	(1)
Royal Blue	$1800.00 – 2200.00	(1)	$1400.00 – 1700.00	(1)

ELK, PORTLAND — Circa 1917

As the price below indicates, this is the rarest of the Elk items with only one example known at the present time. Also it is the highest priced item in the realm of Fenton carnival glass.

	Bell	Rarity
Royal Blue	$20,000.00 – 23,000.00+	(1)

DRAGON & LOTUS
Royal Blue

DRAGON & LOTUS
Violet

DRAGON & LOTUS
Green

DRAGON & LOTUS
Red

DRAGON & STRAWBERRY
Violet

DRAGON'S TONGUE
Golden

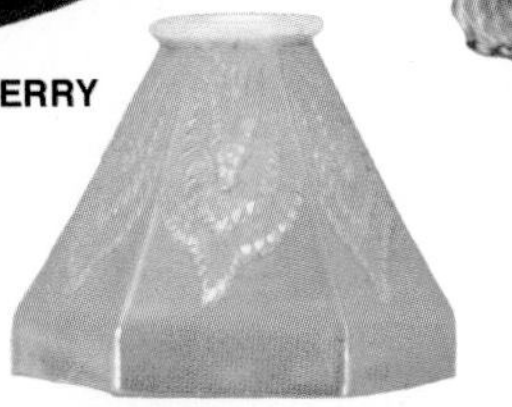

DRAGON'S TONGUE
Golden Iridescence over Milk

ATLANTIC CITY ELK
Royal Blue

ATLANTIC CITY ELK
Royal Blue

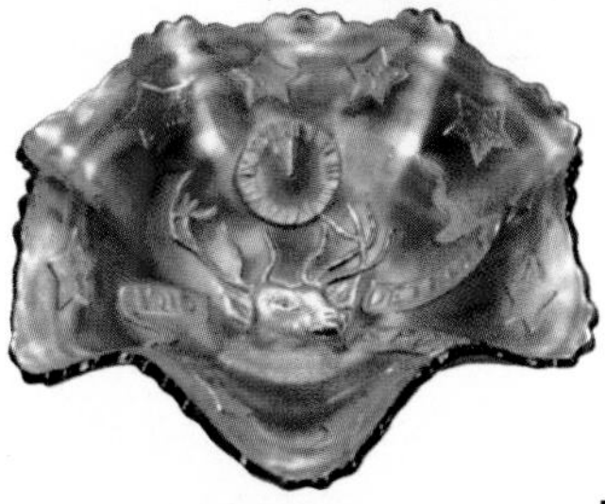

DETROIT ELK
Green

PARKERSBURG ELK
Royal Blue

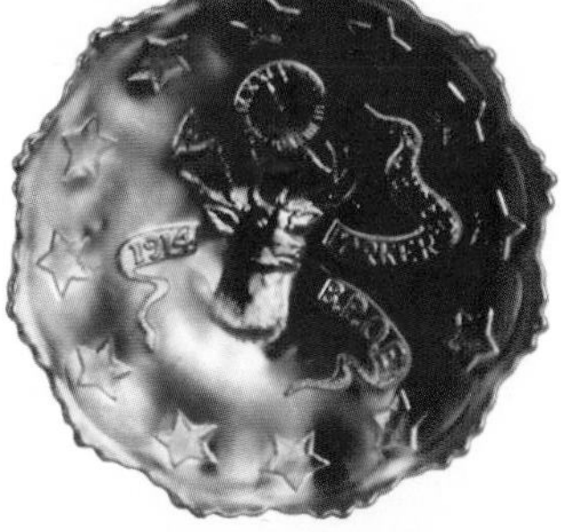

PARKERSBURG ELK
Royal Blue

FANTAIL (PEACOCK TAIL AND DAISY) — Circa 1911

Fantail may often be found as the interior pattern of Butterfly and Berry bowls. The pattern is formed from a series of peacock tails radiating from a central point which produces the appearance of a slowly rotating propeller. At the present time, only a few plates are known in the golden and royal blue colors.

	Bowl, 5"	Rarity	Bowl, 9"	Rarity	Comport	Rarity	Plate	Rarity
Golden	$75.00 – 85.00	(5)	$90.00 – 100.00	(5)	$100.00 – 125.00	(5)	$5000.00+	(1)
Green	$300.00 – 350.00	(4)	$290.00 – 320.00	(4)	$240.00 – 275.00	(4)		
Royal Blue	$200.00 – 250.00	(5)	$275.00 – 300.00	(4)	$200.00 – 250.00	(5)	$2000.00 – 2200.00	(2)
White	$150.00 – 200.00	(5)	$200.00 – 250.00	(4)				

FEATHER STITCH — Circa 1910

This pattern is similar in appearance to Coin Dot. Bowls varying in size from 8" to 10" and a 9¼" plate have been found.

	Bowl, 8"–10"	Rarity		Bowl, 8"–10"	Rarity
Golden	$50.00 – 60.00	(5)	Violet	$90.00 – 120.00	(5)
Green	$95.00 – 110.00	(5)	Aqua	$180.00 – 220.00	(3)
Royal Blue	$80.00 – 90.00	(5)			

FEATHERED SERPENT #437 (FEATHERED SCROLL) — Circa 1910

Berry sets are found with an exterior Honeycomb and Clover pattern. A green spittoon whimsey fashioned from a small berry bowl is also known.

	Bowl, 5½"	Rarity	Bowl, 9"	Rarity
Golden	$25.00 – 30.00	(5)	$65.00 – 75.00	(5)
Green	$50.00 – 60.00	(5)	$80.00 – 90.00	(5)
Royal Blue	$35.00 – 45.00	(5)	$55.00 – 65.00	(5)
Violet	$35.00 – 40.00	(5)	$65.00 – 75.00	(5)

FENTON'S FLOWERS #1401 (AURORA) — Circa 1911

This pattern has flowers which are very similar those of the Orange Tree pattern. The most noticeable difference between the two patterns is the band of leaves around the Fenton's Flowers pieces. The plate is rare. The rose bowl has been one of Fenton's most popular items for re-issue. It reappeared as the #8223 Leaf and Orange Tree rose bowl in August of 1970 in amethyst carnival. Orange carnival, blue satin, custard satin, and lime sherbet satin were also produced in 1973. It was made in Independence Blue in 1976 and in ruby iridescent and Rosalene in 1976 and 1977. The bowl was reissued in 1988 in the teal marigold color. The pattern was also used for the exterior of the Lion 8½" basket made in Red Carnival in 1994 and Spruce Carnival in 1999.

	Bowl, 6" flared	Rarity	Rose Bowl	Rarity
Golden	$40.00 – 50.00	(5)	$55.00 – 65.00	(5)
Green			$145.00 – 160.00	(5)
Red			$2000.00 – 2500.00	(4)
Royal Blue	$75.00 – 90.00	(5)	$60.00 – 70.00	(5)
Violet			$70.00 – 80.00	(5)

FENTON'S RIB #916 (FINE RIB)

Circa 1911

Swung vases from 9" to 11" high were made in this pattern. This pattern is also called Fine Rib. The 10" to 12" vase was reissued in 1930 in transparent green and pink. There are similar ribbed patterns made by Dugan and Northwood.

	Vase, 9"-12" swung	Rarity
Golden	$30.00 – 32.00	(5)
Green	$65.00 – 75.00	(5)
Red	$450.00 – 525.00	(4)
Royal Blue	$45.00 – 50.00	(5)
Violet	$65.00 – 75.00	(3)
Amberina	$100.00 – 120.00	(5)
Aqua	$70.00 – 80.00	(3)
Aqua Opalescent	$500.00 – 600.00	(2)
Celeste Blue	$180.00 – 220.00	(3)
Lime Green Opalescent	$450.00 – 550.00	(3)
Smoke	$325.00 – 375.00	(3)
Teal	$150.00 – 200.00	(4)
Topaz Opalescent	$300.00 – 350.00	(2)

FANTAIL
Royal Blue

FEATHER STITCH
Royal Blue

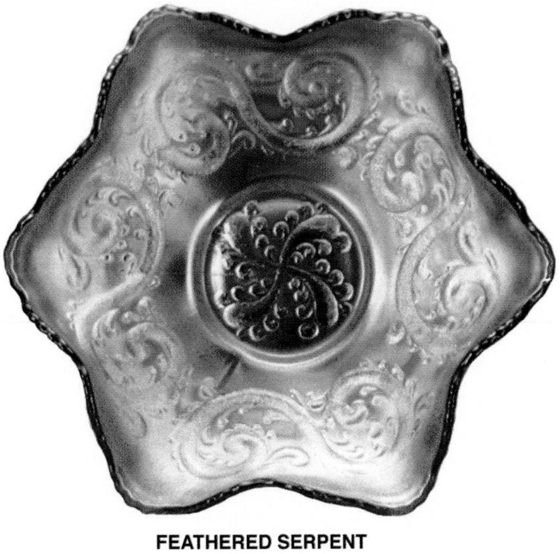

FEATHERED SERPENT
Green

FENTON'S FLOWERS
Golden

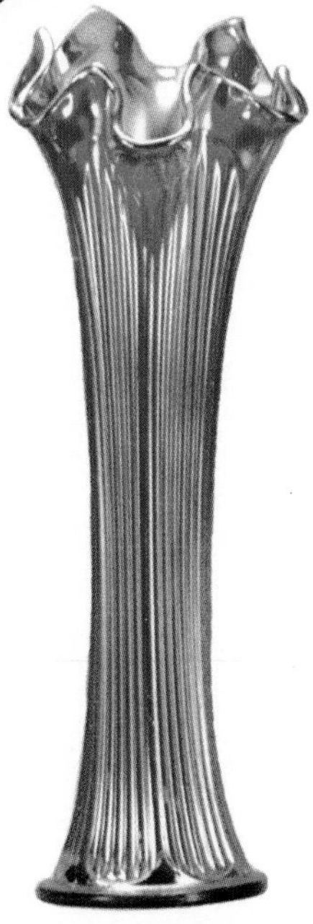

FENTON'S RIB
Red

FENTONIA (DIAMOND AND CABLE)

Circa 1913

Fentonia is a carnival glass pattern with a large number of pieces, most of which can be obtained at reasonable prices. Water sets and full table sets were made. Most items will be found in golden or royal blue, but some pieces were made in other colors.

	Golden	Rarity	Green	Rarity	Royal Blue	Rarity	Violet	Rarity
Bowl, 6" ftd.	$25.00 – 30.00	(5)	$40.00 – 45.00	(5)	$30.00 – 40.00	(5)	$40.00 – 50.00	(5)
Bowl, 10" ftd.	$60.00 – 70.00	(5)	$90.00 – 110.00	(5)	$150.00 – 170.00	(4)	$75.00 – 85.00	(5)
Butter	$100.00 – 120.00	(5)			$175.00 – 200.00	(5)		
Creamer	$60.00 – 70.00	(5)			$75.00 – 95.00	(5)		
Pitcher	$375.00 – 420.00	(5)			$595.00 – 650.00	(4)		
Spooner	$60.00 – 70.00	(5)			$75.00 – 95.00	(5)		
Sugar and lid	$80.00 – 90.00	(5)			$90.00 – 110.00	(5)		
Tumbler	$35.00 – 45.00	(5)	$75.00 – 85.00	(4)				

FENTONIA FRUIT #1134 (CHERRY AND SCALE)

Circa 1925

Fentonia Fruit is a variation from the Fentonia molds that has fruit replacing the diamond pattern. However, only berry sets and water sets were made in this pattern. The tumbler is especially hard to find and the vase is a whimsy. This pattern was also made in custard glass where collectors refer to it as Cherry and Scale.

	Bowl, 6" ftd.	Rarity	Bowl, 10" ftd.	Rarity
Golden	$45.00 – 55.00	(4)	$100.00 – 125.00	(4)
Royal Blue	$80.00 – 100.00	(4)	$130.00 – 150.00	(4)

	Pitcher	Rarity	Tumbler	Rarity	Vase	Rarity
Golden	$550.00 – 600.00	(2)	$140.00 – 160.00	(3)	$160.00 – 180.00	(1)
Royal Blue	$600.00 – 750.00	(1)	$250.00 – 300.00	(1)	$200.00 – 220.00	(1)

FERN PANELS

A hat-shape bonbon in various colors is the only piece that has been found in Fern Panels.

	Bonbon, hat-shape	Rarity
Golden	$30.00 – 40.00	(5)
Green	$65.00 – 75.00	(5)
Red	$425.00 – 500.00	(3)
Royal Blue	$45.00 – 50.00	(5)
Amber	$65.00 – 75.00	(5)
Golden Irid over WMG	$220.00 – 240.00	(4)

FLORAL & GRAPE VARIANT #1012

Circa 1911

Water sets are the only items available in this pattern. A similar pattern called Floral and Grape was produced by Dugan. The easiest way to determine the maker is to examine the banded area. Dugan pieces have heavy horizontal bands above and below the vertical ribs. Fenton pieces lack this horizontal border.

	Pitcher	Rarity	Tumbler	Rarity
Golden	$140.00 – 160.00	(5)	$25.00 – 30.00	(5)
Green	$300.00 – 350.00	(3)	$65.00 – 75.00	(3)
Royal Blue	$240.00 – 270.00	(5)	$30.00 – 35.00	(5)
Purple	$240.00 – 260.00	(4)		
Violet	$200.00 – 240.00	(5)	$30.00 – 35.00	(5)
White	$290.00 – 335.00	(4)	$60.00 – 70.00	(3)

FLOWERING DILL (MICHIGAN BEAUTY)

Circa 1915

The Flowering Dill pattern was used only on a deep bonbon novelty. Numerous colors were made and edge shapes of the bonbon include tulip, hat, and flared crimped.

	Bonbon	Rarity		Bonbon	Rarity
Golden	$30.00 – 35.00	(5)	Aqua	$75.00 – 90.00	(5)
Green	$45.00 – 50.00	(5)	Golden Irid over WMG	$125.00 – 150.00	(4)
Red	$600.00 – 650.00	(3)	Moonstone	$150.00 – 175.00	(4)
Royal Blue	$35.00 – 40.00	(5)			

FENTONIA
Royal Blue

FENTONIA
Golden

FENTONIA
Golden

FENTONIA
Golden

FENTONIA
Golden

FENTONIA FRUIT
Royal Blue

FENTONIA
Golden

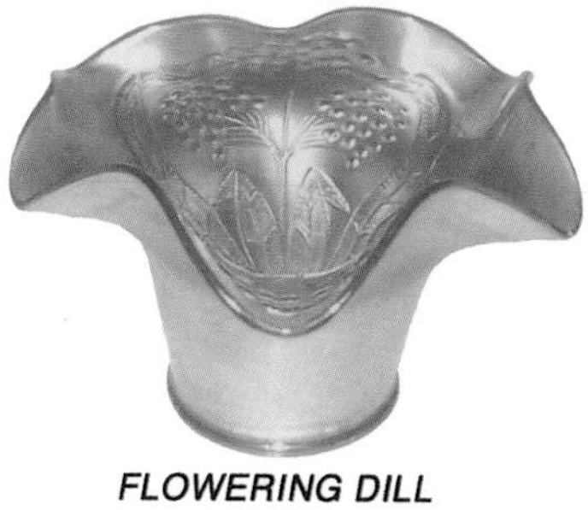

FLOWERING DILL
Golden

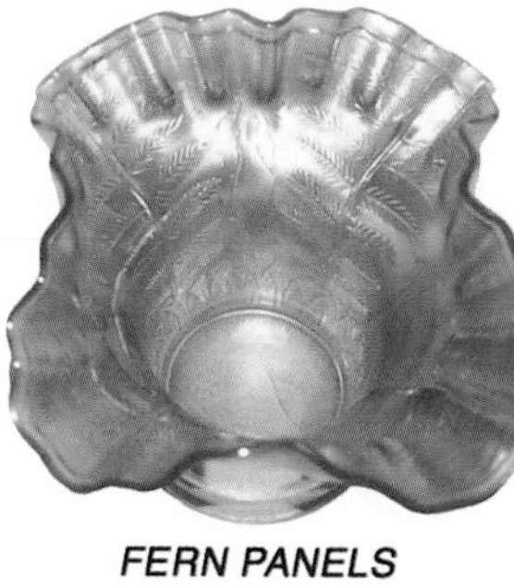

FERN PANELS
Golden

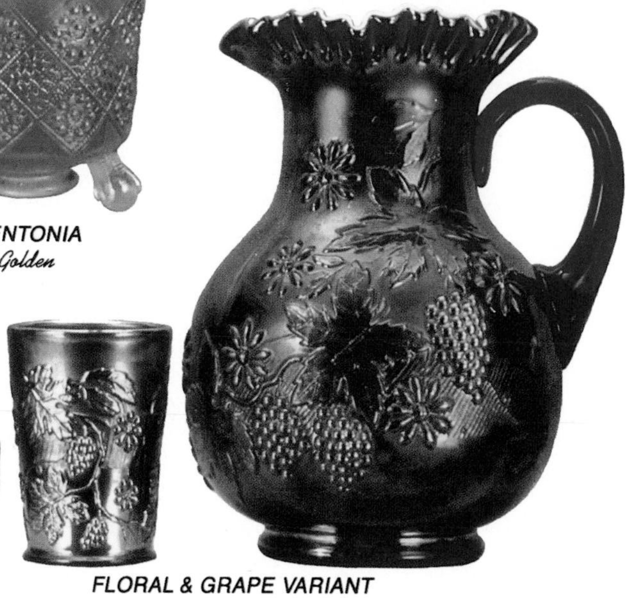

FLORAL & GRAPE VARIANT
Royal Blue

FLUFFY PEACOCK — Circa 1910

Fluffy Peacock is a pattern found only on water sets. The colors are usually vibrant, and the pattern is strong. This combination produces a very desirable set.

	Pitcher	Rarity	Tumbler	Rarity
Golden	$400.00 – 450.00	(5)	$45.00 – 50.00	(5)
Green	$700.00 – 800.00	(4)	$90.00 – 110.00	(4)
Royal Blue	$700.00 – 800.00	(4)	$65.00 – 75.00	(3)
Violet	$500.00 – 550.00	(4)	$60.00 – 70.00	(5)
Purple	$300.00 – 375.00	(4)		

FRENCH KNOTS

A hat-shaped bonbon is the only item found in the French Knots pattern. It is relatively common and inexpensive in all the brilliant colors.

	Bonbon, hat-shape	Rarity		Bonbon, hat-shape	Rarity
Golden	$30.00 – 35.00	(5)	Royal Blue	$35.00 – 45.00	(5)
Green	$45.00 – 55.00	(5)	Violet	$40.00 – 50.00	(5)

GARLAND #525 — Circa 1911

A three-footed rose bowl is the only piece adorned with this pattern of floral wreaths. Golden and royal blue are the most frequently found colors.

	Rose Bowl	Rarity		Rose Bowl	Rarity
Golden	$45.00 – 55.00	(5)	Royal Blue	$70.00 – 90.00	(5)
Green	$300.00 – 350.00	(2)	Violet	$295.00 – 325.00	(2)

GODDESS OF HARVEST

Goddess of Harvest is a very elusive pattern. The only pieces available are 9½" crimped bowls and plates.

	Bowl, 9½"	Rarity	Plate	Rarity
Golden	$5200.00 – 5800.00	(1)		
Royal Blue	$6800.00 – 7500.00	(1)		
Violet	$6800.00 – 7500.00	(1)	$10,000.00+	(1)

GRAPE AND CABLE (GRAPE) — Circa 1921 – 1925

Fenton's Grape and Cable pattern consists primarily of a variety of footed and flat bowls. The large 3-footed orange bowl may be found with a plain interior or with a Persian Medallion interior. It has also been found in golden and royal blue with advertising. Most of the smaller bowls will be found in two styles — cupped or flared crimped. This pattern is very similar to the Northwood and Dugan patterns with the same name. The easiest way to tell the two patterns apart is to look for the Northwood trademark — an "N" in a circle — which is present in many of the Northwood examples. The large 3-footed orange bowl is the only piece on which Fenton used the Grape and Cable pattern as an exterior pattern. The ribbed toes on the Fenton orange bowl are the easiest feature to distinguish the Fenton orange bowl from the Northwood orange bowl, which has plain toes. The smaller Fenton crimped bowl with the interior Grape and Cable pattern has bunches of grapes with the top row of grapes hanging over the right side of the bunch. A similar bowl made by Dugan has grapes with the top row hanging over the left side of the bunch. The golden plate on the right in the bottom row on page 61 is probably an example of Dugan Grape and Cable pattern.

	Bowl, 8" flat	Rarity	Bowl, 8½" 3-ftd.	Rarity	Bowl, 10" 3-ftd.	Rarity	Plate, 9" ftd.	Rarity
Golden	$45.00 – 55.00	(5)	$60.00 – 80.00	(5)	$110.00 – 125.00	(5)	$130.00 – 140.00	(5)
Green	$90.00 – 100.00	(5)	$100.00 – 120.00	(5)	$220.00 – 260.00	(5)	$165.00 – 190.00	(5)
Red	$800.00 – 1000.00	(4)	$1600.00+	(1)	$1600.00 – 2000.00	(2)		
Royal Blue	$70.00 – 80.00	(5)	$650.00 – 800.00	(3)	$200.00 – 250.00	(5)	$190.00 – 220.00	(4)
Violet	$60.00 – 70.00	(3)	$85.00 – 95.00	(5)	$200.00 – 250.00	(5)	$200.00 – 250.00	(5)
Amberina	$450.00 – 550.00	(2)						
Aqua Opal	$850.00 – 1000.00	(2)						
Blue Opal			$1500.00 – 1700.00	(3)				
Brick Red	$450.00 – 550.00+	(4)						
Ice Green							$700.00 – 800.00	(4)
Lime Green	$75.00 – 100.00	(4)						
Purple			$90.00 – 100.00	(5)				
Smoke			$175.00 – 225.00	(4)				
Topaz	$95.00 – 115.00	(3)	$100.00 – 150.00	(4)				
White	$140.00 – 180.00	(4)	$175.00 – 225.00	(4)				

FLUFFY PEACOCK
Violet

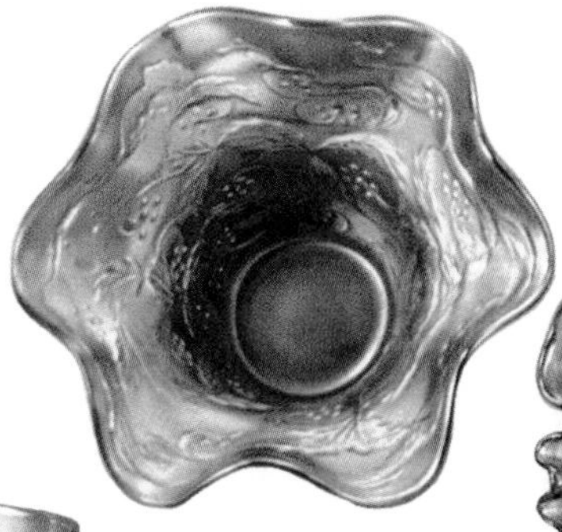

FRENCH KNOTS
Royal Blue

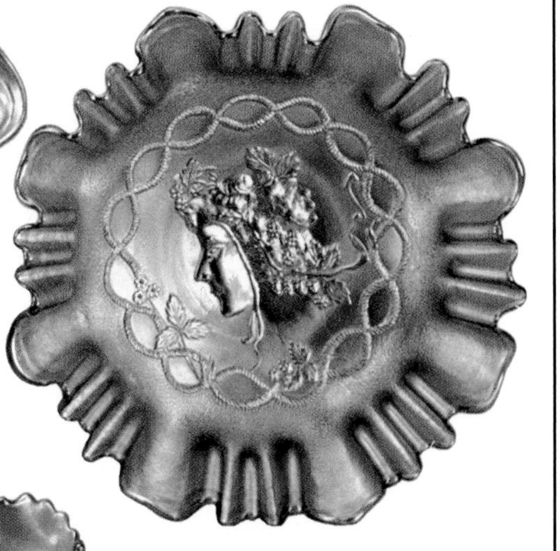

GODDESS OF HARVEST
Violet

GRAPE AND CABLE
Green

GRAPE AND CABLE
Violet

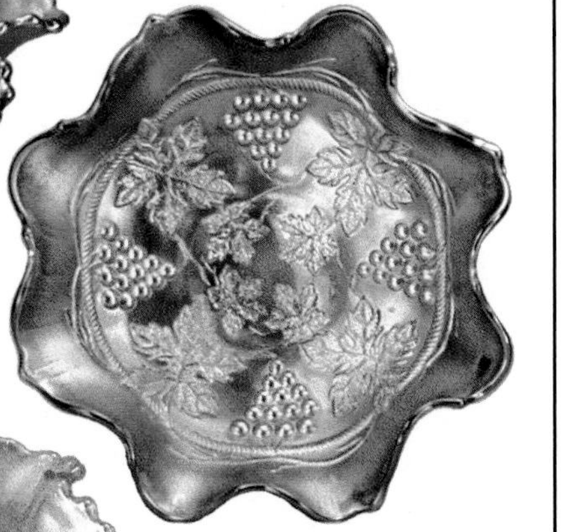

GRAPE AND CABLE
Violet

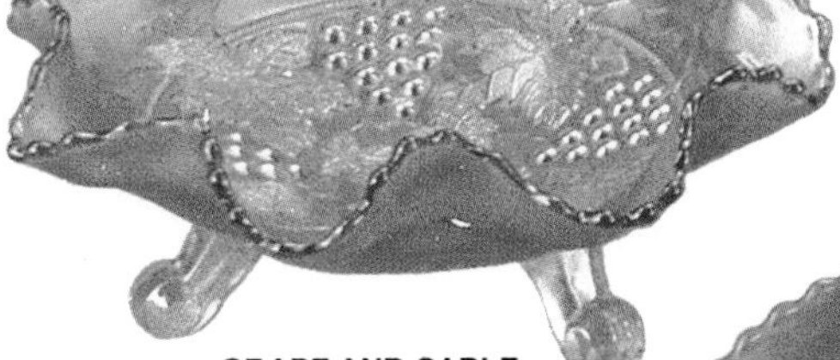

GRAPE AND CABLE
Golden

GRAPE AND CABLE
Green

GARLAND
Royal Blue

GRAPE AND CABLE
(DUGAN)

HEART AND HORSESHOE (FENTON'S GOOD LUCK)

Fenton modified the Heart and Vine pattern by adding a horseshoe and lettering to produce an elusive pattern called Heart and Horseshoe. Golden color bowls are scarce, and the possibility of a plate does exist.

	Bowl, 9"	Rarity
Golden	$1500.00 – 1800.00	(2)

HEART AND VINE

Bowls may sometimes be found with a Bearded Berry exterior, and the plate may be found with advertising. The 8½" bowl reappeared in 1973 in amethyst carnival. Newer pieces are marked with the Fenton logo.

	Bowl, 8½"	Rarity	Plate, 9"	Rarity
Golden	$80.00 – 90.00	(5)	$300.00 – 350.00	(3)
Green	$110.00 – 130.00	(5)	$400.00 – 500.00	(2)
Royal Blue	$100.00 – 120.00	(5)	$450.00 – 500.00	(2)
Violet	$120.00 – 140.00	(4)	$450.00 – 550.00	(2)
Purple	$250.00 – 300.00	(4)		

HEARTS AND TREES

This pattern is sometimes used as the interior pattern of footed Butterfly and Berry large 3-footed bowls. The Golden color is seen most often.

	Bowl, 8½" 3-ftd.	Rarity
Golden	$270.00 – 300.00	(3)
Green	$340.00 – 375.00	(1)
Royal Blue	$310.00 – 335.00	(2)

HEAVY HOBNAIL #517 — Circa 1911

This pattern consists of large hobnailed short vases which are the result of Rustic pattern vases which have not been swung. These vases are elusive.

	Vase, 5"-7"	Rarity
Violet	$600.00 – 675.00	(2)
White	$500.00 – 600.00	(2)

HEAVY PINEAPPLE

Although Fenton's Pineapple pattern is scarce in carnival, non-iridized examples from the 1930s are seen fairly often. The Pineapple pattern is found in numerous shapes in crystal satin, rose satin, and ruby, but the large 3-footed bowl is the only piece that has been found in carnival. This bowl is known with several different styles of crimping in Golden, Royal Blue, and white. For more information about non-iridized pieces, see the Satin Glass Patterns section of this book.

	Bowl, 3-ftd., 9"-11"	Rarity
Golden	$1000.00+	(1)
Royal Blue	$600.00 – 675.00	(3)
White	$500.00 – 600.00	(3)

HONEYCOMB AND CLOVER

Circa 1908

This pattern is used primarily as an exterior pattern for Feathered Serpent pieces. However, it has also been found as the main pattern on a comport and some bonbons. See the Early Opalescent Glass and Pattern Glass sections of this book for non-iridized examples of this pattern.

	Bonbon	Rarity	Comport	Rarity	Plate, 6"	Rarity
Golden	$40.00 – 45.00	(5)	$32.00 – 37.00	(5)	$290.00 – 335.00	(3)
Green	$55.00 – 65.00	(5)	$57.00 – 67.00	(5)		
Royal Blue	$50.00 – 60.00	(5)	$52.00 – 62.00	(5)		
Violet	$55.00 – 65.00	(5)	$47.00 – 57.00	(5)		
Amber	$70.00 – 80.00	(5)				

HONEYCOMB & CLOVER
Golden

HEARTS AND TREES
Golden

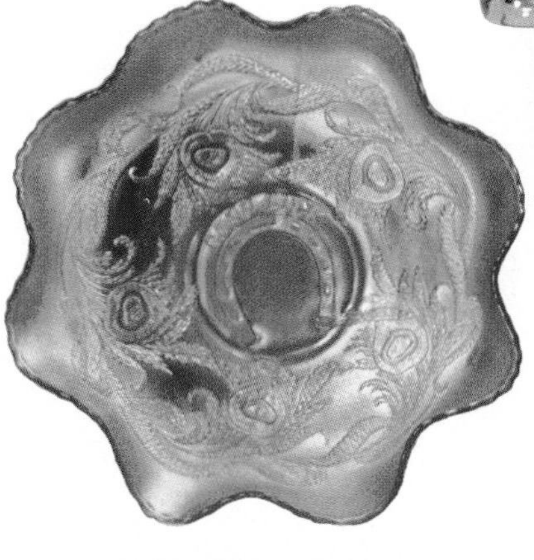

HEART AND HORSESHOE
Golden

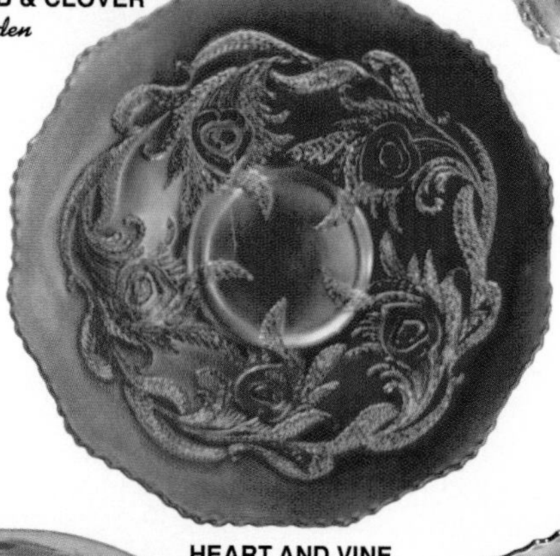

HEART AND VINE
Royal Blue

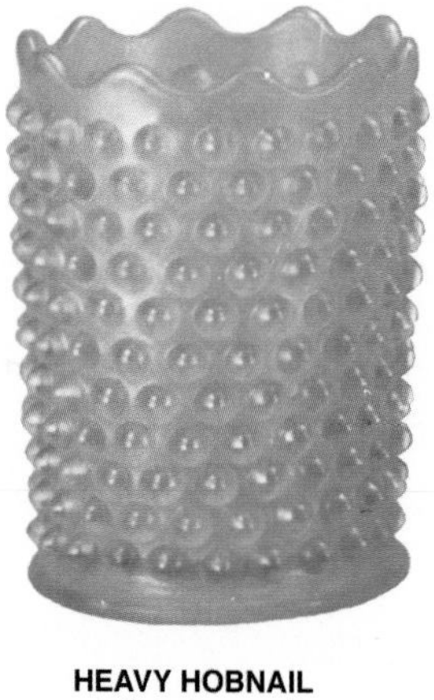

HEAVY HOBNAIL
White Carnival

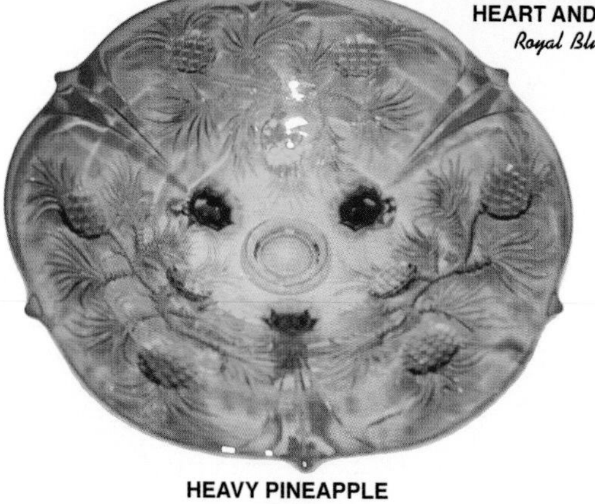

HEAVY PINEAPPLE
Golden

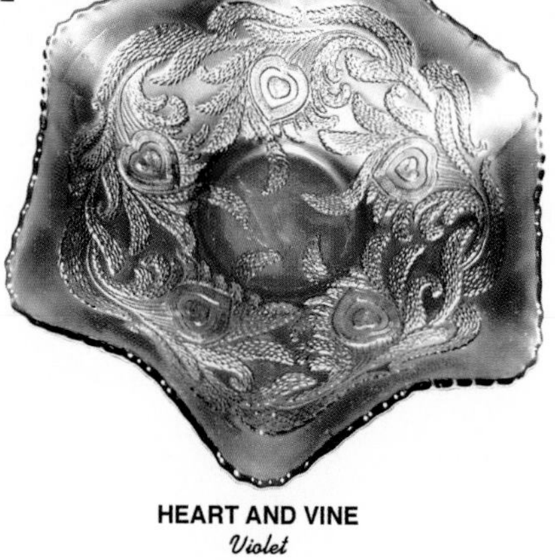

HEART AND VINE
Violet

HOLLY (HOLLY AND BERRIES)

Fenton's Holly pattern is very simple. Sprigs of holly are separated by wide spaces of brilliant iridescence. The top of the deep bonbon was pulled into several shapes — oval, tulip, square, and flared crimped. The larger bowls may have either a cupped, scalloped, or a flared crimped edge. One ice blue plate has surfaced. The 9¼" bowl was re-issued in 1930 in a transparent pink color. The 8¼" bowl was re-issued in 1971 in amethyst carnival. This bowl, with a handle attached to form a basket, was produced in Red Carnival for Fenton's 90th anniversary in 1995. A Red Carnival 9½" plate was made in the year 2000 to commemorate Frank M. Fenton's 85th birthday.

	Bonbon, 6⅛"	Rarity	Bowl, 8¼"	Rarity	Bowl, 9¼"	Rarity
Golden	$30.00 – 35.00	(5)	$65.00 – 75.00	(5)	$65.00 – 80.00	(5)
Green	$60.00 – 70.00	(5)	$90.00 – 110.00	(5)	$110.00 – 130.00	(5)
Red	$375.00 – 425.00	(4)	$1400.00 – 1600.00	(3)	$1600.00 – 1800.00	(3)
Royal Blue	$42.00 – 52.00	(5)	$85.00 – 95.00	(5)	$85.00 – 120.00	(5)
Violet	$37.00 – 42.00	(5)	$85.00 – 95.00	(5)	$85.00 – 100.00	(5)
Amber	$42.00 – 47.00	(3)	$100.00 – 130.00	(3)	$130.00 – 155.00	(3)
Amberina	$290.00 – 325.00	(2)	$750.00 – 850.00	(2)	$775.00 – 850.00	(2)
Aqua	$175.00 – 200.00	(3)	$300.00 – 350.00	(2)		
Blue Opal			$1300.00 – 1500.00	(2)		
Brick Red			$750.00 – 850.00	(4)	$700.00 – 800.00	(2)
Celeste Blue			$3000.00 – 4000.00	(1)		
Lime Green	$45.00 – 55.00	(5)	$100.00 – 150.00	(5)	$120.00 – 160.00	(4)
Golden Irid. over WMG			$600.00 – 700.00	(2)		
Moonstone			$350.00 – 500.00	(4)	$300.00 – 400.00	(4)
White			$175.00 – 195.00	(4)	$165.00 – 185.00	(4)
Topaz	$50.00 – 65.00	(3)	$180.00 – 220.00	(4)	$180.00 – 220.00	(5)

	Comport, flared	Rarity	Comport (goblet shape)	Rarity	Plate, 9½"	Rarity
Golden	$40.00 – 50.00	(5)	$40.00 – 45.00	(5)	$250.00 – 300.00	(5)
Green	$75.00 – 100.00	(5)	$75.00 – 85.00	(5)	$1100.00 – 1500.00+	(3)
Red	$700.00 – 800.00	(3)	$800.00 – 900.00	(3)	$2800.00 – 3200.00	(2)
Royal Blue	$50.00 – 60.00	(5)	$55.00 – 65.00	(5)	$325.00 – 375.00	(4)
Violet	$45.00 – 55.00	(5)	$50.00 – 60.00	(5)	$600.00 – 700.00	(4)
Amber	$110.00 – 130.00	(5)				
Amberina	$350.00 – 500.00	(4)				
Aqua	$90.00 – 110.00	(5)				
Clambroth					$130.00 – 150.00	(4)
Ice blue					$13,000.00+	(1)
Lavender	$150.00 – 200.00	(4)				
Lime Green	$75.00 – 90.00	(5)	$40.00 – 60.00	(5)		
Lime Green Opal	$550.00 – 650.00	(3)	$550.00 – 650.00	(3)		
Pink	$170.00 – 200.00	(4)				
Topaz	$75.00 – 100.00	(5)	$70.00 – 90.00	(5)		
White	$120.00 – 140.00	(5)	$90.00 – 110.00	(5)	$200.00 – 250.00	(4)

	Rose Bowl	Rarity	Vase, 6"	Rarity
Golden	$250.00 – 275.00	(3)		
Green	$1000.00 – 1100.00	(2)	$45.00 – 55.00	(5)
Red			$425.00 – 475.00	(4)
Royal Blue	$300.00 – 350.00	(2)		
Amber			$55.00 – 65.00	(5)
Amberina			$275.00 – 325.00	(4)
Aqua			$65.00 – 80.00	(5)
Brick Red			$325.00 – 375.00	(4)
Golden Irid. over WMG			$250.00 – 300.00	(3)
Lime Green			$55.00 – 65.00	(5)
Moonstone			$300.00 – 350.00	(3)
Teal			$65.00 – 80.00	(5)
Topaz			$100.00 – 120.00	(5)

Holly

Golden

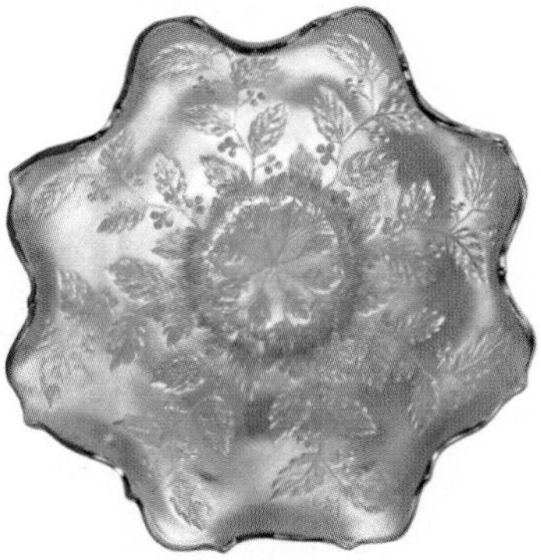

Green

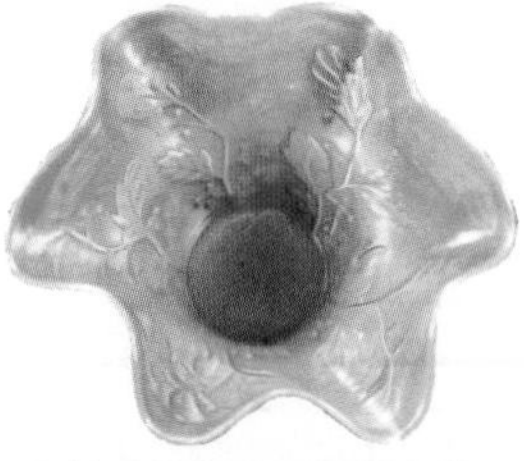

Golden Iridescence over Milk

White Carnival

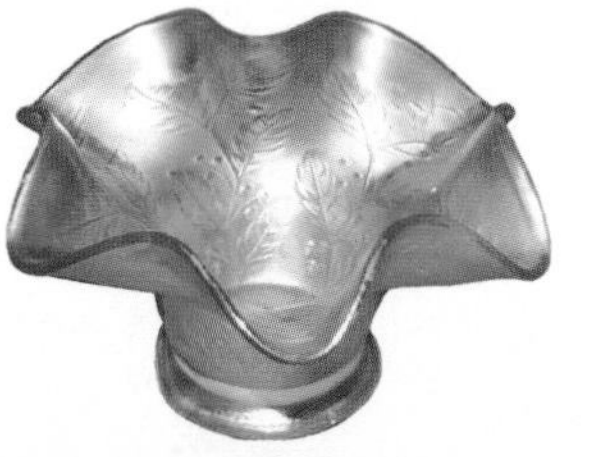

Golden

Royal Blue

Photo Below: Courtesy Of:

Holly Catalog Reprint Composite-Circa 1911 **The Fenton Art Glass Museum**

#508- 6 1/8" HOLLY
Tulip Bon Bon

#508- 6 1/8" HOLLY
Oval Bon Bon

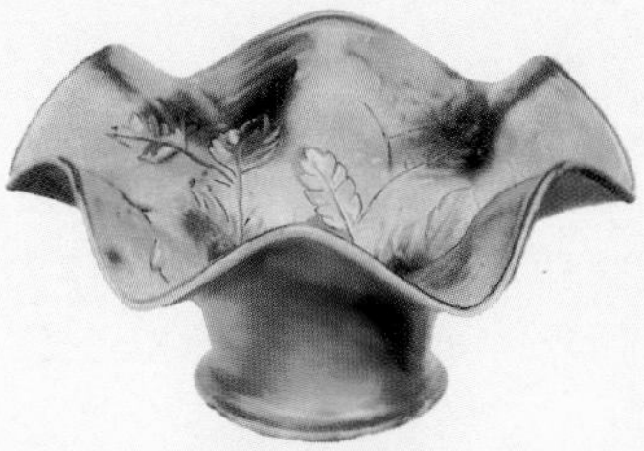

#508- 6" HOLLY
Crimped Violet Vase

208-Shallow Bowl-8½"

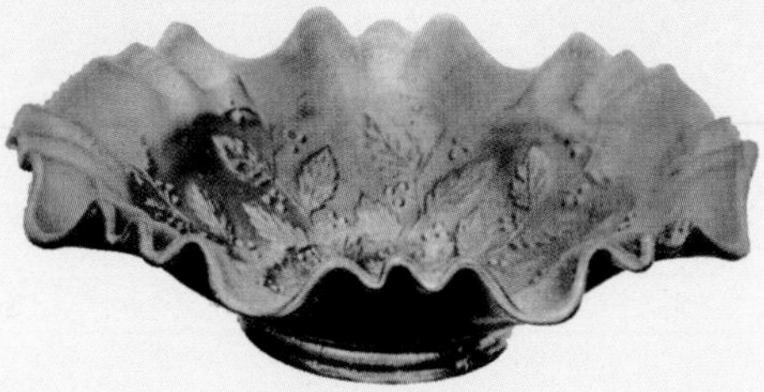

208-Fruit-9½"

208-Crimp Nappy-9"

HORSE MEDALLION #1665 (HORSES' HEADS) — Circa 1912 – 1920

Horse Medallion is sometimes referred to by the name Horses' Heads. There are a number of different size bowls in this pattern. An elusive plate and rose bowl may also be found. There are only two known plates in violet. The rose bowl is three footed and has the pattern on the inside of the bowl. Bowls may be flat or footed and were made in all the usual Fenton shapes — cupped, tulip and flared crimped. The 7½" plates and 7" bowls were produced in custard glass about 1915. They may also be found decorated with nutmeg or green trim. The 6½" deep-footed nut bowl was reissued in 1930 in a pink transparent color.

	Bowl, 6½" ftd. nut	Rarity	Bowl, 7½" ftd.	Rarity	Bowl, 7½" flat	Rarity
Golden	$100.00 – 130.00	(4)	$95.00 – 120.00	(5)	$70.00 – 90.00	(5)
Green	$250.00 – 290.00	(4)	$300.00 – 350.00	(4)	$300.00 – 350.00	(4)
Red	$1400.00 – 1600.00	(3)	$1200.00 – 1400.00	(3)	$1100.00 – 1300.00	(3)
Royal Blue	$140.00 – 160.00	(5)	$275.00 – 325.00	(5)	$200.00 – 250.00	(4)
Violet	$250.00 – 300.00	(4)	$200.00 – 250.00	(4)	$450.00 – 500.00	(3)
Amber	$140.00 – 175.00	(3)	$150.00 – 200.00	(3)		
Amberina					$500.00 – 600.00	(3)
Aqua	$380.00 – 425.00	(4)				
Brick Red	$1200.00 – 1400.00				$500.00 – 600.00	(3)
Celeste Blue			$2000.00+	(2)		
Topaz	$350.00 – 400.00	(4)	$225.00 – 275.00	(5)		
White			$400.00 – 450.00	(3)	$325.00 – 375.00	(4)

	Bowl, ftd. Tulip-style	Rarity	Plate, 8"	Rarity	Rose bowl	Rarity
Golden	$85.00 – 100.00	(5)	$250.00 – 300.00	(5)	$150.00 – 185.00	(5)
Green	$250.00 – 300.00	(4)				
Royal Blue	$120.00 – 140.00	(5)	$800.00 – 1100.00	(3)	$275.00 – 325.00	(4)
Red					$5000.00+	(1)
Violet			$3500.00+	(1)		
Teal	$250.00 – 300.00+	(4)				
Topaz	$225.00 – 250.00	(3)			$550.00 – 600.00	(4)

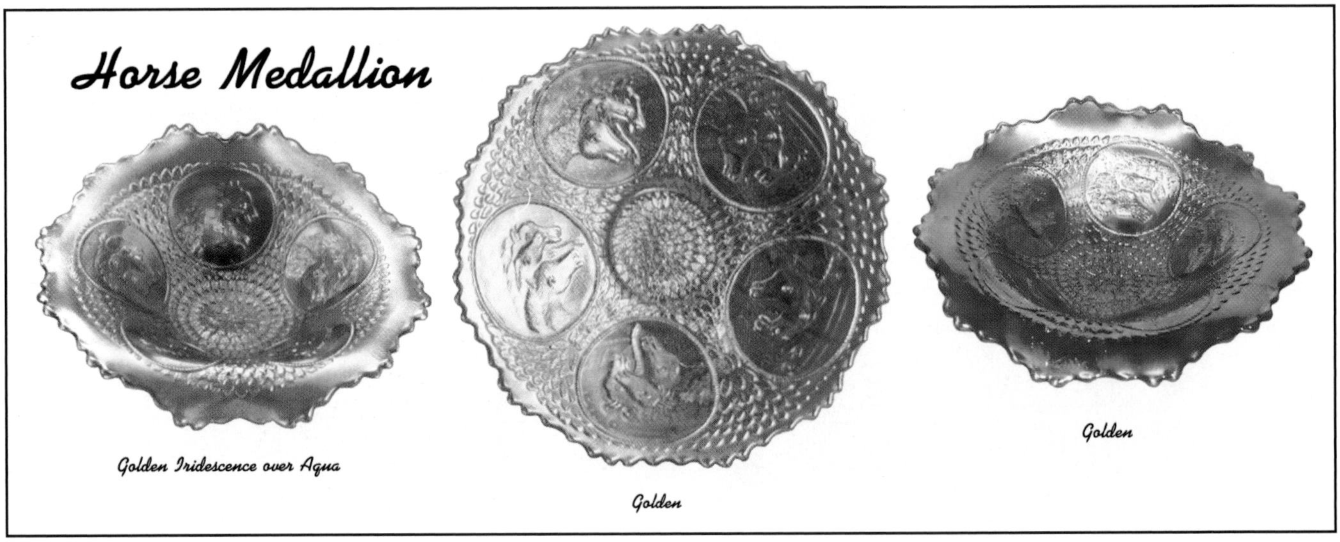

Golden Iridescence over Aqua

Golden

Golden

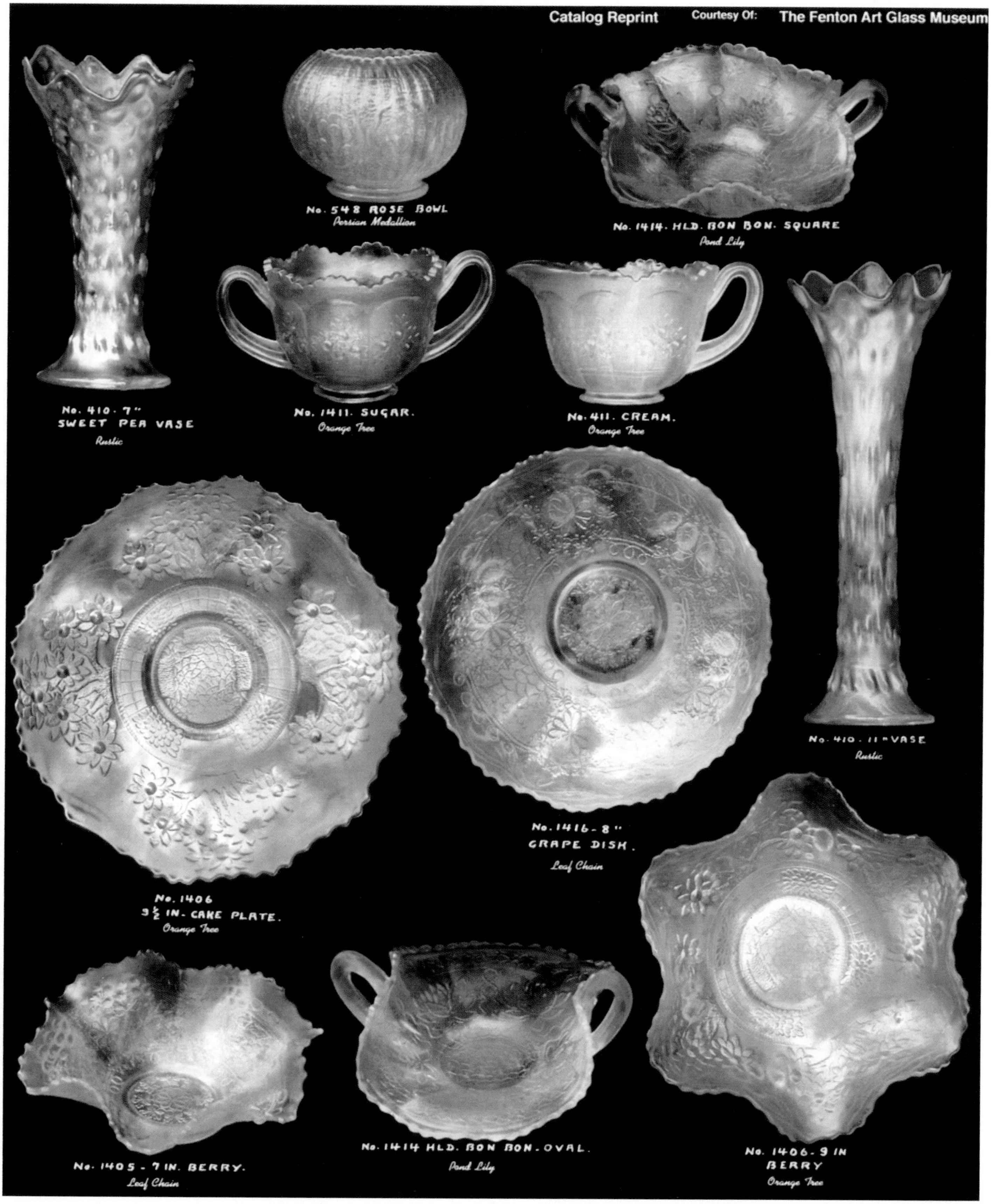
Catalog Reprint Courtesy Of: The Fenton Art Glass Museum

No. 548 ROSE BOWL
Persian Medallion

No. 1414. HLD. BON BON. SQUARE
Pond Lily

No. 410 - 7"
SWEET PEA VASE
Rustic

No. 1411. SUGAR.
Orange Tree

No. 411. CREAM.
Orange Tree

No. 410 - 11" VASE
Rustic

No. 1416 - 8"
GRAPE DISH.
Leaf Chain

No. 1406
9½ IN. CAKE PLATE.
Orange Tree

No. 1405 - 7 IN. BERRY.
Leaf Chain

No. 1414 HLD. BON BON. OVAL.
Pond Lily

No. 1406 - 9 IN
BERRY
Orange Tree

IDYLL (WATERLILY AND CATTAIL WITH BUTTERFLY)

Although carnival glass collectors prefer the name "Idyll" for this scarce vase, it is more appropriately cataloged with Fenton's Water Lily and Cattails group. This 7" tall vase has been found in the Golden and violet carnival colors. Another vase in chocolate in this pattern is pictured on page 29.

	Vase, 7"	Rarity
Golden	$550.00 – 650.00	(2)
Violet	$800.00 – 900.00	(2)

ILLINOIS SOLDIERS AND SAILORS HOME

These Fenton 8" plates feature the Illinois Soldiers' and Sailors' Home of Quincy, Ill. on the top side and have a Berry and Leaf Circle reverse side. Plates were made in Golden and Royal Blue.

	Plate	Rarity
Golden	$1600.00 – 2200.00	(1)
Royal Blue	$2000.00 – 2500.00	(1)

ILLUSION (FENTON'S ARABIC)

Illusion is a floral pattern well endowed with leaves which appears primarily on bonbons, but bowls were also made.

	Bonbon	Rarity	Bowl	Rarity
Golden	$45.00 – 55.00	(5)	$55.00 – 65.00	(5)
Royal Blue	$75.00 – 90.00	(5)	$75.00 – 85.00	(5)

INDIANA SOLDIERS AND SAILORS MONUMENT (Not illustrated)

This Royal Blue carnival rarity depicts the monument from the downtown circle of Indianapolis, Indiana, on the top side and has a Berry and Leaf Circle pattern on the reverse side.

	Plate	Rarity
Golden	$16,000.00+	(1)
Royal Blue	$10,000.00+	(1)

INDIANA STATE HOUSE PLATE

This rare plate features the Indiana State House on the front side and has the Berry and Leaf Circle pattern on the reverse side.

	Plate	Rarity
Golden	$16,000.00+	(1)
Royal Blue	$10,000.00 – 12,000.00	(1)

IRIS

Circa 1910

The Iris pattern consists of buttermilk goblets and small comports. The buttermilk goblet with a floral Iris interior may be found with a clear stem with a golden bowl. This goblet will also be found in a blank version without the Iris pattern

	Comport	Rarity	Goblet, buttermilk	Rarity
Golden	$40.00 – 50.00	(5)	$55.00 – 65.00	(5)
Green	$70.00 – 80.00	(5)	$75.00 – 85.00	(5)
Royal Blue	$150.00 – 200.00	(5)		
Violet	$75.00 – 85.00	(5)	$45.00 – 65.00	(5)
White	$300.00 – 400.00	(3)		
Amber			$75.00 – 85.00	(5)

KITTENS #299

Circa 1918

Kittens is a carnival children's toy pattern with a plate, cup, saucer, spooner, and various shaped bowls. The 3½" cereal bowl is round with a smooth top. The 4½" bowl has a variety of shapes. With two sides up, it forms a banana boat. With four sides up, it may be square or flared with a round and crimped top. A vase (or cuspidor) which was probably fashioned from the cereal bowl is also known to exist.

Kittens	Bowl, 3½"	Rarity	Bowl, 4½"	Rarity	Cup	Rarity
Golden	$225.00 – 270.00	(5)	$175.00 – 200.00	(5)	$120.00 – 140.00	(5)
Royal Blue	$625.00 – 675.00	(4)	$550.00 – 625.00	(4)	$350.00 – 400.00	(2)
Violet			$450.00 – 500.00	(3)		
Aqua			$475.00 – 550.00	(4)		
Lavender	$550.00 – 650.00	(3)				
Teal	$550.00 – 600.00	(4)				

Kittens	Plate, 4"	Rarity	Saucer	Rarity	Vase	Rarity
Golden	$250.00 – 300.00	(5)	$120.00 – 160.00	(5)	$220.00 – 260.00	(5)
Royal Blue	$375.00 – 425.00	(4)	$1000.00+	(2)	$400.00 – 450.00	(4)
Aqua			$250.00 – 275.00	(4)		
Topaz					$500.00 – 550.00	(3)

INDIANA STATE HOUSE
Golden

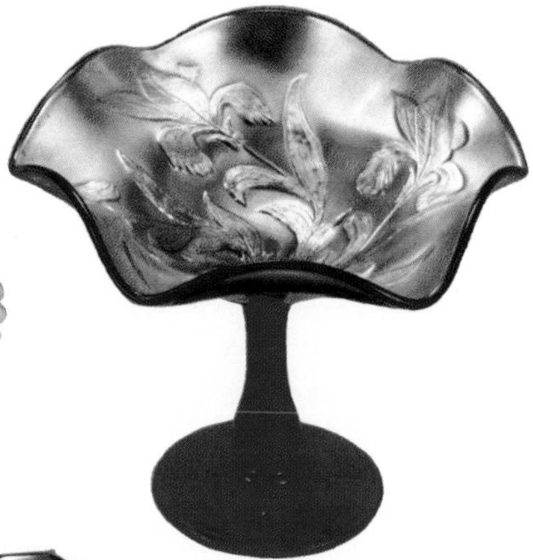

IRIS
Green

ILLINOIS SOLDIERS AND SAILORS HOME
Golden

KITTENS
Golden

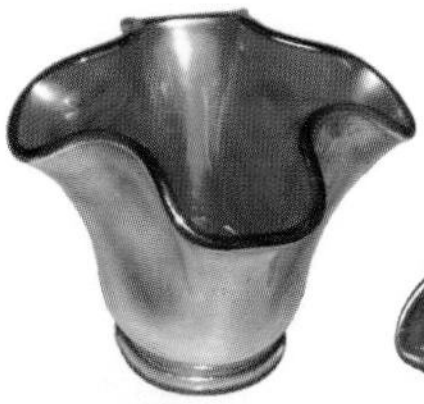

KITTENS
Golden

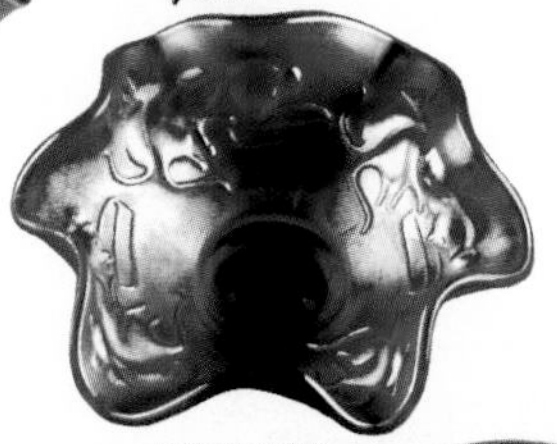

KITTENS
Royal Blue

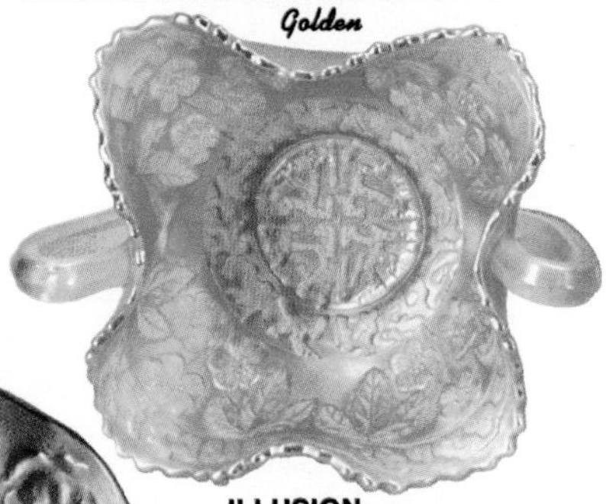

ILLUSION
Golden

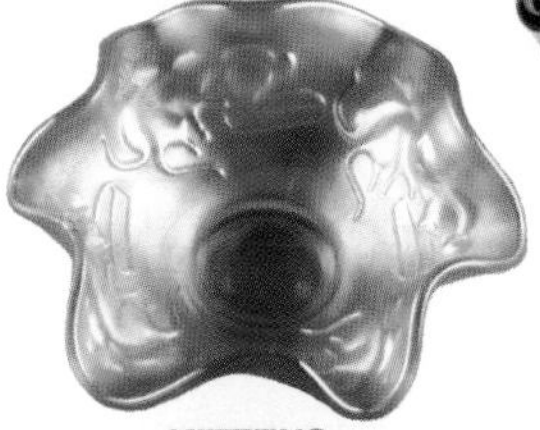

KITTENS
Golden

KITTENS
Royal Blue

KITTENS
Golden

KITTENS
Royal Blue

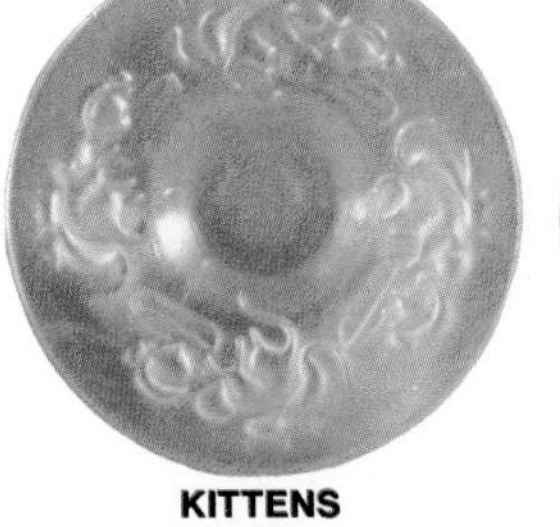

KITTENS
Golden

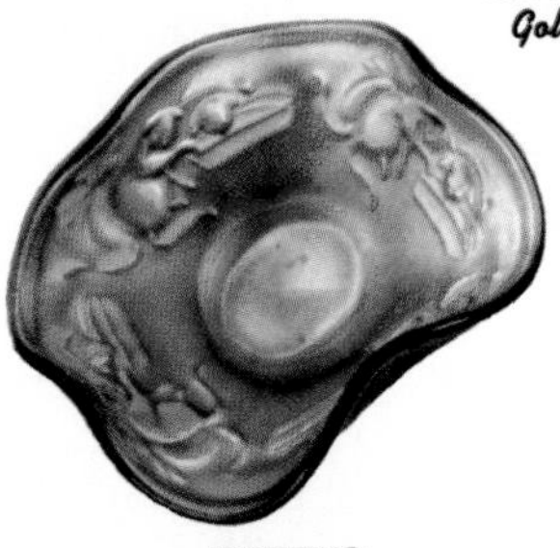

KITTENS
Royal Blue

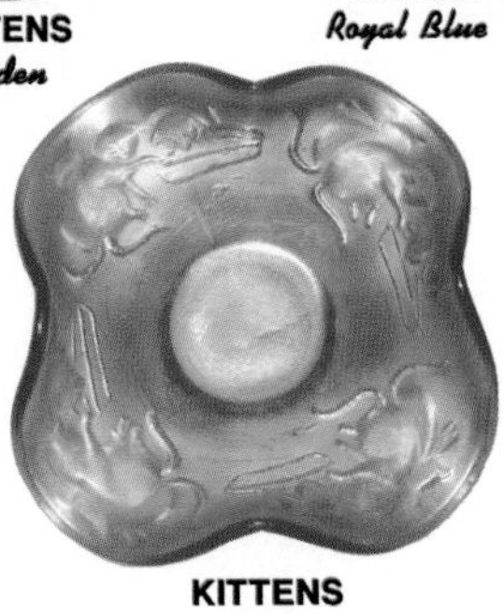

KITTENS
Golden

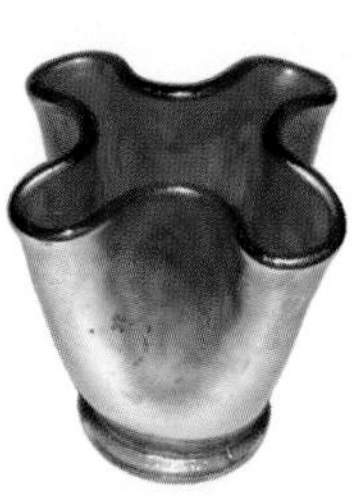

KITTENS
Golden

IRIS
Golden

KNOTTED BEADS #509

Circa 1915

This pattern consists of swung vases with elongated ovals ranging in height from about 4" to 12". Celeste blue and red are difficult colors to find.

	Vase, 4" – 12"	Rarity
Golden	$35.00 – 45.00	(5)
Green	$55.00 – 65.00	(5)
Red	$1200.00+	(2)
Royal Blue	$55.00 – 75.00	(5)
Amber	$200.00 – 325.00	(3)
Celeste Blue	$1000.00+	(3)
Lime Green	$150.00 – 170.00	(4)
Purple	$80.00 – 90.00	(5)
Topaz	$150.00 – 170.00	(3)

LATTICE AND GRAPE #1563 (LATTICE & GRAPEVINE)

Circa 1912 – 1925

Water sets with a large tankard jug and 9-ounce tumblers are available in various colors. These sets were introduced about 1912, but can also be found listed in golden iridescent in Butler Brothers' catalogs from 1925. The wholesale price of a dozen sets of a tankard and six tumblers was $15.00.

	Tankard	Rarity	Tumbler	Rarity
Golden	$150.00 – 200.00	(5)	$25.00 – 30.00	(5)
Green	$400.00 – 450.00	(4)	$50.00 – 60.00	(5)
Royal Blue	$350.00 – 400.00	(4)	$45.00 – 55.00	(5)
Violet	$250.00 – 300.00	(5)	$35.00 – 45.00	(5)
White	$400.00 – 500.00	(3)	$125.00 – 175.00	(3)
Peach Opalescent	$2500.00 – 3000.00	(2)	$550.00 – 600.00	(2)

LEAF CHAIN #1416 (LEAF MEDALLION)

Circa 1921

Leaf Chain has a background pattern with scales and features a cable that has curls. This is similar in style to Fenton's Cherry Chain pattern. However, Cherry Chain features clusters of three cherries arranged in a circular fashion around the item. Leaf Chain substitutes delicate flowers for these cherries. Bonbons, bowls, and plates have been found. Large pieces will be found with a Bearded Berry exterior, and smaller size pieces have the Berry and Leaf Circle exterior.

	Bonbon, 6"	Rarity	Bowl, 7"–8"	Rarity
Golden	$30.00 – 35.00	(5)	$50.00 – 60.00	(5)
Green	$55.00 – 65.00	(5)	$90.00 – 110.00	(4)
Red			$1000.00 – 1100.00	(3)
Royal Blue	$50.00 – 55.00	(5)	$110.00 – 130.00	(5)
Violet	$50.00 – 60.00	(5)	$75.00 – 85.00	(4)
White			$100.00 – 125.00	(5)
Aqua	$100.00 – 110.00	(5)	$75.00 – 100.00	(4)
Aqua Opalescent			$1700.00 – 1900.00	(2)
Ice Green			$3500.00+	(1)
Teal			$90.00 – 110.00	(4)
Topaz			$90.00 – 110.00	(4)

	Plate, 7"	Rarity	Plate, 8"	Rarity	Plate, 9"	Rarity
Golden	$160.00 – 170.00	(5)	$95.00 – 115.00	(5)	$275.00 – 300.00	(4)
Green	$200.00 – 225.00	(4)			$275.00 – 300.00	(4)
Royal Blue	$175.00 – 190.00	(5)	$125.00 – 150.00	(4)	$280.00 – 320.00	(4)
Violet					$2500.00 – 3000.00	(2)
White	$650.00 – 700.00	(3)			$250.00 – 260.00	(4)
Aqua Opalescent					$2500.00 – 3000.00	(2)
Clambroth					$120.00 – 150.00	(4)

LEAF TIERS #1790 (STIPPLED LEAF) — Circa 1914

Leaf Tiers is found primarily in the golden color. Pieces produced include water sets, table sets, berry sets, a vase, and a lamp shade. The unusual twig-shaped feet are a peculiar characteristic of this pattern.

	Golden	Rarity	Green	Rarity	Royal Blue	Rarity	Violet	Rarity
Bowl, 5" 3-ftd.	$25.00 – 30.00	(5)						
Bowl, 10" 3-ftd.	$50.00 – 60.00	(5)						
Butter	$160.00 – 180.00	(5)						
Creamer	$80.00 – 90.00	(5)						
Pitcher	$450.00 – 550.00	(4)	$740.00 – 780.00	(2)	$775.00 – 825.00	(1)	$700.00 – 750.00	(2)
Spooner	$80.00 – 90.00	(5)						
Sugar and lid	$90.00 – 110.00	(5)						
Tumbler	$50.00 – 60.00	(4)	$90.00 – 110.00	(2)	$100.00 – 110.00	(1)	$90.00 – 110.00	(2)

	Gold Irid. over MG	Rarity
Light shade	$60.00 – 70.00	(5)

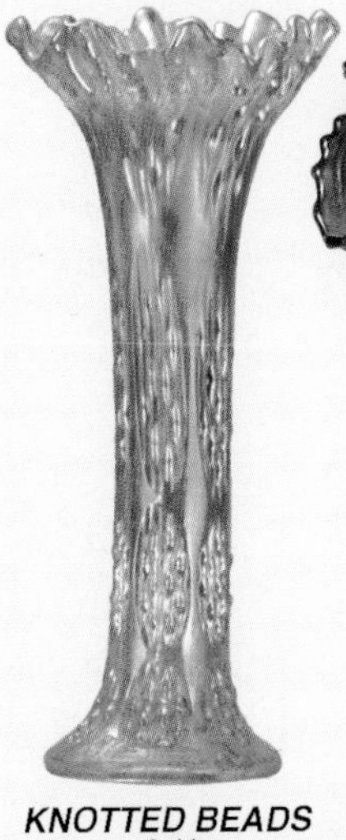

KNOTTED BEADS
Golden

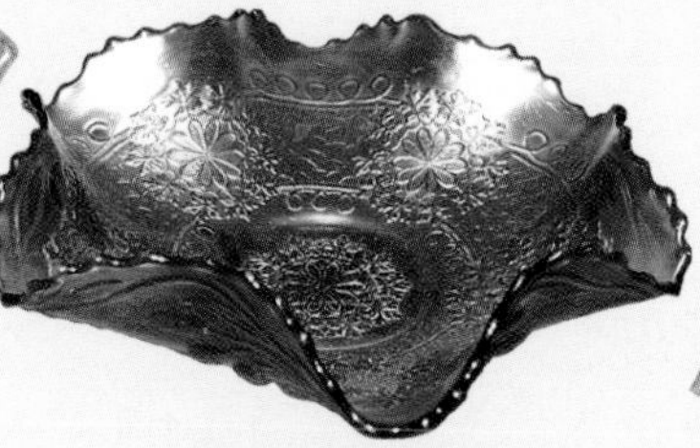

LEAF CHAIN
Green

LEAF TIERS
Golden Iridescence over Milk Glass

LATTICE & GRAPE
Royal Blue

LEAF TIERS
Royal Blue

LEAF TIERS
Golden

LEAF TIERS
Golden

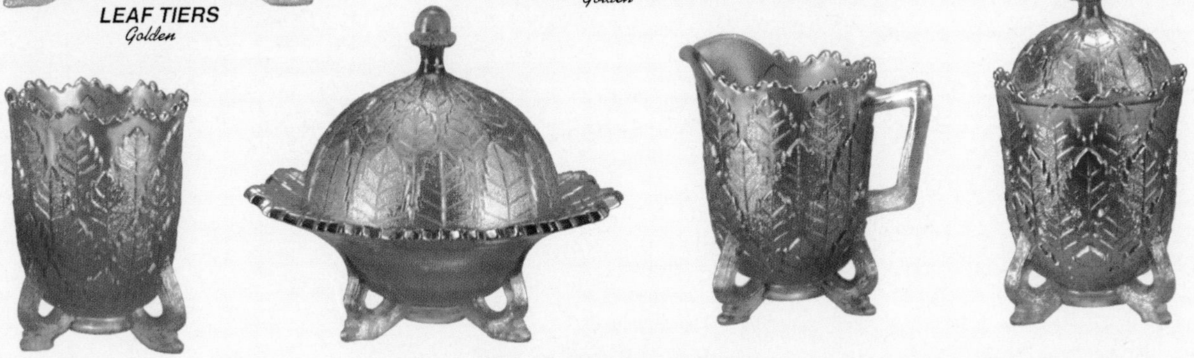

LEAF TIERS TABLE SET
Golden

LILY-OF-THE-VALLEY

Circa 1912 – 1915

Water sets were the only items produced in the elusive Lily-of-the-Valley pattern. The only colors are golden and royal blue.

	Pitcher	Rarity	Tumbler	Rarity
Golden			$500.00 – 600.00	(2)
Royal Blue	$4500.00 – 5000.00	(1)	$225.00 – 300.00	(3)

LION (STALKING LION)

Circa 1912

Bowls and plates may be found in this pattern. Both items are scarce, but plates are found less frequently. The reverse pattern is Berry and Leaf Circle. The 7" plate and bowls were made in custard glass about 1915. They may sometimes be found in custard with green or nutmeg decoration. A recent issue is an 8½" handled basket with the Lion interior and Fenton's Flowers exterior. This piece was made in Red Carnival in 1994 and in Spruce Carnival in 1999.

	Bowl, 7"	Rarity	Plate, 7"	Rarity
Golden	$110.00 – 140.00	(5)	$850.00 – 1000.00	(3)
Royal Blue	$275.00 – 325.00	(4)		

LITTLE DAISIES

Bowls ranging in size from 8" to 9½" with various flared, crimped, and cupped edges may be found in golden and royal blue.

	Bowl, 8"–9"	Rarity
Golden	$825.00 – 950.00	(2)
Royal Blue	$900.00 – 1000.00	(2)

LITTLE FISHES #1607 (SEA LANES)

Circa 1915 – 1921

Little Fishes bowls may be footed or flat, cupped, or flared with a crimped edge. Plates exist in royal blue and white, but they are rare.

	Bowl, 5½"	Rarity	Bowl, 10" 3-ftd.	Rarity	Plate, 10½"	Rarity
Golden	$50.00 – 60.00	(5)	$110.00 – 140.00	(5)		
Green	$300.00 – 325.00	(4)	$350.00 – 400.00	(4)		
Royal Blue	$125.00 – 150.00	(5)	$275.00 – 375.00	(4)	$900.00 – 1100.00	(2)
Aqua	$175.00 – 225.00	(5)				
White	$350.00 – 400.00	(3)	$1000.00 – 1200.00	(3)	$1400.00 – 1600.00	(1)

LITTLE FLOWERS (STIPPLED DIAMOND AND FLOWER)

Circa 1910

Large and small bowls may be found in various colors. The 10½" plates are rare.

	Bowl, 6"	Rarity	Bowl, 9¼"	Rarity	Plate, 6"	Rarity	Plate, 10½"	Rarity
Golden	$35.00 – 45.00	(5)	$60.00 – 75.00	(5)	$300.00 – 350.00	(4)	$800.00 – 1000.00	(2)
Green	$70.00 – 85.00	(5)	$145.00 – 160.00	(5)				
Royal Blue	$80.00 – 90.00	(5)	$160.00 – 200.00	(4)				
Red			$9000.00 – 11,000.00	(2)			$1000.00+	(1)
Violet	$70.00 – 85.00	(5)	$100.00 – 125.00	(5)				
Amber			$150.00 – 160.00	(5)				
Amberina			$800.00 – 1000.00	(3)				
Aqua	$85.00 – 95.00	(5)						

LONG THUMBPRINT

A vase is the only item in this pattern produced by Fenton. Several colors have been found and these vases vary in size from about 7" to 12". Other pieces with a similar elongated Thumbprint pattern, that is also called Long Thumbprint, have been attributed to Dugan by some authorities.

	Vase, 7"-9"	Rarity	Vase, 10"-12"	Rarity
Golden	$40.00 – 45.00	(5)	$35.00 – 40.00	(5)
Green	$30.00 – 35.00	(5)	$35.00 – 40.00	(5)
Violet	$35.00 – 40.00	(5)	$40.00 – 45.00	(5)

LILY-OF-THE-VALLEY
Royal Blue

LION
Royal Blue

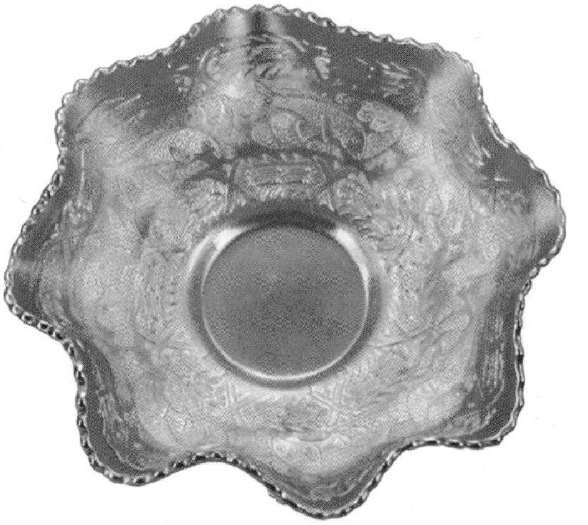

LITTLE FISHES
Golden

LITTLE FISHES
Royal Blue

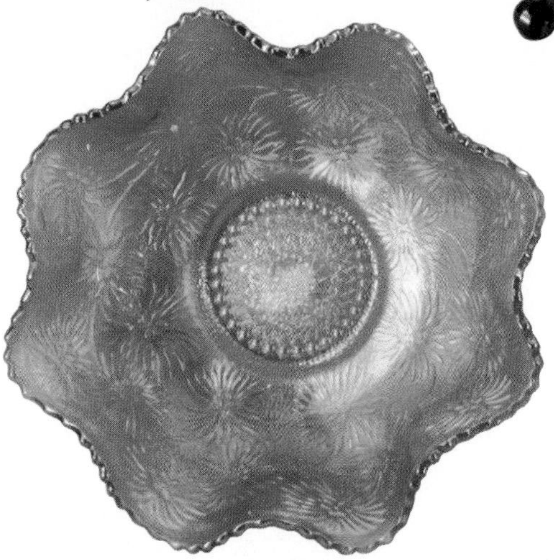

LITTLE DAISIES
Golden

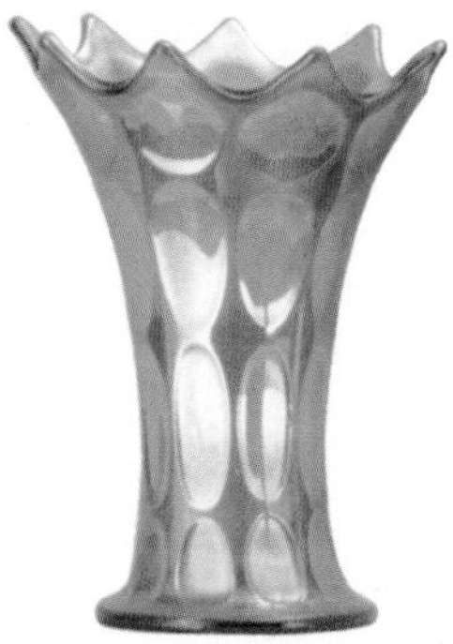

LONG THUMBPRINT
Green

LITTLE FLOWERS
Amberina

LOTUS AND GRAPE AND LOTUS AND GRAPE VARIANT (RUFFLED MAGNOLIA AND GRAPE)

Circa 1911 – 1915

Grapes must have been a favorite subject for designers. Most types of glass from all eras have an abundance of grape patterns, and carnival glass is no exception. This pattern may be found on bonbons, bowls, and plates. The bowls may be footed or flat; plates are elusive. Shapes of the bonbon include oval, square, and card-tray style.

	Bonbon	Rarity	Bowl, 7"	Rarity	Bowl, 9"	Rarity	Plate, 9½"	Rarity
Golden	$35.00 – 40.00	(5)	$50.00 – 60.00	(5)	$50.00 – 60.00	(5)	$400.00 – 500.00	(3)
Green	$100.00 – 130.00	(5)	$80.00 – 90.00	(5)	$90.00 – 110.00	(5)	$1900.00 – 2400.00	(2)
Red	$1000.00 – 1200.00	(3)						
Royal Blue	$90.00 – 110.00	(5)	$65.00 – 75.00	(5)	$80.00 – 90.00	(5)	$1400.00 – 1600.00	(3)
Violet	$60.00 – 80.00	(4)	$65.00 – 75.00	(5)	$50.00 – 65.00	(5)	$1800.00 – 2500.00	(2)
Aqua	$200.00 – 225.00	(4)						
Brick Red	$900.00 – 1000.00	(3)						
Lime Green Opal	$600.00 – 700.00	(3)						
Persian Blue							$400.00 – 500.00	(4)
Teal	$300.00 – 350.00	(4)						
Topaz	$150.00 – 175.00	(4)						

MIKADO

Circa 1912

The only piece Fenton produced with this pattern is a tall comport. The exterior pattern is Fenton's Cherry. The comport and a flattened version described as a tall-footed cake plate were produced in Mandarin red about 1934.

	Comport	Rarity
Golden	$225.00 – 250.00	(5)
Green	$2200.00 – 2400.00	(2)
Red	$7000.00+	(1)
Royal Blue	$400.00 – 450.00	(5)
Violet	$900.00 – 1000.00	(3)
White	$2500.00+	(1)

MILADY #1110

Circa 1910

A water set with a tankard-style pitcher was made by Fenton in the Milady pattern. It is most commonly found in golden, but sets in royal blue, green, and violet also exist. Note the scarcity and price of the green and violet tumblers. Green pitchers with a crimped top and the Fenton family signature are of recent issue.

	Tankard	Rarity	Tumbler	Rarity
Golden	$700.00 – 800.00	(4)	$90.00 – 110.00	(4)
Green	$900.00 – 1100.00	(3)	$400.00 – 450.00	(2)
Royal Blue	$900.00 – 1000.00	(4)	$80.00 – 90.00	(4)
Violet	$750.00 – 850.00	(4)	$300.00 – 400.00	(2)

MIRRORED LOTUS

It will take some searching to find some colors of the bowls and plates which comprise this Fenton pattern. Many collectors are still actively seeking the rare white rose bowl. Cupped 8" bowls and 7½" plates have been found in Celeste blue. The bonbon is a hard-to-find piece in ice blue. Berry and Leaf Circle will be the reverse pattern on many pieces.

	Bonbon	Rarity	Bowl, 8"	Rarity	Plate, 7½"	Rarity	Rose Bowl	Rarity
Golden	$75.00 –85.00	(5)	$50.00 – 60.00	(5)	$500.00 – 600.00	(4)	$500.00 – 550.00	(4)
Green	$120.00 – 140.00	(5)	$90.00 – 110.00	(5)				
Royal Blue	$95.00 – 100.00	(5)	$100.00 – 120.00	(5)	$600.00 – 650.00	(4)	$500.00 – 600.00	(4)
White							$800.00 – 900.00	(3)
Celeste Blue			$900.00 – 1000.00	(2)	$3500.00 – 4000.00	(2)		
Ice Blue	$600.00 – 700.00	(3)						

NORTHERN STAR

Northern Star was an early pressed pattern produced about 1908 in crystal and opalescent colors. Small bowls and plates were also made in the golden carnival color. Plates are not easily found.

	Golden	Rarity
Bowl, 6"–7"	$30.00 – 35.00	(5)
Card tray, 6"	$35.00 – 40.00	(5)
Plate, 6"–7"	$75.00 – 85.00	(3)

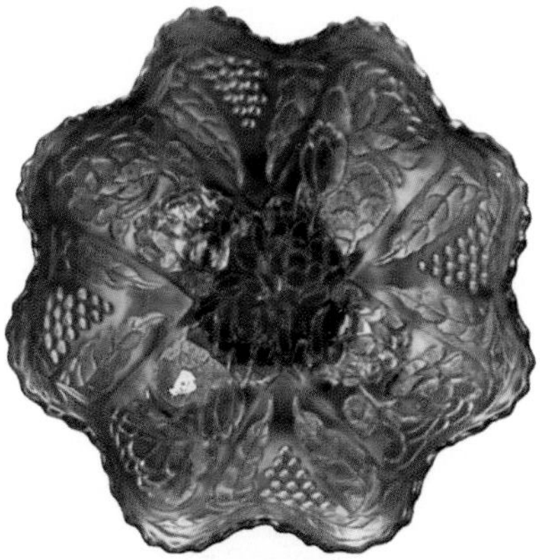

LOTUS & GRAPE
Royal Blue

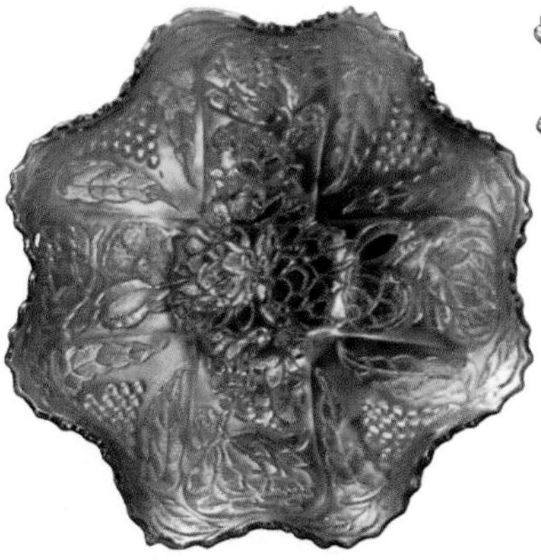

LOTUS & GRAPE VARIANT
Green

MIKADO
Royal Blue

MIKADO
Golden

MIRRORED LOTUS
Green

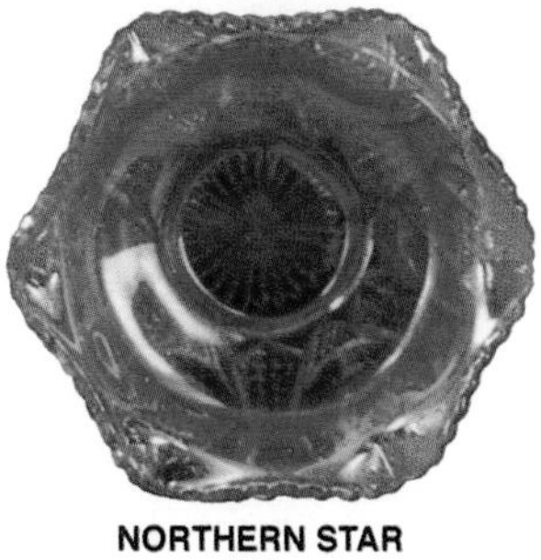

NORTHERN STAR
Golden

MILADY
Golden

MILADY
Golden

ORANGE TREE (FOOTED SMALL ORANGE TREE; SMALL ORANGE TREE) Circa 1911

Orange Tree was one of the most widely produced and one of the most popular of all the Fenton carnival patterns. Other names for this pattern include Footed Small Orange Tree and Small Orange Tree. The 8" bowl may be found flared, crimped, or shallow cupped with an exterior pattern of Bearded Berry. Red bowls were probably made in the mid 1920s. Currently, only a few violet hatpin holders have been found. Chocolate glass collectors treasure hatpin holders in this color. The hatpin holder was made in custard glass about 1915. It may be found in custard with nutmeg or green trim. The 9" 3-footed bowl is the master berry, and the 11" 3-footed bowl is called an orange bowl. Pitchers and tumblers may be found with or without scales. Pieces without scales were made earlier and are much harder to find than the ones with scales. Values for these pieces without scales are about double those indicated below. Notice the breakfast sugar and creamer are not footed, and the sugar does not have a lid; this set is hard to find. There are two sizes of the mug; the larger mug is straight sided and is called a shaving mug; the smaller drinking mug flares slightly outward. During the past several years the hatpin holder has been poorly reproduced by a national importing company. These are available in red and cobalt, but there are no carnival colors. The rose bowl is also called Fenton's Flowers.

	Golden	Rarity	Green	Rarity	Red	Rarity	Royal Blue	Rarity
Bowl, 5½" 3-ftd.	$40.00 – 50.00	(5)	$50.00 – 55.00	(5)	$1000.00 – 1200.00	(2)	$50.00 – 55.00	(5)
*Bowl, 8" flat	$50.00 – 60.00	(5)	$275.00 – 300.00	(4)	$2000.00 – 2500.00+	(3)	$90.00 – 100.00	(5)
Bowl, 9" 3-ftd.	$50.00 – 65.00	(5)	$150.00 – 175.00	(5)			$120.00 – 140.00	(5)
Bowl, 11" 3-ftd.	$95.00 – 125.00	(5)	$450.00 – 500.00	(4)			$190.00 – 220.00	(5)
Butter	$190.00 – 220.00	(5)					$320.00 – 360.00	(4)
**Comport, 5¾"	$40.00 – 45.00	(5)	$95.00 – 115.00	(4)			$55.00 – 65.00	(4)
Creamer	$35.00 – 40.00	(5)					$60.00 – 70.00	(5)
Creamer, breakfast	$100.00 – 120.00	(5)	$120.00 – 140.00	(5)			$100.00 – 120.00	(5)
***Cup, loving	$175.00 – 200.00	(5)	$350.00 – 425.00	(4)			$250.00 – 300.00	(5)
Goblet, water	$60.00 – 70.00	(5)						
****Goblet, wine	$24.00 – 28.00	(5)	$250.00 – 300.00	(4)			$75.00 – 90.00	(4)
Hatpin holder	$200.00 – 225.00	(5)	$600.00 – 650.00	(4)			$225.00 – 250.00	(5)
*****Mug, lg.	$45.00 – 55.00	(5)	$1000.00 – 1200.00	(3)	$400.00 – 500.00	(4)	$75.00 – 85.00	(5)
#Mug, sm.	$40.00 – 50.00	(5)	$750.00 – 850.00	(3)	$450.00 – 500.00	(4)	$60.00 – 70.00	(5)
##Pitcher	$200.00 – 250.00	(5)					$375.00 – 425.00	(5)
###Plate, 9"	$300.00 – 325.00	(5)			$4000.00+	(2)	$400.00 – 550.00	(4)
Puff box	$75.00 – 90.00	(5)	$550.00 – 600.00	(3)			$120.00 – 135.00	(5)
####Punch bowl and base	$140.00 – 180.00	(5)	$450.00 – 600.00	(4)			$250.00 – 275.00	(5)
Punch cup	$27.00 – 30.00	(5)	$38.00 – 42.00	(4)			$30.00 – 32.00	(5)
Rose bowl	$55.00 – 65.00	(5)	$145.00 – 160.00	(5)	$2000.00 – 2500.00	(2)	$60.00 – 70.00	(5)
Sherbet	$25.00 – 30.00	(5)					$35.00 – 40.00	(5)
Spooner	$35.00 – 40.00	(5)					$60.00 – 70.00	(5)
Sugar & lid	$55.00 – 65.00	(5)					$70.00 – 80.00	(5)
Sugar, breakfast	$90.00 – 110.00	(5)	$120.00 – 140.00	(5)			$110.00 – 120.00	(5)
Tumbler	$35.00 – 45.00	(5)					$55.00 – 65.00	(5)

*Moonstone iridized, $525.00 – 625.00, (4); Celeste Blue, $2500.00+, (3); Clambroth $60.00 – 75.00, (5); Peach Opalescent $2200.00+, (1); Gold Iridescence over WMG $500.00 – 700.00, (3); Ice Green $7000.00+, (1); Topaz $200.00 – 250.00, (5).

**Teal $400.00 – 475.00, (3).

***Aqua Opalescent $7000.00+, (1); Peach Opalescent $5000.00+, (1).

****Peach Opalescent $90.00 – 110.00, (4); Topaz $60.00 – 70.00, (4).

*****Amber $225.00 – 275.00, (4); Amberina $350.00 – 400.00, (4); Lime Green $400.00 – 500.00, (4); Topaz $230.00 – 260.00, (4).

#Amber $70.00 – 80.00, (4); Amberina $250.00 – 300.00, (3); Aqua Opalescent $2300.00+, (2); Lime Green $450.00 – 500.00, (3); Sapphire $1200.00+, (3); Teal $100.00 – 125.00, (5); Topaz $100.00 – 120.00, (5).

##Lime Green Opalescent $10,000.00+, (1).

###Aqua Opalescent $14,000.00+, (1); Clambroth $160.00 – 190.00, (4); Ice Green $14,000.00+, (1).

####Moonstone Opalescent $1000.00 – 1200.00, (3).

Orange Tree

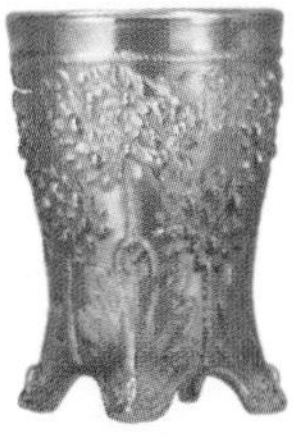
Tumbler
Golden

Pitcher
Golden

Hatpin Holder
Green

Loving Cup
Green

Wine Goblet
Golden

Master Berry
Green

Shaving Mug
Red

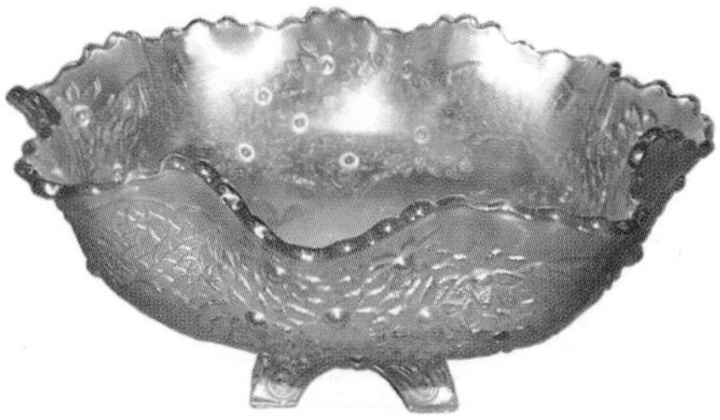
Master Berry
Golden

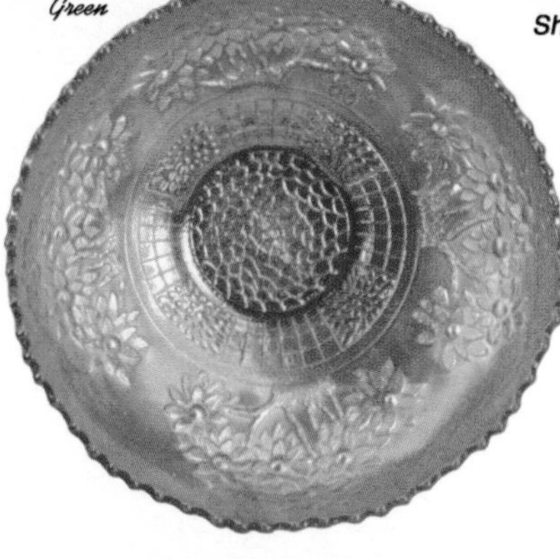
Low Console Bowl
Golden

Crimped Orange Bowl
Golden

ORANGE TREE VARIANT
Green

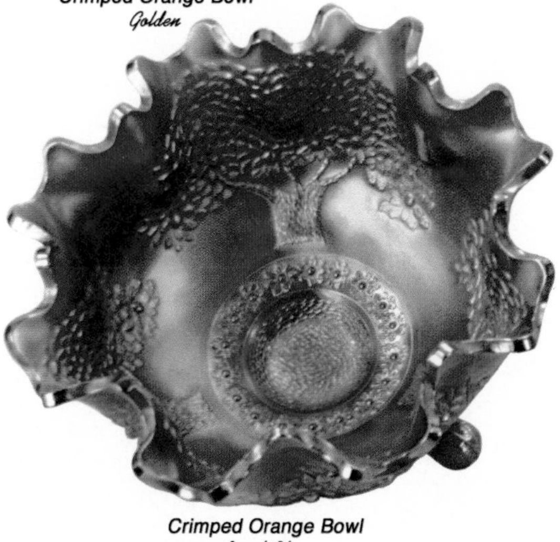
Crimped Orange Bowl
Royal Blue

Orange Tree	Violet	Rarity	White	Rarity	Aqua	Rarity	Purple	Rarity
*Bowl, 8"			$95.00 – 110.00	(5)				
Bowl, 9" 3-ftd.			$160.00 – 220.00	(5)				
Butter			$350.00 – 400.00	(4)				
**Comport, 5¾"	$70.00 – 75.00	(4)					$125.00 – 175.00	(4)
Creamer			$90.00 – 100.00	(5)			$60.00 – 75.00	(5)
Creamer, breakfast	$100.00 – 125.00	(5)	$200.00 – 225.00	(4)				
***Cup, Loving	$425.00 – 500.00	(4)	$700.00 – 800.00	(3)				
Goblet, water					$80.00 – 90.00	(5)		
****Goblet, wine					$60.00 – 70.00	(4)		
Hatpin holder	$1000.00+	(1)	$1000.00+	(3)				
*****Mug, lg.	$175.00 – 190.00	(4)			$220.00 – 240.00	(5)	$200.00 – 250.00	(4)
#Mug, sm.	$60.00 – 70.00	(5)	$1200.00+	(3)	$80.00 – 95.00	(5)	$70.00 – 90.00	(5)
##Pitcher			$800.00 – 900.00	(4)				
###Plate, 9"	$800.00 – 900 .00	(4)	$175.00 – 200.00	(5)				
Puff box	$120.00 – 150.00	(4)	$525.00 – 575.00	(3)				
####Punch bowl & base			$550.00 – 600.00	(4)				
Punch cup			$35.00 – 37.00	(5)				
Rose bowl	$70.00 – 80.00	(5)	$275.00 – 325.00	(4)				
Sherbet			$125.00 – 150.00	(4)				
Spooner			$70.00 – 90.00	(5)			$75.00 – 85.00	(5)
Sugar & lid			$90.00 – 110.00	(5)			$70.00 – 80.00	(5)
Sugar, breakfast	$100.00 – 125.00	(5)	$200.00 – 225.00	(4)				
Tumbler			$80.00 – 95.00	(4)				

See key in value guide on page 76.

9" Plate
Royal Blue

Breakfast Sugar
Green

Breakfast Creamer
Green

Punch Bowl
Green

Punch Cup
Green

Puff Box
Royal Blue

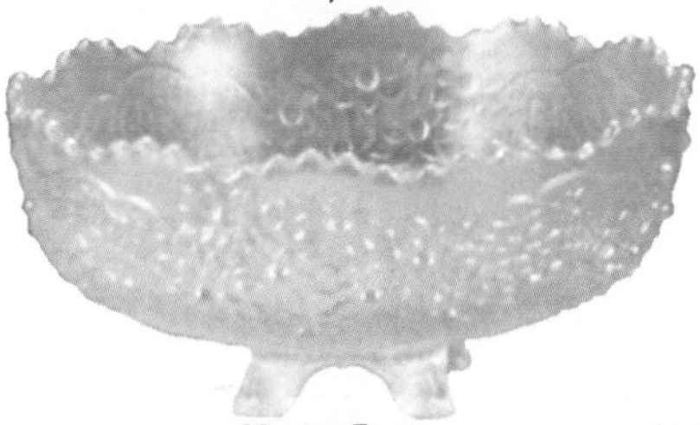
Master Berry
White

Spooner
Royal Blue

Butter
Royal Blue

Sugar & Lid
Royal Blue

Creamer
Royal Blue

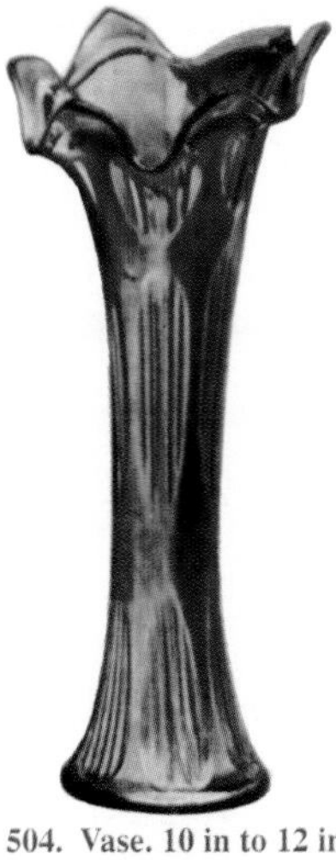

504. Vase. 10 in to 12 in.
Diamond & Rib

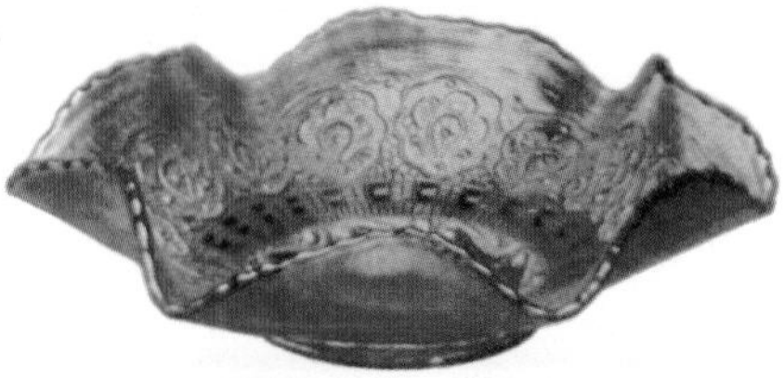

1047. Crimped Nappy
Persian Medallion

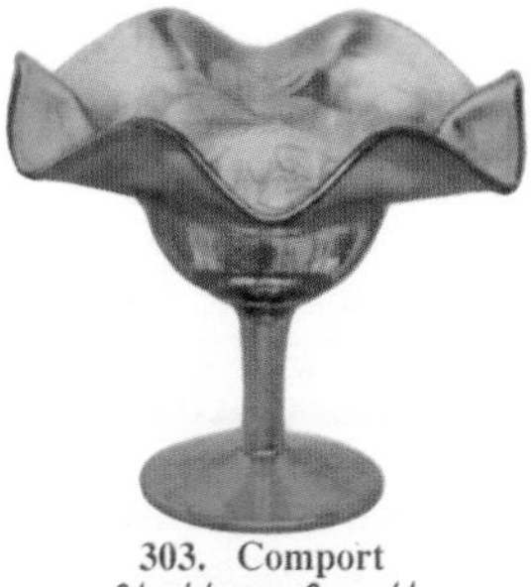

303. Comport
Blackberry Bramble

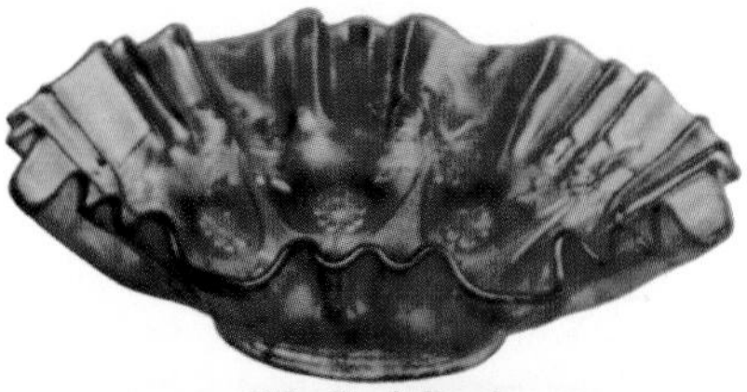

427. Fruit Bowl
Little Flowers

408. Oval Bon Bon
Peacock Tail

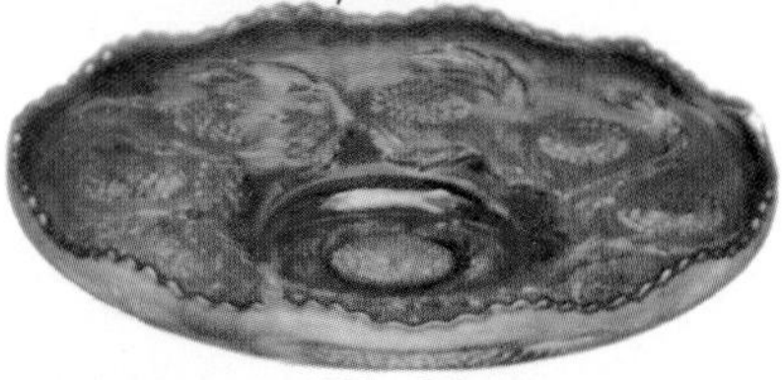

1057. Salver
Ten Mums

916. Vase. 14in. in to 16in.
Fenton's Rib

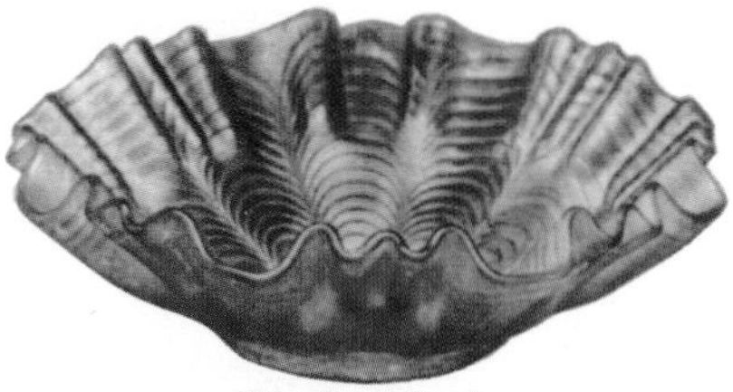

407. Fruit Bowl
Peacock Tail

922. Fern Dish
Vintage

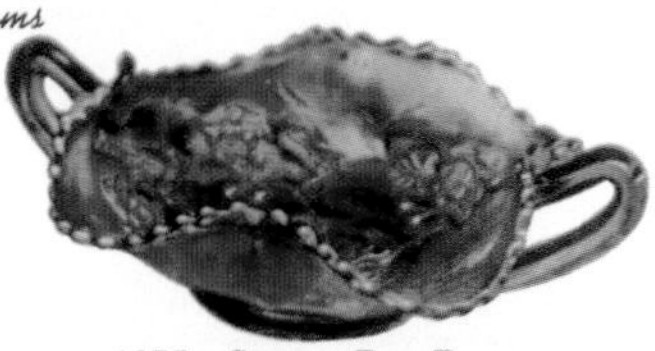

1075. Square Bon Bon
Birds & Cherries

1092. Nut Bowl
Basket w/Open Edge

409. Footed Bon Bon
Peacock Tail

437. Flared Nappy
Feathered Serpent

466. Crimped Nappy
Vintage

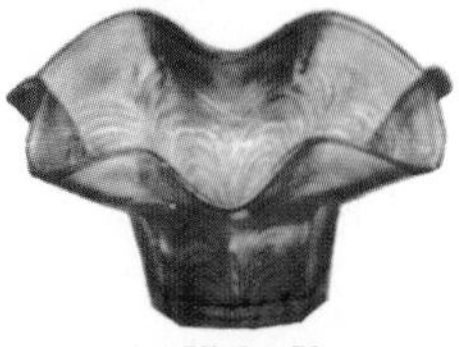

411. Violet Vase
Peacock Tail

231. Comport
Rib & Holly Sprig

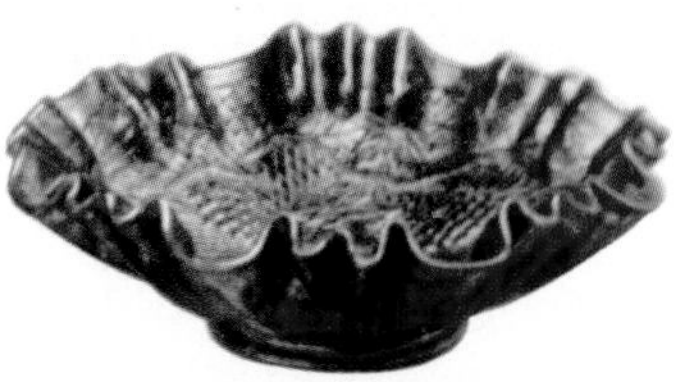

1036. Fruit Bowl
Concord

1057. Salad
Ten Mums

920. Crimped Orange Bowl
Grape & Cable

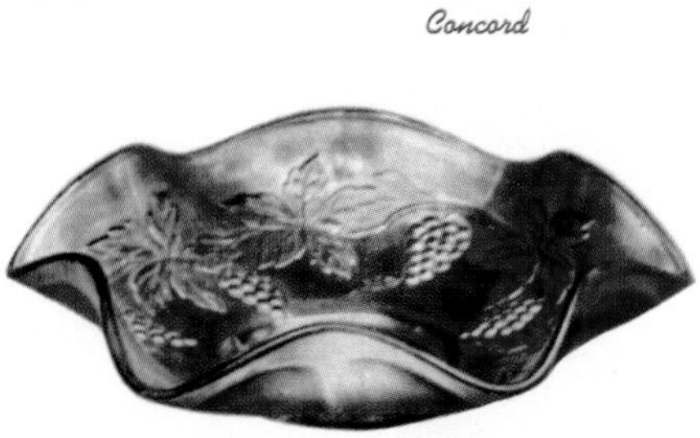

467. Crimped Nappy
Vintage

ORANGE TREE AND SCROLL (ORANGE TREE VARIANT) — Circa 1914

Orange Tree and Scroll was produced as a water set with the tankard-style jug as the star attraction. Look for scrolling near the bottom of the tankard and tumbler to differentiate this pattern from other Fenton Orange Tree patterns.

	Tankard	Rarity	Tumbler	Rarity
Golden	$400.00 – 500.00	(5)	$50.00 – 60.00	(5)
Royal Blue	$800.00 – 900.00	(4)	$70.00 – 80.00	(4)
White			$100.00 – 125.00	(4)

ORANGE TREE ORCHARD (ORANGE TREE AND CABLE) — Circa 1911

Water sets were the only items produced in Orange Tree Orchard. The pitcher is flat and bulbous rather than the footed, straight-sided style of the regular Orange Tree pattern. In this pattern the orange tree extends to the bottom of the piece, and the trees are separated by fancy scroll work. Seven-piece water sets retailed for 55 cents per set in 1914.

	Pitcher	Rarity	Tumbler	Rarity
Golden	$225.00 – 275.00	(5)	$50.00 – 60.00	(5)
Royal Blue	$550.00 – 600.00	(4)	$65.00 – 75.00	(5)
White	$390.00 – 450.00	(4)	$70.00 – 80.00	(4)

PANELED DANDELION — Circa 1910

The Paneled Dandelion pattern is represented by a water set with a tankard-style jug. Royal blue and golden are the most available colors.

	Tankard	Rarity	Tumbler	Rarity
Golden	$300.00 – 400.00	(5)	$40.00 – 45.00	(5)
Green	$650.00 – 750.00	(4)	$65.00 – 70.00	(4)
Royal Blue	$400.00 – 500.00	(5)	$50.00 – 60.00	(5)
Violet	$800.00 – 900.00	(4)	$65.00 – 70.00	(4)

PANELED DIAMOND AND BOWS — Circa 1910

Fenton produced vases from 6" high to about 12" high in this pattern. These are six-paneled vases with alternating vertical rib panels, and panels decorated the diamond and bow pattern.

	Vase	Rarity
Golden	$65.00 – 90.00	(4)
Green	$85.00 – 125.00	(4)
Royal Blue	$60.00 – 70.00	(5)
Lime Green	$150.00 – 175.00	(4)
Lime Green Opalescent	$250.00 – 350.00	(3)
Purple	$70.00 – 90.00	(5)

PANTHER — Circa 1914

Panther may be found as the interior pattern of a footed berry set which uses Butterfly and Berry as the exterior pattern. Notice the different crimping on the small bowls. The large 3-footed bowl has been found in chocolate glass. The small bowl may occasionally be found in red and other scarce colors such as aqua and green.

Panther	Bowl, 5" 3-ftd.	Rarity	Bowl, 10" 3-ftd.	Rarity
Golden	$40.00 – 50.00	(5)	$125.00 – 150.00	(5)
Green	$400.00 – 450.00	(3)	$550.00 – 650.00	(4)
Red	$1100.00 – 1300.00	(3)		
Royal Blue	$90.00 – 125.00	(5)	$300.00 – 375.00	(4)
Violet	$200.00 – 230.00	(4)		
Aqua	$175. 00 – 200.00	(3)	$400.00 – 500.00	(3)
Clambroth	$125.00 – 150.00	(5)		
Nile Green			$7000.00+	(1)
Purple	$200.00 – 250.00	(4)		
White			$950.00+	(3)

PANTHER
Royal Blue

PANTHER
Golden

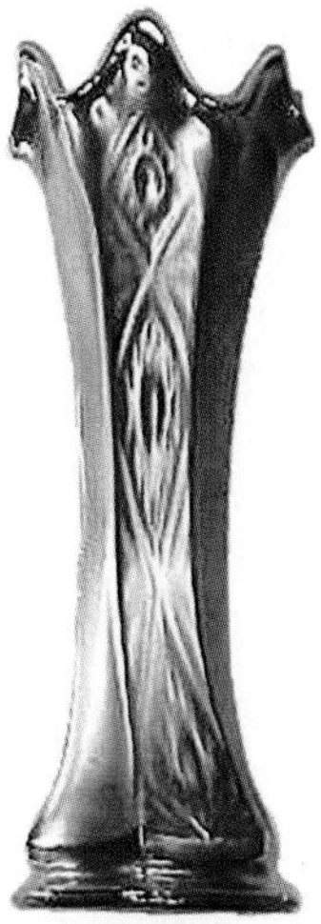

PANELED DIAMOND & BOWS
Royal Blue

PANTHER
Royal Blue

ORANGE TREE & SCROLL
Royal Blue

ORANGE TREE ORCHARD
Royal Blue

PANELED DANDELION
Violet

PEACOCK AND DAHLIA #1645 — Circa 1912

Peacock and Dahlia has the Berry and Leaf Circle pattern on the reverse side. Bowls and plates are the only items known, and plates are more difficult to find. A handle was added to this bowl in 1992 to produce a basket in Red Carnival.

	Bowl, 7"	Rarity	Plate, 8"	Rarity
Golden	$45.00 – 50.00	(5)	$375.00 – 425.00	(4)
Green	$110.00 – 125.00	(5)		
Royal Blue	$90.00 – 110.00	(5)		
Aqua	$100.00 – 125.00	(5)		
Lime Green	$40.00 – 50.00	(4)		
Topaz	$200.00 – 250.00	(4)		
White	$130.00 – 150.00	(5)		

PEACOCK AND GRAPE #1646 — Circa 1911

Peacock and Grape is a pattern with bowls and plates similar in design to Peacock and Dahlia. The bowl may be either flat or 3-footed and has been found in a wide variety of colors with red and amberina bringing the highest prices. The high prices of the plates reflect the difficulty in finding them.

	Bowl, 7¾"- 9"	Rarity	Plate, 9"	Rarity
Golden	$50.00 – 60.00	(5)	$325.00 – 375.00	(4)
Green	$180.00 – 225.00	(5)	$425.00 – 525.00	(4)
Red	$900.00 – 1100.00	(4)		
Royal Blue	$100.00 – 120.00	(5)	$400.00 – 500.00	(4)
Violet	$150.00 – 175.00	(5)	$350.00 – 400.00	(3)
Amber	$125.00 – 150.00	(4)		
Amberina	$500.00 – 600.00	(4)		
Aqua	$100.00 – 125.00	(5)		
Black	$100.00 – 125.00	(4)		
Gold Iris over WMG	$350.00 – 450.00	(4)		
Lavender	$80.00 – 90.00	(5)		
Lime Green	$200.00 – 225.00	(4)		
Lime Green Opalescent	$300.00 – 400.00	(4)		
Peach Opalescent	$350.00 – 450.00	(4)		
Purple	$70.00 – 80.00	(5)	$500.00 – 600.00+	(3)
Smoke	$400.00 – 500.00	(3)		
Topaz	$110.00 – 130.00	(5)		
Topaz Opalescent	$400.00 – 500.00	(4)		

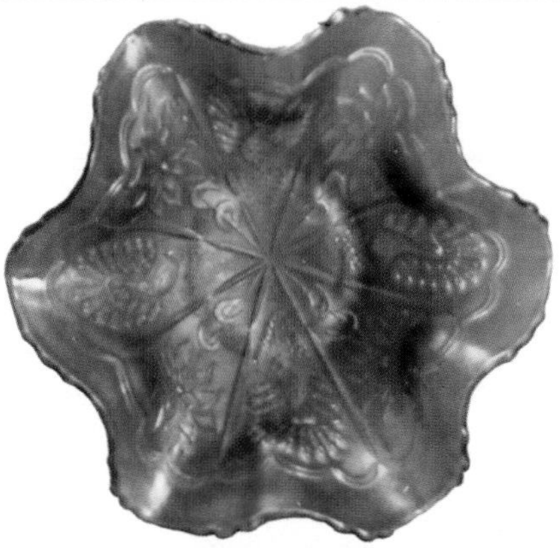

PEACOCK & DAHLIA
Golden

PEACOCK & GRAPE
Golden

PEACOCK & GRAPE
Golden

PEACOCK & GRAPE
Violet

Catalog Reprint Circa 1915 Courtesy Of The Fenton Art Glass Museum

1125 6" FOOTED NAPPY CRIMPED
Butterfly & Berry

1430 MUG
Orange Tree

1605 SQ. BON BON
Flowering Dill

231 COMPORT CRIMPED
Rib & Holly Sprig

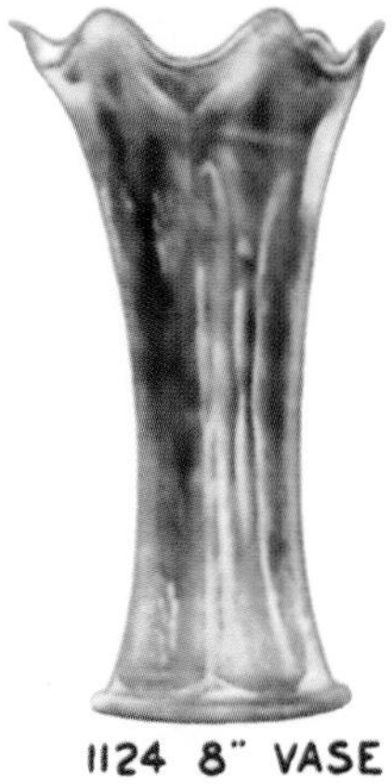

1124 8" VASE
Butterfly & Berry

1606 TULIP BON BON
Flowering Dill

1604 BON BON
Flowering Dill

1802 WINE
Sailboats

1125 5" 3 FOOTED FLARED NAPPY
Panther Interior w/Butterfly & Berry Exterior

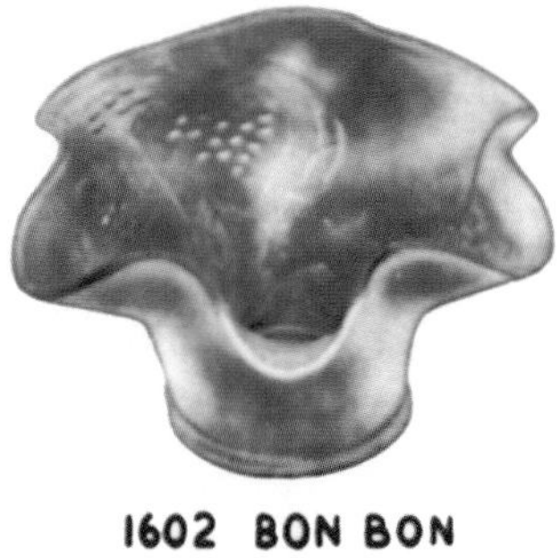

1602 BON BON
Flowering Dill

231 FOOTED COMPORT
Rib & Holly Sprig

1412 GOBLET
Orange Tree

PEACOCK AND URN

Circa 1915

Fenton's Peacock and Urn pattern is very similar to patterns with the same name produced by Millersburg and Northwood. To tell the difference between the makers, first look for Northwood's trademark — the "N" in a circle. Next check for a reverse pattern of Bearded Berry or Orange Tree which will identify the piece as Fenton. If none of this helps, examine the urn on the face of the piece closely. The Millersburg pattern has three variations — no horizontal beading, two rows or three rows of beads; the Fenton pattern has two rows of beads, and the Northwood design has three rows of beads. If a piece has two rows of beads, it is then either Fenton or Millersburg. The only confirmed piece of Millersburg which has been found with two rows of beading is an 8½" bowl in two styles, either a ruffled or crimped top. For final confirmation to attribute this bowl to Fenton, check the position and size of the bee by the peacock's beak. Fenton items will have the body of the bee clearly away from the beak with the bottom of the bee's wings close to the beak; the Millersburg pattern has the beak of the peacock close to the point where the wings and the body of the bee meet. The size of the Millersburg bee is much smaller than the Fenton bee.

	Bowl, 8½"	Rarity	Comport	Rarity	Plate, 9"	Rarity
Golden	$125.00 – 150.00	(5)	$50.00 – 60.00	(5)	$300.00 – 400.00	(5)
Green	$325.00 – 350.00	(5)	$200.00 – 250.00	(4)		
Red	$5000.00 – 6000.00	(4)	$2000.00+	(3)		
Royal Blue	$325.00 – 350.00	(5)	$80.00 – 100.00	(5)	$450.00 – 550.00	(5)
Violet	$220.00 – 260.00	(5)	$150.00 – 175.00	(4)		
Aqua w/Gold Irid.			$145.00 – 170.00	(5)		
Gold Irid. over WMG			$2700.00+	(1)		
Lime Green			$150.00 – 170.00	(3)		
Moonstone	$2200.00+	(3)				
Persian Blue	$1300.00 – 1500.00	(2)				
Teal			$220.00 – 240.00	(4)		
Topaz	$400.00 – 450.00	(4)	$150.00 – 185.00	(5)		
White	$200.00 – 250.00	(5)	$130.00 – 150.00	(5)	$300.00 – 400.00	(5)

PEACOCK TAIL #409 (FLOWERING ALMONDS)

Circa 1911

Peacock Tail is similar to the Northwood Nippon pattern. Bowls and plates in the Fenton pattern have peacock feathers extending outward from a point at the very center of the piece. Northwood's Nippon pattern has a central blossom surrounded by a clear area with no pattern before the peacock-like pattern begins. The hat-shaped violet vase has been found with various advertising around the inside of the base.

	Golden	Rarity	Green	Rarity	Royal Blue	Rarity	Violet	Rarity
Bonbon, 2-hdld. ftd.	$60.00 – 70.00	(5)	$85.00 – 95.00	(5)	$50.00 – 60.00	(4)	$65.00 – 75.00	(5)
*Bowl, 5 – 6½"	$35.00 – 45.00	(5)	$55.00 – 65.00	(5)	$50.00 – 55.00	(5)	$45.00 – 55.00	(5)
**Bowl, 9"	$37.00 – 42.00	(5)	$58.00 – 65.00	(5)	$50.00 – 55.00	(5)	$52.00 – 57.00	(5)
Hat	$25.00 – 35.00	(5)	$40.00 – 45.00	(5)	$45.00 – 50.00	(5)		
Plate, 6"	$300.00 – 400.00	(3)	$250.00 – 300.00	(4)	$1200.00 – 1400.00	(2)	$400.00 – 500.00	(3)
Plate, 9"	$1000.00 – 1200.00	(3)						

*Peach Opalescent $800.00 – 900.00, (3); Red $1900.00 – 2000.00, (2).
**Red $1700.00 – 1900.00, (3).

PEACOCK TAIL VARIANT

The center of Peacock Tail Variant pattern is similar in design to the Peacock Tail pattern. However, the Peacock Tail pieces have feathers which scallop almost to the edge of the piece, and the Peacock Tail Variant only has scalloped feathers near the center. Extending from the central band of scalloped feathers are stippled rays separated by narrow bands of scrawny feathers.

	Golden	Rarity	Green	Rarity	Royal Blue	Rarity	Violet	Rarity	White	Rarity
Comport, 6"	$40.00 – 55.00	(5)	$88.00 – 90.00	(5)	$57.00 – 62.00	(5)	$50.00 – 55.00	(5)	$60.00 – 75.00	(5)

PEACOCK & URN
Golden

PEACOCK & URN
Golden over Aqua

PEACOCK & URN
Golden

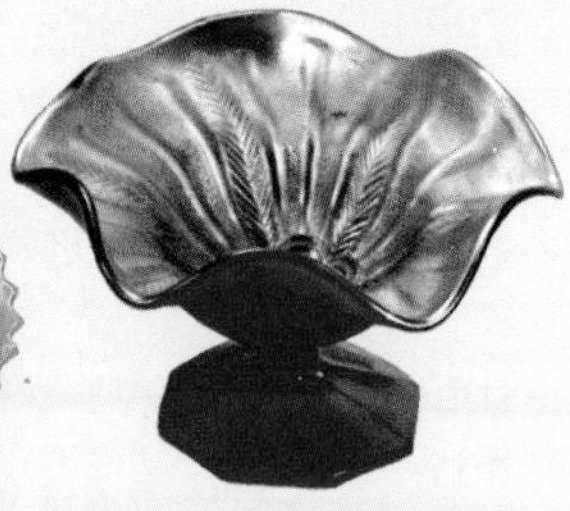

PEACOCK TAIL VARIANT
Violet

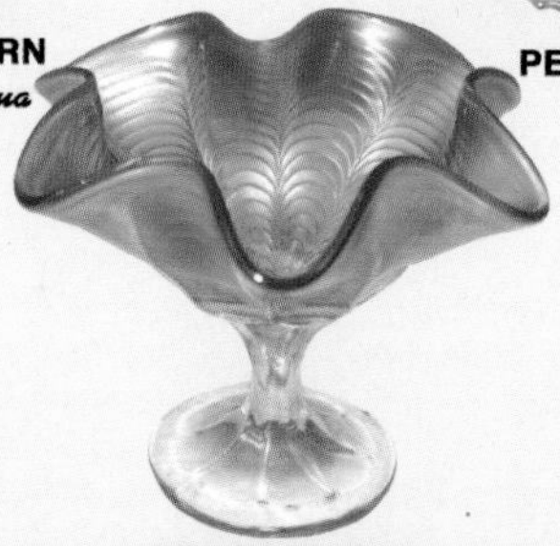

PEACOCK TAIL
Golden

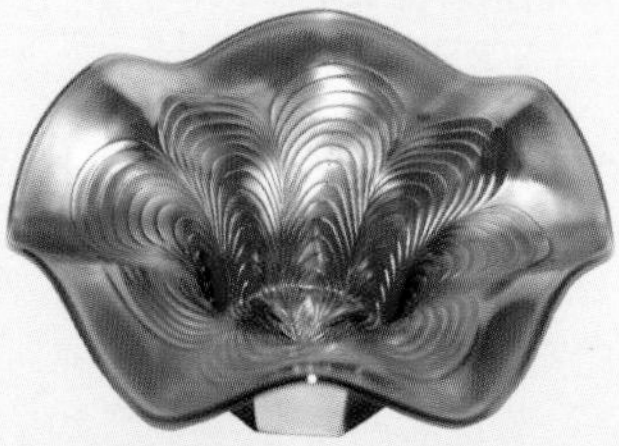

PEACOCK TAIL
Violet

Catalog Reprint Circa 1914 Courtesy Of: The Fenton Art Glass Museum

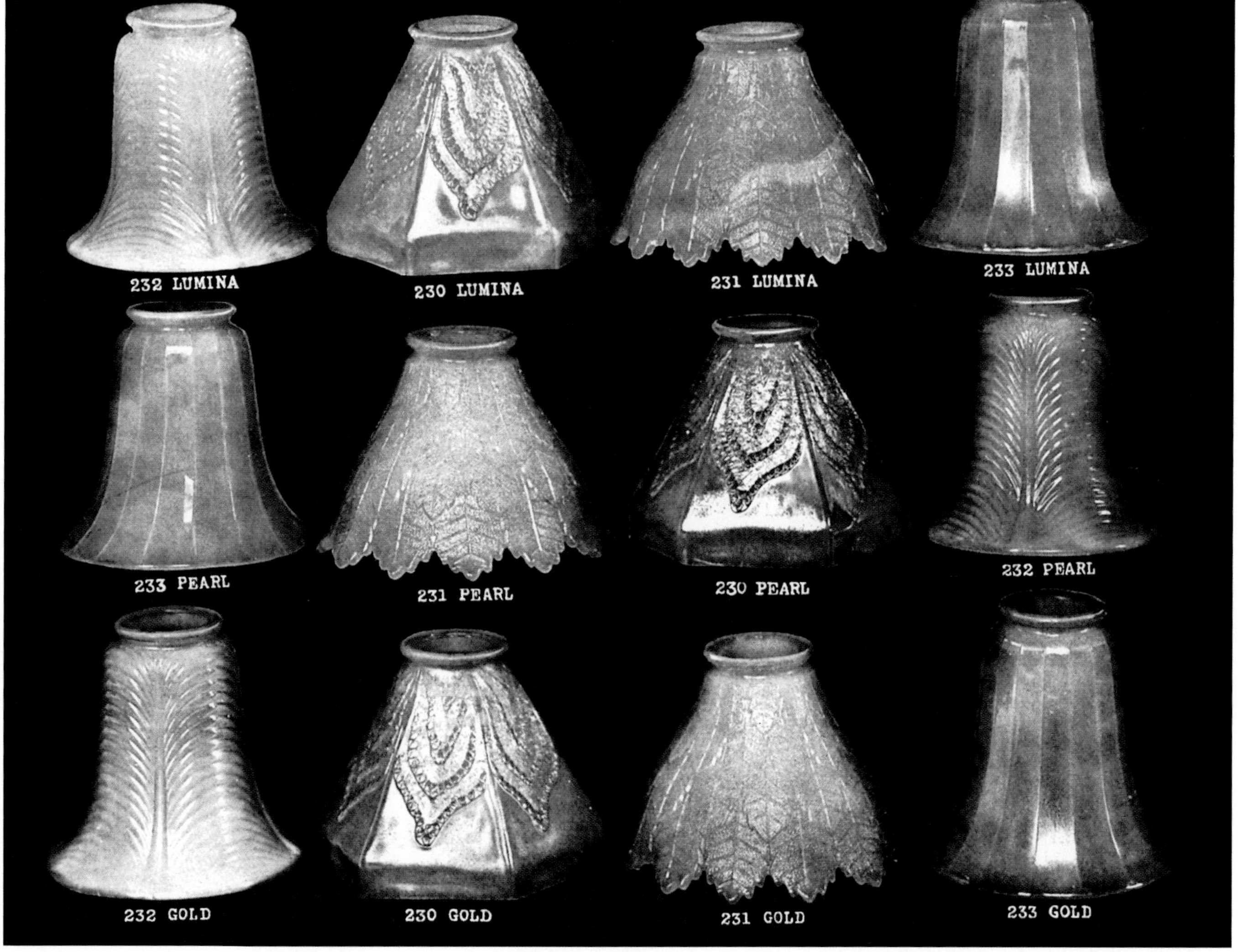
232 LUMINA
230 LUMINA
231 LUMINA
233 LUMINA
233 PEARL
231 PEARL
230 PEARL
232 PEARL
232 GOLD
230 GOLD
231 GOLD
233 GOLD

PERSIAN MEDALLION #1044 Circa 1911

Persian Medallion was a popular pattern with an Oriental motif. In addition to being used on bowls, plates, and comports, it is an interior pattern of the Wreath of Roses punch bowl and punch cup and was used for the exterior pattern of the Stream of Hearts comport. There are two sizes of carnival Persian Medallion comports. The larger one has both an interior and exterior Persian Medallion decoration. The smaller comport has an interior Persian Medallion design and an exterior Wide Panels pattern. The rose bowl was made in custard glass and Persian blue about 1915. Some of the custard glass pieces were decorated with green or nutmeg trim. The 8½" crimped bowl reappeared in 1970 in amethyst carnival, and orange carnival was added in July of 1971. A handle was later added to this bowl to form a basket. The basket was made in Independence Blue in 1976 and ruby iridescent in 1977. In 1971, the 10" plate appeared in amethyst carnival. The large comport was made in 1976 in Independence Blue and ruby carnival. Later in the 1970s and in the 1980s, the comport was made in numerous non-iridescent colors. New Persian Medallion items not produced in the original issue include a chalice and a fairy light. These later items may be found in both iridescent and non-iridescent colors.

	Golden	Rarity	Green	Rarity	Red	Rarity	Royal Blue	Rarity
*Bonbon, 2-hdld.	$43.00 – 47.00	(5)	$140.00 – 160.00	(5)	$900.00 – 1100.00+	(3)	$70.00 – 90.00	(5)
Bowl, 6"	$47.00 – 50.00	(5)	$40.00 – 45.00	(5)	$900.00 – 1100.00	(4)	$57.00 – 62.00	(5)
Bowl, 8½"	$55.00 – 60.00	(5)	$100.00 – 125.00	(5)	$2800.00 – 3000.00	(2)	$125.00 – 150.00	(5)
Bowl, 10"	$80.00 – 90.00	(5)	$350.00 – 425.00	(4)			$375.00 – 400.00	(4)
**Bowl, ftd. orange	$200.00 – 310.00	(5)	$450.00 – 575.00	(5)			$290.00 – 340.00	(5)
Chop plate							$600.00 – 700.00	(4)
Comport, lg.	$75.00 – 80.00	(5)	$260.00 – 310.00	(5)			$95.00 – 105.00	(5)
Comport, sm.	$65.00 – 75.00	(5)	$195.00 – 240.00	(5)			$80.00 – 90.00	(5)
Cup, punch	$22.00 – 25.00	(5)	$35.00 – 40.00	(5)			$27.00 – 30.00	(5)
Hair receiver	$55.00 – 65.00	(5)					$110.00 – 135.00	(5)
***Plate, 6"	$50.00 – 60.00	(5)	$500.00 – 600.00	(3)			$120.00 – 145.00	(5)
Plate, 7"	$50.00 – 55.00	(5)	$290.00 – 310.00	(5)			$110.00 – 130.00	(5)
Plate, 9½"	$300.00 – 350.00	(5)	$4000.00+	(1)			$450.00 – 600.00	(5)
Punch bowl w/base	$260.00 – 290.00	(5)	$520.00 – 575.00	(4)			$650.00 – 700.00	(5)
****Rose bowl	$65.00 – 75.00	(5)	$240.00 – 270.00	(5)			$120.00 – 150.00	(5)

	Violet	Rarity	White	Rarity	Aqua	Rarity	Topaz	Rarity
*Bonbon, 2-hdld.	$80.00 – 95.00	(5)			$120.00 – 135.00	(5)	$145.00 – 170.00	(5)
Bowl, 6"	$50.00 – 55.00	(5)			$70.00 – 85.00	(5)		
Bowl, 8½"	$120.00 – 150.00	(5)						
Bowl, 10"	$330.00 – 400.00	(4)						
**Bowl, ftd. orange	$300.00 – 350.00	(4)						
Comport, lg.	$450.00 – 500.00	(3)	$200.00 – 225.00	(4)				
Comport, sm.	$200.00 – 250.00	(4)	$200.00 – 250.00	(4)				
Cup, punch	$30.00 – 35.00	(5)						
Hair receiver			$250.00 – 275.00	(4)				
***Plate, 6"	$150.00 – 200.00	(4)					$400.00 – 500.00	(3)
Plate, 7"	$240.00 – 260.00	(4)						
Plate, 9½"			$900.00 – 1000.00	(3)				
Punch bowl w/base	$450.00 – 475.00	(4)						
****Rose bowl	$190.00 – 225.00	(4)	$90.00 – 105.00	(5)				

*Amberina $350.00 – 500.00, (4); Celeste Blue $1000.00 – 1200.00+, (3); Moonstone $700.00 – 800.00, (3); Sapphire $600.00 – 700.00, (3).
**Green with Grape & Cable exterior $1700.00 – 1900.00, (1).
***Black Amethyst $200.00 – 250.00+, (4); Purple $150.00 – 200.00, (4).
****Amber $400.00 – 450.00, (3).

PETER RABBIT

Circa 1912

Although large bowls and plates were produced in Peter Rabbit, they are very difficult to find today. The background pattern is similar to that used with Little Fishes, and the exterior pattern is Bearded Berry.

	Bowl, 9"	Rarity	Plate, 10"	Rarity
Golden	$1200.00 – 1400.00	(4)	$2500.00 – 2700.00	(2)
Green	$1500.00 – 1800.00	(4)	$3500.00+	(2)
Royal Blue	$1200.00 – 1400.00	(4)	$3500.00+	(2)

PILLAR AND DRAPE

Circa 1914

Catalog evidence indicates Fenton produced iridescent glass shades for lights about 1914. The photo below pictures a shade in the Pillar and Drape pattern with Golden iridescence over a milk glass base. For other examples of iridescent glass shades, see the catalog reprint at the bottom of page 85 and the Dragon's Tongue pattern on page 55.

	Shade
Golden Iridescence over MG	$50.00 – 60.00

PERSIAN MEDALLION
Golden

PERSIAN MEDALLION
Green

PERSIAN MEDALLION
Green

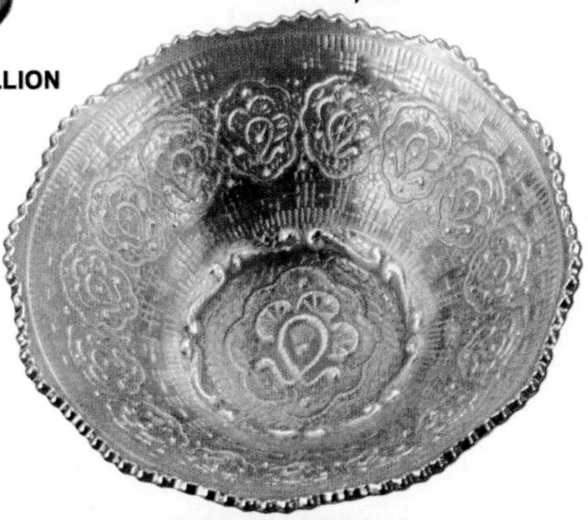

PERSIAN MEDALLION
Golden

PERSIAN MEDALLION
Golden

PERSIAN MEDALLION
Green

PERSIAN MEDALLION
Royal Blue

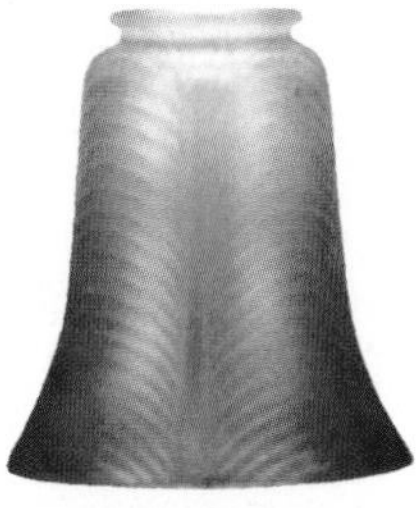

PILLAR & DRAPE
Golden Iridescence over Milk

PETER RABBIT
Green

PINE CONE #1064 (PINE CONE WREATH)

Circa 1911

Pieces of Pine Cone are limited to plates and small bowls.

	Bowl, 5½"	Rarity	Plate, 6¼"	Rarity	Plate, 7½"	Rarity
Golden	$90.00 – 110.00	(5)	$90.00 – 125.00	(5)	$350.00 – 400.00	(4)
Green	$300.00 – 350.00	(5)	$245.00 – 290.00	(5)	$325.00 – 390.00	(4)
Royal Blue	$190.00 – 210.00	(5)	$220.00 – 280.00	(5)	$250.00 – 325.00	(4)
Violet	$225.00 – 250.00	(5)	$180.00 – 225.00	(4)	$380.00 – 425.00	(4)
White	$225.00 – 250.00	(5)				
Amber					$550.00 – 650.00	(3)

PLAID (GRANNY'S GINGHAM)

Circa 1925

Both deep and shallow variations of Plaid bowls may be found. However, plates are very difficult to acquire. In 1930, the 8½" shallow bowl was reissued in transparent pink.

	Bowl, 8½"	Rarity	Plate, 9"	Rarity
Golden	$125.00 – 140.00	(5)	$350.00+	(3)
Green	$425.00 – 460.00	(4)		
Red	$3500.00 – 4000.00	(3)	$7000.00+	(1)
Royal Blue	$200.00 – 225.00	(5)	$550.00+	(3)
Violet	$400.00 – 450.00	(4)		
Celeste Blue	$3500.00+	(2)		
Lavender	$450.00 – 500.00	(4)		

PLUME PANELS

A vase is the only item Fenton produced in this pattern. Sizes range from about 6" to 12". There are six panels that alternate between plain panels and panels with feathers.

	Vase, 6" – 9"	Rarity	Vase, 10" – 12"	Rarity
Golden	$30.00 – 35.00	(5)	$40.00 – 45.00	(5)
Green	$62.00 – 77.00	(5)	$85.00 – 125.00	(5)
Red	$400.00 – 500.00	(3)	$600.00 – 800.00	(3)
Royal Blue	$60.00 – 85.00	(5)	$80.00 – 110.00	(5)
Violet	$50.00 – 65.00	(5)	$70.00 – 90.00	(5)
White	$70.00 – 80.00	(4)	$95.00 – 115.00	(4)

POND LILY #1414

Circa 1915 – 1923

The Pond Lily design incorporates a Lotus type flower with fancy scroll work. The only shape reported is a 2-handled bonbon. This bonbon has also been found in a rare light opaque blue iridescent color which is slightly different from the opaque blue which Fenton was producing during this time period.

	Bonbon, 2-hdld.	Rarity
Golden	$42.00 – 47.00	(5)
Green	$75.00 – 85.00	(5)
Royal Blue	$55.00 – 60.00	(5)
Violet	$55.00 – 65.00	(4)
White	$85.00 – 100.00	(5)
Opaque Blue	$250.00 – 300.00	(3)

PRAYER RUG

A 2-handled bonbon in custard glass with golden iridescence is the only item found in this pattern. Catalog evidence from about 1915 shows numerous pieces of custard glass Prayer Rug, therefore it is possible other pieces with golden iridescence may surface. The example shown is a custard glass bonbon with gold paint.

	Bonbon, 2-hdld.	Rarity
Custard with golden iridescence	$700.00 – 850.00	(3)

PRISM BAND #1014 (THREE BAND) — Circa 1912

Prism Band is an enameled water set with a tankard-style jug. The jug and the tumbler have horizontal banding. This set is found most often in golden or royal blue colors with an enameled forget-me-not style floral decoration. White carnival sets have been found with matching enameled tumblers that lack the band.

	Tankard	Rarity	Tumbler	Rarity
Golden	$150.00 – 175.00	(5)	$27.00 – 32.00	(5)
Green	$375.00 – 400.00	(5)	$50.00 – 55.00	(5)
Royal Blue	$380.00 – 410.00	(5)	$50.00 – 55.00	(5)
Violet	$330.00 – 360.00	(5)	$45.00 – 50.00	(5)
White	$340.00 – 360.00	(5)	$80.00 – 90.00	(4)
Ice Green	$350.00 – 400.00	(5)		

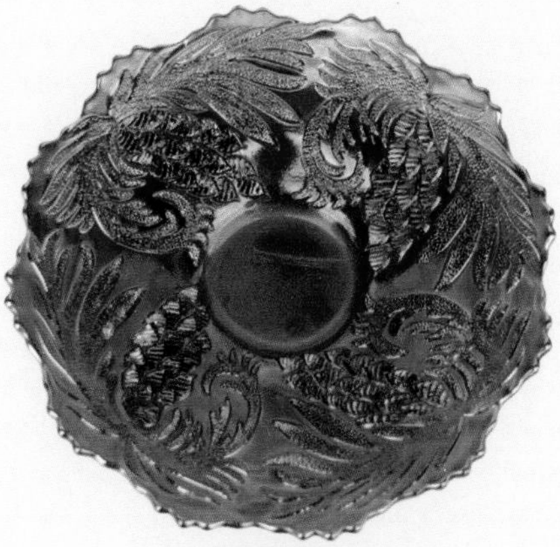

PINECONE
Violet

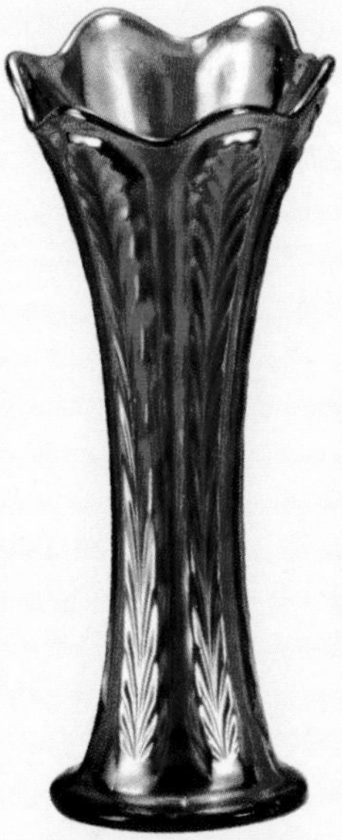

PLUME PANELS
Red

PRISM BAND
Royal Blue

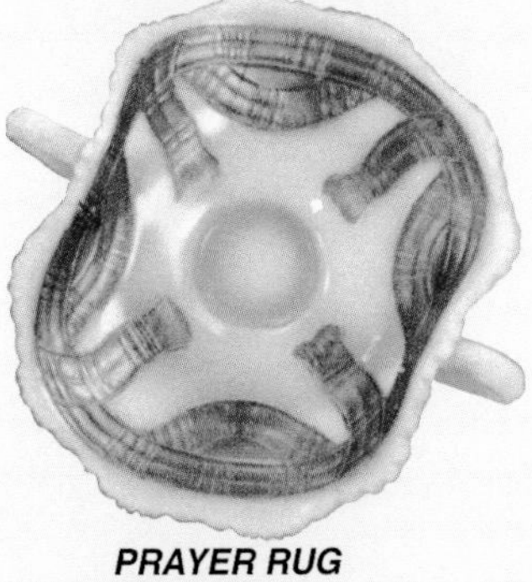

PRAYER RUG
Golden Iridescence over Custard Glass

POND LILY
Golden

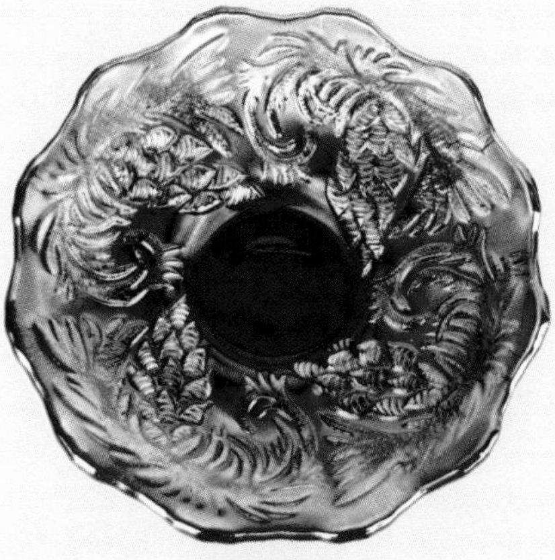

PINECONE
Green

PLAID
Royal Blue

RAGGED ROBIN

Circa 1910

An 8½" bowl that was made in several colors is the only piece known in the Ragged Robin pattern. The pattern consists of a single flower with large petals in the center of the base. This flower is repeated in a circular pattern around the center of the bowl.

	Bowl, 8½"	Rarity
Golden	$95.00 – 125.00	(5)
Green	$150.00 – 170.00	(4)
Royal Blue	$110.00 – 140.00	(5)
Violet	$130.00 – 160.00	(5)
White	$150.00 – 170.00	(4)

RIB AND HOLLY SPRIG (RIBBED HOLLY)

Circa 1925

Rib and Holly Sprig is Fenton's Holly pattern with ribbing added. It is found in flared, crimped, and goblet-style comports. The flared version of this comport was reissued in 1930 in transparent pink and green.

	Comport, 6" flared	Rarity	Comport, goblet-style	Rarity
Golden	$50.00 – 50.00	(5)	$70.00 – 75.00	(5)
Red	$350.00 – 400.00	(4)	$400.00 – 425.00	(4)
Royal Blue	$60.00 – 65.00	(5)	$80.00 – 90.00	(5)
Violet	$70.00 – 75.00	(5)	$80.00 – 90.00	(5)

RIBBON TIE (COMET)

Circa 1911

Large bowls and plates are found in this pattern. Red plates are elusive and very expensive.

	Bowl, 9"	Rarity	Plate, 9"	Rarity
Golden	$50.00 – 55.00	(5)		
Green	$70.00 – 80.00	(5)		
Red	$4500.00 – 5000.00	(1)	$7000.00 – 7500.00	(1)
Royal Blue	$120.00 – 140.00	(5)	$160.00 – 195.00	(5)
Violet	$75.00 – 95.00	(5)		
Purple			$200.00 – 225.00	(4)

ROSE SPRAY

Fenton's Rose Spray pattern consists of comports with various shapes of bowls — tulip, crimped, and flared. There is a lightly embossed rose with leaves on the interior of one side of the bowl. These comports are found most often in Fenton's stretch glass colors such as Celeste Blue and Florentine Green, but some Golden examples also exist.

	Comport	Rarity
Golden	$30.00 – 45.00	(5)
Celeste Blue	$70.00 – 100.00	(5)
Ice Green	$100.00 – 125.00	(5)
White	$140.00 – 180.00	(4)

ROSE TREE

Rose Tree is the interior pattern of a 10" bowl with the Orange Tree exterior pattern. Both ruffled and ice cream shapes have been found.

	Bowl, 10"	Rarity
Golden	$1000.00 – 1100.00	(2)
Royal Blue	$1100.00 – 1300.00	(2)

RUSTIC (MARYLAND) — Circa 1911

Numerous sizes and colors of vases are found in the Rustic pattern. These vases were pulled from Fenton's Hobnail pattern. Vases about 6" tall are considered to be the Hobnail pattern.

	Vase, 7" – 9"	Rarity	Vase, 10" – 15"	Rarity	Vase, 16" – 22"	Rarity
Golden	$40.00 – 45.00	(5)	$42.00 – 50.00	(5)	$750.00 – 850.00	(2)
Green	$60.00 – 70.00	(5)	$60.00 – 80.00	(5)	$1700.00 – 1900.00	(2)
Red	$3000.00 – 3500.00	(2)	$3500.00 – 4000.00	(2)		
Royal Blue	$55.00 – 60.00	(5)	$55.00 – 75.00	(5)	$1800.00 – 2000.00	(3)
Violet	$60.00 – 65.00	(5)	$50.00 – 65.00	(5)	$1800.00 – 2000.00	(2)
Lime Green Opal			$900.00 – 1000.00	(3)		
Peach Opalescent			$1200.00 – 1300.00	(1)		
Purple					$700.00 – 800.00	(3)
White	$70.00 – 75.00	(5)	$70.00 – 80.00	(5)	$2400.00 – 2600.00	(3)

RIBBON TIE
Violet

RIB & HOLLY SPRIG
Royal Blue

RAGGED ROBIN
Violet

RUSTIC
White

RIBBON TIE
Royal Blue

ROSE TREE
Royal Blue

RUSTIC
Green

ROSE SPRAY
Golden Iridescence over Royal Blue

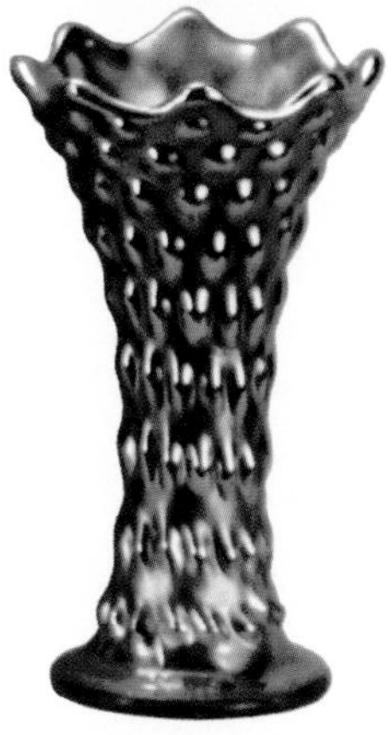

RUSTIC
Royal Blue

SAILBOATS #1774 (SAILBOAT AND WINDMILL) — Circa 1911

Small bowls, comports, goblets, and plates may be found in this pattern. The goblets and comports may be found with iridized bowls and crystal frosted or colored stems. The small bowl may be flared, crimped, or square. The comport and goblet were also made in custard glass.

	Bowl, 5½"	Rarity	Comport	Rarity	Goblet, water	Rarity
Golden	$35.00 – 37.00	(5)	$60.00 – 65.00	(5)	$65.00 – 75.00	(5)
Green	$85.00 – 100.00	(5)			$300.00 – 350.00	(3)
Red	$550.00+	(3)				
Royal Blue	$55.00 – 60.00	(5)	$135.00 – 160.00	(5)	$60.00 – 70.00	(5)
Violet	$55.00 – 65.00	(5)			$250.00 – 275.00	(3)
Amber	$140.00 – 165.00	(4)				
Amberina	$200.00 – 225.00	(4)				
Aqua	$90.00 – 120.00	(5)				
Brick Red	$300.00 – 325.00	(4)				
Topaz	$225.00 – 250.00	(4)				

	Goblet, wine	Rarity	Plate, 6"	Rarity
Golden	$32.00 – 35.00	(5)	$425.00 – 500.00	(4)
Royal Blue	$80.00 – 90.00	(5)	$550.00 – 600.00	(2)

SCALE BAND #212 (TWO BAND) — Circa 1908 – 1925

The Scale Band pattern is found as an exterior pattern on small bowls, large bowls, and small plates. It is the major pattern on a scarce water set found primarily in golden and royal blue.

	Golden	Rarity	Red	Rarity	Royal Blue	Rarity	Peach Opalescent	Rarity
Bowl, 6"	$32.00 – 35.00	(5)					$80.00 – 90.00	(4)
Bowl, 9"–10"	$65.00 – 70.00	(4)			$120.00 – 170.00	(4)		
Pitcher	$135.00 – 170.00	(5)			$390.00 – 445.00	(4)		
Plate, 6½"	$40.00 – 45.00	(5)	$500.00 – 600.00	(3)				
Tumbler	$50.00 – 60.00	(5)			$300.00 – 350.00	(3)		

SILVER QUEEN (Not illustrated)

This is an enameled water set pattern featuring a white scroll pattern, usually on a golden background.

	Pitcher	Rarity	Tumbler	Rarity
Golden	$190.00 – 210.00	(5)	$65.00 – 70.00	(5)

SMALL RIB

Cupped and flared comports have been found. Golden iridescence on the bowl is usually accompanied by a non-iridized stem and base.

	Comport, cupped	Rarity	Comport, flared	Rarity
Golden	$35.00 – 40.00	(5)	$35.00 – 40.00	(5)
Golden Irid. over Aqua	$40.00 – 45.00	(5)	$40.00 – 45.00	(5)
Green	$45.00 – 50.00	(5)	$42.00 – 47.00	(5)

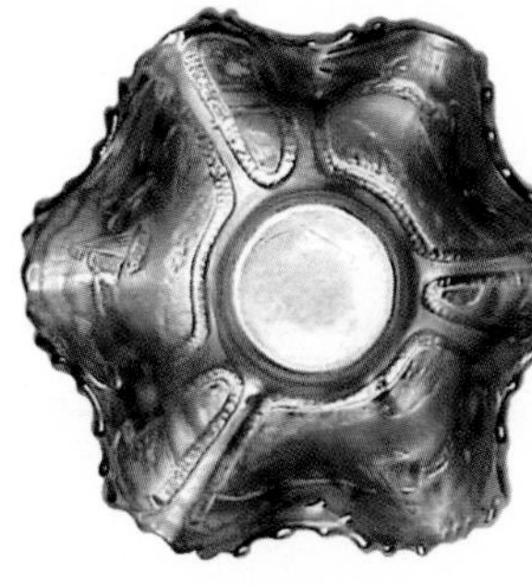

SAILBOATS
Royal Blue

SAILBOATS
Golden

SCALE BAND
Golden

SCALE BAND
Golden

SAILBOATS
Golden

SAILBOATS
Golden

SMALL RIB
Golden Iridescence over Green

SMALL RIB
Golden

Computer Colorized Catalog Reprint Circa 1911

Courtesy Of: The Fenton Art Glass Museum

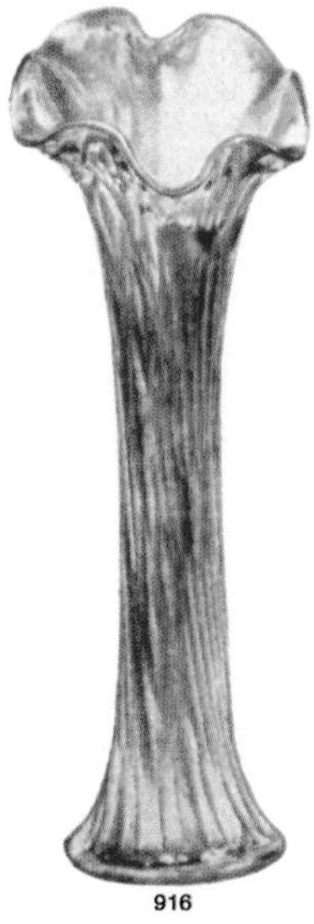

916
Fenton's Rib 16"

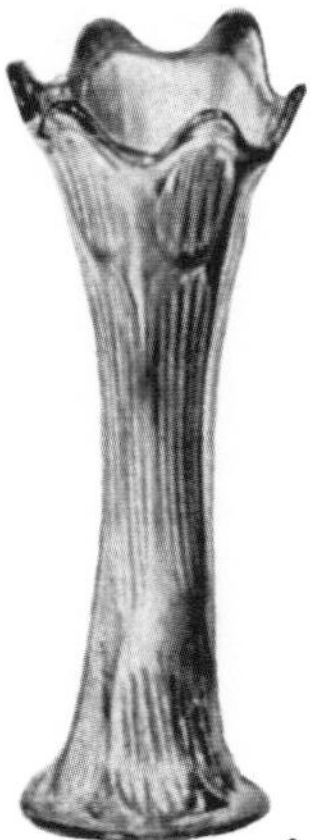

504
Diamond & Rib 12"

32
Paneled Diamond & Bows 9"

517
Rustic 21"

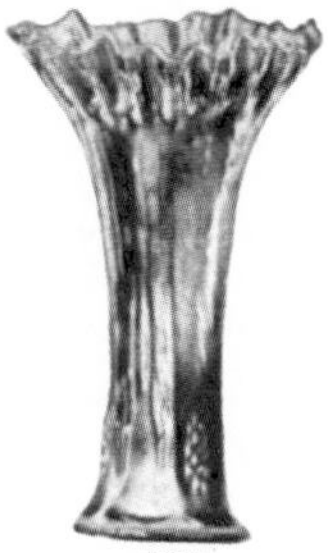

1124
Butterfly & Berry 9"

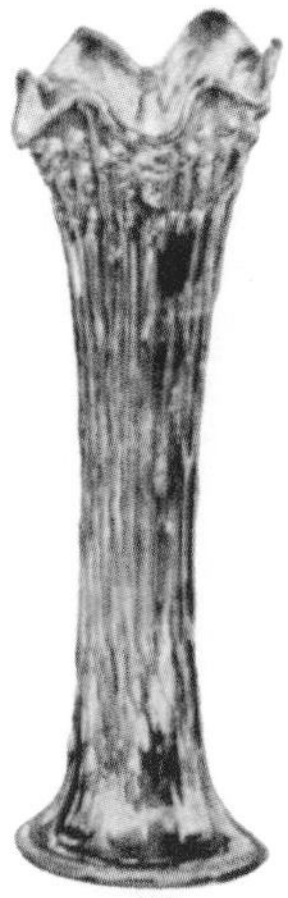

412
April Showers 12"

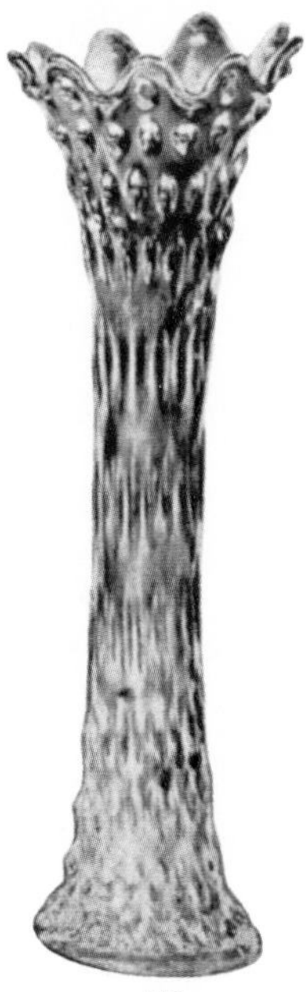

507
Rustic 16"

STAG AND HOLLY

Circa 1912

The rose bowl is a very large, 3-footed bowl which has the pattern on the inside. The bowls may be found flared and crimped or cupped with a scalloped edge. A variation of bowls has spade-type feet. During the last decade, a poor quality reproduction of the large 3-footed bowl has appeared in cobalt, ruby, and iridized white opalescent. Fenton never produced this pattern in these colors. Current production also includes non-iridized colors, and it is possible other iridized colors of this reproduction bowl may be found.

	Bowl, 7" 3-ftd	Rarity	Bowl, 10"	Rarity	Plate, 13"	Rarity	Plate, 9"	Rarity
Golden	$70.00 – 85.00	(5)	$100.00 – 115.00	(5)	$950.00 – 1100.00	(4)	$800.00 – 900.00	(4)
Green	$140.00 – 180.00	(5)	$900.00 – 1000.00	(3)				
Red	$2500.00 – 2700.00	(3)	$3000.00 – 3500.00	(2)				
Royal Blue	$125.00 – 140.00	(5)	$250.00 – 300.00	(4)			$1500.00+	(3)
Violet	$125.00 – 135.00	(5)	$250.00 – 300.00	(4)			$3000.00+	(1)
Aqua			$500.00 – 550.00	(4)				

	Plate, 6½"	Rarity	Rose bowl	Rarity
Golden	$600.00 – 675.00	(3)	$325.00 – 370.00	(3)
Violet	$2500.00+	(2)		

STARFLOWER

Circa 1911

The only item found in this pattern is a pitcher. No tumblers have been found. If tumblers ~~do exist, they are~~ extremely rare.

	Pitcher	Rarity
Golden	$3000.00+	(1)
Royal Blue	$2500.00 – 2700.00	(2)
White	UND	(1)

STIPPLED RAYS

Circa 1908

Imperial and Northwood also had patterns with this name. The exterior pattern on the Fenton version is Scale Band.

	Bonbon	Rarity	Bowl, 5½"	Rarity	Bowl, 10"	Rarity	Comport	Rarity
Golden	$32.00 – 35.00	(5)	$38.00 – 40.00	(5)	$39.00 – 42.00	(5)	$32.00 – 35.00	(5)
Green	$50.00 – 55.00	(5)	$52.00 – 57.00	(5)	$55.00 – 60.00	(5)	$45.00 – 50.00	(5)
Red	$450.00 – 500.00	(3)	$350.00 – 400.00	(4)	$450.00 – 500.00	(3)		
Royal Blue	$38.00 – 42.00	(5)	$45.00 – 50.00	(5)	$45.00 – 50.00	(5)	$42.00 – 45.00	(5)
Violet	$43.00 – 47.00	(5)	$45.00 – 50.00	(5)	$47.00 – 52.00	(5)	$42.00 – 45.00	(5)
Amberina			$225.00 – 250.00	(4)	$300.00 – 350.00	(3)		
Celeste Blue							$300.00 – 350.00	(3)
Lime Green							$60.00 – 75.00	(4)
White							$90.00 – 100.00	(4)

	Creamer	Rarity	Plate, 7"	Rarity	Sugar	Rarity
Golden	$27.00 – 30.00	(5)	$45.00 – 50.00	(5)	$27.00 – 30.00	(5)
Green	$55.00 – 60.00	(5)	$90.00 – 100.00	(5)	$55.00 – 60.00	(5)
Red	$375.00 – 415.00	(4)			$390.00 – 415.00	(4)
Royal Blue	$45.00 – 50.00	(5)	$50.00 – 65.00	(5)	$45.00 – 50.00	(5)
Violet	$50.00 – 55.00	(5)	$75.00 – 85.00	(5)	$40.00 – 45.00	(5)

STRAWBERRY

Circa 1917 – 1922

The only item made in the Strawberry pattern by Fenton was a 6" 2-handled bonbon. Other companies which made a variety of pieces with a Strawberry pattern include Dugan, Northwood, and Millersburg.

	Bonbon	Rarity
Golden	$50.00 – 55.00	(5)
Green	$70.00 – 85.00	(5)
Red	$400.00 – 450.00	(3)
Royal Blue	$95.00 – 110.00	(5)
Violet	$55.00 – 60.00	(5)
Amber	$50.00 – 60.00	(5)
Amberina	$300.00 – 350.00	(4)
Lime Green Opalescent	$425.00 – 475.00	(3)
Reverse Amberina	$350.00 – 400.00	(3)
Topaz	$90.00 – 110.00	(5)

STAG & HOLLY
Golden

STIPPLED RAYS
Violet

STIPPLED RAYS
Violet

STARFLOWER
Royal Blue

STIPPLED RAYS
Green

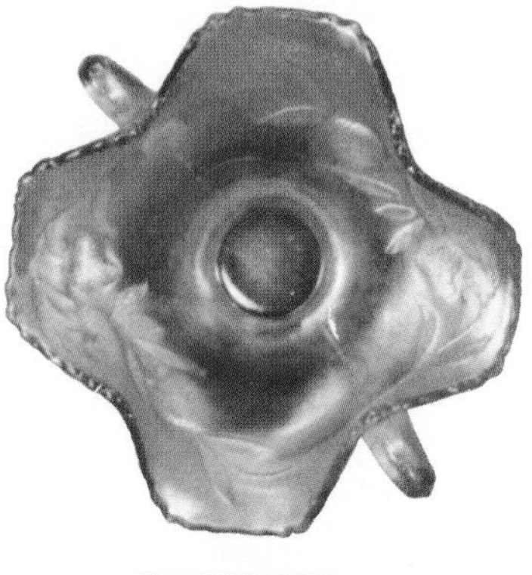

STRAWBERRY
Golden

1656 FOOTED CRIMPED
Dragon& Lotus

1606 FOOTED CRIMPED
Stag & Holly

1656 FOOTED SHALLOW
Dragon& Lotus

1606 FOOTED SHALLOW
Stag & Holly

1746 FOOTED CRIMPED
Grape & Cable

1746 FOOTED SHALLOW
Grape & Cable

STRAWBERRY SCROLL (STRAWBERRY AND SCROLL BAND) Circa 1912

Strawberry Scroll is a fancy water set with the same shape as the Blueberry water set.

	Pitcher	Rarity	Tumbler	Rarity
Golden	$3000.00 – 3500.00	(3)	$125.00 – 150.00	(4)
Royal Blue	$2500.00 – 3500.00	(3)	$175.00 – 225.00	(3)

STREAM OF HEARTS Circa 1915

The exterior pattern on the comport is Persian Medallion. Goblets, found to date only in the golden color, are very difficult to find.

	Bowl, 10" ftd	Rarity	Comport	Rarity	Goblet	Rarity
Golden	$70.00 – 80.00	(5)	$95.00 – 110.00	(5)	$300.00 – 350.00	(1)
Royal Blue	$90.00 – 100.00	(5)				

SWAN (PASTEL SWAN) Circa 1926

Fenton and Dugan both made similar swans. The Fenton mold from the 1920s has tail feathers which come to a point. The early Dugan swan has larger tail feathers, defined nostrils, and a longer neck than the Fenton version. However, Fenton acquired the Dugan mold and began using it in the 1930s to produce satin pieces. This same mold was used for the later clear issues.

	Swan	Rarity		Swan	Rarity
Golden	$150.00 – 200.00	(4)	Lime Green	$375.00 – 425.00	(3)
Green	$150.00+	(3)	Olive Green	$500.00 – 600.00	(3)
Violet	$200.00 – 225.00	(4)	Peach Opalescent	$250.00 – 300.00	(4)
Aqua	$250.00 – 300.00	(3)	Teal	$300.00 – 350.00	(3)
Ice Blue	$35.00 – 40.00	(5)	Topaz	$300.00 – 350.00	(3)
Ice Green	$35.00 – 40.00	(5)	White	$600.00 – 700.00	(3)

TEN MUMS #1057 (DOUBLE CHRYSANTHEMUM; CHRYSANTHEMUM WREATH) Circa 1911

	Bowl, 10"	Rarity	Pitcher, 9"	Rarity	Tumbler	Rarity
Golden	$85.00 – 95.00	(5)	$400.00 – 475.00	(4)	$55.00 – 65.00	(5)
Green	$240.00 – 265.00	(5)				
Royal Blue	$270.00 – 320.00	(5)	$650.00 – 750.00	(4)	$75.00 – 85.00	(4)
Violet	$200.00 – 250.00	(5)				
Purple	$350.00 – 400.00	(4)				
White			$2500.00+	(1)	$300.00 – 350.00	(1)

THISTLE (CARNIVAL THISTLE) Circa 1911

	Bowl, 9"	Rarity	Plate, 9"	Rarity
Golden	$85.00 – 95.00	(5)	$6000.00+	(1)
Green	$150.00 – 165.00	(5)	$3500.00+	(3)
Royal Blue	$130.00 – 150.00	(5)		
Violet	$125.00 – 140.00	(5)	$4000.00+	(2)
Aqua	$350.00 – 400.00	(4)		
Topaz	$300.00 – 350.00	(4)		

THISTLE AND LOTUS Circa 1920

	Bowl, 7"	Rarity
Golden	$75.00 – 80.00	(5)

THISTLE BANANA BOAT (FENTON'S THISTLE) Circa 1911

This is a pattern exclusive to the 4-footed oval banana boat shape. The exterior pattern is Water Lily and Cattails.

	Banana boat	Rarity
Golden	$100.00 – 125.00	(5)
Green	$345.00 – 390.00	(5)
Royal Blue	$250.00 – 300.00	(5)
Violet	$240.00 – 290.00	(5)

STRAWBERRY SCROLL
Golden *Royal Blue*

STREAM OF HEARTS
Golden

SWAN
Aqua

SWAN
Rose

THISTLE
Violet

TEN MUMS
Royal Blue

TEN MUMS
Golden

TEN MUMS
Green

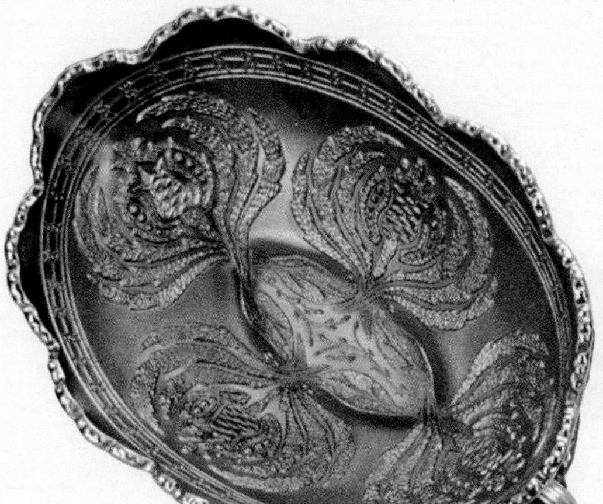

THISTLE BANANA BOAT
Green

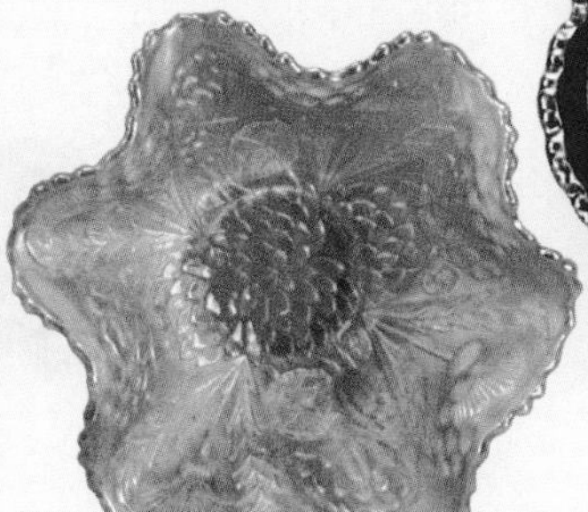

THISTLE & LOTUS
Golden

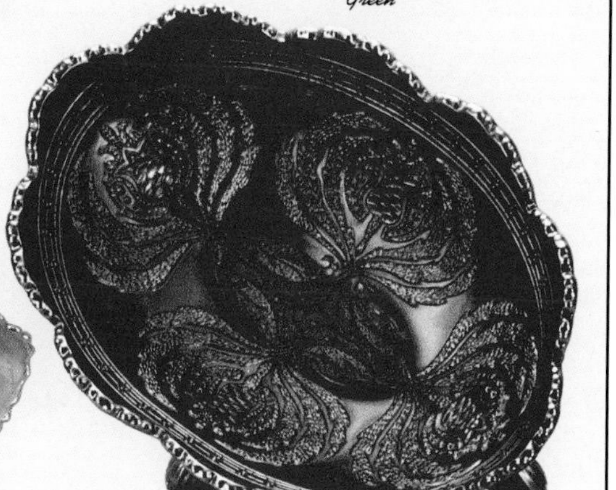

THISTLE BANANA BOAT
Royal Blue

TWO FLOWERS (DOGWOOD AND MARSH LILY)

Circa 1915

	Bowl, 5"-7", ftd.	Rarity	Bowl, 9"-10", 3-ftd.	Rarity	Bowl, 11", 3-ftd.	Rarity
Golden	$50.00 – 55.00	(5)	$50.00 – 60.00	(5)	$70.00 – 80.00	(5)
Green	$60.00 – 70.00	(5)	$240.00 – 260.00	(4)	$265.00 – 310.00	(4)
Red	$1200.00+	(1)	$1500.00 – 1800.00	(3)	$1900.00 – 2200.00	(2)
Royal Blue	$50.00 – 55.00	(5)	$260.00 – 300.00	(4)	$290.00 – 320.00	(4)
Violet	$65.00 – 75.00	(5)	$150.00 – 170.00	(5)	$170.00 – 195.00	(5)
Amberina			$700.00 – 800.00	(3)		
Aqua	$165.00 – 190.00	(4)			$200.00 – 250.00	(4)
Lime Green	$200.00 – 225.00	(4)			$200.00 – 250.00	(4)
Sapphire					$3500.00+	(1)
Topaz	$80.00 – 100.00	(4)			$150.00 – 175.00	(4)

	Plate, 9", ftd.	Rarity	Plate, 13"	Rarity	Rose Bowl	Rarity
Golden	$450.00 – 500.00	(4)	$2000.00+	(2)	$180.00 – 195.00	(5)
Green					$200.00 – 225.00	(5)
Royal Blue					$180.00 – 200.00	(5)

TWO FRUITS (APPLE AND PEAR)

Circa 1912

The only known piece in this pattern is a four-part, #1695 – 5½" 2-handled bonbon. Each section of the bonbon contains a large single fruit — an apple or a pear. This bonbon was re-issued in 1930 in transparent pink.

	Bonbon	Rarity		Bonbon	Rarity
Golden	$60.00 – 70.00	(5)	Violet	$80.00 – 90.00	(5)
Green	$100.00 – 120.00	(5)	Topaz	$100.00 – 125.00	(5)
Royal Blue	$80.00 – 90.00	(5)	White	$110.00 – 125.00	(5)

VINTAGE (GRAPE DELIGHT)

Circa 1910

Dugan, Millersburg, and U. S. Glass also made patterns with the same name. The bowls may be cupped or flared. The flared version will sometimes be found double crimped. The epergne is 4¾" high and 6" in diameter. The exterior pattern of the punch bowl and punch cups is Wreath of Roses. A Vintage 7½" handled basket was made in Red Carnival in 1993.

	Golden	Rarity	Green	Rarity	Red	Rarity	Royal Blue	Rarity	Violet	Rarity
Bowl, 5½"-6"	$22.00 – 27.00	(5)	$35.00 – 40.00	(5)	$7000.00+	(1)	$35.00 – 40.00	(5)	$32.00 – 37.00	(5)
*Bowl, 6½" -7"	$27.00 – 30.00	(5)	$40.00 – 45.00	(5)	$2000.00+	(2)	$40.00 – 45.00	(5)	$37.00 – 40.00	(5)
**Bowl, 8"-9"	$37.00 – 40.00	(5)	$45.00 – 50.00	(5)	$2000.00+	(2)	$45.00 – 50.00	(5)	$34.00 – 37.00	(5)
Bowl, 10"	$42.00 – 47.00	(5)	$85.00 – 95.00	(5)	$2000.00+	(2)	$110.00 – 125.00	(5)	$55.00 – 60.00	(5)
Comport, 6"	$35.00 – 40.00	(5)	$55.00 – 65.00	(5)			$55.00 – 60.00	(5)	$45.00 – 50.00	(5)
Cup, punch	$22.00 – 25.00	(5)	$32.00 – 35.00	(5)			$35.00 – 40.00	(5)	$32.00 – 35.00	(5)
Epergne	$80.00 – 105.00	(5)	$130.00 – 145.00	(5)			$135.00 – 150.00	(5)	$105.00 – 115.00	(5)
Fern bowl, 3-ftd.	$50.00 – 55.00	(5)	$90.00 – 105.00	(5)	$950.00 – 1100.00	(3)	$90.00 – 100.00	(5)	$60.00 – 70.00	(5)
Plate, 6"	$130.00 – 160.00	(5)							$120.00 – 130.00	(5)
Plate, 6½"	$500.00 – 550.00	(1)								
Plate, 7"			$175.00 – 200.00	(5)			$125.00 – 140.00	(5)	$135.00 – 150.00	(5)
Plate, 7½"-8"	$120.00 – 140.00	(5)	$125.00 – 140.00	(5)			$125.00 – 140.00	(5)	$135.00 – 150.00	(5)
Plate, 9"							$1500.00+	(1)	$1500.00+	(1)
Punch bowl and base	$270.00 – 300.00	(5)	$450.00 – 500.00	(4)			$430.00 – 475.00	(4)	$400.00 – 440.00	(5)
Rose bowl	$50.00 – 60.00	(5)					$50.00 – 60.00	(5)		

*Aqua Opalescent $800.00 – 900.00, (3).

**Amber $200.00 – 225.00, (4); Aqua Opalescent $950.00 – 1200.00, (3).

	Bonbon, 6", 3-ftd.	Rarity	Bowl, 5", 3-ftd.	Rarity	Bowl, 10", 3-ftd.	Rarity
Golden	$50.00 – 55.00	(5)	$45.00 – 50.00	(5)	$80.00 –90.00	(5)
Green	$48.00 – 52.00	(5)	$170.00 – 190.00	(5)	$350.00 – 390.00	(4)
Red			$800.00 – 900.00	(3)	$12,000.00+	(1)
Royal Blue	$48.00 – 52.00	(5)	$90.00 – 105.00	(5)	$225.00 – 250.00	(5)
Violet	$48.00 – 52.00	(5)	$80.00 – 90.00	(5)	$125.00 – 135.00	(5)
Amber	$37.00 – 40.00	(5)				
Amberina			$400.00 – 500.00	(4)		
Aqua			$110.00 – 125.00	(5)		
Red Opalescent			$1000.00 – 1200.00	(1)		
Lime Green Opal			$700.00 – 800.00	(3)		
Red Amberina Opal			$1000.00 – 1200.00	(3)		
Teal					$350.00 – 375.00	(3)
Topaz			$90.00 – 110.00	(5)		
White	$80.00 – 100.00	(5)				

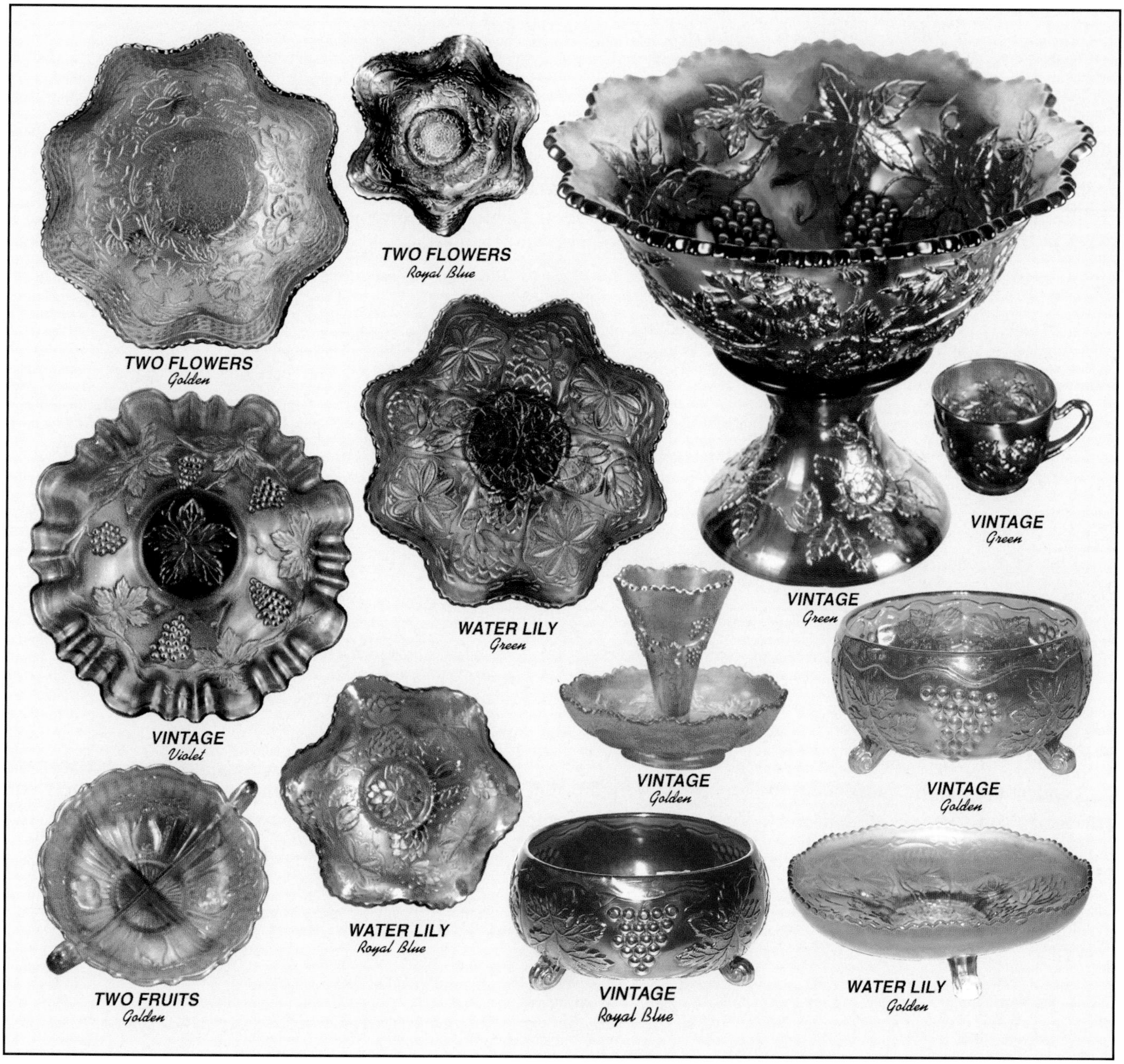

TWO FLOWERS
Golden

TWO FLOWERS
Royal Blue

WATER LILY
Green

VINTAGE
Green

VINTAGE
Green

VINTAGE
Violet

VINTAGE
Golden

VINTAGE
Golden

TWO FRUITS
Golden

WATER LILY
Royal Blue

VINTAGE
Royal Blue

WATER LILY
Golden

WATER LILY AND CATTAILS #8 (CATTAILS AND WATER LILY) Circa 1911

This is the exterior pattern of the Thistle Banana Boat. A table set, water set, and bowls in several sizes were also produced. Most pieces are only available in the golden color and the spittoon whimsy is rare. For other shapes and non-iridescent colors in this pattern see the Early Opalescent, Chocolate Glass, and Early Pattern Glass sections in Part I: Early Glassware.

	Golden	Rarity	Royal Blue	Rarity	Violet	Rarity	Aqua	Rarity
Bowl, 5"	$32.00 – 35.00	(5)	$45.00 – 50.00	(5)	$150.00 – 170.00	(4)	$150.00 – 200.00	(4)
Bowl, 7"-9"	$45.00 – 50.00	(4)						
Bowl, Banana Boat			$130.00 – 150.00	(4)				
Butter	$150.00 – 175.00	(5)						
Creamer	$60.00 – 70.00	(5)						
Pitcher	$325.00 – 350.00	(5)						
Spittoon whimsy	$2000.00+	(1)						
Spooner	$60.00 – 70.00	(5)						
Sugar	$90.00 – 100.00	(5)						
Toothpick	$70.00 – 80.00	(5)						
Tumbler	$85.00 – 95.00	(4)						

WIDE PANEL (Not illustrated) Circa 1920

Wide Panel is primarily an exterior pattern which Fenton used on numerous pieces. For purposes of identification and pricing, see the appropriate interior patterns. A 7" tall vase was made in the Wide Panel pattern. It is pictured in a 1920 Butler Brother's catalog. A similar carnival pattern with this same name was also made by other companies such as Northwood, Dugan, Imperial, and Westmoreland.

	Vase, 7"	Rarity
Golden	$25.00 – 30.00	(5)
Green	$30.00 – 35.00	(5)
Red	$600.00 – 700.00	(3)
Royal Blue	$45.00 – 55.00	(5)
Violet	$35.00 – 45.00	(5)

WILD BLACKBERRY

The Wild Blackberry pattern has four leaves and three blackberries per branch. The exterior pattern is Wide Panel. Some bowls may be found with advertising.

	Bowl, 8½"	Rarity
Golden	$80.00 – 90.00	(4)
Green	$190.00 – 225.00	(4)
Violet	$100.00 – 125.00	(4)

WINE AND ROSES #922 (CABBAGE ROSE AND GRAPE) Circa 1915

The Wine and Roses pattern consists of a pitcher and wine goblet which make up a wine set. The pitcher is elusive.

	Goblet, wine	Rarity	Pitcher	Rarity
Golden	$80.00 – 90.00	(4)	$625.00 – 675.00	(3)
Royal Blue	$100.00 – 125.00	(4)		

WREATH OF ROSES (ROSE WREATH; AMERICAN BEAUTY ROSES) Circa 1910

A pattern with the same name was made by Dugan. The punch sets — both bowl and cups — may be found with either the Persian Medallion or Vintage interior pattern. Two styles of bowls have been found. One style is deep, and the other less common style is shallow and wide. The 2-handled bonbon may be found in two styles — flat or footed with a short stem.

	Golden	Rarity	Green	Rarity	Royal Blue	Rarity	Violet	Rarity
Bonbon, 2-hdld.	$37.00 – 40.00	(5)	$45.00 – 50.00	(5)	$40.00 – 45.00	(5)	$40.00 – 45.00	(5)
Comport	$40.00 – 45.00	(5)	$45.00 – 50.00	(5)	$45.00 – 50.00	(5)	$47.00 – 52.00	(5)
Cup, punch	$15.00 – 20.00	(5)	$25.00 – 30.00	(5)	$25.00 – 30.00	(5)	$20.00 – 25.00	(5)
Punch bowl/base	$400.00 – 450.00	(4)	$650.00 – 750.00	(4)	$400.00 – 450.00	(4)	$370.00 – 425.00	(5)

ZIG-ZAG #1015 — Circa 1912

This embossed pattern is found on a water set with an enameled floral decoration. A Prism Band tumbler is used to complete the set. A pressed pattern with the same name was made by Millersburg.

	Pitcher	Tumbler
Golden	$225.00 – 250.00	$30.00 – 35.00
Royal Blue	$400.00 – 450.00	$40.00 – 45.00
Violet	$400.00 – 450.00	$40.00 – 45.00
Ice Green	$500.00 – 550.00	$60.00 – 70.00

WATER LILY and CATTAILS *Violet*

WREATH OF ROSES VINTAGE INTERIOR *Violet*

WREATH OF ROSES *Violet*

WILD BLACKBERRY *Royal Blue*

WILD BLACKBERRY *Green*

WREATH OF ROSES *Violet*

WINE and ROSES *Golden*

WREATH OF ROSES PERSIAN MEDALLION INTERIOR *Royal Blue*

WREATH OF ROSES *Royal Blue*

ZIG-ZAG *Green*

OFF HAND ART GLASS

In the early 1920s a group of highly professional European glassworkers was hired by Imperial and later Durand to produce off hand art glass. This experiment with free-form glass shapes was not successful, and the group soon became unemployed.

In 1925, this same contingent of skilled European glassworkers was contracted for one year to produce off hand art glass shapes at the Fenton factory. Fenton either had not heard about the difficulties involved in selling this type of glass or they were convinced their successful run of carnival glass empowered them with a superior marketing ability.

Since these workers were previously employed at other American glasshouses such as Durand and Imperial, the colors and shapes of the art glass produced at these different factories will bear many similarities. In addition to the photographs, drawings by James D. Fenton of some of the more elusive shapes have been reproduced on the following pages. They provide a valuable insight into the production of some of the hardest to find glassware produced by Fenton and help to identify these pieces as Fenton.

These off hand art forms were blown to a general shape without the use of molds. As the piece was reheated, colored glass bits used for the designs were worked into the form to produce the pattern; patterns included Hanging Hearts, Hanging Vine, Mosaic Inlaid, and Pulled Feather. Some pieces may also be found with floral decorations. Production colors of the new glass shapes were Karnak red, Oriental ivory, antique green, and turquoise blue, but a few shapes have appeared in jade green and lilac. Handled pieces usually were accented with dark blue or black handles, and footed pieces were commonly produced with dark blue feet.

Vases of all sizes and shapes were the most numerous types of pieces produced. Bowls, candlesticks, and covered candies were also in the line. There are also line drawings of a tobacco jar and a tall 2-piece jardiniere.

This experiment with Tiffany-style art glass lasted only one year. The cost involved in producing these special pieces resulted in glassware which was too expensive for the times. At the end of the contract period, there was so much of this glassware on hand that it was offered for sale to employees at fifty cents per piece. As a result of this short production, examples are seldom found in the marketplace today, and prices are becoming astronomical.

Line Drawings by James D. Fenton-Circa 1920's
Courtesy Of: The Fenton Art Glass Museum

Mosaic Inlaid Plain
mosaic inlaid
3046
3054
3060 Tobacco Jar.
3053
3023

	Hanging Hearts Hanging Vine	Mosaic	Pulled Feather	Plain Karnak
Tobacco jar, #3060		$2000.00+		$2000.00+
Urn, #3046, ftd.	$1800.00 – 2000.00			
*Vase, #3053-10", 3-ftd.	$1800.00 – 2000.00	$1800.00 – 2000.00	$1400.00 – 1600.00	
Vase, #3054, ftd.		$1100.00 – 1300.00		
Vase, #3023			$1200.00 – 1400.00	

*Lilac with Hanging Hearts design $2500.00+

Examples of the #3024 Egyptian style vase are shown on the opposite page. Pieces range in size from 8" to 21" in the Mosaic, Hanging Hearts, and Hanging Vine patterns. Finding the larger sizes of these vases is extremely difficult.

The line drawings below are from 1920s illustrations by James D. Fenton. They show patterns or shapes which are not pictured elsewhere.

	Hanging Hearts Hanging Vine	Mosaic	Pulled Feather
Row 1:			
Vase, #3024-15"	$3000.00+	$3000.00+	
Vase, #3024-8"or 9"	$900.00 – 1000.00	$850.00 – 950.00	
Vase, #3024-12"	$1600.00 – 1800.00	$1600.00 – 1800.00	
Row 2:			
Vase, #3024-10"	$1200.00 – 1400.00	$1200.00 – 1300.00	
Row 3:			
Vase, #3003-6½"	$750.00 – 900.00	$700.00 – 850.00	
Vase, #3024-21"	$4000.00+	$3500.00+	
Vase, #3003-6½"	$750.00 – 900.00	$700.00 – 850.00	
Drawings below:			
Vase, #3022			$1200.00 – 1400.00
Vase, #3031	$1200.00 – 1350.00		
Bonbon, #3038	$1100.00 – 1200.00		
Vase, #3013 ivy ball	$750.00 – 800.00	$700.00 – 750.00	$750.00 – 800.00
Candlestick, #3019 ea.	$650.00 – 700.00		$600.00 – 650.00
Vase, #3020	$750.00 – 900.00	$700.00 – 850.00	$750.00 – 850.00

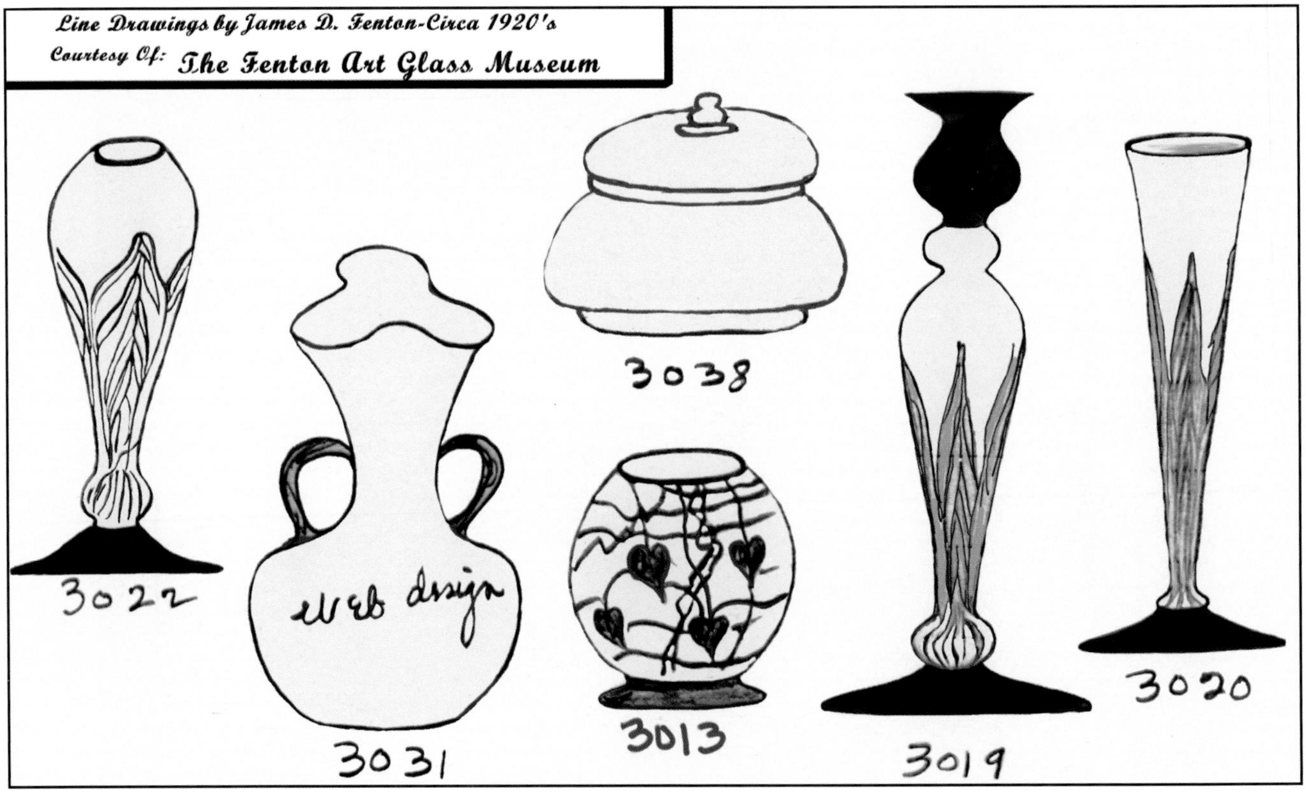
Line Drawings by James D. Fenton-Circa 1920's
Courtesy Of: The Fenton Art Glass Museum
3022
3031
3038
3013
3019
3020

#3024-15" Egyptian Vase

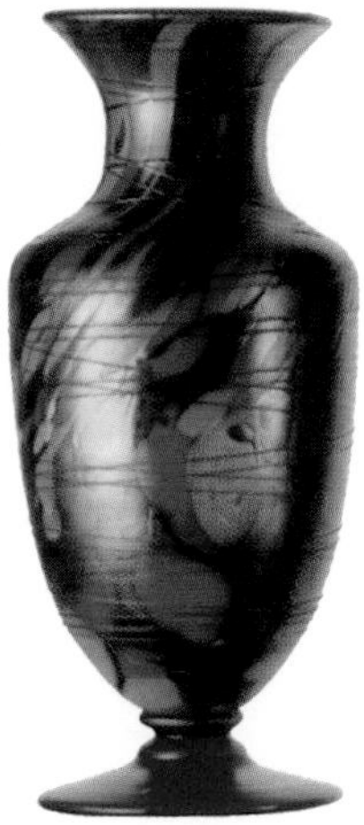

#3024-8" Egyptian Vase

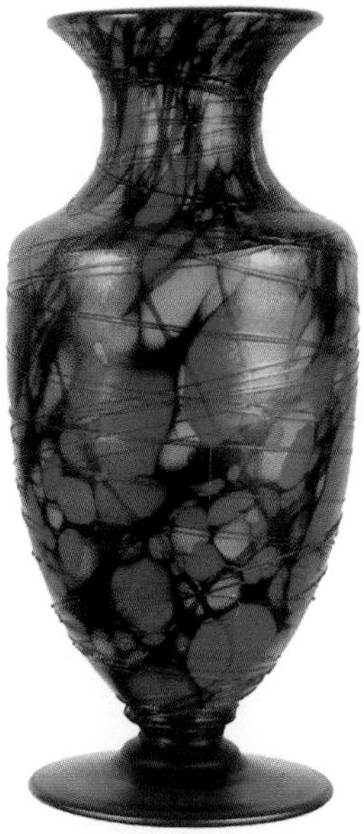

#3024-12" Egyptian Vase

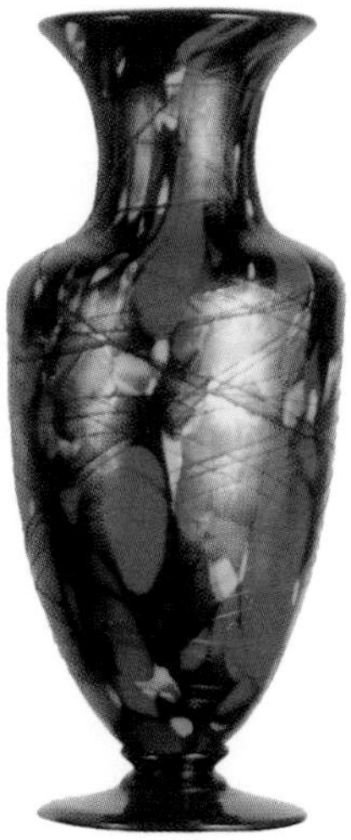

#3024-9" Egyptian Vase

#3024-15" Egyptian Vase

#3024-10" Egyptian Vase

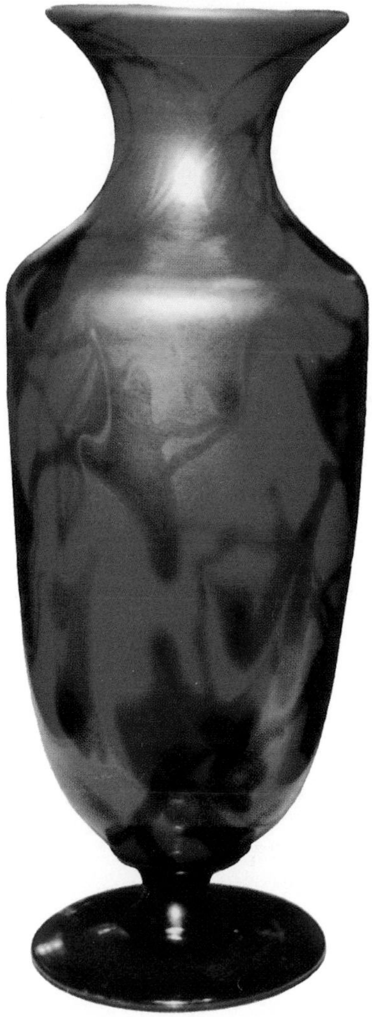

#3024-21" Egyptian Vase

#3024-10" Egyptian Vase

#3003-6 1/2" Footed Vase

#3003-6 1/2" Footed Vase

All pieces on the opposite page are pictured in the Mosaic pattern. Notice the variation in pattern and the glass threading on some pieces. Numerous powder boxes and the #53 cologne with a Mosaic pattern are featured in the drawing below.

	Hanging Hearts Hanging Vine	Mosaic	Plain Pulled Feather	Karnak
Row 1:				
Vase, #3051–10½"		$1200.00 – 1400.00		
Vase, #3021–11¼"		$550.00 – 600.00		
Vase, #3008–11"	$1000.00 – 1200.00	$1100.00 – 1200.00		
Vase, #3010 – 7½"	$1200.00 – 1400.00	$950.00 – 1100.00		
Row 2:				
Comport, #3055 – 7" oval		$600.00 – 800.00		
Vase, #3043–6" wall pocket	$1800.00+			
Candlestick, #3027–5¼"	$700.00 – 750.00	$650.00 – 750.00		
Bonbon base, #3049–5¾"	$250.00 – 300.00	$300.00 – 350.00		
Row 3:				
Vase, #3005-5½"	$600.00 – 700.00	$600.00 – 750.00		
Vase, #3039–6"	$950.00 – 1100.00	$850.00 – 1050.00	$1100.00 – 1300.00	
Vase, #3001–5½"	$500.00 – 550.00	$500.00 – 600.00	$700.00 – 800.00	
Vase, #3014–4"	$550.00 – 650.00	$500.00 – 600.00	$800.00 – 1000.00	
Drawings Below:				
Puff box, #3041	$850.00 – 950.00	$750.00 – 850.00		
Puff box, #3036	$850.00 – 950.00	$750.00 – 850.00		
Puff box, #3040	$900.00 – 1000.00	$800.00 – 900.00		
Bud vase, #3042	$400.00 – 550.00	$400.00 – 550.00		$350.00 – 400.00
Bowl, #3017–8½"	$900.00 – 950.00	$900.00 – 950.00		
Puff box, #542	$800.00 – 850.00	$750.00 – 800.00		
Cologne, #53		$1000.00 – 1200.00		

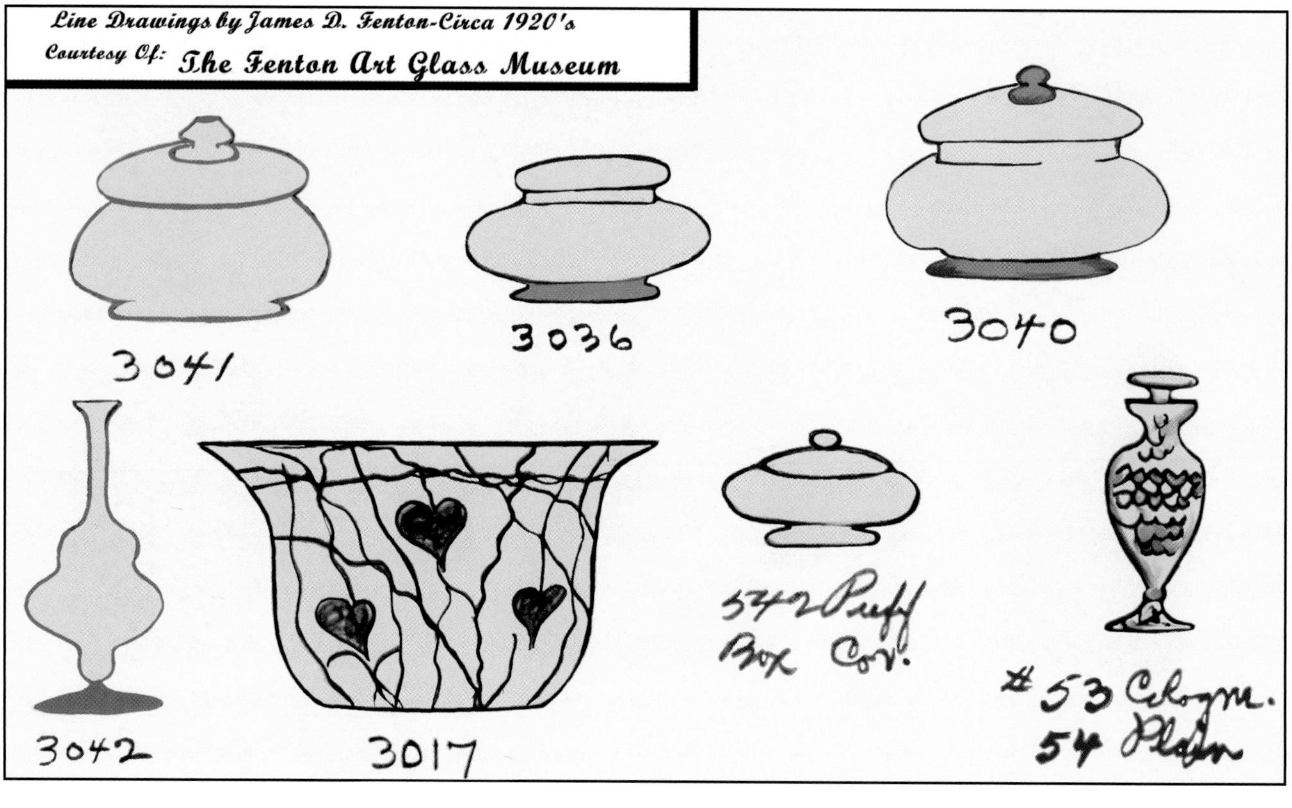
Line Drawings by James D. Fenton-Circa 1920's
Courtesy Of: The Fenton Art Glass Museum
3041
3036
3040
3042
3017
542 Puff Box Cov.
#53 Cologne.
54 Plain

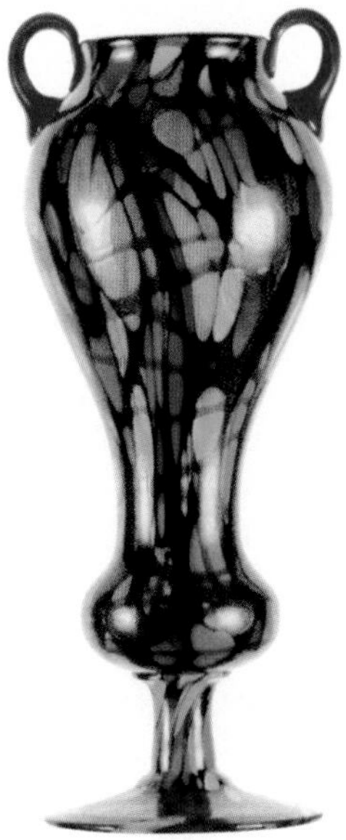

#3051-10 1/2" Vase

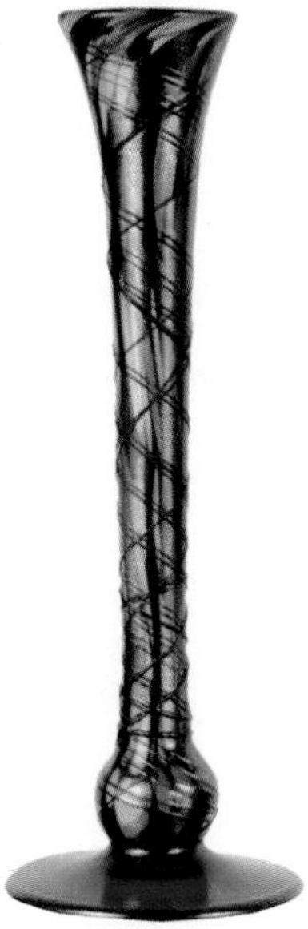

#3021-11 1/4"
Tall Bud Vase

#3021-11 1/4"
Tall Bud Vase

#3008-11" Tall Vase

#3010-7 1/2" Handled Vase

#3010-7 1/2" Vase

#3055-7" Footed
Oval Comport

#3043-6" Wall Vase

#3027-5 1/4" Candlestick

#3049-5 3/4" Bon-bon Base

#3005-5 1/2" Vase

#3039-6" Footed Vase

#3001-5 1/2" Squat Vase

#3014-4" Vase

Some of the shapes associated with off hand glassware will be found in plain Karnak red. Notice the tulip decoration on the third vase in the top row on the opposite page. The lilac color of the 3-footed vase at the top left illustrates an unusual color for this type of glass.

	Hanging Hearts Hanging Vine	Mosaic	Pulled Feather	Plain Karnak
Row 1:				
*Vase, #3053–10"	$1200.00 – 1500.00	$1000.00 – 1200.00		$1000.00 – 1200.00
**Vase, #3006–10½"	$850.00 – 900.00	$850.00 – 950.00		$850.00 – 900.00
Row 2:				
Vase, #3007–9½"	$750.00 – 800.00	$750.00 – 800.00		$600.00 – 700.00
Vase, #3012 – 4"	$650.00 – 750.00	$550.00 – 750.00		
Row 3:				
Vase, #3005 – 5½"	$600.00 – 700.00	$600.00 – 750.00		
Photo Below:				
Vase, tall bulbous	$2000.00+			
Vase, #3020 – 12⅝"	$750.00 – 900.00	$700.00 – 850.00	$750.00 – 850.00	
Candlestick, #3018–12"	$650.00 – 700.00	$650.00 – 700.00	$600.00 – 650.00	
Candlestick, #3019–12"	$650.00 – 700.00		$600.00 – 650.00	
Vase, 8½" trumpet	$850.00 – 950.00	$800.00 – 900.00		

*Lilac with Hanging Hearts decoration, $2000.00+.
**With tulip decoration, $1300.00 – 1500.00.

Tall Bulbous Ftd. Vase — #3020-12 5/8" Vase — #3018-12" Candlestick — #3019-12" Candlestick — 8 1/2" Trumpet Vase

Experimental Off Hand Glassware

Candlestick, 9 1/2"

Pig Whimsy, 8 1/2"

Vase, 10 1/2" 2-Handled

#3053-10" 3-Ftd. Vase

#3006-10 1/2" Vase

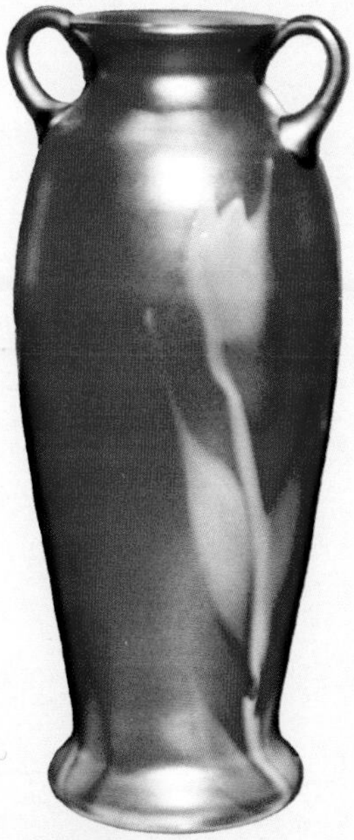

#3006-10 1/2" Vase

#3006-10 1/2" Vase

#3007-9 1/2" Vase

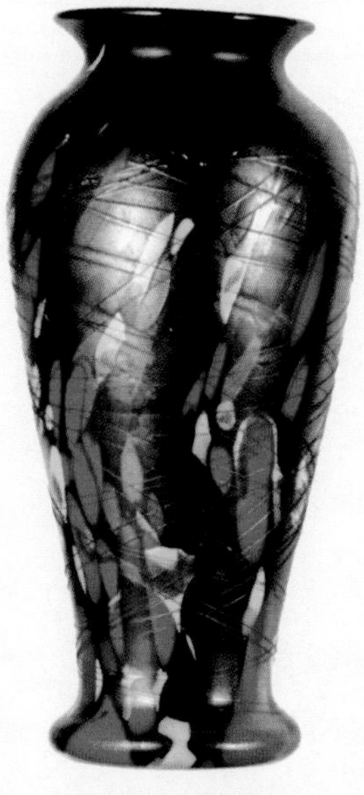

#3007-9 1/2" Vase

#3007-9 1/2" Vase

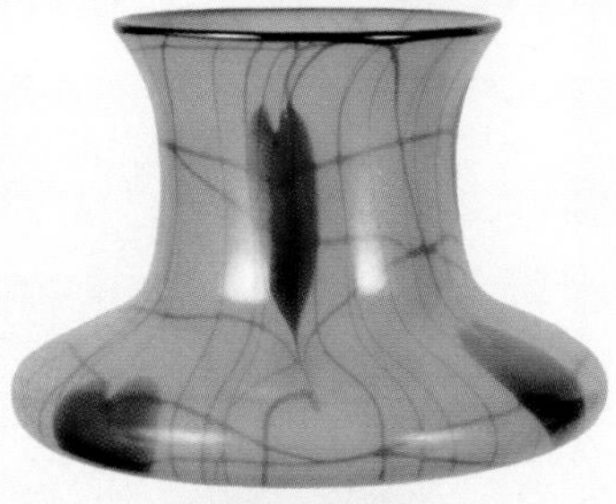

#3012-4" Vase

#3005-5 1/2" Vase

#3005-5 1/2" Vase

#3005-5 1/2" Vase

#3005-5 1/2" Vase

Notice the drawings on the opposite page of the jardiniere and the punch bowl. Although we have not seen these pieces, the drawings indicate they were made.

	Hanging Hearts Hanging Vine	Mosaic	Pulled Feather
Drawings opposite page:			
Jardiniere, #3052–1	$10,000.00+		
Punch bowl and base, #3048–1	$8000.00+		
Pitcher, #3044			$1800.00 – 2200.00
Vase, #3034			$1100.00 – 1200.00
Vase, #3033	$950.00 – 1050.00	$900.00 – 1100.00	
Photo below:			
Bowl, #3016–9" flared			$900.00 – 1100.00
Bowl, #3017–8½" flared			$900.00 – 1000.00
Vase, 6½"	$800.00 – 900.00	$700.00 – 800.00	
Vase, #3002–6½"	$850.00 – 950.00	$800.00 – 900.00	

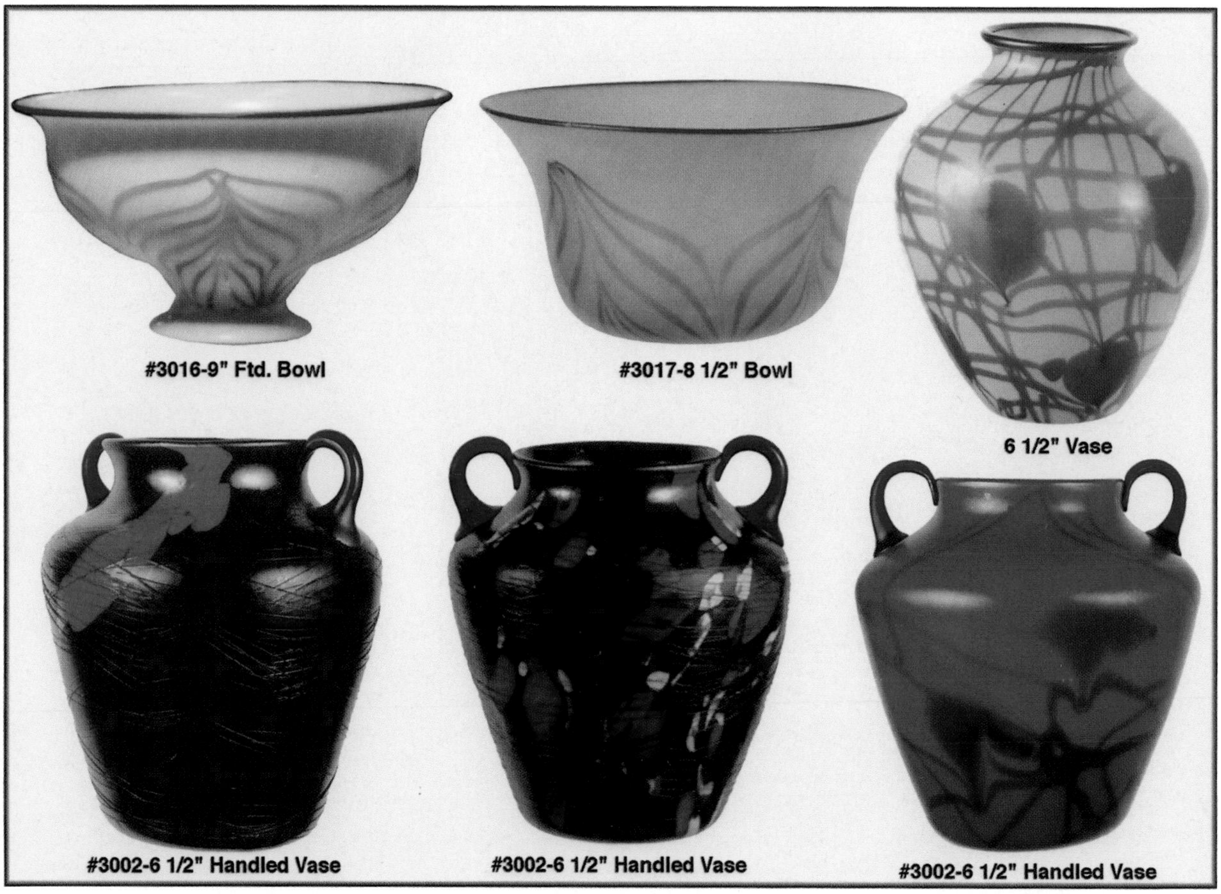

#3016-9" Ftd. Bowl

#3017-8 1/2" Bowl

6 1/2" Vase

#3002-6 1/2" Handled Vase

#3002-6 1/2" Handled Vase

#3002-6 1/2" Handled Vase

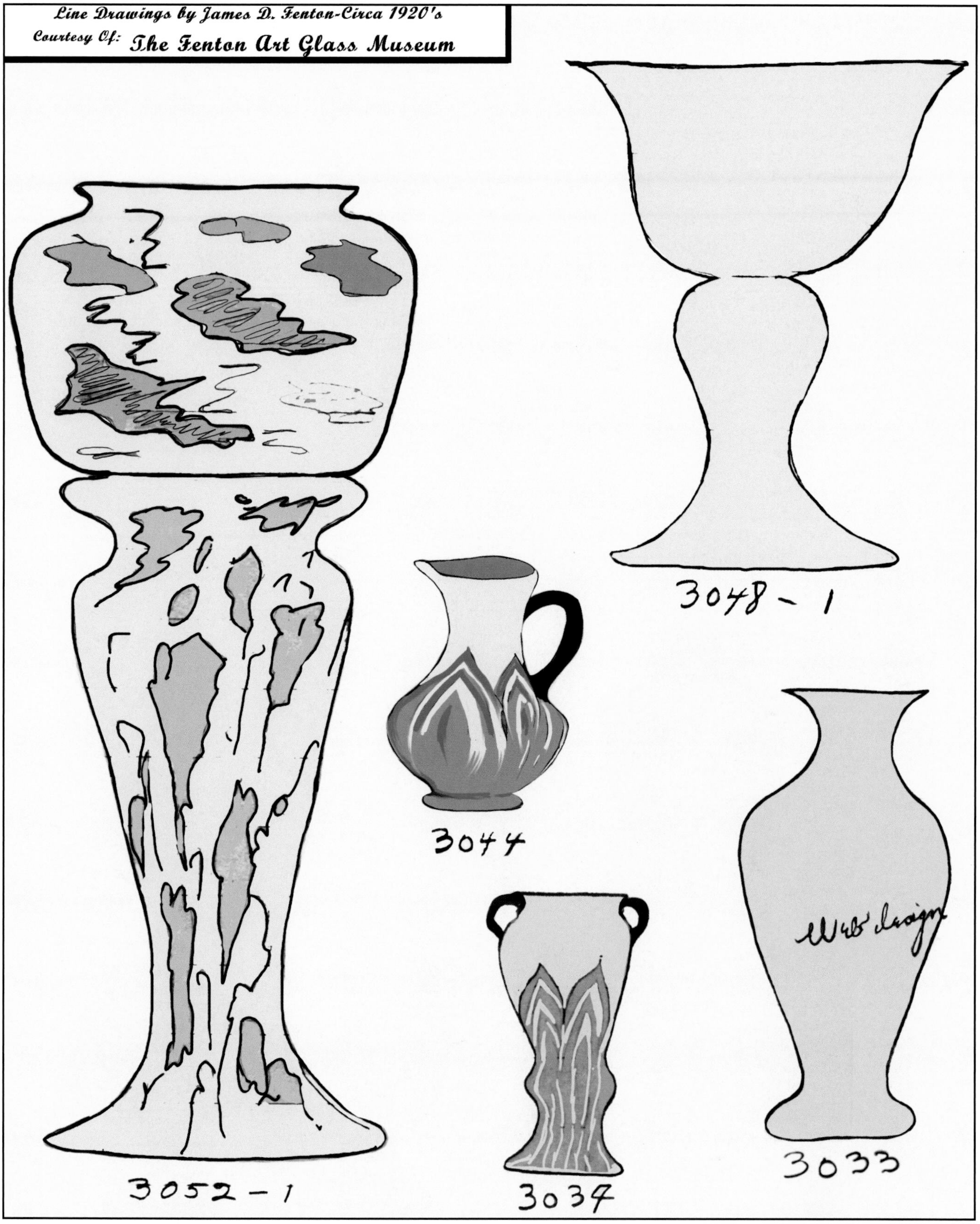
Line Drawings by James D. Fenton-Circa 1920's
Courtesy Of: The Fenton Art Glass Museum
3048-1
3044
3052-1
3034
3033

The handled mug was not an item in the regular line. It is dated 1925 and has the following inscription on the bottom: "MOSAIC INLAID WHEAT by FRITZ ALBERG FOR OTT WELLS."

	Hanging Hearts Hanging Vine	Mosaic	Pulled Feather
Catalog reprint opposite page:			
Vase, #3000 – 11"	$1200.00 – 1400.00	$1000.00 – 1200.00	
Bowl, #30169" ftd.	$1150.00 – 1250.00	$800.00 – 900.00	$850.00 – 950.00
Vase, #3012 – 4"	$650.00 – 750.00	$550.00 – 750.00	
Vase, 3039 ftd.	$1000.00 – 1200.00	$950.00 – 1150.00	$1100.00 – 1200.00
Vase, #3002 – 6¾"	$850.00 – 950.00	$800.00 – 900.00	
Vase, #3014 – 4"	$550.00 – 650.00	$500.00 – 600.00	$800.00 – 1000.00
Bonbon, #3037	$900.00 – 1000.00	$850.00 – 950.00	
Bonbon, #3035 high ftd.	$1800.00+	$1800.00+	
Vase, #3045 – 14"	$1500.00 – 1800.00	$1400.00 – 1700.00	
Vase, #3030 – 12"	$1200.00 – 1400.00	$1100.00 – 1300.00	
Photo below:			
Row 1:			
Vase, #3029-8"	$800.00 – 900.00	$800.00 – 900.00	$750.00 – 850.00
Mug, handled			$600.00 – 700.00
Cream pitcher, handled		$450.00 – 550.00	
Row2:			
Vase, 12" 2-handled	$1600.00 – 1800.00	$1100.00 – 1200.00	
Vase, #3000 – 11"	$900.00 – 1200.00	$800.00 – 900.00	
Urn, #3046-11" ftd.	$1400.00 – 1600.00		
Bonbon, #3035 high ftd.	$1800.00+	$1800.00+	

#3029-8" Vase
Handled Creamer
Handled Mug
#3029-8" Vase
12" 2-Handled Vase
#3000-11" Vase
#3046-11" Ftd. Urn
#3035 High Ftd. Bon-bon

Colorized Reprint Composite From Original Catalog Circa 1926 Courtesy Of: **The Fenton Art Glass Museum**

No. 3000 11" Vase

No. 3016
9" Footed Bowl

No. 3012 4" Vase

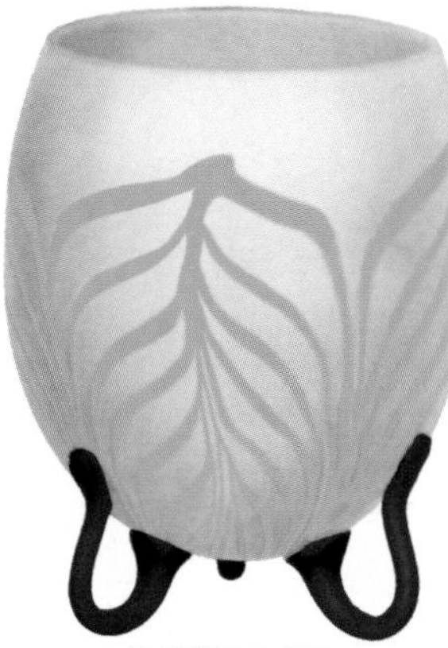

No. 3039 Footed Vase

No. 3002 6 3/4" 2 Hld.Vase

No. 3014 4" Vase

No. 3037 Cov. Bon Bon

No. 3035
High Footed Bon Bon

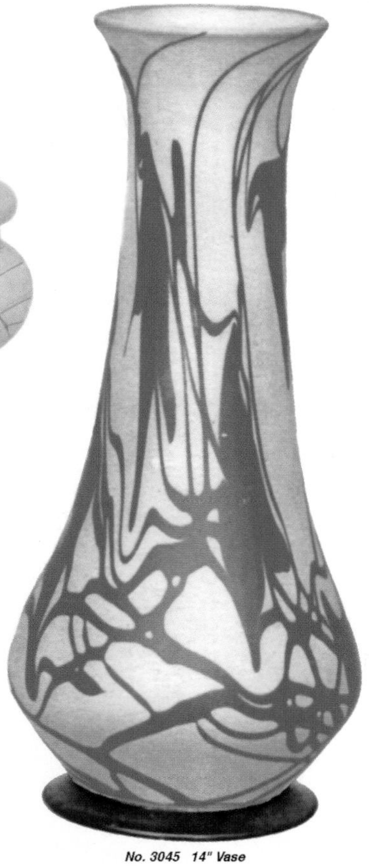

No. 3045 14" Vase

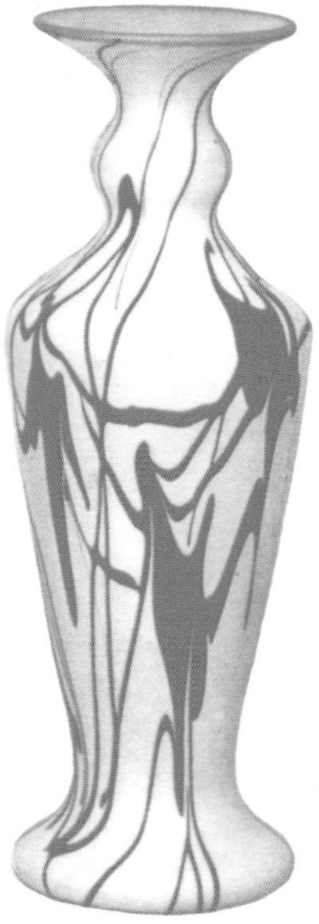

No. 3030 12" Vase

The #3026 – 11" footed bowl shown on opposite page is also listed in an 8" size. In addition to the round shape, it may also be found oval. Notice the jade #3001 vase shown below. Jade is not a commonly found color in the off hand line.

	Hanging Hearts/ Hanging Vine	Mosaic	Tulip	Pulled Feather
Catalog reprint opposite page:				
Row 1:				
Vase, #3028 – 8" fan	$1400.00 – 1650.00	$1300.00 – 1400.00		
Bowl, #3026 – 11" ftd.	$1400.00 – 1650.00	$1200.00 – 1400.00		
Bowl, #3025 covered	$1400.00 – 1500.00	$1300.00 – 1400.00		
Row 2:				
Vase, #3004 – 9"	$950.00 – 1100.00	$900.00 – 1050.00		
Vase, #3028 – 8" fan	$1400.00 – 1650.00	$1300.00 – 1400.00		
Candlestick, #3027	$650.00 – 750.00	$650.00 – 700.00		
Vase, #3009 – 10"	$850.00 – 950.00	$850.00 – 950.00		
Row 3:				
Vase, #3004 – 9"	$950.00 – 1100.00	$900.00 – 1050.00		
Vase, #3008 – 11"	$1000.00 – 1200.00	$1100.00 – 1200.00		
Basket, #3015	$1100.00 – 1200.00	$1000.00 – 1100.00		
Candlestick, #3018 – 12"	$650.00 – 700.00	$650.00 – 700.00		$600.00 – 650.00
Photo below:				
Row 1:				
Vase, #3013 – 6"	$750.00 – 900.00	$700.00 – 850.00	$950.00 – 1000.00	$870.00 – 900.00
Vase, #3001 – 6" (Jade)				$1200.00 – 1450.00
Row 2:				
Vase, #3001 – 6"	$500.00 – 550.00	$500.00 – 600.00		$600.00 – 650.00
Vase, 8"	$900.00 – 1000.00	$825.00 – 950.00		

#3013-6" Vase

#3013-6" Vase

#3001-6" Vase

#3001-6" Vase and Base

#3003-6 1/2" Ftd. Vase

8" Vase

Reprint Composite From Original Catalog Circa 1926 Courtesy Of: **The Fenton Art Glass Museum**

No. 3028-8"
Fan Vase

No. 3026-11"
Footed Bowl

No. 3025 Covered Bowl

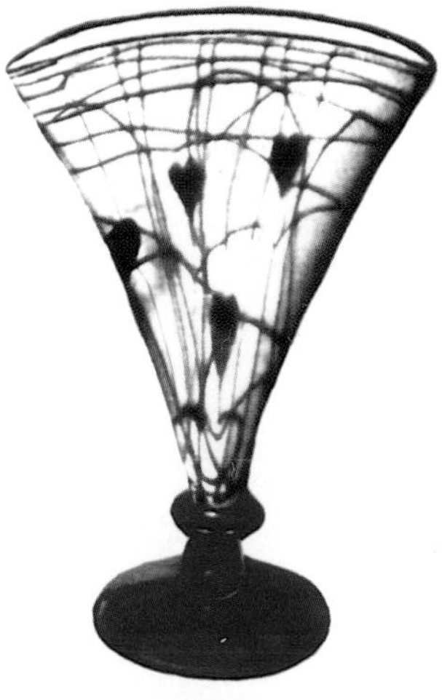

No. 3028-8"
Fan Vase

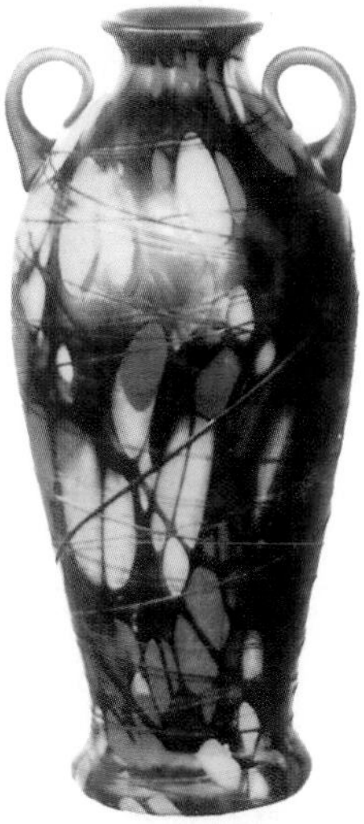

No. 3009-10" Hld. Vase

No. 3004-9"
2-Hdl. Vase

No. 3027 Candlestick

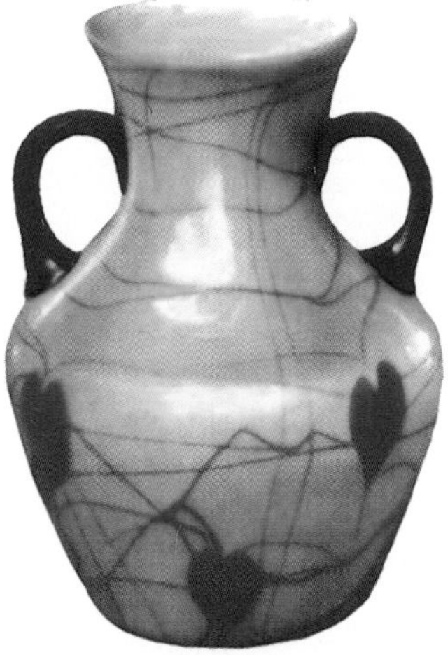

No. 3004-9"
2-Hdl. Vase

No. 3008-11"
Tall Vase

No. 3015 Handled
Basket

No. 3018-12" Candlestick

SUNG KO

Sung Ko is a special type of glassware that looks almost like pottery that enjoyed limited production about 1935. The mottled effect is produced by encasing the glassware in clay in which metallic salts have been embedded. The wrapped glassware is then heated, and the chemical effects of the salts on the glassware produce the various colors.

This glassware is elusive and expensive. The listing below includes the shapes we have seen. Due to the nature of the decoration, each piece will be unique.

Item	Value	Item	Value
Bowl, #1562 – 2 – 14" oval	$500.00 – 600.00	Vase, #621 – 8" cupped	$500.00 – 600.00
Ginger jar, #893 – 8½"	$1400.00 – 1600.00	Vase, #894 – 10"	$750.00 – 800.00
Vase, #200 – 7"	$550.00 – 650.00	Vase, #1934 – 7¾" bud	$550.00 – 650.00

#893-8 1/2" Ginger Jar

#894-10" Vase

#200-7" Vase

#1934-7 3/4" Bud Vase

#1562-2-14" Oval Bowl

#621-8" Cupped Vase

Fenton Art Glass

A distinctive American product developed through years of study and experiment.

The artists who designed the beautiful shapes, the chemist who discovered and perfected the wide range of colors, (more colors we believe, than are made by any one other glass factory in the world) and the skilled craftsmanship of the trained glass worker have all contributed in making Fenton Art Glass a product that rivals in beauty the famous glass wares of Venice and Bohemia.

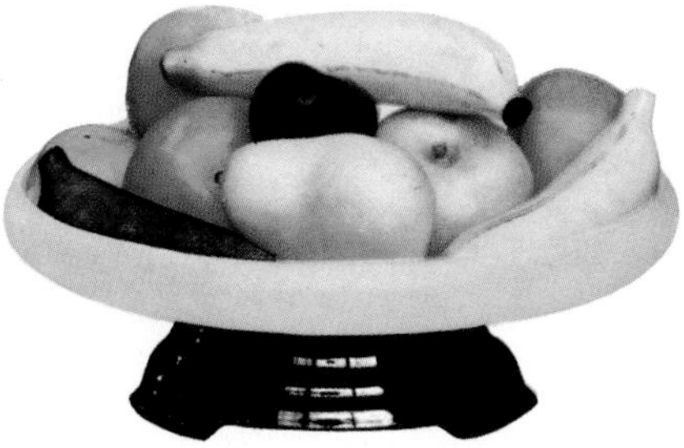

Unlike most other lines of colored glass Fenton Art Glass does not depend upon staining or painting for its wonderful color effects. *All the colors are in the glass.*

Nothing to wear off or fade. A piece of Fenton Art Glass will retain all of its glorious colorings forever.

Stretch Glass Catalog Reprints Circa 1921 Courtesy Of: ***The Fenton Art Glass Museum***

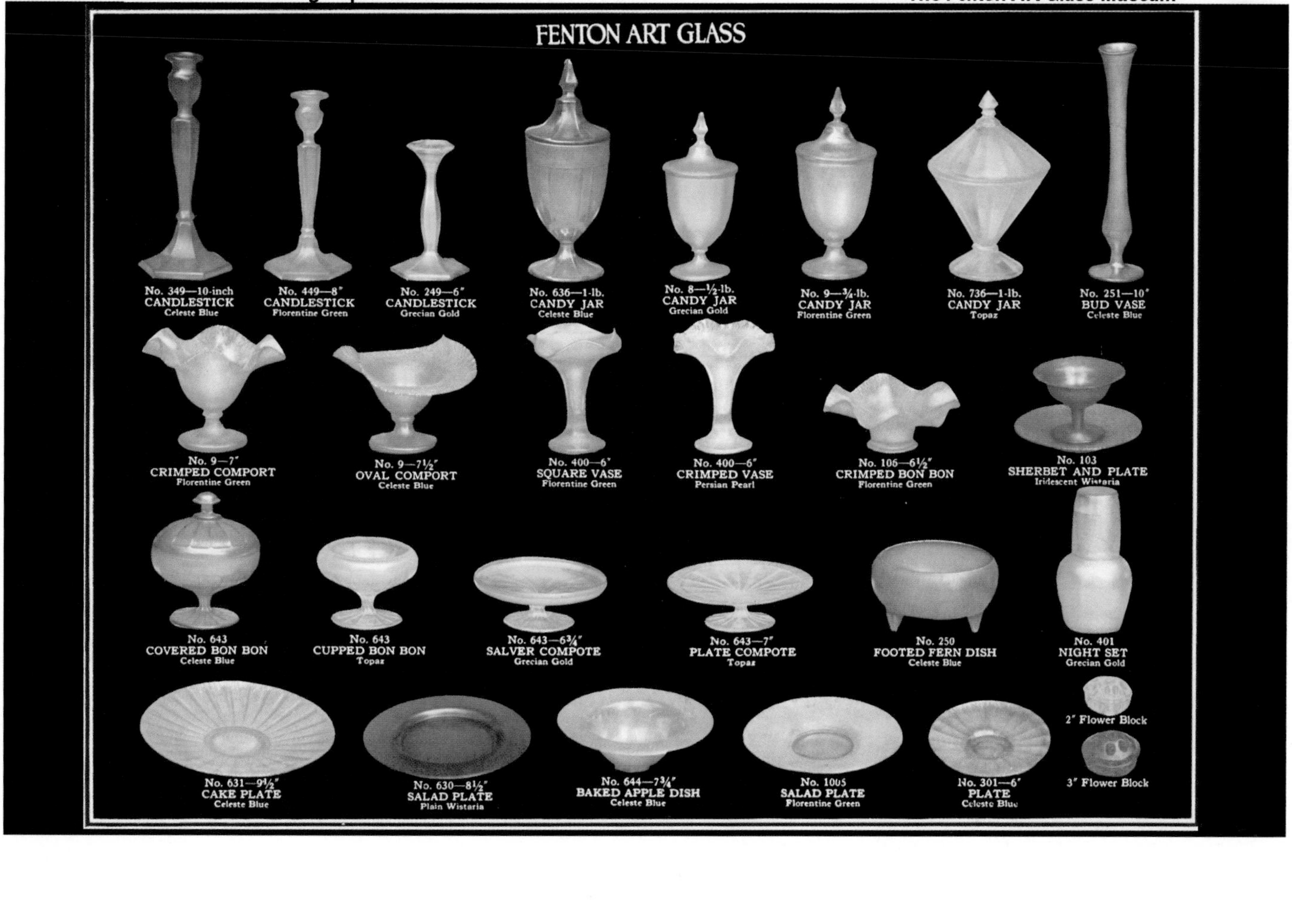

INTRODUCTION

After the phenomenal success of carnival glass, it would only be natural to assume that Fenton should try to achieve success again with another type of iridescent glassware. Fenton began to experiment with plain iridescent glassware about 1917. By 1921, as the interest in carnival glass began to decline, Fenton began to aggressively market plain iridescent glassware which is referred to as "stretch" by today's collectors. This new type of glassware was welcomed by eager buyers and was produced in vast quantities until close to the end of the decade.

Original iridescent colors were Celeste blue, Florentine green, Persian pearl, iridescent wisteria, and topaz iridescent. The amber iridescent color called Grecian Gold was also carried over from its previous role in the decoration of glassware with cut decorations. Limited amounts of iridescent ruby were produced between 1924 and 1928. Velva rose (an iridescent pink) and iridescent tangerine colors were made between 1926 and 1929. Some iridescent colors such as aquamarine, Persian pearl, and rare examples of cameo opalescent were continued into the early 1930s.

IDENTIFICATION OF SHAPES

Fenton produced numerous different shapes of bowls, comports, candies, plates, vases, and other items in stretch glass. All of these items are identified by a line number which describes the mold shape or pattern of the item. It is impossible for anyone to remember all the numbers for these shapes, but they are essential for identification. To help with identification, all the identifiable pieces pictured have their line number below them on the photos. Of course, not all the pieces can be shown in every color, but the same shapes were frequently used for

These color designations are from an early 1920s Fenton stretch glass catalog.

Every stretch glass item shown on the following pages may be had in any of the colors described below.

Celeste Blue
A beautiful sapphire blue with iridescent rainbow finish.

Turquoise
A light blue opaque color of great beauty, exceptionally rich.

Royal Blue
A deep rich dark blue tone, very dignified.

Florentine Green
A delicate shade of green with iridescent rainbow finish.

Persian Pearl
A rich pearl color showing all the iridescence of mother-of-pearl.

Iridescent Wisteria
A wonderful rich effect dark in tone with rainbow iridescent finish.

Plain Wisteria
A transparent color reminding one of rich old Burgundy, sparkling with life and fire.

Grecian Gold
A rich amber iridescent effect with a golden sheen.

Topaz
A rich greenish amber color with rainbow iridescent finish.

Jade Yellow
A rich opaque yellow color that makes a very pleasing combination when used with black stands.

Ebony
A rich black glass with a brilliant mirror-like finish. Ebony glass is becoming very popular and makes wonderful flower bowls, candlesticks, and pieces that are used mainly for decoration.

Ruby
The idea has long prevailed that this exceptionally rich color could only be obtained from Bohemia or Venice, much to the despair of the ordinary glassworker.
We have succeeded in producing a ruby that for richness, depth of color, and fire will compare favorably with the best product of the famous old world glassmakers.
Our color is not stained, painted, or cased, it is in the glass, ruby all the way through.

more than one color. If the item is not pictured in the color in which it is priced, check the other stretch glass colors. There is also a catalog reprint section at the end of the stretch glass section which lists many shapes in alphabetical order. If the item cannot be found in the stretch glass section, check the non-iridescent colors and pattern sections. Many of the same shapes will be found in these sections also.

Some of the items made such as bowls, vases, or comports are available in more than one style from the same mold. The difference in shape is achieved by finishing the edge in a different manner. For example, a bowl may be found 1. crimped; 2. shallow cupped; 3. flared; 4. flared cupped; 5. cupped; 6. special roll rim; 7. rolled edge. Vases styles are generally 1. flared; 2. fan; 3. crimped; 4. cupped; 5. flared cupped; 6. rolled rim.

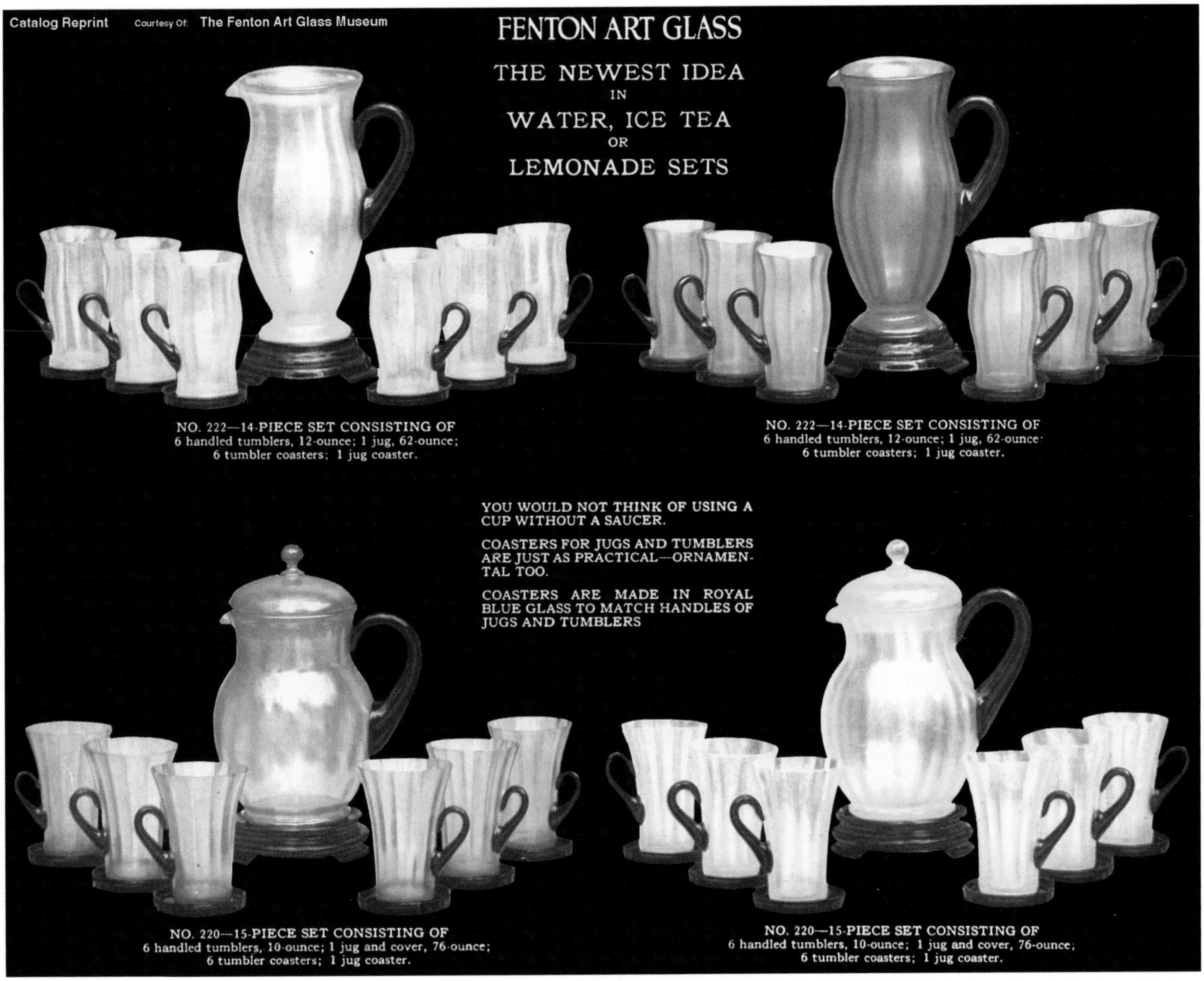

AQUAMARINE

Aquamarine is the name for the pale blue iridescent glassware Fenton produced during the last half of the 1920s and the early 1930s. Production was limited to a relatively small number of pieces, and finding examples of this color is difficult for collectors. Many of the pieces made were in Fenton's popular Dolphin line.

Item	Value
Basket, #1502 Diamond Optic	$175.00 – 200.00
Basket, #1620 – 6" Plymouth w/metal handle	$320.00 – 350.00
Bonbon, 7" 3-footed Sheffield	$50.00 – 60.00
Bowl, #349 – 9" regular	$250.00 – 300.00
Bowl, #349 – 10½" flared	$250.00 – 300.00
Bowl, #604 – 10" cupped	$180.00 – 210.00
Bowl, #847 – 7½" flared	$45.00 – 55.00
Bowl, #848 – flared or cupped	$100.00 – 125.00
Bowl, #857 – 9½" flared crimped	$75.00 – 95.00
Bowl, #857-10" special roll rim	$85.00 – 100.00
Bowl, #1502 – A– 9" dolphin crimped	$195.00 – 250.00
Bowl, #1504-A – 10" flared dolphin	$220.00 – 240.00
Bowl, #1562 – 1 – 13" oval	$225.00 – 250.00
Bowl, #1562 – 2 – 14" oval	$225.00 – 250.00
Bowl, #1602 – 10 ¼" crimped ftd. w/dolphins	$225.00 – 240.00
Bowl, #1604 – 11" oval ftd. w/dolphins	$195.00 – 220.00
Bowl, #1608 – 10½" deep oval footed	$225.00 – 250.00
Bowl, #1663 – 11½" flared	$105.00 – 125.00
Bowl, #1663 – 11½" tulip	$125.00 – 150.00
Candlestick, #950 – 5½" cornucopia	$125.00 – 150.00
Candy jar, #736, 1 lb.	$100.00 – 125.00
Candy jar, #835, ½ lb.	$95.00 – 110.00
Candy jar, #844, 1 lb. w/flower finial	$220.00 – 250.00
Candy jar, #1533 – A w/dolphin handles	$160.00 – 185.00
Comport, #736 – 6½" cupped	$45.00 – 50.00
Comport, #1533 – 6" crimped w/dolphins	$120.00 – 130.00
Creamer, #3	$25.00 – 27.00
Creamer, #1502 Diamond Optic	$135.00 – 145.00
Flower block, #3 – 3"	$15.00 – 20.00
Ice pail, #1616	$125.00 – 150.00
Sugar #3	$25.00 – 27.00
Sugar, #1502 Diamond Optic	$135.00 – 145.00
Tray, #1502 – A –10" handled sandwich w/dolphin	$190.00 – 210.00
Tray, #1562 – 3 – 15" oval	$225.00 – 250.00
Vase, #573 – 8" crimped	$85.00 – 100.00
Vase, #574 – 6" crimped	$40.00 – 50.00
Vase, #847 – 6" fan	$65.00 – 75.00
Vase, #857 – 8" fan	$45.00 – 50.00
Vase, #1502 – 8" Diamond Optic	$85.00 – 95.00
Vase, #1532– A– 5¼" fan	$115.00 – 125.00
Vase, #1533 – 6" fan	$115.00 – 125.00
Vase, #1700 – 8½" flared Sheffield	$235.00 – 285.00
Vase, #1800 – 10½" roll rim Sheffield	$260.00 – 290.00

#1533-6" Ftd.
Crimped Comport

#1602-10" Ftd.
Crimped Bowl

#1533-6"Ftd.
Fan Vase

#857-8" Fan Vase

#574-6" Crimped
Vase or Bonbon

#844-1 lb. Candy Jar

#3 Sugar

847-7 1/2" Flared Bowl

#3 Creamer

#736-1 lb. Candy Jar

#1502-A-10" Handled Sandwich Tray

CELESTE BLUE

Judging by the number of different pieces made in this color, the rich blue iridized color Fenton named "Celeste" must have been a favorite among the glass enthusiasts during the 1920s. Pieces in this color were introduced in 1917, and various pieces were added or deleted from the line throughout most of the rest of the next decade. Some of the more desirable and elusive items include aquariums, the punch set, the high standard comport, colognes, and the handled guest set. Basket Weave with Open Edge pieces which are also sought after by carnival glass collectors bring premium prices.

The #316 cheese comport & underplate and the #757 – 7¼" plate may be found with a Laurel Leaf engraving. The 7½" vase shown in the photo is from the Fenton Art Glass Museum and is not listed in existing Fenton catalogs. The five-part relish with the comport in the photo is Fenton's #1647 sweetmeat set.

In 1995, as part of its 90th anniversary celebration, Fenton re-introduced the Celeste blue color in the 90th Anniversary Collection. The pitcher and tumbler set are a modification of the old Lincoln Inn pattern molds. Some of the new pieces are decorated with a hand-painted floral design called Coralene. These new pieces should be marked with the Fenton logo in an oval. A list of these new items is in the box below.

Basket, #1142 – 7" footed
Logo, #9499 oval
Basket, #1135 – 9½" Diamond
Pitcher, #9001
Bell, #9667 – 7" Aurora
Top hat, #1137 – 4¼"
Candlestick, #2911 – 3"
Tumbler, #9049 – 4½"
Candy box, #9488 – 10¼"
Vase, #2767 – 5¼"
Bowl, #2990 – 9½" w/nymph
Vase, #1136 – 6" fan
Comport, #1134 – 5¼"
Vase, #1140 – 7¼" with cobalt base
Epergne set, #7601 – 13" 5-piece

Celeste Blue
Iridescent Candles
#449-8 1/2"
#349-10"
#449-8 1/2"
w/cutting
#649-10"
#549-8 1/2"
w/Ebony base

10 1/4" High Standard Comport

#222 Ice Tea Tumbler

#222 Ice Tea Pitcher

#572-8" Fan Vase

#736 1 lb. Candy

#847-6" Fan Vase

#249-6" Candlestick

7 1/2" Vase

#738-6 1/2" Flared Cupped Comport

#1561-10" Oval Handled Tray

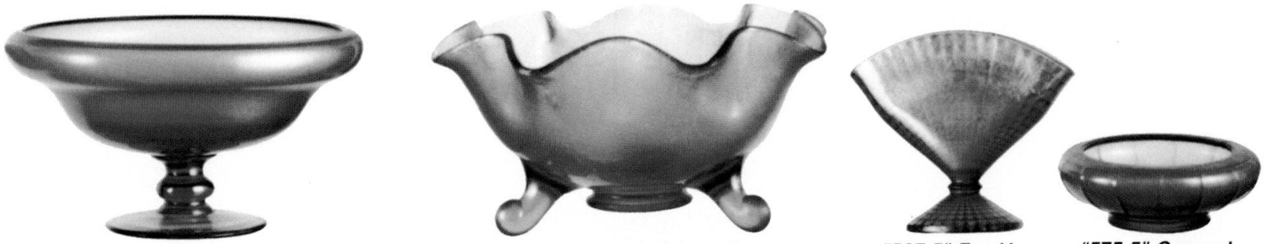

#917-11" Ftd. Flared Cupped Bowl

#603-10" Ftd. Crimped Orange Bowl

#567-5" Fan Vase

#575-5" Cupped Lily Bowl

#607-9" Shallow Cupped Bowl

Cheese Comport with Five Part Relish

#9-7 1/2" Oval Ftd. Comport

#643-5 1/4" Cupped Comport

#943 1/2 lb. Bonbon

#554 Cigarette Holder

#202-5 Piece Ashtray Set

#56 Cologne

#59 Cologne

Celeste Blue	Value
Ashtray Set, #202, 5-pc.	$140.00 – 160.00
Basket, #1093 – 6½"	$350.00 – 400.00
Bathroom set, 4-pc., #16 – 17 – 54	$250.00 – 300.00
Bonbon, #106 – 6½" crimped	$32.00 – 37.00
Bonbon, #543 covered	$75.00 – 95.00
Bonbon, #643 – 5" covered	$75.00 – 95.00
Bonbon, #643 open, cupped	$38.00 – 40.00
Bonbon, #943, ½ lb.	$75.00 – 95.00
Bonbon, #1043, 1 lb. covered, footed	$200.00 – 225.00
Bowl, #109 – 4¼" shallow	$22.00 – 25.00
Bowl, #109 – 5½" shallow	$25.00 – 28.00
Bowl, #231 – 8" footed deep cupped	$80.00 – 90.00
Bowl, #231– 9 ½" shallow cupped	$85.00 – 95.00
Bowl, #312 – 7" cupped	$75.00 – 85.00
Bowl, #347 – 10¾" flared, cupped	$85.00 – 95.00
Bowl, #545 – 5" cupped lily	$35.00 – 40.00
Bowl, #545 – 6½" shallow cupped	$30.00 – 35.00
Bowl, #575 – 5" cupped lily	$30.00 – 32.00
Bowl, #550 – 11" shallow, cupped	$100.00 – 125.00
Bowl, #550 – 12" flared	$100.00 – 125.00
Bowl, #550 – 10 ¼" flared cupped	$100.00 – 125.00
Bowl, #575 – 5" cupped lily	$30.00 – 35.00
Bowl, #600 – 7" cupped	$30.00 – 35.00
Bowl, #600 – 8" cupped	$40.00 – 45.00
Bowl, #600 – 9" flared salad	$60.00 – 65.00
Bowl, #600 – 10" flared salad	$60.00 – 67.00
Bowl, #600 – 10" rolled rim	$65.00 – 75.00
Bowl, #601 – 10" shallow cupped	$75.00 – 82.00
Bowl, #603 – 9" footed, cupped	$225.00 – 250.00
Bowl, #603 – 10" footed, crimped orange	$240.00 – 275.00
Bowl, #604 – 10" cupped	$195.00 – 220.00
*Bowl, #604 – 12" flared (punch bowl)	$400.00 – 450.00
Bowl, #604 – 14" shallow cupped	$70.00 – 75.00
Bowl, #606 – 7½" shallow cupped	$50.00 – 55.00
Bowl, #607 – 8" cupped	$55.00 – 65.00
Bowl, #607 – 8" rolled rim	$50.00 – 60.00
Bowl, #607 – 9" shallow, cupped	$50.00 – 60.00
Bowl, #638 – 8" shallow cupped	$50.00 – 55.00
Bowl, #640 – 7" flared, cupped	$40.00 – 50.00
Bowl, #640 – 7½" rolled rim	$45.00 – 50.00
Bowl, #644 – 7¾" baked apple	$50.00 – 55.00
Bowl, #647 – 8½" cupped (Aquarium)	$160.00 – 185.00
Bowl, #647 – 10¾" flared, cupped	$100.00 – 110.00
Bowl, #647 – 11" rolled rim	$82.00 – 92.00
Bowl, #647 – 13" flared	$90.00 – 110.00
Bowl, #647 – 13" flared w/No. 2 dec.	$100.00 – 125.00
Bowl, #647 – 15" flared	$100.00 – 120.00
Bowl, #750 – 9¼" octagonal	$160.00 – 180.00
Bowl, #846 – 8" flared cupped	$50.00 – 60.00
Bowl, #847 – 7" shallow cupped	$50.00 – 60.00
Bowl, #847 – 7½" flared	$65.00 – 75.00
Bowl, #848 – 8½" tulip	$125.00 – 150.00
Bowl, #857 – 8" cupped	$60.00 – 65.00
Bowl, #857 – 11" flared	$75.00 – 85.00
Bowl, #857 – 11" flared cupped	$70.00 – 77.00

**With base $600.00 – 700.00*

#251-10" Bud Vase

#735-1/2 lb. Candy Jar

#643-5" Covered Bonbon

#9-3/4 lb. Candy Jar w/Grape Cutting and Gold Trim

#316 Candlestick

#712-7" Ftd. Cupped Comport

#57 Puff Box

#743 Puff Box

#315 Princess Candle

#103 Ftd. Sherbet w/Rose Spray Decoration

#556 Cigarette Holder

Fan Vase Made From #53 Cologne

#601-10" Shallow Cupped Bowl

#1502 Night Set

Celeste Blue	Value
Bowl, #917 – 9¼" flared cupped	$125.00 – 150.00
Bowl, #917 – 10¼" rolled rim	$125.00 – 150.00
Bowl, #917 – 11" footed flared	$125.00 – 150.00
Bowl, #1093 – 8" Basket Weave w/Open Edge	$800.00 – 900.00
Bowl, #1512 – 8"	$65.00 – 80.00
Bowl, #2005 – 6½" shallow cupped	$32.00 – 35.00
Bowl, #2006 – 6" cupped	$32.00 – 35.00
Bowl, #2006 – 7½" shallow cupped	$32.00 – 35.00
Bowl, #2007 – 9" shallow cupped	$37.00 – 45.00
Cake plate, #631 – 9½"	$75.00 – 85.00
Candlestick, #232 – 8½"	$70.00 – 80.00
Candlestick, #249 – 6"	$60.00 – 65.00
Candlestick, #314	$20.00 – 25.00
Candlestick, #315 princess	$45.00 – 50.00
Candlestick, #316	$35.00 – 40.00
Candlestick, #349 – 10"	$110.00 – 120.00
Candlestick, #449 – 8½"	$95.00 – 110.00
Candlestick, #549 – 8½"	$90.00 – 95.00
Candlestick, #549 – 2 – 8½" w/black base	$120.00 – 130.00
Candlestick, #649 – 10"	$110.00 – 120.00
Candlestick, #749 – 12"	$120.00 – 130.00
Candy bowl, #844, 1 lb.	$250.00 – 300.00
Candy jar, #8, ½ lb.	$45.00 – 50.00
Candy jar, #9, ¾ lb.	$50.00 – 55.00
Candy jar, #636, 1 lb.	$65.00 – 75.00
Candy jar, #735, ½ lb.	$57.00 – 62.00
Candy jar, #736, 1 lb.	$75.00 – 85.00
Candy jar, #943, ½ lb.	$70.00 – 80.00
Cheese comport, #316/underplate	$75.00 – 85.00
Cigarette box, #665	$250.00 – 300.00
Cigarette holder, #554 round	$125.00 – 150.00
Cigarette holder, #556 oval	$125.00 – 150.00
Coaster	$18.00 – 22.00
Cologne, #53 Diamond Optic	$150.00 – 170.00
Cologne, #54	$150.00 – 170.00
Cologne, #55	$195.00 – 220.00
Cologne, #55½ with flower stopper	$250.00 – 275.00
Cologne, #56	$225.00 – 250.00
Cologne , #59	$245.00 – 270.00
Comport, #9 – 7½" oval footed	$60.00 – 70.00
Comport, #103 – 4¾" oval	$60.00 – 65.00
Comport, #260 – 7" tall footed	$75.00 – 85.00
Comport, #312 – 7" cupped, low footed	$65.00 – 75.00
Comport, #312 – 8" flared footed	$55.00 – 65.00
Comport, #500 footed oval	$60.00 – 65.00
Comport, #643 – 5¼" cupped	$45.00 – 55.00
Comport, #643 – 6¾" salver	$40.00 – 50.00
Comport, #643 – 7" plate	$45.00 – 55.00
Comport, #712 – 7" cupped footed	$65.00 – 75.00
Comport, #736 – 6½" cupped	$45.00 – 55.00
Comport, #736 – 8" flared cupped	$60.00 – 70.00
Comport, #737 – 7" flared cupped	$45.00 – 55.00
Comport, #738 flared, cupped	$50.00 – 55.00
Comport, scalloped w/Stippled Ray interior	$250.00 – 300.00
Compote, Hi-Standard	$250.00 – 275.00
Creamer, #2	$50.00 – 60.00

FENTON ART GLASS COMPANY, WILLIAMSTOWN, W. VA.

Catalog Reprint
Courtesy Of:
The Fenton Art Glass Museum

1925
SUPPLEMENT OF
FLORENTINE CATALOG.

NEW ENGRAVED LINE.

681. 8 in. Salad Plate.
Celeste Blue.
Decoration No. 3

647. 13 in Center Bowl and Base.
Celeste Blue.
Decoration No. 2

681. 8 in. Salad Plate.
Florentine Green
Decoration No. 3

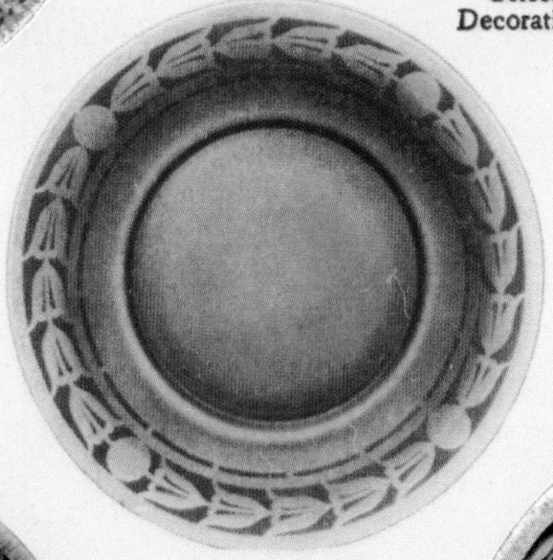

681. 8 in. Salad Plate.
Grecian Gold.
Decoration
No. 2

681. 8 in. Salad Plate.
Florentine Green.
Decoration No. 2

681 8 in. Salad Plate
Celeste Blue.
Decoration
No. 2

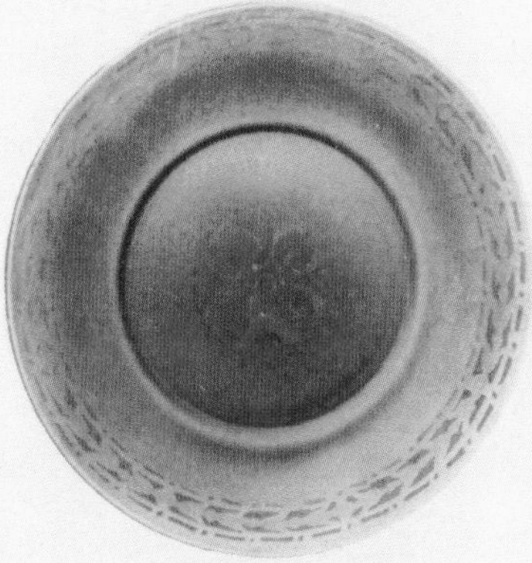

681. 8 in. Salad Plate.
Grecian Gold.
Decoration No. 3

682. 9 in. Service Plate.
Grecian Gold.
Decoration No. 2

682. 9 in. Service Plate.
Florentine Green.
Decoration No. 2

682. 9 in. Service Plate.
Celeste Blue.
Decoration No. 2

Celeste Blue	Value
Creamer, #3	$40.00 – 50.00
Creamer, #1502 Diamond Optic	$55.00 – 65.00
Cup, #1502 Diamond Optic	$55.00 – 65.00
Cup and saucer, plain	$100.00 – 125.00
Fern bowl ,#250 three-footed	$105.00 – 120.00
Flower block, #2	$18.00 – 20.00
Flower block, #3 – 3"	$25.00 – 30.00
Guest set, #200 handled	$320.00 – 370.00
Jar, #60 bath (smelling) salts	$200.00 – 250.00
Mayonnaise & ladle, #923	$55.00 – 65.00
Mug, #1630 shaving	$350.00 – 400.00
Night set, #401	$140.00 – 165.00
Nite set, #1502	$190.00 – 225.00
Nut bowl, #1192 Basket Weave w/Open Edge	$350.00 – 400.00
Nut cup, #923 individual	$35.00 – 40.00
Pen holder	$200.00 – 220.00
Pitcher, #215 grape juice	$220.00 – 240.00
Pitcher, #222 iced tea	$270.00 – 310.00
Pitcher & lid, #220 – 9¼"	$320.00 – 360.00
Plate, #103 sherbet	$22.00 – 24.00
Plate, #301 – 6"	$30.00 – 35.00
Plate, #600 – 11½"	$75.00 – 85.00
Plate, #630 – 8½" salad	$18.00 – 20.00
Plate, #631 – 11½" sandwich	$80.00 – 90.00
Plate, #680 – 6"	$30.00 – 35.00
Plate, #681 – 8" salad	$40.00 – 45.00
Plate, #681 – 8" salad w/No. 2 or No. 3 dec.	$50.00 – 60.00
Plate, #682 – 9" service	$40.00 – 45.00
Plate, #681 – 9" service w/No. 2 or No. 3 dec.	$55.00 – 65.00
Plate, #750 – 11¾"octagonal	$75.00 – 85.00
Plate, #756 – 6" octagonal	$14.00 – 16.00
Plate, #757 – 7¼" octagonal/w Laurel Leaf dec.	$40.00 – 50.00
Plate, #758 – 8½" octagonal	$18.00 – 20.00
Plate, #1502 – 8" octagonal Diamond Optic	$50.00 – 65.00
Puff box, #53	$75.00 – 95.00
Puff box, #54	$75.00 – 95.00
Puff box, #57	$100.00 – 130.00
Puff box, #743	$120.00 – 140.00
Punch cup # 604	$35.00 – 40.00
Salver, #1043 – 7¼" footed	$45.00 – 55.00
Salver, #1043 – 9" footed	$50.00 – 60.00
*Sherbet, #103	$28.00 – 32.00
Sign, "Fenton Art Glass" logo	$900.00 – 1000.00
Sweetmeat set, #1647, 2-pc. w/cheese comport	$100.00 – 110.00
Sugar, #2	$50.00 – 60.00
Sugar, #3	$40.00 – 50.00
Sugar, #1502 Diamond Optic	$55.00 – 65.00
Tray, #53 vanity set	$50.00 – 60.00
Tray, #66 lemon or butter	$50.00 – 60.00
Tray, #317 – 10" handled sandwich	$65.00 – 75.00
Tray, #318 – 7" oval handled butter	$60.00 – 70.00
Tray, #1561 – 10" oval handled	$75.00 – 85.00
Tumbler, #215 grape juice	$25.00 – 30.00
Tumbler, #220 handled	$40.00 – 50.00
Tumbler, #222 handled	$40.00 – 50.00
Vanity set, #53, 4-pc.	$425.00 – 495.00
Vanity set, #54, 4-pc.	$425.00 – 495.00
with Rose Spray decoration	*$70.00 – 100.00*

Celeste Blue	Value
Vase, 7½" blown w/cutting	$85.00 – 110.00
Vase, #99 – 7" bud	$40.00 – 45.00
Vase, #251 – 10" bud	$50.00 – 65.00
Vase, #562 – 8" flared rib optic	$65.00 – 75.00
Vase, #565 – 6" fan	$55.00 – 65.00
Vase, #567 – 5" fan	$45.00 – 50.00
Vase, #572 – 8" fan	$50.00 – 55.00
Vase, #574 – 6" crimped (comport)	$50.00 – 60.00
Vase, #602 – 10" flared	$90.00 – 110.00
Vase, #611 – 6½" cupped	$50.00 – 60.00
Vase, #612 – 6½" flared	$50.00 – 60.00
Vase, #621 – 8" flared	$120.00 – 140.00
Vase, #622 – 7½" flared	$80.00 – 90.00
Vase, #847 – 6" fan	$45.00 – 55.00
Vase, #857 – 8" fan	$60.00 – 75.00
Vase, #891 – 12"	$400.00 – 450.00
Vase, #1502 – 6" Diamond Optic	$50.00 – 60.00
Vase, #1531 – 15" Ring Optic	$175.00 – 225.00
Vase, #1533 – 6" fan w/dolphins	$175.00 – 200.00
Vase, 4¼" fan from #53 Diamond Optic cologne	$180.00 – 200.00

#60 Bath Salts Jar

#54 Vanity Set

#55 Cologne

FLORENTINE GREEN

Iridescent light Florentine green glassware was introduced in 1917. Numerous pieces were made until the color was phased out about 1928. Among the more popular items in this color were bowls, candlesticks, vases, and candy jars. Hard-to-find pieces include the punch set, the logo display sign, and handled guest sets. The Basket Weave with Open Edge pieces are especially desirable among carnival glass collectors.

Florentine Green	Value
Ashtray Set, #202 – 5-pc.	$130.00 – 150.00
Basket, #1093 tulip crimped	$375.00 – 400.00
Basket, #1620 Plymouth w/metal handle	$120.00 – 145.00
Bathroom Set #16–17–54–4-pc.	$200.00 – 250.00
Bonbon, #106 – 6½" crimped	$25.00 – 27.00
Bonbon, #543 covered	$50.00 – 55.00
Bonbon, #643 – 5" covered	$62.00 – 70.00
Bonbon, #643 open, cupped	$32.00 – 34.00
Bonbon, #1043, 1 lb. covered, footed	$145.00 – 160.00
Bonbon, #1621 – 6½" w/dolphins	$50.00 – 60.00
Bowl, #109 – 4¼" shallow	$18.00 – 20.00
Bowl, #545 – 5" cupped lily	$30.00 – 35.00
Bowl, #545 – 6½" shallow cupped	$27.00 – 30.00
Bowl, #601 – 10" flared salad	$60.00 – 65.00
Bowl, #601 – 10" shallow cupped	$60.00 – 65.00
Bowl, #603 – 9" footed, cupped	$180.00 – 200.00
Bowl, #604 – 10" cupped	$190.00 – 210.00
*Bowl, #604 – 11¼" crimped (punch bowl)	$275.00 – 300.00
*Bowl, #604 – 12" flared (punch bowl)	$275.00 – 300.00
Bowl, #604 – 14" shallow cupped	$60.00 – 65.00
Bowl, #640 – 7" flared, cupped	$37.00 – 42.00
Bowl, #647 – 10¾" flared, cupped	$75.00 – 85.00
Bowl, #846 – 8" flared cupped	$37.00 – 45.00
Bowl, #847 – 7½" flared	$40.00 – 45.00
Bowl, #847 – 7" shallow cupped	$35.00 – 40.00
Bowl, #857 – 8" cupped	$45.00 – 50.00
Bowl, #857 – 11" flared	$55.00 – 60.00
Bowl, #857 – 11" flared cupped	$55.00 – 60.00
Bowl, #857 – 8" cupped	$50.00 – 55.00
Bowl, #1093 – 8" Basket Weave w/Open Edge	$275.00 – 325.00
Bowl, #1502 – 13" dolphin flared	$200.00 – 230.00
Bowl, #1502– A-9" crimped w/dolphins	$200.00 – 230.00
Bowl, #1503 – A-10" dolphin flared	$200.00 – 230.00
Bowl, #1504 – A-10" crimped w/dolphins	$200.00 – 230.00
Bowl, #1604 – 11" oval footed w/dolphins	$190.00 – 210.00
Bowl, #1608 – 10½" deep oval footed	$190.00 – 210.00
Bowl, #2006 – 6" cupped	$27.00 – 30.00
Bowl, #2007 – 9" shallow cupped	$37.00 – 42.00
Candlestick, #232 – 8½"	$70.00 – 85.00
Candlestick, #249 – 6"	$45.00 – 50.00
Candlestick, #314	$18.00 – 20.00
Candlestick, #315 princess	$32.00 – 37.00
Candlestick, #316	$28.00 – 32.00
Candlestick, #317	$28.00 – 32.00
Candlestick, #318	$28.00 – 32.00
Candlestick #349 – 10"	$125.00 – 140.00
Candlestick, #449 – 8½"	$95.00 – 100.00
Candlestick, #649 – 10"	$115.00 – 125.00
Candlestick, #749 – 12"	$150.00 – 175.00
Candlestick, #1623 w/dolphins	$100.00 – 120.00
Candle vase, #1673 – 8"	$250.00 – 300.00
Candy bowl, #844, 1 lb.	$200.00 – 250.00
Candy jar, #8, ½ lb.	$40.00 – 47.00
Candy jar, #9, ¾ lb.	$47.00 – 52.00
Candy jar, #568, ½ lb.	$45.00 – 55.00
Candy jar, #736, 1 lb.	$55.00 – 65.00
Candy jar, #835, ½ lb.	$45.00 – 55.00

**with base, $300.00 – 350.00*

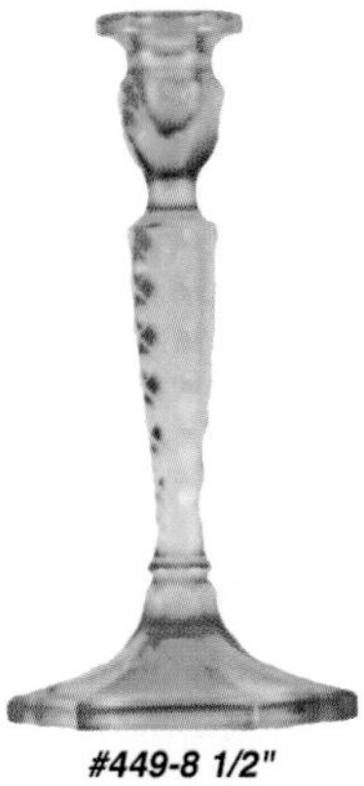
#449-8 1/2" Candlestick w/Cutting

#232-8" Candlestick

"Fenton Art Glass" Display Sign

#604-12" Crimped Punch Bowl w/Base

#215 Juice Tumbler

#215 Juice Pitcher

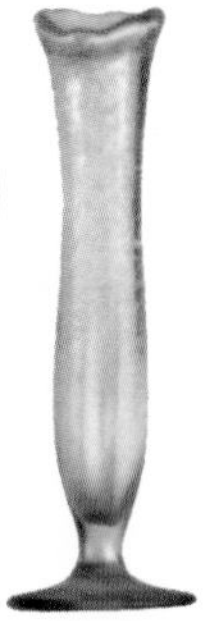
#354-8" Bud Vase

#570-5" Fan Vase w/Gold Decoration

#744 Powder Jar

#844-1 lb. Candy Jar

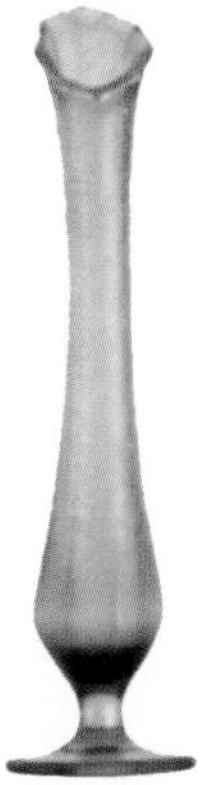
#251-10" Bud Vase

#681-8" Salad Plate w/Decoration #2

#9-7" Crimped Comport

#743 Puff Box

#66 Handled Lemon Tray

#3 Sugar and Creamer

#567-5" Fan Vase

11" Oval Ftd. Bowl with Dolphins

#554 Cigarette Holder

#314 Candlestick

#9, 3/4 lb. Candy Jar

#556 Cigarette Holder

#1623 Candlestick

#315 Candlestick

#317 Candlestick

Florentine Green	Value
Candy jar, #1532 w/dolphins	$125.00 –150.00
Cheese comport/under plate, #316	$50.00 – 60.00
Cigarette holder, #554 round	$85.00 – 100.00
Cigarette holder, #556 oval	$85.00 – 100.00
Cologne, #55	$140.00 – 160.00
Cologne, #55½ with flower finial	$225.00 – 270.00
Cologne, #56	$135.00 – 160.00
Comport, #9 – 7" crimped	$35.00 – 40.00
Comport, #260 – 7" tall footed	$45.00 – 50.00
Comport, #312 – 7" cupped, low footed	$30.00 – 35.00
Comport, #312 – 8" flared footed	$30.00 – 35.00
Comport, #400 – 6" square	$32.00 – 37.00
Comport, #500 footed crimped	$35.00 – 40.00
Comport, #643 – 6¾" salver	$22.00 – 27.00
Comport, #643 – 7" plate	$22.00 – 27.00
Comport, #712 – 7" cupped footed	$35.00 – 40.00
Comport, #736 – 8" flared cupped	$35.00 – 40.00
Comport, #737 – 7" flared cupped	$35.00 – 40.00
Comport, No. 1502 – A Diamond Optic	$90.00 –100.00
Comport, #1533- A– 6" crimped w/dolphins	$90.00 –100.00
Comport, scalloped top w/Stippled Ray interior	$150.00 – 175.00
*Creamer, #2	$50.00 – 60.00
Creamer, #3	$40.00 – 45.00
Creamer, #1502 Diamond Optic	$50.00 – 60.00
*Guest set, #200 handled	$320.00 – 360.00
Jar, #60 bath (smelling) salts	$160.00 – 190.00
Marmalade, #76	$100.00 – 120.00
Mayonnaise & ladle, #923	$45.00 – 50.00
Mayonnaise & under plate, #2005	$40.00 – 50.00
Night set, #401	$145.00 – 185.00
Nut bowl, #1192 Basket Weave w/Open Edge	$200.00 – 250.00
Nut cup, #923 individual	$27.00 – 30.00
Pitcher, #215 grape juice	$170.00 – 190.00
Pitcher & lid, #220 – 9¼"	$245.00 – 270.00
Pitcher, 9¼"	$150.00 – 175.00
Plate, #103 – sherbet	$18.00 – 20.00
Plate, #647 – 14"	$50.00 – 60.00
Plate, #680 – 6"	$22.00 – 25.00
Plate, #681 – 8" salad	$30.00 – 35.00
Plate, #681 – 8" salad w/No. 2 or No. 3 dec.	$40.00 – 45.00
Plate, #682 – 9" service	$30.00 – 35.00
Plate, #682 – 9" service w/No. 2 or No. 3 dec.	$45.00 – 50.00
Plate, #756 – 6" octagonal	$9.00 – 11.00
Plate, #757 – 7¼" octagonal/w Laurel Leaf dec.	$65.00 – 75.00
Plate, #758 – 8½" octagonal	$11.00 – 14.00
Plate, #1006 – 8" salad	$14.00 – 16.00
Plate, #2005 – 8"	$18.00 – 20.00
Plate, #2007 – 11"	$25.00 – 30.00
Puff box, 4¾"	$65.00 – 75.00
Puff box, #57	$70.00 – 80.00
Puff box, #743	$80.00 – 90.00
Puff box, #744 with flower finial	$150.00 – 200.00
Rose bowl, #847	$45.00 – 55.00
Sherbet, #103	$24.00 – 28.00
Sign, "Fenton Art Glass" logo	$700.00 – 900.00
*Sugar, #2	$50.00 – 60.00
Sugar, #3	$40.00 – 45.00
Sugar, #1502 Diamond Optic	$60.00 – 75.00
Tray, #66 lemon or butter	$45.00 – 50.00
Tray, #317 – 10" handled sandwich	$55.00 – 60.00
Tray, #318 – 7" oval handled	$50.00 – 60.00
Tray, #1502 – A–10" handled sandwich	$125.00 – 150.00
Tray, #1557 – 6½" cheese w/dolphin handle	$120.00 – 140.00
Tumbler, #215 grape juice	$25.00 – 30.00
Tumbler, 5⅛" flat	$25.00 – 30.00
Vase, #251 – 10" bud	$45.00 – 55.00
Vase, #354 – 8" bud	$22.00 – 25.00
Vase, #400 – 6" square, crimped	$30.00 – 32.00
Vase, #565 – 6" fan	$40.00 – 50.00

** with cobalt handle add 20%*

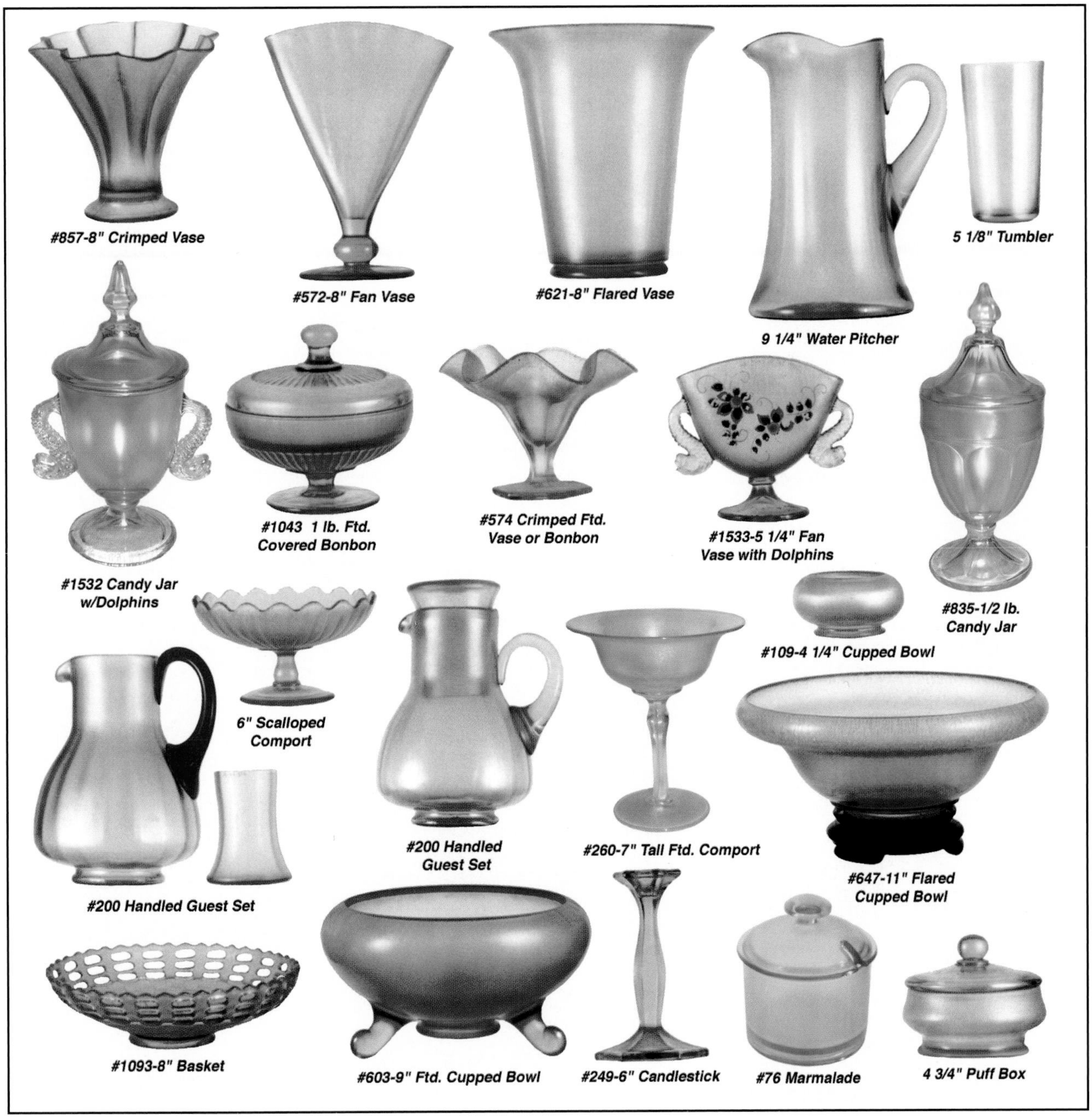

#857-8" Crimped Vase · #572-8" Fan Vase · #621-8" Flared Vase · 9 1/4" Water Pitcher · 5 1/8" Tumbler · #1532 Candy Jar w/Dolphins · #1043 1 lb. Ftd. Covered Bonbon · #574 Crimped Ftd. Vase or Bonbon · #1533-5 1/4" Fan Vase with Dolphins · #835-1/2 lb. Candy Jar · 6" Scalloped Comport · #200 Handled Guest Set · #260-7" Tall Ftd. Comport · #109-4 1/4" Cupped Bowl · #647-11" Flared Cupped Bowl · #200 Handled Guest Set · #1093-8" Basket · #603-9" Ftd. Cupped Bowl · #249-6" Candlestick · #76 Marmalade · 4 3/4" Puff Box

Florentine Green	Value
Vase, #567 – 5" fan	$40.00 – 50.00
Vase, #570 – 5" fan	$30.00 – 35.00
Vase, #572 – 8" fan	$40.00 – 45.00
Vase, #574 – 6" crimped (comport)	$30.00 – 35.00
Vase, #602 – 10" flared	$70.00 – 80.00
Vase, #611 – 6½" cupped	$40.00 – 45.00
Vase, #612 – 6½" flared	$40.00 – 50.00
Vase, #621 – 8" flared	$60.00 – 70.00
Vase, #622 – 7½" flared	$45.00 – 55.00
Vase, #736 – 7" fan	$40.00 – 50.00
Vase, #847 – 6" fan	$45.00 – 55.00
Vase, #857 – 8" crimped	$95.00 – 125.00
Vase, #857 – 8" fan	$55.00 – 65.00
Vase, #1502 – A Diamond Optic w/dolphins	$90.00 – 100.00
Vase, #1533, 6¼" fan w/dolphins	$110.00 – 125.00

GRECIAN GOLD AND GOLD IRIDIZED CRYSTAL

A golden iridescent finish was applied to crystal engraved glassware beginning about 1915. Then starting in the early 1920s, stretch glass was produced in a golden amber color called Grecian Gold. To collectors of stretch glass the two finishes are technically different since the earlier glassware does not have a stretch effect. Prices and demand for Grecian Gold are generally lower than for other colors of stretch glass. Therefore, collectors who like this color may find some bargains available. Both Grecian Gold and gold iridized crystal pieces are included in the following price guide.

Item	Value	Item	Value
Ashtray Set, #202 – 5-pc.	$70.00 – 85.00	Bowl, #857 – 11" flared cup	$45.00 – 50.00
Bathroom set, 4-pc., #16 – 17 – 54	$140.00 – 160.00	Bowl, #857 – 8" cupped	$32.00 – 37.00
Bonbon, #543 covered	$45.00 – 50.00	Bowl, #917 – 11" footed flared	$65.00 – 75.00
Bonbon, #643 – 5" covered	$40.00 – 45.00	Bowl, #1604 – 11" oval w/dolphins	$185.00– 200.00
Bonbon, #1043, 1 lb. covered, ftd.	$50.00 – 55.00	Bowl, #2005 – 6½" shallow cup	$22.00 – 25.00
Bowl, #231 – 8" footed, deep cup	$65.00 – 75.00	Bowl, #2007 – 7½" shallow cup	$25.00 – 27.00
Bowl, #231 – 10" ftd, shallow cup	$40.00 – 45.00	Candlestick, #232 – 8½"	$40.00 – 45.00
Bowl, #347 – 10¼" flared cup	$75.00 – 85.00	Candlestick, #249 – 6"	$35.00 – 40.00
Bowl, #545 – 5" cupped lily	$12.00 – 15.00	Candlestick, #314	$10.00 – 12.00
Bowl, #545 – 6½" shallow cup	$14.00 – 17.00	Candlestick, #349 – 10"	$50.00 – 55.00
Bowl, #550 – 12" flared	$70.00 – 80.00	Candlestick, #449 – 8½"	$40.00 – 45.00
Bowl, #550 – 12" flared cup	$70.00 – 80.00	Candlestick, #549 – 8½"	$40.00 – 45.00
Bowl, #575 – 5" cupped lily	$12.00 – 15.00	Candlestick, #549 – 2 – 8½"	$55.00 – 65.00
Bowl, #601 – 10" shallow cup	$50.00 – 55.00	with Persian pearl base	$100.00 – 110.00
Bowl, #604 – 12" flared cup	$150.00 – 175.00	*Candlestick, #649 – 10"	$50.00 – 55.00
Bowl, #607 – 9" shallow, cup	$40.00 – 45.00	Candlestick, #749 – 12"	$65.00 – 75.00
Bowl, #640 – 7" flared, cup	$18.00 – 22.00	Candy jar, #8, ½ lb.	$32.00 – 35.00
Bowl, #647 – 10¼" flared, cup	$50.00 – 55.00	Candy jar, #9, ¾ lb.	$30.00 – 35.00
Bowl, #647 – 13" shallow salver	$50.00 – 55.00	Candy jar, #636, 1 lb.	$32.00 – 37.00
Bowl, #846 – 8¼" cupped	$30.00 – 35.00	Candy jar, #735, ¼ lb.	$30.00 – 35.00
Bowl, #846 – 8" flared cup	$32.00 – 35.00	Cheese comport/underplate, #316	$45.00 – 55.00
Bowl, #847 – 7½" flared	$32.00 – 35.00	Cigarette holder, #556	$85.00 – 95.00
Bowl, #847 – 8" shallow cup	$30.00 – 32.00	Cologne, #55	$110.00 – 125.00
Bowl, #857 – 11" flared	$45.00 – 50.00	* *with Persian pearl base*	$130.00 – 150.00

#3700-8" Vase w/Floral Cutting

#55 Cologne

#3700 Water Set w/Grape Cutting

#56 Cologne

#3700 Water Set w/Floral Cutting

#57 Puff Box

#56 Cologne w/#55 1/2 Stopper

#349-10" Candlestick

#401 Night Set
#9-3/4 lb. Candy Jar
#9-3/4 lb. Candy Jar
#636-1lb. Candy Jar
#735-1/2 lb. Candy Jar
9" Vase
#543 Covered Bonbon
#60 Bath Salts
#260 High Ftd. Comport
#17 Bathroom Bottle
#3600 Jug
#16 Bathroom Bottle
10 1/4 " High Standard Comport
#317 Candlestick

Item	Value	Item	Value
Cologne, #55½ w/flower finial	$240.00 – 270.00	Plate, #682 – 9" w/ No. 2/3 dec	$30.00 – 35.00
Cologne, #56	$115.00 – 130.00	Plate, #757 – 7¼" octagonal	$9.00 – 11.00
Cologne, #56 w/55½ stopper	$220.00 – 250.00	Plate, #758 – 8½" octagonal	$10.00 – 12.00
Comport, #260 – 7" tall footed	$45.00 – 55.00	Puff box, #57	$35.00 – 45.00
Comport, #312 – 7" cup, low footed	$22.00 – 27.00	Puff box, #743	$50.00 – 60.00
Comport, #643 – 6¼" salver	$28.00 – 30.00	Rose Bowl, #847	$40.00 – 45.00
Comport, #643 – 7" plate	$22.00 – 27.00	Sherbet, #103	$25.00 – 30.00
Comport, #712 – 7" cupped footed	$25.00 – 30.00	Sugar, #3	$28.00 – 30.00
Comport, #736 – 6½" cupped	$27.00 – 30.00	Tray, #317 – 10" handled sandwich	$40.00 – 45.00
Comport, #737 – 6½" cupped	$22.00 – 27.00	Tumbler, #3700	$8.00 – 10.00
Comport, #737 – 7" flared cupped	$22.00 – 27.00	Tumbler, #3600	$8.00 – 10.00
Compote, Hi-Standard	$180.00 – 200.00	Vase, #99 – 7" bud	$8.00 – 10.00
Creamer, #3	$28.00 – 30.00	Vase, #251 – 10" bud	$12.00 – 15.00
Flower block, #3 – 3"	$10.00 – 12.00	Vase, #562 – 8" fan	$27.00 – 30.00
Flower pot and base, #1555	$65.00 – 75.00	Vase, #567 – 5" fan	$22.00 – 25.00
**Guest set, #200 handled	$150.00 – 200.00	Vase, #602 – 10" flared	$30.00 – 40.00
Jar, #60 bath (smelling) salts	$110.00 – 130.00	Vase, #611 – 6½" cupped	$22.00 – 25.00
Jug, #3600	$45.00 – 55.00	Vase, #612 – 6½" flared	$22.00 – 25.00
Jug, #3700	$45.00 – 55.00	Vase, #622 – 7½" flared	$30.00 – 35.00
Night set, #401	$40.00 – 50.00	Vase, #791 peacock	$750.00 – 800.00
Plate, #103 sherbet	$18.00 – 22.00	Vase, #847 – 6" fan	$30.00 – 35.00
Plate, #680 – 4"	$8.00 – 9.00	Vase, #857 – 8" fan	$37.00 – 40.00
Plate, #681 – 8" salad	$27.00 – 30.00	Vase, #901–8½" flared crimped	
Plate, #681 – 8" w/No. 2/3 dec.	$30.00 – 35.00	Dancing Ladies	$3000.00 – 3500.00
Plate, #682 – 9" service	$30.00 – 32.00	Vase, #3700 – 8"	$18.00 – 20.00
		***with blue handle*	$200.00 –240.00

PERSIAN PEARL

Persian pearl stretch glass results from the application of an iridescent spray over crystal glassware. Many of the prices for this color glassware are still reasonable. However, a few of the elusive pieces such as the punch bowl and the handled guest set are beginning to get expensive. Basket Weave with Open Edge items bring high prices among the carnival glass crowd. The #901 Dancing Ladies piece are listed in this color. However, only two examples, an oval bowl and a fan shape vase have been reported by collectors.

Item	Value	Item	Value
Basket, #1620 Plymouth	$235.00 – 260.00	Candlestick, #549 – 2 – 8½" with black base	$100.00 – 110.00
Bonbon, #106 – 6½" crimped	$22.00 – 25.00	Candlestick, #649 – 10"	$100.00 – 110.00
Bonbon, #643 open, cupped	$22.00 – 25.00	Candlestick, #749 – 12"	$100.00 – 110.00
Bonbon, #643 – 5" covered	$35.00 – 40.00	Candlestick, #950 – 5½"	$25.00 – 30.00
Bowl, #109 – 4¼" shallow	$18.00 – 22.00	Candy jar, #8, ½ lb.	$35.00 – 45.00
Bowl, #109 – 5½ shallow	$20.00 – 22.00	Candy jar, #9, ¾ lb.	$40.00 – 47.00
Bowl, #349 – 10½" flared	$225.00 – 275.00	Candy jar, #636 – 1 lb.	$45.00 – 55.00
Bowl, #545 – 6 ½" shallow cup	$22.00 – 25.00	Comport, #9 – 7½" oval footed	$30.00 – 35.00
Bowl, #600 – 7" cupped	$22.00 – 27.00	Comport, #400 – 6" crimped	$40.00 – 45.00
Bowl, #601 – 10" shallow cup	$45.00 – 50.00	Comport, #500 footed oval	$50.00 – 60.00
Bowl, #603 – 9" ftd., shallow cup	$150.00 – 175.00	Creamer, #3	$25.00 – 30.00
Bowl, #603 – 9" ftd., crimped	$210.00 – 220.00	Cup, #1502 Diamond Optic	$18.00 – 22.00
Bowl, #603 – 10" ftd., crimped orange	$220.00 – 240.00	Fern bowl, #250 three-footed	$90.00 – 100.00
Bowl, #604 – 12" (punch bowl)	$275.00– 300.00	Ginger jar, #893 w/base & top	$150.00 – 175.00
Bowl, #604 – 14" shallow cup	$170.00 – 190.00	Guest set #200 handled	$220.00 – 240.00
Bowl, #607 – 9" shallow cup	$40.00 – 45.00	Night set, #401	$60.00 – 70.00
Bowl, #640 – 7" flared, cup	$30.00 – 35.00	Nut cup, #923 individual	$30.00 – 35.00
Bowl, #846 – 9" flared	$40.00 – 45.00	Pitcher, #215 grape juice	$160.00 – 175.00
Bowl, #847 – 7½" flared	$40.00 – 45.00	Plate, #103 sherbet	$8.00 – 10.00
Bowl, #857 – 10" crimped	$45.00 – 55.00	Plate, 11"	$15.00 – 17.00
Bowl, #900 – 11" oval D.L.	$350.00 – 400.00	Plate, #301 – 6"	$6.00 – 8.00
Bowl, #920 – 9" 3 – toed cupped orange	$160.00 – 180.00	*Plate, #680 – 8¼"	$7.00 – 9.00
Bowl, #920 – 10" 3 – toed crimped orange	$165.00 – 185.00	Plate, #757 – 7¼" octagonal with Laurel Leaf dec.	$55.00 – 65.00
Bowl, #1093 – 8" "Basket" pattern	$100.00 – 150.00	*Sherbet, #103	$22.00 – 25.00
Bowl, oval, #1562 – 1 – 13"	$125.00 – 140.00	Sugar, #3	$25.00 – 30.00
Bowl, #1562 – 2 – 14" oval	$170.00 – 180.00	Tray, #1562 – 3 – 15" oval	$125.00 – 150.00
Bowl, #1663 – 10½" tulip	$45.00 – 55.00	Tumbler, #215 grape juice	$25.00 – 30.00
Bowl, #1663 – 10" square	$45.00 – 55.00	Vase, #400 – 6" crimped	$32.00 – 35.00
Bowl, #1663 – 12" flared	$50.00 – 55.00	Vase, #567 – 5" fan	$30.00 – 35.00
Bowl, #1663 – 9" oval	$40.00 – 45.00	Vase, #572 – 8" fan	$40.00 – 45.00
Bowl, #1790 – 10" flared	$250.00 – 300.00	Vase, #573 – 8" flared trumpet	$27.00 – 32.00
Bowl, #1790 – 8" cupped	$250.00 – 300.00	Vase, #620 – 10" flared	$35.00 – 45.00
Bowl, #1790 – 9" crimped	$250.00 – 300.00	Vase, #621 – 8" flared	$30.00 – 37.00
Bowl, #2005 – 6½" shallow cup	$27.00 – 30.00	Vase, #901 – 8½" flare D. L.	$450.00 – 475.00
Bowl, #2006 – 7½" shallow cup	$27.00 – 30.00	Vase, #901 – 8½" sq. D. L.	$400.00 – 550.00
Candlestick, #249 – 6"	$30.00 – 35.00	Vase, #901 – 9½" fan D. L.	$450.00 – 500.00
*Candlestick, #316	$27.00 – 30.00	Vase, #1531 – 14"	$130.00 – 150.00
Candlestick, #318	$27.00 – 30.00	Vase, #1533 – 5¼" fan w/dolphins	$130.00 – 140.00
Candlestick, #349 – 10"	$100.00 – 110.00		
Candlestick, #449 – 8½"	$95.00 – 100.00		
Candlestick, #549 – 8½"	$80.00 – 85.00		

**with cobalt trim add 20%*

#8-1/2 lb. Candy

#621-8" Flared Vase

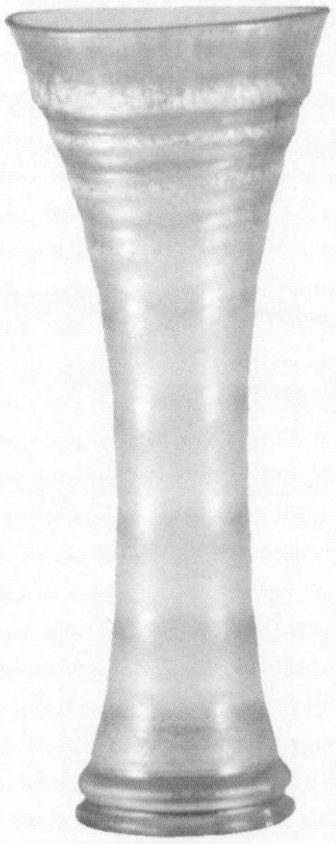

#1531-14" Swung Vase

#572-8" Fan Vase

#8-1/2 lb. Candy

#567-5" Fan Vase

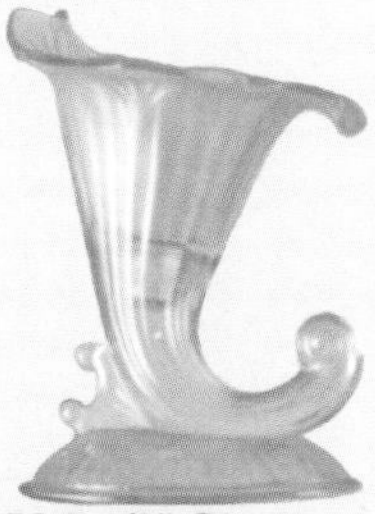

#950-5 1/2" Cornucopia Candlestick

#643-5" Covered Bonbon

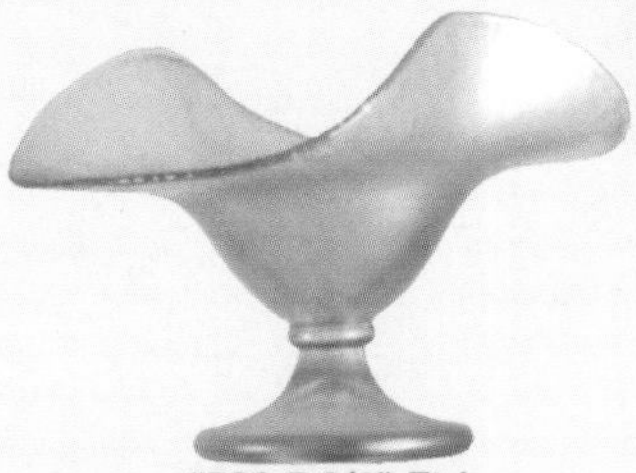

#500-7 3/4" Ftd. Oval Bonbon

#603-9 1/2" Ftd. Shallow Cupped Bowl

#1562-2-14" Oval Bowl and #1562-3 Oval Tray

#680-8 1/4" Salad Plate

#604-12" Flared Punch Bowl

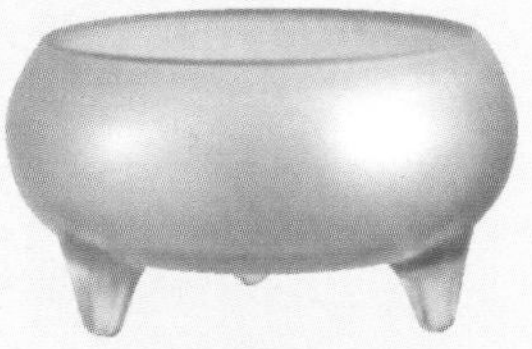

#250 Fern Bowl

#3 Sugar and Creamer

#1502 Cup

#316 Candlestick

RUBY

Pieces of ruby stretch glass are treasured by all dedicated stretch glass collectors. The color was in limited production through the 1920s, and not many pieces are available in the marketplace today. Some pieces will be found with iridescence on only one surface.

A 6" fan vase with dolphin handles has been made recently in limited quantities. This newer vase is marked with the Fenton logo.

Item	Value
Bonbon, #543 covered	$240.00 – 275.00
Bowl, #109 cupped or flared	$200.00 – 225.00
Bowl, #600 – 10" flared salad	$275.00 – 300.00
Bowl, #601 – 10" shallow	$250.00 – 275.00
Bowl, #603 – 10" footed, crimped orange	$600.00 – 650.00
Bowl, #603 – 9" footed, cupped	$575.00 – 600.00
Bowl, #604 – 10" crimped	$275.00 – 325.00
Bowl, #604 – 12" flared (punch bowl)	$450.00 – 500.00
Bowl, #604 – 11¼" crimped (punch bowl) w/ ruby base	$3000.00 – 3200.00
Bowl, #604 – 14" shallow cupped	$275.00 – 300.00
Bowl, #606 – 6" cupped	$190.00 – 225.00
Bowl, #606 – 7½" shallow cupped	$200.00 – 250.00
Bowl, #638 – 8" shallow cupped	$225.00 – 250.00
Bowl, #647 – 11" rolled rim	$200.00 – 250.00
Bowl, #1504 – A – 7" crimped w/dolphins	$700.00 – 800.00
Bowl, #1006 cupped	$165.00 – 185.00
Bowl, #2006 – 7½" shallow cupped	$165.00 – 185.00
Bowl, #2007 – 9" shallow cupped	$175.00 – 200.00
Candlestick, #249 – 6"	$150.00 – 175.00
*Candlestick, #349 – 10"	$200.00 – 250.00
Candlestick, #449 – 8½"	$150.00 – 175.00
Candy jar, #9, ¾ lb.	$240.00 – 285.00
Candy jar, #736, 1 lb.	$450.00 – 500.00
Comport, #500 – 6 ½" footed crimped	$225.00 – 250.00
Comport, #643 – 7" plate	$180.00 – 200.00
Comport, #1533 – 7" crimped w/dolphins	$700.00 – 800.00
Plate, #103 sherbet	$45.00 – 55.00
Plate, #604 – 16¾"	$300.00 – 400.00
Plate, #607 – 6"	$45.00 – 55.00
Plate, #1006 – 8"	$80.00 – 90.00
Plate, #2006 – 8"	$80.00 – 90.00
Plate, #2007 – 11"	$110.00 – 125.00
Sherbet, #103	$50.00 – 60.00
Vase, #602 – 10" flared	$400.00 – 500.00
Vase, #612 – 6½" flared	$350.00 – 400.00
Vase, #621 – 8" cupped	$200.00 – 250.00
Vase, #621 – 8" flared	$300.00 – 350.00
Vase, #1533 – 5¼" crimped w/dolphins	$500.00 – 600.00
**with cut oval*	$300.00 – 400.00

9-3/4 lb. Candy Jar

#604 Punch Bowl with Black Base

#603-10" Crimped Orange Bowl

#603-9" Cupped Orange Bowl

#606-6" Shallow Cupped Bowl

#621-8" Flared Vase

#604-12" Flared Cupped Bowl

TANGERINE

Tangerine is an orange colored iridescent glass which was introduced in 1927 and produced through 1929. As a result of this late introduction and the short period of production, there is a shortage of tangerine stretch glass on many collectors' shelves. Also, notice that the listing below is not very lengthy, and many of the pieces are in the Diamond Optic and Dolphin patterns. The general scarcity of this color has caused prices to remain at elevated levels in comparison to the other colors of stretch glass.

Item	Value
Bowl, #231 – 10" footed shallow cupped	$120.00 – 140.00
Bowl, #600 – 10" rolled rim	$100.00 – 110.00
Bowl, #647 – 10¾" flared cupped	$110.00 – 130.00
Bowl, #647 – 12" rolled console	$105.00 – 120.00
Bowl, #647 – 12" shallow cupped	$100.00 – 110.00
Bowl, #846 – 8" flared cupped	$80.00 – 90.00
Bowl, #848 – 9" flared	$150.00 – 175.00
Bowl, #857 – 9½" flared cupped	$90.00 – 100.00
Bowl, #857 – 10" flared, rolled rim	$90.00 – 100.00
Bowl, #857 – 10" special roll	$85.00 – 95.00
Bowl, #857 – 11" flared	$90.00 – 100.00
Bowl, #857 – 8" cupped	$75.00 – 85.00
Bowl, #1502 – 9½" flared Diamond Optic	$110.00 – 125.00
Bowl, #1502 – 13" special roll rim Diamond Optic	$125.00 – 150.00
Bowl, #1512 – 10½" shallow cupped	$110.00 – 125.00
Bowl, #1512 – 8½" special roll	$110.00 – 125.00
Bowl, #1512 – 8" flared	$110.00 – 125.00
Bowl, #1512 – 9½" flared	$100.00 – 125.00
Bowl, #1512 – 9½" shallow	$100.00 – 125.00
Bowl, 10" octagonal w/Laurel Leaf rim	$125.00 – 150.00
Candlestick, #316	$40.00 – 45.00
Candlestick, #317	$40.00 – 45.00
Candlestick, #318	$40.00 – 45.00
Candy jar, #844, 1 lb.	$350.00 – 400.00
Candy jar, #10	$150.00 – 200.00
Candy jar, #835, ½ lb.	$75.00 – 85.00
Candy jar, #1532 –A – ½ lb. w/dolphins	$150.00 – 175.00
Cigarette holder, #556 oval	$140.00 – 160.00
Cologne, #53 Diamond Optic	$190.00 – 210.00
Cologne, #55	$210.00 – 225.00
Cologne, #55½ with flower finial	$250.00+
Comport, #260 – 7" tall footed	$95.00 – 110.00
Comport, #1502 –A – 5" flared Diamond Optic	$100.00 – 125.00
Comport, #1533 – 6" round w/dolphins	$120.00 – 135.00
Creamer, #3	$55.00 – 65.00
Flower pot and saucer, #1554	$100.00 – 120.00
Guest set, #200 handled	N.D.
Plate, #103, sherbet	$18.00 – 22.00
Plate, #1043 – 9" footed	$55.00 – 65.00
Plate, 13" octagonal w/Laurel Leaf rim	$110.00 – 130.00
Salver, #1043 – 7¼" footed	$75.00 – 85.00
Sherbet, #103	$30.00 – 35.00
Sherbet, low footed	$35.00 – 40.00
Sugar, #3	$55.00 – 65.00
Tray, #66 lemon or butter	$60.00 – 65.00
Tray, #317 – 10" handled	$120.00 – 135.00
Tray, #318 – 7" oval handled butter	$65.00 – 75.00
Tray, #1561 – 10" oval handled	$95.00 – 115.00
Vase, #251 – 10" bud	$50.00 – 55.00

Low Footed Sherbet
#556 Cigarette Holder
#318 Candlestick
#857-8" Fan Vase
#835-1/2 lb. Candy Jar
#573-8" Flared Vase
#200 Guest Set
#1531-14" Vase
#251-12" Bud Vase
#1533-6" Fan Vase
#1533-6" Ftd. Comport
#1043 Ftd. Plate
#260 Tall Ftd. Comport
#318-7" Oval Handled Butter or Lemon Tray
#316 Candlestick
#857-8" Cupped Bowl
#1512-9" Flared Bowl
#1561-10" Oval Handled Tray
#621-8" Flared Vase
#1512-9 1/2" Shallow Bowl
#231-10" Shallow Cupped Ftd. Bowl
#857-11" Flared Bowl

Item	Value
Vase, #251 – 12" bud	$55.00 – 65.00
Vase, #835 – 6" crimped	$57.00 – 67.00
Vase, #572 – 8" fan	$65.00 – 70.00
Vase, #573 – 8" crimped	$65.00 – 70.00
Vase, #573 – 8" flared trumpet	$70.00 – 75.00
Vase, #612 – 6 ½" flared	$60.00 – 70.00
Vase, #621 – 8" flared	$70.00 – 80.00
Vase, #847 – 5" shell-shaped crimp	$45.00 – 55.00
Vase, #857 – 8" fan	$80.00 – 85.00
Vase, #1502 – 8" flared Diamond Optic	$90.00 – 95.00
Vase, #1530 – 12"	$140.00 – 150.00
Vase, #1531 – 14"	$175.00 – 190.00
Vase, #1531 – 16"	$195.00 – 210.00
Vase, #1533 – 5¼" fan w/dolphins	$130.00 – 150.00

TOPAZ

Fenton's topaz stretch glass is a yellow-green color which some people refer to as vaseline. Topaz stretch glass was introduced in 1921 and remained in production for most of the decade. Unusual shapes shown in the photo include the banana bowl, the cornucopia vase, and the scalloped comport. The 3" puff box is similar in style to one produced by Fenton, but the one in the picture may not have been made by Fenton.

Item	Value
Ashtray Set, #202, 5-piece	$140.00 – 160.00
Bonbon, #543 covered	$65.00 – 75.00
Bonbon, #643 open, cupped	$32.00 – 35.00
Bonbon, #643 – 5" covered	$90.00 – 120.00
Bonbon, #1043, 1 lb. covered, footed	$115.00 – 130.00
Bowl, #545 – 5" cupped lily	$30.00 – 35.00
Bowl, #545 – 6½" shallow cupped	$27.00 – 32.00
Bowl, #550 – 11" shallow, cupped	$45.00 – 55.00
Bowl, #550 – 12" flared	$60.00 – 65.00
Bowl, #601 – 10" shallow cupped	$55.00 – 60.00
Bowl, #601 – 11" rolled edge	$60.00 – 65.00
Bowl, #604 – 10" cupped	$200.00 – 225.00
Bowl, #604 – 12" flared (punch bowl)	$300.00 – 350.00
Bowl, #604 – 14" shallow cupped	$85.00 – 95.00
Bowl, #604 – 9" cupped	$65.00 – 75.00
Bowl, #606 – 6" cupped	$30.00 – 35.00
Bowl, #608 – 11" hat-shaped	$75.00 – 85.00
Bowl, #640 – 8" shallow	$35.00 – 40.00
Bowl, #604 – 14" shallow cupped	$55.00 – 65.00
Bowl, #647 – 10" deep w/rolled rim	$50.00 – 60.00
Bowl, #647 – 11" shallow cupped	$50.00 – 65.00
Bowl, #847 – 6" cupped	$37.00 – 40.00
Bowl, #847 – 7½" flared	$40.00 – 45.00
Bowl, #847 – 7" shallow cupped	$40.00 – 45.00
Bowl, #848 – 8½" tulip	$75.00 – 90.00
Bowl, #857 – 9" banana	$50.00 – 55.00
Bowl, #1604 – 11" oval ftd. w/dolphins	$175.00 – 200.00
Bowl, #2007 – 7½" shallow cupped	$30.00 – 32.00
Candlestick, #232 – 8½"	$45.00 – 55.00
Candlestick, #314	$22.00 – 25.00
Candlestick, #315 princess	$30.00 – 32.00
Candlestick, #317	$30.00 – 32.00
Candlestick, #318	$30.00 – 32.00
Candlestick, #349 – 10"	$125.00 – 140.00
Candlestick, #449 – 8½"	$125.00 – 135.00
Candlestick, #549 – 8½"	$60.00 – 70.00
Candlestick, #549 – 2 – 8½" w/Celeste blue base	$110.00 – 125.00
*Candlestick, #649 – 10"	$100.00 – 110.00
Candlestick, #749 – 12"	$120.00 – 140.00
Candlestick, #1623 w/dolphins	$110.00 – 130.00
Candy jar, #9, ¾ lb.	$65.00 – 70.00
Candy jar, #636, 1 lb.	$60.00 – 70.00
Candy jar, #735, ½ lb.	$50.00 – 60.00
Candy jar, #736, 1 lb.	$55.00 – 65.00
Cheese comport/underplate, #316	$50.00 – 55.00
Cigarette box, #500	$100.00 – 125.00
Cigarette box, #655	$150.00 – 175.00
Cigarette holder, #556 oval	$95.00 – 110.00
Cologne, #53 Diamond Optic	$120.00 – 140.00
Cologne, #55	$150.00 – 170.00
Cologne, #55½ w/flower finial stopper	$220.00 – 250.00
Cologne, #56	$130.00 – 150.00
with ebony base	$160.00 – 175.00

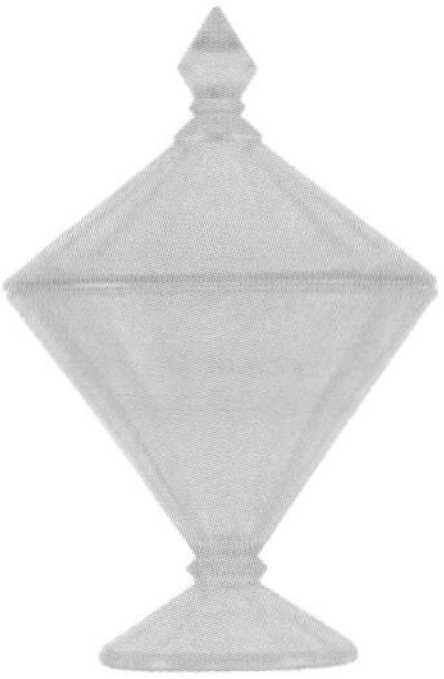
#735-1/2 lb.
Candy Jar

#1043-1 lb.
Bonbon

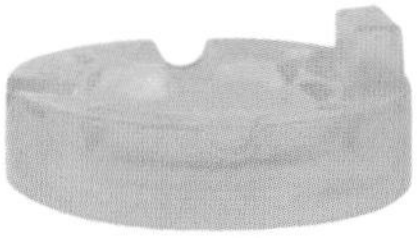
#203 Ashtray

#220 Pitcher & Lid

#222 Ice Tea
Tumbler

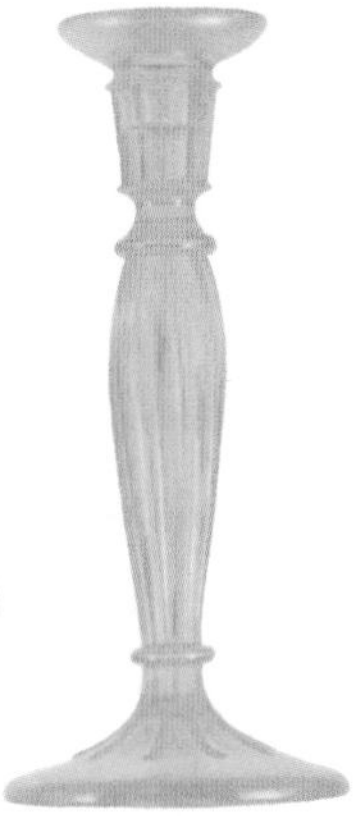
#232-8 1/2"
Candlestick

#2 Creamer

#655 Cigarette Box

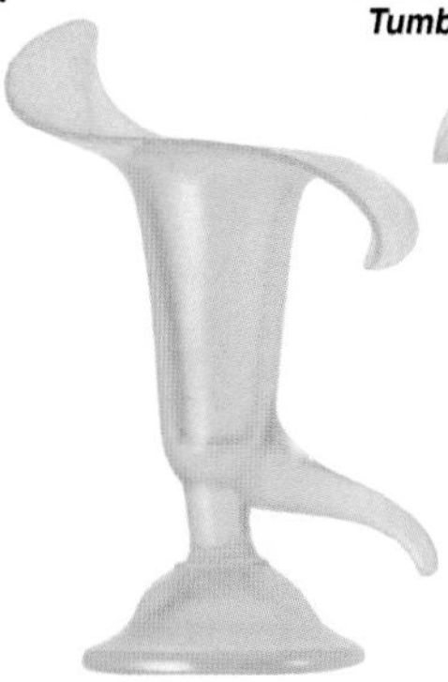
7 3/4" Cornucopia
Vase

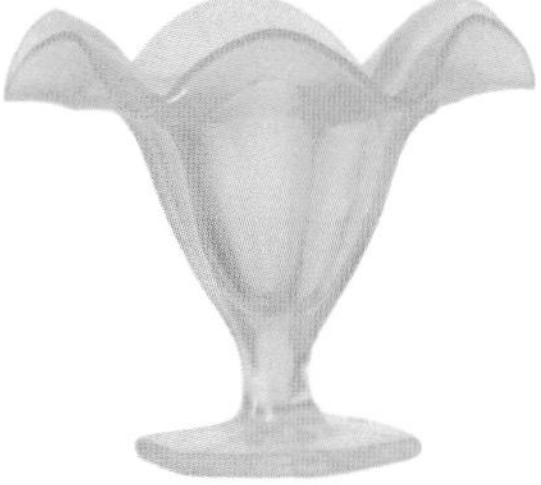
#574-6" Crimped
Vase

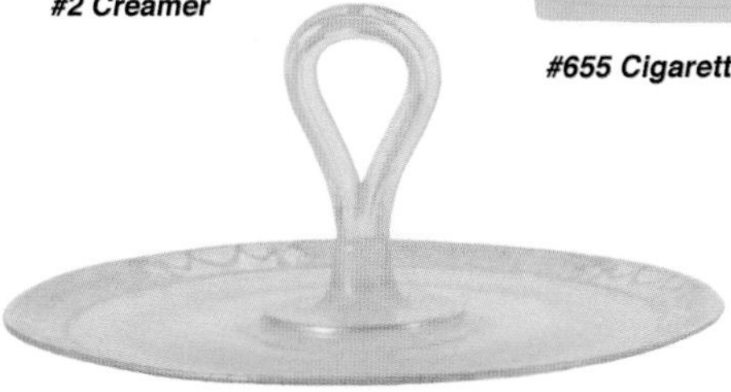
#317-10" Handled Tray

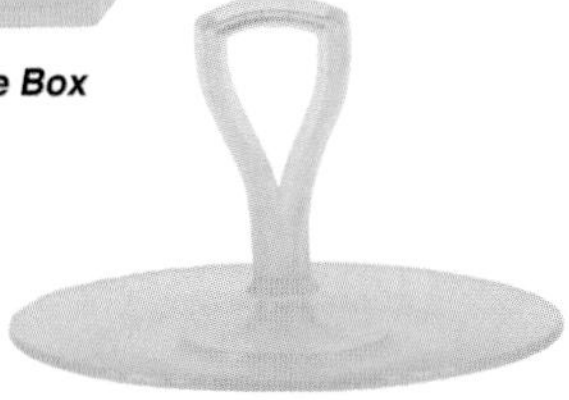
#318 Handled Oval
Butter or Lemon Tray

6" Scalloped Comport

#712-7" Ftd.
Cupped Comport

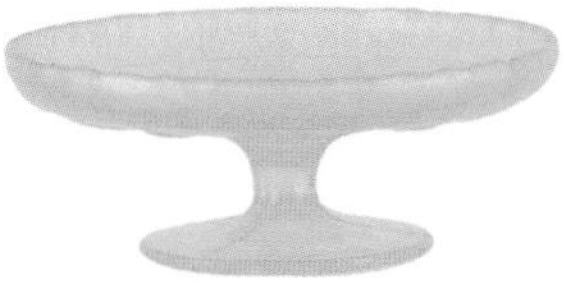
#643-6 3/4" Ftd.
Salver Comport

#103 Ftd. Sherbet

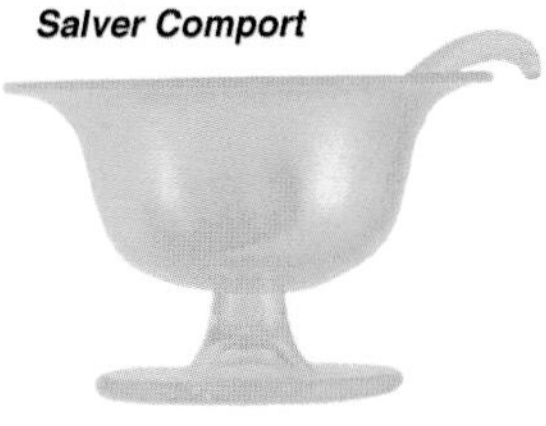
#923 Mayonnaise & Ladle

#556 Cigarette Holder

#923 Individual
Nut Cup

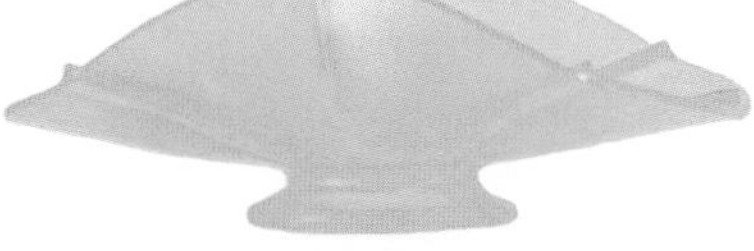
#857-9" Banana Bowl

3" Puff Box

#53 Puff Jar

#59 Cologne

#55 Cologne

#743 Puff Box

#55 1/2 Cologne

#401 Night Set

Item	Value
Cologne, #59	$120.00 – 140.00
Comport, #9 – 7" crimped	$50.00 – 55.00
Comport, #260 – 7" tall footed	$55.00 – 65.00
Comport, #312 – 7" cupped, low footed	$60.00 – 65.00
Comport, #312 – 8" flared footed	$50.00 – 55.00
Comport, #643 – 5¾" cupped	$32.00 – 37.00
Comport, #643 – 6¾" salver	$35.00 – 40.00
Comport, #643 – 7" plate	$40.00 – 50.00
Comport, #712 – 7" cupped footed	$40.00 – 45.00
Comport, #737 – 7" flared cupped	$40.00 – 50.00
Comport, #738 flared, cupped	$37.00 – 42.00
Comport, #1533 – 5" round w/dolphins	$85.00 – 95.00
Comport, #1533 – 7" oval	$90.00 – 100.00
Comport, scalloped top w/Stippled Rays interior	$200.00 – 250.00
Creamer, #2	$75.00 – 80.00
Fern bowl, #250 three-footed	$120.00 – 130.00
Flower block, #2 – 2"	$20.00 – 25.00
*Guest set, #200 handled	$350.00 – 400.00
Jar, #60 (smelling) bath salts	$175.00 – 200.00
Mayonnaise & ladle, #923	$55.00 – 60.00
Mug, #1630 shaving	$350.00 – 400.00
Night set, #401	$145.00 – 175.00
Nut cup, #923 individual	$30.00 – 35.00
Pitcher, #222 iced tea	$250.00 – 275.00
Pitcher & lid, #220	$300.00 – 325.00
Plate, #103 sherbet	$14.00 – 16.00
Plate, #631 – 11½" sandwich	$70.00 – 80.00
Plate, #680 – 6"	$22.00 – 25.00
Plate, #681 – 8" salad	$25.00 – 30.00
Plate, #682 – 9" service	$30.00 – 35.00
Plate, #756 – 6" octagonal	$20.00 – 25.00
Plate, #757 – 7¼" octagonal	$22.00 – 27.00
Plate, #758 – 8½" octagonal	$25.00 – 30.00
Plate, #1502 – 8" octagonal Diamond Optic	$50.00 – 65.00
Puff box, #53 Diamond Optic	$60.00 – 70.00
Puff box, #57	$70.00 – 80.00
Puff box, #743	$80.00 – 90.00
Puff box, #744	$150.00 – 200.00
Salver, #601 – 12"	$50.00 – 60.00
Sherbet, #103	$28.00 – 32.00
Sugar, #2	$75.00 – 80.00
Tray, #53 vanity set	$40.00 – 50.00
Tray, #66 lemon or butter	$45.00 – 50.00
Tray, #317 – 10" handled sandwich	$60.00 – 70.00
Tray, #318 – 7" oval or rd. handled butter	$45.00 – 50.00
Tumbler, #220 handled	$40.00 – 50.00
Tumbler, #222 handled iced tea	$75.00 – 95.00
Vanity Set, #53, 4-pc.	$340.00 – 400.00
Vase, #99 – 7" bud	$35.00 – 40.00
Vase, #251 – 10" bud	$40.00 – 50.00
Vase, #354 – 8" bud	$32.00 – 37.00
Vase, #400 – 6" square	$45.00 – 50.00
Vase, #574 – 6" crimped	$45.00 – 50.00
Vase, #602 – 10" flared	$65.00 – 75.00
Vase, #611 – 6½" cupped	$45.00 – 50.00
Vase, #612 – 6½" flared	$45.00 – 50.00
Vase, #622 – 7½" flared	$55.00 – 60.00
Vase, 7#/4" cornucopia	$120.00 – 150.00
Vase, #847 – 5" shell-shaped crimp	$40.00 – 45.00
Vase, #891 – 12"	$300.00 – 350.00
Vase, #1533 – 5¼" fan/w dolphins	$125.00 – 135.00
**with cobalt handle*	$375.00 – 425.00

VICTORIA TOPAZ

Victoria Topaz was Fenton's early name for yellow opalescent glassware. Yellow opalescent stretch glass pieces are available in the Curtain Optic (Drapery) and Rib Optic patterns. Some pieces may be accented with blue trim. All pieces in both patterns are difficult to find. The amber iridescent basket is one of the few pieces Fenton produced in that color. An 11" flared cupped bowl has also been found in amber stretch glass.

Item	Rib Optic	Curtain Optic
Guest Set, #200		$600.00 – 650.00
Pitcher, #222	$550.00 – 600.00	$550.00 – 600.00
Pitcher, 8¼" 4-rib base	$550.00 – 600.00	$500.00 – 550.00
Tumbler, #222	$100.00 – 125.00	$100.00 – 125.00
Vase, 9" 4-rib base	$600.00 – 650.00	$600.00 – 650.00
Vase, 9" 4-rib base w/cob handles	$650.00 – 750.00	$650.00 – 750.00

#222 Lemonade Pitcher

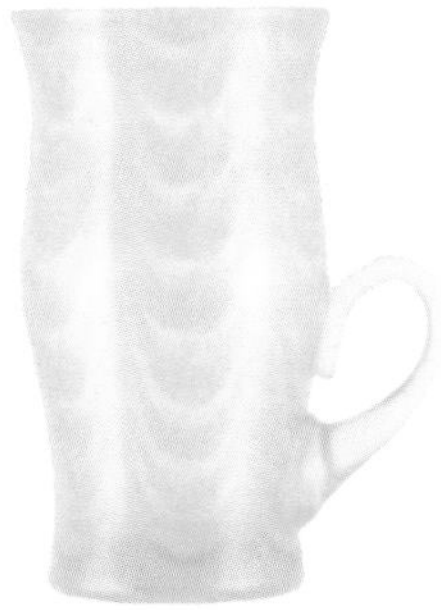

#222 Lemonade Tumbler

10 1/4" Lemonade Pitcher

#200 Guest Set

9" Vase

AMBER STRETCH GLASS

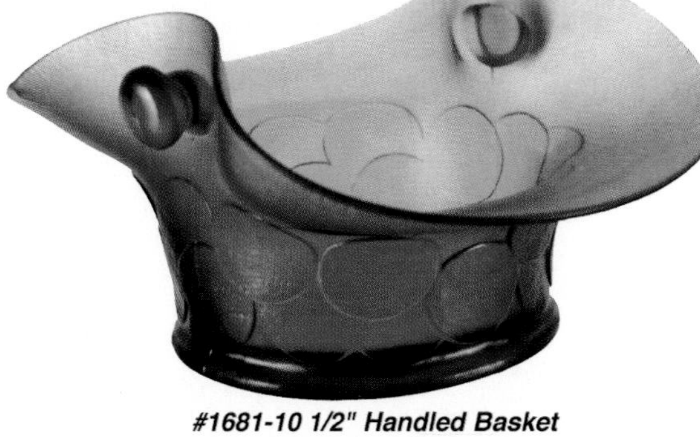

#1681-10 1/2" Handled Basket

9" Vase

VELVA ROSE

Fenton's name for pink glassware is rose, therefore, it seems perfectly logical they called their iridescent pink glassware Velva rose. Velva rose was not introduced into the line until 1926 and was only produced for about two years. Although this color is not as common as some of the other colors, the prices generally do not reflect the lack of availability, and most prices are reasonable. The covered pitcher, guest set, and large dolphin handled bowls are creeping upward in price. The colognes in the #55½ vanity set have rosebud stoppers.

Item	Value
Basket, #1615 – 6" Diamond Optic w/metal handle	$90.00 – 100.00
Basket, #1616 – 8" Diamond Optic w/metal handle	$125.00 – 150.00
Bathroom set, #16 – 17 – 54, 4 pc. set	$200.00 – 250.00
Bonbon, #106– 6½" crimped	$25.00 – 30.00
Bonbon, #543 covered	$45.00 – 50.00
Bonbon, #643 – 5" covered	$50.00 – 55.00
Bonbon, #943 covered	$50.00 – 55.00
Bonbon, #1043, 1 lb. covered, footed	$125.00 – 150.00
Bonbon, #1502 round Bridge w/metal handle	$55.00 – 65.00
Bowl, #500 – 12" flared	$85.00 – 100.00
Bowl, #550 – 10¼" flared cupped	$85.00 – 100.00
Bowl, #550 – 12" flared	$90.00 – 110.00
Bowl, #604 – 15" w/optic rolled rim	$95.00 – 115.00
Bowl, #640 – 7½" rolled rim	$27.00 – 32.00
Bowl, #847 – 6½" nut	$27.00 – 32.00
Bowl, #847 – 7" shallow cupped	$28.00 – 32.00
Bowl, #848 – 8½" tulip	$85.00 – 95.00
Bowl, #857 – 10" deep rolled rim	$50.00 – 60.00
Bowl, #857 – 11" flared	$50.00 – 60.00
Bowl, #857 – 11" flared cupped	$50.00 – 55.00
Bowl, #857 – 8" crimped	$45.00 – 55.00
Bowl, #857 – 9½" deep cupped	$50.00 – 55.00
Bowl, #1502 – 10" shallow cupped Diamond Optic	$60.00 – 70.00
Bowl, #1502 – 12" Diamond Optic/special rolled rim	$65.00 – 75.00
Bowl, #1502 – A-10" Diamond Optic w/dolphins	$195.00 – 210.00
Bowl, #1504 – A-10" crimped w/dolphins	$200.00 – 225.00
Bowl, #1504 – A-10" flared w/dolphins	$200.00 – 225.00
Bowl, #1504 – A-10" rolled rim w/dolphins	$190.00 – 220.00
Bowl, #1512 – 8" flared	$90.00 – 100.00
Bowl, #1515 oval pickle	$60.00 – 70.00
Bowl, #1563 – 17" oval handled	$185.00 – 225.00
Bowl, #1600 – 10" dolphin, rolled rim	$180.00 – 200.00
Bowl, #1602 – 10¼" crimped ftd. w/dolphins	$170.00 – 195.00
Bowl, #1608 – 10½" deep oval footed	$190.00 – 220.00
Candlestick, #314	$16.00 – 18.00
Candlestick, #316	$30.00 – 35.00
Candlestick, #317	$28.00 – 32.00
Candlestick, #318	$30.00 – 35.00
Candlestick, #349 – 10"	$75.00 – 85.00
Candlestick, #449 – 8½"	$90.00 – 100.00
Candlestick, #1502 Diamond Optic	$20.00 – 25.00
Candlestick, #1623 w/dolphins	$100.00 – 125.00
Candy jar, #9, ¾ lb.	$45.00 – 55.00
Candy jar, #10	$125.00 – 160.00
Candy jar, #568, ½ lb. covered	$55.00 – 60.00
Candy jar, #635, ½ lb.	$55.00 – 60.00

#572-8" Fan Vase

#251-12"
Bud Vase

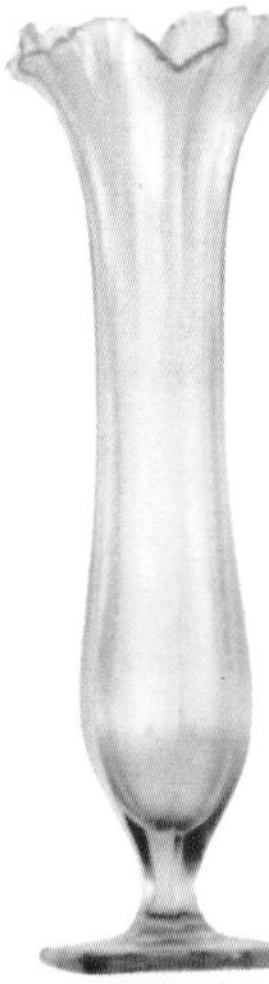

#574-12"
Swung Vase

#857-8" Crimped vase

#574-6" Crimped Ftd.
Vase or Bonbon

Hi-Standard Oval
Comport

Lamp, Ftd.
Flared Cupped

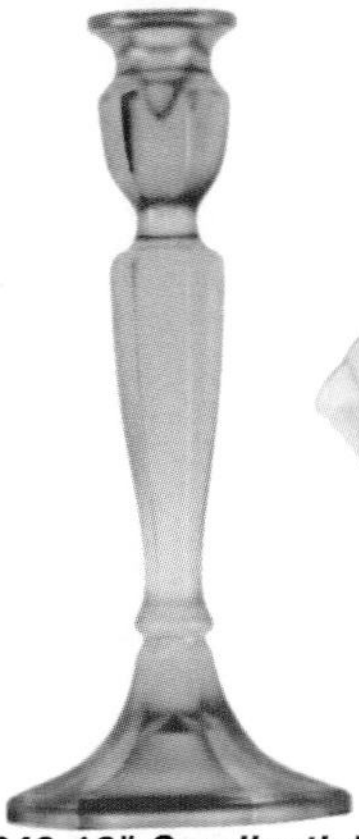

#349-10" Candlestick

#857-8" Fan Vase

#630-8 1/2" Salad Plate

#923 Mayonnaise
and Ladle

#3 Open Creamer and Sugar

#1043-7 1/2"
Ftd. Salver Comport

#1043-7 1/2" Ftd. Flared
Rolled Rim Comport

#316 Cheese
Comport

#314 candlestick

#848-9"
Flared Bowl

#550-12" Ftd.
Flared Bowl

#1602-10 1/4" Ftd.
Crimped Bowl

Item	Value
Candy jar, #636, 1 lb.	$55.00 – 60.00
Candy jar, #735, ½ lb.	$50.00 – 55.00
Candy jar, #835, ½ lb.	$70.00 – 75.00
Candy jar, #844, 1 lb.	$200.00 – 250.00
Candy jar, #1532 w/dolphins	$120.00 – 140.00
Cheese comport/under plate, #316	$45.00 – 55.00
Cigarette box, #500	$100.00 – 120.00
Cigarette box, #655	$125.00 – 150.00
Cigarette holder, #554 round	$110.00 – 125.00
Cigarette holder, #556 oval	$120.00 – 140.00
Cologne, #53 Diamond Optic	$120.00 – 140.00
Cologne, #54	$115.00 – 135.00
Cologne, #55	$130.00 – 150.00
Cologne, #55½	$220.00 – 270.00
Cologne, #59	$150.00 – 170.00
Comport, #643 – 6¾" salver	$37.00 – 40.00
Comport #1043 – 7½" flared, rolled rim	$35.00 – 40.00
Comport, #1502 – 7" oval Diamond Optic w/dolphins	$90.00 – 100.00
Comport, #1502 – 7" square Diamond Optic w/dolphins	$90.00 – 100.00
Comport, #1536 – 6¾" tall flared, ftd.	$70.00 – 80.00
Compote, Hi-Standard oval-shape	$175.00 – 200.00
Creamer, #3	$45.00 – 55.00
Creamer, #1502 Diamond Optic	$45.00 – 55.00
Cup, plain	$70.00 – 80.00
Flower pot and base, #1554	$90.00 – 100.00
Flower pot and base, #1555	$90.00 – 100.00
Goblet, #1502 Bridge, Diamond Optic	$80.00 – 90.00
Guest set, #200 handled	$320.00 – 360.00
Lamp, ftd. flared cupped	$250.00 – 300.00
Mayonnaise & ladle, #923	$45.00 – 50.00
Night set, #401	$145.00 – 185.00
Nut cup, #923 individual	$30.00 – 35.00
Pitcher & lid, #220	$300.00 – 350.00
Plate, #630 – 8½" salad	$30.00 – 32.00
Plate, #1502 – 8" octagonal Diamond Optic	$40.00 – 50.00
Puff box, #53 Diamond Optic	$50.00 – 60.00
Puff box, #54	$45.00 – 55.00
Puff box, #57	$50.00 – 60.00
Puff box, #744	$220.00 – 250.00
Salver, #1043 – 7½" footed	$40.00 – 45.00
Salver, #1043 – 9" footed	$50.00 – 55.00
Saucer	$16.00 – 18.00
Sherbet, #1502 Diamond Optic	$27.00 – 30.00
Sugar, #3	$45.00 – 55.00
Sugar, #1502 Diamond Optic	$45.00 – 55.00
Tray, #53 vanity set	$50.00 – 60.00
Tray, #66 lemon	$30.00 – 35.00
Tray, #317 – 10" handled sandwich	$60.00 – 65.00
Tray, #318 – 7" oval handled butter tray	$40.00 – 45.00
Tray, #1502 – A 10" handled sandwich	$145.00 – 160.00
Tray, #1557 dolphin handled cheese	$135.00 – 150.00
Tray, #1561 – 10" oval handled	$75.00 – 85.00
Vanity set, #53, 4-pc.	$340.00 – 400.00
Vanity set, #54, 4-pc.	$355.00 – 415.00
Vanity set, #55½/744, 3-pc.	$660.00 – 790.00

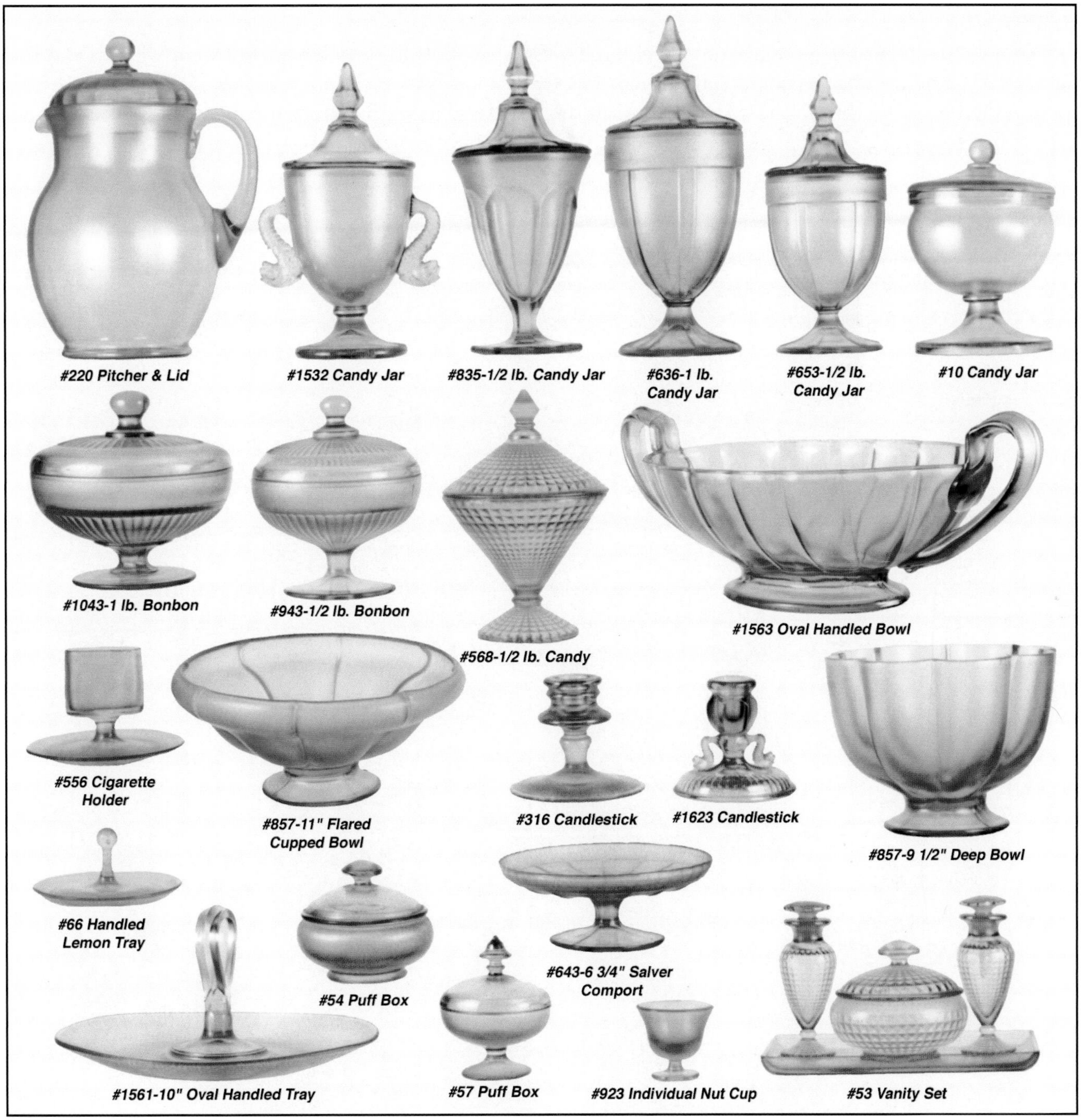

#220 Pitcher & Lid
#1532 Candy Jar
#835-1/2 lb. Candy Jar
#636-1 lb. Candy Jar
#653-1/2 lb. Candy Jar
#10 Candy Jar
#1043-1 lb. Bonbon
#943-1/2 lb. Bonbon
#568-1/2 lb. Candy
#1563 Oval Handled Bowl
#556 Cigarette Holder
#857-11" Flared Cupped Bowl
#316 Candlestick
#1623 Candlestick
#857-9 1/2" Deep Bowl
#66 Handled Lemon Tray
#54 Puff Box
#643-6 3/4" Salver Comport
#1561-10" Oval Handled Tray
#57 Puff Box
#923 Individual Nut Cup
#53 Vanity Set

Item	Value
Vase, #251 – 10" bud	$30.00 – 40.00
Vase, #251 – 12" bud	$40.00 – 45.00
Vase, #562 – 8" fan	$50.00 – 55.00
Vase, #572 – 8" fan	$50.00 – 55.00
Vase, #573 – 8" crimped	$50.00 – 55.00
Vase, #574 – 12" crimped top	$65.00 – 75.00
Vase, #574 – 6" crimped top	$45.00 – 50.00
Vase, #857 – 8" fan	$55.00 – 60.00
Vase, #1502 – 5" fan, Diamond Optic w/dolphins	$100.00 – 110.00
Vase, #1502 – 6" Diamond Optic w/dolphins	$100.00 – 110.00
Vase, #1533 – 5¼" fan w/dolphins	$120.00 – 130.00
Vase, #1533 – 6" fan w/dolphins	$125.00 – 140.00

WISTERIA

Wisteria stretch glass is a deep burgundy colored glass with an iridescent finish. Iridescent wisteria was introduced in 1921, and production continued through 1928.

Note the bath salts jar and the crimped bowl in the picture. These are two of the more unusual stretch glass pieces in this color.

Item	Value	Item	Value
Ashtray Set, #202 – 5-pc.	$170.00 – 190.00	Candy jar, #736, 1 lb.	$75.00 – 95.00
Bonbon, #543 covered	$90.00 – 100.00	Cheese comport/underplate, #316	$50.00 – 55.00
Bonbon, #643 covered	$90.00 – 100.00	Cigarette holder, #556 oval	$150.00 – 175.00
Bonbon, #643 open, cupped	$42.00 – 45.00	Cologne, #55	$165.00 – 185.00
Bowl, #545 – 6½" shallow cupped	$40.00 – 45.00	Cologne, #55½ w/flower finial	$250.00 – 300.00
Bowl, #550 – 7½" cupped	$250.00 – 300.00	Cologne, #56	$140.00 – 160.00
Bowl, #550 – 11" shallow, cupped	$185.00 – 220.00	Comport, #260 – 6" flared	$100.00 – 125.00
Bowl, #575 – 5" cupped lily	$40.00 – 45.00	Comport, #312 – 7" cup, low ftd.	$50.00 – 60.00
Bowl, #601 – 10" shallow cupped	$70.00 – 80.00	Comport, #312 – 8" flared footed	$55.00 – 65.00
Bowl, #604 – 10" cupped	$270.00 – 300.00	Comport, #643 – 6¾" salver	$50.00 – 55.00
Bowl, #604 – 12" flared cupped	$250.00 – 275.00	Comport, #712 – 7" cupped footed	$50.00 – 60.00
Bowl, #604 – 7½" cupped	$55.00 – 65.00	Comport, #737 – 7" flared cupped	$50.00 – 60.00
Bowl, #604 – 9" cupped	$110.00 – 130.00	Compote, Hi-Standard	$300.00 – 325.00
Bowl, #606 – 7½" shallow cupped	$70.00 – 80.00	Jar, #60 bath (smelling) salts	$160.00 – 180.00
Bowl, #607 – 7½" cupped	$70.00 – 80.00	Night set, #401	$120.00 – 135.00
Bowl, #607 – 8" rolled rim	$75.00 – 85.00	Nut cup, #923 individual	$40.00 – 45.00
Bowl, #607 – 9" shallow, cupped	$75.00 – 85.00	Pen holder	$200.00 – 225.00
Bowl, #647 – 11" shallow cupped	$95.00 – 100.00	Pitcher & lid, #220	$350.00 – 400.00
Bowl, #647 – 13" shallow flared	$110.00 – 120.00	Pitcher, #222 iced tea	$300.00 – 350.00
Bowl, #847 – 7" shallow cupped	$55.00 – 60.00	Plate, #103 sherbet	$30.00 – 35.00
Bowl, #848 – 9" shallow cupped	$100.00 – 125.00	Plate, #630 – 8½" salad	$35.00 – 40.00
Bowl, #1522 – 10" double crimped	$110.00 – 120.00	Plate, #680 – 4"	$18.00 – 20.00
Bowl, #1602 – 10¼" crimped		Plate, #681 – 8" salad	$35.00 – 40.00
w/dolphins	$220 .00 – 240.00	Plate, #756 – 6" octagonal	$20.00 – 22.00
Bowl, #1604 – 11" oval ftd.		Plate, #757 – 7¼" octagonal with	
with dolphins	$210.00 – 230.00	Laurel Leaf dec.	$75.00 – 85.00
Bowl, #1608 – 10¼" crimped		Plate, #758 – 8½" octagonal	$45.00 – 55.00
w/dolphins	$200.00 – 220.00	Puff box, #743	$65.00 – 75.00
Candlestick, #232 – 8½"	$100.00 – 125.00	Puff box, #744	$200.00 – 250.00
Candlestick, #315 princess	$50.00 – 55.00	Sherbet, #103	$50.00 – 60.00
Candlestick, #349 – 10"	$90.00 – 100.00	Tray, #317 – 10" handled sandwich	$75.00 – 85.00
Candlestick, #449 – 8½"	$70.00 – 75.00	Tumbler, #222 handled iced tea	$50.00 – 60.00
Candlestick, #549 – 2 – 8½" with		Vanity Set, #55½/744, 3-pc.	$700.00 – 850.00
Persian pearl base	$140.00 – 160.00	Vase, #251 – 10"	$40.00 – 50.00
Candlestick, #649 – 10"	$95.00 – 120.00	Vase, #251 – 12"	$50.00 – 60.00
Candlestick, #749 – 12"	$120.00 –150.00	Vase, #602 – 10" cupped	$75.00 – 85.00
Candlestick, #1623 w/dolphins	$110.00 – 130.00	Vase, #611 – 6½" cupped	$60.00 – 65.00
Candy jar, #8, ½ lb.	$65.00 – 70.00	Vase, #612 – 6½" flared	$60.00 – 65.00
Candy jar, #9, ¾ lb.	$65.00 – 75.00	Vase, #622 – 7½" flared	$60.00 – 70.00
Candy jar, #735, ½ lb.	$65.00 – 70.00	Vase, #736 – 7" fan	$60.00 – 70.00

#612-6 1/2" Flared Vase

#449-8 1/2" Candlestick

#222 Pitcher and Base

#222 Handled Tumbler and #220 Coaster

 # 9, 3/4 lb. Candy

#401 Night Set

#643-6 3/4" Salver Comport

#643-5 1/4" Cupped Comport

#60 Bath Salt Jar

#55 Cologne

9 1/2" Double Crimped Bowl

#848-9"Shallow Cupped Bowl

#556 Cigarette Holder

#315 Candlestick

#604-7 1/2" Cupped Bowl

#757-7 1/4" Salad Plate

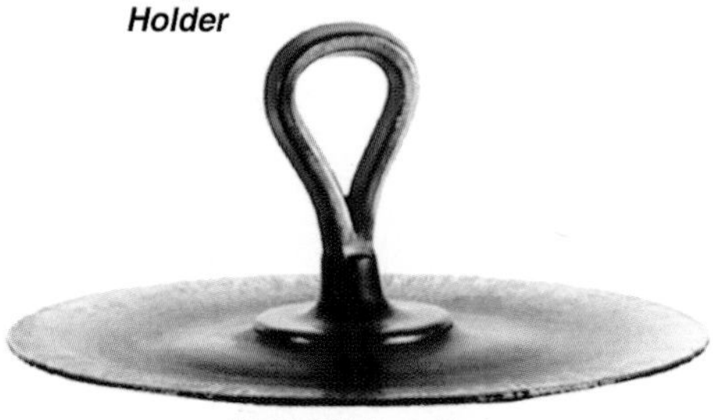

#317-10" Handled Sandwich Tray

#604-12" Flared Cupped Bowl

#647-11" Shallow Cupped Bowl

#923 Individual Nut Cup

STRETCH GLASS SHAPES FROM ORIGINAL CATALOGS

#1620-6" Diamond Optic Basket

#1620-6" Plymouth Basket

#1502 Round Bridge Bon bon

#543 Bon bon

#106 Bon bon

231-10" Shallow Cupped Footed Bowl

#231-8" Deep Cupped Bowl

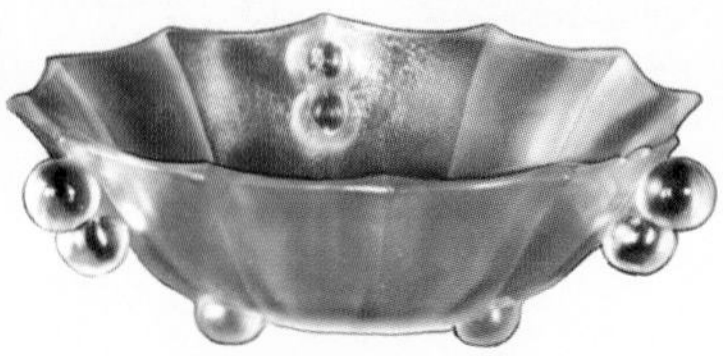
#349-10 1/2" Flared Bowl

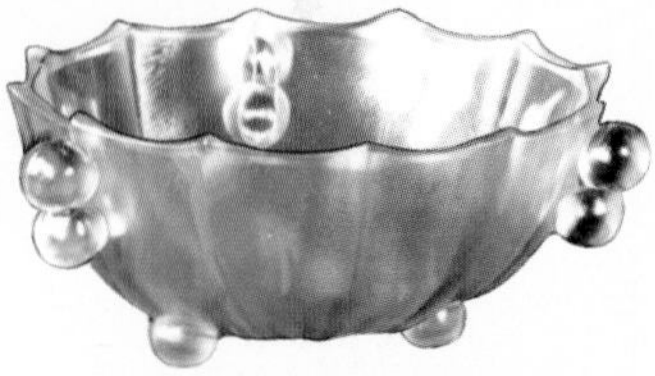
#349-10 1/2" Regular Bowl

#500-12" Flared Footed Bowl

#545-6 1/2" Shallow Cupped Bowl

#550-12" Flared Bowl

#550-11" Shallow Cupped Bowl

#545-5" Cupped Lily

#600-7" Cupped Bowl

#600-10" Rolled Rim Bowl

#600-10" Flared Salad Bowl

#600-8" Shallow Rolled Rim Bowl

#600-8" Deep Cupped Bowl

#601-10" Flared Cupped Bowl

#601-10" Shallow Cupped Bowl

#846-8 3/4" Flared Cupped Bowl

#846-9" Flared Bowl

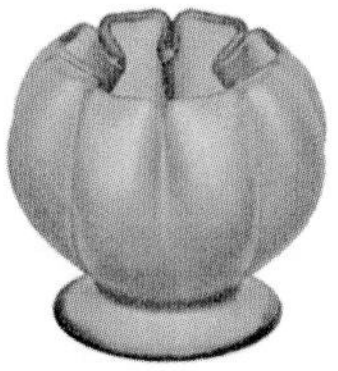
#847 Rose Bowl

#847 -6 1/2" Nut Bowl

#847 -6" Cupped Bowl

#847 -7 1/2" Flared Bowl

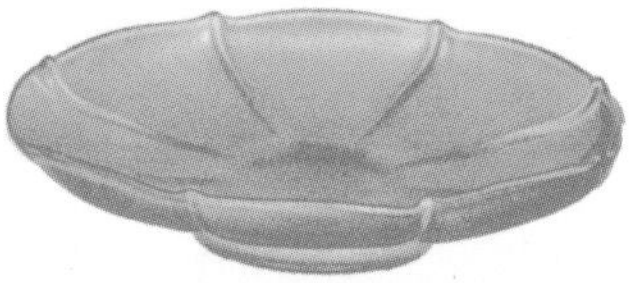
#847 -8" Shallow Cupped Bowl

#857-10" Special Rolled Rim Bowl

#857-10" Rolled Rim Bowl

#917-11" Footed Flared Bowl

#920-9" Cupped Bowl

#920-10" Crimped Orange Bowl

#950-10" Tulip Bowl

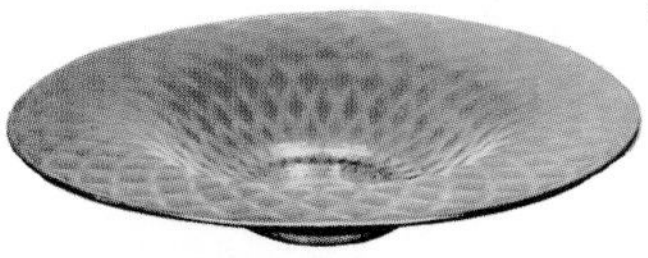
#1502-A-9" Dolphin Flared Bowl

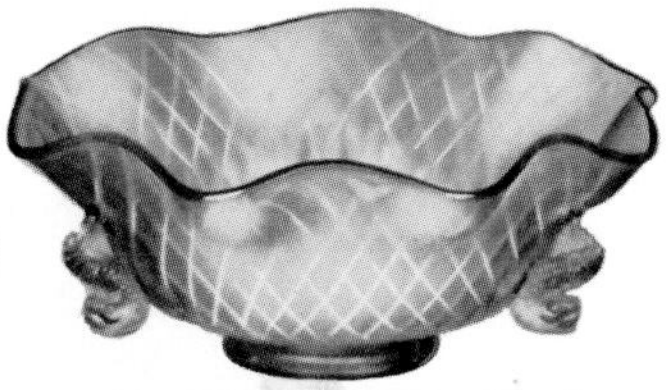
#1502-A-9" Dolphin Crimped Bowl

#1503-A-10" Dolphin Flared Bowl

#1504-A-10" Dolphin Rolled Rim Bowl

#1512-8" Flared Bowl

#1512-8 1/2" Special Rolled Rim Bowl

#1515 Oval Pickle

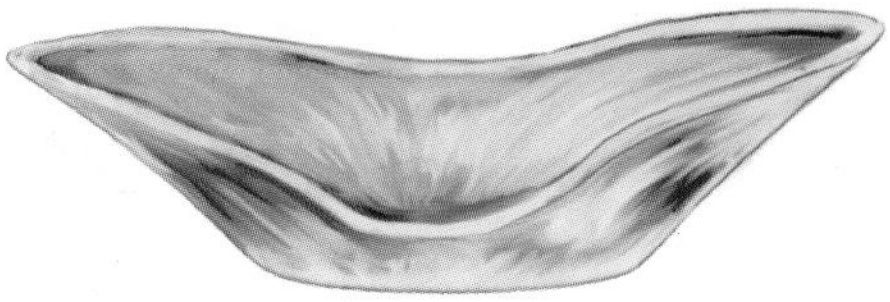
#1562-1-13" Oval Bowl

#1600-10" Dolphin Rolled Rim Bowl

#1608-10 3/4" Dolphin Flared Bowl

#1608-10 1/2" Dolphin Deep Oval Bowl

#601-12" Salver Bowl

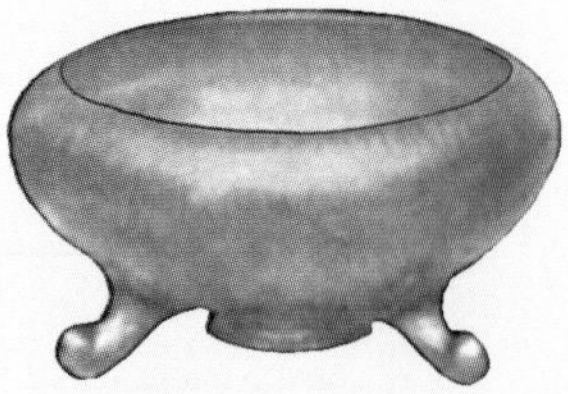
#603-9" Cupped Footed Orange Bowl

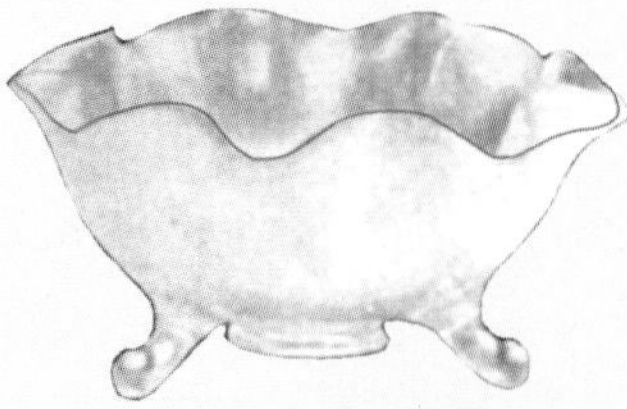
#603-10" Crimped Footed Orange Bowl

#604-14" Shallow Cupped Bowl

#604-10" Deep Cupped Bowl (Aquarium)

#604-15" Optic Rolled Rim Bowl

#604-12" Flared Cupped Bowl

#604-12" Flared Bowl

#606-7 1/2" Shallow Cupped Bowl

#606-6" Cupped Bowl

#607-8" Rolled Rim Bowl

#607-7 1/2" Shallow Cupped Bowl

#607-7 1/2" Cupped Bowl

#608-11" Hat-shaped Bowl

#638-8" Shallow Cupped Bowl

#640-7" Flared Cupped Bowl

#640-7 1/2" Rolled Rim Bowl

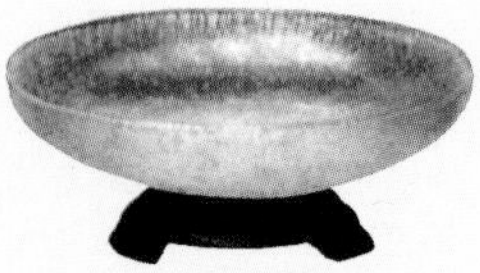
#640-8" Shallow Bowl

#644-7 3/4" Baked Apple

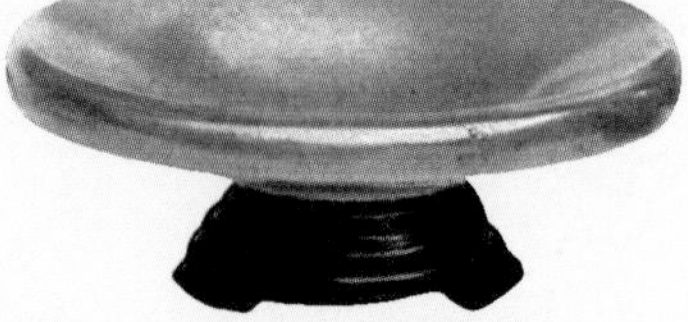
#647-11" Rolled Rim Bowl

#647-10" Deep Rolled Rim Bowl

#647-8 1/2" Deep Cupped Bowl (Aquarium)

#647-13" Shallow Flared Bowl

#647-13" Flared Bowl

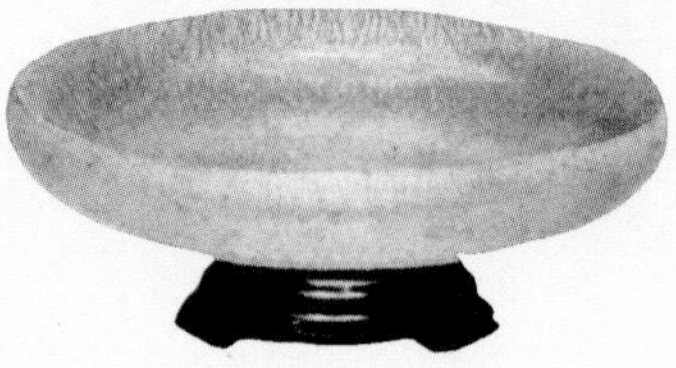
#647-12" Shallow Cupped Bowl

#647-13" Salver Bowl

#1663-10" Square Bowl

#1663-11 1/2" Tulip Console Bowl

#1663-10 1/2" Tulip Console Bowl

#1663-10 1/2" Flared Bowl

#1663-10 1/2" Flared Bowl

#1663-9" Oval Bowl

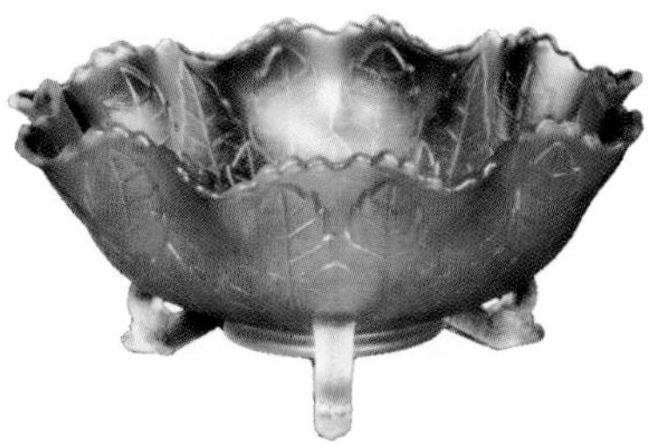
#1790-9" Crimped Bowl

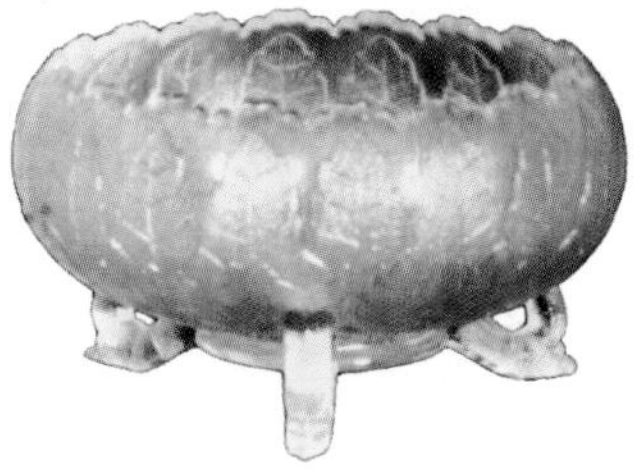
#1790-10" Cupped Bowl

#1790-10" Flared Bowl

#2005-6 1/2" Shallow Cupped Bowl

#2006-7 1/2" Cupped Bowl

#2006-7 1/2" Shallow Cupped Bowl

#2007-9" Shallow Cupped Bowl

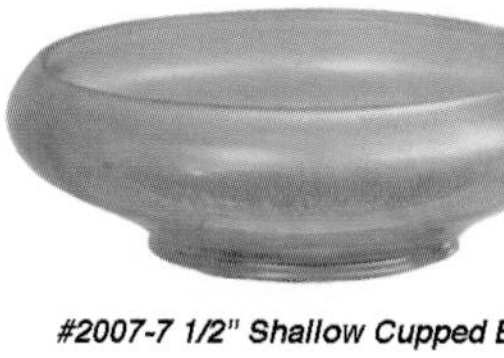
#2007-7 1/2" Shallow Cupped Bowl

#2007-7 1/2" Cupped Bowl

#649-10" Candlestick | #749-12" Candlestick | #349-10" Candlestick | #449-8" Candlestick | #249-6" Candlestick | #950 Candlestick | #314 Candlestick | #315 Candlestick

#500 Cigarette Box | #655 Cigarette Box w/Cutting | #1569 Cigarette Box/Ashtray | #312-8" Flared Comport | #312-7" Cupped Comport

#9-7" Crimped Comport | #9-7 1/2" Oval Comport | #260-7" High Comport | #500 Crimped Comport | #500 Crimped Comport

#574-6" Crimped Comport (Vase) | #643-7" Salver Comport | #712 Footed Comport | #736-6 1/2" Comport | #737-7" Comport

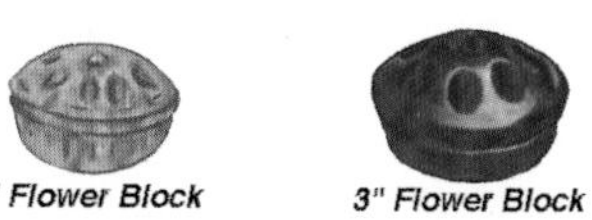

2" Flower Block | 3" Flower Block

#1554 Flower Pot and Base | #893 Ginger Jar | #1616 Icepack | #76 Marmalade | #2005 Mayonnaise | #401 Night Set

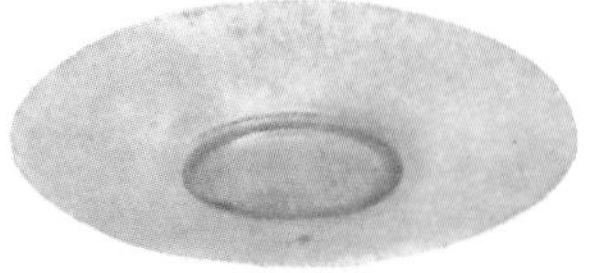

#103-6" Plate

#301-6" Plate

#600-11 1/2" Plate and Base

#630-8 1/2" Plate

#631-9 1/2" Cake Plate

#631-11 1/2" Plate

#681-8" Plate
Decoration No. 2

#681-8" Plate
Decoration No. 3

#682-9" Service Plate
Decoration No. 2

#756-6" Plate

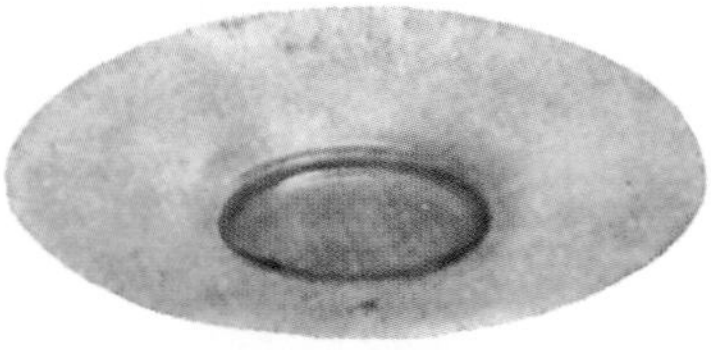

#1005-8" Plate

#1006-8" Plate

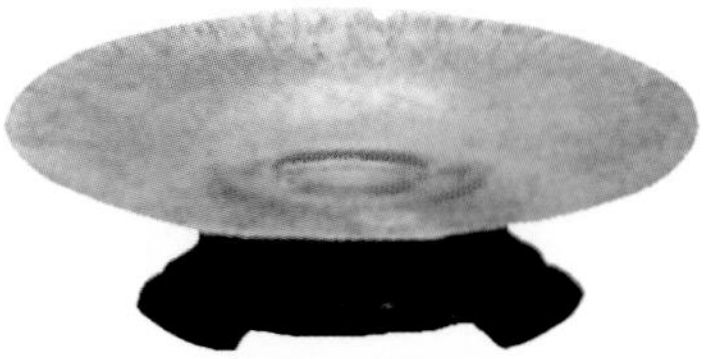

2005-8" Plate

#2007-11" Plate

#1043-7 1/2" Footed Salver

#643-6 1/2" Footed Salver

#99-6 1/2" Bud Vase

#251-10" Bud Vase

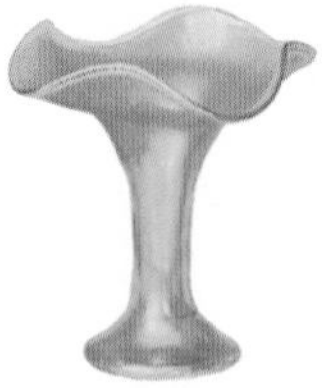
#400-6" Square Vase

#573-8" Flared Vase

#573-8" Crimped Vase

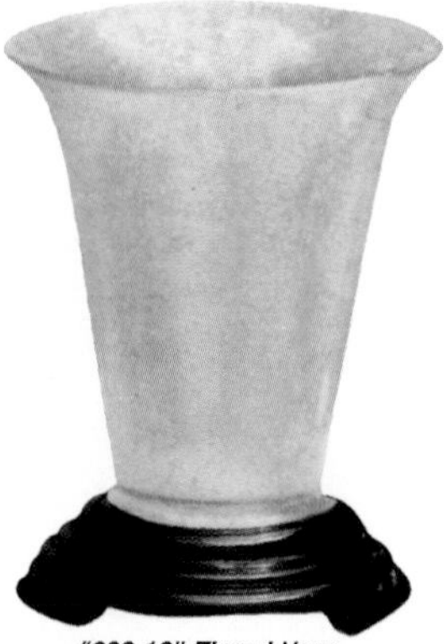
#602-10" Flared Vase

#602-10" 1/2 Cupped Vase

#567-5" Fan Vase

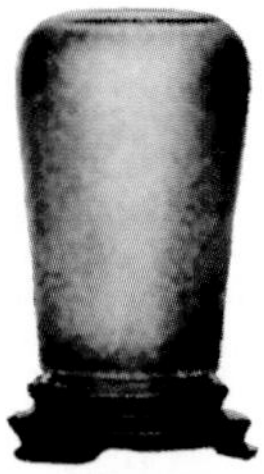
#611-6 1/2" Cupped Vase

#620-10" Flared Vase

#622-7 1/2" Flared Vase

#847-5" Shell-shaped Vase

#847-6" Fan Vase

#857-8" Fan Vase

#885-5" Paste Mold Vase

#886-6" Paste Mold Vase

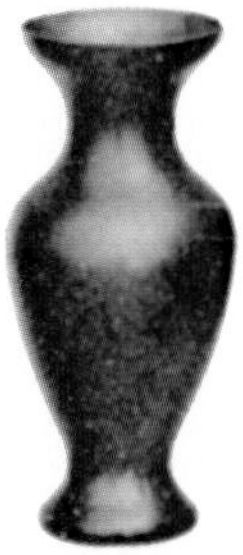
#887-8" Vase

#888-10" Vase

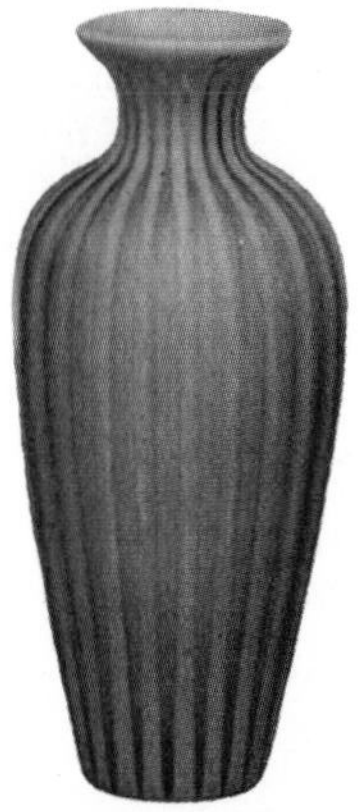
#891-12" Vase

#901-Flared Vase

#901 Square Vase

#1502-8" Flared Vase

#1530-12" Vase

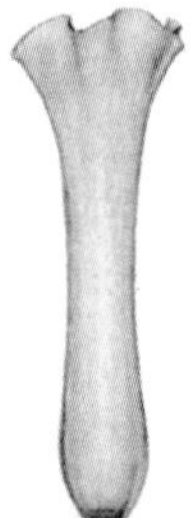
#1535-10" Bud Vase

#1700-8 1/2" Flared Vase

Sets and Combinations

#16-17-54-4 Pc. Bath Room Set

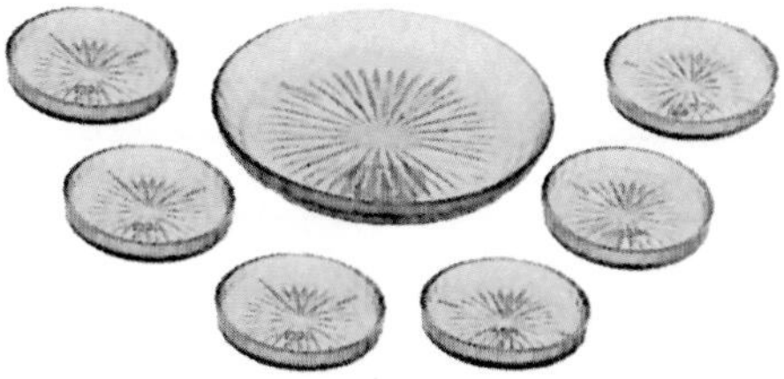

#230-7 Pc. Coaster Set

#103 Sherbet & Plate

#316 Cheese & Cracker Set

#220-15 Pc. Covered Beverage Set

#222-14 Pc. Beverage Set

#2005 Mayonaisse Set

#923-7 Pc. Nut Set

#1647-5 Part Relish/Comport Set

#403-2 Pc. Sherbet & Plate

#55 1/2/744 Vanity Set

#54 Vanity Set

NON-IRIDESCENT COLORS

INTRODUCTION

Colored Fenton pattern glass and colored iridescent glassware are featured earlier in this book. The following pages picture non-iridescent colored glassware produced by Fenton from about 1921 to 1939. Many of the pieces represented are plain — without a pattern. Fenton produced many plain and patterned colored bowls, comports, candies, candlesticks, and vases. Plain colored glassware, items with dolphin handles, and patterns with only a few pieces will be priced in this section. For information and pricing of Fenton's major patterns such as Lincoln Inn, Georgian, or Plymouth see the chapter on Fenton Patterns.

Colors in this section are arranged alphabetically according to Fenton's or researcher's names. Opaque and transparent colors of the same hue are listed on separate pages, but they are alphabetized according to their name in the section. Experimental colors and variations are shown on the last page of this chapter.

Pieces which are known to exist but are not pictured will also be priced. All known variations of each shape are listed. For example, when they are known to exist, bowls will be listed as crimped, flared, flared cupped, cupped, shallow cupped, rolled edge, special roll rim, or rose bowl. Since Fenton is a hand operation, any of these resulting shape variations may be produced from a piece of glassware coming from a single mold. The size differences for pieces with the same number are a result of this hand shaping.

Pricing for most of the shapes of items produced from the same mold will usually be similar. On occasion, special circumstances will result in a particular shape that may be more unusual, and the price for that shape may be substantially different. All pieces, including candlesticks and shakers, are priced individually.

Items in each listing are arranged alphabetically by category, such as bowl, candy, or vase, etc.; each category is arranged in ascending numerical order according to Fenton's line numbers. There are times when Fenton used the same number for more than one item. Therefore, a name or as much of a description as possible has been included in the listings to help eliminate confusion.

To identify pieces which are not pictured, first check the other colors in this section. If the piece is not shown in this section, it may appear in the Stretch Glass section. Pay special attention to the numerous shapes shown in the catalog reprints at the end of Stretch Glass.

The non-iridescent colors listed on the next page were produced at some time during the years 1921 to 1939. The dates which appear are confirmed years of production for a particular color. All pieces found in each color were not necessarily made for the entire time. Dates found after the items in the price listing are the year(s) of production that can be confirmed from catalog, price lists, or inventory records. However, records for this time period are not complete, and this information should only be used as a guide. It is possible that some items were made for a number of years before or after the indicated date.

Color	Years of Production	Comments
Amber	1926 – 1939	is usually a deep brown color with an orange or red cast.
Aquamarine	1927	is a light transparent blue color.
Aqua Opalescent	1927 – 1928	is a light transparent blue glass with milky opal edges.
Azure Blue		is a term for a light blue color that appears in catalogs that Fenton used at times instead of aquamarine.
Black	1911 – 1939	largest production was between 1924 and 1936.
Cameo Opalescent	1926 – 1927	is a transparent beige color with opalescent edges.
Celeste Blue	1921 – 1928	is a transparent sapphire color.
Chinese Yellow	1922 – 1932	is a translucent bright yellow color that was introduced as jade yellow. The name was supposedly changed to Chinese yellow in 1932, but inventory records refer to Chinese yellow as early as 1924.
Flame	1924 – 1926	is a bright red-orange opaque color that is more orange than Venetian red.
Green Transparent	1921 – 1939	is a clear color which consists of at least four shade variations — light green, medium green, dark green (emerald), and a light blue green.
Jade Green	1921 – 1939	is a translucent green color.
Jade Yellow	1921 – 1924	is an early 1920s name for Chinese yellow.
Lilac	1932 – 1933	is a translucent lavender color that was used in limited production.
Mandarin Red	1932 – 1935	used the same formula as Venetian red. Marbled color differences were a result of the gathering process during pressing.
Mermaid Blue	1934	is a very light steel-blue color that was made for a very short time.
Milk Glass	1924 & 1933 – 1939	is opaque white glass.
Mongolian Green	1934 – 1935	is an opaque blue-green color with a marbled appearance.
Moonstone	1932 – 1934	is a translucent opaline color used frequently in toiletry items.
Orchid	1927 – 1928	is a transparent lavender color used mainly with Diamond Optic and dolphin related pieces that were made for only a few years.
Pekin Blue	1932 – 1933	is a translucent light blue color that is probably the same as or very similar to a color Fenton called turquoise in the 1920s.
Periwinkle Blue	1943 – 1934	is an opaque dark cobalt blue color with a marbled appearance.
Rose	1927 – 1939	is Fenton's name for transparent pink.
Royal Blue	1907 – 1939	is a transparent cobalt color.
Ruby	1907 – 1939	is a transparent deep red color.
Tangerine		is a transparent orange color.
Venetian Red	1922 – 1926	is an opaque dark red color made with the same formula as Mandarin red.
Wisteria	1933 – 1939	was called amethyst in pattern glass and violet in the carnival glass era.
Wisteria Opalescent	1933 – 1935	is often called amethyst opalescent.

AMBER

Fenton's production of amber glassware began in the mid 1920s and continued through much of the 1930s in a limited capacity. This color must not have been a favorite at Fenton since only a few different items were produced. Production of the number of amber items increased during the mid 1930s when the color was introduced into the pattern lines such as Georgian, Lincoln Inn, Plymouth, and Sheffield. For a listing of pieces in these patterns and the Swan novelty bonbons, see the appropriate pattern listing later in this book.

Two of the more unusual items found in amber include the Big Cookies basket and macaroon jar. The decanter sets which were produced after the demise of Prohibition are a nice addition to a collection. The mixing bowls were only produced for a short time and are elusive.

Amber	Value	Date
Ashtray, U. S.	$11.00 – 13.00	1933
Basket, #1681 – 10½" Big Cookies	$90.00 – 110.00	1933
Bonbon, #1621 – 6½" sq. or crimped	$18.00 – 22.00	1936
Bowl, #6 – 11½" Swan	$75.00 – 85.00	
Bowl, #456 – 1 mixing	$18.00 – 22.00	1933
Bowl, #456 – 2 mixing	$25.00 – 30.00	1933
Bowl, #456 – 3 mixing	$30.00 – 35.00	1933
Bowl, #950 – 11" oval	$35.00 – 40.00	1935 – 1936
Bowl, #950 – 11" tulip	$40.00 – 50.00	1935 – 1937
Bowl, #1933 – 5" cupped	$8.00 – 10.00	
Bowl, #1933 – 7" flared	$12.00 – 15.00	
Candlestick, #950 cornucopia	$10.00 – 15.00	1935
Coaster, #1590 – 4"	$4.00 – 6.00	1933
Cologne, #54	$40.00 – 45.00	1926
Decanter, #1934 w/flower stopper	$85.00 – 100.00	1935
Decanter, #1935 Franklin	$60.00 – 70.00	1935
Flower Block, #4	$6.00 – 8.00	1927
Ivy ball, #706	$25.00 – 30.00	1933
Macaroon jar, #1681 – 7" Big Cookies	$200.00 – 225.00	1933 – 1934
Mug, #2010 – 10 oz.	$10.00 – 15.00	1933
Mug, #4009	$10.00 – 15.00	1933
Nappy, 5" "Sailboats"	$30.00 – 35.00	
Plate, #758 – 8½" octagonal	$7.00 – 8.00	1927
Puff box, #54	$20.00 – 25.00	1926
Shell, 3½" or 4½"	$6.00 – 8.00	1936
Tumbler, #1933	$7.00 – 9.00	1932
Tumbler, #1934 whiskey (goblet)	$8.00 – 10.00	1935 – 1936
Tumbler, #1935 1 oz. whiskey Franklin	$7.00 – 9.00	1935
Vanity set, #54	$100.00 – 125.00	1926
Vase, #180 Hyacinth	$30.00 – 35.00	1935
Vase, #184 – 10"	$25.00 – 30.00	1935 – 1936
Vase, #184 – 12"	$30.00 – 35.00	1933 – 1935
Vase, #1668 – 8" flip	$40.00 – 50.00	1933

#950 Console Set with #950-11" Oval Bowl and #950-5 1/2" Cornucopia Candlesticks

#6-11 1/2" Oval Swan Bowl

#1933-7" Flared Bowl

#1681-7" Macaroon Jar
"Big Cookies"

#1934 Liquor Set

AQUAMARINE

Aquamarine is one term that is frequently used to describe Fenton's light blue transparent color. On occasion, catalogs also refer to this color as azure blue. As far as anyone can determine, both these names are describing the same color. This color was introduced about 1927, and was used heavily, especially in the Diamond Optic line, through the mid 1930s. Many aquamarine Diamond Optic items were also decorated with cuttings. Dolphin handles were also popular decorative additions.

Another light blue color — mermaid blue — which is more of a steel gray, was produced for a very short period in about 1933. An example of an item in this color is the elephant bottle pictured on page 236.

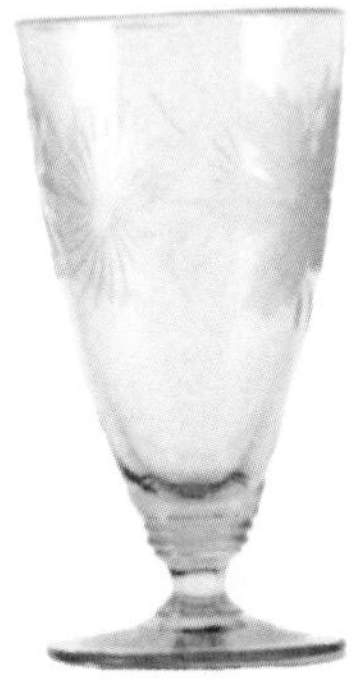

#1641 11 oz. Tumbler w/#1702 Cutting

#1634 Jug

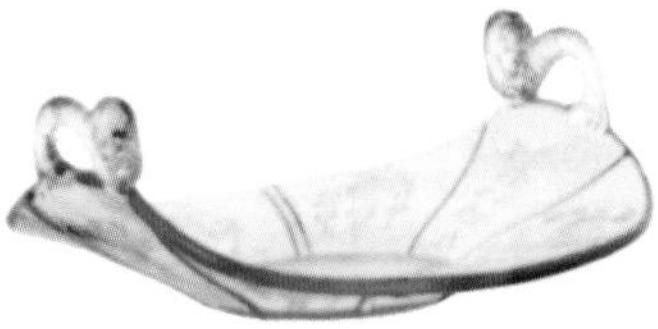

1621 Square Bonbon w/#1703 Cutting

#1502 Flared Basket w/#1702 Cutting

#1600-10 1/2" Rolled Edge Bowl

#1530-12" Vase

#1616 Ice Pack w/#1702 Cutting

#1621-10" Deep Oval Bowl w/#1703 Cutting

#1533-A Fan Vase w/#1702 Cutting

Item	*Value	Date
Basket, #1502 Diamond Optic	$28.00 – 37.00	1927
Basket, #1615 – 5" w/metal handle	$43.00 – 47.00	1928
Basket, #1615 – 6" w/metal handle	$60.00 – 65.00	1928
Basket, #1616 – 8" Diamond Optic	$60.00 – 65.00	1928
Basket, #1616 – 1702 cut Diamond Optic	$85.00 – 95.00	1928
Basket, #1616 – 1709 cut Diamond Optic	$95.00 – 115.00	1928
Bonbon, #1621/1702 cut-6½" crimped; flared; square	$22.00 – 27.00	1928
Bowl, #349 – 10" club, flared, or reg.	$35.00 – 40.00	1932
Bowl, #1502 – A-9" crimped w/dolphins Diamond Optic	$40.00 – 50.00	1927
Bowl, #1504 – A-9½" flared cupped w/#1702 cut w/dolp.	$50.00 – 55.00	1928
Bowl, #1504 – A-9" flared w/#1702 cut w/dolphins	$50.00 – 55.00	1928
Bowl, #1562 – 1 – 13½" oval	$75.00 – 85.00	1932
Bowl, #1562 – 2 – 13" oval	$75.00 – 85.00	1932
Bowl, #1600 – 10" rolled rim ft., w/dolphins	$100.00 – 140.00	1929
Bowl, #1608 – 10½" deep oval ft. w/dolphins	$120.00 – 150.00	1927
Bowl, #1621 – 10" deep oval w/dolphins	$45.00 – 55.00	1928
Bowl, #1621 – 10" deep oval w/dolphins, cut	$55.00 – 65.00	1928
Bowl, #1621 – 9" shallow oval w/dolphin handle	$40.00 – 50.00	1928
Bowl, #1663 – 12" flared; tulip	$90.00 – 110.00	1932
Candlestick, #318 – 1702 cut	$22.00 – 24.00	1928
Candlestick, #950 cornucopia	$20.00 – 22.00	1932
Candy, #1533 – A w/dolphins	$110.00 – 130.00	1928
Cologne, #1502 Diamond Optic	$100.00 – 125.00	1927
Creamer, #1502 Diamond Optic	$30.00 – 35.00	1927
Cup, #1502 Diamond Optic	$10.00 – 12.00	1927
Flower block, #2	$18.00 – 20.00	1933
Flower block, #3 – 3"	$10.00 – 12.00	1933
Goblet, #1502 11 oz. bridge Diamond Optic	$20.00 – 22.00	1930
Goblet, #1502 Hi ft. Diamond Optic	$22.00 – 25.00	1933
Goblet, #1640 – 1702 cut 9 oz. Bridge	$15.00 – 18.00	1928
Goblet, #1642 – 1702 cut	$20.00 – 25.00	1928
Ice pack, #1614 Diamond Optic	$65.00 – 70.00	1928
Ice pail, #1616 – 6½" Diamond Optic	$65.00 – 70.00	1927
Ice tub, #1502 – 4" Diamond Optic	$25.00 – 35.00	1928
Ice tub, #1616 – 1702 cut Diamond Optic	$65.00 – 75.00	1928
Ice tub, #1616 – 1709 cut Diamond Optic	$65.00 – 75.00	1928
Night set, #1502– 2-pc. Diamond Optic	$125.00 – 145.00	1928
Nymph, #1645 Sept. Morn.	$250.00 – 300.00	
Pitcher, #1634 – 1702 cut Diamond Optic	$65.00 – 75.00	1928
Pitcher, #1635 – 1702 cut Diamond Optic	$75.00 – 95.00	1928
Pitcher, #1636 – 1702 cut Diamond Optic	$100.00 – 120.00	1928
Puff box, #1502 Diamond Optic	$50.00 – 60.00	1927
Sherbet, #1502 Diamond Optic	$12.00 – 14.00	1927
Sugar, #1502 Diamond Optic	$30.00 – 35.00	1927
Tray, #1502 dresser Diamond Optic	$35.00 – 40.00	1927
Tray, #1502 – 10" handled sandwich Diamond Optic	$58.00 – 62.00	1927
Tray, #1562 – 3	$55.00 – 60.00	1932
Tumbler, #1502 – 5 oz. orange juice Diamond Optic	$12.00 – 14.00	1928
Tumbler, #1502 – 9 oz. ft. Diamond Optic	$15.00 – 17.00	1928
Tumbler, #1634 w/#1702 cut Diamond Optic	$11.00 – 15.00	1928
Tumbler, #1635 – 1702 cut 10 oz. Diamond Optic	$18.00 – 20.00	1928
Tumbler, #1636 – 1702 cut 12 oz. Diamond Optic	$22.00 – 25.00	1928
Tumbler, #1641 – 11 oz.	$14.00 – 16.00	1928
Tumbler, #1641 – 1702 cut 11 oz. ice tea	$15.00 – 18.00	1928
Vase, #857 – 8" fan	$35.00 – 40.00	1927
Vase, #1502 – 8½" flared Diamond Optic	$40.00 – 45.00	1927
Vase, #1502 – 8" flip w/#1702 cut Diamond Optic	$50.00 – 60.00	1928
Vase, #1530 – 12"	$65.00 – 75.00	
Vase, #1532 – A-5½" w-dolphins	$47.00 – 58.00	1928
Vase, #1533 – A-6" fan w/dolphins	$52.00 – 58.00	1928

**Add 20% to regular value for all cut items not included in value guide.*

BLACK

The first notation of black glassware in Fenton's inventory records shows up in 1911. Although production of pieces in black increased during the early 1920s, it appears as if most items, except bases for bowls and vases, were produced sparingly in this color until about 1928. Production in the color continued to increase until it peaked about 1933. Some pieces have lids or stoppers that were accented with a color such as jade green, lilac, or moonstone. Look for this mixing of colors in the cologne sets and in the #1639 line.

Numerous sizes of bases for bowls and vases were produced in black. It was common during this era for Fenton to sell bowls and vases with an accompanying base. Bowls and vases in black were commonly sold with a moonstone color base. Notice from the listing the multitude of bowls and vases that were produced. The #184 vase may sometimes be found with a cut decoration. The candy jar and some of the bowls and vases were produced with dolphin handles. Molds from the popular Basket Weave w/Open Edge pattern of the carnival and stretch glass eras were also used to produce bowls in black.

Unusual items found in black include the Rose Spray mug and the Butterfly and Berry vase which were made from carnival glass molds about 1916. Other items that are elusive are the elephant flower bowl, both reamers with jugs, the 4-piece bathroom set, and the Mikado pieces.

The same number for the two #1608 bowls in the listing is somewhat confusing. The number is a shape designation used for the deep oval bowl with dolphins and is a pattern number for the early pattern glass pattern Stag & Holly.

For additional pieces in black, check the listing in the Patterns section under Georgian and Lincoln Inn.

Item	Value	Date
Ashtray, #848 – 3 ft.	$16.00 – 19.00	1933 – 1936
Ashtray Set, #202, 5-pc.-#1,2,3,4,	$53.00 – 58.00	
Base, ft. notched	$32.00 – 37.00	
Base, 5-legged	$74.00 – 83.00	
Base, #539 – 10" rnd.	$25.00 – 30.00	1933
Base, #542 – 10" oval	$25.00 – 30.00	1933
Base, #544 – 5½" rnd.	$22.00 – 27.00	1933
Base, #706 diamond-shaped	$48.00 – 58.00	1933
Basket, #1502	$30.00 – 35.00	1928
Basket, #1615 – 6½"	$70.00 – 80.00	1930
Basket, #1681 – 10½" Big Cookies	$115.00 – 130.00	1933
Basket, #1684 w/wicker handle	$80.00 – 95.00	1933 – 1934
*Bathroom Set, #16 – 17 – 54, 4-pc.	$250.00 – 275.00	1929
Batter set, #1639 Batter Jug/Syrup/Tray Elizabeth	$345.00 – 405.00	1930
Bonbon, #1565 Turtle, covered	$240.00 – 260.00	
Bonbon, #1565 Turtle, open	$158.00 – 210.00	
Bonbon, #1621 – 6½" sq. or crimped	$22.00 – 27.00	1928
Bookend, #711 Peacock ea.	$180.00 – 205.00	1935
Bowl, #100 – 5" 3-toed Wide Rib	$13.00 – 15.00	1930
Bowl, #100 – 7½" 3-footed round Wide Rib	$19.00 – 25.00	1930
Bowl, #100 – 8" octagonal 3-footed Wide Rib	$25.00 – 30.00	1930
Bowl, #456 – 1 mixing	$29.00 – 37.00	1933
Bowl, #456 – 2 mixing	$37.00 – 42.00	1933
Bowl, #456 – 3 mixing	$42.00 – 53.00	1933
Bowl, #543 lily	$26.00 – 32.00	1924
Bowl, #601 – 10" shallow cupped	$37.00 – 42.00	1933
Bowl, #606 – 8" rolled rim	$22.00 – 27.00	1924
Bowl, #607 – 8" cupped	$22.00 – 27.00	1924

**with flower stopper, $250.00 – 300.00*

#9. 3/4lb. Candy

#1600-10" Dolphin Rolled Rim Bowl

#60 Lamp Base

#1532 Candy Jar

#844-1lb. Candy Jar

#1639 Batter Set

Roll Edge Vase "Butterfly & Berry"

#1673-8" Candle Vase

#1561-10" Vase "Apple Tree"

#848 Cupped Bowl & #1645 Nymph Figure

#1681-7" Macaroon Jar "Big Cookies"

#1618 Elephant Flower Bowl

#2318 Candelabra

#57 Puff Box

"Rose Spray" Mug

Item	Value	Date
Bowl, #607 – 8" rolled rim	$22.00 – 27.00	1924
Bowl, #607 – 9" shallow, cupped	$22.00 – 27.00	1924
Bowl, #647 – 11½" shallow cupped	$45.00 – 50.00	1921
Bowl, #647 – 10¾" flared cupped	$45.00 – 50.00	1921
Bowl, #647 – 10" flared	$45.00 – 50.00	1921
Bowl, #647 – 11" rolled rim	$45.00 – 55.00	1924
Bowl, #647 – 13" flared	$45.00 – 55.00	1924
Bowl, #848 – 6" cupped	$22.00 – 27.00	1933
Bowl, #848 – 8½" flared	$22.00 – 27.00	1933 – 1936
Bowl, #857 – 11" flared or flared cupped	$45.00 – 50.00	1931
Bowl, #857 – 7" cupped footed	$22.00 – 27.00	1932
Bowl, #919 – 7" rnd. Mikado orange bowl (comport)	$180.00 – 200.00	1916
Bowl, #1039 – 6" deep crimp	$25.00 – 30.00	1935
Bowl, #1092 – 5½" Basket Weave w/Open Edge	$27.00 – 32.00	1935 – 1936
Bowl, #1093 – 8" shallow Basket Weave w/Open Edge	$37.00 – 42.00	1935
Bowl, #1093 – 9" shallow crimped Basket Weave	$42.00 – 45.00	1935
Bowl, #1504 – A-9" cupped w/dolphins	$60.00 – 70.00	1928
Bowl, #1504 – A-9" shallow cupped w/dolphins	$70.00 – 75.00	1928
Bowl, #1504 – A-10" rolled rim or flared w/dolphins	$70.00 – 80.00	1928
Bowl, #1504 – A-6" cupped w/dolphins	$35.00 – 40.00	1928
Bowl, #1562 – 13" oval	$50.00 – 60.00	1933
Bowl, #1563 – 14" sq.	$70.00 – 80.00	1933
Bowl, #1563 – 17" oval handled	$70.00 – 80.00	1933
Bowl, #1600 – 10" rolled rim ft., w/dolphins	$70.00 – 80.00	1929
Bowl, #1601 – 11" flared ft. w/dolphins	$70.00 – 80.00	1929
Bowl, #1608 – 10½" deep oval ft. w/dolphins	$130.00 – 150.00	1934
Bowl, #1608 – 10" rolled rim Stag & Holly	$130.00 – 155.00	1916
Bowl, #1663 – 12" flared	$55.00 – 65.00	1933
Bowl, #1663 – 9" oval	$35.00 – 40.00	1933
Bowl, #1790 – 10" flared Leaf Tiers	$145.00 – 155.00	
Bowl, 10½" rolled rim Chrysanthemum	$125.00 – 170.00	
Candelabra, #2318 – 6"	$35.00 – 45.00	1927
Candle vase, #1673 – 8"	$50.00 – 60.00	1933
Candleholder, #848/1234 – 3 ft.	$12.00 – 15.00	1933
Candlestick, #1091 Basket Weave w/Open Edge	$47.00 – 55.00	1936
Candlestick, #316	$15.00 – 18.00	
Candlestick, #318	$13.00 – 15.00	1933
Candlestick, #349 – 10"	$115.00 – 125.00	1921
Candlestick, #349 – 10" w/cutting	$135.00 – 145.00	1921
Candlestick, #449 – 8½"	$95.00 – 100.00	1925
Candlestick, #649 – 10"	$110.00 – 120.00	1925
Candlestick, #749 – 12"	$150.00 – 175.00	
Candlestick, #1672 flared or rolled edge	$19.00 – 22.00	1933
Candy Jar, #636, 1 lb.	$58.00 – 63.00	
Candy jar, #835, ½ lb.	$39.00 – 43.00	
Candy jar, #844, 1 lb. w/flower finial	$250.00 – 300.00	1931
Candy jar, #9, ¾ lb.	$35.00 – 40.00	1925
Candy jar, #1532, ½ lb. w/dolphins	$60.00 – 65.00	1928
Cigarette holder, #556	$48.00 – 52.00	
Coaster, #1590 – 4"	$19.00 – 22.00	1932 – 1933
Cologne, #53	$110.00 – 150.00	1927
Comport, #260 – 7" tall footed	$35.00 – 40.00	1924

#184-10" Vase with Cutting

#919-7" Mikado Comport

#349-10" Candlestick

#349-10" Candlestick

#649-10" Candlestick

#607-8" Cupped Bowl

#649-10" Candlestick

Peacock Tail Footed Comport

#848 Candlestick

#1608-10" Rolled Rim Stag & Holly Bowl

#1619 Reamer & Handled Jug

#1504-A-9" Cupped Bowl and Base

#1684 Basket

#1615-6" Basket

Item	Value	Date
Comport, #712 – 7" cupped footed	$32.00 – 35.00	
Comport, #737 flared cupped	$32.00 – 35.00	
Comport, #1536	$75.00 – 95.00	1934
Comport, Peacock Tail ft.	$48.00 – 53.00	1916
Creamer, #100 Wide Rib	$20.00 – 28.00	1930
Creamer, #1502 Diamond Optic	$25.00 – 30.00	1928
Cup, #1502 Diamond Optic	$10.00 – 12.00	1927
Flower block, #1234 for nymph figure	$20.00 – 23.00	1933
Flower bowl, #1618 elephant	$420.00 – 460.00	1928
Flower pot, #1554 w/underplate	$53.00 – 58.00	1932
Flower Pot, #1555 w/underplate	$69.00 – 78.00	1932
Goblet, #1502 11 oz. bridge Diamond Optic	$22.00 – 25.00	1930
Goblet, #1502 9 oz. bridge Diamond Optic	$22.00 – 25.00	1928
Goblet, #1502 Hi ft. Diamond Optic	$27.00 – 32.00	1928
Hat, #1921 – 10"	$145.00 – 155.00	
Ice jar, #1615 (flower pot w/handles) Diamond Optic	N.D.	
Ice pack, #1616 – 6½" Diamond Optic	$53.00 – 60.00	1928
Ice tub, #1502 – 4" Diamond Optic	$27.00 – 32.00	1928
Ivy Ball, #706	$27.00 – 32.00	1933
Jug, #100 Wide Rib	$105.00 – 130.00	1930
Jug #1639 Batter w/lid Elizabeth	$190.00 – 225.00	1930
Jug, #1639 Syrup w/lid Elizabeth	$90.00 – 125.00	1930
Jug, #1639 – 3 pint Elizabeth	$90.00 – 110.00	1930
Lamp Base, #60	$95.00 – 130.00	
Macaroon Jar, #1681 – 7" Big Cookies	$130.00 – 150.00	1933
Macaroon jar, #1684 – 6½"	$80.00 – 90.00	1933
Mayonnaise, #2005	$52.00 – 65.00	1924
Mayonnaise & ladle, #923	$42.00 – 47.00	
Mug, Rose Spray	$63.00 – 66.00	1916
Nymph, #1645 September Morn	$220.00 – 245.00	1933
Plate, #301 – 6"	$4.00 – 5.00	1924
Plate, #543	$10.00 – 12.00	1924
Plate, #607	$7.00 – 9.00	1924
Plate, #630 – 8½" salad	$9.00 – 10.00	1924
Plate, #631 – 11½" sandwich	$21.00 – 23.00	1924
Plate, #1502 – 6" octagonal Diamond Optic	$6.00 – 7.00	1928
Plate, #1502 – 8" octagonal Diamond Optic	$8.00 – 10.00	1928
Plate, #1639 – 6" Elizabeth	$7.00 – 8.00	1933
Plate, #1639 – 8" Elizabeth	$12.00 – 14.00	1933
Puff box, #53	$30.00 – 35.00	
Puff box, #57	$50.00 – 55.00	
Puff box, #743 covered	$58.00 – 62.00	
Puff box, #1229	$34.00 – 40.00	1933
Razor sharpener	$20.00 – 25.00	1933
Reamer, #1619 w/handled jug	$1150.00 – 1300.00	1933
Refrigerator dish, #457 rectangular	$25.00 – 30.00	1933
Salver, #606	$15.00 – 20.00	1924
Salver, #647 – 13" ftd.	$48.00 – 53.00	1921
Salver, #2005	$14.00 – 16.00	1925
Shaving mug, W-111, 112, 113	$50.00 – 55.00	1933
Shell, 3½" – 4½"	$10.00 – 12.00	1936

Item	Value	Date
Sugar, #1502 Diamond Optic	$25.00 – 30.00	1927
Sugar & lid, #100 Wide Rib	$30.00 – 35.00	1930
Tumbler, #19 – 10 oz.	$10.00 – 12.00	1930
Tray, #23	$45.00 – 55.00	1933
Tray, #53 vanity	$45.00 – 50.00	1927
Tumbler, #100 Wide Rib	$20.00 – 22.00	1930
Tumbler, #1502 – 5 oz. orange juice Diamond Optic	$12.00 – 14.00	1930
Tumbler, #1502 – 9 oz. ftd. Diamond Optic	$15.00 – 17.00	1928
Tumbler, #1639 ft. Elizabeth	$65.00 – 75.00	1931
Vase, #107 tulip–6½"	$22.00 – 25.00	1932
Vase, #183	$25.00 – 30.00	1931
Vase, #184 – 10"	$48.00 – 57.00	1933 – 1936
Vase, #184 – 10" w/cutting	$100.00 – 115.00	1933
Vase, #184 – 12"	$58.00 – 62.00	1933
Vase, #184 – 12" w/cutting	$115.00 – 145.00	1933
Vase, #184 – 8"	$42.00 – 47.00	1936
Vase, #184 – 8" w/cutting	$75.00 – 90.00	1933
Vase, #349 oval	$32.00 – 37.00	
Vase, #354 – 8" bud	$19.00 – 23.00	1932 – 1939
Vase, #354 – 9" bud	$19.00 – 23.00	1932 – 1939
Vase, #519 – 20"	$65.00 – 75.00	1933
Vase, #562 – 8" fan	$21.00 – 25.00	1926
Vase, #602 – 10" cupped	$69.00 – 75.00	1921
Vase, #602 – 10" flared	$69.00 – 75.00	1921
Vase, #612 – 6½" flared	$37.00 – 42.00	
Vase, #621 – 6"	$27.00 – 30.00	
Vase, #621 – 8" flared, cupped or square top	$32.00 – 37.00	
Vase, #857 flared	$37.00 – 45.00	1934
Vase, #857 – 8" fan	$37.00 – 42.00	
Vase, #897 – 8"	$37.00 – 45.00	1933
Vase, #898 – 11½"	$79.00 – 85.00	1933 – 1934
Vase, #992	$42.00 – 46.00	1935 – 1936
Vase, #1124 – 5" Butterfly & Berry	$130.00 – 150.00	1916
Vase, #1502 – 8½" flared Diamond Optic	$45.00 – 50.00	
Vase, #1531 – 16"	$55.00 – 65.00	1933
Vase, #1532 – A-5¼" fan w/dolphins	$45.00 – 50.00	
Vase, #1533 – A–6" fan w/dolphins	$47.00 – 52.00	
Vase, #1561 – 10" reg., crimped or flared Apple Tree	$175.00 – 200.00	

Chrysanthemum 10 1/2" Rolled Rim Bowl

#857-8" Fan Vase

#1790-12" Flared Leaf Tiers Bowl

CAMEO OPALESCENT

Cameo opalescent is a beige opalescent color that Fenton produced from 1926 to 1927. The darker hexagonal sugar and creamer shown in the bottom left of the photo are examples of an early trial of this color called amber opalescent. These were made in about 1916. In addition to the pieces produced with the normal opalescent effect toward the edge, the #2 sugar and creamer, and the "twin rib" and #200 guest sets were produced in the Rib Optic pattern. This pattern has vertical stripes that alternate between the cameo color and opalescence.

Fenton re-introduced cameo opalescent in January, 1979, and production of the color continued until 1982. Items were made in Hobnail, Spiral Optic, and pattern glass shapes. The list of newer pieces includes:

Hobnail Pattern
Basket, #3837 – 7"
Bell, #3667
Candy box, #3802
Comport, #3628
Fairy light, #3608
Lamp w/globe shade, #3907 – 26"
Vase, #3950 – 10" bud
Vase, #3854 – 4½"

Spiral Optic Pattern
Basket, #3137
Candy box, #3180
Fairy light, #3100
Pitcher, 10 oz. #3166
Pitcher, 44 oz. #3164
Vase, #3157 – 6½"

Pattern Glass Item	Pattern Glass Design
Basket, #8437	Lily-of-the-Valley
Bell, #8263	Lily-of-the-Valley
Bowl, ftd. #8451	Lily-of-the-Valley
Bowl, #8454	Curtain
Cake plate, #8411 – 12½"	Lily-of-the-Valley
Candy box, #8439	Lily-of-the-Valley
Candy box, ftd., #8434	Lily-of-the-Valley
Comport, #8431	Water Lily
Fairy light, #8404	Lily-of-the-Valley
Nappy, #8225	Grape
Nut dish (comport), #8248	Scroll and Eye
Rose bowl, #8453	Lily-of-the-Valley
Toothpick, #8294	Paneled Daisy
Vase, #8458 bud	Lily-of-the-Valley

Item	Value	Date
Bonbon, #643 – 5" covered	$60.00 – 80.00	
Bonbon, #1043 covered, ftd.	$75.00 – 95.00	
Bowl, #847 – 6½" nut	$15.00 – 22.00	1926
Bowl, #847 – 6" cupped	$15.00 – 22.00	1926
Bowl, #847 – 7½" flared	$30.00 – 35.00	1929
Bowl, #848 – 8½" flared	$75.00 – 95.00	
Bowl, #857 – 10" crimped, ft.	$65.00 – 75.00	
Bowl, #857 – 11" flared or flared cupped	$65.00 – 70.00	1929
Bowl, #857 – 8" cupped footed	$40.00 – 45.00	
Bowl, #1512 – 9" flared	$40.00 – 45.00	1926
Candlestick, #314	$15.00 – 18.00	1926
Candlestick, #316	$15.00 – 18.00	1926
Candlestick, #318	$20.00 – 25.00	1926
Candy jar, #735, ½ lb.	$40.00 – 45.00	
Candy jar, #736, 1 lb.	$75.00 – 90.00	1926
Candy jar, #835, ½ lb.	$55.00 – 70.00	1926
Candy jar, #1532, ½ lb. with dolphins	$110.00 – 125.00	1927
Cheese comport and underplate, #316	$50.00 – 65.00	1928
Cigarette holder, #556	$125.00 – 145.00	
Cologne, #53 – 5"	$110.00 – 125.00	1927
Comport, #1043 – 8½" plate,	$25.00 – 35.00	
Comport, #1533 6" round flared	$65.00 – 80.00	1929
Comport, #1533 – 7" oval with dolphins	$75.00 – 85.00	1929
Creamer, #2	$30.00 – 35.00	1926
Creamer, #3	$25.00 – 30.00	
Creamer, Hexagonal	$32.00 – 35.00	1916
Flower pot, #1554 w/underplate	$90.00 – 100.00	
Flower pot, #1555 w/underplate	$100.00 – 125.00	
Guest set, #200 handled	$290.00 – 350.00	1938
Jug, 7"	$250.00 – 300.00	
Mayonnaise & ladle, #923	$55.00 – 65.00	
Night set, "twin rib"	$150.00 – 170.00	
Puff box, #53	$60.00 – 65.00	1927
Sugar, #2	$30.00 – 35.00	1926
Sugar, #3	$25.00 – 30.00	
Sugar, Hexagonal	$32.00 – 35.00	1916
Tray, #53 for vanity set	$45.00 – 50.00	
Tray, #1561 – 10" oval handled	$65.00 – 70.00	
Vanity set, #53, 4-pc.	$325.00 – 465.00	1927
Vase, #572 – 8" fan	$40.00 – 45.00	
Vase, #573 – 8" trumpet	$45.00 – 48.00	1926
Vase, 8" Peacock (iridescent)	$500.00 – 600.00	1926
Vase, #847 – 6" fan	$35.00 – 40.00	
Vase, #847 – 6½" crimped	$35.00 – 40.00	
Vase, #1530 – 12"	$65.00 – 75.00	
Vase, #1531 – 16"	$70.00 – 90.00	1927
Vase, #1533 – A-6" fan w/dolphins	$65.00 – 75.00	

#572-8" Fan Vase

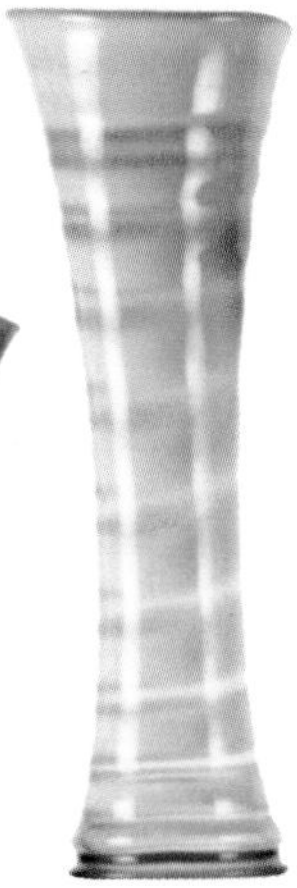

#1530-12" Vase

#573-8" Trumpet Vase

#847-6" Fan Vase

#1533-5 1/2" Fan Vase with Dolphins

#923 Mayonnaise and Ladle

#857-8" Cupped Bowl

#847-6 1/2" Nut Bowl

#857-11" Flared Bowl

#1512-9" Flared Bowl

#735-1/2 lb. Candy Jar

#835-1/2 lb. Candy Jar

#1532 Candy Jar

#643-5" Covered Bon-bon

#316 Cheese Comport

#1561-10" Oval Handled Tray

#1043-8 1/2" Plate Comport

#316 Candlestick

#318 Candlestick

#314 Candlestick

Hexagonal Open Sugar and Creamer

#3 Open Creamer and Sugar

#556 Cigarette Holder

#1554/1555 Flower Pot Saucer

CHINESE YELLOW

Fenton's bright translucent yellow color was originally introduced in the early 1920s as jade yellow. By as early as 1924, this color was referred to as Chinese yellow in inventory records and the name was popularized with the introduction of other colors with Oriental derivations in the early 1930s.

Especially desirable items in this color include the two-piece reamer sets, the nymph figure, tall cut candlesticks, Dancing Ladies urns, and the ginger jar.

Item	Value	Date
Basket, #1681 – 10½" Big Cookies	$200.00 – 210.00	
Bonbon, #543 covered	$90.00 – 95.00	1925
Bonbon, #643 – 5" covered	$98.00 – 105.00	
Bonbon, #643 open, cupped	$27.00 – 30.00	1925
Bowl, #456 – 1 mixing	$58.00 – 66.00	1932
Bowl, #456 – 2 mixing	$42.00 – 48.00	1932
Bowl, #456 – 3 mixing	$68.00 – 77.00	1932
Bowl, #543 lily	$20.00 – 25.00	1924
Bowl, #550 – 7½" cupped	$65.00 – 75.00	1933
Bowl, #550 – 10" flared cupped	$85.00 – 125.00	1933
Bowl, #550 – 11" shallow, cupped	$85.00 – 95.00	1933
Bowl, #550 – 12" flared	$85.00 – 125.00	1933
Bowl, #600 – 7" cupped	$35.00 – 45.00	1924
Bowl, #607 – 8" cupped	$42.00 – 47.00	1925
Bowl, #607 – 8" rolled rim	$42.00 – 47.00	1924
Bowl, #607 – 9" shallow cupped	$42.00 – 47.00	
Bowl, #638 – 8" shallow cupped	$47.00 – 52.00	1925
Bowl, #640 – 7" flared, cupped	$35.00 – 45.00	1924–25
Bowl, #647 – 10¾" flared cupped	$55.00 – 65.00	1925
Bowl, #647 – 8"	$40.00 – 45.00	1926
Bowl, #846 – 6" cupped	$40.00 – 45.00	1933
Bowl, #846 – 8½" flared cupped	$75.00 – 85.00	1933
Bowl, #846 – 8½" flared or cupped	$42.00 – 47.00	1933
Bowl, #847 – 7½" flared	$37.00 – 42.00	
Bowl, #848 – 6" cupped	$37.00 – 42.00	
Bowl, #848 – 8½" flared	$58.00 – 67.00	1933
Bowl, #857 – 8" cupped footed	$48.00 – 52.00	
Bowl, #900 – 11" oval Dancing Ladies	$300.00 – 375.00	1932
Bowl, #1504 – A-9" cupped with dolphins	$75.00 – 85.00	1929
Bowl, #1504 – A-9" shallow cupped with dolphin	$75.00 – 85.00	1929
Bowl, #1504 – A-6" cupped with dolphins	$40.00 – 50.00	1932–33
Bowl, #1663 – 12" flared; tulip	$100.00 – 125.00	1932
Bowl, #1663 – 12" Reg.	$100.00 – 125.00	1932
Bowl, #1663 – 9" oval	$100.00 – 125.00	1932
Bowl set, for electric mixer	$63.00 – 68.00	1933
Candleholder, #848/1234 – 3 ft.	$22.00 – 27.00	1933
Candlestick, #314	$22.00 – 27.00	1925
Candlestick, #315 – 3½" princess	$27.00 – 30.00	1925
Candlestick, #318	$32.00 – 37.00	1933
Candlestick, #349 – 10"	$100.00 – 110.00	1924
Candlestick, #349 – 10" with cutting	$150.00 – 170.00	1924
Candlestick, #549 – 8½"	$60.00 – 70.00	1926
*Candlestick, #649 – 10"	$90.00 – 100.00	1924–25
Candy jar, #636, 1 lb.	$175.00 – 200.00	1925
Candy jar, #736, 1 lb.	$150.00 – 180.00	1925
Ginger jar and lid, #893	$280.00 – 320.00	1933
Jug, #400	$85.00 – 95.00	1932
Jug, 6" ft.	$210.00 – 250.00	
Macaroon jar, #1681 – 7" Big Cookies	$290.00 – 325.00	1933
Nymph, #1645 September Morn	$250.00 – 325.00	1933
Plate, #103 – 6"	$12.00 – 14.00	1924
Plate, #301 – 6"	$12.00 – 14.00	1924
Plate, #543	$15.00 – 17.00	1924
Plate, #630 – 8½" salad	$22.00 – 27.00	1925
Plate, #638	$17.00 – 20.00	1924
Plate, #200	$22.00 – 25.00	1924
Reamer, #1619 w/handled jug	$1500.00 – 1800.00	1933
Salver, #543	$23.00 – 27.00	1924
Salver, #647 – 13" ft.	$125.00 – 150.00	1924
Sherbet, #103	$22.00 – 27.00	1924
Urn, #901 – 12" covered Dancing Ladies	$900.00 – 1200.00	1932
Urn, #901 – 7" covered Dancing Ladies	$600.00 – 700.00	
Vase, #184 – 10"	$90.00 – 115.00	
Vase, #184 – 12"	$100.00 – 125.00	
Vase, #184 – 8"	$80.00 – 95.00	
Vase, #611 – 6½" cupped	$55.00 – 70.00	1925
Vase, #612 – 6½" flared	$55.00 – 70.00	1925
Vase, #621 – 6"	$37.00 – 42.00	1933
Vase, #621 – 8" flared, cupped or square top	$50.00 – 55.00	1933
Vase, #857 – 8" fan	$200.00 – 250.00	
Vase, #894 – 10" triangle; square; flared; tulip; or reg.	$100.00 – 110.00	1924
Vase, #901 – 5" (handled urn base) Dancing Ladies	$250.00 – 300.00	
Vase, #1668 – 8" flip	$90.00 – 110.00	1933
with ebony base	$100.00 – 110.00	

#1681-7" Macaroon Jar
"Big Cookies"

#894-10" Regular Vase

#621-6 1/2" Flared Vase

6" Jug

#550-12" Flared Cupped Bowl

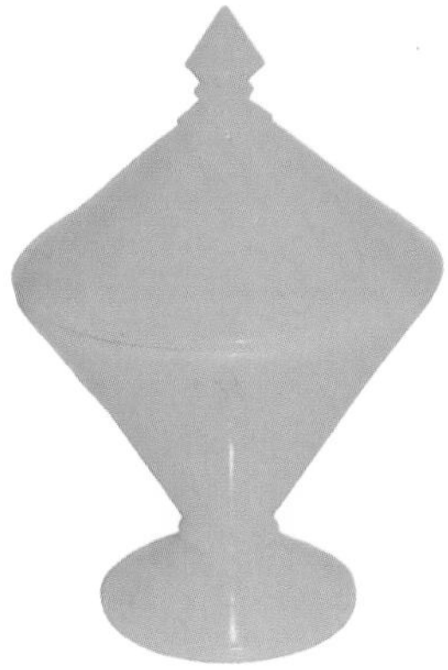

#736-1 lb. Candy Jar

#315-3 1/2" Candlestick

#848 Flared Bowl &
#1645 Nymph Figure

#1668-8" Flip Vase

#53 Cologne

#846-8" Flared Bowl
w/5-legged Base

#846-6 1/2" Cupped Bowl
w/5-legged Base

#349-10" Candlestick

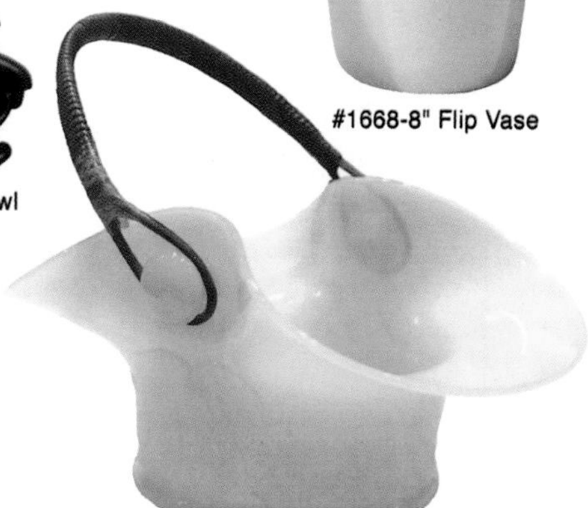

#1681-10 1/2" Basket
"Big Cookies"

#1663-12" Flared Bowl

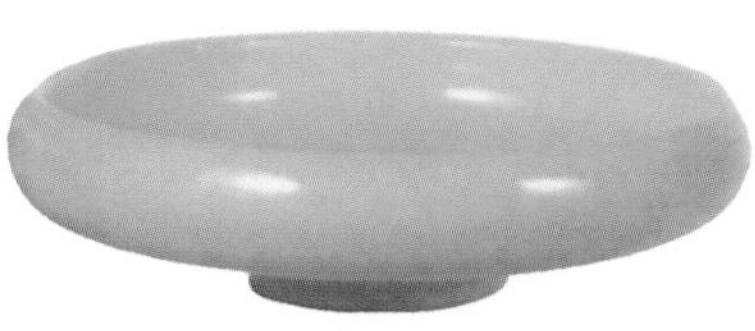

#607-8" Cupped Bowl

#456-3-9" Mixing Bowl

#1504-A-9" Cupped Bowl

CELESTE BLUE

Catalog and inventory records are too incomplete to confirm the number of different pieces made in Celeste blue. The very limited list below only includes the pieces we have seen. If the number of pieces made in this color in iridescent can be used as an indication, more items in this color will appear in the coming years.

Item	Value
Ashtray set, #202, 5-pc., #1,2,3,4,	$68.00 – 85.00
Ashtray, #1566	$95.00 – 120.00
Bonbon, #643 – 5" covered	$55.00 – 60.00
Candlestick, #449 – 8½"	$37.00 – 40.00
Candlestick, #449 – 8½" w/oval cut	$85.00 – 95.00
Candlestick, #549 – 8½"	$37.00 – 42.00
Candlestick, #649 – 10"	$50.00 – 55.00
Cologne , #59	$75.00 – 85.00
Cup, #1502 Diamond Optic	$25.00 – 28.00
Pitcher, #220 covered	$250.00 – 290.00
Puff Box, #743	$45.00 – 55.00
Vase, #857 – 8" fan	$40.00 – 50.00

#643-5" Covered Bonbon

#649-10" Candlestick

#449-8 1/2" Candlestick

#857-8" Fan Vase

CRYSTAL & CRYSTAL SATIN

Examples of early Fenton crystal and crystal cut glassware are illustrated on pages 21 – 23. The listing below describes shapes of many of the Fenton crystal pieces made during the 1930s. For more information about other crystal Fenton production, see the Patterns and Satin Patterns chapters of this book.

Item	Value	Date
Ashtray, #304 oblong	$3.00 – 400	1933
Ashtray, #309 – 301 – 312	$3.00 – 4.00	1935 – 1936
Ashtray, #848– 3-ftd.	$6.00 – 8.00	1936 – 1939
Base, Diamond-shape for ivy ball	$35.00 – 40.00	1937 – 1938
Basket, #1681 – 10½" Big Cookies	$70.00 – 80.00	1933 – 1938
Basket, #1684	$70.00 – 80.00	1935 – 1937
Bonbon, #389 Hobnail	$4.00 – 5.00	1939
Bonbon, #1235 triangle, cupped	$4.00 – 5.00	1935 – 1937
Bonbon, #1595	$4.00 – 5.00	1938
Bookend, #711 pr.	$150.00 – 175.00	1935
Bowl, #349 – 7"	$16.00 – 18.00	1936 – 1937
Bowl. #349 – 10" club	$22.00 – 27.00	1937
Bowl, #349 – 11"	$22. 00 – 27.00	1936 – 1937
Bowl, #604 –10" shallow	$16.00 – 18.00	1935
Bowl, #705 flower	$15.00 – 18.00	1935 – 1936
Bowl, #750	$18.00 – 20.00	1935
Bowl, #843	$12.00 – 14.00	1935
Bowl, #846 – 6" cupped	$18.00 – 20.00	1934 – 1938
Bowl, #847 – 6" crimped, cupped, flared	$16.00 – 18.00	1937
Bowl, #848/1234 – 8½" flared	$17.00 – 20.00	1935 – 1936
Bowl, #857 –10" crimped, flared	$16.00 – 18.00	1936 – 1937
Bowl, #1595 – 3½"	$3.00 – 5.00	1933 – 1934
Bowl, #900 – 11" oval Dancing Ladies	$100.00 – 110.00	1934
Bowl, #950 – 8" oval, tulip	$18.00 – 22.00	1935 – 1938
Bowl, #1000 – 10" Silvertone	$16.00 – 22.00	1936
Bowl, #1000 – 11" Silvertone	$16.00 – 22.00	1936
Bowl, #1092 – 5"	$4.00 – 6.00	1935
Bowl, #1093 – 6" deep crimped	$6.00 – 7.00	1935
Bowl, #1093 – 7¼" shallow, 8½" crimped	$7.00 – 9.00	1937
Bowl, #1562 oval	$20.00 – 25.00	1936 – 1937
Bowl, #1563 boat shape	$20.00 – 25.00	1935
Bowl, #1663 tulip, cloverleaf	$12.00 – 14.00	1937 – 1938
Bowl, #1790 – 4½" Leaf Tiers	$22.00 – 24.00	1934 – 1936
Bowl, #1790 – 10" cupped, 12" flared Leaf Tiers	$37.00 – 45.00	1935 – 1936
Bowl, #1932-6¼" 3-ftd. flared, shallow cupped	$10.00 – 12.00	1933 – 1936
Bowl, #1932-7½" 3-ftd. crimped	$10.00 – 12.00	1933 – 1936
Candelabra, #2318 – 6"	$22.00 – 25.00	1935
Candleholder, #314	$4.00 – 6.00	1933
Candleholder, #349	$10.00 – 12.00	1936
Candleholder, #751	$10.00 – 12.00	1935 – 1936
Candleholder, #848/1234 – 3-ftd.	$12.00 – 14.00	1933
Candleholder, #950 cornucopia	$12.00 – 14.00	1935 – 1938
Candleholder, #1000 Silvertone	$8.00 – 12.00	1936
Candleholder, #1523	$8.00 – 10.00	1936
Candleholder, #1790 Leaf Tiers	$10.00 – 12.00	
Candleholder, #1800	$9.00 – 11.00	1936 – 1937
Candleholder #6000	$10.00 – 12.00	1935
Candy jar, #844 w/flower finial	$55.00 – 65.00	1936 – 1938
Coaster, #1590 – 4"	$2.00 – 3.00	1932 – 1933
Creamer, #349	$5.00 – 7.00	1937
Decanter, #1935 Franklin	$60.00 – 70.00	1935 – 1938
Dog novelty figure, #307	$22.00 – 25.00	1937
Cup, #604	$4.00 – 5.00	1935
Fish novelty figure, #306	$22.00 – 25.00	1937

Item	Value	Date
Flower block, #2	$5.00 – 6.00	1932
Flower block, #1643 for nymph figure	$5.00 – 7.00	1933
Ginger jar and lid, #893	$40.00 – 45.00	1935 – 1937
Hat, #1920 – 1921	$7.00 – 10.00	1938
Hat, #1922 – 1923 – 1924	$20.00 – 28.00	1938
Ice pack, #1616	$18.00 – 22.00	1935 – 1937
Ivy ball, #706	$8.00 – 10.00	1936
Jug, #1352	$25.00 – 40.00	1937 – 1938
Jug, #1355	$30.00 – 45.00	1937
Mug, #2010 – 12 oz.	$8.00 – 10.00	1933
Night set, #200	$40.00 – 50.00	1937 – 1938
Nymph, #1645 September Morn	$85.00 – 95.00	1933
Paper vase	$12.00 – 15.00	1933
Plate, #175-8" Leaf	$14.00 – 16.00	1935 – 1938
Plate, #175 – 11" Leaf	$18.00 – 22.00	1935 – 1938
Plate, #681 – 8"	$5.00 – 7.00	1934 – 1938
Plate, #1000 – 12"	$18.00 – 20.00	1936
Plate, #1093 – 9"	$10.00 – 12.00	1937
Plate, #1790 – 6" Leaf Tiers	$8.00 – 10.00	1935 – 1936
Plate, #1790 – 11" Leaf Tiers	$20.00 – 22.00	1935 – 1937
Punch bowl, #930	$40.00 – 60.00	1938
Punch cup, #604	$4.00 – 6.00	1937
Punch cup, #920	$4.00 – 6.00	1938
Punch cup, #930	$4.00 – 6.00	1938 – 1939
Reamer, #1209 – 2-piece	$20.00 – 25.00	1939
Reamer, #1210 – 2-piece	$20.00 – 25.00	1935 – 1939
Refrigerator dish, #457 rectangular w/lid	$16.00 – 18.00	1935
Relish, #2	$14.00 – 16.00	1935 – 1937
Relish, #1688	$14.00 – 16.00	1935 – 1936
Shaker, #33	$8.00 – 10.00	1937
Shell, 3½ – 4½"	$2.00 – 5.00	1936
Sugar, #349	$5.00 – 7.00	1937
Tumbler, #33	$5.00 – 7.00	1935 – 1938
Tumbler, #35 – 1 oz. whiskey	$7.00 – 9.00	1935 – 1938
Tumbler, #35 – 4 oz.	$7.00 – 9.00	1935 – 1938
Tumbler, #200	$6.00 – 8.00	1937
Tumbler, #1352 ice tea	$8.00 – 10.00	1935
Tumbler, #1353 – 12 oz. ice tea	$8.00 – 10.00	1936
Tumbler, #1933	$5.00 – 7.00	1932 – 1934
Tray, #957 fan	$10.00 – 12.00	1937– 1938
Tray, #1689	$14.00 – 16.00	1936
Urn, #901 – 12" covered Dancing Ladies	$250.00 – 300.00	1935
Urn, #901 – 7"covered Dancing Ladies	$175.00 – 225.00	1935
Vanity set, #389 Hobnail	$75.00 – 85.00	1939
Vase, #182 flared	$12.00 – 14.00	1937
Vase, #184 – 8"	$13.00 – 15.00	1937
Vase, #184 – 10" or 12"	$20.00 – 25.00	1936 – 1937
Vase, #349 fan, flared	$18.00 – 20.00	1937 – 1938
Vase, #354 bud	$7.00 – 9.00	1933 – 1936
Vase, #519 – 20"	$20.00 – 25.00	1933
Vase, #621 flared	$10.00 – 12.00	1937
Vase, #847 crimped, fan	$16.00 – 18.00	1937 – 1938
Vase, #857 fan	$20.00 – 22.00	1937 – 1938
Vase, #901 – 5" Dancing Ladies	$65.00 – 75.00	1936
Vase, #901 – 9" Dancing Ladies	$225.00 – 300.00	1934
Vase, #922	$12.00 – 14.00	1935
Vase, #1126 – 10" Fenton's Rib	$18.00 – 22.00	1933 – 1936
Vase, #1561 – 10" reg., crimped, or flared Apple Tree	$35.00 – 50.00	1933
Vase, #1562 Blueberry	$30.00 – 40.00	1933
Vase, #1563	$18.00 – 22.00	1933

FLAME

Flame is an opaque bright orange color that was produced from about 1922 to 1924. Catalog records are not complete enough to establish the number of different pieces that were produced. Inventory records and items in collections suggest the pieces listed below should be available.

The tall candles may be found either in solid flame or with a royal blue base. The Big Cookies macaroon jar may not actually be flame since the mold for this piece did not exist until a number of years after the time that flame was produced. The orange color of the jar is a good imitation of flame, but it is probably the result of a weak colored batch of Mandarin red.

Flame	Value	Date
Bonbon, #1043, 1 lb. covered, footed	\$100.00 – 300.00	
Bowl, #231, cupped	\$125.00 – 150.00	
Bowl, #601 – 10" shallow cupped	\$70.00 – 80.00	1924
Bowl, #2007 – 9" shallow cupped	\$60.00 – 70.00	1924
Candlestick, #549 – 8½"	\$120.00 – 130.00	1924
Candlestick, #549 – 8½" w/blue base	\$120.00 – 140.00	1924
Candlestick, #649 – 10"	\$145.00 – 160.00	1924
Candlestick, #649 – 10" w/blue base	\$150.00 – 165.00	1924
Candy jar, #636, 1 lb.	\$100.00 – 125.00	1924
Macaroon jar, #1681 – 7" Big Cookies	\$400.00 – 500.00	
Vase, #857 – 8"	\$150.00 – 200.00	
Vase, #857 – 6"	\$120.00 – 150.00	

#857-8" Fan Vase

#1681-7" Macaroon Jar "Big Cookies"

#636-1 lb. Candy

#549-8" Candlestick

#2007-9" Shallow Cupped Bowl

#549-8" Candlestick

GREEN TRANSPARENT

Fenton began making transparent green glassware in the early 1920s and production increased and continued through the late 1930s. Shades of transparent green range from light green through blue-green to emerald green. Some of the patterns such as Lincoln Inn and Georgian were made in more than one shade of transparent green. Dolphin and Diamond Optic pieces usually tend to run toward blue-green.

Many of the Diamond Optic items and some of the vases will be found with cuttings. Add about 20 per cent to the prices listed below for any items found with cuttings if they are not already priced in the listing. Most of the bonbons, bowls, comports, and vases are common and very inexpensive. The #1932 bowl, shown with the nymph figure in the photo, comes with or without the candleholder center.

The elephant flower bowl, the large 2-piece reamer, and the turtle-based aquariums are the items at the top of the rarity list in transparent green. Also, the ginger jar and the large punch bowl are elusive.

Item	Value	Date
Aquarium, #1538 – 1565 turtle base w/opal Coin Spot top	$700.00 – 800.00	1929
Aquarium, #1538 – 1565 turtle base w/Button & Braids top	$700.00 – 800.00	1929
Aquarium, #1538 – 1565 turtle base w/crys. Bubble Optic top	$500.00 – 600.00	1929
Ashtray, #305	$8.00 – 10.00	1932
Ashtray, #848 – 3-ftd.	$9.00 – 11.00	1933
Basket, #1502	$25.00 – 30.00	1928
Basket, #1615 cut	$55.00 – 65.00	1938
Basket, #1616 -8" w/metal handle	$53.00 – 55.00	1933
Basket, #1616 – 1702 cut	$55.00 – 65.00	1931
Basket, #1616 – 1709 cut	$55.00 – 60.00	1928
Basket, #1617	$55.00 – 65.00	1933
Basket, #1617 cut	$65.00 – 75.00	1933
Basket, #1681 – 10½" Big Cookies	$125.00 – 175.00	1933
Basket, #1684 w/wicker handle	$70.00 – 85.00	1935
Bonbon, #74	$15.00 – 18.00	1933
Bonbon, #846 – 5" covered	$50.00 – 55.00	1935
Bonbon, Blackberry Banded	$25.00 – 32.00	
Bonbon, #1216 Blackberry Spray	$25.00 – 32.00	
Bonbon, #1235 cupped	$12.00 – 14.00	1936
Bonbon, #1235 flared	$12.00 – 14.00	1935
Bonbon, #1235 triangle	$12.00 – 14.00	1935
Bonbon, #1502 – 6" flared	$32.00 – 37.00	1927
Bonbon, #1502 – 7½" crimped	$32.00 – 37.00	1927
Bonbon, #1502 – 7½" oval	$42.00 – 46.00	1927
Bonbon, #1502 – 7½" round w/dolphins	$42.00 – 47.00	1927
Bonbon, #1565 turtle w/flower frog	$170.00 – 190.00	1929
Bonbon, #1565 turtle open	$150.00 – 175.00	1929
Bonbon, #1621/1702 cut-6½" crimped; flared; square	$20.00 – 22.00	1928
Bookend, #1711 Peacock pr.	$160.00 – 185.00	1935
Bowl, #100 – 5" 3-toed	$12.00 – 14.00	1930
Bowl, #100 – 7½" 3-footed round	$20.00 – 23.00	1930
Bowl, #100 – 8" octagonal 3-footed	$25.00 – 30.00	1930
Bowl, #456 – 1 mixing	$20.00 – 23.00	1933
Bowl, #456 – 2 mixing	$20.00 – 25.00	1933
Bowl, #456 – 3 mixing	$20.00 – 25.00	1933
Bowl, #750 reg., flared	$27.00 – 32.00	1935
Bowl, #846 – 8½" flared cupped	$22.00 – 25.00	1935
Bowl, #846 – 8½" flared or cupped	$22.00 – 25.00	1935
Bowl, #847 – 7½" flared	$20.00 – 22.00	
Bowl, #848 – 6" cupped	$37.00 – 45.00	

#1645 Nymph Figure w/ #1932-6 1/2" Bowl

#1641-11 oz. Ice Tea Tumbler

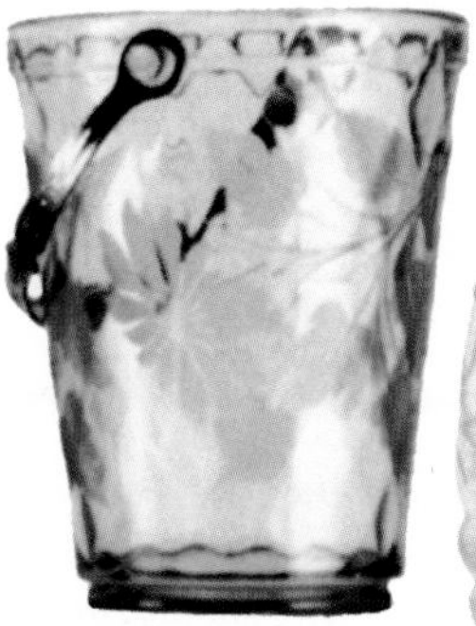
#1502 Ice Pail

#1634 Water Set

#1681-7" Macaroon Jar "Big Cookies"

#1684-6 1/2" Macaroon Jar

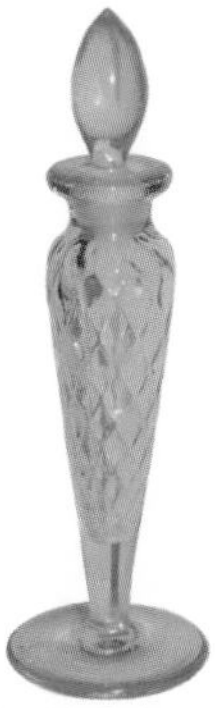
#1502 Cologne

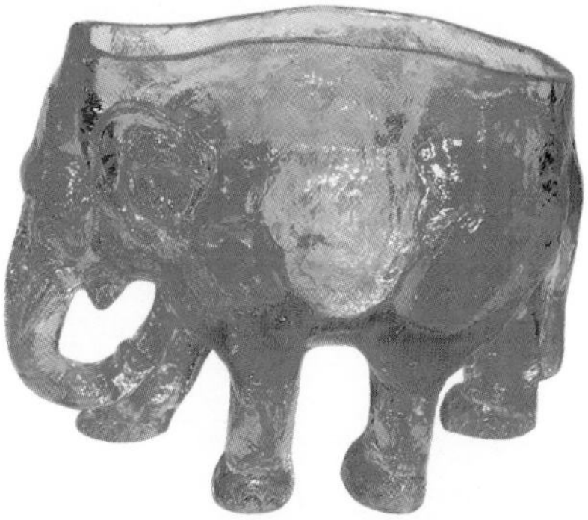
#1618 Elephant Flower Bowl

#1565-9 1/2" Turtle w/ Flower Block Insert

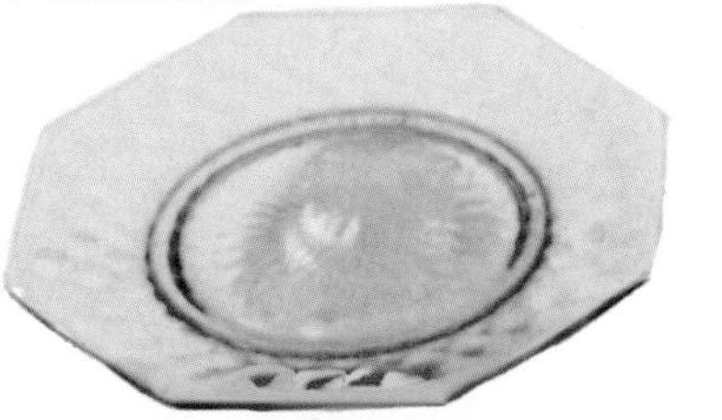
#1502-8" Octagonal Plate

#1503-A-7" Cupped Bowl

#1790 Leaf Tiers Candlestick

#1502-A-7" Cupped Bowl

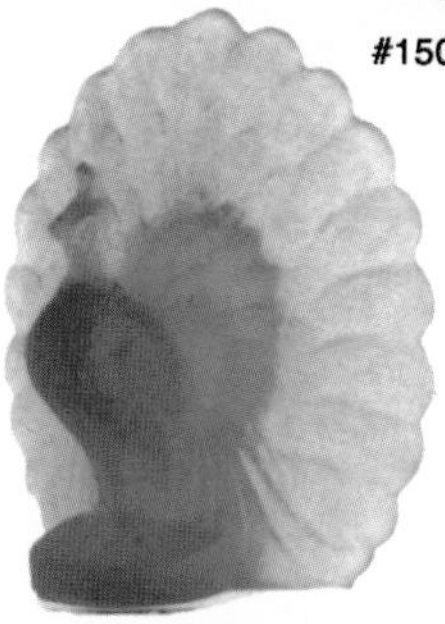
#1711-5 3/4" Peacock Bookend

#1532 Candy Jar

#231 Rib & Holly Sprig Comport

#1502 Basket

#1700 Lincoln Inn Tumbler

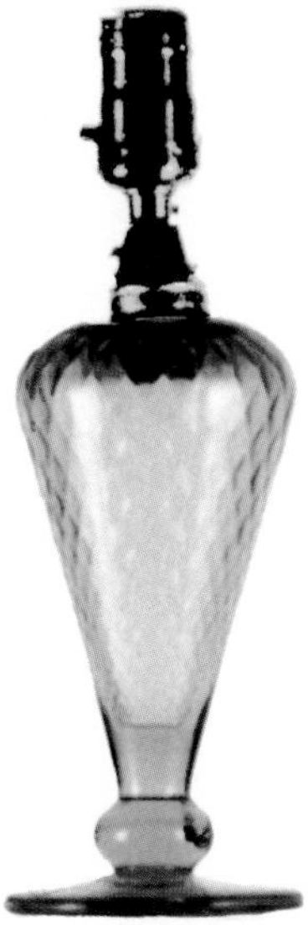
#1502 Lamp

Item	Value	Date
Bowl, #848 – 8½" flared	$55.00 –60.00	1933
Bowl, #950 – 11" oval	$30.00 – 35.00	1935 – 1936
Bowl, #950 – 11" tulip	$30.00 – 35.00	1935
Bowl, #1039 – 6" deep crimp	$20.00 – 23.00	1935
Bowl, #1092 – 5½" Basket Weave w/Open Edge	$12.00 – 15.00	1936
Bowl, #1093 – 9" shallow crimped Basket Weave w/Open Edge	$25.00 – 30.00	1935
Bowl, #1234 – 9" flared	$55.00 – 65.00	1935 – 1936
Bowl, #1235 – 5"	$8.00 – 10.00	1932
Bowl, #1237 – 10" crimped	$37.00 – 42.00	1933
Bowl, #1245 – 5"	$8.00 – 10.00	1932
Bowl, #1502 finger	$13.00 – 16.00	1928
Bowl, #1502 – 10" shallow cupped	$25.00 – 30.00	1927
Bowl, #1502 – 10" special roll rim	$30.00 – 35.00	1927
Bowl, #1502 – 12" shallow cupped	$27.00 – 32.00	1927
Bowl, #1502 – 12" special roll rim	$30.00 – 35.00	1927
Bowl, #1502 – 13" flared	$32.00 – 37.00	1927
Bowl, #1502 – 14" special rolled rim	$35.00 – 40.00	1928
Bowl, #1502 – 8" deep cupped	$27.00 – 30.00	1928
Bowl, #1502 – 8" flared cupped	$27.00 – 30.00	1928
Bowl, #1502 – A-9" crimped w/dolphins	$30.00 – 35.00	1928
Bowl, #1502 – A-10" flared w/dolphins	$32.00 – 37.00	1928
Bowl, #1502 – A-7" cupped w/dolphins	$30.00 – 35.00	1928
Bowl, #1502 – A-8½" roll rim w/dolphins	$30.00 – 35.00	1928
Bowl, #1502 – A-8" cupped w/dolphins	$30.00 – 35.00	1928
Bowl, #1502 – A-8½" flared cupped w/dolphins	$30.00 – 35.00	1928
Bowl, #1503 – 10" flared	$27.00 – 30.00	1927
Bowl, #1503 – A-10" flared w/dolphins	$30.00 – 35.00	1927
Bowl, #1503 – A-7" cupped w/dolphins	$27.00 – 30.00	1928
Bowl, #1503 – A-8½" roll edge w/dolphins	$27.00 – 32.00	1928
Bowl, #1503 – A-9" shallow cupped or crimped	$30.00 – 35.00	1928
Bowl, #1504 – A-9½" flared cupped w/#1702 cut	$47.00 – 55.00	1928
Bowl, #1504 – A-9" flared w/#1702 cut	$47.00 – 55.00	1928
Bowl, #1608 – 10" shallow or crimped Stag & Holly	$45.00 – 45.00	1932
Bowl, #1663 – 10½" tulip	$40.00 – 45.00	1935
Bowl, #1932 – 6½" flared or cupped	$15.00 – 17.00	1933 – 1936
Bowl, #1932 – 7½" crimped	$15.00 – 17.00	1933 – 1936
Bowl, #1933 – 7" flared	$15.00 – 17.00	
Candle, #1502	$15.00 – 17.00	1927
Candleholder, #848 – 3-ftd.	$22.00 – 25.00	1935
Candlestick, #314	$12.00 – 15.00	1932
Candlestick, #316	$12.00 – 15.00	
Candlestick, #318	$14.00 – 16.00	
Candlestick, #318 w/#1702 cut	$25.00 – 27.00	1928
Candlestick, #950 – 5½" cornucopia	$25.00 – 27.00	
Candlestick, #1091 Basket Weave w/Open Edge	$20.00 – 22.00	1936
Candlestick, #1234	$20.00 – 25.00	
Candlestick, #1623 w/dolphins	$20.00 – 22.00	1932
Candy jar, #844, 1 lb. w/flower finial	$250.00 – 295.00	1933
Candy jar, #1533 – A w/dolphins	$65.00 – 75.00	1928
Candy jar, #1532, ½ lb. w/dolphins	$47.00 – 52.00	1928
Coaster, #1590 – 4"	$12.00 – 15.00	1932
Cologne, #53 – 4"	$125.00 – 150.00	
Cologne, #53 – 5"	$90.00 – 100.00	
Cologne, #1502 Diamond Optic	$120.00 – 145.00	1927
Comport, #231 Rib & Holly Sprig	$18.00 – 22.00	

Catalog Reprint Circa 1937
Courtesy Of:
The Fenton Art Glass Museum
S. S. KRESGE COMPANY
DETROIT, MICH.
NOVELTY GLASSWARE
354 – 8"–9" BUD VASE
Crystal – Green – Rose – Black
1126 – 10" VASE
Crystal – Rose – Green
1234 – CANDLEHOLDER
Crystal – Green – Royal Blue – Jade – Black and Ruby
1234 – 9" Flared Console Bowl
1234 – Flower Block
1234 – Nymph Figure
Crystal – Green – Royal Blue – Jade – Black and Ruby
1234 – CANDLEHOLDER
Crystal – Green – Royal Blue – Jade – Black and Ruby
1093 – 7¾" Shallow Fancy Nappy
Crystal – Royal Blue – Ruby and Opalescent
1093 – 8¾" Crimp Fancy Nappy
Crystal – Royal Blue – Ruby and Opalescent
1093 – 9" Plate – Same Colors
307 – NOVELTY DOG
Sparkling Eyes – Royal Blue – Ruby – Jade – Crystal Etched – Plain Green
306 – NOVELTY FISH
Sparkling Eyes – Royal Blue – Ruby Jade – Crystal Etched – Plain Green
304 – Oblong Ash Tray
Royal Blue – Jade – Ruby – Plain Green – Crystal Etched
47 – TEA BELL
Crystal – Ruby – Royal Blue
FENTON ART GLASS COMPANY, WILLIAMSTOWN, W. VA.

Item	Value	Date
Comport, #1502 cheese & cracker	$35.00 – 40.00	1927
Creamer, #1502 Diamond Optic	$20.00 – 25.00	1927
Creamer, #4	$18.00 – 22.00	1933
Decanter, #1935 Franklin	$80.00 – 90.00	1934
Dog, #307 novelty	$42.00 – 47.00	1933
Dresser set, #1502 3-pc.	$270.00 – 325.00	1927
Dresser set, #1502 4-pc. (with tray)	$295.00 – 355.00	1927
Fish, #306 novelty	$42.00 – 47.00	1933
Flower block, #2	$8.00 – 10.00	1932
Flower block, #1234 for nymph figure	$15.00 – 17.00	1933
Flower block, #1564 turtle	$42.00 – 47.00	1927
Flower bowl, #1618 elephant	$450.00 – 500.00	1929
Ginger jar and lid, #893	$200.00 – 225.00	1935
Goblet, #1412 – 5" Orange Tree	$16.00 – 18.00	1933
Goblet, #1502 – 11 oz. bridge Diamond Optic	$13.00 – 15.00	1930
Goblet, #1502 – 9 oz. bridge Diamond Optic	$13.00 – 15.00	1933
Goblet, #1502 Hi ft. Diamond Optic	$16.00 – 18.00	1927
Goblet, #1503 – 9 oz. Spiral Optic	$15.00 – 20.00	1928
Goblet, #1640 – 9 oz. bridge w/#1702 cutting	$23.00 – 27.00	1928
Goblet, #1642 w/#1702 cutting	$27.00 – 30.00	1928
Ice pack, #1614	$27.00 – 35.00	1928
Ice pack, #1616 – 6½"	$32.00 – 37.00	1928
Ice pack, #1616 – 1702 cut	$43.00 – 47.00	1928
Ice pack, #1616 – 1709 cut	$32.00 – 47.00	1928
Ice tub, #1502 – 4" Diamond Optic	$22.00 – 27.00	1928 - 1933
Ivy ball, #706	$20.00 – 25.00	1933
Lamp, #1502	$110.00 – 130.00	1927
Macaroon jar, #1681 – 7" Big Cookies	$240.00 – 260.00	1933
Macaroon jar, #1684 – 6½"	$150.00 – 200.00	1935
Mayonnaise and ladle, #1502	$35.00 – 40.00	1927
Mint jar and cover, #1639 Elizabeth	$170.00 – 195.00	
Mug, #1430 Orange Tree	$22.00 – 27.00	
Mug, #2010 – 10 oz.	$14.00 – 16.00	1933
Mug, #4009	$12.00 – 15.00	1933
Night set, #401	$50.00 – 65.00	1935
Night set, #1502 – 2-pc.	$75.00 – 85.00	1928
Nymph, #1645 September Morn	$180.00 – 200.00	1933
Pitcher, #1634 Diamond Optic	$65.00 – 75.00	1927
Pitcher, #1634 w/#1702 cut	$75.00 – 100.00	1928
Pitcher, #1635 "Diamond Optic	$65.00 – 75.00	1927
Pitcher, #1635 w/#1702 cut	$75.00 – 100.00	1928
Pitcher, #1636	$57.00 – 67.00	1927
Pitcher, #1636 w/#1702 cut	$60.00 – 80.00	1928
Plate, #750 – 14"	$22.00 – 27.00	1935
Plate, #750 – 8"	$8.00 – 9.00	1935
Plate, 757 cut #2	$20.00 – 22.00	1933
Plate, 757 cut #4	$20.00 – 22.00	1933
Plate, #758 – 8½" octagonal	$9.00 – 11.00	1927
Plate, #1235	$14.00 – 16.00	1935
Plate, #1502 w/indent for cheese comport	$18.00 – 20.00	1927
Plate, #1502 – 8" octagonal	$10.00 – 12.00	1928
Plate, #1502 – 6" octagonal	$6.00 – 7.00	1927
Puff box, #53	$27.00 – 32.00	
Puff box, #1502 Diamond Optic	$30.00 – 35.00	1927
Punch bowl & base, #1400 Orange Tree	$240.00 – 270.00	1933
Reamer, #1210 – 2-handled	$150.00 – 180.00	1936
Reamer, #1619 w/handled jug	$2000.00 – 2500.00	1933

Item	Value	Date
Refrigerator set, #1502 3-pc.	$100.00 – 125.00	1930
Shaker, #1502	$22.00 – 25.00	1933
Shell, 3½ – 4½"	$8.00 – 10.00	1936
Sherbet, #103	$8.00 – 10.00	1924
Sherbet, #1502	$9.00 – 11.00	1927
Sherbet, #1503	$8.00 – 10.00	1928
Sugar, #4	$18.00 – 22.00	1933
Sugar, #1502 Diamond Optic	$20.00 – 25.00	1927
Tray, #53 vanity	$25.00 – 30.00	
Tray, #1502 dresser set	$25.00 – 30.00	1927
Tray, #1502 – 10" handled sandwich	$25.00 – 30.00	1927
Tray, #1502 – A-10" w/dolphin handle	$65.00 – 70.00	1927
Tumbler, #1352 – 5¼" ice tea	$18.00 – 20.00	1935
Tumbler, #1502 – 5 oz. orange juice Diamond Optic	$12.00 – 15.00	1928
Tumbler, #1502 – 9 oz. ft. Diamond Optic	$13.00 – 16.00	1928
Tumbler, #1634	$10.00 – 12.00	1928
Tumbler, #1634 w/#1702 cut	$12.00 – 15.00	1928
Tumbler, #1636 – 12 oz.	$10.00 – 12.00	1928
Tumbler, #1636 – 12 oz. w/#1702 cutting	$22.00 – 25.00	1928
Tumbler, #1641 – 11 oz.	$12.00 – 15.00	1928
Tumbler, #1641 – 11 oz. ice tea w/#1702 cutting	$25.00 – 30.00	1928
Tumbler, #1933	$8.00 – 10.00	1932 – 1935
Tumbler, #1935 – 1 oz. whiskey Franklin	$8.00 – 10.00	1934
Underplate, #1502 finger bowl	$5.00 – 6.00	1928
Vanity set, #53 – 4-pc.	$235.00 – 262.00	
Vase, #107 tulip-6½"	$20.00 – 22.00	1933
Vase, #184 – 10"	$35.00 – 40.00	1932 – 1937
Vase, #184 – 12"	$50.00 – 55.00	1935
Vase, #184 – 8"	$30.00 – 35.00	1932
Vase, #184 – 8" w/cutting	$50.00 – 60.00	1932
Vase, #1923 square; tulip; triangle; crimped	$28.00 – 32.00	1939
Vase, #32 Boggy Bayou	$37.00 – 42.00	1932
Vase, #349 oval	$37.00 – 42.00	1932
Vase, #354 – 8" bud	$10.00 – 12.00	1933 – 1939
Vase, #354 – 9" bud	$10.00 – 12.00	1933 – 1939
Vase, #519 – 20"	$45.00 – 55.00	1933 – 1935
Vase, #621 – 6"	$16.00 – 20.00	
Vase, #621 – 8" flared, cupped or square top	$27.00 – 32.00	1935
Vase, #912 – 12"	$27.00 – 32.00	1933
Vase, #916 – 14"-16" Fenton's Rib	$47.00 – 57.00	1927
Vase, #992	$25.00 – 27.00	1936
Vase, #1126 – 9" Fenton's Rib	$38.00 – 42.00	1927 – 1936
Vase, #1219	$25.00 – 27.00	1932
Vase, #1235 – 5"	$10.00 – 12.00	1933
Vase, #1502 – 10" Diamond Optic	$42.00 – 45.00	1927
Vase, #1502 – 5" fan w/dolphins Diamond Optic	$30.00 – 35.00	1927
Vase, #1502 – 6" fan w/dolphins Diamond Optic	$32.00 – 37.00	1927
Vase, #1502 – 7" roll edge Diamond Optic	$43.00 – 48.00	1927
Vase, #1502 – 8½" flared Diamond Optic	$37.00 – 42.00	1927
Vase, #1502 – 8" crimped Diamond Optic	$37.00 – 42.00	1927
Vase, #1502 – 8" flip w/#1702 cut Diamond Optic	$45.00 – 50.00	1927
Vase, #1502 – 8½" fan Diamond Optic	$42.00 – 47.00	1927
Vase, #1532 – A-5½" fan w/dolphins	$32.00 – 37.00	1928
Vase, #1533 – A-6" fan w/dolphins	$37.00 – 46.00	1928
Vase, #1562 – 10" Blueberry	$55.00 – 65.00	1933

JADE GREEN

Judging by the number of different pieces made in jade green, either someone at Fenton was partial to this color or it was at the top of the sales charts. Initial production of jade green began in 1921. The number of items made in this color gradually increased through the 1920s until there was a virtual explosion of jade green items during the early to mid 1930s. The number of unusual items available in this color is enough to make any avid collector drool.

Unusual pieces include the #1565 turtle with any top. Flower block or bonbon tops are difficult to find. Any of the aquarium tops that fit onto the turtle bases are rare. If you have a chance at one, don't be too particular about style.

The nymph figure has been dubbed September Morn. If you must have one, jade green is one of the easier colors to find. She was also made in numerous other colors, some of which are rare. For more on this lady, see page 322.

Some items which have lids or stoppers will be found with tops in black or lilac. Black tops are more common, especially with the #1639 batter set, the colognes, and the bath set. The colognes and bath bottles will sometimes be found with black flower bud stoppers.

Other pieces any collector might be proud to own include the ginger jar with the dragon decoration, the two-piece reamer set, and the #1618 elephant flower bowl. Of course, if your pocketbook is bottomless, you might try to land one of the elusive Dancing Ladies urn lamps.

In 1980, Fenton revived the jade green color with the introduction into the line of the following pieces:

Basket, #7537 – 7"
Bell, #7564
Bird figure, #5163
Bowl, #7523 rolled rim
Boy and Girl figures, #5100
Bud vase, #9054
Bunny figure, #5162
Candle, #7572
Cat figure, #5165
Comport, #7528
Fairy light, #7500
Nut dish, #7529
Owl figure, #5168
Temple jar, #7488
Temple jar, #7588 tall
Vase, #7550 – 7"
Vase, #7557 – 10"
Vase, #8251 Mandarin
Vase, #8252 Empress

For other items in jade, see the sections on Lincoln Inn and Georgian in Fenton Patterns, and lamps in Specialty Items.

Item	Value	Date
Aquarium, #1538 – 1565 turtle base w/opal Coin Spot top	$750.00 – 850.00	1929
Aquarium, #1538 – 1565 turtle base w/Button & Braids top	$750.00 – 850.00	1929
Aquarium, #1538 – 1565 turtle base w/crystal Bubble Optic top	$600.00 – 700.00	1929
Ashtray, #304 rectangular	$12.00 – 15.00	1934
Ashtray, #848 – 3-ftd.	$15.00 – 18.00	1933 – 1936
Ashtray set, #202, 5-pc., #1,2,3,4,	$57.00 – 62.00	
Base, #539 – 10" rnd.	$30.00 – 35.00	1933
Base, ftd., notched	$45.00 – 50.00	
Basket, #1502 Diamond Optic	$30.00 – 35.00	1928
Basket, #1615 – 6" Diamond Optic	$70.00 – 80.00	1928
Basket, #1681 – 10½" Big Cookies	$100.00 – 120.00	1931 – 1934
Basket, #1684 w/wicker handle	$80.00 – 90.00	1931
*Bathroom set, #16 – 17 – 54, 4-pc.	$175.00 – 200.00	1929
Batter set, #1639 Batter jug/syrup/tray Elizabeth	$345.00 – 405.00	1931
Bonbon, #543 covered	$58.00 – 67.00	
Bonbon, #543 open	$22.00 – 25.00	
Bonbon, #643 open, cupped	$25.00 – 30.00	1931
with flower stoppers	$250.00 – 300.00	

#1681-7" Macaroon Jar "Big Cookies"

#1531-16" Vase

#901-18" Urn Lamp "Dancing Ladies"

#184-12" Vase

#1561-10" Vase "Apple Tree"

#1673-8" Candle Vase

#2318 Candelabra

#848 Cupped Bowl & #1645 Nymph Figure

#1619 2-pc Reamer Set

#1565-1538 Turtle Aquarium

#3 Sugar and Creamer

W-111 Shaving Mug

#308 Cigarette Box

#59 Cologne

#847 Rose Bowl

#1502 Round Bridge Bonbon

#1672 Flared Candlesticks

#848 Candlesticks

#1564 Turtle Flower Block

#643 Covered Bonbon

#1563-17" Oval Handled Bowl

#1563 Square Handled Bowl

Item	Value	Date
Bonbon, #643 – 5" covered	$60.00 – 65.00	1924
Bonbon, #943, ½ lb. covered	$63.00 – 72.00	1931
Bonbon, #1502 – 6" flared Diamond Optic	$45.00 – 50.00	1927
Bonbon, #1502 – 7½" crimped Diamond Optic	$45.00 – 50.00	1927
Bonbon, #1502 – 7½" oval Diamond Optic	$45.00 – 50.00	1927
Bonbon, #1502 – 7½" round w/dolphins Diamond Optic	$45.00 – 50.00	1927
Bonbon, #1565 turtle w/flower frog	$210.00 – 260.00	1929
Bonbon, #1565 turtle open	$195.00 – 240.00	1929
Bonbon, #1621 oval	$25.00 – 30.00	1928
Bonbon, #1621/#1702 cut-6½" crimped, flared, square	$25.00 – 30.00	1928
Bottle, #100 w/assorted lettering	$120.00 – 140.00	
Bowl, #100 – 5" 3-toed Wide Rib	$18.00 – 22.00	1930
Bowl, #100 – 7½" 3-footed round Wide Rib	$25.00 – 30.00	1930
Bowl, #100 – 8" octagonal 3-footed Wide Rib	$30.00 – 35.00	1933
Bowl, # 231 shallow cupped	$27.00 – 32.00	1931
Bowl, #456 – 1 mixing	$30.00 – 35.00	1936
Bowl, #456 – 2 mixing	$27.00 – 32.00	1936
Bowl, #456 – 3 mixing	$32.00 – 37.00	1936
Bowl, #535 – 5" cupped lily	$22.00 – 27.00	1924
Bowl, #543 lily	$18.00 – 22.00	1924
Bowl, #550 rolled rim	$45.00 – 50.00	1924
Bowl, #550 – 10" flared cupped	$47.00 – 55.00	1924
Bowl, #550 – 12" flared	$50.00 – 55.00	1924
Bowl, #600 shallow cupped	$20.00 – 25.00	1926
Bowl, #600 – 7" cupped	$20.00 – 25.00	1924
Bowl, #600 – 8" flared	$20.00 – 25.00	1924
Bowl, #601 – 10" shallow cupped	$35.00 – 38.00	1933 – 1934
Bowl, #606 – 8" rolled rim	$25.00 – 30.00	1924
Bowl, #607 – 8" cupped	$25.00 – 30.00	1924
Bowl, #607 – 8" rolled rim	$25.00 – 30.00	1924 – 1931
Bowl, #607 – 9" shallow, cupped	$32.00 – 37.00	1924
Bowl, #638 – 8" shallow cupped	$25.00 – 30.00	1924
Bowl, #640 shallow	$30.00 – 35.00	1924
Bowl, #640 – 7½" rolled rim	$27.00 – 32.00	1924
Bowl, #640 – 7" flared, cupped	$27.00 – 32.00	1924
Bowl, #647 – 11½" shallow cupped	$45.00 – 50.00	1924
Bowl, #647 – 10¾" flared cupped	$45.00 – 50.00	1924
Bowl, #647 – 10" flared	$45.00 – 50.00	1933
Bowl, #647 – 11" rolled rim	$47.00 – 52.00	1924
Bowl, #647 – 12" w/special rolled rim	$47.00 – 52.00	1924
Bowl, #647 – 13" flared	$47.00 – 52.00	1921
Bowl, #647 – 8"	$30.00 – 35.00	1931 – 1934
Bowl, #647 – 8½" cupped (aquarium)	$60.00 – 67.00	1924
Bowl, #846 special rolled rim	$30.00 – 32.00	1931
Bowl, #846 – 6" cupped	$22.00 – 27.00	1933
Bowl, #846 – 8½" flared cupped	$27.00 – 32.00	1933
Bowl, #846 – 9¼" deep fruit	$35.00 – 40.00	1933
Bowl, #847 – 6" crimped	$22.00 – 25.00	1934
Bowl, #847 – 6" cupped	$22.00 – 25.00	1932
Bowl, #847 – 7½" flared	$22.00 – 27.00	1931
Bowl, #847 – 7" shallow cupped	$22.00 – 27.00	1933
Bowl, #847 – 8½" crimped, ftd.	$25.00 – 30.00	1931
Bowl, #848 – 6" cupped	$22.00 – 25.00	1933
Bowl, #848 – 8½" flared	$25.00 – 30.00	1933 – 1937

#1536-6" Comport

#100 Tumbler

#100 Jug

#100 Creamer and Sugar

7 1/2" Strawberry Jar

#844-1lb. Candy Jar

#543 Covered Bonbon

#893 Ginger Jar

#736-1 lb. Candy Jar

#835-1/2 lb.
Candy Bottom

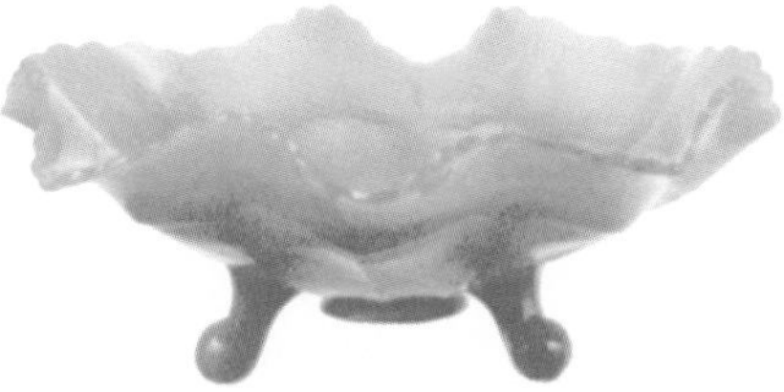
11" 3-ftd Stag & Holly Bowl

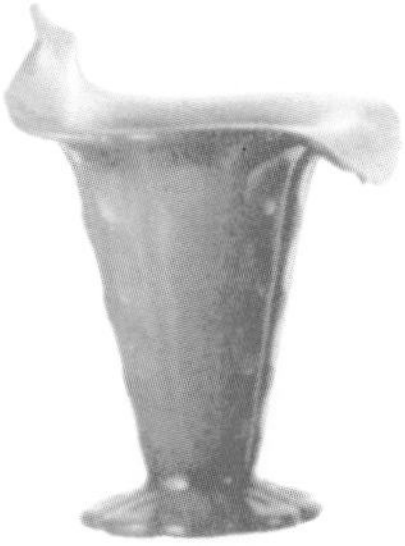
107-6 1/2" Tulip Vase

#574-6" Crimped
Vase or Bonbon

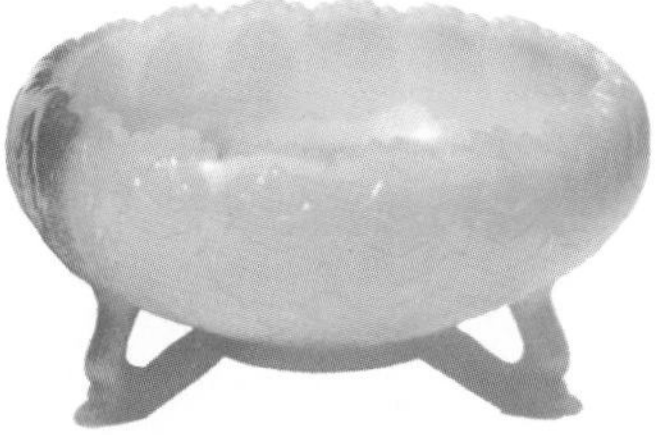
#1790-8" Cupped Bowl
"Leaf Tiers"

#1562 Square Bowl

#1554 Flower Pot
And Base

#316 Candlesticks

5 1/2" Fan Vase Flower Block

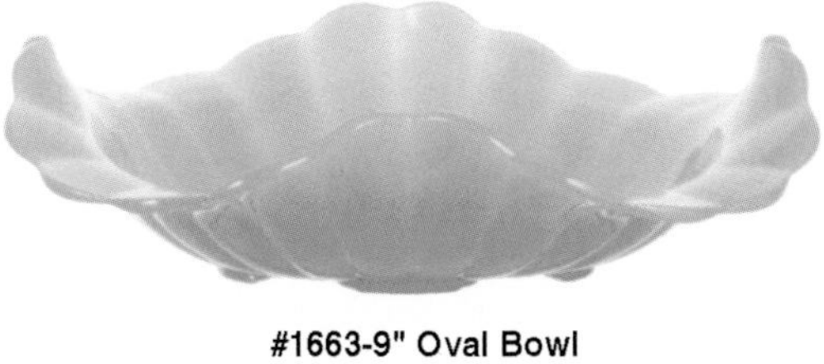
#1663-9" Oval Bowl

#231 Shallow Cupped Bowl

#3-3" Base

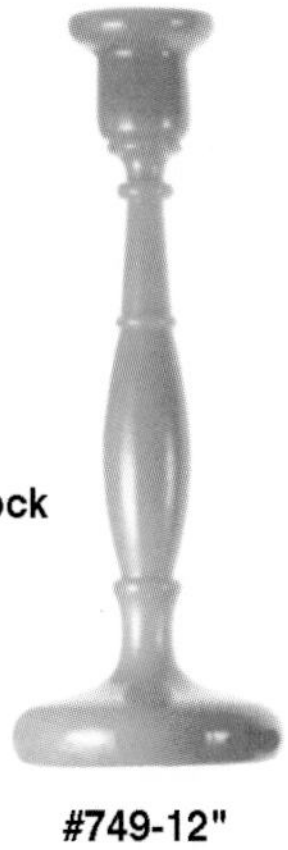
#749-12"
Candlestick

Item	Value	Date
Bowl, #857 – 10" crimped, ftd.	$47.00 – 57.00	1927
Bowl, #857 – 10" rolled rim	$45.00 – 50.00	1927
Bowl, #857 – 11" flared, ftd.	$50.00 – 55.00	1928
Bowl, #857 – 11" flared cupped	$52.00 – 57.00	1931
Bowl, #857 – 7" cupped footed	$52.00 – 57.00	1932
Bowl, #857 – 8" cupped footed	$52.00 – 57.00	1934
Bowl, #900 – 11" oval Dancing Ladies	$275.00 – 325.00	1932
Bowl, #917 – 10" special rolled rim	$75.00 – 95.00	1931
Bowl, #918 flared footed	$75.00 – 100.00	1924
Bowl, #950 – 11" tulip	$47.00 – 52.00	1934
Bowl, #950 – 12" flared, handled	$52.00 – 57.00	1933 – 1935
Bowl, #1093 – 6" deep crimp	$30.00 – 37.00	1935
Bowl, #1093 – 9" shallow crimped Basket Weave w/Open Edge	$47.00 – 55.00	1935
Bowl, #1235 – 5"	$12.00 – 15.00	1933
Bowl, #1237 – 10" crimped	$30.00 – 32.00	1931
Bowl, #1237 – 7" cupped, 3-ftd.	$20.00 – 25.00	1931
Bowl, #1245 – 5"	$12.00 – 15.00	1933
Bowl, #1502 finger Diamond Optic	$18.00 – 20.00	1928
Bowl, #1502 – 10" special roll rim Diamond Optic	$40.00 – 45.00	1928
Bowl, #1502 – 12" shallow cupped Diamond Optic	$40.00 – 45.00	1928
Bowl, #1502 – 12" special roll rim Diamond Optic	$45.00 – 50.00	1928
Bowl, #1502 – 13" flared Diamond Optic	$45.00 – 50.00	1928
Bowl, #1502 – 14" special rolled rim Diamond Optic	$45.00 – 55.00	1928
Bowl, #1502 – A – 8" flared cupped w/dolphins Diamond Optic	$55.00 – 60.00	1928
Bowl, #1504 – A – 9" cupped w/dolphins	$60.00 – 65.00	1928
Bowl, #1504 – A – 9" shallow cupped w/dolphins	$47.00 – 50.00	1928
Bowl, #1504 – A – 10" rolled rim or flared w/dolphins	$80.00 – 85.00	1928
Bowl, #1504 – A – 6" cupped w/dolphins	$35.00 – 37.00	1928 – 1934
Bowl, #1504 – A – 8½" rolled rim w/dolphins	$53.00 – 60.00	1928
Bowl, #1512 – 9" flared	$42.00 – 45.00	
Bowl, #1562 – 13" oval	$47.00 – 55.00	1931
Bowl, #1562 square	$47.00 – 55.00	1931
Bowl, #1563 – 14" square	$70.00 – 75.00	1931
Bowl, #1563 – 17" oval handled	$95.00 – 120.00	1931 – 1933
Bowl, #1600 – 10" rolled rim ftd. w/dolphins	$70.00 – 80.00	1929
Bowl, #1601 – 11" flared ftd. w/dolphins	$105.00 – 125.00	1928
Bowl, #1602 – 10¼" crimped w/dolphins	$90.00 – 100.00	1929
Bowl, #1608 – 10½" deep oval ftd. w/dolphins	$105.00 – 125.00	1929
Bowl, #1608 – 10" shallow or crimped Stag & Holly	$260.00 – 310.00	1929
Bowl, #1621 – 10" deep oval w/dolphins	$45.00 – 50.00	1928
Bowl, #1663 – 10½" tulip	$60.00 – 67.00	1935
Bowl, #1663 – 12" flared or tulip	$60.00 – 67.00	1933 – 1935
Bowl, #1663 – 12" regular	$60.00 – 67.00	1932
Bowl, #1663 – 9" oval	$45.00 – 50.00	1932
Bowl, #1790 – 8" cupped Leaf Tiers	$110.00 – 130.00	1935
Bowl, #1933 – 7" flared	$20.00 – 22.00	
Bowl, #2005 – 6½" shallow cupped	$20.00 – 22.00	1921
Bowl, #2006 – 7½" shallow cupped	$20.00 – 22.00	1924
Bowl, #2007 – 9" shallow cupped	$32.00 – 37.00	1924
Candelabra, #2318 – 6"	$45.00 – 55.00	1933
Candelabra, #2398	$32.00 – 37.00	1933 – 1935
Candle vase, #1673 – 8"	$42.00 – 47.00	1933
Candleholder, #848/1234 – 3-ftd.	$12.00 – 15.00	1933 – 1936
Candlestick, #249 – 6"	$22.00 – 27.00	

Catalog Reprints Circa 1931 Courtesy Of: The Fenton Art Glass Museum

JADE GREEN
THE FENTON ART GLASS CO.
WILLIAMSTOWN, W.VA.
622-8" Flared Vase & Base.
918-12" Flared Footed Bowl.
736-1 lb. Candy Jar.
260-6½" Footed Comport.
917-10" Special Roll Rim Footed Bowl.
923-Mayonnaise And Ladle.
231-10" Shallow Cup. Footed Bowl.
317-10" Handled Sandwich Tray.
943 Covered Bon Bon.
743-Covered Puff Box.
314 C. Stick.
846-Special Roll Rim Bowl.
314 C. Stick.
66 Lemon Tray.
251-10" Bud Vase.
680-6¼" Bread & Butter or Ice Cream Plate.
758-9" Octagon Salad Plate.
354-8" Bud Vase.
No. 1 Jade Asst.
857-10" Fld. Cup. No. 1- Jade Asst.
316 Candlesticks. No. 1- Jade Asst.
857-11" Fld. No. 1- Jade Asst
1681-10½" Basket No. 1- Jade Asst.
1237-10" Crimp. No. 1. Jade Asst.
1504-A-10" Fld. No. 1- Jade Asst.
1608-10" Dup. Oval No. 1 Jade Asst.

Item	Value	Date
Candlestick, #314	$14.00 – 16.00	1931
Candlestick, #315 – 3½" princess	$20.00 – 22.00	
Candlestick, #316	$14.00 – 16.00	1931
Candlestick, #318	$14.00 – 16.00	1933 – 1935
Candlestick, #349 – 10"	$115.00 – 125.00	1924
Candlestick, #449 – 8½"	$95.00 – 105.00	1924
Candlestick, #549 – 8½"	$80.00 – 97.00	1924
Candlestick, #549 – 8½" w/moonstone base	$105.00 – 130.00	
Candlestick, #649 – 10"	$147.00 – 165.00	1924
Candlestick, #749 – 12"	$180.00 – 190.00	1924
Candlestick, #950 cornucopia	$40.00 – 50.00	1932
Candlestick, #1091 Basket Weave w/Open Edge	$50.00 – 55.00	1936
Candlestick, #1623 w/dolphins	$22.00 – 27.00	1928
Candlestick, #1672 flared or rolled edge	$20.00 – 22.00	1931
Candlestick, #2000 – 5½" double branch	$45.00 – 60.00	1936
Candy jar, #735, ½ lb.	$45.00 – 50.00	
Candy jar, #736, 1 lb.	$55.00 – 65.00	1931
Candy jar, #835, ½ lb.	$45.00 – 50.00	1931 – 1932
Candy jar, #844, 1 lb. w/flower finial	$270.00 – 300.00	1931 – 1932
Candy jar, #1532, ½ lb. w/dolphins	$75.00 – 90.00	
Cheese comport and underplate, #316	$42.00 – 47.00	
Cigarette box, #308	$80.00 – 90.00	1934
Cigarette holder, #556	$85.00 – 95.00	
Coaster, #1590 – 4"	$12.00 – 14.00	1931 – 1933
Cologne, #53 – 5"	$140.00 – 165.00	1931
Cologne, #55	$200.00 – 225.00	1924
Cologne , #59	$200.00 – 225.00	1929
Comport, #260 high ftd.	$45.00 – 50.00	1923
Comport, #260 – 7" tall footed	$45.00 – 50.00	1931
Comport, #312 – 7" cupped, low footed	$25.00 – 27.00	
Comport, #643 – 6¾" salver	$22.00 – 27.00	
Comport, #712 – 7" cupped footed	$25.00 – 30.00	
Comport, #737 flared cupped	$25.00 – 27.00	1934
Comport, #1502 cheese & cracker Diamond Optic	$50.00 – 55.00	1928
Comport, #1533 – 7" oval w/dolphins	$45.00 – 50.00	1931 – 1934
Comport, #1536	$27.00 – 32.00	1928
Creamer, #3	$20.00 – 25.00	
Creamer, #100 Wide Rib	$20.00 – 25.00	1930
Creamer, #1502 Diamond Optic	$22.00 – 27.00	1927
Creamer, #1639 Elizabeth	$50.00 – 55.00	1930
Cup, #31	$9.00 – 10.00	1931
Cup, #1502 Diamond Optic	$10.00 – 12.00	1927
Dog, #307 novelty	$42.00 – 47.00	1933
Fish, #306 novelty	$37.00 – 47.00	1933
Flower block, #2	$15.00 – 18.00	1933
Flower block, #1234/1645 for nymph figure	$15.00 – 18.00	1931 – 1934
Flower block, #1564 turtle	$75.00 – 85.00	1929
Flower block for fan vase	$25.00 – 32.00	
Flower bowl, #1618 elephant	$450.00 – 500.00	1928
Flower pot, #1554 w/underplate	$60.00 – 75.00	1932 – 1933
Flower pot, #1555 w/underplate	$75.00 – 95.00	1931 – 1932
*Ginger jar and lid, #893	$210.00 – 250.00	1933 – 1935
Goblet, #139	$10.00 – 12.00	1931
Goblet, #1502 – 11 oz. bridge Diamond Optic	$18.00 – 22.00	1928
decorated	$400.00 – 500.00	

Item	Value	Date
Goblet, #1502 – 9 oz. bridge Diamond Optic	$18.00 – 22.00	1928
Goblet, #1502 Hi ftd. Diamond Optic	$22.00 – 27.00	1928
Ice jar, #1615 (flower pot w/handles) Diamond Optic	N.D.	1932
Ice pack, #1614 Diamond Optic	$45.00 – 55.00	1928
Ice tub, #1502 – 4" Diamond Optic	$27.00 – 30.00	1928
Jar, #60 smelling salts	$185.00 – 200.00	1926
Jug, #1639 batter w/lid black/jade combo Elizabeth	$190.00 – 225.00	1931 – 1932
Jug #1639 batter w/lid Elizabeth	$190.00 – 225.00	1931
Jug, #1639 syrup w/lid Elizabeth	$150.00 – 175.00	1931
Jug, #1639 – 3 pint Elizabeth	$150.00 – 175.00	1931
Jug, 6" ftd.	$125.00 – 175.00	
Lamp, #1502 Diamond Optic	$110.00 – 145.00	1928
Macaroon jar, #1681 – 7" Big Cookies	$120.00 – 145.00	1931 – 1934
Macaroon jar, #1684 – 6½"	$90.00 – 105.00	1931
Mayonnaise, #109	$27.00 – 32.00	1924
Mayonnaise, #2005	$27.00 – 32.00	1924
Mayonnaise & ladle, #923	$37.00 – 45.00	1931
Mint jar and cover, #1639 Elizabeth	$175.00 – 200.00	
Night set, #1502 – 2-pc. Diamond Optic	$190.00 – 225.00	1928
Nymph, #1645 September Morn	$170.00 – 200.00	1931 – 1934
Pitcher, #100 Wide Rib	$100.00 – 130.00	1933
Pitcher, #219	$85.00 – 90.00	1933
Pitcher, #1635 w/#1702 cut Diamond Optic	$125.00 – 150.00	1930
Pitcher, #1636 Diamond Optic	$135.00 – 160.00	1928
Plate, #103 – 6"	$7.00 – 9.00	1924
Plate, #175 – 11½" Leaf	$65.00 – 70.00	1936
Plate, #175 – 8" Leaf	$32.00 – 35.00	1934
Plate, #1790 – 12" Leaf Tiers	$90.00 – 110.00	1935
Plate, #2006 – 8"	$8.00 – 10.00	1924
Plate, #2007 – 11"	$30.00 – 35.00	1924
Plate, #301 – 6"	$7.00 – 8.00	1924
Plate, #607	$7.00 – 8.00	1924
Plate, #638	$7.00 – 8.00	1924
Plate, #680 – 6"	$7.00 – 8.00	1927
Plate, #681 – 8"	$7.00 – 8.00	1927
Plate, #682 – 9"	$12.00 – 14.00	
Plate, #758 – 8½" octagonal	$12.00 – 14.00	1931
Plate, #1006	$8.00 – 10.00	1924
Plate, #1043 – 8½" comport	$22.00 – 27.00	1927
Plate, #1502 w/indent for cheese comport Diamond Optic	$12.00 – 14.00	1927
Plate, #1502 – 6" octagonal Diamond Optic	$7.00 – 9.00	1927
Plate, #1502 – 8" octagonal Diamond Optic	$12.00 – 14.00	1927
Plate, #1639 – 12" 2-handled Elizabeth	$45.00 – 55.00	1931 – 33
Plate, #1639 – 6" Elizabeth	$8.00 – 10.00	1931
Plate, #1639 – 8" Elizabeth	$12.00 – 14.00	1931
Puff box, #53	$30.00 – 35.00	
Puff box, #57	$48.00 – 55.00	
Puff box, #61	$30.00 – 35.00	1931
Puff box, #743 covered	$55.00 – 60.00	1931
Puff box, #1229	$30.00 – 40.00	1932 – 1933
Reamer, #1619 w/handled jug	$1000.00 – 1200.00	1933
Refrigerator dish, #457 rectangular w/lid	$45.00 – 50.00	1934
Refrigerator set, #1502 3-pc. Diamond Optic	$110.00 – 135.00	1928
Rose bowl, #847 – 5"	$22.00 – 27.00	

Item	Value	Date
Salver, #647 – 13" ftd.	$45.00 – 55.00	1924
Salver, #2005	$37.00 – 42.00	1924
Shaker, #1502 Diamond Optic	$58.00 – 66.00	1928
Shaving mug, W-111, 112, 113	$35.00 – 45.00	1933
Sherbet, #1639 Elizabeth	$40.00 – 45.00	1931
Strawberry jar	$165.00 – 185.00	
Sugar, #3	$20.00 – 25.00	
Sugar, #1502 Diamond Optic	$22.00 – 27.00	1931
Sugar, #1639 – 3½" Elizabeth	$45.00 – 55.00	1931
Sugar & lid , #100 Wide Rib	$27.00 – 37.00	1930
Tray, #23	$22.00 – 27.00	1931 – 33
Tray, #66 center handle lemon	$27.00 – 32.00	1926
Tray, #317 – 10" handled sandwich	$37.00 – 42.00	1931
Tray, #53 vanity set	$30.00 – 35.00	1927
Tray, #1561 – 10" oval handled	$30.00 – 35.00	
Tray, #1639 , batter set Elizabeth	$47.00 – 57.00	1931
Tumbler, #100 Wide Rib	$20.00 – 25.00	1931
Tumbler, #1502 – 5 oz. orange juice Diamond Optic	$15.00 – 16.00	1928
Tumbler, #1502 – 9 oz. ftd. Diamond Optic	$15.00 – 17.00	1928
Tumbler, #1634	$12.00 – 14.00	1930
Tumbler, #1634 w/#1702 cut Diamond Optic	$14.00 – 16.00	1930
Tumbler, #1635 – 10 oz.	$20.00 – 25.00	1930
Tumbler, #1635 – 10 oz. w/#1702 cut Diamond Optic	$20.00 – 25.00	1930
Tumbler, #1636 ice tea	$24.00 – 30.00	1930
Tumbler, #1639 ftd. Elizabeth	$65.00 – 70.00	1931
Tumbler, #1641 – 11 oz.	$15.00 – 17.00	1928
Underplate, #1502 finger bowl Diamond Optic	$7.00 – 9.00	1928
Urn, #901 – 12" covered Dancing Ladies	$800.00 – 1000.00	1933
Urn, #901 – 7" covered Dancing Ladies	$450.00 – 550.00	1933
Urn lamp, #901 – 18" Dancing Ladies	$3500.00+	
Vanity set, #53, 4-pc.	$340.00 – 400.00	1927
Vase, #32	$25.00 – 30.00	1932
Vase, #107 tulip-6½"	$27.00 – 32.00	1932 – 1933
Vase, #183 – 10" tulip, triangle, flared, square, special	$37.00 – 48.00	1931
Vase, #184 – 10"	$50.00 – 60.00	1933 – 1936
Vase, #184 – 12"	$60.00 – 70.00	1931 – 1935
Vase, #184 – 12" w/cutting	$100.00 – 125.00	1933
Vase, #184 – 6"	$35.00 – 40.00	1934
Vase, #184 – 8"	$42.00 – 47.00	1931
Vase, #251 – 10" bud	$22.00 – 27.00	1931
Vase, #251 – 12" bud	$27.00 – 30.00	1922
Vase, #252 bud	$22.00 – 27.00	1931
Vase, #349 oval	$48.00 – 55.00	1932
Vase, #354 – 8" bud	$22.00 – 27.00	1932
Vase, #611 – 6½" cupped	$25.00 – 28.00	
Vase, #612 – 6½" flared	$25.00 – 28.00	1933
Vase, #621 – 6"	$25.00 – 27.00	1933 – 1935
Vase, #621 – 8" flared, cupped or square top	$27.00 – 32.00	1933
Vase, #622 – 7½" flared	$25.00 – 28.00	
Vase, #835 – 6" crimped	$27.00 – 30.00	1931
Vase, #847 – 6½" crimped	$27.00 – 32.00	1931
Vase, #847 – 6" fan	$27.00 – 32.00	1931
Vase, #857 – 8" flared	$32.00 – 35.00	1934 – 1935

Item	Value	Date
Vase, #857 – 8" fan	$40.00 – 45.00	1934
Vase, #888 – 10"	$150.00 – 200.00	
Vase, #897	$45.00 – 55.00	1933
Vase, #898 – 11½"	$55.00 – 60.00	1933 – 1934
Vase, #901 – 5" (handled urn base) Dancing Ladies	$150.00 – 190.00	1933
Vase, #901 – 9" crimped Dancing Ladies	$600.00 – 650.00	1933 – 1935
Vase, #901 – 9" flared Dancing Ladies	$600.00 – 650.00	1932 – 1933
Vase, #901 – 9" square Dancing Ladies	$600.00 – 700.00	1933
Vase, #1502 – 5" fan w/dolphins Diamond Optic	$32.00 – 37.00	1928
Vase, #1502 – 6" fan w/dolphins Diamond Optic	$37.00 – 42.00	1928
Vase, #1502 – 8½" flared Diamond Optic	$45.00 – 50.00	1928
Vase, #1504 – A-6" cupped w/dolphins	$35.00 – 40.00	1931
Vase, #1530 – 12"	$85.00 – 95.00	
Vase, #1531 – 16"	$90.00 – 120.00	1931 – 1934
Vase, #1533 – 6½" square w/dolphins	$35.00 – 40.00	1931
Vase, #1533 – A-6" fan w/dolphins	$37.00 – 42.00	1931
Vase, #1561 – 10" reg., crimped or flared Apple Tree	$170.00 – 200.00	1933
Vase, #1681 – 9" flared	$42.00 – 47.00	1933 – 1935

#1636 Ice Tea

#1636 Pitcher

11" Compartment Plate

#100-6" Flared Bowl

#835-1/2 lb. Candy Jar

#1619 Flared Jug

#1504-A-6" Cupped Bowl

#1640-9 Oz. Bridge Goblet

LILAC

Lilac is a translucent lavender colored glassware that Fenton produced for a short time in about 1933. Pieces in this color are both elusive and desirable. Many of the items have dolphin handles. Some items, such as the Elizabeth pieces, the bathroom set, and the colognes and puff boxes, are often found combined with lids or stoppers of other colors. Favorite combinations used with lilac were jade green, black, or moonstone.

Item	Value	Date
Basket, #1681 – 10½" Big Cookies	$270.00 – 300.00	1933
Basket, #1684 w/wicker handle	$250.00 – 290.00	1933
*Bathroom set, #16 – 17 – 54, 4-pc.	$220.00 – 250.00	1933
*Batter set, #1639 batter jug/syrup/tray Elizabeth	$575.00 – 700.00	1933
Bonbon, #1621/#1702 cut-6½" crimped, flared, square	$35.00 – 42.00	1933
Bowl, #848 – 6" cupped	$65.00 – 85.00	1932
Bowl, #848 – 8½" flared	$75.00 – 90.00	1933
Bowl, #857 – 10" crimped, ftd.	$80.00 – 85.00	
Bowl, #857 – 8" cupped, footed	$52.00 – 57.00	
Bowl, #1504 – A-9" cupped w/dolphins	$100.00 – 120.00	1933
Bowl, #1504 – A-6" cupped w/dolphins	$50.00 – 55.00	1933
Bowl, #1562 – 13" oval	$80.00 – 85.00	1933
Bowl, #1608 – 10½" deep oval ftd. w/dolphins	$160.00 – 175.00	1933
Bowl, #1676, 11½" flared	$150.00 – 165.00	1933
Candelabra, #2318 – 6"	$65.00 – 75.00	1933
Candlestick, #1672 flared or rolled edge	$67.00 – 73.00	1933
Candy jar, #844-1 lb. w/flower finial	$450.00 – 550.00	
*Cologne, #53 – 5"	$200.00 – 225.00	1933
Comport, #1536	$115.00 – 130.00	1933
Flower block, #2	$55.00 – 60.00	1933
Flower pot, #1554 w/underplate	$130.00 – 150.00	1933
Flower pot, #1555 w/underplate	$130.00 – 150.00	1933
Jug, #1639 batter w/lid Elizabeth	$300.00 – 350.00	1933
Jug, #1639 syrup w/lid Elizabeth	$200.00 – 250.00	1933
Macaroon jar, #1681 – 7" Big Cookies	$550.00 – 600.00	1933
Macaroon jar, #1684 – 6½"	$650.00 – 700.00	1933
Nymph, #1645 September Morn	$750.00 – 850.00	1933
*Puff box, #53	$75.00 – 95.00	1933
*Puff box, 4¾"	$75.00 – 95.00	1933
Tray, #1639 , batter set Elizabeth	$75.00 – 90.00	1933
Tray, #53 vanity	$45.00 – 50.00	1933
**Tumbler, #1639 ftd. Elizabeth	$70.00 – 75.00	1933
*Vanity set, #53 4-pc.	$520.00 – 595.00	1933
Vase, #847 – 6" fan	$50.00 – 55.00	1932
Vase, #857 – 8" fan	$65.00 – 75.00	1933
Vase, #894, bottle shape	$150.00 – 200.00	

**May have jade green, black or moonstone lids or stoppers*
***Has a moonstone foot*

#1684-6 1/2" Macaroon Jar

#844-1 lb. Candy

#848 Flared Bowl &
#1645 Nymph Figure

#857-8" Fan Vase

#857-10" Crimped Bowl

#848 Cupped Bowl &
5-legged Base

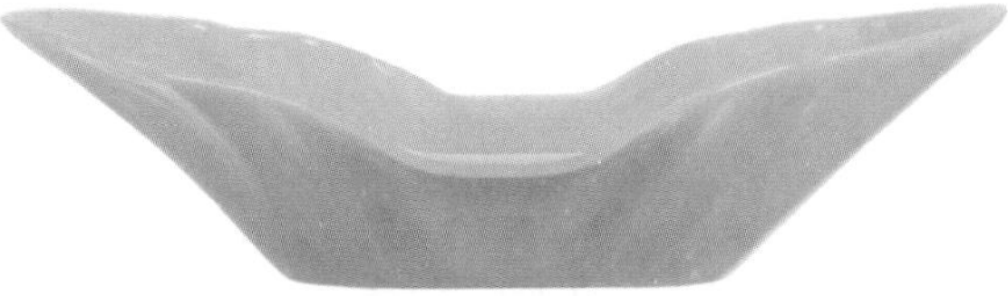
#1562-2-14" Oval Bowl

4 3/4" Puff Box

#53 Cologne

#53 Puff Box

#16 & 17 Bathroom Jars
on Diamond Optic Rectangular Tray

#1639-3 Pint Covered Jug

#1639-4 3/4" Covered Jug

#2318 Candelabra

#1554 Flower Pot & Base

#1536-6" Comport

#847-6" Fan Vase

#1608-10 1/2" Dolphin Handle
Deep Oval Bowl

#1681-7" Macaroon Jar
"Big Cookies"

MANDARIN RED & VENETIAN RED

Mandarin red and Venetian red are both deep red colored opaque glassware. Although they were made at different times, they are both included in this section because the formula used to produce these two colors was the same. The listing and price guide below will separate the two periods of production.

Venetian red was made from about 1924 through 1927. Many of the same shapes found in stretch glass were also made in Venetian red. A few pattern glass pieces such as the Grape and Cable bowl, the Flowering Dill vase, and the Lotus and Grape bonbon may also be found in this early color.

Mandarin red was made from 1933 through 1935. The difference in appearance between the two colors is the marbling effect in the Mandarin red color. This effect is a result of the way the molten glass is gathered when a piece is being made. To achieve the marbled appearance, the gatherer simply does not clean the excess glass from his punty when he gathers molten glass for a new piece. The difference in temperature of the old glass and the new glass produces different shades of red glass which are spread throughout the piece when the glass is pressed in a mold.

Mandarin red pieces causing the greatest excitement among collectors include the Mikado comports and the Dancing Ladies vases. The ginger jar is especially nice when found with a gold decoration. In addition to the design pictured, it may also be found with a gold dragon decoration similar to the one shown on the Jade ginger jar in the Jade photo. Some pieces which were produced over a long period of time like the #549 – 8½" candles and the Grape and Cable bowls may be found in both Venetian red and Mandarin red.

In honor of the American Bicentennial, the Mandarin red formula was revived in 1975 to produce a color Fenton called Patriot red. Bicentennial pieces produced in this color include the #8476 Jefferson covered comport, the #8446 stein, the #8467 patriot's bell, the #9418 eagle plate, and the #8470 eagle paperweights.

Item – Mandarin Red	Value	Date
Ashtray, #308	$50.00 – 60.00	
Basket, #1681 – 10½" Big Cookies	$120.00 – 150.00	1933 – 1935
Basket, #1684 w/wicker handle	$125.00 – 155.00	1933 – 1935
Bonbon, #1093 – 5¾"	$125.00 – 150.00	
Bowl, #535 cupped lily	$45.00 – 50.00	
Bowl, #601 – 10" shallow cupped	$80.00 – 95.00	1933
Bowl, #647 – 10¾" flared cupped	$80.00 – 95.00	1933
Bowl, #846 – 6" cupped	$50.00 – 55.00	1933
Bowl, #846 – 8½" flared cupped	$62.00 – 67.00	1933 – 1935
Bowl, #846 – 8½" flared or cupped	$62.00 – 67.00	1933 – 1935
Bowl, #846 – 9¼" deep fruit	$95.00 – 115.00	1933
Bowl, #846 – 9" crimped	$90.00 – 105.00	1934
Bowl, #847 – 6" crimped	$50.00 – 55.00	1934
Bowl, #847 – 6" cupped	$50.00 – 55.00	1933
Bowl, #847 – 7½" flared ftd.	$60.00 – 65.00	1934
Bowl, #848 cupped or flared	$150.00 – 200.00	
Bowl, #857 – 11" flared or flared cupped	$80.00 – 95.00	1935
Bowl, #919 – 7" ftd. Mikado orange bowl (comport)	$300.00 – 350.00	1934
Bowl, #920 – 10" crimped Grape & Cable	$210.00 – 250.00	1933
Bowl, #950 – 11" tulip	$90.00 – 115.00	1935
Bowl, #1093 – 8" shallow Basket Weave w/Open Edge	$125.00 – 150.00	1934
Bowl, #1663 – 12" flared or tulip	$80.00 – 95.00	1932
Bowl, #1663 – 12" Reg.	$85.00 – 95.00	1932
Bowl, #1790 – 8" cupped Leaf Tiers	$150.00 – 185.00	1935
Bowl, #2007 – 9" shallow cupped	$80.00 – 85.00	1933
Cake plate, #919 high ftd. Mikado	$350.00 – 400.00	1934
Cake plate, #1790 – 10¼"-12" Leaf Tiers	$150.00 – 200.00	1934
Candlestick, #318	$42.00 – 47.00	1933 – 1934
Candlestick, #950 cornucopia	$47.00 – 52.00	1934
Candy, #735	$250.00 – 300.00	
Cigarette box, #308	$175.00 – 200.00	
Comport, #737 – 6½" cupped	$55.00 – 65.00	
Compote, Hi-Standard	$205.00 – 250.00	
Ginger jar and lid, #893	$190.00 – 225.00	1933
Macaroon jar, #1681 – 7" Big Cookies	$220.00 – 285.00	1933
Macaroon jar, #1684 – 6½"	$225.00 – 275.00	1933 – 1935
Pipe ashtray with advertising on bottom	$145.00 – 160.00	1933
Nymph, #1645 September Morn	$300.00 – 350.00	1933

#1684-9" Basket

#893 Ginger Jar

#1681-10 1/2" Basket "Big Cookies"

#1684-6 1/2" Macaroon Jar

#621-6" Flared Vase

#846-9" Crimped Fruit Bowl

#1663-12" Flared Bowl

#847-6" Flared Crimped Vase

#621-8" Flared Vase

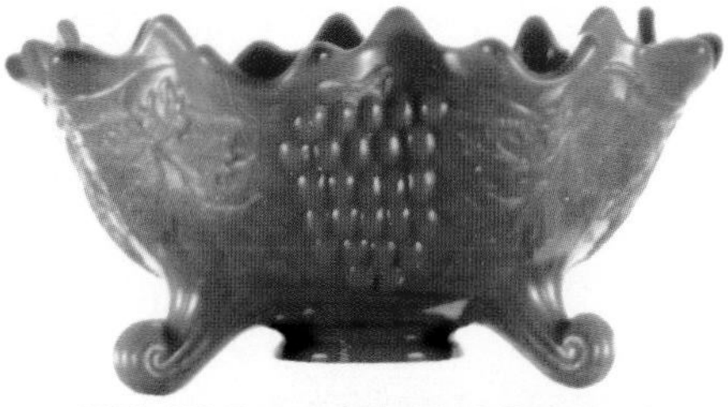
#920-11" Grape & Cable 3-Ftd. Bowl

#180 Hyacinth Vase

10 1/4" Flared High Standard Comport

#318 Candlestick

#549-8 1/2" Candlestick

#735-1/2 lb. Candy Jar

#184-12" Vase

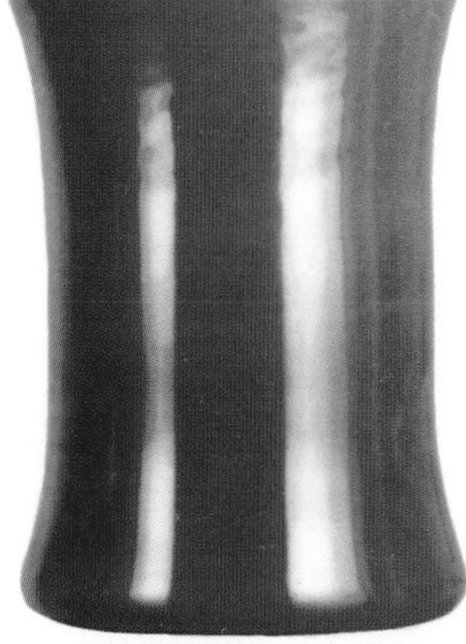
10" Wide Straight Vase

#888-10" Vase

#251-12" Bud Vase

Item – Mandarin Red	Value	Date
Vase, #180 Hyacinth	$300.00 – 350.00	1935
Vase, #184 – 10"	$125.00 – 135.00	1933 – 1934
Vase, #184 – 12"	$140.00 – 170.00	1933 – 1934
Vase, #184 – 8"	$85.00 – 95.00	1933
Vase,, #200 – 7"	$80.00 – 90.00	
Vase, #251 – 10" bud	$47.00 – 52.00	1933
Vase, #251 – 12" bud	$57.00 – 67.00	1933
Vase, #621 – 6"	$57.00 – 67.00	1932 – 1933
Vase, #621 – 8" flared, cupped or square top	$75.00 – 85.00	1932 – 1933
Vase, #791 – 8" Peacock flared or cupped	$280.00 – 325.00	1934
Vase, #791 – 10" Peacock	$390.00 – 420.00	
Vase, #847 – 6½" crimped	$55.00 – 60.00	1935
Vase, #847 – 6" fan	$50.00 – 55.00	1935
Vase, #857 – 8" fan	$70.00 – 85.00	1933 – 1934
Vase, #888 – 10"	$350.00 – 400.00	1933
Vase, #891 – 12"	$100.00 – 110.00	1933
Vase, #901 – 9" crimped Dancing Ladies	$500.00 – 550.00	1934
Vase, #901 – 8½" cupped Dancing Ladies	$550.00 – 590.00	1934
Vase, #901 – 9" fan Dancing Ladies	$550.00 – 600.00	1934
Vase, #901 – 9" flared Dancing Ladies	$500.00 – 550.00	1934
Vase, #901 – 9" square Dancing Ladies	$500.00 – 550.00	1934
Vase, #1093 – 5½" flared Basket Weave w/Open Edge	$150.00 – 200.00	1933
Vase, #1502 – 10" Diamond Optic	$100.00 – 120.00	1933
Vase, #1668 – 8" flip	$120.00 – 135.00	1935
Vase 10"wide straight	$450.00 – 500.00	

#791-8" Flared Vase "Peacock"

#919-10" Comport Mikado

6" Deep Flared Bon-bon Flowering Dill

6" 2-Handled Bon-bon Lotus and Grape

5 1/2" Flared Vase "Basket Weave w/Open Edge"

#1790-8" 3-Ftd. Cupped Bowl Leaf Tiers

#847-5 1/2" Fan Vase

#901-9" Fan Vase "Dancing Ladies"

#1790-10 1/4" 3-Ftd. Plate Leaf Tiers

#1681-7" Macaroon Jar "Big Cookies"

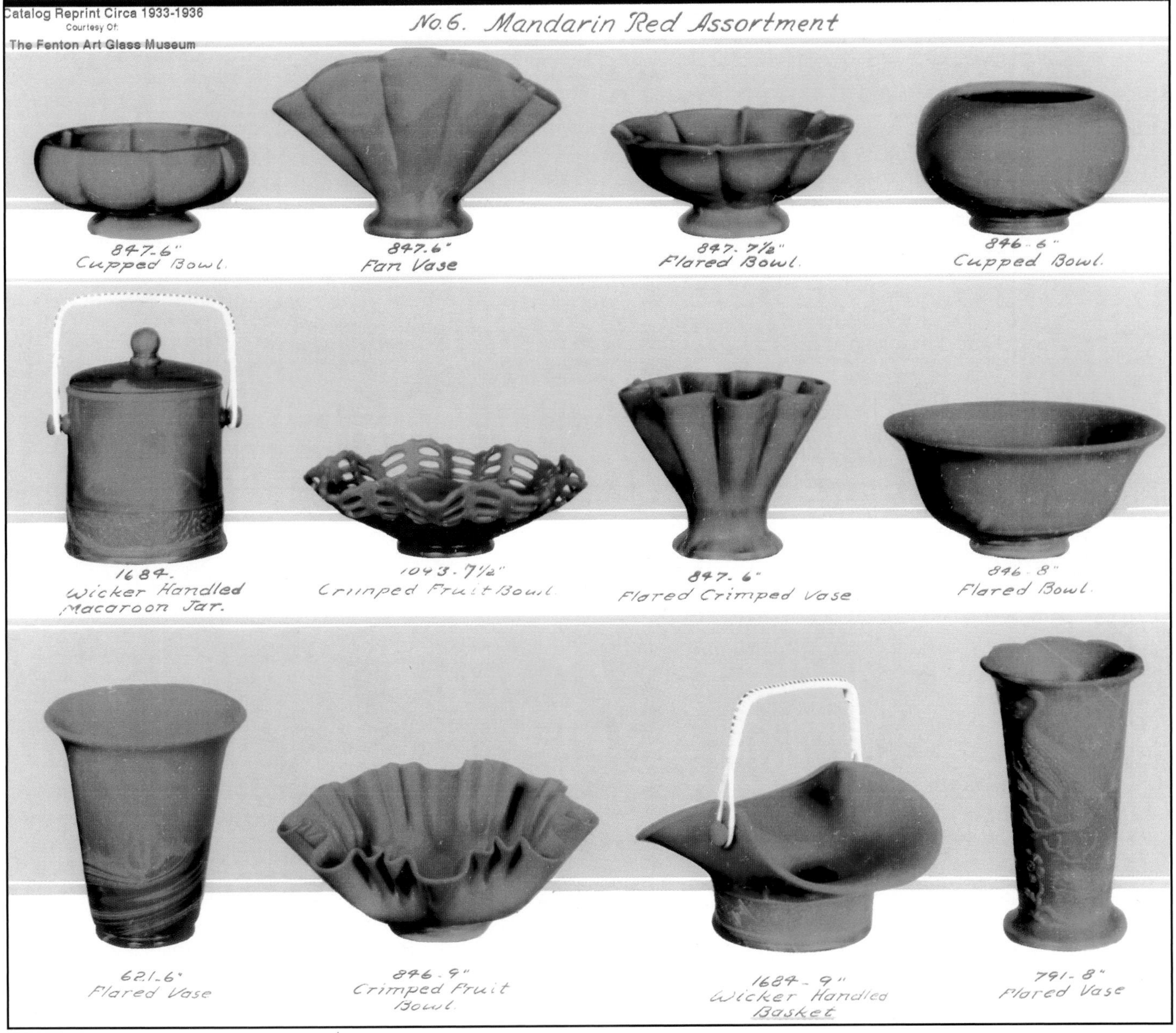
Catalog Reprint Circa 1933-1936
Courtesy Of:
The Fenton Art Glass Museum
No. 6. Mandarin Red Assortment
847-6" Cupped Bowl.
847.6" Fan Vase
847. 7½" Flared Bowl.
846-6" Cupped Bowl.
1684. Wicker Handled Macaroon Jar.
1043. 7½" Crimped Fruit Bowl.
847. 6" Flared Crimped Vase
846-8" Flared Bowl.
621-6" Flared Vase
846-9" Crimped Fruit Bowl.
1684-9" Wicker Handled Basket
791-8" Flared Vase

Item – Venetian Red	Value	Date
Ashtray, #1566	$67.00 – 85.00	1927
Bonbon, #643 open, cupped	$30.00 – 35.00	1925
Bonbon, #643 – 5" covered	$100.00 – 125.00	1924
Bonbon, 6" 2-handled Lotus & Grape	$130.00 – 150.00	
Bowl, #543 lily	$30.00 – 35.00	1924
Bowl, #547 lily	$30.00 – 35.00	1924
Bowl, #600 – 7" cupped	$40.00 – 45.00	1924
Bowl, #600 – 8" flared	$45.00 – 55.00	1924
Bowl, #601 – 10" shallow cupped	$65.00 – 75.00	1924
Bowl, #606 cupped	$42.00 – 47.00	1924
Bowl, #607 – 8" cupped	$50.00 – 60.00	1924
Bowl, #607 – 8" rolled rim	$50.00 – 60.00	1924
Bowl, #607 – 9" shallow, cupped	$55.00 – 65.00	1924
Bowl, #638 – 8" shallow cupped	$50.00 – 60.00	1924 – 1925
Bowl, #640 – 7½" rolled rim	$37.00 – 40.00	1924 – 1926
Bowl, #640 – 7" flared or cupped	$42.00 – 47.00	1925
Bowl, #647 – 11½" shallow cupped	$55.00 – 65.00	1924
Bowl, #647 – 10¾" flared or cupped	$60.00 – 75.00	1926
Bowl, #647 – 11" rolled rim	$60.00 – 75.00	1924
Bowl, #846 – 8½" flared or cupped	$45.00 – 55.00	1926
Bowl, #920 – 11" flared or crimped Grape & Cable	$300.00 – 350.00	
Bowl, #2005 – 6½" shallow cupped	$27.00 – 30.00	1926
Candlestick, #249 – 6"	$45.00 – 55.00	1924
Candlestick, #315 – 3½" princess	$40.00 – 47.00	1924 – 1925
Candlestick, #349 – 10"	$140.00 – 160.00	1924
Candlestick, #349 – 10" w/cutting	$165.00 – 180.00	1924
Candlestick, #449 – 8½"	$115.00 – 130.00	1924 – 1929
Candlestick, #549 – 8½"	$100.00 – 110.00	1924 – 1925
Candlestick, #649 – 10"	$200.00 – 250.00	1924
Candy jar, #8, ½ lb.	$110.00 – 130.00	1924
Candy jar, #636, 1 lb.	$95.00 – 100.00	1925
Candy jar, #735, ½ lb.	$80.00 – 95.00	1926
Lamp base, cut	$310.00 – 400.00	1926
Plate, #301 – 6"	$14.00 – 16.00	1924
Plate, #2007	$22.00 – 27.00	1924
Salver, #647 – 13" ftd.	$75.00 – 95.00	1924
Vase, #251 – 10" bud	$65.00 – 75.00	1924 – 1925
Vase, 6" deep Flowering Dill	$110.00 – 130.00	

#1093-5 3/4" Crimped Basket Weave w/Open Edge Bonbon

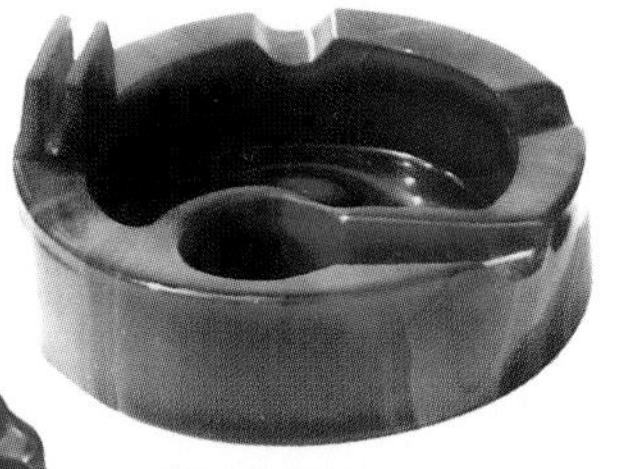

Pipe Ashtray

#950 Cornucopia Candlestick

#200-7" Vase

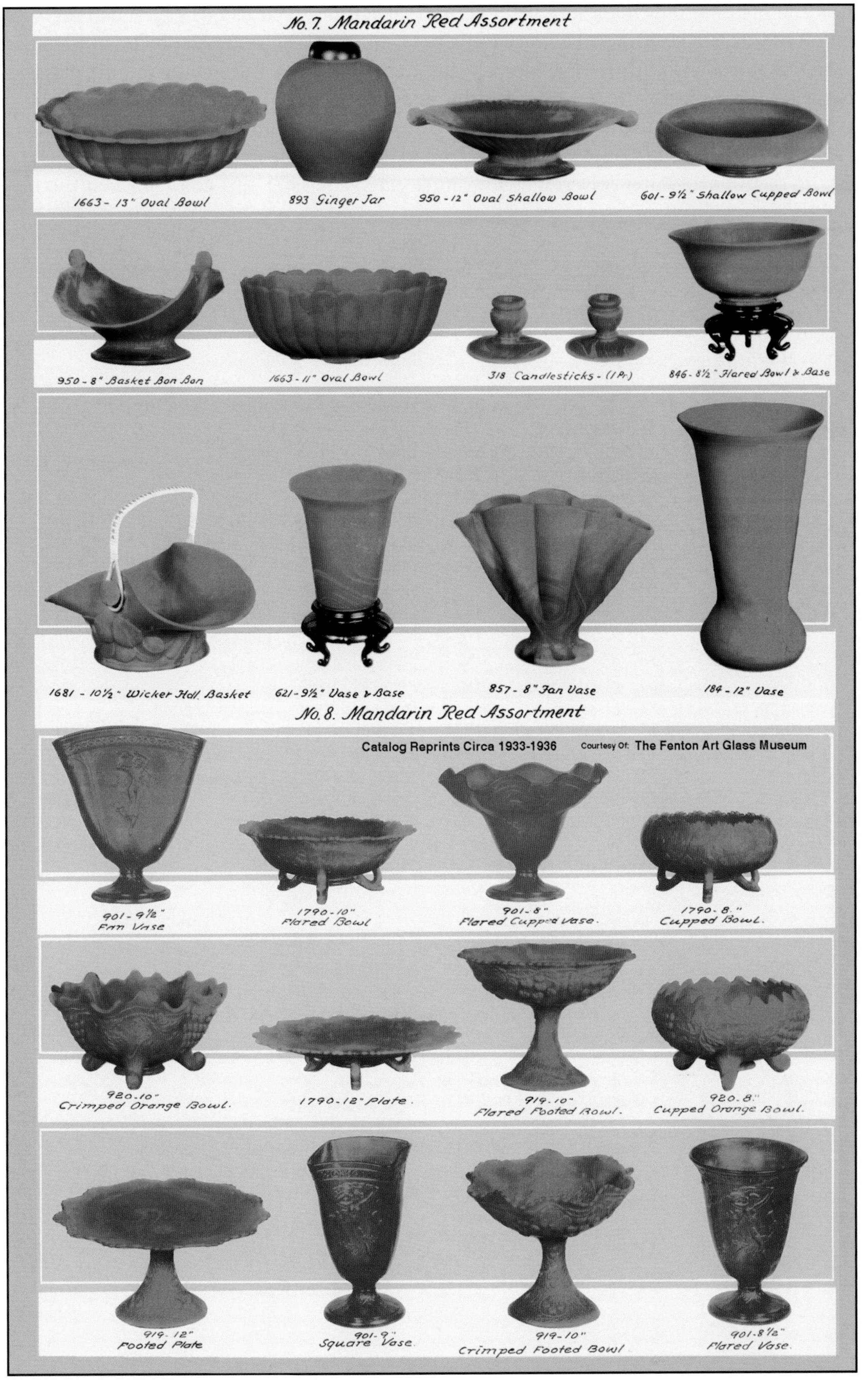
No. 7. Mandarin Red Assortment
1663 - 13" Oval Bowl
893 Ginger Jar
950 - 12" Oval Shallow Bowl
601 - 9½" Shallow Cupped Bowl
950 - 8" Basket Bon Bon
1663 - 11" Oval Bowl
318 Candlesticks - (1 Pr)
846 - 8½" Flared Bowl & Base
1681 - 10½" Wicker Hdl. Basket
621 - 9½" Vase & Base
857 - 8" Fan Vase
184 - 12" Vase
No. 8. Mandarin Red Assortment
Catalog Reprints Circa 1933-1936
Courtesy Of: The Fenton Art Glass Museum
901 - 9½" Fan Vase
1790 - 10" Flared Bowl
901 - 8" Flared Cupped Vase.
1790 - 8" Cupped Bowl.
920 - 10" Crimped Orange Bowl.
1790 - 12" Plate.
919 - 10" Flared Footed Bowl.
920 - 8" Cupped Orange Bowl.
919 - 12" Footed Plate
901 - 9" Square Vase.
919 - 10" Crimped Footed Bowl
901 - 8½" Flared Vase.

MILK GLASS

A few bowls and plates in milk glass appear on Fenton's inventory records in 1924. Then there appears to be a gap in production of this white opaque glassware until 1933. In 1933, the assortment shown in the catalog reprint on the next page was introduced. Also, some kitchenware items and bases were made in milk glass during the next few years. Carnival glass collectors may recognize the revival of some of the older molds for the production of milk glass items. Perhaps the economies forced on the company by the pressures of the Great Depression caused the Mikado, Milady, Lattice and Grape, and Apple Tree molds to be pressed into service to make new items. In 1938, some of the swan novelty items were made in milk glass, and later this color formed the backbone of the Hobnail line.

Item	Value	Date
Base, #1522	$13.00 – 16.00	1939
Base, #160	$13.00 – 16.00	1937
Base, #706 diamond-shaped	$42.00 – 52.00	
Base, #8	$13.00 – 16.00	1938
Bonbon, #1093 – 7" Basket Weave with Open Edge	$32.00 – 37.00	1934
Bonbon, #6 – 5½" crimped Swan	$45.00 – 50.00	1938
Bonbon, #6 – 5" square Swan	$45.00 – 50.00	1938
Bonbon, #6 – 6" flared Swan	$45.00 – 50.00	1938
Bowl, #456 – 1 mixing	$30.00 – 35.00	1936 – 38
Bowl, #456 – 2 mixing	$27.00 – 32.00	1936
Bowl, #456 – 3 mixing	$37.00 – 40.00	1936
Bowl, #601 – 10" shallow cupped	$27.00 – 32.00	1924
Bowl, #607 – 8" cupped	$22.00 – 27.00	1924
Bowl, #647 – 11½" shallow cupped	$35.00 – 40.00	1924
Bowl, #647 – 10¾" flared cupped	$37.00 – 42.00	1924
Bowl, #846 – 10½" oval fruit	$37.00 – 42.00	1933
Bowl, #846 – 10" square	$37.00 – 45.00	1933
Bowl, #846 – 10¼" crimped	$37.00 – 45.00	1933
Bowl, #846 – 9¼" deep fruit	$37.00 – 45.00	1933
Bowl, #847 – 7½" flared	$25.00 – 27.00	1933
Bowl, #848 – 6" cupped	$22.00 – 25.00	
Bowl, #848 – 8½" flared	$27.00 – 32.00	
Bowl, #900 – 11" oval Dancing Ladies	$130.00 – 160.00	1933
Bowl, #919 – 7" ftd. Mikado orange bowl (comport)	$150.00 – 175.00	1933 – 34
Bowl, #920 oval Grape & Cable	$90.00 – 100.00	1933 – 35
Bowl, #920 – 10" crimped Grape & Cable	$85.00 – 95.00	1933
Bowl, #920 – 9" cupped Grape & Cable	$75.00 – 85.00	1933
Bowl, #922 cupped Vintage	$42.00 – 45.00	1933
Bowl, #922 flared Vintage	$45.00 – 55.00	1933
Bowl, #930 orange	$65.00 – 75.00	1933
Bowl, #1091 – 4½" Basket weave with Open Edge	$20.00 – 22.00	1933
Bowl, #1092 – 5½" Basket Weave with Open Edge	$25.00 – 27.00	1933
Bowl, #1093 – 6½" flared cupped Basket Weave w/Open Edge	$32.00 – 36.00	1933
Bowl, #1093 – 8" shallow Basket Weave w/Open Edge	$42.00 – 47.00	1933
Bowl, #1093 – 9" shallow crimped Basket Weave w/Open Edge	$22.00 – 27.00	1933
Bowl, #1120 – 11" oval Thistle banana boat	$95.00 – 110.00	1934
Bowl, #1790 – 10" crimped Leaf Tiers	62.00 – 72.00	1933
Bowl, #1790 – 10" flared Leaf Tiers	$62.00 – 72.00	1934 – 36
Bowl, #1790 – 8" cupped Leaf Tiers	$67.00 – 75.00	1933
Candle, #1576	$18.00 – 20.00	1933 – 34
Candleholder, #6 Swan	$57.00 – 65.00	1938
Flower block, #1234 for nymph	$20.00 – 22.00	1933
Flower block, #1522	$9.00 – 11.00	1939
Ginger jar and lid, #893	$180.00 – 200.00	
Hurricane base, #170	$27.00 – 30.00	1939
Nymph, #1645 September Morn	$140.00 – 175.00	1939
Plate, #175 – 11½" Leaf	$40.00 – 45.00	1936
Plate, #175 – 8" Leaf	$22.00 – 25.00	1936
Plate, #1093 – 9" Basket Weave with Open Edge	$27.00 – 32.00	1933
Plate, #1790 – 12" Leaf Tiers	$150.00 – 175.00	1933
*Reamer, #1210 w/2-handled base	$75.00 – 80.00	1939
Salver, #647 – 13" ftd.	$40.00 – 45.00	1924
Shell, 3½ – 4½"	$9.00 – 11.00	1936
Swan, #4	$43.00 – 47.00	1938
Tumbler, #1561	$8.00 – 10.00	1933 – 34
Vase, #107 tulip – 6½"	$20.00 – 23.00	1933 – 35
Vase, #107 – 6½" cupped flared	$20.00 – 25.00	1933
Vase, #107 – 6½" flared	$27.00 – 30.00	1933
Vase, #791 – 10" flared cupped Peacock	$210.00 – 260.00	1934
Vase, #791 – 4" Peacock	$190.00 – 235.00	1933 – 34
Vase, #791 – 6" Peacock	$165.00 – 175.00	1933
Vase, #791 – 8" Peacock flared or cupped	$70.00 – 75.00	1933
Vase, #1093 – 5½" flared Basket Weave with Open Edge	$30.00 – 33.00	1933
Vase, #1110 – 11" flared; crimped Milady	$45.00 – 55.00	1935
Vase, #1561 – 10" reg., crimped or flared Apple Tree	$85.00 – 95.00	1933 – 36
Vase, #1563 – 11" flared Lattice & Grape	$85.00 – 95.00	1933 – 36
*with enameled decoration	$175.00 – 225.00	

#1790-8" Cupped Leaf Tiers Bowl

#1561-10" Apple Tree Vase

#1120-11" Oval Thistle Banana Boat

#1290-2-piece Reamer w/Enameled Teddy Bear and Balloons" Decoration

#1290-2-piece Reamer w/Enameled "Rabbit Playing Ball with Puppy" Decoration

#1290-2-piece Reamer w/ Enameled "Rabbit Dreaming About Carrot" Decoration

#1290-2-piece Reamer w/Enameled "Jack & Jill" Decoration

#922 Vintage Fern Dish

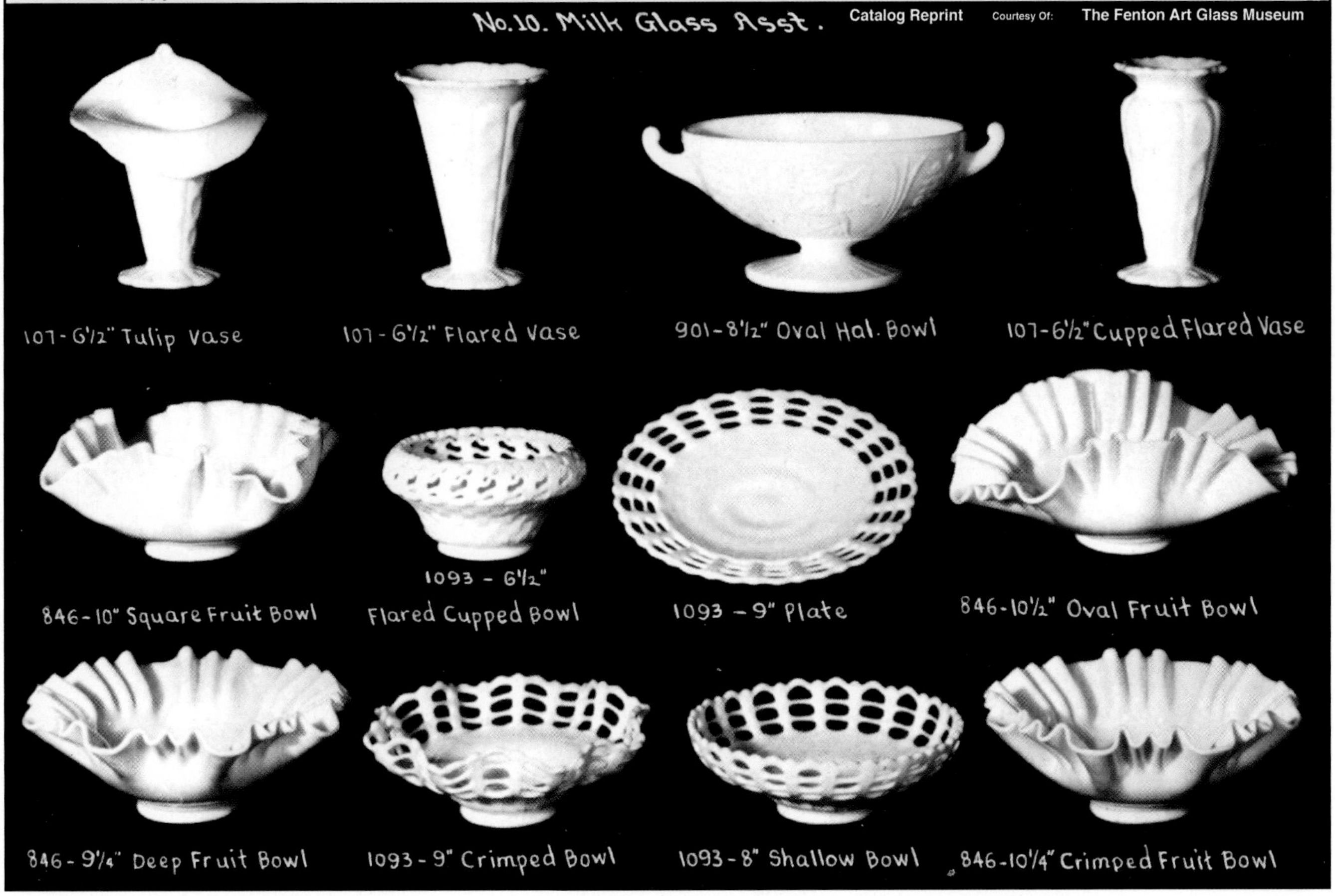
No.10. Milk Glass Asst.
107-6½" Tulip Vase
107-6½" Flared Vase
901-8½" Oval Hal. Bowl
107-6½" Cupped Flared Vase
846-10" Square Fruit Bowl
1093 - 6½" Flared Cupped Bowl
1093 - 9" Plate
846-10½" Oval Fruit Bowl
846-9¼" Deep Fruit Bowl
1093-9" Crimped Bowl
1093-8" Shallow Bowl
846-10¼" Crimped Fruit Bowl

Catalog Reprint Courtesy Of: The Fenton Art Glass Museum

MONGOLIAN GREEN

Mongolian green is an opaque dark blue-green colored glassware that is sometimes called slag glass by collectors. The color was made by Fenton in 1934 and 1935, and the marbleized effect is obtained by the same process as explained in the Mandarin red section.

The ginger jar and the Dancing Ladies vases are the star attractions in this color. The cigarette box and ashtray are elusive.

Item	Value	Date
Ashtray, #308 w/flower	$37.00 – 45.00	
Basket, #1684 w/wicker handle	$200.00 – 240.00	1935
Bonbon, #1093, 5¾"	$90.00 – 100.00	
Bowl, #600 – 7" cupped	$37.00 – 40.00	1935
Bowl, #600 – 8" flared	$45.00 – 55.00	1934
Bowl, #846 – 6" cupped	$37.00 – 42.00	1934
Bowl, #846 – 8½" flared or cupped	$47.00 – 55.00	1934
Bowl, #847 – 11" flared	$70.00 – 85.00	1934
Bowl, #847 – 6" crimped	$37.00 – 42.00	1934
Bowl, #847 – 6" cupped	$37.00 – 42.00	1934
Bowl, #847 – 7½" flared	$47.00 – 55.00	1935
Bowl, #847 – 7" shallow cupped	$47.00 – 55.00	1934
Bowl, #950 – oval	$85.00 – 105.00	
Candlestick, #950 cornucopia	$47.00 – 60.00	1934
Cigarette box, #308	$105.00 – 125.00	1934
Ginger jar and lid, #893	$220.00 – 250.00	1934 – 1935
Macaroon jar, #1684 – 6½"	$260.00 – 300.00	1935
Rose bowl, #847 – 5"	$47.00 – 55.00	1934
Vase, #602 – 10" flared	$110.00 – 150.00	1935
Vase, #621 – 6"	$42.00 – 45.00	1934 – 1935
Vase, #621 – 8" flared, cupped or square top	$52.00 – 55.00	1934 – 1935
Vase, #791 – 8" Peacock flared or cupped	$220.00 – 260.00	1935
Vase, #847 – 6½" crimped	$47.00 – 52.00	1935
Vase, #847 – 6" fan	$47.00 – 56.00	1935
Vase, #847 – 8½" crimped	$57.00 – 65.00	1934
Vase, #857 – 8" fan	$57.00 – 65.00	1935
Vase, #901 – 8½" cupped Dancing Ladies	$400.00 – 450.00	1934
Vase, #901 – 9" crimped Dancing Ladies	$400.00 – 450.00	1934
Vase, #901 – 9" flared Dancing Ladies	$450.00 – 500.00	1934
Vase, #901 – 9" Sq. Dancing Ladies	$450.00 – 550.00	1934
Vase, #1093, 5½" flared	$90.00 – 100.00	

#308 Ashtray w/Flower Back

#847-5" Rose Bowl

#950-11" Oval Tulip Bowl

#1684 Macaroon Jar

#1684-9 1/2" Basket

#847-5 1/2" Fan Vase

#847-8 1/2" Crimped Bowl

Photo Below: **Mongolian Green Catalog Reprint Composite Circa 1934-1935** Courtesy Of: **The Fenton Art Glass Museum**

#893 Ginger Jar

#901-9" Crimped Vase
Dancing Ladies

#901-8 1/2" Cupped Vase
Dancing Ladies

#791-8" Flared Vase
Peacock

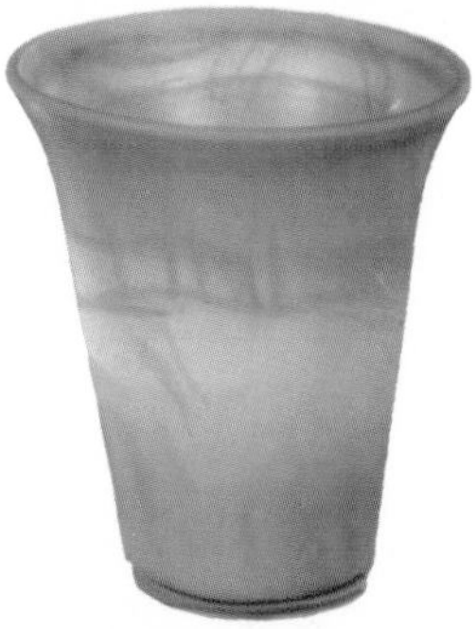
#621-6" Flared Vase

#846-8" Cupped Bowl

#847-6" Cupped Bowl

#847-6" Flared Crimped Vase

#846-8" Flared Bowl

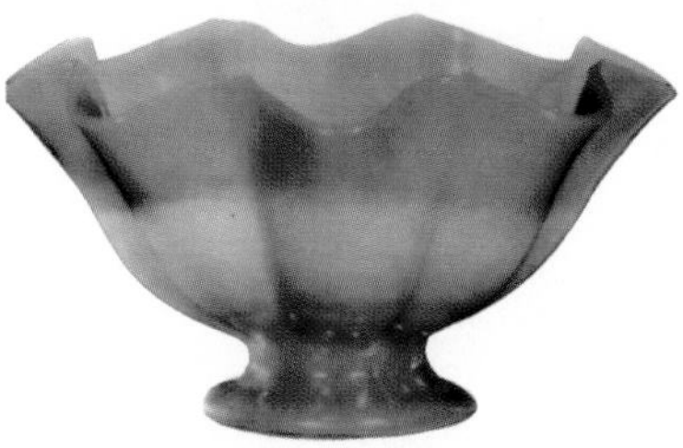
#847-8 1/2" Flared
Crimped Bowl

#847-11" Flared Bowl

#846-8" Flared Bowl

MOONSTONE

Moonstone is a translucent opaline color that Fenton made between 1932 and 1934. In addition to bowls and vases from the regular line, Fenton produced a line of toiletries in moonstone. For more information, see the reprint on page 310.

Moonstone was a popular color for use as stoppers or lids of jade, black, or lilac colognes, bath bottles or covered jugs. The Dancing Ladies tall covered urn, ginger jar, and nymph figure are elusive. Also, this is one of the few colors where the Big Cookies pieces are hard to find.

Item	Value	Date
Barber bottle	$60.00 – 80.00	1933
Basket, #1681 – 10½" Big Cookies	$300.00 – 350.00	1933
Bathroom set, #16 – 17 – 54	$185.00 – 200.00	
Bottle, #100 w/assorted lettering	$60.00 – 80.00	1934
Bottle, #105 – 108	$30.00 – 35.00	1933
Bowl set, #456 – 3-pc. mixing	$75.00 – 90.00	
Bowl, #846 – 6" cupped	$22.00 – 27.00	1934
Bowl, #848 – 8½" flared	$35.00 – 40.00	1933
Bowl, #900 – 11" oval Dancing Ladies	$220.00 – 240.00	1933
Bowl, #1663 – 9" oval	$45.00 – 55.00	1933
Candelabra, #2318 – 6"	$32.00 – 37.00	1933
Candleholder, #848 – 3 ftd.	$22.00 – 25.00	1933
*Candlestick, #549 – 8½"	$55.00 – 65.00	1924
**Candlestick, #649 – 10"	$80.00 – 90.00	
Candlestick, #950 cornucopia	$50.00 – 60.00	1933
Coaster, #1590 – 4"	$12.00 – 15.00	1932 – 1933
Cologne, #53 – 5"	$110.00 – 130.00	1933
Cream jar, #114	$20.00 – 25.00	1934
Cup, #123 sanitary paper soap	$45.00 – 50.00	1933
Cup, #1502 Diamond Optic	$12.00 – 15.00	1933
Flower block, #1234/1634 for nymph figure	$16.00 – 18.00	1933
Ginger jar and lid, #893	$230.00 – 260.00	1933
Goblet, Diamond Optic	$16.00 – 18.00	1933
Jug, #400	$75.00 – 85.00	1932
Macaroon jar, #1681 Big Cookies	$210.00 – 250.00	1933
Mug, #1630	$22.00 – 25.00	1931 – 1934
Nymph, #1645 September Morn	$165.00 – 200.00	1933
Paper soap holder, #122	$45.00 – 50.00	1933
Paper vase	$75.00 – 100.00	1933
Plate, #1639 – 8" Elizabeth	$14.00 – 16.00	1933
Puff box, #53	$37.00 – 45.00	1933
Puff box, #57	$48.00 – 55.00	1933
Puff box, #1229	$40.00 – 50.00	1933
Refrigerator dish, #457 rectangular w/lid	$35.00 – 40.00	1933 – 1934
Shaving mug, W-111,112,113	$35.00 – 40.00	193
Shell, 3½ – 4½"	$10.00 – 12.00	1933
Sterilizer, #116	$85.00 – 95.00	1933
Tray, #53 for vanity set	$42.00 – 45.00	1933
Urn, #901 – 12" covered Dancing Ladies	$800.00 – 1000.00	1933
Urn, #901 – 7" covered Dancing Ladies	$400.00 – 500.00	1933
Vanity set, #53, 4-pc.	$300.00 – 350.00	1933
Vase, #115	$37.00 – 42.00	1934
Vase, #184 – 10"	$80.00 – 90.00	1933
Vase, #184 – 12"	$90.00 – 100.00	1933
Vase, #621 – 6"	$25.00 – 30.00	1933
Vase, #621 – 8" flared, cupped, or square top	$35.00 – 40.00	1933
Vase, #847 – 6½" crimped, fan	$67.00 – 75.00	1933
Vase, #901 – 5" (handled urn base) Dancing Ladies	$125.00 – 145.00	1933
Vase, #1502 – 10" Diamond Optic	$50.00 – 60.00	1933
Vase, #1561 – 10" reg., crimped, or flared Apple Tree	$125.00 – 160.00	1933
*with ebony base	$100.00 – 110.00	
**with ebony base	$115.00 – 125.00	

#1681-7" Macaroon Jar
"Big Cookies"

#549-8 1/2" Candlestick

#1561-10" Vase
"Apple Tree"

#621-8" Vase w/Moonstone Base

#2318 Candelabra

#621-6" Flared Vase

#846-6" Cupped Bowl

#900-11 1/2" Oval Bowl
"Dancing Ladies"

#901-12" Covered Urn

#16-17-54 4 Piece
Bath Room Set

53 4 Pc. Dresser Set

#1645 Nymph Figure
w/#848-8" flared Bowl

#1639-7 1/2" Salad Plate

ORCHID

Orchid is a transparent lavender color that Fenton introduced in 1927. The color was used mainly in the Diamond Optic, Spiral Optic, and Dolphin lines and was discontinued after 1928. A few rare examples of orchid with a stretch finish have been found.

Item	Value	Date
Bonbon, #1502 – 6" flared Diamond Optic	$35.00 – 40.00	1927
Bonbon, #1502 – 7½" crimped Diamond Optic	$43.00 – 48.00	1927
Bonbon, #1502 – 7½" oval Diamond Optic	$43.00 – 48.00	1927
Bonbon, #1502 – 7½" round w/dolphins Diamond Optic	$43.00 – 48.00	1927
Bowl, #100 – 8" octagonal 3 – footed Wide Rib	$25.00 – 32.00	1928
Bowl, #1502 finger Diamond Optic	$13.00 – 15.00	1928
Bowl, #1502 – 10" shallow cupped Diamond Optic	$27.00 – 32.00	1928
Bowl, #1502 – 10" special roll rim Diamond Optic	$40.00 – 45.00	1927
Bowl, #1502 – 12" shallow cupped Diamond Optic	$45.00 – 50.00	1927
Bowl, #1502 – 12" special roll rim Diamond Optic	$45.00 – 50.00	1927
Bowl, #1502 – 13" flared Diamond Optic	$50.00 – 55.00	1927
Bowl, #1502 – 14" special rolled rim Diamond Optic	$45.00 – 55.00	1927
Bowl, #1502 – 8" deep cupped Diamond Optic	$30.00 – 35.00	1928
Bowl, #1502 – 8" flared cupped Diamond Optic	$30.00 – 35.00	1928
Bowl, #1502 – A-9" crimped w/dolphins Diamond Optic	$45.00 – 50.00	1928
Bowl, #1502 – A-10" flared w/dolphins Diamond Optic	$50.00 – 60.00	1928
Bowl, #1502 – A-7" cupped Diamond Optic	$47.00 – 50.00	1928
Bowl, #1502 – A-8½" roll edge Diamond Optic	$45.00 – 50.00	1928
Bowl, #1502 – A-8" flared cupped w/dolphins Diamond Optic	$47.00 – 52.00	1928
Bowl, #1503 – 10" flared Spiral Optic	$30.00 – 35.00	1928
Bowl, #1503 – A-10" flared w/dolphins Spiral Optic	$47.00 – 50.00	1928
Bowl, #1503 – A-7" cupped w/dolphins Spiral Optic	$42.00 – 47.00	1928
Bowl, #1503 – A-8½" roll edge w/dolphins Spiral Optic	$47.00 – 55.00	1928
Bowl, #1503 – A-9" shallow cupped or crimped Spiral Optic	$35.00 – 45.00	1928
Candle, #1502 Diamond Optic	$16.00 – 18.00	1927
Candlestick, #1623 w/dolphins	$20.00 – 25.00	1927
Cologne, #53 – 5"	$110.00 – 125.00	1927
Comport, #1502 cheese & cracker Diamond Optic	$45.00 – 50.00	1927
Creamer, #1502 Diamond Optic	$22.00 – 27.00	1927
Flower block, #1564 turtle	$80.00 – 90.00	1927
Flower bowl, #1618 elephant	$500.00 – 550.00	
Goblet, #1502 11 oz. bridge Diamond Optic	$15.00 – 18.00	1928
Goblet, #1502 9 oz. bridge Diamond Optic	$15.00 – 18.00	1927
Goblet, #1502 Hi ftd. Diamond Optic	$22.00 – 27.00	1927
Mayonnaise and ladle, #1502 Diamond Optic	$50.00 – 55.00	1927
Pitcher, #1635 w/#1702 cut Diamond Optic	$85.00 – 95.00	1928
Plate, #1502 w/indent for cheese comport Diamond Optic	$22.00 – 25.00	1927
Plate, #1502 – 6" octagonal Diamond Optic	$7.00 – 9.00	1928
Plate, #1502 – 8" octagonal Diamond Optic	$10.00 – 12.00	1928
Puff box, #53	$50.00 – 55.00	1927
Tray, #53 vanity	$35.00 – 40.00	1927
Tray, #1502 –A –10" Dolphin handled	$65.00 – 75.00	
Underplate, #1502 finger bowl Diamond Optic	$7.00 – 8.00	1928
Vanity set, #53, 4-pc.	$305.00 – 350.00	1927
Vase, #1502 – 5" fan w/dolphins Diamond Optic	$35.00 – 40.00	1927
Vase, #1502 – 6" fan w/dolphins Diamond Optic	$37.00 – 42.00	1927
Vase, #1502 – 8½"	$70.00 – 80.00	

#1502-A-10" Flared Bowl

#1502-6" Fan Vase

#1623 Candlestick

#1502-7 1/2" Oval Bon-bon

#1502-A-10" Handled Sandwich Tray

#1502 Candlestick

#1503-A-10" Flared Bowl

#1503-A-7" Cupped Bowl

PEKIN BLUE

Pekin blue is an translucent color that Fenton introduced in 1932. Production of the color continued through 1933. The earlier pieces, such as the candlesticks and bowls which appear to be this color, are probably what Fenton originally called turquoise. Turquoise probably became the more alluring Pekin blue as marketing experts tried to entice housewives to part with money they could ill afford to spend on expensive luxuries during the depths of the Great Depression. Both the lack of consumer cash and difficulties in producing the color contributed to the short term of production.

Most pieces of this color are scarce on the resale market. Even the bowls, vases, and Big Cookies pieces which are frequently seen in other colors are hard to find in Pekin blue.

Items with stoppers or lids such as the bath bottles, colognes, the Big Cookies macaroon jar, or the refrigerator jar will often be found with moonstone tops. The tray to the bath set may also be moonstone.

Prize pieces to own in this color include the two-piece reamer set, the Dancing Ladies covered urn, and the nymph figure.

In the late 1960s Fenton produced a number of sample items for a contemplated revival of the Pekin blue color. However, production difficulties prevented these items from becoming a part of the regular line. Another attempt was made to produce the color in 1980. This time a successful run was made and the production items were marketed for a brief period. The new color was called Peking blue. Again the color proved to be very hard to make, and Peking blue was discontinued after only a few months.

Items from this 1980 production include:
Basket, #7537 – 7"
Bell, #7564
Bird figure, #5163
Bowl, #7523 rolled rim
Boy and Girl figures, #5100
Bud vase, #9054
Bunny figure, #5162
Cat figure, #5165
Comport, #7528
Fairy light, #7500
Nut dish, #7529
Owl figure, #5168
Temple jar, #7488
Temple jar, #7588 tall
Vase, #7550 – 7"
Vase, #7557 – 10"
Vase, #8251 Mandarin
Vase, #8252 Empress

Item	Value	Date
Basket, #1681 – 10½" Big Cookies	$250.00 – 300.00	1933
Bathroom set, #16 – 17 – 54, 4-pc.	$230.00 – 260.00	1933
Bonbon, #543 covered	$95.00 – 115.00	1933
Bowl, #456 – 1 mixing	$37.00 – 48.00	1933
Bowl, #456 – 2 mixing	$47.00 – 52.00	1933
Bowl, #456 – 3 mixing	$68.00 – 72.00	1933
Bowl, #640 – 7" flared, cupped	$37.00 – 45.00	
Bowl, #846 – 6" cupped	$37.00 – 45.00	1933
Bowl, #846 – 8½" flared cupped	$50.00 – 55.00	1933
Bowl, #846 – 8½" flared or cupped	$50.00 – 55.00	1933
Bowl, #848 – 6" cupped	$75.00 – 95.00	1932
Bowl, #848 – 8½" flared	$100.00 – 125.00	1933
Bowl, #900 – 11" oval Dancing Ladies	$350.00 – 400.00	1932
Bowl, #1504 – A 9" cupped w/dolphins	$75.00 – 85.00	1932
Bowl, #1504 – A-9" shallow cupped w/dolphins	$75.00 – 85.00	1932
Bowl, #1504 – A-6" cupped w/dolphins	$45.00 – 55.00	1932
Bowl, #1663 – 12" flared or tulip	$95.00 – 125.00	1933
Bowl, #1663 – 12" reg.	$90.00 – 110.00	1932
Bowl, #1663 – 9" oval	$80.00 – 90.00	1933
Candlestick, #318	$47.00 – 50.00	1933
Candlestick, #349 – 10"	$110.00 – 115.00	
Candlestick, #349 – 10" w/oval cutting	$125.00 – 140.00	
Candlestick, #549 – 8½"	$80.00 – 85.00	1924
Candlestick, #649 – 10"	$100.00 – 125.00	
Candlestick, #749 – 12"	$150.00 – 175.00	
Cologne, #53 – 5"	$200.00 – 225.00	1932
Comport, #643 – 6¾" salver	$35.00 – 40.00	1924
Flower block, #1234 for nymph figure	$22.00 – 25.00	1933
Jug, #400	$115.00 – 135.00	1932
Jug, 6" ftd.	$250.00 – 300.00	1932
Macaroon jar, #1681 – 7" Big Cookies	$350.00 – 400.00	1933
Nymph, #1645 September Morn	$350.00 – 400.00	1933
Puff box, #53	$60.00 – 65.00	1932
Reamer, #1619 with handled jug	$2200.00 – 2500.00	1933
Refrigerator bowl, #457 rectangular w/cover	$60.00 – 65.00	1933
Urn, #901 – 7" covered Dancing Ladies	$600.00 – 700.00	1933
Urn, #901 – 12" covered Dancing Ladies	$900.00 – 1200.00	1933
Tray, #53 vanity	$50.00 – 55.00	
*Vanity set, #53, 4-pc.	$510.00 – 570.00	1933
Vase, #621 – 6"	$45.00 – 50.00	1933
Vase, #621 – 8" flared, cupped, or square top	$75.00 – 85.00	1933
Vase, #901 – 5" (handled urn base) Dancing Ladies	$250.00 – 300.00	1933

**May have moonstone stoppers, lid, and tray.*

#846-6 1/2" Cupped Bowl & #1645 Nymph Figure

#621-6 1/2" Flared Vase

#549-8 1/2" Candlestick

6" Jug

#53 Vanity Set

Puff Box

#640-7" Flared Cupped Bowl

#543 Bon-bon

#318 Candlestick

#647-10 3/4" Flared Cupped Bowl

2-Pc. Reamer Set

#643-7" Salver Comport

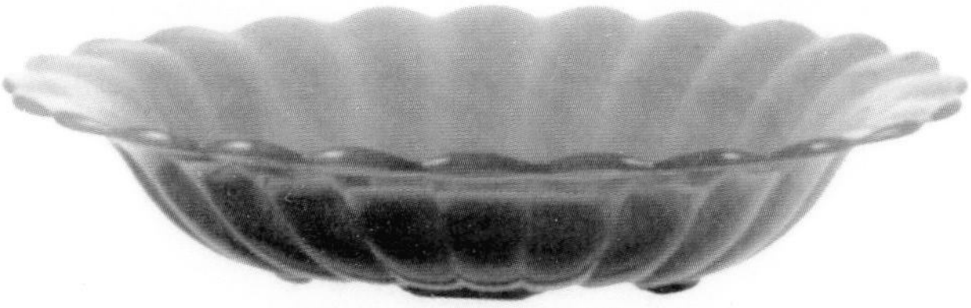

#1663-10 1/2" Flared Bowl

#1681-7" Macaroon Jar "Big Cookies"

PERIWINKLE BLUE

In an attempt to produce desirable items and saleable products in the midst of the Great Depression, Fenton kept experimenting with new colors. Periwinkle blue was introduced in 1933, and continued in the line through 1935. The slag effect of the glass is produced by allowing the excess glass from the previous piece to remain on the gatherer's punty (the rod which is used to remove the molten glass from the furnace). The lower temperature of the old glass produces a slightly different color when the piece is pressed.

In addition to common bowls and vases, Fenton made an elephant bottle and Peacock and Dancing Ladies vases. These latter items always bring premium prices when they are offered for sale.

Item	Value	Date
Ashtray set, #202, 5-pc., #1, 2, 3, 4,	$70.00 – 85.00	
Basket, #1684 w/wicker handle	$210.00 – 250.00	1935
Bonbon, #1043, 1 lb. covered, footed	$210.00 – 250.00	1934
Bowl, #600 – 7" cupped	$40.00 – 45.00	1935
Bowl, #846 – 6" cupped	$50.00 – 55.00	1935
Bowl, #846 – 8½" flared or cupped	$50.00 – 55.00	1935
Bowl, #847 – 6" cupped	$40.00 – 50.00	1935
Bowl, #847 – 7½" flared	$45.00 – 50.00	1935
Bowl, #847 – 8½" crimped, ftd	$45.00 – 55.00	1935
Bowl, #955 shallow cupped	$50.00 – 55.00	1935
Bowl, #1504 – A-10" clover w/dolphins	$240.00 – 265.00	1935
Bowl, #1602 – 10¼" crimped w/dolphins	$220.00 – 240.00	1934
Bowl, #1663 – 12" reg. or flared	$90.00 – 125.00	1933
Elephant bottle	$600.00 – 700.00	1935
Macaroon jar, #1684 – 6½"	$320.00 – 370.00	1935
Rose bowl, #847 – 5"	$42.00 – 45.00	1935
Vase, #621 – 6"	$47.00 – 55.00	1934
Vase, #621 – 8" flared, cupped or square top	$58.00 – 65.00	1934
Vase, #791 – 8" Peacock flared or cupped	$260.00 – 290.00	1935
Vase, #847 – 6½" crimped	$47.00 – 52.00	1935
Vase, #847 – 6" fan	$47.00 – 55.00	1935
Vase, #847 – 8½" crimped	$47.00 – 55.00	1935
Vase, #857 – 8" fan	$65.00 – 75.00	1935
Vase, #901 – 8½" cupped Dancing Ladies	$475.00 – 500.00	1934
Vase, #901 – 9" crimped Dancing Ladies	$480.00 – 525.00	1934
Vase, #901 – 9" flared Dancing Ladies	$500.00 – 525.00	1934
Vase, #901 – 9" sq. Dancing Ladies	$500.00 – 525.00	1934

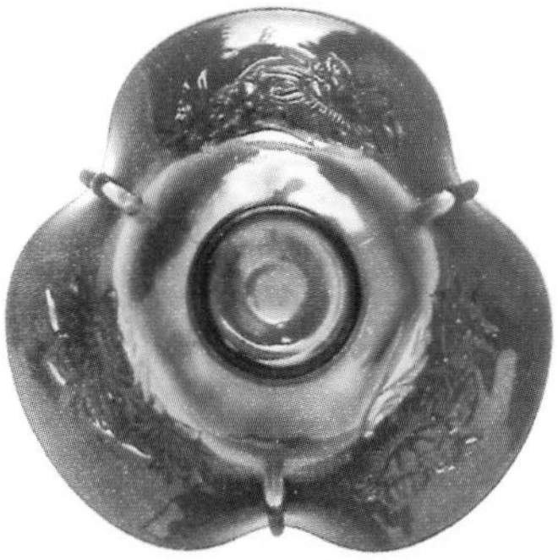

#1504-A-10" Clover Bowl

#847-8 1/2" Crimped Bowl

Elephant Bottle

#1684-6 1/2" Macaroon Jar

#1684-9" Handled Basket

#857-8" Fan Vase

Photo Below: **Periwinkle Blue Catalog Reprint Composite** Courtesy Of: **The Fenton Art Glass Museum**

No. 621-8"
Flared Vase

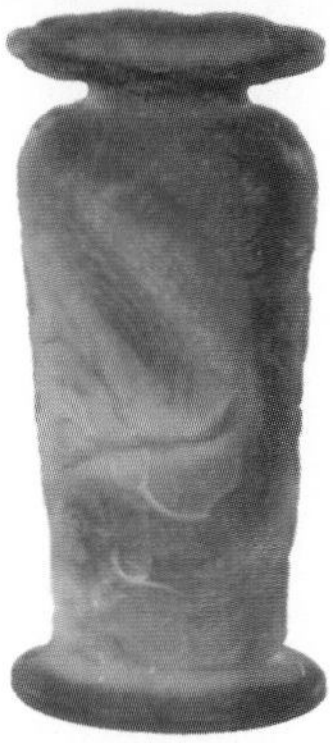

No. 791-7 1/2"
Vase-Cupped
Flared

No. 791-8"
Flared Vase

No. 901-8 1/2"
Cupped Vase

No. 901-9"
Flared Vase

No. 846-6" Cupped
Bowl and Base

No. 847-5"
Rose Bowl

No. 846-8"
Flared Bowl

ROSE

Fenton added a transparent pink color to its line in 1927. This new color was called rose. Much of the early production of pink glassware was iridized and may be found in the stretch glass section. However, clear pink items were also made. Besides plain bowls and vases, some of the first items made in clear pink were dolphin decorated items and patterns like Diamond Optic and Spiral Optic. During the early to mid 1930s production of transparent pink glassware increased sharply as kitchenware items and new lines such as Lincoln Inn and Georgian were made in this color.

The elephant flower bowl and the turtle based aquariums are eagerly sought after by collectors. Notice the unusual Diamond Optic bonbon with the crimped top in the photo.

Item	Value	Date
Aquarium, #1538 – 1565 turtle base w/crys. Bubble Optic top	$500.00 – 600.00	1929
Ashtray, #305	$10.00 – 12.00	1932
Ashtray, #311	$10.00 – 12.00	1936
Basket, #1502 Diamond Optic	$25.00 – 30.00	1933
Basket, #1615 cut Diamond Optic	$53.00 – 60.00	1933
Basket, #1616 -6½" Diamond Optic	$47.00 – 57.00	1933
Basket, #1616 – 1702 cut Diamond Optic	$55.00 – 65.00	1933
Basket, #1616 – 1709 cut Diamond Optic	$55.00 – 65.00	1933
Basket, #1617	$55.00 – 65.00	1933
Basket, #1617 cut	$65.00 – 70.00	1933
Basket, #1681 – 10½" Big Cookies	$125.00 – 175.00	1933
Basket, #1684 w/wicker handle	$80.00 – 95.00	1935
Bonbon, #846 – 5" covered	$48.00 – 55.00	1935
Bonbon, Blackberry Banded	$25.00 – 32.00	
Bonbon, #1216 Blackberry Spray	$25.00 – 32.00	
Bonbon, #1235 cupped, flared, triangular	$14.00 – 16.00	1936 – 1937
Bonbon, #1426 – 6½" Cherry Circles	$25.00 – 30.00	
Bonbon, #1502 bridge Diamond Optic	$48.00 – 55.00	1928
Bonbon, #1502 – 6" flared Diamond Optic	$32.00 – 37.00	1927
Bonbon, #1502 – 7½" crimped Diamond Optic	$32.00 – 37.00	1927
Bonbon, #1502 – 7½" oval Diamond Optic	$42.00 – 46.00	1927
Bonbon, #1502 – 7½" round w/dolphins Diamond Optic	$42.00 – 47.00	1927
Bonbon, #1565 turtle w/flower frog	$180.00 – 200.00	1929
Bonbon, #1565 turtle open	$160.00 – 185.00	1929
Bonbon, #1621/1702 cut-6½" crimped, flared, square	$22.00 – 27.00	1928
Bonbon, #1695-6" 2-hdld. Two Fruits	$25.00 – 30.00	
Bonbon, #2000 – A-5½" flat club, regular	$27.00 – 32.00	1938
Bookend, #711 Peacock pr.	$180.00 – 200.00	1935
Bowl, #100 – 5" 3-toed Wide Rib	$12.00 – 15.00	1930
Bowl, #100 – 7½" 3-footed round Wide Rib	$20.00 – 23.00	1930
Bowl, #100 – 8" octagonal 3-footed Wide Rib	$27.00 – 32.00	1930
Bowl, #750 reg., flared	$20.00 – 22.00	1935
Bowl, #846 – 8½" flared cupped	$22.00 – 27.00	1935
Bowl, #846 – 8½" flared or cupped	$22.00 – 27.00	1935
Bowl, #848 – 8½" flared	$70.00 – 75.00	1933
Bowl, #857 – 10" rolled rim	$52.00 – 55.00	1927
Bowl, #857 – 11" flared or flared cupped	$45.00 – 50.00	1927
Bowl, #920 – 11" rolled edge; flared Grape & Cable	$190.00 – 225.00	
Bowl, #950 – 11" tulip; oval	$32.00 – 37.00	1935 – 1938
Bowl, #1124 Butterfly & Berry 3-ftd. master berry	$50.00 – 60.00	
Bowl, #1235 – 5"	$15.00 – 17.00	1932
Bowl, #1237 – 10" crimped	$45.00 – 50.00	1933

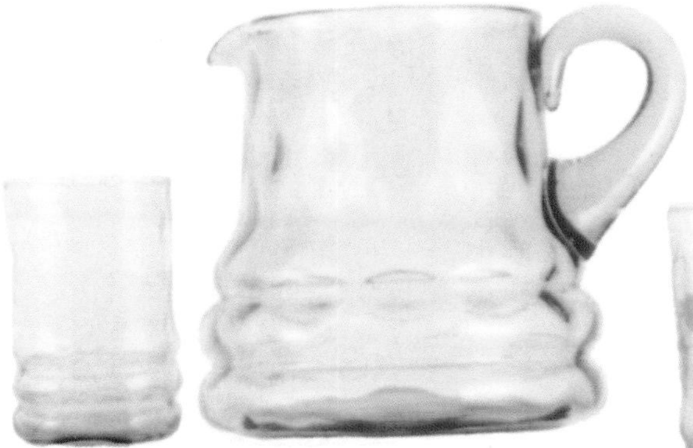
#1635 Water Set

#1636 Ice Tea Set w/#1702 Cutting

#1684 Macaroon Jar

#1502-A-7" Cupped Bowl

#1634 Tumbler

#1502 Sugar and Creamer

#1565-1538 Turtle Aquarium

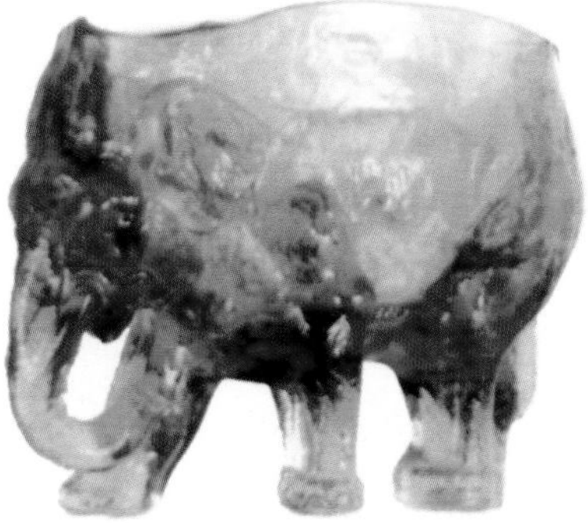
#1618 Elephant Flower Bowl

#1503-A-9" Crimped Bowl

#1502 4-Piece Dresser Set

#1502 Bridge Bonbon

#100-8 1/2" Octagonal Bowl

#920 Rolled Edge
Grape & Cable Bowl

100-7 1/2" Round Bowl

Item	Value	Date
Bowl, #1245 – 5"	$16.00 – 18.00	1932 – 1933
Bowl, #1502 finger Diamond Optic	$13.00 – 16.00	1928
Bowl, #1406 – 8" Orange Tree	$30.00 – 40.00	
Bowl, #1502 – 10" shallow cupped Diamond Optic	$25.00 – 30.00	1927
Bowl, #1502 – 10" special roll rim Diamond Optic	$30.00 – 35.00	1927
Bowl, #1502 – 12" shallow cupped Diamond Optic	$27.00 – 32.00	1927
Bowl, #1502 – 12" special roll rim Diamond Optic	$30.00 – 35.00	1927
Bowl, #1502 – 13" flared Diamond Optic	$32.00 – 37.00	1927
Bowl, #1502 – 14" special rolled rim Diamond Optic	$35.00 – 40.00	1928
Bowl, #1502 – 8" deep cupped Diamond Optic	$22.00 – 26.00	1928
Bowl, #1502 – 8" flared cupped Diamond Optic	$22.00 – 26.00	1928
Bowl, #1502 – A -9" crimped w/dolphins Diamond Optic	$38.00 – 42.00	1928 – 1933
Bowl, #1502 – A-10" flared w/dolphins Diamond Optic	$35.00 – 40.00	1928
Bowl, #1502 – A-7" cupped Diamond Optic	$30.00 – 35.00	1928
Bowl, #1502 – A-8½" roll edge Diamond Optic	$30.00 – 35.00	1928
Bowl, #1502 – A-8" cupped Diamond Optic	$32.00 – 40.00	1928
Bowl, #1502 – A-8" flared cupped w/dolphins Diamond Optic	$30.00 – 35.00	1928
Bowl, #1503 – 10" flared Spiral Optic	$25.00 – 30.00	1928
Bowl, #1503 – A-10" flared w/dolphins Spiral Optic	$44.00 – 47.00	1928
Bowl, #1503 – A-7" cupped w/dolphins Spiral Optic	$38.00 – 42.00	1928
Bowl, #1503 – A-8½" roll edge w/dolphins Spiral Optic	$38.00 – 42.00	1928
Bowl, #1503 – A-9" shallow cupped or crimped Spiral Optic	$37.00 – 45.00	1928
Bowl, #1504 – A-9½" flared cupped w/#1702 cut & dolphins	$45.00 – 55.00	1928
Bowl, #1504 – A-9" flared w/#1702 cut and dolphins	$45.00 – 55.00	1928
Bowl, #1600 – 10" rolled rim ftd. w/dolphins	$55.00 – 60.00	1928
Bowl, #1608 – 10" shallow or crimped Stag & Holly	$45.00 – 55.00	1932
Bowl, #1665 – 6½" 3-ftd. Horse Medallion	$40.00 – 50.00	
Bowl, #1621 – 10" deep oval w/dolphins	$40.00 – 45.00	1928
Bowl, #1621 – 10" deep oval w/dolphins, cut	$45.00 – 55.00	1928
Bowl, #1621 – 9" shallow oval w/dolphin handle	$40.00 – 47.00	1928
Bowl, #1932 – 6½" flared or cupped	$13.00 – 15.00	1933 – 1936
Bowl, #1932 – 7½" crimped	$17.00 – 20.00	1933 – 1936
Bowl, #1933 – 5" cupped	$9.00 – 11.00	1932
Bowl, #1933 – 7" flared	$16.00 – 18.00	
Bowl, #2000 – A-11" crimped Pineapple	$60.00 – 65.00	1938
Candlestick, #314	$14.00 – 16.00	1932
Candlestick, #316	$13.00 – 15.00	1928
Candlestick, #318	$14.00 – 16.00	1928
Candlestick, #318 w/#1702 cut	$24.00 – 26.00	1928
Candlestick, #950 cornucopia	$25.00 – 27.00	1932
Candlestick, #1234	$18.00 – 22.00	1933
Candlestick, #1502 Diamond Optic	$15.00 – 17.00	1927
Candlestick, #1623 w/dolphins	$22.00 – 25.00	1928
Candlestick, #2000 – 5½" double branch Pineapple	$55.00 – 60.00	1938
Candy, #1533 – A w/dolphins	$75.00 – 95.00	1928
Coaster, #1590 – 4"	$13.00 – 15.00	1936
Cologne, #53 – 5"	$90.00 – 100.00	1927
Cologne, #1502 Diamond Optic	$120.00 – 145.00	1927
Comport, #231 Rib & Holly Sprig	$22.00 – 27.00	
Comport, #1502 cheese & cracker Diamond Optic	$35.00 – 40.00	1927
Creamer, #4	$20.00 – 22.00	1933
Creamer, #1502 Diamond Optic	$20.00 – 25.00	1927

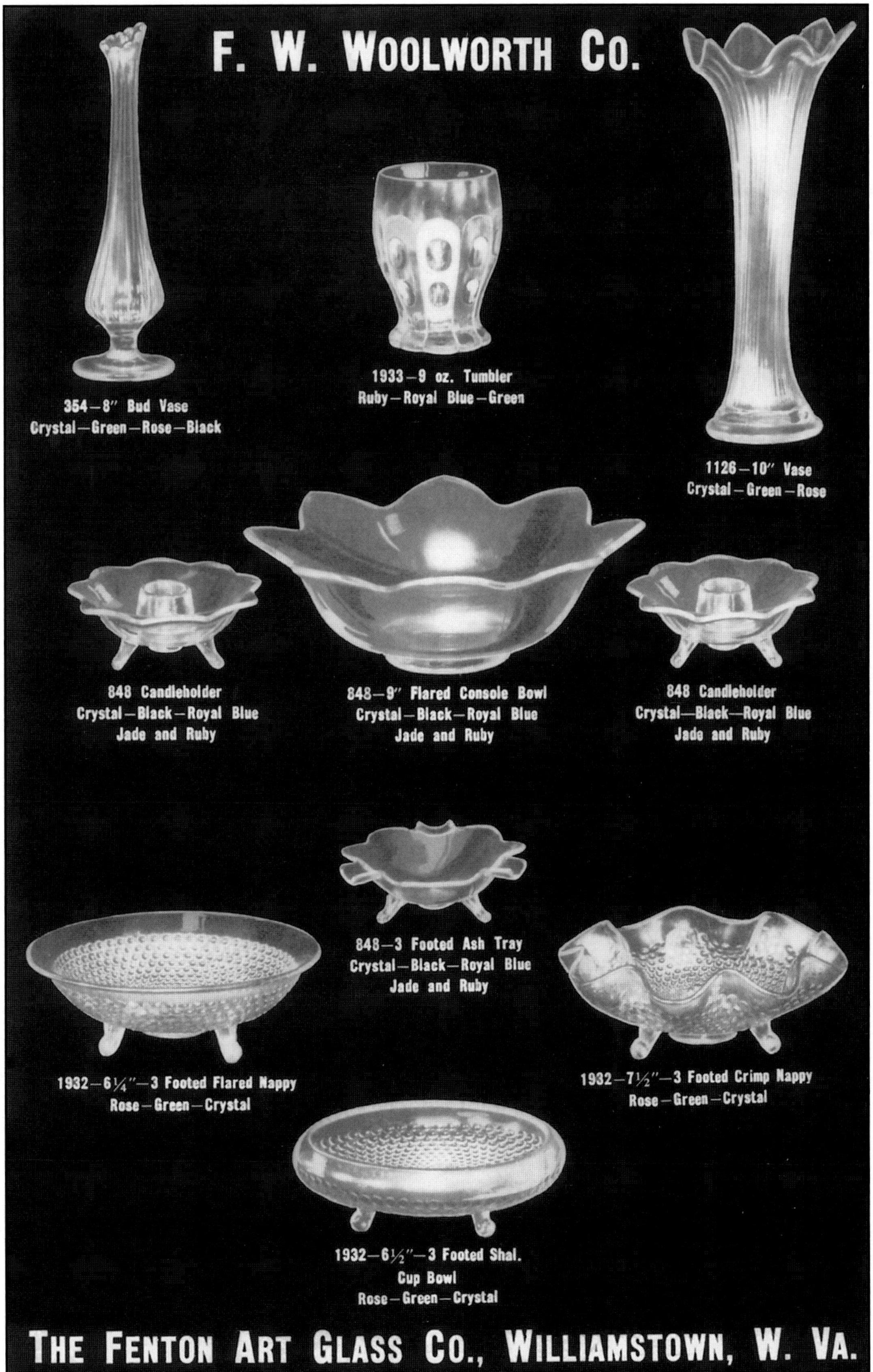
F. W. WOOLWORTH CO.
354—8" Bud Vase
Crystal—Green—Rose—Black
1933—9 oz. Tumbler
Ruby—Royal Blue—Green
1126—10" Vase
Crystal—Green—Rose
848 Candleholder
Crystal—Black—Royal Blue
Jade and Ruby
848—9" Flared Console Bowl
Crystal—Black—Royal Blue
Jade and Ruby
848 Candleholder
Crystal—Black—Royal Blue
Jade and Ruby
848—3 Footed Ash Tray
Crystal—Black—Royal Blue
Jade and Ruby
1932—6¼"—3 Footed Flared Nappy
Rose—Green—Crystal
1932—7½"—3 Footed Crimp Nappy
Rose—Green—Crystal
1932—6½"—3 Footed Shal.
Cup Bowl
Rose—Green—Crystal
THE FENTON ART GLASS CO., WILLIAMSTOWN, W. VA.

Catalog Reprint Circa 1933-1936 Courtesy Of: The Fenton Art Glass Museum

Item	Value	Date
Cup, #1502 Diamond Optic	$10.00 – 12.00	1927
Decanter, 1935 Franklin	$80.00 – 90.00	1934
Flower block, #2	$14.00 – 18.00	1932
Flower block, #4	$18.00 – 20.00	1927
Flower block, #1234/1643 for nymph	$18.00 – 22.00	
Flower block, #1564 turtle	$43.00 – 48.00	1927
Flower bowl, #1618 elephant	$450.00 – 500.00	1929
Flower pot, #1555 w/underplate	$80.00 – 90.00	1927
Ginger jar and lid, #893	$200.00 – 220.00	1936
Goblet, #1412 – 5" Orange Tree	$16.00 – 18.00	1930
Goblet, #1502 – 11 oz. bridge Diamond Optic	$13.00 – 15.00	1928
Goblet, #1502 – 9 oz. bridge Diamond Optic	$13.00 – 15.00	1928
Goblet, #1502 Hi ftd. Diamond Optic	$16.00 – 18.00	1927
Goblet, #1503 – 9 oz.	$20.00 – 22.00	1928
Goblet, #1640 – 9 oz. bridge w/#1702 cutting	$21.00 – 25.00	1928
Goblet, #1642 w/#1702 cutting	$21.00 – 25.00	1928
Ice pack, #1614 Diamond Optic	$32.00 – 35.00	1928
Ice pack, #1616 – 6½" Diamond Optic	$32.00 – 37.00	1928
Ice pack, #1502 – 4" Diamond Optic	$22.00 – 27.00	1928
Ice pack, #1616 – 1702 cut Diamond Optic	$43.00 – 47.00	1928
Ice pack, #1616 – 1709 cut Diamond Optic	$43.00 – 47.00	1928
Ivy ball, #706	$22.00 – 27.00	1933 – 1935
Lamp, #1502 Diamond Optic	$110.00 – 125.00	1928
Macaroon jar, #1684 – 7" Big Cookies	$230.00 – 245.00	1933
Mug, #1430 Orange Tree	$22.00 – 27.00	
Nappy, 5" 3-ftd. "Chrysanthemum"	$25.00 – 30.00	
Night set, #401	$50.00 – 65.00	1927
Night set, #1502 2-pc. Diamond Optic	$75.00 – 85.00	1928
Nymph, #1645 September Morn	$175.00 – 195.00	1931 – 1933
Pitcher, #1353 – 9½" Thumbprint	$115.00 – 135.00	1936
Pitcher, #1634 w/#1702 cut Diamond Optic	$75.00 – 95.00	1928
Pitcher, #1635 w/#1702 cut Diamond Optic	$75.00 – 95.00	1928
Pitcher, #1636 Diamond Optic	$57.00 – 67.00	1930
Pitcher, #1636 w/#1702 cut Diamond Optic	$60.00 – 80.00	1928
Plate, #750 – 14"	$22.00 – 27.00	1935
Plate, #750 – 8"	$8.00 – 10.00	1935
Plate, 757 Cut #2	$20.00 – 24.00	1933
Plate, 757 Cut #4	$20.00 – 24.00	1933
Plate, #758 – 8½" octagonal	$9.00 – 11.00	1927
Plate, #848	$75.00 – 80.00	
Plate, #1235	$14.00 – 16.00	1936
Plate, #1502 w/indent for cheese comport Diamond Optic	$18.00 – 20.00	1927
Plate, #1502 – 6" octagonal Diamond Optic	$6.00 – 7.00	1927
Plate, #1502 – 8" octagonal Diamond Optic	$10.00 – 12.00	1928
Puff box, #53	$27.00 – 32.00	1927
Puff box, #1502 Diamond Optic	$30.00 – 35.00	1927
Punch bowl & base, "Orange Tree"	$230.00 – 265.00	1933
Reamer, #1210 w/2-handled bottom	$155.00 – 180.00	1935
Reamer, #1619 w/handled jug	$1800.00 – 2000.00	1933
Refrigerator set, #1502 3 pc. Diamond Optic	$90.00 – 115.00	1933
Shaker, #1502 Diamond Optic ea.	$22.00 – 25.00	1928
Shell, 3½" – 4½"	$9.00 – 11.00	1936

Item	Value	Date
Sherbet, #1502 Diamond Optic	$9.00 – 11.00	1927
Sherbet, #1503	$9.00 – 10.00	1928
Sugar, #4	$18.00 – 22.00	1933
Sugar, #1502 Diamond Optic	$20.00 – 25.00	1927
Tray, #53 vanity	$25.00 – 30.00	1927
Tray, #1502 vanity Diamond Optic	$25.00 – 30.00	1927
Tray, #1502 – 10" handled sandwich Diamond Optic	$25.00 – 30.00	1927
Tray, #1502 – A-10" w/dolphin handle Diamond Optic	$65.00 – 70.00	1927
Tumbler, #19 – 12 oz. ice tea	$11.00 – 13.00	1933
Tumbler, #20 – 12 oz. ice tea	$11.00 – 13.00	1932
Tumbler, #1352 – 5¼" ice tea Thumbprint	$20.00 – 22.00	1935
Tumbler, #1502 – 5 oz. orange juice Diamond Optic	$12.00 – 15.00	1928
Tumbler, #1502 – 9 oz. ftd Diamond Optic	$13.00 – 16.00	1928
Tumbler, #1634	$10.00 – 12.00	1930
Tumbler, #1634 w/#1702 cut Diamond Optic	$12.00 – 15.00	1930
Tumbler, #1636 – 12 oz. ice tea	$10.00 – 12.00	1930
Tumbler, #1636 – 12 oz. w/#1702 cut Diamond Optic	$22.00 – 25.00	1928
Tumbler, #1641 – 11 oz.	$12.00 – 15.00	1928
Tumbler, #1641 – 11 oz. ice tea w/#1702 cutting	$25.00 – 30.00	1928
Tumbler, #1935 – 1 oz. whiskey Franklin	$8.00 – 10.00	1934
Underplate, #1502 finger bowl Diamond Optic	$5.00 – 6.00	1928
Vanity set, #53	$235.00 – 262.00	1927
Vanity set, #1502 Diamond Optic	$130.00 – 155.00	1927
Vanity set, #1502 4-pc. (with tray) Diamond Optic	$295.00 – 355.00	1928
Vase, #32	$22.00 – 27.00	1932
Vase, #107 tulip – 6½"	$22.00 – 24.00	1933
Vase, #184 – 10"	$35.00 – 45.00	1933 – 1937
Vase, #184 – 12"	$50.00 – 55.00	1935 – 1937
Vase, #184 – 8"	$37.00 – 40.00	1933
Vase, #184 – 8" w/cutting	$48.00 – 55.00	1933
Vase, #349 oval	$38.00 – 42.00	1932
Vase, #354 – 8" bud	$11.00 – 13.00	1933 – 1936
Vase, #354 – 9" bud	$12.00 – 14.00	1933 – 1936
Vase, #412-12" April Showers	$30.00 – 35.00	
Vase, #519 – 20"	$43.00 – 46.00	1932 – 1933
Vase, #621 – 6"	$15.00 – 22.00	1935
Vase, #621 – 8" flared, cupped or square top	$27.00 – 30.00	1935
Vase, #1126 – 9" Fenton's Rib	$32.00 – 36.00	1933 – 1936
Vase, #1219	$27.00 – 32.00	1932 – 1933
Vase, #1235 – 5"	$10.00 – 12.00	1933
Vase, #1502 – 10" Diamond Optic	$42.00 – 45.00	1927
Vase, #1502 – 5" fan w/dolphins Diamond Optic	$30.00 – 35.00	1927
Vase, #1502 – 6" fan w/dolphins Diamond Optic	$32.00 – 37.00	1927
Vase, #1502 – 7" roll edge Diamond Optic	$43.00 – 48.00	1927
Vase, #1502 – 8½" flared Diamond Optic	$37.00 – 42.00	1927
Vase, #1502 – 8" crimped Diamond Optic	$37.00 – 42.00	1927
Vase, #1502 – 8" flip w/#1702 cut Diamond Optic	$45.00 – 50.00	1927
Vase, #1502 – 8½" fan Diamond Optic	$42.00 – 47.00	1927
Vase, #1532 – A-5½" fan w/dolphins	$32.00 – 37.00	1928
Vase, #1533 – A-6" fan w/dolphins	$37.00 – 46.00	1928

ROYAL BLUE

Royal blue is a transparent cobalt color that has been associated with Fenton since the early carnival glass production. In 1917, the color continued in the line with the introduction of stretch glass, and production of clear royal blue has been confirmed as early as 1924. Production of the number of pieces in this color increased steadily through the years, and the color was extended into the pattern lines during the 1930s.

In the early 1930s Fenton revived a few of the old carnival glass molds for the production of some items in Royal Blue. Some of the more interesting of these items include a Milady vase, Mikado comports and a footed cake plate, Leaf Tiers bowls and plates, and Grape and Cable bowls. Among the more desirable and more expensive pieces are the Dancing Ladies vases.

Royal Blue	Value	Date
Ashtray set, #202, 5-pc., #1, 2, 3, 4,	$60.00 – 75.00	1936
Ashtray, #304 w/flower in bottom	$48.00 – 50.00	1934
Ashtray, #848 – 3 ftd.	$22.00 – 27.00	1933 – 1939
Baked apple, #650	$10.00 – 14.00	1924
Base, #2	$20.00 – 25.00	1924
Base, pitcher	$40.00 – 45.00	
Basket, #1681 – 10½" Big Cookies	$150.00 – 175.00	1935
Bonbon, #543 covered	$90.00 – 100.00	1924
Bonbon, #643 open, cupped	$27.00 – 32.00	1924
Bonbon, #643 – 5" covered	$80.00 – 85.00	1924
Bonbon, #943, ½ lb. covered	$110.00 – 125.00	1924
Bonbon, #1621 – 6½" sq. w/#1621 etch w/dolphins	$45.00 – 55.00	1936
Bowl, #208 – 8" Holly	$90.00 – 100.00	
Bowl, #600 – 7" cupped	$32.00 – 35.00	1924 – 1932
Bowl, #601 – 10" shallow cupped	$47.00 – 50.00	1924
Bowl, #604 – 10" cupped	$80.00 – 85.00	1924
Bowl, #607 – 9" shallow, cupped	$37.00 – 45.00	1924
Bowl, #638 – 8" shallow cupped	$32.00 – 35.00	1924
Bowl, #640 – 8½" shallow	$22.00 – 28.00	1924
Bowl, #640 – 7½" rolled rim	$22.00 – 30.00	1924
Bowl, #640 – 7" flared, cupped	$22.00 – 30.00	1924
Bowl, #647 – 11½" shallow cupped	$45.00 – 55.00	1924
Bowl, #647 – 10¾" flared cupped	$45.00 – 55.00	1924
Bowl, #647 – 10" flared	$45.00 – 55.00	1933
Bowl, #647 – 11" rolled rim	$45.00 – 55.00	1924
Bowl, 8½" crimped, Peacock & Urn	$150.00 – 170.00	
Bowl, #846 – 6" cupped	$37.00 – 45.00	1938
Bowl, #846 – 8½" flared cupped	$42.00 – 46.00	1933
Bowl, #846 – 8½" flared or cupped	$42.00 – 46.00	1933
Bowl, #848 – 8½" flared	$37.00 – 42.00	1936
Bowl, #900 – 11" oval Dancing Ladies	$250.00 – 300.00	1933
Bowl, #919 – 7" ftd. Mikado Orange Bowl (comport)	$300.00 – 330.00	1935
Bowl, #920 – 10" crimped Grape & Cable	$165.00 – 180.00	1935
Bowl, #950 – 11" tulip; oval	$60.00 – 65.00	1934
Bowl, #1092 – 5½" Basket Weave w/Open Edge	$32.00 – 37.00	1935 – 36
Bowl, #1093 – 8" shallow Basket Weave w/Open Edge	$45.00 – 50.00	1933
Bowl, #1093 – 9" shallow crimped Basket Weave w/Open Edge	$47.00 – 55.00	1935
Bowl, #1234 – 9"	$45.00 – 50.00	1935 – 1936
Bowl, #1502 – 12" special roll rim Diamond Optic	$55.00 – 65.00	1928
Bowl, #1621 – 9½" sq. w/#1621 etch	$70.00 – 75.00	1936
Bowl, #1639 – 10" flared 2-handled Elizabeth	$35.00 – 40.00	1933
Bowl, #1790 – 10" flared Leaf Tiers	$110.00 – 125.00	1935
Bowl, #1790 – 8" cupped Leaf Tiers	$90.00 – 110.00	1934
Cake plate, #919 high ftd. Mikado	$300.00 – 325.00	1935
Cake plate, #1790 – 10¼"-12" Leaf Tiers	$160.00 – 180.00	1935
Candleholder, #848 – 3 ftd.	$22.00 – 25.00	1933 – 1936
Candlestick, #349 – 10"	$75.00 – 80.00	1924
Candlestick, #349 – 10" w/oval cut	$80.00 – 90.00	1924
Candlestick, #549 – 8½"	$65.00 – 70.00	1924
Candlestick, #649 – 10"	$100.00 – 125.00	
Candlestick, #950 cornucopia	$50.00 – 55.00	1934

#1681-10 1/2" Basket
"Big Cookies"

#349-8" Vase

#1645 Nymph Figure
& Flower Block

#1934 Decanter

#848 Ashtray

#1934 Goblet

#208-8" Shallow Cupped Holly Bowl

6" Bonbon
w/#1621 Etch

Shell Ashtray

#107-6" Vase

#1561-10" Apple Tree Vase

#950-11" Oval Bowl

#950-5" Candlestick

#1933-4 1/2" Tumbler

#1502 Sugar & Creamer

#848 Candlestick

Item	Value	Date
Candy jar, #636, 1 lb.	$63.00 – 68.00	1924
Candy jar, #736, 1 lb.	$100.00 – 110.00	1924
Coaster, #1590 – 4"	$20.00 – 22.00	1932
Comport, #260 – 7" tall footed	$40.00 – 45.00	1924
Comport, #643 – 6¾" salver	$25.00 – 30.00	1924
Creamer, #1502 Diamond Optic	$27.00 – 32.00	1927
Creamer, #1639 Elizabeth	$35.00 – 40.00	1930
Cup, #1502 Diamond Optic	$13.00 – 15.00	1927
Cup, #1639 Elizabeth	$13.00 – 15.00	1930
Decanter, #1934	$150.00 – 180.00	1925
Decanter, 1935 Franklin	$125.00 – 150.00	1935
Dog, #307 novelty	$50.00 – 55.00	1933
Fish, #306 novelty	$45.00 – 50.00	1933
Flower block, #4	$18.00 – 20.00	1927
Flower block, #1234 for nymph figure	$25.00 – 35.00	1933
Goblet, #1502 9 oz. bridge Diamond Optic	$20.00 – 22.00	1928
Ice pail, #1616 – 6½" Diamond Optic	$110.00 – 120.00	1933
Ivy ball, #706	$50.00 – 55.00	1933
Jug, #1639 – 3 pint Elizabeth	$150.00 – 175.00	1930
Lamp, #1502 Diamond Optic	$130.00 – 150.00	
Lamp, #1561 Apple Tree	$180.00 – 200.00	1937
Lamp, #1563 Lattice & Grape	$180.00 – 190.00	1937
Mint jar & cover, #1639 Elizabeth	$165.00 – 185.00	1930
Nymph, #1645 September Morn	$225.00 – 250.00	1933
Pitcher, #1635 w/#1702 cut Diamond Optic	$160.00 – 185.00	1933
Pitcher, #1636 Diamond Optic	$150.00 – 175.00	1932
Plate, #103 – 6"	$8.00 – 10.00	1924
Plate, #175 – 8" Leaf	$40.00 – 45.00	1938
Plate, #175 – 11½" Leaf	$55.00 – 65.00	1938
Plate, #600 – 8"	$10.00 – 12.00	1924
Plate, #631 – 11½" sandwich	$27.00 – 30.00	1924
Plate, #638	$43.00 – 48.00	1924
Plate, #758 – 8½" octagonal	$12.00 – 15.00	1927
Plate, #1093 – 9" Basket Weave w/Open Edge	$32.00 – 37.00	1930
Plate, #1639 – 6" Elizabeth	$8.00 – 12.00	1930
Plate, #1639 – 8" Elizabeth	$15.00 – 18.00	1930
Puff box, #743 covered	$75.00 – 85.00	1924
Salver, #606	$12.00 – 14.00	1924
Salver, #647 – 13" ftd.	$35.00 – 50.00	1924
Shell, 3½" – 4½"	$12.00 – 14.00	1936
Sugar, #1502 Diamond Optic	$27.00 – 32.00	1927
Sugar, #1639 – 3½" Elizabeth	$34.00 – 37.00	1930
Tea bell, #47 Daisy Cut	$40.00 – 45.00	1933
Tumbler, #1635 10 oz. w/#1702 cut Diamond Optic	$22.00 – 28.00	1933
Tumbler, #1933	$8.00 – 10.00	1933 – 37
Tumbler, #1934 whiskey (goblet)	$12.00 – 14.00	1935 – 36
Tumbler, #1935 1 oz. whiskey Franklin	$12.00 – 14.00	1935
Vase, #107 6½" tulip	$27.00 – 30.00	1932
Vase, #184 – 10"	$85.00 – 90.00	1933
Vase, #184 – 12"	$90.00 – 110.00	1934
Vase, #184 – 12" w/cutting	$110.00 – 120.00	1933
Vase, #349 oval	$55.00 – 65.00	1932
Vase, #519 – 20"	$95.00 – 110.00	1932
Vase, #901 – 9" crimped Dancing Ladies	$600.00 – 650.00	1935
Vase, #901 – 9" flared Dancing Ladies	$600.00 – 650.00	1935
Vase, #901 – 9" sq. Dancing Ladies	$600.00 – 700.00	1934
Vase, #912 – 12"	$45.00 – 50.00	1927
Vase, #916 – 16" Fenton's Rib	$80.00 – 85.00	1927
Vase, #1110 – 11" flared Milady	$100.00 – 125.00	1935
Vase, #1561 – 10" Apple Tree	$225.00 – 270.00	1935
Vase, #1562 – 10" Blueberry	$140.00 – 160.00	1935

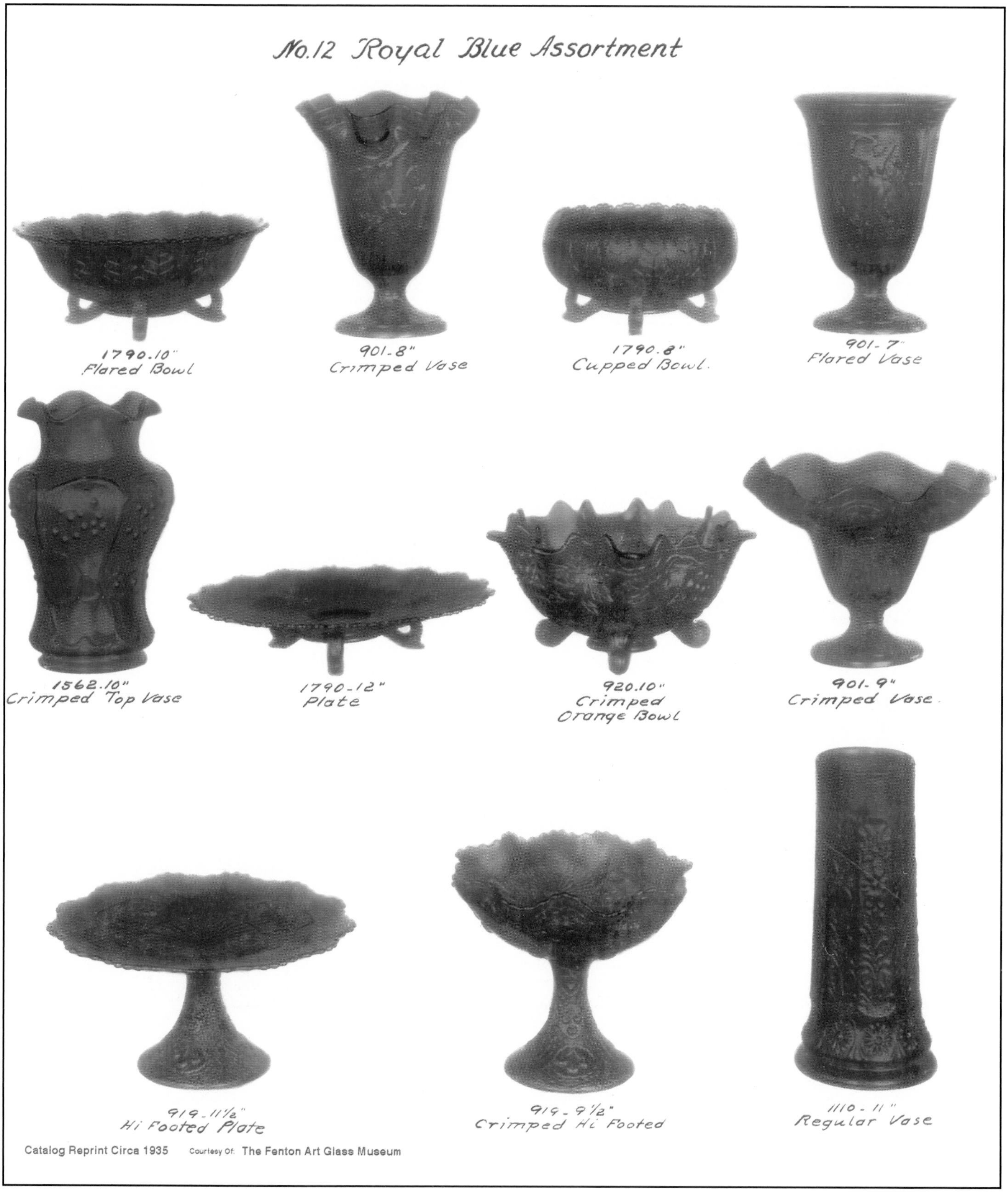
No.12 Royal Blue Assortment
1790.10" Flared Bowl
901-8" Crimped Vase
1790.8" Cupped Bowl.
901-7" Flared Vase
1562.10" Crimped Top Vase
1790-12" Plate
920.10" Crimped Orange Bowl
901-9" Crimped Vase.
919-11½" Hi Footed Plate
919-9½" Crimped Hi Footed
1110-11" Regular Vase

Catalog Reprint Circa 1935 Courtesy Of: The Fenton Art Glass Museum

RUBY

Fenton started making transparent ruby bowls, candlesticks, and vases in 1921. Production expanded into the Dolphin and Diamond Optic lines in the late 1920s and continued into the other pattern and kitchenware lines throughout the 1930s.

A few of the more unique pieces pictured are the Big Cookies macaroon jar with the cut decoration and the Dancing Ladies covered urn without the tab handles. Some of the #1540 – #1542 vases shown in the reprint on page 229 are not commonly found in other colors.

The mixer attachment is probably similar to the attachments and mixer bowls that were made for the A. F. Dormeyer Co. of Chicago. Catalog records do not show pictures of the exact styles of the items which were made for Dormeyer, but the company was one of Fenton's largest customers during the lean years of the Great Depression.

Item	Value	Date
Ashtray, #304 w/flower in bottom	$50.00 – 55.00	1933
Ashtray, #848 – 3 ftd.	$20.00 – 22.00	1933
Ashtray set, #202, 5-pc., #1, 2, 3, 4,	$58.00 – 75.00	1936
Base, #1	$14.00 – 16.00	1926
Basket, #1681 – 10½" Big Cookies	$110.00 – 130.00	1933 – 1935
Basket, #1684 w/wicker handle	$90.00 – 115.00	1933
Bonbon, #543 covered	$90.00 – 100.00	1924
Bonbon, #643 open, cupped	$27.00 – 32.00	1925
Bonbon, #1093 – 6½" Basket Weave w/Open Edge	$32.00 – 37.00	1932
Bonbon, #1502 – 6" flared Diamond Optic	$85.00 – 110.00	1930
Bonbon, #1720 Flower Windows	$35.00 – 45.00	
Bowl, #100 – 5" 3-toed Wide Rib	$33.00 – 37.00	1933
Bowl, #109 cupped	$22.00 – 24.00	1924
Bowl, #231 – 8" footed deep cupped	$48.00 – 52.00	1929
Bowl, #456 – 1 mixing	$75.00 – 80.00	1933
Bowl, #456 – 2 mixing	$70.00 – 75.00	1933
Bowl, #456 – 3 mixing	$75.00 – 85.00	1933
Bowl, #550 – 11" shallow, cupped	$60.00 – 65.00	1925
Bowl, #600 – 10" flared	$50.00 – 60.00	1933
Bowl, #600 – 7" cupped	$32.00 – 36.00	1932
Bowl, #600 – 8" cupped	$35.00 – 40.00	1930
Bowl, #600 – 8" flared	$35.00 – 40.00	1934
Bowl, #601 – 10" shallow cupped	$70.00 – 80.00	1930
Bowl, #603 – 10" footed, crimped orange	$130.00 – 150.00	1925
Bowl, #603 – 9" footed, cupped	$110.00 – 125.00	1924
Bowl, #607 – 8" cupped	$38.00 – 42.00	1925
Bowl, #607 – 8" rolled rim	$37.00 – 42.00	1924
Bowl, #607 – 9" shallow cupped	$43.00 – 50.00	1925
Bowl, #638 – 8" shallow cupped	$43.00 – 47.00	1925
Bowl, #640 – 7" flared or cupped	$32.00 – 37.00	1925
Bowl, #647 – 10¾" flared cupped	$45.00 – 50.00	1925
Bowl, #647 – 10" flared	$45.00 – 50.00	1924
Bowl, #647 – 11" rolled rim	$48.00 – 55.00	1924
Bowl, #647 – 12" w/special rolled rim	$50.00 – 55.00	1930
Bowl, #647 – 13" flared	$60.00 – 65.00	1924
Bowl,#846 – 8½" flared cupped	$30.00 – 35.00	1930
Bowl,#846 – 8½" flared or cupped	$30.00 – 35.00	1934
Bowl, #847 – 6"cupped	$25.00 – 28.00	1932
Bowl, #847 – 7" shallow cupped	$40.00 – 42.00	1933
Bowl, #848 – 8½" flared	$30.00 – 35.00	1933
Bowl, #857 – 11" flared, ftd.	$63.00 – 68.00	1933
Bowl, #857 – 11" flared or flared cupped	$55.00 – 65.00	1933 – 1935

#1562-1-13" Oval Bowl

#1561-10" Apple Tree Vase

#184-12" Cut Vase

#1681-7" Macaroon Jar "Big Cookies"

#901-9" Flared Vase

#1934 Decanter

#1934 Goblet

#1935 Whiskey

#1935 Decanter

#107-6 1/2" Vase

#901-12" Covered Urn

#1502 Diamond Optic Lamp

#1619 Reamer & Handled Jug

#1720 Ftd. Tumbler "Flower Windows"

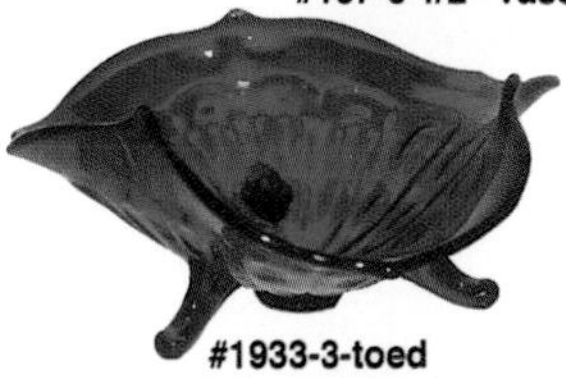
#1933-3-toed Crimped Bowl

Mixer Attachment

#1720 Wine Goblet "Flower Windows"

#950-5" Candlestick

#848 Candlestick

#56 Cologne

#307 Novelty Dog

#621-8" Flared Vase

#349-10" Oval Cut Candlestick

#848 Bowl & Nymph Figure

#1502-11 1/2" Diamond Optic Roll Rim Bowl

Item	Value	Date
Bowl, #857 – 7" cupped footed	$30.00 – 32.00	1930
Bowl, #900 – 11" oval Dancing Ladies	$400.00 – 450.00	1933
Bowl, #1093 – 8" shallow Basket Weave w/Open Edge	$45.00 – 50.00	1935
Bowl, #1093 – 9" shallow crimped Basket Weave w/Open Edge	$45.00 – 55.00	1936
Bowl, #1234 – 6"	$25.00 – 28.00	1934
Bowl, #1235 – 5"	$22.00 – 24.00	1937
Bowl, #1237 – 10" crimped	$40.00 – 45.00	1933
Bowl, #1504 – A 9" cupped w/dolphins	$45.00 – 55.00	1930
Bowl, #1504 – A- 9" shallow cupped w/dolphins	$45.00 – 55.00	1930
Bowl, #1504 – A-6" cupped w/dolphins	$32.00 – 37.00	1932
Bowl, #1562 – 13" oval	$55.00 – 65.00	1933
Bowl, #1563 – 17" oval handled	$150.00 – 175.00	1933
Bowl, #1608 – 10½" deep oval ftd. w/dolphins	$160.00 – 175.00	1933
Bowl, #1639 – 10" flared 2-handled Elizabeth	$50.00 – 55.00	1933
Bowl, #1676 – 11½" flared	$70.00 – 75.00	
Bowl, #1932 – 6½" flared or cupped	$22.00 – 27.00	1933
Bowl, #1932 – 7½" crimped	$27.00 – 30.00	1933 – 1934
Bowl, #1933 – 7" flared	$20.00 – 23.00	1933
Bowl, #2000 – 7" Pineapple	$30.00 – 35.00	1938
Bowl, #2000 – A-11" crimped Pineapple	$70.00 – 90.00	1937
Bowl, mixing attachment	$22.00 – 25.00	
Candelabra, #2318 – 6"	$43.00 – 45.00	1933
Candle vase, #1673 – 8"	$55.00 – 60.00	1932
Candleholder, #848 – 3 ftd.	$15.00 – 18.00	1933 – 1936
Candlestick, #249 – 6"	$25.00 – 27.00	1925
Candlestick, #314	$20.00 – 22.00	1925
Candlestick, #316	$20.00 – 22.00	1933
Candlestick, #318	$20.00 – 22.00	1933
Candlestick, #349 – 10"	$90.00 – 95.00	1925
Candlestick, #349 – 10" w/oval cut	$95.00 – 110.00	1925
Candlestick, #449 – 8½"	$70.00 – 75.00	1922
Candlestick, #549 – 8½"	$70.00 – 75.00	1925
Candlestick, #749 – 12"	$160.00 – 170.00	1924 – 1926
Candlestick, #1091 Basket Weave w/Open Edge	$50.00 – 55.00	1936
Candlestick, #1623 w/dolphins	$27.00 – 32.00	1930 – 1937
Candlestick, #1672 flared or rolled edge	$20.00 – 23.00	1933
Candy jar, #8, ½ lb.	$40.00 – 45.00	1925
Candy jar, #9, ¾ lb.	$50.00 – 60.00	1925
Candy jar, #636, 1 lb.	$55.00 – 65.00	1925
Candy jar, #735, ½ lb.	$55.00 – 60.00	1925
Candy jar, #736, 1 lb.	$100.00 – 105.00	1925
Cheese comport and underplate, #316	$60.00 – 65.00	
Cigarette box, #308	$105.00 – 125.00	1934
Coaster, #201	$18.00 – 20.00	1926
Coaster, #1590 – 4"	$18.00 – 20.00	1932 – 1933
Cologne, #55	$125.00 – 150.00	1925
Cologne, #56	$150.00 – 190.00	1925
Cologne, #1502 Diamond Optic	$150.00 – 180.00	1927
Comport, #100 tulip	$30.00 – 33.00	1924
Comport, #260 – 7" tall footed	$45.00 – 50.00	1925
Comport, #737 – 6½" cupped	$32.00 – 37.00	1921
Creamer, #1502 Diamond Optic	$30.00 – 37.00	1927
Creamer, #1639 Elizabeth	$35.00 – 45.00	1930
Cup, #1502 Diamond Optic	$14.00 – 16.00	1933
Decanter, #1934	$150.00 – 180.00	
Decanter, 1935 Franklin	$125.00 – 150.00	1934

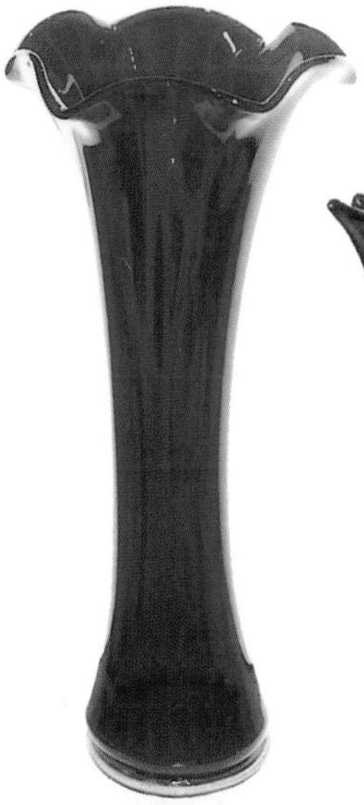

#916-14" Vase

#1673-8" Candle Vase

#895-10" Flared Vase

#621-8" Square Top Vase

#184-6" Vase

Catalog Reprint Circa 1930 Courtesy Of: The Fenton Art Glass Museum

THE FENTON ART GLASS CO.
WILLIAMSTOWN, W. VA.
PLAIN RUBY
602-10" Vase & Base.
1542-9" Flared Vase.
1542-8 1/2" Roll Rim Vase.
1541-6" Fld. Vase.
1541-7" Crimp. Vase.
1540-6" Crimp. Vase.
1541-8" Roll Rim Vase.
1541-9" Fld. Vase
1540-7 3/4" Flared Vase.
1540-8 1/4" Crimp. Vase.
1540-7 1/4" Flared Vase.
1540-5" Fld. Vase.
857-7" Cupped Footed Bowl.
600-8" Cupped Bowl & Base.
601-10" Shallow Cup. Bowl & Base.
846-8 1/2" Flared Cup Bowl & Base.
857-7" Regular Footed Bowl.
570-5" Fan Vase.
543 Covered Bon Bon.
316-C.S.
647-12" Special Roll Rim Bowl.
316-C.S.
847-8" Plate.
640-7" Fld. Cup Bowl & Base.

Item	Value	Date
Dog, #307 novelty	$42.00 – 46.00	1933
Fern bowl, #250 three-footed	$40.00 – 45.00	1924 – 1925
Fish, #306 novelty	$53.00 – 58.00	1933
Flower block, #1234 for nymph figure	$20.00 – 25.00	1933 – 1934
Goblet, #1502 – 11 oz. bridge Diamond Optic	$20.00 – 22.00	1937
Goblet, #1502 – 9 oz. bridge Diamond Optic	$20.00 – 22.00	1937
Goblet, #1502 Hi ftd. Diamond Optic	$22.00 – 27.00	1937
Goblet, 1934	$16.00 – 18.00	
Goblet, #1720 cocktail Flower Windows	$37.00 – 42.00	1937 – 1938
Goblet, #1720 water Flower Windows	$45.00 – 50.00	1937
Ice pail, #1616 – 6½" Diamond Optic	$90.00 – 110.00	1933
Ivy ball, #705	$42.00 – 48.00	1933
Ivy ball, #706	$42.00 – 48.00	1933
Lamp, #1502 Diamond Optic	$140.00 – 170.00	
Lamp, #1561 Apple Tree	$170.00 – 195.00	1937
Lamp, #1563 Lattice & Grape	$170.00 – 185.00	1937
Macaroon jar, #1681 – 7" Big Cookies	$140.00 – 165.00	1933
Mayonnaise, #109	$38.00 – 42.00	1924
Mayonnaise, #2005	$37.00 – 42.00	1924
Nymph, #1645 September Morn	$225.00 – 250.00	1933 – 1934
Pitcher, #1635 w/#1702 cut Diamond Optic	$160.00 – 185.00	1930
Pitcher, #1636 Diamond Optic	$150.00 – 175.00	1932
Pitcher, #1653	$150.00 – 175.00	
Plate, #103 – 6"	$6.00 – 8.00	1924
Plate, #175 – 11½" Leaf	$70.00 – 85.00	1936
Plate, #175 – 8" Leaf	$40.00 – 45.00	1936
Plate, #680 – 8"	$10.00 – 12.00	1927
Plate, #682 – 9"	$12.00 – 14.00	1926 – 1938
Plate, #847 – 8" round	$10.00 – 12.00	1930
Plate, #1093 – 9" Basket Weave w/Open Edge	$25.00 – 30.00	1930
Plate, #1502 – 6" octagonal Diamond Optic	$7.00 – 9.00	1928
Plate, #1502 – 8"octagonal Diamond Optic	$12.00 – 14.00	1928
Plate, #1639 – 12" 2-handled Elizabeth	$60.00 – 70.00	1933
Plate, #1639 – 6" Elizabeth	$10.00 – 12.00	1933
Plate, #1639 – 8" Elizabeth	$15.00 – 18.00	1932
Puff box, #57	$60.00 – 65.00	1925
Puff box, #743 covered	$75.00 – 100.00	1925
Puff box, #1502 Diamond Optic	$75.00 – 100.00	1933
Reamer, #1619 w/handled jug	$1000.00 – 1200.00	1933
Salver, #647 – 13" ftd.	$80.00 – 85.00	1924
Saucer, #1502 Diamond Optic	$5.00 – 6.00	1933
Shaker, #1502 Diamond Optic	$60.00 – 70.00	1937
Shell, 3½ – 4½"	$13.00 – 15.00	1936
Sherbet, #1502 Diamond Optic	$15.00 – 18.00	1933
Sherbet, #1720 Flower Windows	$32.00 – 35.00	1937 – 1938
Sherbet, #316	$9.00 – 11.00	1925
Sugar, #1502 Diamond Optic	$30.00 – 37.00	1933
Sugar, #1639 – 3½" Elizabeth	$35.00 – 45.00	1930
Tea bell, #47 Daisy Cut	$45.00 – 55.00	1933
Tray, #1502 vanity Diamond Optic	$27.00 – 32.00	1933
Tray, #1502 – 10" handled sandwich Diamond Optic	$55.00 – 65.00	1933
Tumbler, #1502 – 5 oz. orange juice Diamond Optic	$15.00 – 19.00	1933
Tumbler, #1502 – 9 oz. ftd Diamond Optic	$16.00 – 20.00	1934 – 1935
Tumbler, #1635 – 10 oz. w/#1702 cut Diamond Optic	$22.00 – 25.00	1930
Tumbler, #1653	$25.00 – 30.00	
Tumbler, #1720 ice tea, Flower Windows	$50.00 – 55.00	1937 – 1938
Tumbler, #1933	$8.00 – 10.00	1933 – 1935

Item	Value	Date
Tumbler, #1934 whiskey (goblet)	$12.00 – 14.00	1935 – 1936
Tumbler, #1935 1 oz. whiskey Franklin	$12.00 – 14.00	1934
Urn, #901 – 12" covered Dancing Ladies	$800.00 – 1000.00	1933
Vanity set, #1502 3-pc. Diamond Optic	$375.00 – 460.00	1933
Vanity set, #1502 4-pc. (with tray) Diamond Optic	$400.00 – 495.00	1933
Vase, 10" (bottle shape)	$70.00 – 85.00	
Vase, #107 tulip – 6½"	$27.00 – 30.00	1932 – 1934
Vase, #183 – 10" tulip; triangle; flared; square; special	$60.00 – 65.00	1932
Vase, #183 – 12"	$65.00 – 70.00	1933
Vase, #184 – 10"	$65.00 – 75.00	1934
Vase, #184 – 10" w/cutting	$100.00 – 150.00	1933
Vase, #184 – 12"	$85.00 – 95.00	1933
Vase, #184 – 12" w/cutting	$150.00 – 175.00	1931 – 1933
Vase, #184 – 6"	$37.00 – 45.00	1931
Vase, #184 – 6" w/cutting	$40.00 – 50.00	1931
Vase, #184 – 8"	$40.00 – 50.00	1931
Vase, #184 – 8" w/cutting	$75.00 – 85.00	1931
Vase, #185 – 6"	$32.00 – 42.00	1933 – 1934
Vase, #251 – 10" bud	$37.00 – 42.00	1925
Vase, #349 oval	$55.00 – 65.00	1932
Vase, #349 – 8" fan	$63.00 – 70.00	1936
Vase, #519 – 20"	$75.00 – 85.00	
Vase, #560 fan	$42.00 – 46.00	1925
Vase, #561 fan	$42.00 – 46.00	1925
Vase, #562 – 8" fan	$45.00 – 50.00	1926
Vase, #570 – 5" fan	$42.00 – 48.00	1930
Vase, #602 – 10" flared	$53.00 – 56.00	1925
Vase, #611 – 6½" cupped	$30.00 – 35.00	1925
Vase, #612 – 6½" flared	$30.00 – 35.00	1925
Vase, #621 – 6"	$42.00 – 45.00	1925 – 1933
Vase, #621 – 8" flared, cupped, or square top	$45.00 – 50.00	1925
Vase, #622 – 7½" flared	$32.00 – 35.00	1925
Vase, #835 – 6" crimped	$32.00 – 35.00	1937
Vase, #857 – 8" flared	$35.00 – 45.00	1934
Vase, #857 – 8" fan	$40.00 – 47.00	1934 – 1935
Vase, #901 – 9" crimped Dancing Ladies	$600.00 – 625.00	1933
Vase, #901 – 9" square Dancing Ladies	$600.00 – 700.00	1933
Vase, #912 – 12"	$65.00 – 70.00	1927
Vase, #916 – 14"-16" Fenton's Rib	$53.00 – 56.00	1927
Vase, #1126	$40.00 – 50.00	1927
Vase, #1502 – 10" Diamond Optic	$65.00 – 75.00	1932
Vase, #1502 – 8" crimped Diamond Optic	$60.00 – 65.00	1932
Vase, #1502 – 8½" fan Diamond Optic	$60.00 – 65.00	1928
Vase, #1540 – 5" flared	$32.00 – 35.00	1930
Vase, #1540 – 6" crimped	$32.00 – 35.00	1930
Vase, #1540 – 7½" flared	$38.00 – 40.00	1930
Vase, #1540 – 7¾" flared	$38.00 – 40.00	1930
Vase, #1540 – 8¼" crimped	$40.00 – 44.00	1930
Vase, #1541 – 6" flared	$33.00 – 35.00	1930
Vase, #1541 – 7" crimped	$33.00 – 35.00	1930
Vase, #1541 – 8" rolled rim	$40.00 – 50.00	1930
Vase, #1541 – 9" flared	$40.00 – 50.00	1930
Vase, #1542 – 8½" rolled rim	$38.00 – 40.00	1930
Vase, #1542 – 9" flared	$42.00 – 50.00	1930
Vase, #1561 – 10" Apple Tree	$180.00 – 220.00	
Vase, #1611 – 6" crimped violet	$35.00 – 40.00	1932
Vase, #1668 – 8" flip	$80.00 – 95.00	1933

TANGERINE

Fenton's tangerine is a deep orange color. Much of Fenton's tangerine production was iridized and will be found in the Stretch Glass section. Most of the clear tangerine was made in 1927, and just about all of this will be found in the Diamond Optic pattern.

Item	Value	Date
Bonbon, #1502 – 6" flared Diamond Optic	$95.00 – 125.00	1927
Bonbon, #1502 – 7½" crimped Diamond Optic	$100.00 – 125.00	1927
Bonbon, #1502 – 7½" oval Diamond Optic	$100.00 – 125.00	1927
Bonbon, #1502 – 7½" round w/dolphins Diamond Optic	$95.00 – 125.00	1927
Bowl, #1502 – 10" special roll rim Diamond Optic	$55.00 – 65.00	1927
Bowl, #1502 – 12" special roll rim Diamond Optic	$65.00 – 75.00	1927
Candle, #1502 Diamond Optic	$25.00 – 30.00	1927
Candy jar, #1533–A	$150.00 – 165.00	
Comport, #1502, Hi ftd. Diamond Optic	$235.00 – 260.00	1928
Comport, #1533 – 7" oval w/dolphins	$125.00 – 135.00	1928
Comport, #643 – 6¾" salver	$37.00 – 40.00	
Creamer, #1502 Diamond Optic	$35.00 – 40.00	1927
Cup, #1502 Diamond Optic	$43.00 – 48.00	1927
Mayonnaise and ladle, #1502 Diamond Optic	$95.00 – 110.00	1927
Plate, #1502 – 8" octagonal Diamond Optic	$33.00 – 37.00	1927
Saucer, #1502 Diamond Optic	$12.00 – 15.00	1927
Sugar, #1502 Diamond Optic	$37.00 – 42.00	1927
Tray, #1502 – 10" handled sandwich Diamond Optic	$75.00 – 85.00	1927
Vase, #1502 – 5" fan w/dolphins Diamond Optic	$80.00 – 90.00	1927
Vase, #1502 – 6" fan w/dolphins Diamond Optic	$85.00 – 95.00	1927
Vase, #1502 – 7" roll edge Diamond Optic	$100.00 – 110.00	1927
Vase, #1502 – 8" crimped Diamond Optic	$90.00 – 95.00	1927
Vase, #1502 – 8½" fan Diamond Optic	$95.00 – 110.00	1927
Vase, #1530 – 12"	$135.00 – 150.00	1928

#1502 High Ftd. Comport

#1533-7" Oval Bon-bon

#1502-7" Roll Top Vase

#1502-10" Handled
Sandwich Tray

#1502 Mayonnaise

#643-6 3/4" Ftd.
Salver Comport

#1502 Sugar and Creamer

#1502-6" Fan Vase

WISTERIA & WISTERIA OPALESCENT

Fenton's wisteria color is probably more readily recognized as amethyst by collectors. Fenton produced large quantities of this color in carnival glass and stretch glass through the mid 1920s. The fact that some of this glass was made without an iridescent finish is not surprising. However, there does not appear to be a significant amount of this color available in either quantity or number of different pieces made. It is possible this color swan bowl may have been made by Dugan before Fenton acquired the mold. There is no written evidence to support Fenton's production of this color swan.

Notice the pieces of wisteria opalescent in the photo. This is a reappearance of a color produced in the early pattern glass era of about 1910. The vanity tray in the photo below has not yet been confirmed as Fenton. Color and ring size of the indentations lend credence to the possibility that this is a Fenton piece.

Item	Wisteria	Wisteria Opalescent	Date
Bonbon, hat-shaped Fern Panels		$55.00 – 65.00	
Bowl, #100 – 7½" 3-footed round Wide Rib		$30.00 – 35.00	
Bowl, #6 – 11" square, oval or tulip swan	$90.00 – 100.00		
Bowl, #607 – 8" rolled rim	$38.00 – 42.00		1924
Bowl, #647 – 11" rolled rim	$45.00 – 55.00		1924
Bowl, #847 – 6" cupped	$35.00 – 50.00		
Bowl, oval Grape & Cable	$140.00 – 160.00		
Candlestick, #349 flared	$25.00 – 27.00		
Candlestick, #749 – 12"	$148.00 – 160.00		1924
Candy jar, #636, 1 lb.	$80.00 – 90.00		
Cologne, #56	$170.00 – 190.00		
Flower block, #4	$17.00 – 19.00		1927
Night set, #401	$110.00 – 130.00		
Pitcher, #215 grape juice		$235.00 – 260.00	
Pitcher, #222 iced tea	$210.00 – 260.00		
Pitcher, #1353 Spiral Optic		$700.00 – 800.00	
Plate, #103 – 6"	$5.00 – 7.00		1924
Plate, #2006	$20.00 – 22.00		1924
Tumbler, #222 handled	$20.00 – 22.00		
Tumbler, 4" Thumbprint		$45.00 – 50.00	
Vase, 9" – 12" "Boggy Bayou"		$50.00 – 60.00	
Vase, 10" flared		$55.00 – 62.00	

Fern Panels Hat-shaped Bonbon

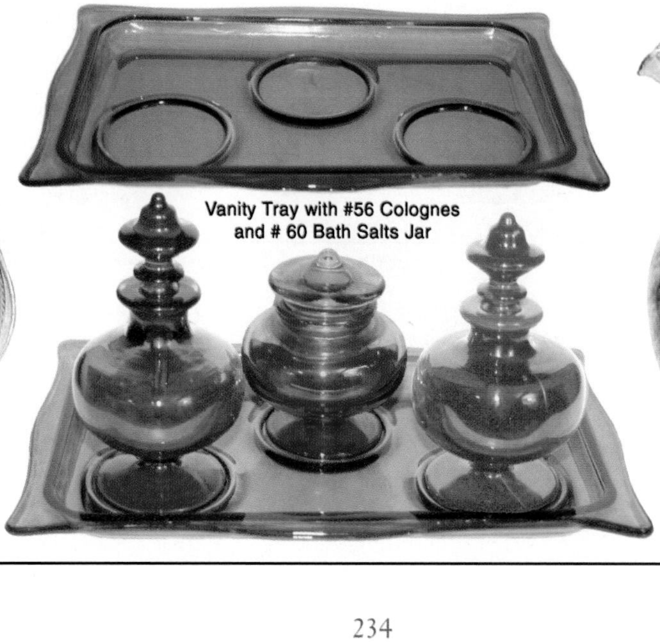

Vanity Tray with #56 Colognes and # 60 Bath Salts Jar

#1353 Spiral Optic Pitcher

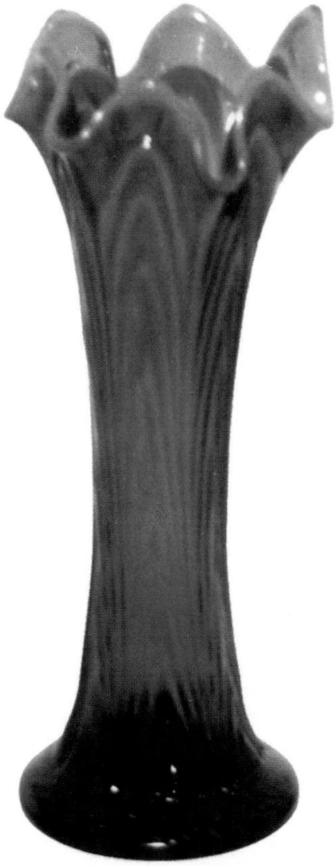

12" Boggy Bayou Vase

#636-1lb. Candy

#215 Grape Juice Pitcher

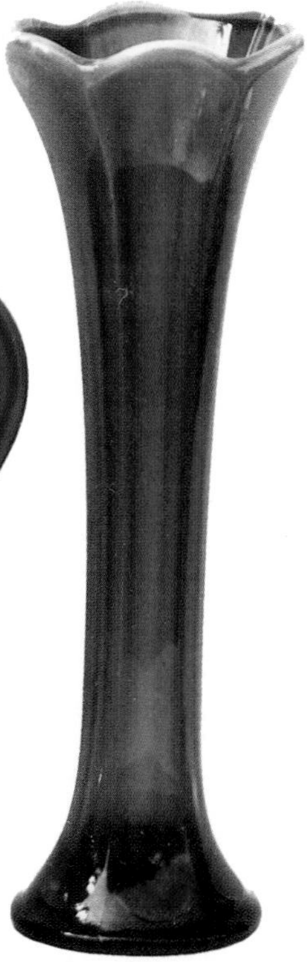

10" Flared Vase

4" Thumbprint Tumbler

#222 Handled Ice Tea Tumbler

#401 Night Set

EXPERIMENTAL COLORS AND UNUSUAL DECORATIONS

Pictured are a few sample items or items with limited production that are almost impossible to evaluate accurately. Fenton, like most other companies, periodically made sample items to assess the feasibility of producing an item. Some of these items have found their way into collectors' hands through one means or another. Other items have remained in the company archives. In either case, too few of these items exist to be able to establish any kind of an accurate value. Some of these items are pictured here merely to provide examples of some of the unique shapes, colors, and decorations that were contemplated. Unfortunately, very few collectors will ever be able to own these items.

Left to right

Row 1:

A. #898 – 11½" vase cased blue over white; cut floral decoration, circa 1935.
B. #893 ginger jar with mottled periwinkle blue shade color, circa 1935.
C. #1110 – 11" vase in unusual green collectors refer to as kitchen green.

Row 2:

A. #621 – 6½" flared vase with hand-painted Oriental scene.
B. 7" footed bowl in what appears to be a dark lilac and moonstone combination.

Row 3:

A. #848 – 8" flared bowl, unusual in blue opalescent.
B. #1562 – 13" oval bowl in an opaque orange-yellow color, with black decoration.
C. Elephant whiskey bottle with stopper in mermaid blue.

#893 Ginger Jar
#1110-11" Crimped Top Vase
#898-11 1/2" Vase
7" Footed Bowl
#621-6 1/2" Flared Vase
#848-8" Flared Bowl
#1562-13" Oval Bowl
Elephant Whiskey Bottle

FENTON PATTERNS

INTRODUCTION

Much of Fenton's production prior to the late 1920s was devoted to novelty and accessory pieces. Bowls, candy jars, comports, candlesticks, and vases were ideally suited to a labor intensive environment, whereas dinnerware production was not. Most of the early Fenton lines have concentrated on these larger items and production of smaller pieces such as cups and saucers and plates has been very limited. Fenton had also established its niche in the marketplace as a major producer of iridescent glassware.

Starting in 1927, with the introduction of Diamond Optic and Spiral Optic, Fenton's philosophy seemed to change. Interest in iridescent glassware was declining, and the uncertain economic times forced Fenton's management to become more conservative. For about the next ten years Fenton seemed willing to compete with the other contemporary glass factories by producing luncheon, dinnerware, and basic utilitarian kitchenware items. Production of items essential to everyday life at competitive prices seemed to be the key to the company's survival during these lean times. Also, a large account from A. H. Dormeyer, a major maker of electric kitchen appliances from Chicago, to produce mixing bowls for their electric mixers helped tremendously.

Other patterns followed soon after these first two. Lincoln Inn appeared in 1928, #1639 Elizabeth followed in 1930, and Georgian came on line in 1931. Most of these patterns were made in crystal and a variety of colors throughout the 1930s. A pattern which collectors call Daisy and Button was introduced into the Fenton line in 1937.

The Basket Weave with Open Edge pieces included in this section are a continuation of the intermittent production of items in this pattern from early carnival glass molds. This pattern has been one of the most heavily produced by Fenton with pieces appearing in carnival, stretch glass, transparent, and opaque colors.

We have cheated slightly by including Dolphin as a pattern. Although technically this is not a pattern, the dolphin-handle decoration was used on a number of different patterns and plain items in both iridescent and non-iridescent production. Therefore, since there are a number of collectors who collect only Dolphin items, it seemed appropriate to group everything together in one area and organize all the different types of glassware made with this decoration.

Collectors will face a challenge in finding many of the pieces to these patterns. Since Fenton was a hand operation, they simply did not crank out the quantities of items that were produced in patterns by contemporary machine-made glass companies.

The patterns in this section are arranged alphabetically by name. Most of the illustrations are mixed with original catalog reprints from the era. The known colors are listed in each pattern, and an attempt has been made to show pieces in as many colors as possible.

BASKET WEAVE WITH OPEN EDGE

Colors: Mandarin red; green opalescent; ruby; golden iridescent; topaz opalescent; blue opalescent; jade green; ruby iridescent; black; crystal; green transparent; royal blue; milk glass, Mongolian green.

Small bonbons, bowls, and vases in this pattern appear to be among Fenton's favorite items. The first records of this pattern are from 1911, when pieces of blue and gold carnival were made. Production continued through the early 1920s when items were added in stretch glass and other carnival glass colors. During the 1930s, pieces were made in black, milk glass, Mandarin red, jade green, crystal, Mongolian green, and opalescent colors. Fenton is currently making a Basket Weave pattern tall vase which does not have the open edge.

Inventory records indicate that milk glass pieces were introduced in 1933. Other colors of Basket Weave followed in 1935. Milk glass pieces were no longer listed by 1936, and by 1937 all the Basket Weave pieces had disappeared from the records. The absence of Basket Weave from the line continued until 1970, when pieces were once again made in new colors. Look for the Fenton logo to verify these newer items.

For listings and prices of these items in carnival glass and stretch glass, see the appropriate listings in these sections earlier in this book.

Item	Black	Jade/ Ruby	Green Opalescent	Blue Opalescent	Crystal	Green
Basket, 6" crimped				$32.00 – 38.00		
Basket, 7½" oval				$40.00 – 42.00		
Bonbon, 5¾"	$27.00 – 32.00	$32.00 – 37.00	$32.00 – 36.00	$32.00 – 40.00	$21.00 – 26.00	$12.00 – 15.00
Bowl, 6½" flared cupped	$23.00 – 28.00	$30.00 – 37.00	$33.00 – 35.00			$20.00 – 23.00
Bowl, 7" deep ft.		$31.00 – 36.00				
Bowl, 8" shallow	$37.00 – 42.00	$45.00 – 50.00				
Bowl, 9" shallow crimped	$42.00 – 45.00	$45.00 – 55.00	$42.00 – 46.00		$20.00 – 22.00	$25.00 – 30.00
Candlestick	$47.00 – 55.00	$50.00 – 55.00	$42.00 – 46.00			$20.00 – 22.00
Mayonnaise/underplate				$58.00 – 65.00		
Plate, 9"		$25.00 – 30.00			$32.00 – 35.00	

Item	Royal Blue	Milk Glass	Mandarin Red	Topaz Opalescent	French Opalescent	Mongolian Green
Basket, 6" crimped				$45.00 – 55.00	$30.00 – 35.00	
Bonbon, 5¾"	$32.00 – 37.00	$32.00 – 37.00	$125.00 – 150.00	$32.00 – 40.00	$28.00 – 32.00	$90.00 – 100.00
Bowl, 4½"		$20.00 – 22.00				
Bowl, 5"		$25.00 – 27.00				
Bowl, 6½" flared cupped		$32.00 – 36.00				
Bowl, 7½" shallow flared	$45.00 – 50.00		$125.00 – 150.00	$32.00 – 40.00		
Bowl, 9" shallow crimped	$47.00 – 55.00	$22.00 – 27.00				
Plate, 9"	$32.00 – 37.00	$25.00 – 32.00				
Vase, 5½" flared		$30.00 – 33.00	$150.00 – 200.00			$90.00 – 100.00

5 1/2" Flared Vase
Mandarin Red

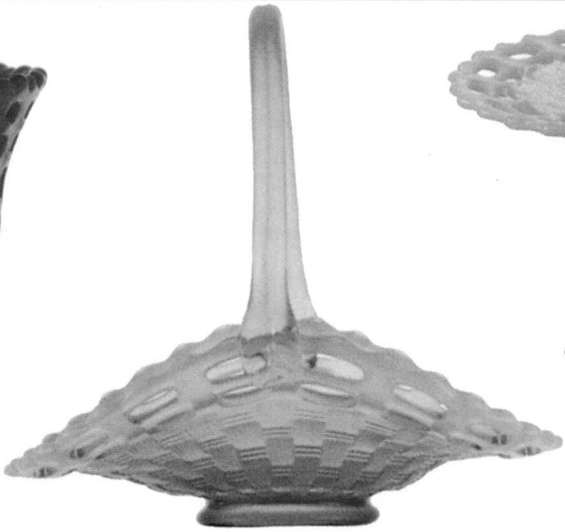

7 1/2" Oval Basket
Blue Opalescent

7 1/2" Shallow Flared Bowl
Topaz Opalescent

5 3/4" Oval Bonbon
Golden Iridescent

7 1/4" Footed Deep Bowl
Jade Green

9" Shallow Crimped Bowl
Ruby

5" Candlestick
Jade Green

5 3/4" Mayonnaise
& 7 3/4" Underplate
Blue Opalescent

5 3/4" Crimped Bonbon
Ruby Iridescent

6 1/2" Crimped Bonbon
Ruby Iridescent

6" Crimped Basket
Blue Opalescent

5" Candlestick
Transparent Green

DAISY AND BUTTON #1900 (CAPE COD) 1937 – 1939

Colors: amber; aqua; crystal; gold; Cape Cod green; colonial blue; royal blue; rose, ruby; vaseline; wisteria.

The pattern which is called Daisy and Button by collectors was introduced as the #1900 Cape Cod Crystal Line in 1937. Later, Fenton also referred to this pattern as Daisy and Button. Between 1937 and 1939 this line was offered in crystal and transparent colors. In 1953 the pattern was reissued in opaque colors.

New colors brought into the line for the first time and used with this pattern are Cape Cod green and Colonial blue. Cape Cod green was originally introduced into the line as Stiegel green. After a few years in the line this color became known as Cape Cod green. Colonial blue is a transparent copper blue that is darker than aquamarine. When Colonial blue was remade in the 1960s, the later version was darker than the Colonial blue from the 1930s. Some of the crystal items will have colored decorative panels. An example is the 9½" flared bowl shown in the photo. The fan-shaped tray used with the dresser set, #957, has a different number from the rest of the line.

	Crystal	Royal Blue	Ruby	Vaseline
Ashtray	$5.00 – 6.00	$10.00 – 12.00	$9.00 – 11.00	$6.00 – 8.00
Basket, #2			$27.00 – 30.00	
Basket, #3			$32.00 – 34.00	
Bell	$13.00 – 15.00			
Bootee	$12.00 – 15.00	$27.00 – 32.00	$25.00 – 30.00	
Bottle, cologne	$38.00 – 42.00	$100.00 – 125.00	$110.00 – 125.00	
Bowl, 7½" regular			$8.00 – 10.00	
Bowl, 10" flared	$20.00 – 22.00			
Bowl, 11" handled square; clover leaf	$22.00 – 24.00			$30.00 – 33.00
Bowl, 12" handled boat; flared	$22.00 – 25.00			
Candelabra	$20.00 – 22.00			
Creamer	$6.00 – 8.00	$14.00 – 16.00		$8.00 – 10.00
Cup	$4.00 – 5.00	$10.00 – 12.00		$6.00 – 7.00
Hat, #1 small	$9.00 – 10.00	$14.00 – 16.00	$12.00 – 15.00	$10.00 – 14.00
Hat, #2 medium			$12.00 – 15.00	
Hat, #3			$14.00 – 16.00	
Plate, 8"	$9.00 – 11.00			
Powder box	$22.00 – 24.00	$65.00 – 70.00		$60.00 – 65.00
Rose bowl, 7"	$20.00 – 22.00			
Saucer	$1.50 – 2.00	$2.00 – 2.50		$1.50 – 2.00
Slipper ashtray	$11.00 – 13.00	$18.00 – 20.00	$18.00 – 20.00	$15.00 – 18.00
Sugar	$5.00 – 7.00	$12.00 – 15.00		$8.00 – 10.00
Tray, #957 fan	$11.00 – 13.00	$30.00 – 35.00		$25.00 – 30.00
Underplate, 13½" for 10" bowl	$15.00 – 18.00			
Vanity set	$75.00 – 80.00	$190.00 – 210.00		$170.00 – 195.00
Vase, 10" fan	$15.00 – 18.00			$75.00 – 95.00
Vase, hand	$15.00 – 16.00			$28.00 – 30.00

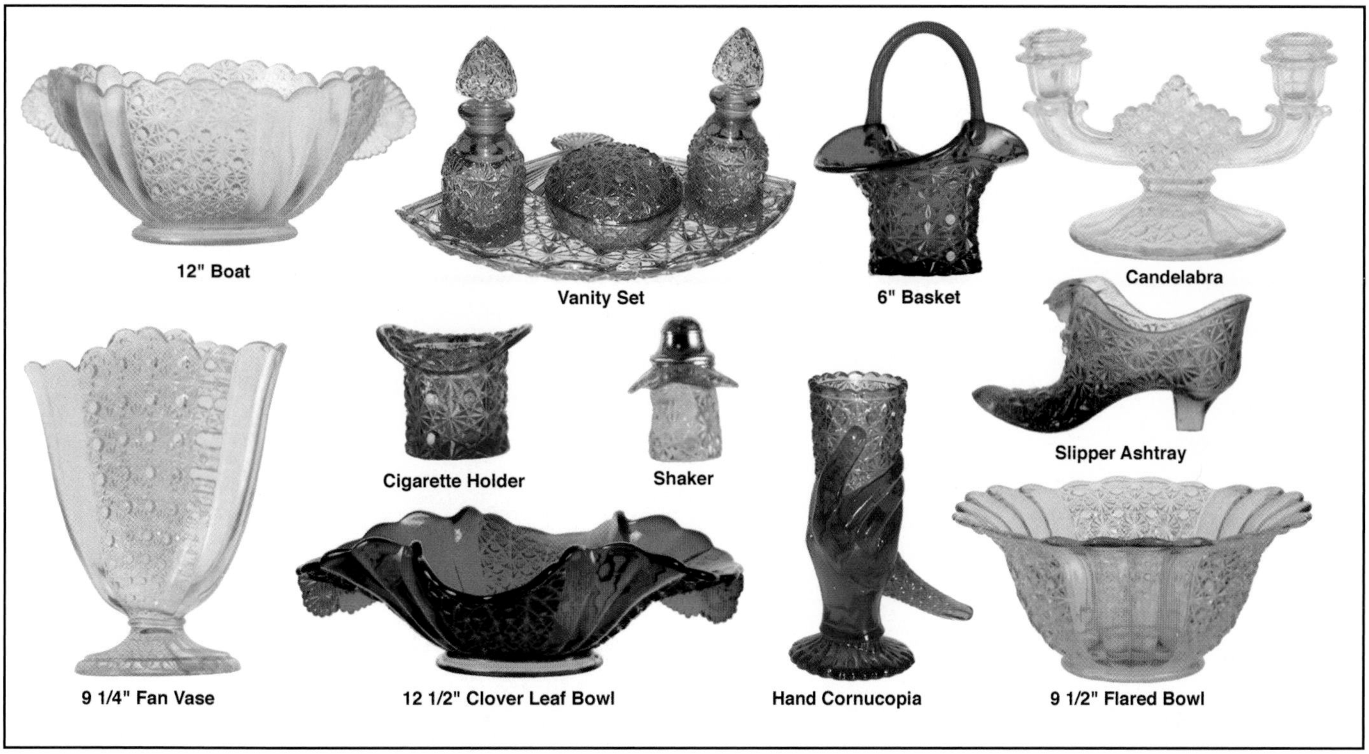
12" Boat
Vanity Set
6" Basket
Candelabra
Slipper Ashtray
Cigarette Holder
Shaker
9 1/4" Fan Vase
12 1/2" Clover Leaf Bowl
Hand Cornucopia
9 1/2" Flared Bowl

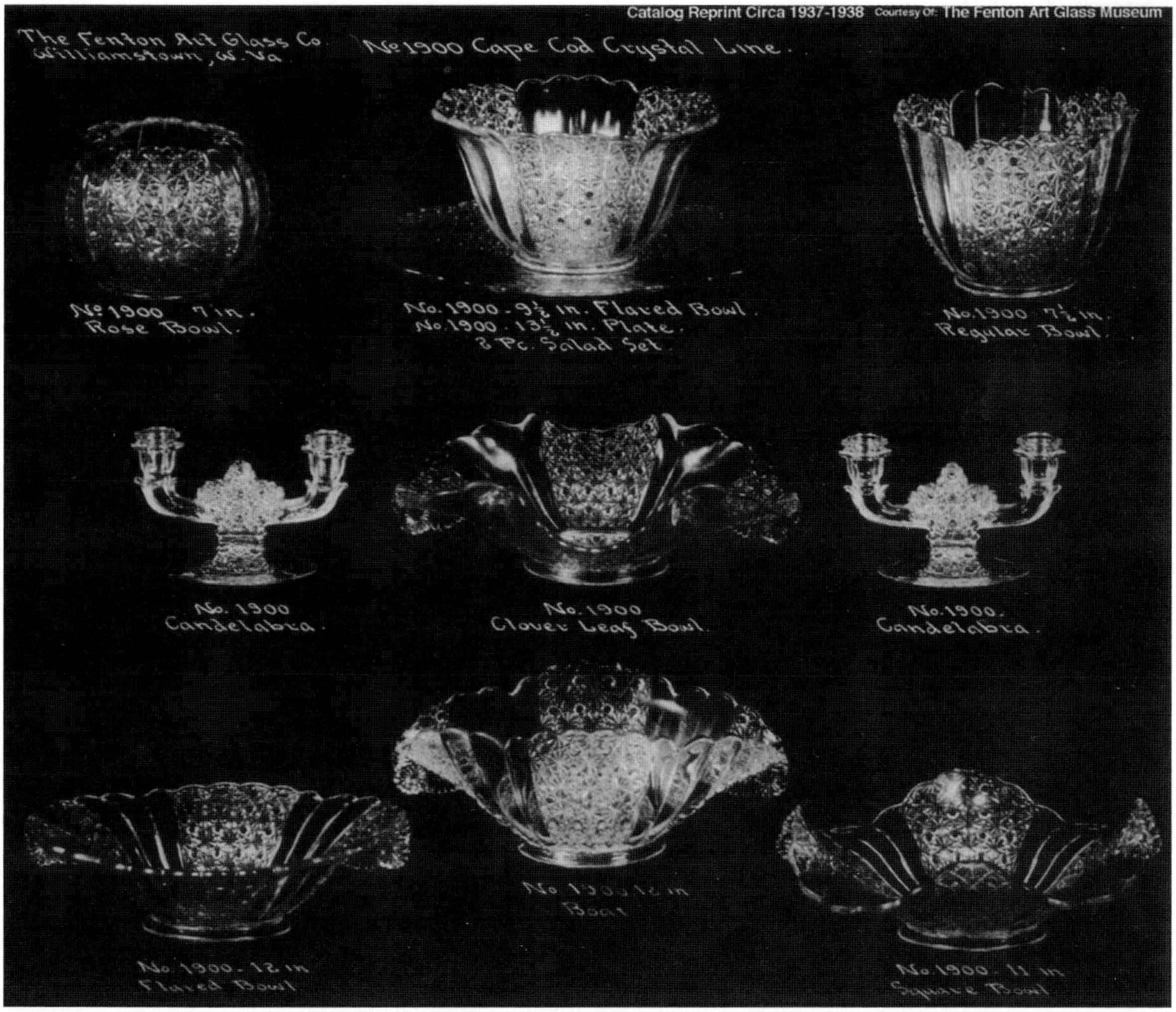
Catalog Reprint Circa 1937-1938 Courtesy Of: The Fenton Art Glass Museum
The Fenton Art Glass Co.
Williamstown, W. Va.
No 1900 Cape Cod Crystal Line.
No 1900 7 in. Rose Bowl.
No. 1900 - 9½ in. Flared Bowl.
No. 1900 - 13½ in. Plate.
3 Pc. Salad Set.
No. 1900 7½ in. Regular Bowl.
No. 1900 Candelabra.
No. 1900 Clover Leaf Bowl.
No. 1900. Candelabra.
No 1900 12 in Boat
No. 1900 - 12 in Flared Bowl
No. 1900. 11 in Square Bowl

Daisy & Button	Amber/ Gold/Rose	Cape Cod Green	Colonial Blue	Aqua	Wisteria
Ashtray	$9.00 – 11.00	$8.00 – 10.00	$7.00 – 9.00	$7.00 –9.00	$7.00 – 8.00
Basket, #2			$20.00 – 22.00	$22.00 – 25.00	
Basket, #3			$22.00 – 27.00	$25.00 – 28.00	
Bell				$22.00 – 24.00	
Bootee				$26.00 – 31.00	
Bottle, cologne	$70.00 – 75.00			$78.00 – 85.00	$80.00 – 85.00
Bowl, 12" handled boat; flared	$20.00 – 24.00				
Candelabra					$28.00 – 35.00
Creamer	$8.00 – 10.00			$20.00 – 23.00	
Cup	$6.00 – 7.00			$12.00 – 15.00	
Hat, #1 small	$8.00 – 10.00	$8.00 – 10.00	$13.00 – 15.00	$12.00 – 15.00	$15.00 – 18.00
Hat, #2 medium	$8.00 – 10.00	$12.00 – 15.00	$13.00 – 15.00	$12.00 – 15.00	$15.00 – 18.00
Hat, #3					$14.00 – 17.00
Plate, 8"	$4.00 – 6.00			$10.00 – 12.00	
Powder box	$32.00 – 37.00			$43.00 – 46.00	$46.00 – 48.00
Rose bowl, 7"					
Shaker					$18.00 – 20.00
Saucer	$1.00 – 2.00			$3.00 – 4.00	
Slipper ashtray	$10.00 – 12.00	$18.00 – 20.00	$20.00 – 22.00	$18.00 – 20.00	$20.00 – 22.00
Sugar	$8.00 – 10.00			$18.00 – 22.00	
Tray, #957 fan	$18.00 – 22.00			$25.00 – 30.00	$27.00 – 30.00
Vanity set	$120.00 – 130.00			$150.00 – 160.00	$150.00 – 160.00
Vase, 10" fan	$22.00 – 25.00	$22.00 – 25.00	$26.00 – 28.00		
Vase, hand	$22.00 – 27.00	$22.00 – 27.00	$28.00 – 32.00		$28.00 – 33.00

DANCING LADIES #900 – 901

1932 – 1935

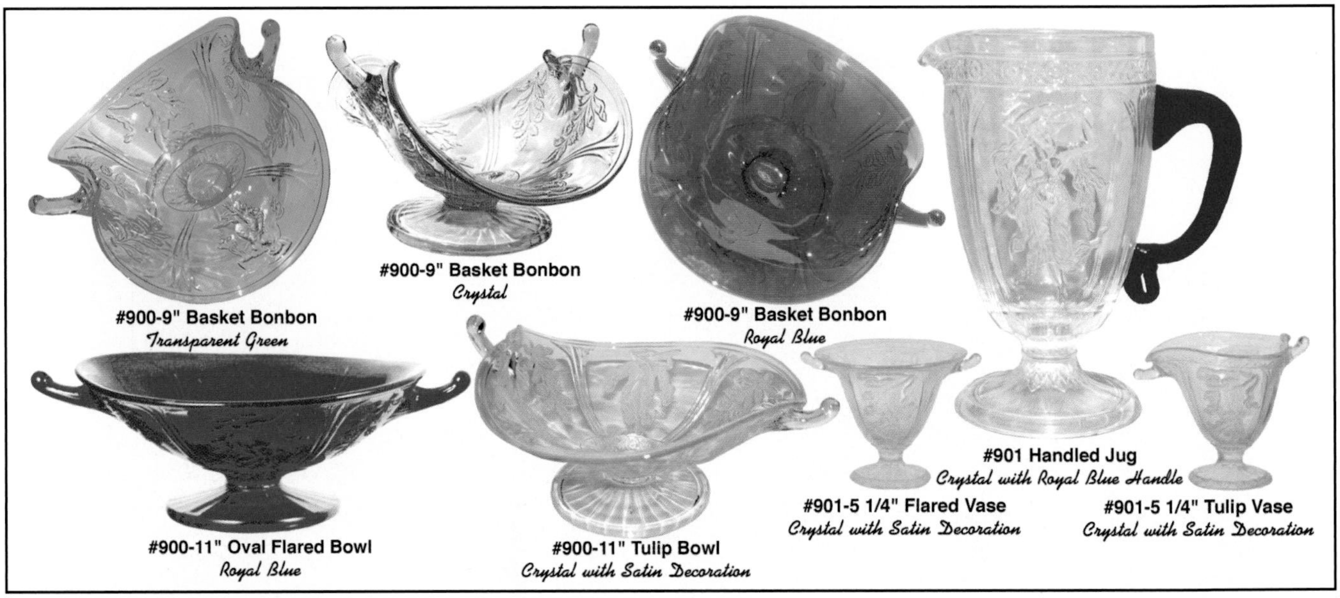

#900-9" Basket Bonbon *Transparent Green*

#900-9" Basket Bonbon *Crystal*

#900-9" Basket Bonbon *Royal Blue*

#901 Handled Jug *Crystal with Royal Blue Handle*

#900-11" Oval Flared Bowl *Royal Blue*

#900-11" Tulip Bowl *Crystal with Satin Decoration*

#901-5 1/4" Flared Vase *Crystal with Satin Decoration*

#901-5 1/4" Tulip Vase *Crystal with Satin Decoration*

Dancing Ladies	Crystal	Crystal/w Satin	Green	Royal Blue
Bonbon, #900 – 9½" basket shape	$110.00 – 125.00	$100.00 – 125.00	$150.00 – 175.00	$160.00 – 185.00
Bowl, #900 – 11" oval shape	$100.00 – 110.00	$110.00 – 120.00		$250.00 – 300.00
Bowl, #900 – 11" tulip shape	$100.00 – 110.00	$110.00 – 120.00		$250.00 – 300.00
Pitcher	$3000.00+			
Vase, #901 – 5¼" flared, tulip	$65.00 – 75.00	$75.00 – 85.00		

DANCING LADIES #900 – 901 1932 – 1935

Colors: Chinese yellow; crystal; crystal with satin pattern; crystal satin; French opalescent; Mongolian green; Mandarin red; Pekin blue; periwinkle blue; Persian pearl; jade green; royal blue; ruby; topaz opalescent; Grecian gold; transparent green, amber/gold; and milk glass.

Fenton's Dancing Ladies pattern consists of vases, bowls, and urns which feature a decorative figure of a dancing nude lady. Pieces in this pattern were produced from about 1932 to 1935. Vases in Persian pearl are shown in the catalogs, but collectors are reporting this color is nearly impossible to find. The only reported Persian Pearl pieces in collections are an oval bowl and a fan shape vase.

Rare items include a water pitcher (labeled as handled jug in the photo on page 242) and the urn-style lamp which is shown in the picture on page 244. The water pitcher is not a listed production item. The large Fenton covered urn/lamp has only appeared in jade green, and production problems resulted in very few of these being made. Other colors of large urns in this pattern are attributed to Northwood before Fenton acquired the mold.

The 12" covered urns are scarce in all colors. A rare gold amber urn is shown on page 247. The strange color of this piece is darker than Fenton's gold, but lighter than amber. However, it appears to be more amber than gold.

The jade green 12" urn shown on page 244 differs from normal urns of this size. Notice there are no tab handles at the top of the base. A similar urn base is known to exist in ruby. Small 7" covered urns are found more often. Since they are frequently found without lids and are then considered vases, the urn bases will also be priced separately in the listings. This size base may also be found with a flared or tulip-shape top, upon which a lid will not fit.

Numerous size differences may be found in catalog references for the various vases. A multitude of shapes were fashioned from the basic molds, and the size variations are a result of the shape of the item. The large vase mold was used for the 9" flared vase, the 9½" fan vase, the 8½" crimped vase, the 8" flared cupped vase, and the 8½" cupped vase. Notice the odd 9½" octagonal-top vase with the flashed decoration pictured on page 249. This shape has not been found in Fenton's catalogs.

The small urn base mold was used to make the 5¼" square vase, the 5¼" flared vase, and the 5¼" tulip vase. Although we have only seen these vases made from the small urn base mold, these sizes and shapes may appear without handles if the information in the catalogs is correct.

The 14" flared vase is only known in jade. This flared piece was formed from the large urn base. The #900 bowl appears most commonly in the 11" oval flared form. However, it may be found in additional shapes such as triangular, basket, or boat. These bowls are found most often in crystal, jade green, or milk glass, but also exist in other colors such as Chinese yellow, Pekin blue, royal blue, moonstone, and transparent green.

No. 901-12" Urn
Jade Green..
No. 901-12" Urn.
Chinese Yellow
No. 901-12" Urn
Pekin. Blue.
No. 901-12" Urn
Moonstone.

Dancing Ladies 12" Covered Urns Reprint Courtesy Of The Fenton Art Glass Museum

#900-11" Oval Flared Bowl
Pekin Blue

#901-18" Urn Lamp
Green Jade

 # 901-8 1/2" Crimped Vase
Green Jade

#901-9" Flared Vase
Jade Green

#901-7" Covered Urn
Jade Green

#901-7" Covered Utn
Moonstone

#901-12" Handled Covered Urn
Chinese Yellow

#901-12" Covered Urn
Green Jade

#901-12" Handled Covered Urn
Pekin Blue

Fenton's
Jades

901-12" Covered Urn
Moonstone

#901-7" Covered Urn
Chinese Yellow

#900 -11" Oval Bowl
Jade Green

#900-11" Oval Bowl
Milk

#900-11" Oval Bowl
Chinese Yellow

#901-7" Covered Urn
Pekin Blue

#900-11" Oval Bowl
Moonstone

Dancing Ladies	Chinese Yellow	Jade Green	Moonstone	Pekin Blue
*Bowl, #900-11" oval shape	$300.00 – 375.00	$275.00 – 325.00	$220.00 – 240.00	$350.00 – 400.00
Urn, #901-5" open	$250.00 – 300.00	$150.00 – 190.00	$100.00 – 125.00	$250.00 – 300.00
Urn and lid, #901-7"	$600.00 – 700.00	$450.00 – 550.00	$400.00 – 500.00	$600.00 – 700.00
Urn, #901-9" open		$350.00 – 400.00		
Urn, #901-9" open, handled	$400.00 – 450.00	$300.00 – 350.00	$300.00 – 350.00	$400.00 – 450.00
Urn & lid, #901-12"		$800.00 – 1000.00		
Urn &lid, #901-12" handled	$900.00 – 1200.00	$900.00 – 1100.00	$850.00 – 950.00	$900.00 – 1200.00
Urn lamp, #901-18"		$3500.00+		
Vase, #901-9" crimped		$600.00 – 650.00		
Vase, #901-9" cupped		$600.00 – 700.00		
Vase, #901-9" flared		$600.00 – 650.00		
Vase, #901-9" square		$600.00 – 700.00		
Vase, #901-14" flared		$1800.00+		
**Milk glass*	$90.00 – 100.00			

Dancing Ladies

#901-9" Flared Vase
Royal Blue

#901- 8 1/2" Crimped Vase
Royal Blue

#901-8 1/2" Crimped Vase
Ruby

#901-12" Covered Urn
Ruby

#901-9" Flared Vase
Ruby

#901-8 1/2" Cupped Vase
Mongolian Green

#901-9" Flared Vase
Ruby

#901-8 1/2" Crimped Vase
Mongolian Green

#901-9" Flared Crimped Vase *French Opalescent*

#901-9" Flared Crimped Vase *Topaz Opalescent*

#901-9" Flared Cupped Vase *Topaz Opalescnet*

#901-9" Square Vase *Topaz Opalescent*

#901-9 1/2" Fan Vase *French Opalescent*

#901-9" Square Vase */French Opalescent*

#901-9" Flared Vase *Topaz Opalescent*

901-12" Covered Urn *Gold Amber*

Dancing Ladies	Mongolian Green	Royal Blue	Ruby	Topaz Opalescent
Urn, #901-9" open			$350.00 – 400.00	
Urn & lid, #901-12			$800.00 – 1000.00	
Vase, #901-9" crimped	$400.00 – 450.00	$600.00 – 650.00	$600.00 – 625.00	$600.00 – 700.00
Vase, #901-9" cupped	$400.00 – 450.00			
Vase, #901-9" flared	$450.00 – 500.00	$600.00 – 650.00	$600.00 – 625.00	$600.00 – 650.00
Vase, #901-9" flared cupped				$700.00 – 750.00
Vase, #901-9" flared crimped				$700.00 – 750.00
Vase, #901-9" square	$450.00 – 550.00	$600.00 – 700.00	$600.00 – 700.00	$650.00 – 700.00

Dancing Ladies	French Opalescent	Gold Amber
Urn, #901-9" handled, open		$350.00 – 400.00
Urn & lid, #901-12 handled		$1200.00+
Vase, #901-9" crimped	$450.00 – 500.00	
Vase, #901-9" flared	$400.00 – 450.00	
Vase, #901-9" flared crimped	$450.00 – 550.00	
Vase, #901-9" square	$400.00 – 450.00	
Vase, #901- 9½" fan	$500.00 – 550.00	

#901-8 1/2" Crimped Vase
Mandarin Red

#901-9" Flared Vase
Periwinkle Blue

#901-9" Square Vase
Mandarin Red

#901-8 1/2" Cupped Vase
Periwinkle Blue

#901-9 1/2" Fan Vase
Mandarin Red

#901 8 1/2" Crimped Vase
Periwinkle Blue

#901-8 1/2" Flared Vase
Mandarin Red

#901-9" Flared Vase
Mandarin Red

#901-8 1/2" Cupped Vase
Mandarin Red

#901-9 1/2" Octagonal
Crystal with Flashed and Gold Decoration

#901-9 1/2" Fan Vase
Crystal with Satin Decoration

#901-9" Flared Vase
Crystal Satin Decoration

#901-8 1/2" Crimped Vase
Crystal

#901-8 1/2" Crimped Vase
Crystal Satin

#900-11" Oval Bowl
Persian Pearl

Dancing Ladies	*Crystal	Mandarin Red	Periwinkle Blue	Persian Pearl
Bowl, #900 – 11" oval				$350.00 – 400.00
Vase, #901 – 9" crimped	$250.00 – 300.00	$500.00 – 550.00	$480.00 – 525.00	$400.00 – 450.00
Vase, #901 – 9" cupped		$550.00 – 590.00	$475.00 – 500.00	
Vase, #901 – 9" flared	$225.00 – 250.00	$500.00 – 550.00	$500.00 – 525.00	$400.00 – 450.00
Vase, #901 – 8½" flared cupped		$550.00 – 590.00		
Vase, #901 – 9" square	$225.00 – 250.00	$500.00 – 550.00	$500.00 – 525.00	$450.00 – 475.00
Vase, #901 – 9½" fan		$550.00 – 600.00		$450.00 – 550.00

Dancing Ladies	Crystal/w Satin	Crystal Satin
Vase, #901 – 9" crimped	$250.00 – 300.00	$275.00 – 325.00
Vase, #901 – 9" flared	$250.00 – 275.00	$275.00 – 325.00
Vase, #901 – 9" square	$200.00 – 250.00	

**crystal with flashed color and gold decoration* $300.00 – 350.00.

DIAMOND OPTIC

1927 – 1938

Colors: black; jade; green; rose; aqua; royal blue; ruby; orchid; tangerine; crystal; moonstone.

Fenton introduced the Diamond Optic pattern in 1927. Most pieces were discontinued by 1931. However, a few pieces were still made in jade green, and baskets and ice tubs continued to be made in various colors. A #1502 – 10" vase in Mandarin red was listed in the inventory records in 1933. The 1600 series baskets and ice pails were made from 1929 to as late as 1933. Ruby tumblers were made in 1934, and crystal bowls were listed in 1936.

In 1937, shakers were made in royal blue, ruby, and other colors. Only the 9 oz. goblets, cups, and a 10" vase have been reported in moonstone. Some pieces in Diamond Optic were also made in iridescent colors. For prices of these items, see the listings in the Stretch Glass section.

Numerous bowls and vases with Dolphin handles were made. Rose, green, aqua, and orchid are the most commonly found colors. The tab-handle ice bucket, refrigerator set, and dresser set are difficult to find.

#1502-6" Fan Vase

#1502-12" Special Rolled Edge Console bowl

#1502-7 1/2" Crimp Top Bonbon

#1502-A-10" Sandwich Tray

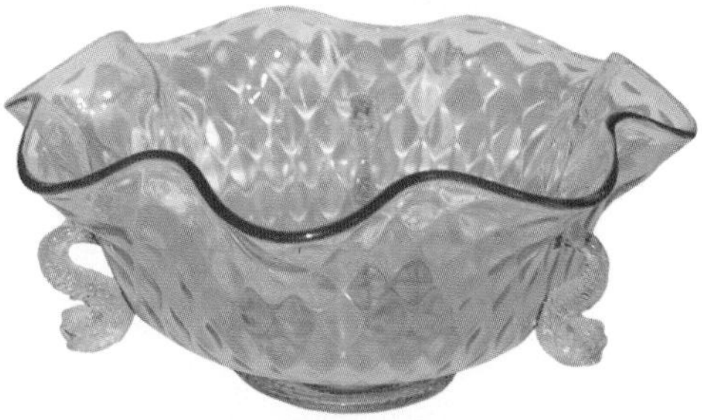

#1502-A-9" Crimped Bowl

#1502 Footed Juice Tumbler

#1502 Lamp

#1502 Round Refrigerator Set

#1502 Night Set Bottle

#1502-8 1/2" Fan Vase

Item	Green/Rose	Orchid	Jade	Aqua
Basket, #1502 w/metal handle	$25.00 – 30.00		$30.00 – 35.00	$28.00 –37.00
*Basket, #1615 – 5" w/metal handle	$42.00 – 46.00			$43.00 – 47.00
*Basket, #1615 – 6" w/metal handle	$47.00 – 57.00		$70.00 – 80.00	$60.00 –65.00
*Basket, #1616 – 8" w/metal handle	$53.00 – 58.00			$60.00 – 65.00
*Basket, #1617 – 10" w/metal handle	$55.00 – 65.00			
Bonbon, #1502 – 5½" w/metal handle	$42.00 – 46.00		$43.00 – 45.00	
Bonbon, #1502 – 6" flared w/dolphin handles	$32.00 – 37.00	$35.00 – 40.00	$45.00 – 50.00	
Bonbon, #1502 – 7½" crimped w/dolphin handles	$32.00 – 37.00	$43.00 – 48.00	$45.00 – 50.00	
Bonbon, #1502 – 7½" comport w/dolphin handles	$42.00 – 47.00	$43.00 – 48.00	$45.00 – 50.00	
Bonbon, #1502 – 7½" oval w/dolphin handles	$42.00 – 46.00	$43.00 – 48.00	$45.00 – 50.00	
Bowl, #1502 finger	$13.00 – 16.00	$13.00 – 15.00	$18.00 – 20.00	
Bowl, #1502 – 10" shallow cupped	$25.00 – 30.00	$27.00 – 32.00		
Bowl, #1502 – 10" special rolled rim	$30.00 – 35.00	$40.00 – 45.00	$40.00 – 45.00	
Bowl, #1502 – 12" shallow cupped	$27.00 – 32.00	$45.00 – 50.00	$40.00 – 45.00	
Bowl, #1502 – 12" special rolled rim	$30.00 – 35.00	$45.00 – 50.00	$45.00 – 50.00	
Bowl, #1502 – 13" flared	$32.00 – 37.00	$50.00 – 55.00	$50.00 – 55.00	
Bowl, #1502 – 14" special rolled rim	$35.00 – 40.00	$45.00 – 55.00	$45.00 – 55.00	
Bowl, #1502 – A-10" flared bowl w/dolphins	$35.00 – 40.00	$50.00 – 60.00		
Bowl, #1502 – A-7" cupped w/dolphins	$30.00 – 35.00	$47.00 – 50.00		
Bowl, #1502 – A-8½" rolled rim w/dolphins	$30.00 – 35.00	$45.00 – 50.00		
Bowl, #1502 – A-8" flared cupped w/dolphins	$30.00 – 35.00	$47.00 – 52.00	$55.00 – 60.00	
Bowl, #1502 – A-9" crimped w/dolphins	$30.00 – 35.00	$45.00 – 50.00		$40.00 – 50.00
Bowl, #1502 – 8½" flared cupped	$27.00 – 30.00	$30.00 – 35.00		
Bowl, #1502 – 8" deep cupped	$27.00 – 30.00	$30.00 – 35.00		
Candlestick, #1502	$15.00 – 17.00	$16.00 – 18.00		
Cologne, #53 – 4"	$125.00 – 145.00			
Cologne, #53 – 5"	$90.00 – 100.00	$110.00 – 125.00		$140.00 – 165.00
Cologne, #1502	$120.00 – 145.00			$100.00 – 125.00
Comport, #1502 cheese	$35.00 – 40.00	$45.00 – 50.00	$50.00 – 55.00	
Comport, #1502 high footed	$85.00 – 90.00			
Creamer, #1502	$20.00 – 25.00	$22.00 – 27.00	$22.00 – 27.00	$30.00 – 35.00
Cup, #1502 ftd.	$10.00 – 12.00		$9.00 – 10.00	$10.00 – 12.00
Dresser set, #1502 3-pc.	$270.00 – 325.00			$250.00 – 310.00
Dresser set, #1502 4-pc.	$295.00 – 355.00			$285.00 – 350.00
Goblet, #1502 – 11 oz. ftd. Bridge	$13.00 – 15.00	$15.00 – 18.00	$18.00 – 22.00	$20.00 – 22.00
Goblet, #1502 – 9 oz. ftd. Bridge	$13.00 – 15.00	$15.00 – 18.00	$18.00 – 22.00	
Goblet, #1502 – 9 oz. high stemmed water	$16.00 – 18.00	$22.00 – 27.00	$22.00 – 27.00	$22.00 – 25.00
Ice jar #1502 (flower pot with handles)			N.D.	
Ice pack, #1614	$27.00 – 35.00		$45.00 – 55.00	$65.00 – 70.00
Ice pack, #1616 – 6½"	$32.00 – 37.00		$45.00 – 55.00	$65.00 – 70.00
Ice tub, #1502 – 4"	$22.00 – 27.00		$22.00 – 27.00	$25.00 – 30.00
Ice pack, #1616 – 6½" w/#1702 cut	$43.00 – 47.00			$65.00 – 75.00
Ice pack, #1616 – 6½" w/#1709 cut	$43.00 – 47.00			$65.00 – 75.00
Lamp, #1502	$110.00 – 130.00		$110.00 – 145.00	
Mayonnaise and ladle	$35.00 – 40.00	$50.00 – 55.00		

*With cut decoration add 20%.

Item	Green/Rose	Orchid	Jade	Aqua
Night set, #1502 – 2-pc.	$75.00 – 85.00		$190.00 – 225.00	$125.00 – 145.00
*Pitcher, #1634	$65.00 – 75.00			$55.00 – 65.00
*Pitcher, #1635	$65.00 – 75.00	$75.00 – 90.00	$100.00 – 125.00	$60.00 – 70.00
*Pitcher, #1636	$57.00 – 67.00	$75.00 – 90.00	$135.00 – 160.00	$70.00 – 75.00
Plate, #1502 – 6" octagonal	$6.00 – 7.00	$7.00 – 9.00	$7.00 – 9.00	
Plate, #1502 – 6" round	$4.00 – 5.00			
Plate, #1502 – 8" octagon salad	$10.00 – 12.00	$10.00 – 12.00	$12.00 – 14.00	
Plate, #1502 – 8" round salad	$8.00 – 9.00			
Plate, finger bowl	$5.00 – 6.00	$7.00 – 8.00	$7.00 – 9.00	
Plate w/indent for cheese comport	$18.00 – 20.00	$22.00 – 25.00	$22.00 – 27.00	
Puff box, #53	$27.00 – 32.00	$50.00 – 55.00	$30.00 – 35.00	
Puff box, #1502	$30.00 – 35.00			$50.00 – 60.00
Refrigerator stack set, #1502 – 3-pc.	$100.00 – 125.00		$110.00 – 135.00	
Saucer, #1502	$4.00 – 6.00			$4.00 – 6.00
Shaker, #1502 ea.	$22.00 – 25.00		$58.00 – 66.00	
Sherbet, #1502 low footed	$9.00 – 11.00			$12.00 – 14.00
Sugar, #1502	$20.00 – 25.00		$22.00 – 27.00	$30.00 – 35.00
Tray, #53 vanity set	$25.00 – 30.00	$35.00 – 40.00	$30.00 – 35.00	
Tray, #1502 – 10" center handled sandwich	$25.00 – 30.00			$58.00 – 62.00
Tray, #1502 – A-10" sandwich, dolphin handle	$65.00 – 70.00	$65.00 – 75.00		
Tray, #1502 dresser set	$25.00 – 30.00			$35.00 – 40.00
Tumbler, #1502 – 5 oz.	$12.00 – 15.00		$15.00 – 16.00	$12.00 – 14.00
Tumbler, #1502 – 9 oz.	$13.00 – 16.00		$15.00 – 17.00	$15.00 – 17.00
*Tumbler, #1634 – 8 oz. flat	$10.00 – 12.00		$12.00 – 14.00	$10.00 – 14.00
*Tumbler, #1635 – 10 oz. flat	$10.00 – 12.00		$20.00 – 25.00	$15.00 – 18.00
*Tumbler, #1636 – 12 oz. flat	$10.00 – 12.00		$24.00 – 30.00	$20.00 – 22.00
Vanity set, #53 – 4-pc.	$235.00 – 262.00	$305.00 – 350.00	$340.00 – 400.00	
Vase, #1502 – 5" fan w/dolphin handles	$30.00 – 35.00	$35.00 – 40.00	$32.00 – 37.00	
Vase, #1502 – 6" fan w/dolphin handles	$32.00 – 37.00	$37.00 – 42.00	$37.00 – 42.00	
Vase, #1502 – 6" flat flared	$25.00 – 30.00			
Vase, #1502 – 7" ftd. w/rolled rim	$43.00 – 48.00			
Vase, #1502 – 8½" flat flared	$37.00 – 42.00		$45.00 – 50.00	$35.00 – 45.00
Vase, #1502 – 8½" ftd. fan	$42.00 – 47.00	$70.00 – 80.00	$50.00 – 55.00	
Vase, #1502 – 8" flared, crimped, ftd.	$37.00 – 42.00			$40.00 – 45.00
Vase, #1502 – 8" flip	$40.00 – 45.00			$45.00 – 55.00
Vase, #1502 – 10"	$40.00 – 45.00			

**with cut decoration add 20%*

Item	Black	Tangerine	Ruby
Basket, #1502 w/metal handle	$30.00 – 35.00		
Basket, #1615 – 6½" w/metal handle	$70.00 – 80.00		
*Basket, #1616 – 8" w/metal handle	$70.00 – 85.00		
Bonbon, #1502 – 6" flared w/dolphin handles	$25.00 – 30.00	$95.00 – 125.00	$85.00 – 110.00
Bonbon, #1502 – 7½" crimped w/dolphin handles			$100.00 – 125.00
Bonbon, #1502 – 7½" comport w/dolphin handles			$95.00 – 125.00
Bonbon, #16502 – 7½" oval w/dolphin handles			$100.00 – 125.00

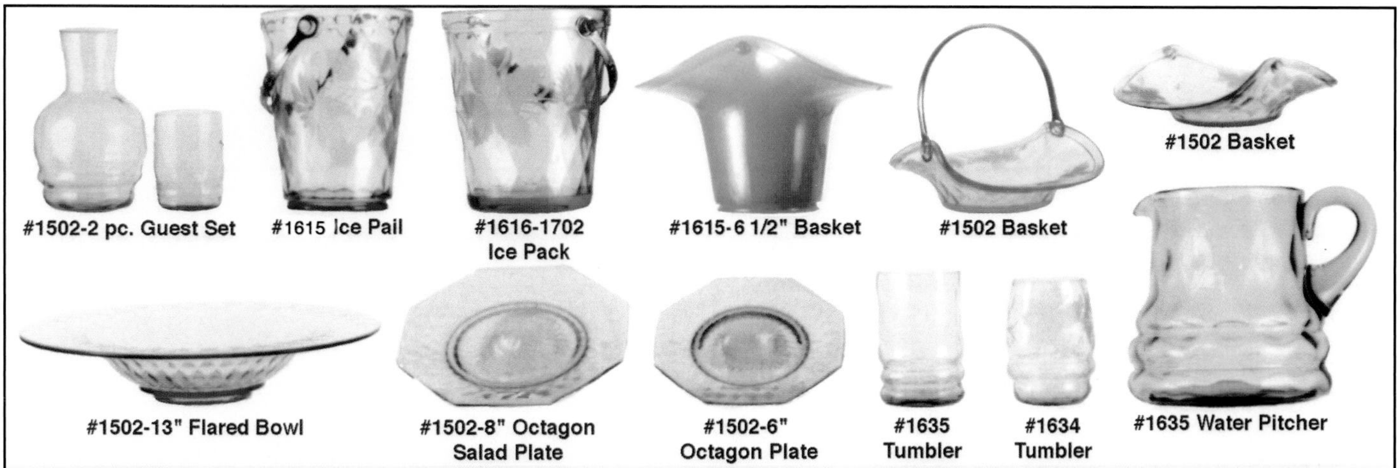

#1502-2 pc. Guest Set | #1615 Ice Pail | #1616-1702 Ice Pack | #1615-6 1/2" Basket | #1502 Basket | #1502 Basket

#1502-13" Flared Bowl | #1502-8" Octagon Salad Plate | #1502-6" Octagon Plate | #1635 Tumbler | #1634 Tumbler | #1635 Water Pitcher

Catalog Reprint
Courtesy Of:
The Fenton Art Glass Museum

THE FENTON ART GLASS COMPANY, WILLIAMSTOWN, W. VA.

No. 1502 DIAMOND OPTIC LINE, MADE ONLY IN PLAIN ROSE, PLAIN GREEN AND ORCHID COLORS.

No. 1502. 7 inch Roll Edge Vase.
No. 1502. 8 inch Crimp Top Vase.
No. 1502. 8½ inch Fan Vase.
No. 1502. 6 inch Dolphin 2 Hdl. Fan Vase.
No. 1502. 5¼ inch Dolphin 2 Hdl. Fan Vase.
No. 1502. 6 inch Flared Vase.
No. 1502. 8¼ inch Flared Vase.

No. 1502. 7½ inch Comport Bon Bon.
No. 1502. 7½ inch Oval Bon Bon.
No. 1502. 6 inch Flared Bon Bon.
No. 1502. 7½ inch Crimp Top Bon Bon.
No. 1502. 3 Piece Dresser Set.

No. 53. 4 Piece Dresser Set.
No. 1502. 12 inch 3 Piece Console Set Special Roll Edge Bowl.

No. 1502. 13 inch Flared Bowl.
No. 1502. 10 inch Cupped
No. 1502. 12 inch Cupped Bowl.
No. 1502. 10 inch Hdl. Sandwich Tray

No. 1502 8 inch Octagon Salad Plate.
No. 1502 Footed Sherbet.
No. 1502 Goblet
No. 1502 Cup and Saucer
No. 1502. Sugar and Cream Set.
No. 1502. Mayonnaise and Ladle.
No. 1502. Cheese and Cracker.

Item	Black	Tangerine	Ruby	Royal Blue
Bowl, #1502 – 10" special rolled rim			$55.00 – 65.00	
Bowl, #1502 – 12" special rolled rim		$65.00 – 75.00	$55.00 – 65.00	$55.00 – 65.00
Candle, #1502			$25.00 – 30.00	
Cologne, #53 – 5"	$110.00 – 150.00			
Cologne, #1502			$150.00 – 180.00	
Comport, #1502 high footed			$235.00 – 260.00	
Creamer, #1502	$25.00 – 30.00	$35.00 – 40.00	$30.00 – 37.00	$27.00 – 32.00
Cup, #1502	$9.00 – 12.00	$43.00 – 48.00	$14.00 – 16.00	$13.00 – 15.00
Dresser set, #1502 3-pc.			$375.00 – 460.00	
Dresser set, #1502 4-pc.			$400.00 – 495.00	
Goblet, #1502 – 11 oz.	$22.00 – 25.00		$20.00 – 22.00	
Goblet, #1502 – 9 oz. ftd. bridge	$22.00 – 25.00		$20.00 – 22.00	$20.00 – 22.00
Goblet, #1502 – 9 oz. high stemmed water	$27.00 – 32.00		$22.00 – 27.00	
Ice jar #1502 (flower pot with handles)	N.D.			
Ice pack, #1614	$53.00 – 55.00			
Ice pack, #1616 – 6½"	$53.00 – 60.00		$90.00 – 110.00	$110.00 – 120.00
Ice tub, #1502 – 4"	$27.00 – 30.00			
Lamp, #1502			$140.00 – 170.00	$130.00 – 150.00
Mayonnaise and ladle, #1502			$95.00 – 110.00	
*Pitcher, #1635			$150.00 – 175.00	$150.00 – 175.00
*Pitcher, #1636			$150.00 – 175.00	$150.00 – 175.00
Plate, #1502 – 6" octagonal	$6.00 – 7.00		$7.00 – 9.00	
Plate, #1502 – 8" octagonal	$8.00 – 10.00	$33.00 – 37.00	$12.00 – 14.00	
Puff box, #53	$30.00 – 35.00			
Puff box, #1502			$75.00 – 100.00	
Saucer, #1502		$12.00 – 15.00	$5.00 – 6.00	
Shaker, #1502 ea.	$58.00 – 65.00		$60.00 – 70.00	$95.00 – 110.00
Sherbet, #1502			$15.00 – 18.00	
Sugar, #1502	$25.00 – 30.00	$37.00 – 42.00	$30.00 – 37.00	$27.00 – 32.00
Tray, #53 vanity set	$45.00 – 50.00			
Tray, #1502 dresser set			$27.00 – 32.00	
Tray, #1502 – 10" center handled sandwich		$75.00 – 85.00	$55.00 – 65.00	
Tumbler, #1502 5 oz.	$12.00 – 14.00		$15.00 – 19.00	
Tumbler, #1502 9 oz.	$15.00 – 17.00		$16.00 – 20.00	
Tumbler, #1635 10 oz.			$22.00 – 25.00	$22.00 – 28.00
Vanity set, #53 – 4-piece	$295.00 – 385.00			
Vase, #1502 – 5" fan w/dolphin handles			$80.00 – 90.00	
Vase, #1502 – 6" fan w/dolphin handles			$85.00 – 95.00	
Vase, #1502 – 7" ftd. w/rolled rim			$100.00 – 110.00	
Vase, #1502 – 8" flared, crimped, ftd.		$90.00 – 95.00	$60.00 – 65.00	
Vase, #1502 – 8½" flat flared	$45.00 – 50.00			
Vase, #1502 – 8½" fan		$95.00 – 110.00	$60.00 – 65.00	

**with cut decoration add 20%*

#1502 Lamp
#1636-1702 Ice Tea Set
#1502-A-10" Sandwich Tray
#1641-11 oz. Ice Tea
#1634 Water Pitcher
#1502 Creamer
#1502-A-7" Cupped Bowl
#1502 Cologne
#1502 Dresser Set
#1502-7 1/2" Oval Bon-bon
#1502-6" Fan Vase

8.00
10.00
3.50
10.00
10.00
10.00
5.00
9.00
5.00
3.50
10.00
9.00
6.60
6.00
16.00
6.00
10.00
4.00
6.00
12.00
6.00
4.40

1502-5" Fan Vase. 1502-6" Fan Vase. 1502-A-7" Cupped Bowl 1502 Sherbet. 1502 Sugar and Cream Set.

1502-7" Square Hdl. Comport. 1502-7" Oval Hdl. Comport. 1502 A-10" 3 Piece Console Set. 1502-7 oz. Bridge Goblet. 1502 Mayonnaise and Ladle.

1502 Cup and Saucer. 1502 Round Bridge Bon Bon. 1502-12" 3 piece Special R. R. Console Set. 1615-6" Hdl. Basket.

1502-6" Round Bread and Butter. 1502-10" Shallow Cup 3 piece Console Set. 1502-8" Round Salad Plate.

DOLPHIN

Dolphin may not actually be a pattern, but it is a decoration that was used by Fenton on enough different patterns and shapes that many collectors are attracted to collecting just Dolphin items. The listing below is separated into sections to provide a better understanding of the variety of pieces available with the dolphin decoration.

Iridescent Colors	Aqua	Green	Rose	Tangerine	Celeste Blue
Bowl, #1502 – 13" flared	$175.00 – 200.00	$200.00 – 230.00			
Bowl, #1502 – A-9" crimped	$195.00 – 250.00	$200.00 – 230.00	$195.00 – 210.00		
Bowl, #1503 – A-10" flared		$200.00 – 230.00			
Bowl, #1504 – A-10" crimped		$200.00 – 223.00	$200.00 – 225.00		
Bowl, #1504 – A-10" flared	$220.00 – 240.00	$190.00 – 225.00	$200.00 – 225.00		
Bowl, #1504 – A-10" rolled rim			$190.00 – 220.00		
Bowl, #1600 – 10" rolled rim			$180.00 – 200.00		
Bowl, #1602 – 10¼" crimped, ft.	$225.00 – 240.00		$170.00 – 195.00		
*Bowl, #1604 – 11" oval, ft.	$195.00 – 220.00	$190.00 – 210.00			
Bowl, #1608 – 10½" deep oval	$225.00 – 250.00	$190.00 – 210.00	$190.00 – 220.00		
Candlestick, #1623		$100.00 – 120.00	$100.00 – 125.00		
Candy jar, #1532		$125.00 – 150.00	$120.00 – 140.00		
Comport, #1533 – 6" round, ft.				$150.00 – 175.00	
Comport, #1533 – 6½" crimped	$120.00 – 130.00	$90.00 – 100.00			
Tray, #1502 – A-10" sandwich	$190.00 – 210.00	$125.00 – 150.00	$145.00 – 160.00		
Tray, #1557 handled cheese		$120.00 – 140.00	$135.00 – 150.00		
**Vase, #1533 – 5¼" fan	$115.00 – 125.00	$110.00 – 125.00	$120.00 – 130.00	$135.00 – 150.00	
Vase, #1533 – 6" fan	$120.00 – 130.00	$110.00 – 125.00	$125.00 – 140.00		$175.00 – 200.00

**Grecian Gold $185.00 – 200.00; wisteria $200.00 – 215.00*
***Persian Pearl $140.00 – 150.00; topaz $130.00 – 140.00*

Opaque Colors	Jade Black	Green	Lilac	Pekin Blue	Periwinkle Blue
Bonbon, #1502 – 6" flared, ft.		$45.00 – 50.00			
Bonbon #1502 – 7½" round, ft.		$45.00 – 50.00			
Bonbon, #1502 – 7½" oval, ft.		$45.00 – 50.00			
Bonbon, #1502 – 7½" sq., ft.		$45.00 – 50.00			
Bonbon, #1533 – 6" square crimped		$35.00 – 45.00			
Bonbon, #1621 flared		$25.00 – 30.00	$35.00 – 40.00		
Bonbon, #1621 – 6½" crimped	$22.00 – 27.00	$25.00 – 30.00	$35.00 – 40.00		
Bowl, #1502 – A-8½" flared cupped		$55.00 – 60.00			
Bowl, #1504 – A-6" cupped	$35.00 – 40.00	$35.00 – 37.00	$50.00 – 55.00	$45.00 – 55.00	
Bowl, #1504 – A-8½" roll rim		$53.00 – 60.00			
Bowl, #1504 – A – 8½" triangle		$53.00 – 60.00			
Bowl, #1504 – A-9" cupped	$60.00 – 70.00	$60.00 – 65.00	$100.00 – $120.00	$75.00 – 85.00	
Bowl, #1504 – A-9" shallow cupped	$70.00 – 75.00	$47.00 – 50.00	$75.00 – 85.00		
Bowl, #1504 – A-10" clover					$210.00 – 250.00
Bowl, #1504 – A-10" flared		$80.00 – 85.00			
Bowl, #1504 – A-10" rolled rim	$70.00 – 80.00	$80.00 – 85.00			
Bowl, #1600 – 10" rolled rim	$70.00 – 80.00	$70.00 – 80.00			
Bowl, #1601 – 10¾" flared ft.	$70.00 – 80.00	$105.00 – 125.00			
Bowl, #1602 – 10¼" crimped		$90.00 – 100.00			$210.00 – 225.00
Bowl, #1604 – 11" oval, ft.		$110.00 – 120.00			
Bowl, #1608 – 10½" deep oval	$130.00 – 150.00	$105.00 – 125.00	$160.00 – 175.00		
Candlestick, #1623		$22.00 – 27.00			
Candy jar, #1532	$60.00 – 65.00	$75.00 – 90.00			
Comport, #1533 – 6" round, ft.		$45.00 – 50.00			

#1532 Candy Jar
Jade Green

#1532 Candy Jar
Velva Rose

#1532 Candy Jar
Ebony

#1532 Candy Jar
Cameo Opalescent

#1532 Candy Jar
Green w/Cutting

#1533-6" Flared Comport
Jade Green

#1533-7" Oval Comport
Tangerine

#1533-6" Crimped Comport
Ruby

#1533-6" Crimped Comport
Florentine Green

#1502-6" Fan Vase
Orchid

#1533-A-1702-6" Cut Fan Vase
Aquamarine

#1533-5" Fan Vase
Jade Green

#1533-6" Fan Vase
Aquamarine Stretch

#1533-6" Square Crimped Bon-bon
Jade Green

#1502-7 1/2" Oval Bon-bon
Orchid

#1621 E. Deep Oval Bowl
Crystal Satin

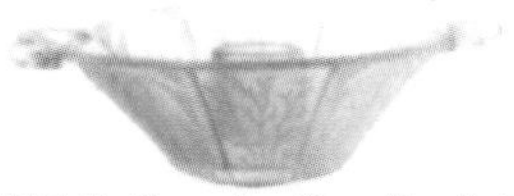
#1621 E. Regular Candlestick
Crystal Satin

#1502-A-10" Handled Sandwich Tray
Aquamarine Stretch

#1557 Handled Cheese Tray
Florentine Green

Oval Comport
Rose

#1623 Candlestick
Velva Rose

#1623 Candlestick
Jade Green

Opaque Colors	Jade Black	Green
Comport, #1533 – 7" oval		$45.00 – 50.00
Vase, #1502 – 5" fan		$32.00 – 37.00
Vase, #1502 – 6" fan		$37.00 – 42.00
Vase, #1504 – A-6" cupped		$35.00 – 40.00
Vase, #1532 – A-5¼" fan	$45.00 – 55.00	
Vase, #1533 – 6" square		$35.00 – 40.00
Vase, #1533 – A-6" fan	$47.00 – 52.00	$37.00 – 42.00

Transparent Non-iridized Colors

	Aqua	Green	Orchid	Rose	Ruby	Tangerine
Bonbon, #1502 – 6" flared, ft.		$32.00 – 37.00	$43.00 – 48.00	$32.00 – 37.00	$85.00 – 100.00	$95.00 – 125.00
Bonbon, #1502 – 7½" crimped, ft.		$32.00 – 37.00	$43.00 – 48.00	$32.00 – 37.00		$100.00 – 125.00
Bonbon #1502 – 7½" round, ft.		$42.00 – 47.00	$43.00 – 48.00	$42.00 – 47.00		$95.00 – 125.00
Bonbon, #1502 – 7½" oval, ft.		$42.00 – 46.00	$43.00 – 48.00	$42.00 – 46.00		$100.00 – 125.00
Bonbon, #1502 – 7½" sq., ft.		$32.00 – 37.00	$43.00 – 48.00	$42.00 – 45.00		
*Bonbon, #1621 – 5½" square	$22.00 – 27.00	$18.00 – 20.00		$22.00 – 27.00		
*Bonbon, #1621 – 6½" crimped	$22.00 – 27.00	$18.00 – 20.00		$22.00 – 27.00		
*Bonbon, #1621 – 6½" oval	$22.00 – 27.00	$18.00 – 20.00		$22.00 – 27.00		
*Bonbon, #1621 – 6½" plate	$20.00 – 25.00	$18.00 – 20.00		$22.00 – 27.00		
*Bonbon, #1621 – 7" flared	$22.00 – 27.00	$18.00 – 20.00		$22.00 – 27.00		
Bowl, #1502 – A-7" cupped		$30.00 – 35.00		$30.00 – 35.00		
Bowl, #1502 – A-8" cupped		$30.00 – 35.00		$32.00 – 40.00		
Bowl, #1502 – 8½" flared cupped		$30.00 – 35.00		$30.00 – 35.00		
Bowl, #1502 – A-8½" rolled rim		$30.00 – 35.00		$30.00 – 35.00		
Bowl, #1502 – A-9" crimped	$40.00 – 50.00	$30.00 – 35.00		$38.00 – 42.00		
Bowl, #1502 – A-10" flared		$32.00 – 37.00		$35.00 – 40.00		
Bowl, #1503 – A-7" cupped		$25.00 – 30.00	$47.00 – 50.00	$38.00 – 42.00		
Bowl, #1503 – 8½" rolled rim		$27.00 – 32.00	$45.00 – 50.00	$38.00 – 42.00		
Bowl, #1503 – A-9" shallow cupped		$30.00 – 35.00	$35.00 – 45.00	$37.00 – 45.00		
Bowl, #1503 – A-10" flared		$30.00 – 35.00	$44.00 – 50.00	$44.00 – 47.00		
Bowl, #1504 – A-6" cupped					$32.00 – 37.00	
Bowl, #1504 – A-9" cupped					$45.00 – 55.00	
Bowl, #1504 – A-9" shallow cupped					$45.00 – 55.00	
Bowl, #1504 – A-9" flared w/#1702 cut	$50.00 – 55.00	$47.00 – 55.00		$45.00 – 55.00		
Bowl, #1504 – A-9½" flared cupped w/#1702 cut	$50.00 – 55.00	$47.00 – 55.00		$45.00 – 55.00	$60.00 – 70.00	
Bowl, #1504 – A-10" crimped						
Bowl, #1054 – A-10" flared					$60.00 – 70.00	
Bowl, #1600 – 10" rolled rim	$100.00 – 140.00			$55.00 – 65.00		
**Bowl, #1602 – 10¼" crimped, ft.						
Bowl, #1608 – 10½" deep oval	$120.00 – 150.00				$150.00 – 175.00	
*Bowl, #1621 – 10" deep oval	$45.00 – 55.00			$40.00 – 45.00		
*Bowl, #1621 – 9" shallow oval	$40.00 – 50.00			$40.00 – 47.00		
Candlestick, #1623		$20.00 – 22.00	$20.00 – 25.00	$22.00 – 25.00	$27.00 – 32.00	
*Candy jar, #1533 – A	$110.00 – 130.00	$65.00 – 75.00		$75.00 – 95.00		$145.00 – 165.00
Comport, #1533 – 7" oval						$100.00 – 125.00
*Tray, #1502 – A-10" sandwich		$65.00 – 70.00	$65.00 – 75.00	$45.00 – 55.00		
Tray, #1557 handled cheese		$27.00 – 30.00				
*Vase, #1502 – 5" fan Diamond Optic		$30.00 – 35.00	$35.00 – 40.00	$27.00 – 30.00		$60.00 – 65.00
*Vase, #1502 – 6" fan Diamond Optic		$32.00 – 37.00	$37.00 – 42.00	$30.00 – 35.00		$75.00 – 85.00

#1608-10 1/2" Oval Footed Bowl
Jade Green

#1602-10 1/4" Crimped Footed Bowl
Crystal

#1604-11" Oval Footed Bowl
Jade Green

#1602-10 1/4" Crimped Footed Bowl
Velva Rose

#1602-10 1/4" Crimped Footed Bowl
Aquamarine Stretch

#1608-10 1/2" Oval Footed Bowl
Lilac

#1502-A-7" Cupped Bowl
Rose

#1504-A-9" Cupped Bowl
Chinese Yellow

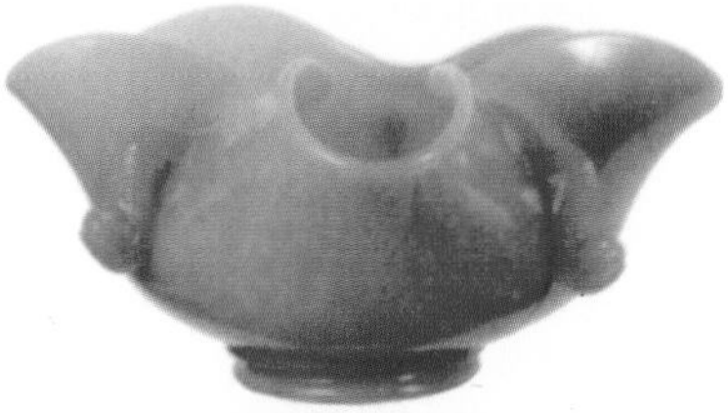

#1504-A-8 1/2" Triangular Bowl
Pekin Blue

#1621--1703-10" Cut Deep Oval Bowl
Aquamarine

#1504-A-9" Cupped Bowl
Ebony

#1504-A-9" Cupped Bowl
Ruby

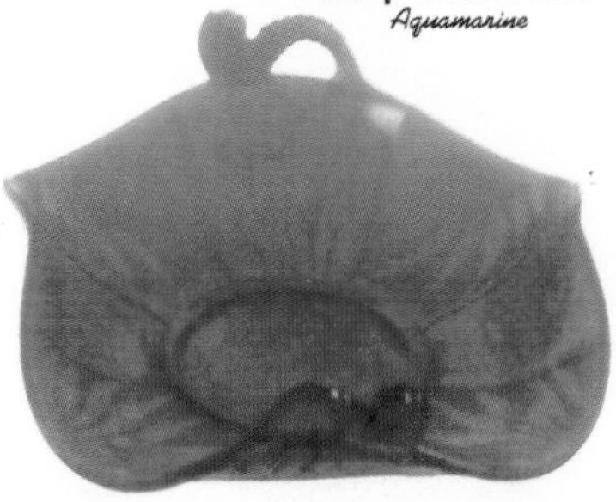

#1621 E. 9 1/2"Oval Bon-bon
Royal Blue

#1621-6 1/2" Bon-bon
Jade Green

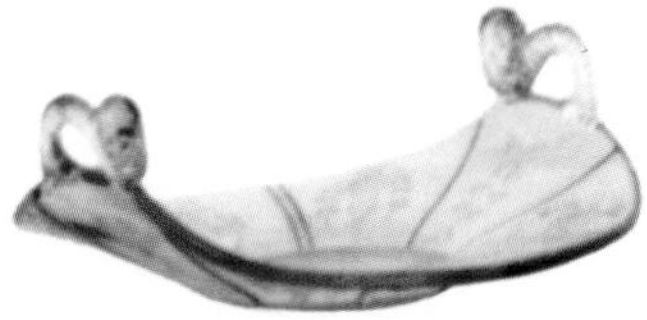

#1621-1703-6 1/2" Cut Bon-bon
Aquamarine

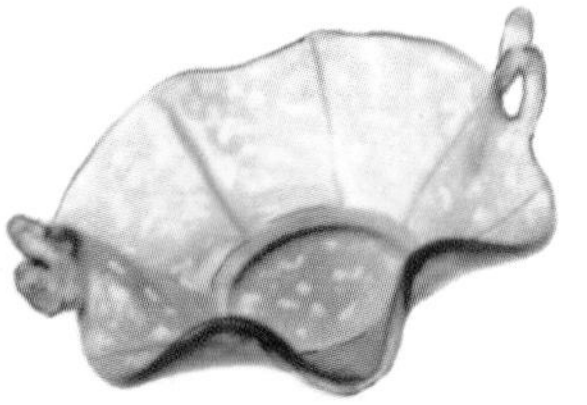

#1621-6 1/2" Bon-bon
Rose

Transparent Non-iridized Colors

	Aqua	Green	Rose
Vase, #1532 – A-5¼" fan	$47.00 – 58.00	$32.00 – 36.00	$32.00 – 37.00
Vase, #1533 – A-6" fan	$52.00 – 58.00	$37.00 – 45.00	$37.00 – 45.00

** with cutting add 20%*
***crystal, $40.00 – 45.00*

Satin Etched	Crystal	Royal Blue
Bonbon, #1621 – 5½" square	$16.00 – 18.00	$40.00 – 50.00
Bonbon, #1621 – 6½" crimped	$16.00 – 18.00	$40.00 – 50.00
Bonbon, #1621 – 6½" oval	$16.00 – 18.00	$40.00 – 50.00
Bonbon, #1621 – 6½" plate	$16.00 – 18.00	$40.00 – 50.00
Bonbon, #1621 – 7" flared	$16.00 – 18.00	$40.00 – 50.00
Bowl, #1621 – 8"	$43.00 – 47.00	
Bowl, #1621 – 9½" crimped	$47.00 – 50.00	$70.00 – 75.00
Bowl, #1621 – 9½" low oval	$47.00 – 50.00	$70.00 – 75.00
Bowl, #1621 – 9½" square crimped	$47.00 – 50.00	$70.00 – 75.00
Bowl, #1621 – 9" flared	$43.00 – 48.00	$60.00 – 70.00
Candlestick, #1621 crimped	$24.00 – 27.00	$34.00 – 36.00
Candlestick, #1621 oval	$24.00 – 27.00	$34.00 – 36.00
Candlestick, #1621 regular (flared)	$24.00 – 27.00	$34.00 – 36.00

Opalescent Colors	Cameo Opalescent	Blue Opalescent
Bowl, #1600 – 10½" rolled edge		$105.00 – 125.00
Candy jar, #1532	$110.00 – 125.00	
Comport, #1533 – 6" round, ft.	$65.00 – 80.00	
Comport, #1533 – 7" oval	$75.00 – 85.00	$105.00 – 125.00
Vase, #1533 – 6" fan	$65.00 – 75.00	$105.00 – 125.00

#1600-10 1/2" Rolled Edge Bowl

#1533-A-1702-6" Cut Fan Vase
Rose

#1533-5" Fan Vase
Blue Opalescent

#1533-7" Oval Comport
Blue Opalescent

#1533-6" Crimped Comport
Amberina

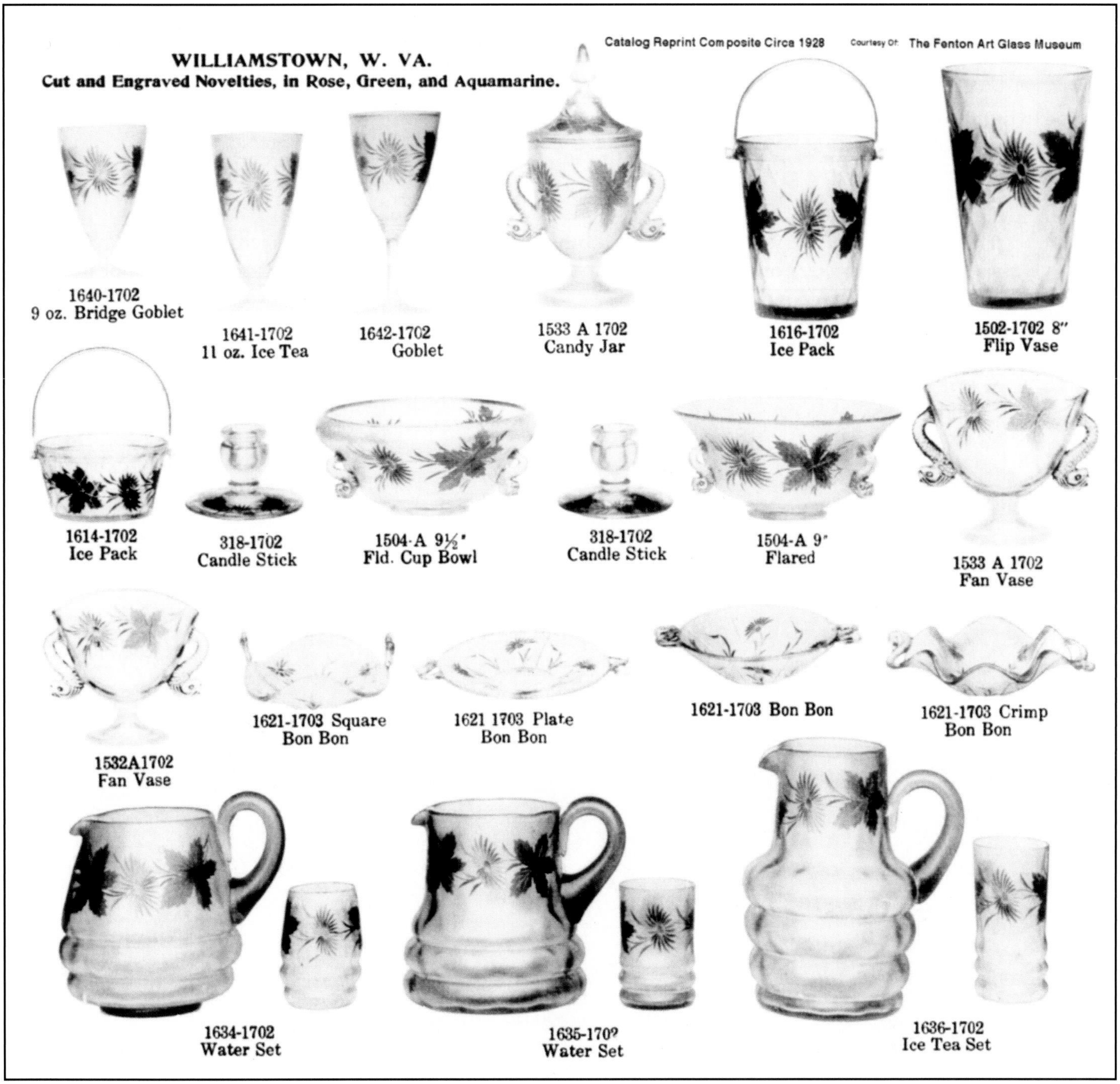
Catalog Reprint Composite Circa 1928
Courtesy Of: The Fenton Art Glass Museum
WILLIAMSTOWN, W. VA.
Cut and Engraved Novelties, in Rose, Green, and Aquamarine.
1640-1702
9 oz. Bridge Goblet
1641-1702
11 oz. Ice Tea
1642-1702
Goblet
1533 A 1702
Candy Jar
1616-1702
Ice Pack
1502-1702 8"
Flip Vase
1614-1702
Ice Pack
318-1702
Candle Stick
1504-A 9½"
Fld. Cup Bowl
318-1702
Candle Stick
1504-A 9"
Flared
1533 A 1702
Fan Vase
1532A1702
Fan Vase
1621-1703 Square
Bon Bon
1621 1703 Plate
Bon Bon
1621-1703 Bon Bon
1621-1703 Crimp
Bon Bon
1634-1702
Water Set
1635-170?
Water Set
1636-1702
Ice Tea Set

ELIZABETH #1639 — 1930 – 1933

Colors: jade green; ruby; black; royal blue; moonstone; lilac; crystal.

Fenton produced this colorful breakfast set from 1930 to 1933. Most of the pieces were made in solid jade green, black, ruby, and royal blue. Combinations of these colors were also used with crystal or moonstone for lids of the batter set or feet of the sherbet, tumbler, and sugar and creamer. Jade green and black combinations were also made. Lilac pieces have been found with moonstone lid or feet combinations.

A complete set has been found in royal blue with a cut decoration. Add 25% to the prices below for pieces with cut designs.

The 3-pint jug in the listing is the batter jug without a lid. This is the same jug that will sometimes fit the large jade or black reamer top. However, most of these jugs flare too wide, and the reamer will not fit. It is still unclear as to whether Fenton actually sold these bases with the reamer top.

It appears that this pattern was never named by Fenton. All of the references to the pattern simply refer to the line number — 1639. Since the other patterns have names, it seemed appropriate that this one should also. Therefore, we have taken the liberty of naming this pattern Elizabeth in honor of the wife of Frank M. Fenton.

Solid colors:

Elizabeth	Black	Jade	Lilac	Ruby	Royal Blue
Batter set, batter jug/syrup/tray	$345.00 – 405.00	$345.00 – 405.00	$575.00 – 790.00		
Bowl, 9½" salad					$30.00 – 35.00
Bowl, 10" flared 2-handled			$50.00 – 55.00	$40.00 – 50.00	
Creamer, 4"		$50.00 – 55.00	$35.00 – 45.00	$35.00 – 40.00	
Cup	$13.00 – 15.00	$12.00 – 14.00		$12.00 – 14.00	$12.00 – 14.00
Jug, batter w/lid	$190.00 – 225.00	$190.00 – 225.00	$300.00 – 350.00		
Jug, syrup w/lid	$90.00 – 125.00	$150.00 – 175.00	$200.00 – 250.00		
Jug, 3 pint open	$90.00 – 110.00	$150.00 – 175.00	$200.00 – 250.00	$150.00 – 175.00	
Mint jar & cover	$150.00 – 165.00	$175.00 – 200.00		$150.00 – 185.00	
Plate, 12" 2-handled	$43.00 – 48.00	$45.00 – 55.00		$60.00 – 70.00	$55.00 – 60.00
Plate, 6"	$7.00 – 8.00	$8.00 – 10.00		$10.00 – 12.00	$8.00 – 12.00
Plate, 8"	$12.00 – 14.00	$12.00 – 14.00		$15.00 – 18.00	$15.00 – 18.00
Sherbet, flared or cupped			$40.00 – 45.00		
Sugar, 3½"			$45.00 – 55.00	$35.00 – 45.00	$34.00 – 37.00
Tray, batter set	$50.00 – 55.00	$45.00 – 55.00	$75.00 – 90.00		
Tray, center handle			$55.00 – 65.00		

In the following listing, the body of the piece is the first color.

Color Combinations	Mint Jar	Tumbler	Sherbet	Batter Jug	Syrup	Cream/Sugar
Royal Blue & Crystal	$150.00 – 165.00	$35.00 – 45.00	$30.00 – 35.00			
Black & Moonstone		$65.00 – 75.00	$45.00 – 50.00			
Jade & Black or Black & Jade	$150.00 – 165.00	$65.00 – 70.00	$45.00 – 50.00	$190.00 – 225.00	$90.00 – 125.00	$53.00 – 60.00
Jade & Moonstone	$125.00 – 150.00	$35.00 – 45.00	$45.00 – 50.00			
Lilac & Moonstone		$85.00 – 100.00	$65.00 – 80.00			
Ruby & Crystal	$150.00 – 165.00	$40.00 – 45.00	$30.00 – 35.00		$32.00 – 34.00	

Color Combinations	Cologne	Puff box
Jade & Moonstone	$200.00 – 225.00	$125.00 – 150.00
Pekin Blue & Moonstone	$225.00 – 250.00	$150.00 – 175.00

Footed Tumbler
Black/Moonstone

Footed Tumbler
Jade/Black

Footed Tumbler
Ruby/Crystal

Batter Set
Black/Jade

Flared Sherbet
Jade/Black

Cupped Sherbet
Ruby/Royal Blue

Cupped Sherbet
Jade/Black

9 1/2" Salad Bowl
Royal Blue

Reamer with Handled Jug
Black/Jade

Mint Jar
Royal Blue/Crystal

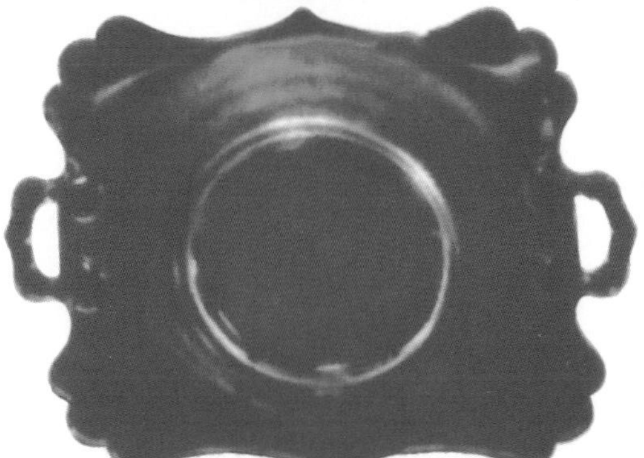

12" Handled Plate
Ruby

Handled Sandwich Tray
Jade

Sugar
Ruby/Crystal

Creamer
Ruby/Crystal

Cologne
Pekin Blue/Moonstone

Vanity Set
Jade/Moonstone

GEORGIAN #1611 (AGUA CALIENTE) 1931 – 1942

Colors: amber; aquamarine; black; crystal; jade green; green; rose; ruby; milk glass.

The pattern which is commonly called Georgian was introduced in 1931 as Agua Caliente. Significant production of most colors continued through 1939. Ruby tumblers, 8" plates, and stems were made through 1942.

Elusive pieces include the cocktail shaker, vase, decanter, and mugs. The 10" plates and ice pail are also desirable. The pitcher may be found with or without an ice lip.

Numerous glass companies — Cambridge, Duncan and Miller, Hocking, Paden City, and Canton — made glassware with a Georgian-style pattern. Trying to distinguish the Fenton Georgian from the others takes some close examination of the pieces. First check the shape, quality, and manner of attachment of the jug handles. The shape of the piece must match the shape of the items in the photo or reprint. Most of the companies made tumblers, so this is the area of greatest confusion. Fenton is handmade glassware, so the difference in the quality of Hocking's machine-made glasses should quickly eliminate them from consideration. The Cambridge tumblers, have an exact diamond in the center of each hex. Duncan's tumblers curve in at the top and will not stack in each other; Fenton's tumblers are straight at the top and stack together easily. Fenton's goblets curve in at the top; the Cambridge and Canton stems are straighter. Goblets which resemble Fenton's more closely were made by Duncan and Miller. In this case, size differences and types of stems help to determine the maker. Fenton made a short wide footed cordial, or in the flared version, a nut cup. Duncan made nothing similar. Fenton made a short bowl claret, and Duncan made a wine goblet. Duncan's goblets also have a wider diameter at the top.

Plates in Georgian were also made by Duncan and Miller. Fenton's plates have a relatively small center banded by a wide area of pattern. Duncan's plates have a wide center surrounded by a narrow band of pattern.

Fenton brought the Georgian line back in 1952 when the 5 ounce, 10 ounce, and 12 ounce tumblers reappeared in the line. The new colors were a pale blue, amber, milk glass, ruby, amethyst, dark green, and light green.

Item	Amber/ Crystal	Black Aquamarine Jade Green	Green/Rose Milk Glass	Ruby Royal Blue
Bonbon, 5"	$6.00 – 7.00	$11.00 – 13.00	$8.00 – 9.00	$8.00 – 10.00
Bowl, cupped	$7.00 – 8.00	$11.00 – 13.00	$8.00 – 9.00	$10.00 – 12.00
Bowl, 7½" flared	$8.00 – 9.00	$14.00 – 15.00	$12.00 – 14.00	$14.00 – 16.00
Bowl, 9" cupped	$8.00 – 10.00	$24.00 – 25.00	$14.00 – 16.00	$22.00 – 25.00
Candlestick	$32.00 – 36.00	$65.00 – 75.00	$27.00 – 29.00	$48.00 – 55.00
Candy jar	$22.00 – 25.00	$85.00 – 90.00	$27.00 – 31.00	$80.00 – 85.00
Cocktail shaker	$37.00 – 45.00			$80.00 – 100.00
Creamer	$10.00 – 12.00	$12.00 – 14.00	$10.00 – 12.00	$12.00 – 15.00
Cup	$4.00 – 5.00	$10.00 – 12.00	$7.50 – 8.50	$12.00 – 12.00
Decanter	$43.00 – 50.00	$125.00 – 135.00		$100.00 – 125.00
Finger bowl	$7.00 – 9.00	$15.00 – 16.00	$8.00 – 10.00	$12.00 – 14.00
Goblet	$9.00 – 10.00	$20.00 – 22.00	$12.00 – 14.00	$16.00 – 18.00
Goblet, cocktail	$9.00 – 10.00	$20.00 – 22.00	$12.00 – 14.00	$16.00 – 18.00
Goblet, cordial	$11.00 – 12.00	$23.00 – 25.00	$14.00 – 16.00	$20.00 – 24.00
Goblet, 4½ oz. claret	$8.00 – 9.00	$17.00 – 19.00	$10.00 – 12.00	$15.00 – 17.00
Ice pail				$105.00 – 130.00
Jug, 54 oz., with or without IL	$48.00 – 55.00	$155.00 – 165.00	$63.00 – 72.00	$85.00 – 90.00
Mug, 10 oz.	$20.00 – 22.00	$37.00 – 40.00	$22.00 – 24.00	$32.00 – 35.00
Mug, 12 oz.	$22.00 – 24.00	$38.00 – 42.00	$22.00 – 25.00	$34.00 – 37.00
Mug, 8 oz.	$16.00 – 18.00	$37.00 – 40.00	$16.00 – 18.00	$30.00 – 32.00
Nut cup	$5.00 – 7.00	$10.00 – 12.00	$6.00 – 8.00	$8.00 – 10.00
Plate, 6"	$3.00 – 3.50	$5.00 – 6.00	$4.00 – 5.00	$5.00 – 6.00
Plate, 8"	$4.00 – 5.00	$12.00 – 15.00	$7.00 – 8.00	$7.00 – 8.00
Plate, 10"	$10.00 – 14.00	$37.00 – 42.00	$22.00 – 25.00	$32.00 – 35.00
Plate, 11" compartment	$9.00 – 10.00	$32.00 – 35.00	$13.00 – 15.00	$23.00 – 26.00

54 Oz. Jug · 9 Oz. Tumbler · 21 Oz. Decanter · 1 Oz. Cordial · 10 Oz. Goblet · High Sherbet

Cupped Sherbet · Sugar & Creamer · Candlestick · Beer Mug

Agua Caliente TABLE SERVICE IN Ruby AND OTHER GORGEOUS COLORS
GOBLET
10 oz.
HIGH SHERBET
6 oz
CLARET
COCKTAIL
COCKTAIL SHAKER 24 oz
Silver Strainer Top
JUG Regular 54 oz
Also Furnished Ice Lipped
DECANTER 21 oz
Ground in Stopper
FOOTED CORDIAL
TABLE TUMBLER
ICE TEA
SUGAR & CREAM SET
CUPPED SHERBET
Also furnished flared
CUP & SAUCER
FOOTED TUMBLER
9 oz
SALT & PEPPER SET
FLARED FOOTED
NUT
FINGER BOWL & PLATE
8" SALAD PLATE
10" SERVICE PLATE
6" BREAD &
BUTTER PLATE
11" COMPARTMENT PLATE
AGUA CALIENTE, the finest of finished pressed glass, can now be had in colors to harmonize with every decorative scheme.
Illustrated is the irresistible and fascinating Ruby, with its glow of life and warmth. Other colors are rich Royal Blue, semi-opaque Jade Green, mirror-black Ebony, sparkling Crystal, delicate Rose, Pale Green, and alluring Amber.
From this gorgeous array of AGUA CALIENTE colors the modern hostess can select a complete service for her table at a most moderate expenditure.
Styled in the spirit of today, but suggesting the charm of Early American days, AGUA CALIENTE glassware lends itself to any type of home furnishing and table setting.
Comprising a complete line of shapes, colors and items you will find an AGUA CALIENTE service for your own particular need.
A price list of the items illustrated is shown on the reverse side of this folder.

Item	Amber/ Crystal	Black/Aquamarine Jade Green	Green/Rose Milk Glass	Ruby Royal Blue
Plate, 12"	$11.00 – 13.00	$27.00 – 30.00	$16.00 – 20.00	$25.00 – 30.00
Shaker	$20.00 – 22.00	$37.00 – 42.00	$20.00 – 22.00	$27.00 – 35.00
Sherbet, cupped; flared	$4.00 – 5.00	$12.00 – 14.00	$6.00 – 8.00	$10.00 – 12.00
Sherbet, Hi ftd.	$5.00 – 8.00	$12.00 – 14.00	$8.00 – 10.00	$10.00 – 12.00
Sugar	$9.00 – 10.00	$12.00 – 14.00	$10.00 – 12.00	$12.00 – 14.00
Tumbler, 12 oz. flat	$5.00 – 8.00	$16.00 – 18.00	$8.00 – 10.00	$14.00 – 16.00
Tumbler, 2½ oz. whiskey	$5.00 – 6.00	$12.00 – 14.00	$8.00 – 10.00	$10.00 – 12.00
Tumbler, 5 oz. flat	$4.00 – 5.00	$9.00 – 11.00	$7.00 – 9.00	$8.00 – 10.00
Tumbler, 9 oz. flat	$4.00 – 6.00	$9.00 – 11.00	$6.00 – 8.00	$8.00 – 10.00
Tumbler, 9 oz. footed	$10.00 – 12.00	$12.00 – 14.00	$10.00 – 12.00	$12.00 – 14.00
Vase, 6" crimped violet	N.D.			

Catalog Reprint
Courtesy Of:
The Fenton Art Glass Museum
THE FENTON ART GLASS CO.
WILLIAMSTOWN, W. VA.
No. 1611 Georgian Tableware Line
Colors - Crystal - Green - Pink - Amber - Ruby - Royal Blue - Topaz - Black
Computer Colorized Reprint
No. 1611 —2½ oz. Tumbler
No. 1611 Decanter
No. 1611 —5 oz. Tumbler
No. 1611—10 oz. Tumbler
No. 1611 —½ Gal. Jug
No. 1611 — 8" Salad Plate
No. 1611 — 6" Salad Plate
No. 1611 — Sherbet
No. 1611 — Goblet
No. 1611 — 12 oz. Ice Tea

LEAF # 175

The #175 Leaf pattern consists of two different sizes of leaf-shaped plates. There are 11" cake plates and 8" salad plates. According to information from Fenton's inventory records, this pattern was introduced in 1934 in jade, transparent green and rose colors. Later in the 1930s the plates were also made in crystal, crystal satin, and royal blue. The French opalescent, blue opalescent, and topaz opalescent colors were added in 1941 and were discontinued about the end of 1943. In 1955 the plates were made in milk, rose pastel, and green pastel. The pastel colors were discontinued by the end of 1956, but the milk plates were made through 1969. Pastel and milk 2-tier metal handled servers were also made with a drilled plate of each size. Roselene 8" Leaf plates were made in 1977.

#175 Leaf	Plate, 8"	Plate, 11"
Blue Opalescent	$35.00 – 40.00	$55.00 – 60.00
Crystal	$14.00 – 16.00	$18.00 – 22.00
Crystal Satin	$15.00 – 18.00	$22.00 – 26.00
Jade Green	$32.00 – 35.00	$65.00 – 70.00
Milk Glass	$22.00 – 25.00	$40.00 – 45.00
Royal Blue	$40.00 – 45.00	$55.00 – 65.00
Ruby	$40.00 – 45.00	$70.00 – 85.00
Topaz Opalescent	$35.00 – 40.00	$55.00 – 60.00

11" Plate
Blue Opalescent

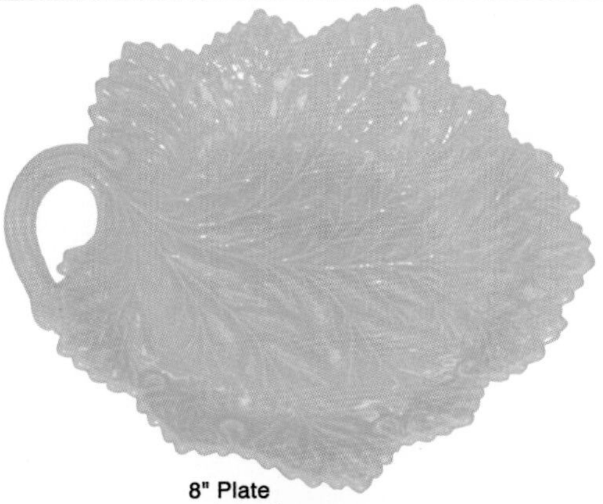

8" Plate
Jade

11" Plate
Milk

8" Plate
Royal Blue

LEAF TIERS #1790

Bowls, candlesticks, and cake plates in the Leaf Tiers pattern were made between 1934 and 1941. Late production from the early 1940s included pieces in opalescent colors.

Some earlier molds from the carnival glass era were borrowed to produce these new Leaf Tiers pieces. Items were made in crystal, crystal satin, milk glass, blue opalescent, topaz opalescent, royal blue, jade green, and Mandarin red.

#1790 Leaf Tiers	Crystal/ Crystal Satin	Royal Blue/ Ruby	Emerald/ Milk	Jade Green/ Black	Mandarin Red	Topaz Opalescent
Bowl, 4½"	$22.00 – 24.00					
Bowl, 8" cupped	$27.00 – 36.00	$90.00 – 110.00	$58.00 – 66.00	$110.00 – 130.00	$158.00 – 185.00	$90.00 – 110.00
Bowl, 9½"-10" crimped	$37.00 – 45.00	$95.00 – 115.00	$63.00 – 75.00	$125.00 – 140.00	$158.00 – 190.00	$95.00 – 115.00
Bowl, 10" flared	$37.00 – 45.00	$110.00 – 125.00	$78.00 – 95.00	$145.00 – 155.00	$158.00 – 200.00	$105.00 – 125.00
*Cake plate, 10"– 12"		$168.00 – 180.00		$90.00 – 110.00	$150.00 – 200.00	
Candle	$18.00 – 20.00	$40.00 – 50.00	$22.00 – 27.00			$35.00 – 45.00

**WMG $150.00 – 175.00*

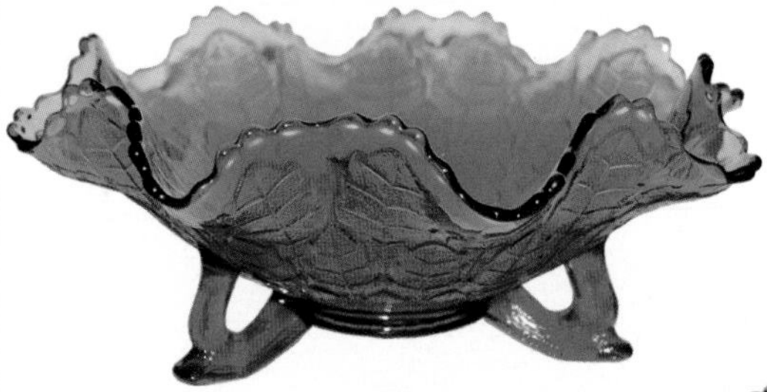

Crimped Bowl
Green

Flared Bowl
Royal Blue

Flared Candlestick
Green

Cupped Bowl
Mandarin Red

10 1/4" Cake Plate
Mandarin Red

Cupped Bowl
Milk

LINCOLN INN #1700 — 1928 – 1940

Colors: gold, aquamarine; black; crystal; emerald green; green opalescent; light green; jade green; rose; royal blue; ruby.

Fenton's #1700 Lincoln Inn pattern was introduced in 1928. Although the pattern was not discontinued until 1940, catalogs and inventory records indicate that the greatest production of this pattern occurred before 1933. After that date, the number of pieces listed in the inventory records starts to decline and eventually only crystal pieces are listed. Notice the crystal Lincoln Inn pieces with the embossed intaglio pattern in the reprint from a 1940 Blackwell Wielandy catalog. In addition to the pieces pictured, small berry bowls and a 7⅝" large berry bowl may also be found in crystal. The 8" plates have also been reported in rose.

There are a number of pieces with the Lincoln Inn line number in the inventory records that are not commonly recognized as belonging to this pattern. A 4-part relish, snack plate, and mayonnaise jar were made in crystal. Be on the lookout for these elusive pieces in crystal.

The pitcher, center-handled server, and 12" vase are the items still lacking from many collections. Finding the 10" plates and shakers will take some diligent searching also. The pitcher was made in aquamarine, ruby, royal blue, and a lighter blue that is possibly mermaid blue. The sandwich tray and vase were made in royal blue and ruby. The vase has been found flared, crimped, and with a square top. A candlestick that was fashioned from a shaker has been found in black.

In 1995, Fenton brought back the pitcher and a restyled 4½" tumbler in iridescent Celeste blue as part of their 90th anniversary celebration.

Cup & Saucer *Royal Blue*

Finger Bowl *Ruby*

Cigarette Holder *Ruby*

Sandwich Plate *Ruby*

Sugar & Creamer *Green Opalescent*

Flared Sherbet *Orchid*

Water Goblet *Orchid*

Item	Amber/ Crystal	Aqua	Black/ Jade Green	Rose/ Green	Ruby/ Royal Blue	Green Opalescent	Emerald Green
*Ashtray	$13.00 – 16.00						
Bonbon, 2-handled oval or square	$10.00 – 12.00	$22.00 – 24.00	$24.00 – 28.00	$18.00 – 20.00	$24.00 – 28.00		
*Bowl, 7⅝"	$10.00 – 12.05						
*Bowl, 9"	$22.00 – 22.00						
Bowl, 10" footed	$20.00 – 25.00	$45.00 – 55.00	$58.00 – 65.00	$30.00 – 35.00	$60.00 – 65.00		
Bowl, 5" fruit	$4.00 – 5.00	$12.00 – 14.00	$15.00 – 18.00	$10.00 – 12.00	$15.00 – 18.00		$7.00 – 9.00
Bowl, 6" cereal	$5.00 – 8.00	$18.00 – 20.00	$25.00 – 28.00	$15.00 – 16.00	$25.00 – 28.00		$12.00 – 15.00
Bowl, 6" crimped	$7.00 – 9.00	$20.00 – 22.00	$24.00 – 28.00	$18.00 – 20.00	$24.00 – 28.00		
Bowl, olive, S-handled	$7.00 – 9.00	$25.00 – 28.00	$28.00 – 30.00	$14.00 – 16.00	$28.00 – 30.00		$10.00 – 14.00
Cigarette holder	$16.00 – 18.00	$35.00 – 40.00			$65.00 – 75.00		
Comport, flat plate	$13.00 – 15.00	$25.00 – 28.00	$40.00 – 50.00	$16.00 – 20.00	$35.00 – 45.00	$40.00 – 50.00	$14.00 – 16.00
Comport, shallow cupped	$13.00 – 15.00	$25.00 – 28.00	$40.00 – 50.00	$16.00 – 20.00	$35.00 – 45.00	$40.00 – 50.00	$14.00 – 16.00
Comport, mint	$10.00 – 12.00	$20.00 – 25.00	$35.00 – 40.00	$18.00 – 20.00	$30.00 – 37.00	$34.00 – 39.00	$14.00 – 16.00
Comport, nut	$11.00 – 13.00	$20.00 – 25.00	$35.00 – 40.00	$18.00 – 20.00	$30.00 – 37.00	$34.00 – 37.00	$14.00 – 16.00
Comport, oval	$11.00 – 13.00	$16.00 – 18.00	$22.00 – 30.00	$16.00 – 18.00	$27.00 – 31.00	$32.00 – 35.00	$10.00 – 12.00
Creamer,	$11.00 – 13.00	$22.00 – 24.00	$27.00 – 30.00	$20.00 – 22.00	$22.00 – 27.00	$30.00 – 32.00	$10.00 – 12.00
Cup,	$5.00 – 6.00	$12.00 – 14.00	$20.00 – 22.00	$8.00 –9.00	$16.00 – 18.00	$22.00 – 25.00	$7.00 – 9.00
Finger bowl	$7.00 – 9.00	$22.00 – 25.00	$25.00 – 30.00	$14.00 – 18.00	$25.00 – 30.00		$10.00 – 12.00
Goblet, V cocktail	$10.00 – 12.00	$27.00 – 30.00	$32.00 – 34.00	$20.00 – 22.00	$27.00 – 30.00	$34.00 – 37.00	$11.00 – 12.00
Goblet, water	$15.00 – 17.00	$27.00 – 30.00	$24.00 – 27.00	$15.00 – 16.00	$24.00 – 27.00	$32.00 – 35.00	$9.00 – 11.00
Goblet, wine	$13.00 – 15.00	$34.00 – 38.00	$40.00 – 42.00	$24.00 – 28.00	$34.00 – 38.00	$40.00 – 45.00	$16.00 – 18.00
*Mayonnaise jar	$12.00 – 14.00						
**Pitcher, 7½"		$550.00 – 650.00			$550.00 – 630.00		
Plate, 6"	$3.00 – 4.00	$6.00 – 7.00	$7.00 – 8.00	$5.00 – 6.00	$5.00 – 6.00	$8.00 – 10.00	$5.00 – 6.00
Plate, 8"	$7.00 – 8.00	$12.00 – 14.00	$18.00 – 20.00	$10.00 – 12.00	$18.00 – 20.00	$18.00 – 22.00	$9.00 – 11.00
Plate, 10"	$16.00 – 18.00	$50.00 – 55.00	$52.00 – 60.00	$25.00 – 35.00	$52.00 – 60.00		$25.00 – 30.00
Plate, 12"	$13.00 – 15.00	$27.00 – 30.00	$32.00 – 35.00	$29.00 – 32.00	$30.00 – 40.00	$40.00 – 50.00	$18.00 – 20.00
Plate, 14"	$22.00 – 25.00	$40.00 – 55.00	$50.00 – 55.00	$35.00 – 40.00	$50.00 – 55.00		$37.00 – 42.00
Plate, finger bowl	$4.00 – 5.00	$8.00 – 10.00	$9.00 – 12.00	$8.00 – 10.00	$12.00 – 14.00	$16.00 – 18.00	$7.00 – 9.00
*Relish, 5 part, 10⅜"	$95.00 – 120.00						
Saucer	$2.00 – 3.00	$4.00 – 5.00	$5.00 – 6.00	$3.00 – 4.00	$6.00 – 7.00		$2.00 – 3.00
Shaker, ea.	$28.00 – 25.00	$70.00 – 75.00	$80.00 – 90.00	$53.00 – 60.00	$105.00 – 130.00		$42.00 – 50.00
Sherbet	$7.00 – 8.00	$20.00 – 22.00	$25.00 – 27.00	$12.00 – 14.00	$25.00 – 27.00	$27.00 – 30.00	$12.00 – 14.00
Sugar	$11.00 – 13.00	$22.00 – 24.00	$27.00 – 30.00	$20.00 – 22.00	$22.00 – 25.00	$30.00 – 32.00	$10.00 – 12.00
Tray, center handle					$125.00 – 150.00		
Tumbler, 4 oz. ft.	$10.00 – 12.00	$32.00 – 35.00	$35.00 – 42.00	$27.00 – 30.00	$32.00 – 35.00	$35.00 – 40.00	$20.00 – 22.00
Tumbler, 5 oz. flat	$9.00 – 10.00	$30.00 – 35.00	$35.00 – 40.00	$12.00 – 14.00	$30.00 – 35.00	$35.00 – 40.00	$11.00 – 12.00
Tumbler, 7 oz. ft.	$13.00 – 14.00	$35.00 – 40.00	$40.00 – 50.00	$27.00 – 32.00	$40.00 – 50.00	$50.00 – 55.00	$20.00 – 22.00
***Tumbler, 9 oz. flat	$9.00 – 10.00	$25.00 – 30.00		$18.00 – 22.00			$18.00 – 20.00
Tumbler, 12 oz. flat	$22.00 – 24.00	$35.00 – 40.00	$40.00 – 50.00	$27.00 – 32.00	$40.00 – 50.00		$27.00 – 29.00
Tumbler, 12 oz. ft.	$16.00 – 18.00	$25.00 – 30.00	$35.00 – 40.00	$22.00 – 25.00	$45.00 – 50.00	$52.00 – 55.00	$22.00 – 24.00
Vase					$200.00 – 250.00		

**crystal only*
***Mermaid blue $550.00 – 650.00*
****Mermaid blue, $40.00 – 45.00*

Cocktail Goblet
Wine Goblet
Salt & Pepper
Oval Comport
Water Goblet
12" Square Crimped Vase
12 Oz. High Ball
12 Oz. Ftd. Tumbler
7 Oz. Ftd. Tumbler
11" Shallow Crimped Bowl

Catalog Reprint
Coutesy Of:
The Fenton Art Glass Museum

FENTON ART GLASS COMPANY

WILLIAMSTOWN, W. VA.

No 1700 Line in Rose, Green, and Aquamarine.

1700 Goblet
1700 Sherbet
1700S Oval
1700S Nut
1700S Mint
1700 Cream
1700 Sugar
1700 Cup and Saucer
1700 Cereal
1700 Hdl. Olive
1700-S Hdl. Bon Bon Square
1700-S Hdl. Bon Bon Oval
1700-C 6" Crimp
1700-12" Plate
1700-8" Plate
1700-G Comport Plate
1700-G Shallow Comport

9" Round Bowl

Matches Holder

7 5/8" Round Bowl
Intaglio Design

Reprint from 1940 Blackwell Wielandy Catalog

214/7439—15 Piece Luncheon Set. Crystal glass, with wide flange cut in Colonial design, with centers of Intaglio pattern assorted fruits. Consists of four 8 inch salad plates, four cups, four saucers, one 11 inch cake plate, sugar and creamer. **Per set $6.00**

Photo Below: Lincoln Inn Catalog Reprint Circa 1928 Courtesy Of: The Fenton Art Glass Museum

Lincoln Inn Line

	List Price Per Dozen Crystal
1700-5 oz. Tumbler Straight	$ 1.80
1700-9 oz. Tumbler Straight	2.00
1700-12 oz. Ice Tea or Hi-Ball-Straight	3.00
1700-7 oz. Ftd. Tumbler	3.50
1700-12 oz. Ftd. Ice Tea	3.50
1700 Goblet	3.50
1700-5 oz. Fruit Juice Low Ftd.	3.50
1700 Cocktail or Wine	3.50
1700 High Ftd. Sherbet	3.50
1700-6" Plate	3.50
1700-8" Plate	5.00
1700-9¼" Plate	7.50
1700-12" Plate	12.00
1700 Sugar & Cream Set	9.00
1700 Cup & Saucer	7.00
1700 Finger Bowl & Plate	9.00
1700-5" Fruit Saucer	3.50
1700 Salt & Pepper	12.00
1700-9¼" Fld. Bowl	7.50
1700-10½" Fld. Bowl	12.00
1700-5 pc. Ash Tray Set ea. set (Gross lots—$1.00 each set)	1.10
1700-2 pc. Snack Set	14.40
1700 Relish	9.60

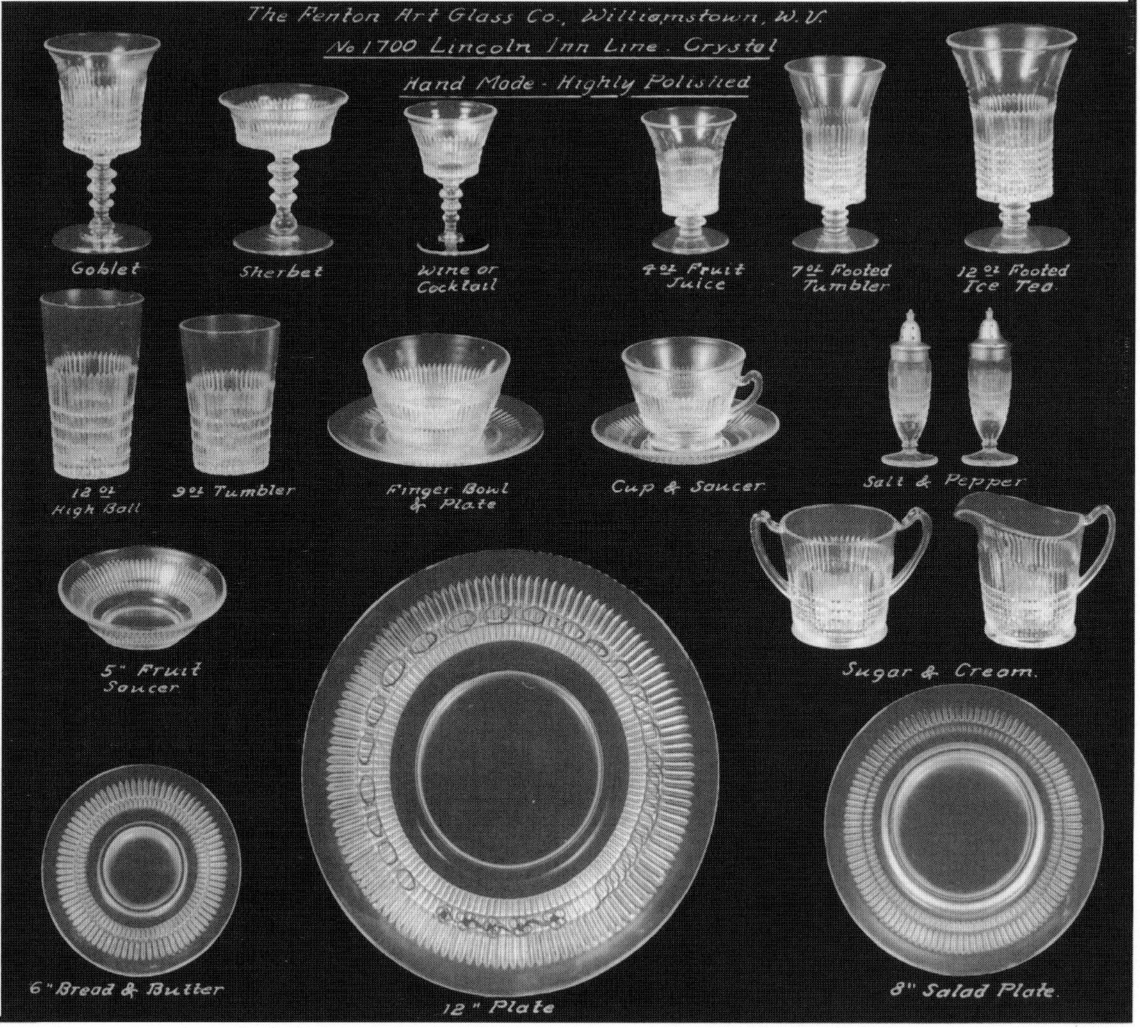
The Fenton Art Glass Co., Williamstown, W.V.
No 1700 Lincoln Inn Line. Crystal
Hand Made - Highly Polished
Goblet
Sherbet
Wine or Cocktail
4 oz Fruit Juice
7 oz Footed Tumbler
12 oz Footed Ice Tea
12 oz High Ball
9 oz Tumbler
Finger Bowl & Plate
Cup & Saucer
Salt & Pepper
Sugar & Cream.
5" Fruit Saucer
6" Bread & Butter
12" Plate
8" Salad Plate.

PEACOCK

Colors: crystal; crystal satin; Mandarin red; milk glass; Mongolian green; periwinkle blue; French opalescent.

Catalog and inventory records indicate Fenton made Peacock vases from 1933 through 1935. The vases were introduced in white milk in 1933, in the 4", 6", and 8" sizes. Inventory records in 1934 include the addition of a 10" vase in white milk glass, Mandarin red, and French opalescent. In 1935, the 8" vase was made in Mandarin red, Mongolian green, and periwinkle blue.

The 8" vase was made in carnival glass in 1973, in opaque blue satin and a green satin opaque color called lime sherbet from 1973 to 1976. An opaque green non-satin color variation was also made as a special club item.

Item	Crystal/ Crystal Satin	Milk Glass	Mongolian Green	Periwinkle Blue	Mandarin Red
Vase, 4" flared, cupped flared		$119.00 – 235.00			
Vase, 6" flared, cupped flared		$165.00 – 175.00			
Vase, 8" flared, cupped flared	$84.00 – 95.00	$70.00 – 75.00	$220.00 – 260.00	$268.00 – 290.00	$280.00 – 325.00
*Vase, 10" flared, cupped flared	$100.00 – 115.00	$210.00 – 260.00			$350.00 – 450.00

**French opalescent $235.00 – 255.00*

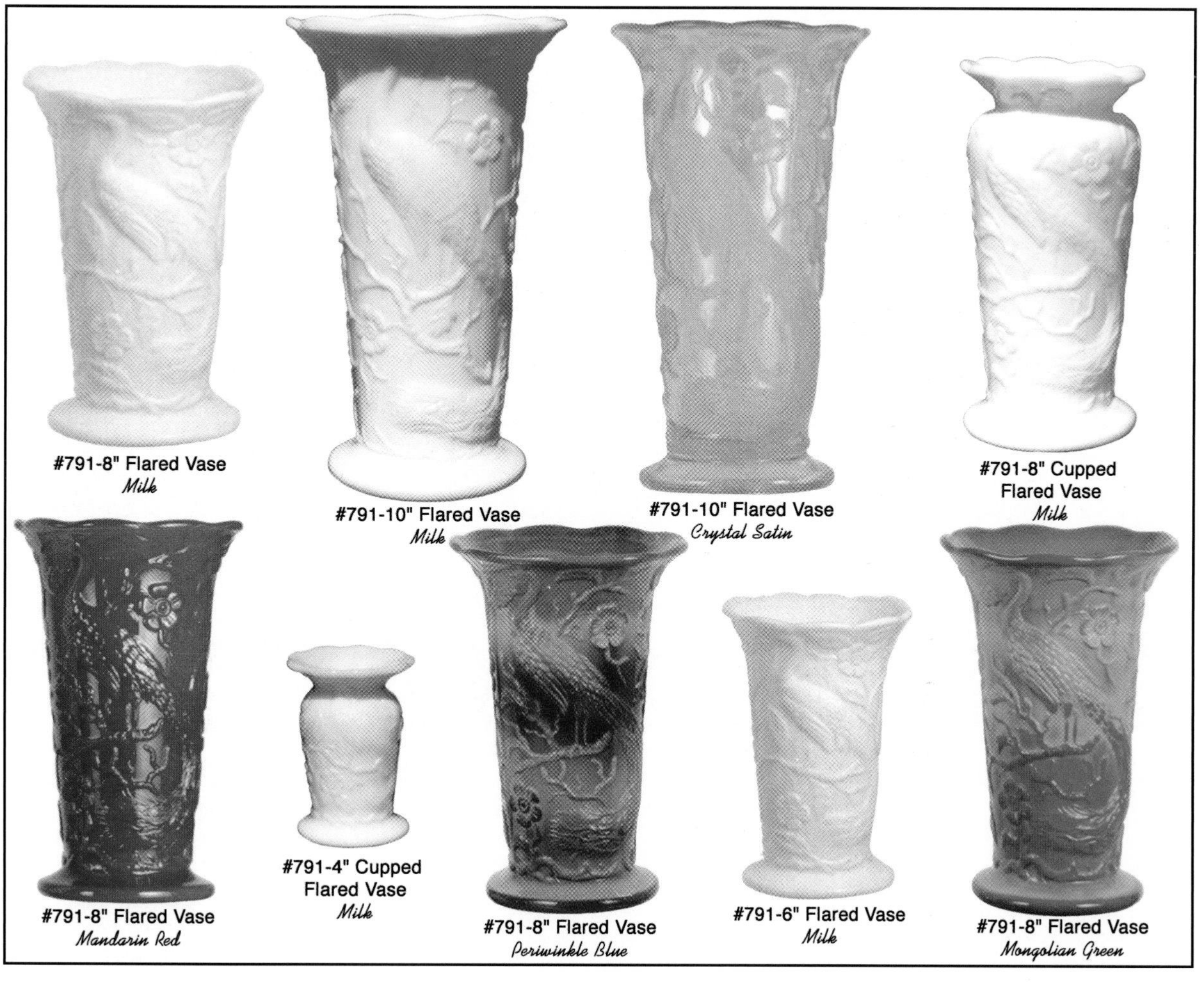

#791-8" Flared Vase *Milk*

#791-10" Flared Vase *Milk*

#791-10" Flared Vase *Crystal Satin*

#791-8" Cupped Flared Vase *Milk*

#791-8" Flared Vase *Mandarin Red*

#791-4" Cupped Flared Vase *Milk*

#791-8" Flared Vase *Periwinkle Blue*

#791-6" Flared Vase *Milk*

#791-8" Flared Vase *Mongolian Green*

PLYMOUTH #1620

Colors: amber; crystal; French opalescent; royal blue; ruby; Stiegel green.

Fenton eagerly welcomed the repeal of Prohibition with a bar and cocktail set — Plymouth. Pieces of this pattern are found most often in ruby and crystal. Some of the pieces were made in amber and French opalescent, but they are not plentiful. Production of royal blue and Stiegel green was very limited, and items in these colors are elusive. Examples of the Stiegel green color are the teal color whiskey and 6" tumbler shown in the photo. Iridescent baskets have been found, but they are uncommon. The crystal satin Ming ice bucket on the Plymouth blank is not too difficult to find.

	Amber	Crystal	French Opalescent	Royal Blue	Ruby	Stiegel Green
Bar bottle		$158.00 – 180.00			$210.00 – 235.00	
*Basket		$37.00 – 47.00		$90.00 – 95.00	$90.00 – 100.00	
Cocktail shaker		$57.00 – 60.00		$210.00 – 235.00	$105.00 – 125.00	
Goblet, 4 oz. wine	$16.00 – 18.00	$12.00 – 14.00	$26.00 – 28.00	$22.00 – 25.00	$24.00 – 27.00	$24.00 – 26.00
Goblet, 5¾"	$8.00 – 9.00	$6.00 – 8.00	$20.00 – 24.00	$12.00 – 14.00	$10.00 – 12.00	$20.00 – 24.00
**Ice pail	$43.00 – 47.00	$27.00 – 29.00		$155.00 – 200.00	$80.00 – 85.00	
Jigger		$24.00 – 26.00		$47.00 – 53.00	$47.00 – 52.00	
Mug, 4½" 10 oz		$22.00 – 25.00				
***Mug, 5¾"			$80.00 – 90.00			
Pilsner, 10 oz.		$22.00 – 25.00	$53.00 – 57.00		$37.00 – 45.00	
Pilsner, 8 oz.		$22.00 – 25.00		$32.00 – 37.00	$32.00 – 36.00	
Plate, 6"	$5.00 – 6.00	$5.00 – 6.00	$6.00 – 8.00	$5.00 – 6.00		$4.00 – 6.00
Plate, 8"	$16.00 – 22.00	$15.00 – 16.00	$30.00 – 32.00	$22.00 – 27.00	$22.00 – 27.00	$20.00 – 25.00
Sherbet, 4¾"	$8.00 – 10.00	$5.00 – 6.00	$13.00 – 15.00	$9.00 – 10.00	$9.00 – 11.00	$12.00 – 14.00
Tumbler, 2½ oz. whiskey	$11.00 – 13.00	$5.00 – 8.00			$15.00 – 18.00	$16.00 – 19.00
Tumbler, 4" 5 oz.	$11.00 – 13.00	$5.00 – 8.00	$17.00 – 19.00		$15.00 – 18.00	$12.00 – 14.00
Tumbler, 7 oz. Old fashion	$16.00 – 18.00	$15.00 – 17.00	$27.00 – 32.00	$60.00 – 65.00	$22.00 – 25.00	
Tumbler, 8 oz. Highball	$15.00 – 16.00	$13.00 – 15.00	$28.00 – 30.00		$22.00 – 24.00	$22.00 – 24.00
Tumbler, 9 oz.	$12.00 – 14.00	$5.00 – 7.00		$22.00 – 25.00	$15.00 – 18.00	
Tumbler, 6", 12 oz.	$12.00 – 14.00	$13.00 – 15.00	$22.00 – 25.00		$20.00 – 22.00	$20.00 – 22.00

**Persian Pearl $235.00 – 260.00; aqua iridescent $320.00 – 350.00; Florentine green $120.00 – 145.00*

***Ming crystal $55.00 – 60.00; Ming green or rose $130.00 – 150.00*

****with blue handle $90.00 – 110.00*

2 Oz. Whiskey
7 Oz. Old Fashioned
Sherbet
4" Tumbler
4 1/2" Mug
Jigger
8 Oz. Highball
6" Tumbler
8 Oz. Pilsner
Cocktail Shaker
Basket
Ice Pail
5 3/4" Mug

Plymouth Reprint Courtesy Of: The Fenton Art Glass Museum

Drink
FROM
PLYMOUTH
CRYSTAL

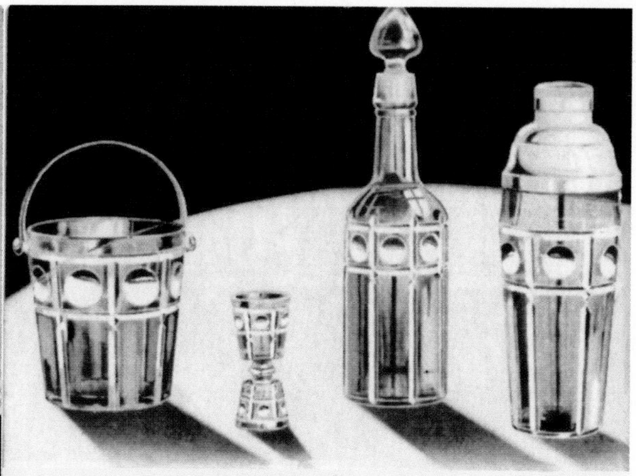

No. 1620 -- Ice Pail
No. 1620 -- Jigger
No. 1620 -- Bar Bottle 32 -- oz.
No. 1620 -- Cocktail Shaker -- 32 oz

No. 1620 -- 8 oz. Pilsner
No. 1620 -- 7 oz. Old Fashioned
No. 1620 -- 9 oz. High Ball
No. 1620 -- 2 oz. Whiskey
No. 1620 -- 4 oz. Wine

SHEFFIELD #1800 — 1936 – 1938

Colors: crystal; crystal satin; aquamarine; mermaid blue; gold; wisteria; ruby; royal blue; amber.
Etched Patterns: Halo; Silvertone.

Sheffield is a vertical ribbed pattern that Fenton introduced in 1936. Much of the production was in crystal and crystal satin, but most pieces can also be found in ruby. Two distinctive pastel blues may be found in this pattern. One is the normal aquamarine and the other is more of a gray-blue. An inventory record which refers to a color in this pattern as "M. blue" suggests this may be the elusive mermaid blue color.

Etched decorations found on this blank include Halo and Silvertone. Halo is usually found on small crystal satin 3-footed bonbons and a large 10" flared bowl. The Silvertone etching is commonly found on crystal satin pieces, but it may also be found on gold or blue. A few pieces, such as the rose bowl in the photo have been found with an iridescent finish. Refer to the next section, page 294, for a listing and prices of Sheffield pieces with Silvertone Etch.

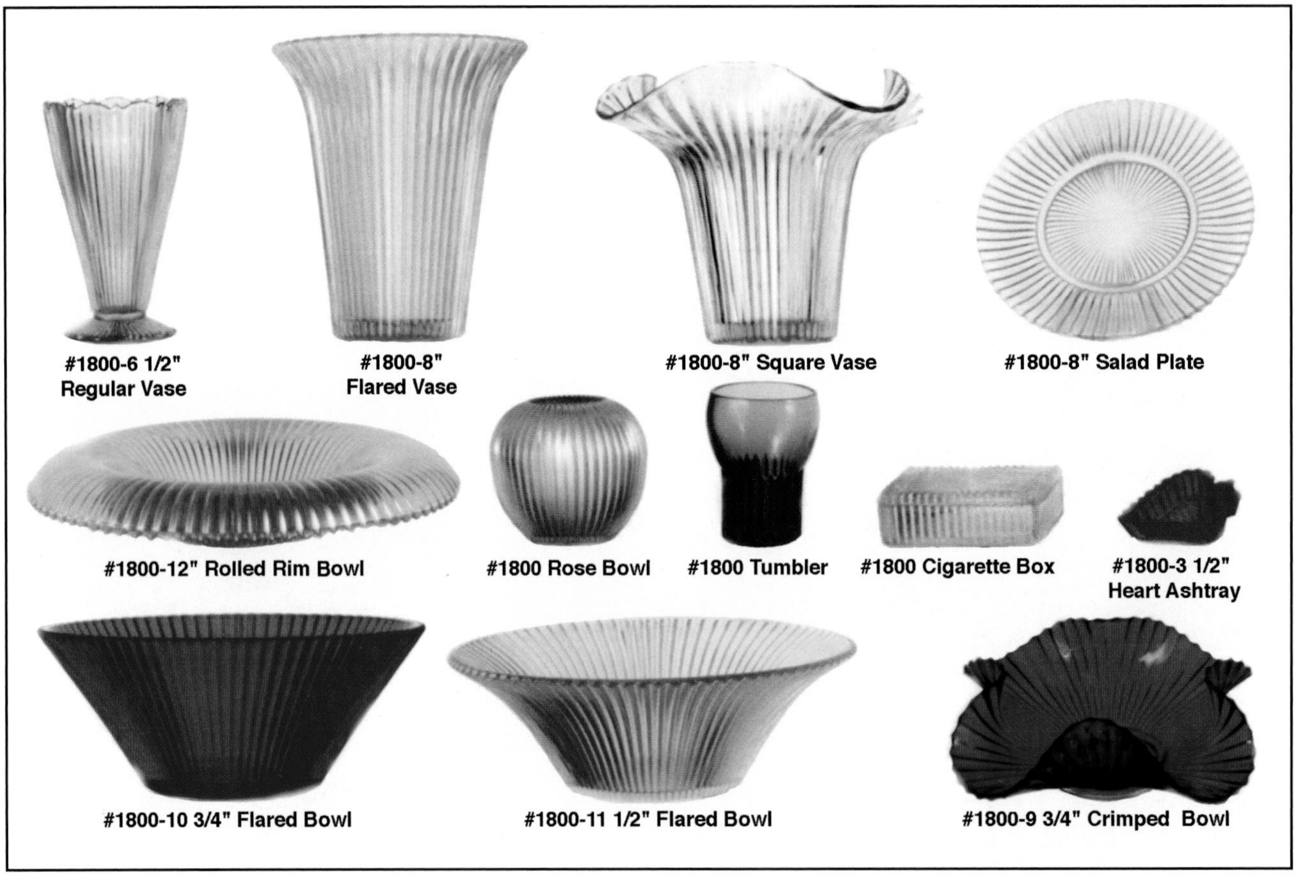

#1800-6 1/2" Regular Vase
#1800-8" Flared Vase
#1800-8" Square Vase
#1800-8" Salad Plate
#1800-12" Rolled Rim Bowl
#1800 Rose Bowl
#1800 Tumbler
#1800 Cigarette Box
#1800-3 1/2" Heart Ashtray
#1800-10 3/4" Flared Bowl
#1800-11 1/2" Flared Bowl
#1800-9 3/4" Crimped Bowl

Sheffield	**Crystal/ Crystal Satin**	**Ruby**	**Aquamarine**	**Wisteria**	**Gold**	**Royal Blue**
Ashtray	$2.00 – 4.00	$5.00 – 6.00	$4.00 – 5.00			$3.00 – 4.00
Bonbon, 6½" club; triangle	$6.00 – 8.00	$20.00 – 22.00	$16.00 – 18.00			$10.00 – 12.00
Bonbon, 7½" 3-ftd. shallow	$7.00 – 9.00	$24.00 – 26.00	$22.00 – 24.00			$10.00 – 12.00
#Bonbon, 7" 3-ftd. flared	$7.00 – 9.00	$24.00 – 26.00	$22.00 – 24.00			$10.00 – 12.00
Bonbon, 7" flat covered			$47.00 – 57.00			$37.00 – 39.00
Bonbon, covered 3-ftd.	$16.00 – 20.00	$47.00 – 49.00	$42.00 – 47.00	$27.00 – 32.00	$22.00 – 25.00	
Bowl, 10"	$20.00 – 22.00	$42.00 – 45.00	$37.00 – 42.00			$24.00 – 26.00
*Bowl, 12" flared or sq. or 11" crimp	$22.00 – 24.00	$47.00 – 49.00	$42.00 – 47.00			$26.00 – 28.00
Candleholder	$10.00 – 12.00	$20.00 – 24.00	$16.00 – 18.00			$12.00 – 14.00
**Cigarette box	$10.00 – 12.00	$27.00 – 32.00	$22.00 – 25.00			$20.00 – 22.00
Creamer	$8.00 – 10.00		$16.00 – 18.00			$11.00 – 13.00
Mayonnaise bowl, 5"	$8.00 – 10.00		$16.00 – 18.00			$11.00 – 13.00
Plate, 6"	$2.00 – 3.00	$5.00 – 6.00			$4.00 – 5.00	$7.00 – 9.00
Plate, 8"	$6.00 – 7.00	$12.00 – 14.00	$12.00 – 13.00			$7.00 – 9.00
Plate, 8¼" 3 – ft.	$10.00 – 12.00					
Plate, 9"	$10.00 – 12.00	$22.00 – 24.50	$20.00 – 22.00			$13.00 – 15.00
Plate, 10"	$12.00 – 14.00	$28.00 – 32.00	$24.00 – 25.00			$15.00 – 17.00
Plate, 14" underplate	$22.00 – 24.00	$37.00 – 40.00	$32.00 – 37.00			$23.00 – 25.00
***Rose bowl, flat	$6.00 – 8.00			$20.00 – 22.00		
Sugar	$10.00 – 12.00		$16.00 – 18.00			$10.00 – 12.00
Tumbler, 12 oz.	$6.00 – 7.00	$20.00 – 22.00	$16.00 – 18.00			$10.00 – 12.00
Tumbler, 9 oz.	$3.00 – 4.00	$10.00 – 12.00	$10.00 – 12.00	$8.00 – 9.00	$7.00 – 8.00	$10.00 – 12.00
Tumbler, 5 oz.			$10.00 – 12.00			
Tumbler, whiskey	$3.00 – 4.00	$15.00 – 17.00	$15.00 – 18.00		$5.00 – 6.00	$15.00 – 17.00
Vase, 6½" flared; regular; tulip; cupped; crimped	$12.00 – 14.00	$27.00 – 29.00	$22.00 – 26.00			$15.00 – 17.00
##Vase, 8" square; flared	$12.00 – 14.00	$27.00 – 30.00	$24.00 – 27.00			$16.00 – 18.00
###Vase, 10" sq.	$22.00 – 24.00	$42.00 – 46.00	$42.00 – 45.00			$26.00 – 31.00

Halo Etch	**Crystal Satin**
Bonbon, 6"– 7"	$8.00 – 10.00
Bowl, 10" flared	$22.00 – 24.00

*French opalescent	$53.00 – 57.00
**Milk Glass	$37.00 – 42.00
#Iridescent Aquamarine	$50.00 – 60.00
***Iridescent Mermaid blue	N.D.
##Iridescent Aquamarine	$235.00 – 285.00
###Iridescent Aquamarine	$275.00 – 300.00

SPIRAL OPTIC #1503

1927 – 1930

Colors: green, orchid, rose, gold.

Fenton produced a rather abbreviated line of swirl items from about 1927 – 1930. The pattern was called Spiral Optic and is a complementary pattern to Diamond Optic which was introduced the same year. The basic style is the same as Diamond Optic, but Spiral Optic must not have been as popular since the assortment of pieces remained very limited. Many of the pieces are adorned with dolphins, and this is an interesting pattern to collect if you are looking for a collection that will not occupy your whole house.

	Green/Gold	Orchid	Rose
Bowl, #1503 – 10" flared	$30.00 – 35.00	$30.00 – 35.00	$25.00 – 30.00
Bowl, #1503 – A-7" cupped w/dolphins	$27.00 – 30.00	$42.00 – 47.00	$38.00 – 42.00
Bowl, #1503 – A-8½" rolled rim w/dolphins	$27.00 – 32.00	$47.00 – 55.00	$38.00 – 42.00
Bowl, #1503 – A-9" shallow cupped w/dolphins	$30.00 – 35.00	$35.00 – 55.00	$37.00 – 45.00
Bowl, #1503 – A-10" flared w/dolphins	$30.00 – 35.00	$47.00 – 50.00	$44.00 – 47.00
*Candlestick, #1623	$20.00 – 22.00	$24.00 – 26.00	$15.00 – 18.00
Goblet, #1503 – 9 oz.	$15.00 – 20.00	$22.00 – 24.00	$20.00 – 22.00
Plate, #1503 – 8" octagonal	$10.00 – 12.00	$12.00 – 14.00	$12.00 – 14.00
Sherbet, #1503	$8.00 – 10.00	$12.00 – 14.00	$9.00 – 10.00
*Ruby $22.00 – 27.00			

#1503-A-7" Cupped Bowl

#1503-A-10" Flared Bowl

#1503-A/#1623 Console Set

#1503-A/#1623 Console Set

#1503-A-9 1/2" Crimped Bowl

#1503-A-7" Cupped Bowl

Catalog Reprint Circa 1928
Courtesy Of:
The Fenton Art Glass Museum

THE FENTON ART GLASS COMPANY
WILLIAMSTOWN, W. VA.

SUPPLEMENTARY
PAGE THIRTEEN

1502 DIAMOND AND 1503 SPIRAL OPTIC LINE.
Plain Colors — Rose — Green — Orchid — Royal Blue — Ruby.

1502 8½" Flared Cup Bowl
1502A-7" Cupped Bowl
1502A-9" Crimp Bowl
1503A-8½" Roll Edge Bowl
1503A-7" Cupped Bowl

1502A-8½" Roll Edge Bowl
1502A-8" Flared Cup Bowl
1502-14" Special Roll Edge Bowl
1503 Candlestick
1503-10" Flared Bowl
1503 Candlestick

1502-10" Special Roll Edge Bowl
1502A-10" Flared Bowl
1502-8" Deep Cup Bowl
1623 Candlestick
1503A-10" Flared Bowl
1623 Candlestick
1503A-9" Shallow Cup Bowl

1502 Cup and Saucer

1502-2 pc. Guest Set
1502-11 oz. Bridge Goblet
1502-9" Bridge Goblet
1502-Finger Bowl and Plate
1502-6" Octagon Plate
1503-8" Spiral Optic Plate
1503-Spiral Optic Sherbet
1503-9 oz. Goblet

SILVERTONE 1934 – 1938

Between 1934 and 1938, a 13-piece assortment of pressed bowls, plates, and candles was made with an embossed design which resembles the veins of a leaf. The pattern was called Silvertone, and the colors made were crystal, amber, and wisteria. Wisteria is Fenton's name for amethyst.

The reprint on the next page shows pieces of this pattern sold by the F. W. Woolworth Company. The two pieces in the lower right side of the photo below have a similar pattern, but there is no catalog evidence to confirm they were made by Fenton.

Don't confuse this pattern with a different Fenton decoration of the same name. The Silvertone pattern listed on page 294 has an acid etched design. To help avoid the name confusion, we will call this embossed pattern Silvertone and the etched decoration will be referred to as Silvertone Etch.

Silvertone	Crystal	Amber	Wisteria
Bowl, #1000 – 10" shallow	$16.00 – 22.00	$24.00 – 26.00	$27.00 – 35.00
Bowl, #1001 – 9" club	$13.00 – 15.00	$22.00 – 24.00	$27.00 – 30.00
Bowl, #1002 – 9" flared	$13.00 – 15.00	$22.00 – 24.00	$27.00 – 30.00
Bowl, #1004 – 7" cupped	$10.00 – 12.00	$17.00 – 19.00	$22.00 – 25.00
Bowl, #1005 – 7" flared	$10.00 – 12.00	$17.00 – 19.00	$22.00 – 25.00
Bowl, #1006 – 7" club	$10.00 – 12.00	$17.00 – 19.00	$22.00 – 25.00
Bowl, #1007 – 5" cupped	$8.00 – 9.00	$13.00 – 16.00	$17.00 – 19.00
Bowl, #1008 – 7" triangular	$12.00 – 13.00	$17.00 – 19.00	$22.00 – 27.00
Bowl, #1000 – 11" club	$16.00 – 24.00	$25.00 – 27.00	$28.00 – 37.00
Cake plate, #1003 – 10"	$16.00 – 22.00	$22.00 – 25.00	$37.00 – 40.00
Candlestick, #1010 flared	$8.00 – 12.00	$15.00 – 18.00	$22.00 – 24.00
Candleholder, #1011 club	$8.00 – 12.00	$15.00 – 18.00	$22.00 – 24.00
Plate, #1009 – 8"	$8.00 – 10.00	$14.00 – 16.00	$17.00 – 19.00

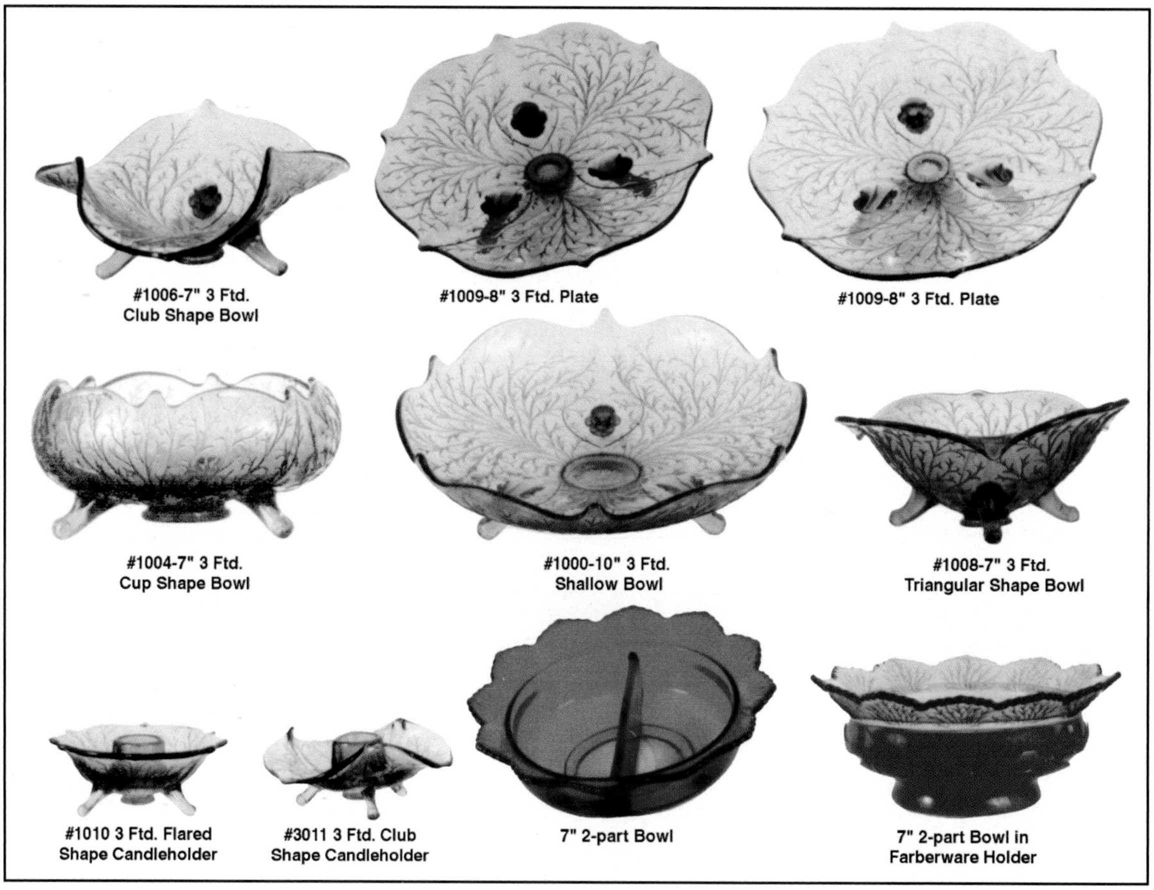

#1006-7" 3 Ftd. Club Shape Bowl

#1009-8" 3 Ftd. Plate

#1009-8" 3 Ftd. Plate

#1004-7" 3 Ftd. Cup Shape Bowl

#1000-10" 3 Ftd. Shallow Bowl

#1008-7" 3 Ftd. Triangular Shape Bowl

#1010 3 Ftd. Flared Shape Candleholder

#3011 3 Ftd. Club Shape Candleholder

7" 2-part Bowl

7" 2-part Bowl in Farberware Holder

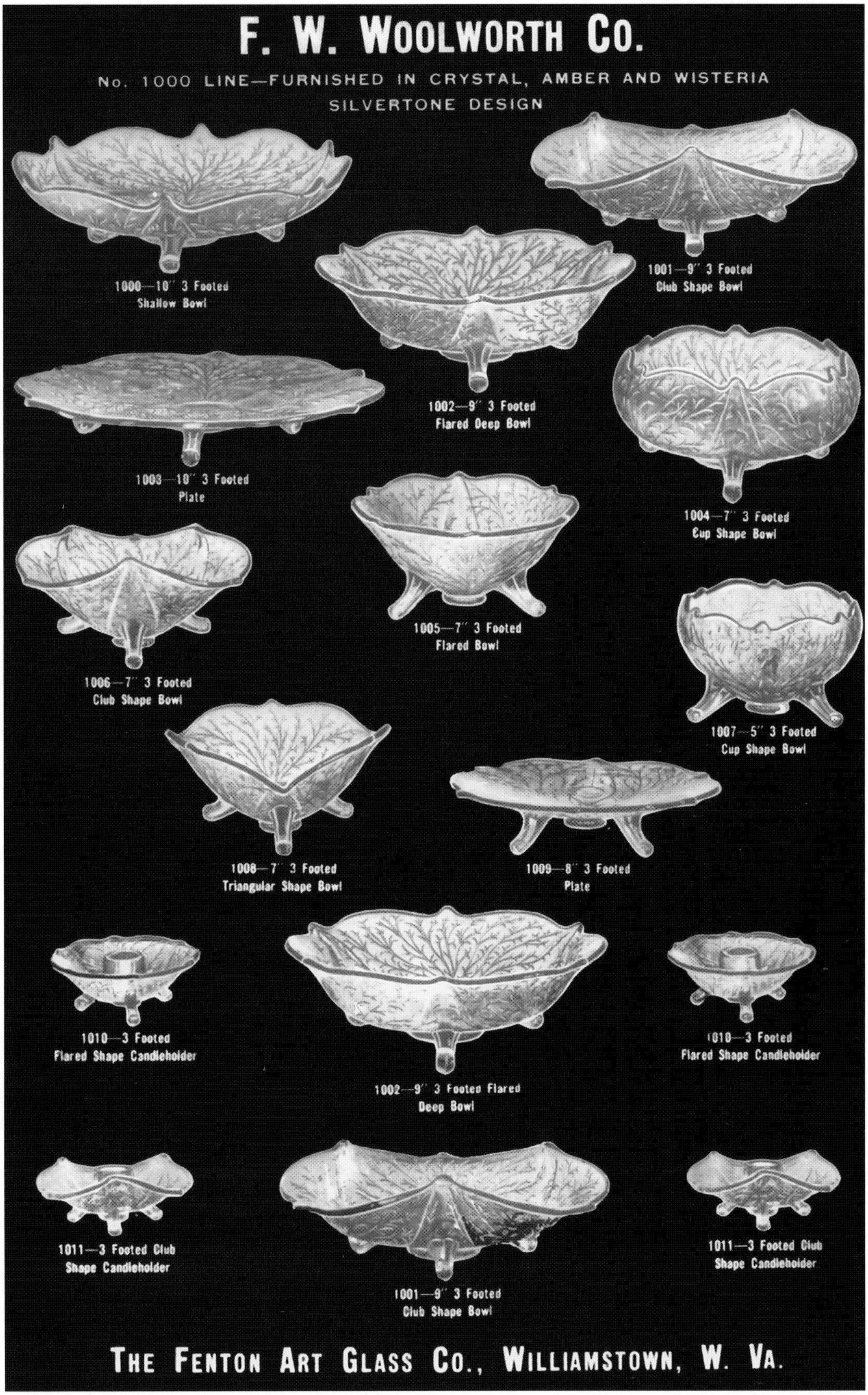
F. W. WOOLWORTH CO.
No. 1000 LINE—FURNISHED IN CRYSTAL, AMBER AND WISTERIA
SILVERTONE DESIGN
1000—10" 3 Footed Shallow Bowl
1001—9" 3 Footed Club Shape Bowl
1002—9" 3 Footed Flared Deep Bowl
1003—10" 3 Footed Plate
1004—7" 3 Footed Cup Shape Bowl
1005—7" 3 Footed Flared Bowl
1006—7" 3 Footed Club Shape Bowl
1007—5" 3 Footed Cup Shape Bowl
1008—7" 3 Footed Triangular Shape Bowl
1009—8" 3 Footed Plate
1010—3 Footed Flared Shape Candleholder
1002—9" 3 Footed Flared Deep Bowl
1010—3 Footed Flared Shape Candleholder
1011—3 Footed Club Shape Candleholder
1001—9" 3 Footed Club Shape Bowl
1011—3 Footed Club Shape Candleholder
THE FENTON ART GLASS CO., WILLIAMSTOWN, W. VA.

INTRODUCTION

Fenton produced a number of acid etched satin glass patterns from 1935 to 1939. Crystal was the primary color, but some patterns also were made in colors.

Patterns such as Ming, San Toy, and Wisteria appear to have been made in large quantities, and some pieces in each pattern are common. Of course, there are rare items in each pattern, too. Items in other patterns like Scenic, Twin Ivy, and Snow Fern are rarely seen.

The patterns on the following pages are illustrated with the aid of catalog reprints which have been reproduced through the courtesy of the Fenton Art Glass Museum. The museum is located in Williamstown, West Virginia, at the site of the plant and is accessible from the Fenton Gift Shop. Any trip to this vicinity should include a visit to this museum. Frank M. Fenton has done an admirable job in procuring and displaying samples of glassware which illustrate the history of his company.

MING 1935 – 1936

Colors: amber satin; crystal satin; green satin; rose satin.

Ming is an acid etched pattern which was produced during 1935 and 1936. A wider variety of pieces may be found in this pattern than in any of the other similar acid etched patterns which were made during this era. Crystal is the most easily found color, and all the listed pieces have been found in crystal. Most pieces may be found in green and rose. Amber pieces are scarce, but there were so few different pieces made that not many collectors attempt to collect this color. The pitchers may be found with either the same color or a black or blue handle.

Scarce items include the hyacinth vase, the stack set, the bath set, the compartment plate, the 5-part relish, the covered mayonnaise jar, and the baby reamer. Matching satin tops for the reamer are almost impossible to find.

Item	Crystal	Green	Rose	Amber
Basket, #1684 – 9" w/wicker handle	$42.00 – 50.00	$90.00 – 95.00	$80.00 – 90.00	
Bath set, (2 – #16, 1 – #17 bottles; #54 tray)	$158.00 – 175.00	$235.00 – 275.00	$235.00 – 275.00	
Bonbon, #846 – 5" covered	$42.00 – 47.00	$80.00 – 85.00	$80.00 – 85.00	
Bonbon, #846 – 5" open	$20.00 – 22.00	$24.00 – 26.00	$24.00 – 26.00	
Bonbon, #1235 flared; cupped, triangular	$11.00 – 13.00			
Bonbon, #1621 – 6½" crimped w/dolphins	$12.00 – 14.00	$12.00 – 14.00	$12.00 – 14.00	
Bowl, #249 – 10½" crimped, 3-toed	$26.00 – 29.00	$37.00 – 45.00	$37.00 – 45.00	
Bowl, #249 – 10½" shallow cupped, 3-toed	$27.00 – 29.00	$37.00 – 45.00	$37.00 – 45.00	
Bowl, #249 – 10" deep flared, 3-toed	$27.00 – 29.00	$37.00 – 45.00	$37.00 – 45.00	
Bowl, #249 – 11½" flared, 3-toed	$27.00 – 29.00	$37.00 – 45.00	$37.00 – 45.00	
Bowl, #249 – 9" crimped, 3-toed	$25.00 – 28.00	$35.00 – 40.00	$35.00 – 40.00	
Bowl, #349 – 11" flared	$30.00 – 32.00			
Bowl, #750 – 9¼" octagonal	$47.00 – 55.00	$90.00 – 95.00	$90.00 – 95.00	
Bowl, #750 flared; regular	$47.00 – 55.00	$85.00 – 90.00	$85.00 – 90.00	
Bowl, #846 – 8½" flared; flared cupped	$20.00 – 25.00	$32.00 – 40.00	$32.00 – 40.00	
Bowl, #857 – 10" crimped ftd.	$27.00 – 29.00	$37.00 – 42.00	$37.00 – 40.00	
Bowl, #857 – 11" flared ftd.	$29.00 – 31.00	$42.00 – 46.00	$42.00 – 46.00	
Bowl, #950 – 11" oval; tulip	$27.00 – 30.00	$70.00 – 75.00	$70.00 – 75.00	
Bowl, #1005 – 5" cupped, 3-toed	$15.00 – 16.00	$22.00 – 24.00	$22.00 – 24.00	
Bowl, #1517 crimped	$30.00 – 32.00			
Bowl, #1663 – 10½" oval; tulip	$37.00 – 45.00	$70.00 – 75.00	$70.00 – 75.00	
Bowl, #1663 – 12" oval; flared; regular	$37.00 – 45.00	$80.00 – 85.00	$80.00 – 85.00	
Bowl, #1700 – 7"	$30.00 – 32.00			
Bowl, #1800 – 11" flared Sheffield	$30.00 – 32.00			
Candelabra, #2000 – 5" Pineapple	$22.00 – 25.00			
Candelabra, #2318 – 6"	$27.00 – 32.00			
Candlestick, #349 – 10" flared	$42.00 – 48.00			
Candlestick, #950 – 5½" cornucopia	$22.00 – 24.00	$32.00 – 40.00	$32.00 – 40.00	$27.00 – 29.00
Candlestick, #1800 Sheffield	$22.00 – 24.00			
Candy jar, #844 1 lb. w/flower finial	$130.00 – 165.00			
Cigarette box, #5889	$80.00 – 85.00			
Coaster, #1590	$11.00 – 13.00	$15.00 – 20.00	$15.00 – 20.00	
Decanter, #1934 w/stopper	$90.00 – 100.00	$150.00 – 175.00	$150.00 – 175.00	$175.00 – 200.00
Ginger jar, #893 w/cover and base	$105.00 – 125.00	$200.00 – 250.00	$200.00 – 250.00	
Ice bucket, #1620 Plymouth	$53.00 – 60.00	$125.00 – 150.00	$125.00 – 150.00	
Ice pail, #1616 – 6"	$63.00 – 75.00			
Ivy ball, #705	$22.00 – 25.00	$42.00 – 45.00	$42.00 – 45.00	
Macaroon jar, #1684 – 6½" w/wicker handle	$57.00 – 65.00	$105.00 – 135.00	$105.00 – 135.00	
Mayonnaise jar	$67.00 – 85.00			

Item	Crystal	Green	Rose	Amber
*Pitcher, #1353 tankard style	$105.00 – 150.00	$158.00 – 185.00	$158.00 – 185.00	
*Pitcher, #1653 – 10"	$105.00 – 150.00	$158.00 – 185.00	$158.00 – 185.00	
Plate, #107 – 8" 3-toed	$13.00 – 15.00	$20.00 – 22.00	$20.00 – 22.00	
Plate, #750 – 14" torte	$37.00 – 42.00	$63.00 – 66.00	$63.00 – 66.00	
Plate, #1235	$15.00 – 17.00			
Plate, #1517 – 14"	$30.00 – 32.00	$42.00 – 46.00	$42.00 – 46.00	
Plate, #1611 – 11" compartment Georgian	$22.00 – 30.00	$42.00 – 46.00	$42.00 – 46.00	
Reamer, #1260	$250.00 – 270.00	$300.00 – 335.00	$310.00 – 350.00	
Refrigerator dish, #457 rectangular w/cover	$22.00 – 27.00			$42.00 – 47.00
Relish set, 5-part divided 10½" tray/3¼" insert	$95.00 – 120.00			
Rose bowl, #846, Lincoln Inn	$20.00 – 22.00	$22.00 – 26.00	$22.00 – 25.00	
Stack set, #457 – 3-pc.	$105.00 – 145.00	$160.00 – 200.00	$158.00 – 200.00	
Tray, #1934 12"	$20.00 – 22.00			
Tumbler, #1934 – 1 oz. whiskey	$9.00 – 10.00	$20.00 – 22.00	$20.00 – 22.00	$18.00 – 22.00
Tumbler, #35 – 5 oz.	$9.00 – 10.00	$16.00 – 18.00	$15.00 – 18.00	
Tumbler, #1353 – 10 oz. flat/curved sides	$12.00 – 14.00	$15.00 – 18.00	$15.00 – 18.00	
Tumbler, #1653 – 10 oz. flat/straight sides	$10.00 – 15.00	$15.00 – 18.00	$16.00 – 18.00	
Tumbler, #1502 – 9 oz. ftd.	$15.00 – 18.00			
Vase, #180 Hyacinth	$27.00 – 35.00	$53.00 – 62.00	$53.00 – 62.00	
Vase, #184 – 8"	$27.00 – 30.00			
Vase, #184 – 10"	$32.00 – 36.00	$68.00 – 75.00	$68.00 – 75.00	
Vase, #184 – 12"	$32.00 – 36.00	$75.00 – 85.00	$77.00 – 87.00	
Vase, #621 – 6½" cupped	$25.00 – 27.00	$38.00 – 45.00	$37.00 – 45.00	
Vase, #621 – 8" cupped; flared; flared cupped	$27.00 – 29.00	$42.00 – 50.00	$42.00 – 50.00	
Vase, 8½" bud	$25.00 – 27.00			
Vase, #847 – 6" fan	$27.00 – 29.00	$42.00 – 46.00	$42.00 – 47.00	
**Vase, #857 – 8" fan	$37.00 – 40.00	$57.00 – 65.00	$58.00 – 65.00	
Vase, #898 – 11½" crystal	$95.00 – 120.00			
Vase, #1110 – 11" crystal	$200.00 – 250.00			
Vase, #1800 – 8" flared; square Sheffield	$37.00 – 42.00	$57.00 – 60.00	$58.00 – 60.00	
Vase, #1800 – 8" straight Sheffield	$34.00 – 37.00	$53.00 – 55.00	$53.00 – 56.00	

** with blue or black handle add 20%*
***in metal mount, add 20%*

#893 Ginger Jar ***#1653 Tumbler*** ***#1653 Pitcher*** ***#1653 Pitcher*** ***#1653 Pitcher*** ***#1934 Decanter*** ***#35 Whiskey***

#621-6 1/2" Cupped Vase ***#184-8" Vase*** ***#184-10" Vase*** ***#1800-8" Flared Vase*** ***#180 Hyacinth Vase*** ***8 1/2" Bud Vase*** ***#857-8" Vase***

#1620 Ice Bucket "Plymouth" ***#1502-11 Oz. Tumbler*** ***#35-5 Oz. Tumbler*** ***#1684 Macaroon Jar*** ***#1684 Macaroon Jar*** ***Stack Set*** ***#249-10" Bowl***

#1005-5" Cupped Bowl ***#1005-5" Cupped Bowl*** ***#750-9 1/4" Octagonal Bowl*** ***#846-6" Cupped Bowl*** ***#846-8" Flared Bowl*** ***#1621-6 1/2" Bonbon***

#349-11" Flared Bowl ***#5889 Cigarette Box*** ***#950-11" Oval Bowl*** ***#950 Candlestick*** ***#1663-10 1/2" Tulip Bowl***

#1611-11" Compartment Plate ***Baby Reamer*** ***#249-11 1/2" Flared Bowl*** ***#107-8" 3-toed Plate*** ***#2000 Candlestick***

PINEAPPLE, #2000 – A

Colors: crystal satin; rose satin; ruby.

Fenton's satinized embossed Pineapple pattern was introduced in 1938. Most of the pieces were made in crystal satin and are relatively inexpensive. However, the candlesticks and some of the bowls were made in colors. The larger colored bowls are priced reasonably, and collectors are finding they make an attractive centerpiece.

	Crystal Satin	Rose Satin	Ruby
Bonbon, 6½" flat btm., triangle; flared; club; crimped	$20.00 – 24.00	$25.00 – 30.00	
Bonbon, 5½" flat club; regular	$16.00 – 20.00	$24.00 – 28.00	
Bonbon and cover (in crystal satin only)	$45.00 – 55.00		
Bowl, 7" berry	$18.00 – 22.00		$30.00 – 35.00
Bowl, 11¼" crimped, 3-footed			$70.00 – 90.00
Bowl, 11¼" flat bottom, flared	$37.00 – 45.00	$60.00 – 65.00	$60.00 – 65.00
Bowl, 13" square	$60.00 – 65.00	$80.00 – 85.00	$80.00 – 85.00
*Candlestick, 5½" double branch	$23.00 – 27.00	$55.00 – 60.00	$60.00 – 65.00
Comport, 5½" footed, crimped	$22.00 – 27.00		
Comport, 5½" low ftd. cupped; regular	$22.00 – 27.00		
Comport, 6½" ftd. crimped; flared; club	$22.00 – 27.00		
Comport, 7" tall, crimped	$38.00 – 45.00		
Plate, 7"	$24.00 – 26.00		
Relish, 12" 3-pt	$37.00 – 42.00		
Salver, 7"	$20.00 – 22.00		
Tray, olive	$20.00 – 22.00		

**Royal Blue* $65.00 – 75.00.

No. 2000-A Pineapple Console Set
3 Shape Bowls
Shallow - Crimp
& Flared
2000A - 3 Pc. Console Set.
Satin Finish - Crystal & Rose
Cataolg Reprint Circa 1938 Courtesy Of: The Fenton Art Glass Museum

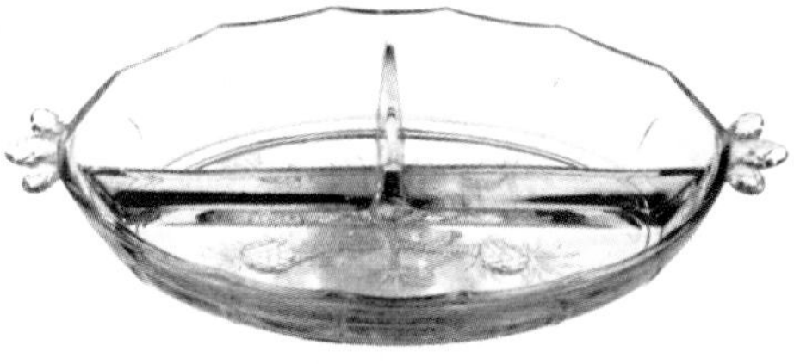

12" 3-part Relish

7" Crimped Comport

Covered Bonbon

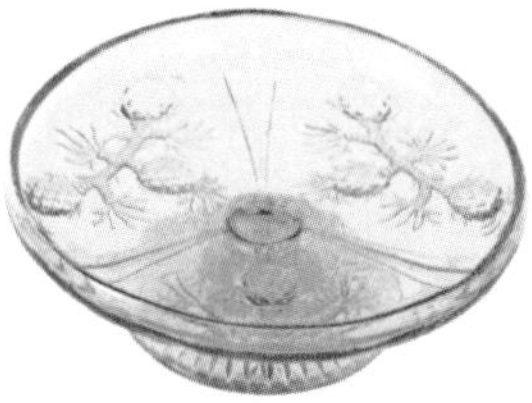

6 1/2" Low Footed Comport

11 1/4" Flared Bowl

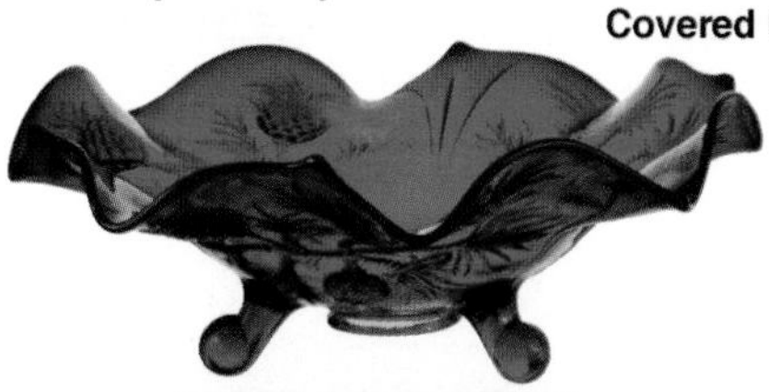

11 1/4" 3-footed Bowl

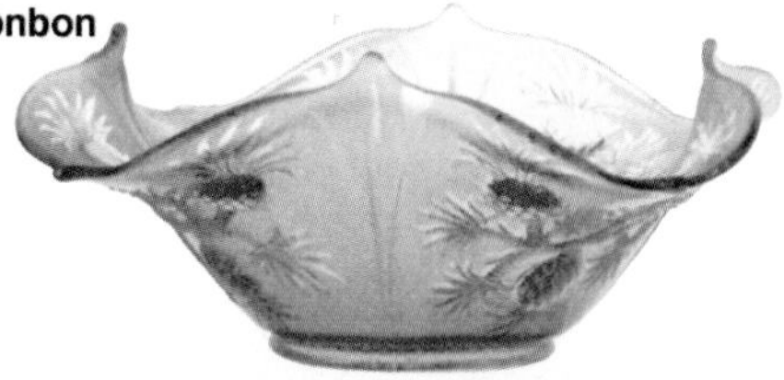

13" Square Bowl

No 2000-A
Bon Bon Assortment

Item	List Price Per Dozen
2000 6½" Fld Bon Bon, S F	$6.00
2000 7" Salver Bon Bon, S F	6.00
2000 5½" Reg Bon Bon, S F	6.00
2000 6½" Crimped Bon Bon, S F	6.00
2000 5½" Cupd Bon Bon, S F	6.00
2000 6½" Club Bon Bon, S F	6.00
2000 6½" Ftd Fld Bon Bon, S F	9.00
2000 6½" Ftd Club Bon Bon, S F	9.00
2000 6½" Ftd Salver Bon Bon, S F	9.00
2000 5½" Ftd Reg Bon Bon, S F	9.00
2000 6½" Ftd Crimped Bon Bon, S F	9.00
2000 5½" Ftd Cupd Bon Bon, S F	9.00

Assortment Price $7.20
Less 50%
Regular Package Charge

Fenton Art Glass Co.
Williamstown, W. Va.
No. 2000A - Bon Bon Assortment.
6½" Ftd. Crimped
6½" Club.
6½" Ftd. Flared
6½" Flared
6¾" Ftd. Plate.
5½" Regular
6½" Ftd. Club.
5½" Club.
5½" Ftd. Regular
6½" Crimped.
5½" Ftd. Cupped.
7" Salver

Catalog Reprint
Courtesy Of:
The Fenton Art Glass Museum

NO. 43 POINSETTIA CRYSTAL SATIN DECORATION

Crystal satin pieces with the No. 43 Poinsettia etching were produced from 1938 through 1939. The short period of production has helped to contribute to the relative scarcity of this pattern. This attractive floral and leaf etching is not known to exist in colors. Among the more attractive pieces are the basket and the large 10" vases.

Item	Value
Basket, #1616 – 9½" handled	$68.00 – 75.00
Bowl, #231 – 11" crimped	$78.00 – 85.00
Bowl, #349 – 10½"	$68.00 – 80.00
Bowl, #950 – 10" oval tulip	$68.00 – 78.00
Bowl, #950 – 11" clover	$73.00 – 78.00
Bowl, #1522 – 8"	$58.00 – 65.00
Bowl, #1562 – 13" oval	$78.00 – 85.00
Bowl, #1663 – 10½" tulip	$73.00 – 80.00
Bowl, #1663 – 11½" flared	$78.00 – 85.00
Candlestick, #950 – 5" cornucopia	$43.00 – 45.00
Plate, #231 – 12"	$58.00 – 65.00
Rose bowl, #894 crimped	$50.00 – 55.00
Vase, #182 – 10" flared	$58.00 – 65.00
Vase, #183 – 7" special	$38.00 – 42.00
Vase, #894 – 10" regular	$58.00 – 65.00
Vase, #894 – 10" square	$68.00 – 75.00
Vase, #895 – 10"	$68.00 – 75.00

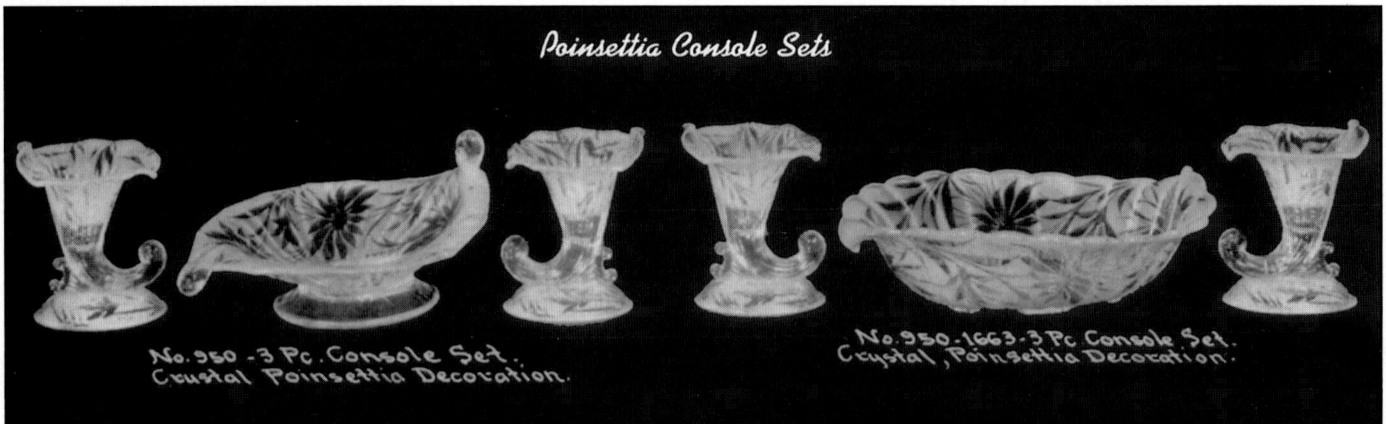
Poinsettia Console Sets
No. 950 -3 Pc. Console Set.
Crystal Poinsettia Decoration.
No. 950-1663-3 Pc Console Set.
Crystal, Poinsettia Decoration.

Cataolg Reprint Circa 1938 Courtesy Of: The Fenton Art Glass Museum

#1616-9 1/2" Handled Basket

#183-7" Special Vase

#950 Oval Bowl

Photo Below:

Poinsettia Catalog Reprint Composite-Circa 1938

Courtesy Of:

The Fenton Art Glass Museum

#231-11" Crimped Bowl

#1522-8" Bowl

#950-11" Clover Bowl

#231-12" Plate

#894 Crimped Rose Bowl

#1562-13" Oval Bowl

#182-10" Flared Vase

#894-10" Regular Vase

#894-10" Square Vase

#895-10" Vase

SAN TOY

Colors: crystal; green; rose.

San Toy is a acid etched satin pattern that was introduced in 1936. The pattern was produced in crystal, green, and rose, but not all pieces were made in colors; most items are scarce in color. A few of the more elusive pieces in crystal include the bathroom set, the candy jar with the flower finial, and the ginger jar.

Item	Crystal	Green	Rose
Base, #706 diamond-shaped	$20.00 – 22.00		
Bathroom set, #16 – 17 – 54, 4-pc.	$158.00 – 175.00	$235.00 – 285.00	$235.00 – 285.00
Bonbon, #107 – 7" flared	$15.00 – 17.00		
Bonbon, #1800 – 6½"	$15.00 – 17.00		
Bowl, #349 – 8½" flared	$30.00 – 32.00		
Bowl, #847 – 6" crimped	$13.00 – 15.00		
Bowl, #847 – 6" cupped	$13.00 – 15.00		
Bowl, #847 – 7½" flared	$15.00 – 17.00		
Bowl, #847 – 8½" crimped, ftd	$20.00 – 22.00		
Bowl, #950 – 11" tulip; oval	$25.00 – 28.00		
Bowl, #1663 – 10½" tulip	$38.00 – 45.00		
Candlestick, #249 – 6"	$22.00 – 24.00		
Candlestick, #349 flared	$43.00 – 47.00		
Candlestick, #950 cornucopia	$22.00 – 24.00		
Candy jar, #844, 1 lb. w/flower finial	$130.00 – 170.00		
Coaster, #1590 – 4"	$10.00 – 12.00		
Cocktail shaker, #33	$27.00 – 30.00		
Ginger jar and lid, #893	$110.00 – 125.00		
Ice pail, #1616 – 6"	$65.00 – 75.00		
Ivy ball, #705	$22.00 – 25.00		
Plate, #107 – 8" 3-footed	$14.00 – 16.00		
Puff box	$48.00 – 55.00		
Tumbler, #35 whiskey	$8.00 – 10.00		
Vase, #180 hyacinth	$26.00 – 35.00		
Vase, #184 – 8"	$26.00 – 30.00		
Vase, #349 oval	$43.00 – 47.00	$79.00 – 95.00	
Vase, #847 – 6½" crimped	$27.00 – 30.00		
Vase, #847 – 6" fan	$27.00 – 30.00		
Vase, #857 – 8" fan	$30.00 – 33.00		
Vase, #898 – 11½"	$33.00 – 37.00		

#16-17-54 Bathroom Set

#1563-17" 2-handled Bowl

#349-8" Flared Vase

#857-8" Fan Vase | #844-6" Bonbon | #893 Ginger Jar | #1616 Ice Pail | #249-6 1/2" Candlestick

#950 Oval Bowl | #705 Flower Ball and Base | #107-7" Flared Bonbon | #1800-6 1/2" Club Bonbon

Photo Below: **San Toy Catalog Reprint Circa 1936** Courtesy Of: **The Fenton Art Glass Museum**

No. 33 — San Toy Crystal Assortment

	Indiv. Price Per Dozen
184-8″ Vase	$15.00
950 Candlesticks (1 pair) doz. pair	12.00
950 Oval Bowl	12.00
180 Hyacinth Vase	5.00
847-6″ Cupd BonBon	12.00
847-6″ Crimped Vase	12.00
847-7½″ Flared Bowl	12.00
847-6″ Regular Bowl	12.00
847-6″ Fan Vase	12.00
705 Flower Ball & Base	12.00
847-8½″ Shal Crpd Bowl	12.00

Regular Pkg. Chg.

Assortment price $10.00

No. 33 - San-Toy Crystal.
12 Piece Assortment
Fenton Art Glass Co., Williamstown, W. Va.
No. 184-8" Vase.
No. 950. Candlestick.
No. 950. Oval Bowl.
No. 950. Candlestick.
Hyacinth Vase.
No. 847-6" Cupped Bon Bon.
No. 847-6" Vase. Crimped.
No. 847-7½" Flared Bowl.
No 847-6" Regular.
No. 847-6" Fan Vase.
No. 705. Flower Ball & Base.
No. 847-8½" Shallow Crimped

SCENIC

Scenic is one of the more intricate of the Fenton satin etched patterns. The pattern, which was made in 1938, is highly collectible today. Unfortunately, not much of this pattern is appearing for sale. The relatively high prices in the listing below are a good indication of the popularity and scarcity of this pattern.

One of the more desirable items is the covered bonbon. As is many times the case with covered pieces, obtaining the bonbon with the lid intact is difficult. Some of the more unusual shapes with this decoration include the #1934 vase and the #1564 square bowl. The #1934 vase was made in both a short 5" size and tall 7½" size.

Item	Value
Bonbon, #846 – 5" covered	$210.00 – 260.00
Bowl, #846 – 6" cupped	$95.00 – 110.00
Bowl, #846 – 8½" cupped	$100.00 – 115.00
Bowl, #846 – 8½" flared	$100.00 – 115.00
Bowl, #1562 – 2 – 13" oval	$105.00 – 115.00
Bowl, #1564 – 5½" square	$78.00 – 85.00
Vase, #200 – 7" flared	$88.00 – 92.00
Vase, #200 – 7" regular	$88.00 – 92.00
Vase, #200 – 7" triangle	$88.00 – 92.00
Vase, #621 – 6½" cupped	$88.00 – 92.00
Vase, #621 – 6½" flared	$88.00 – 92.00
Vase, #1934 – 5" triangle	$88.00 – 92.00
Vase, #1934 – 7½" regular	$95.00 – 110.00
Vase, #1934 – 7½" triangle	$95.00 – 110.00

#200-7" Flared Vase

#1934-5" Triangle Vase

#846 Covered Bonbon

Photo Below:

Velvatone Catalog Reprint Composite-Circa 1938

Courtesy Of:

The Fenton Art Glass Company

#200-7" Triangular Vase

#200-7" Regular Vase

#621-6 1/2" Flared Vase

#621-6 1/2" Cupped Vase

#1934-7 1/2" Regular Vase

#846-8 1/2" Bowl

#1934-7 1/2" Triangle Vase

#1564-5 1/2" Square Bowl

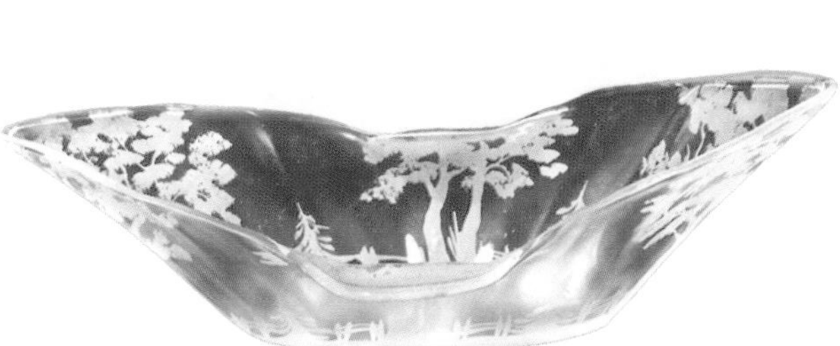

#1562-2-14" Oval Bowl

#846-6" Cupped Bowl

SILVERTONE ETCH

Silvertone Etch is a acid etched satin decoration that was made from 1937 to 1938. Do not confuse this decoration with an embossed pattern called Silvertone. Most of the Silvertone Etch items were produced in crystal, but some pieces on the Sheffield blanks were made in blue or gold.

Item	Crystal	Blue	Gold
Basket, #1681 – 10"handled Big Cookies	$58.00 – 62.00		
Bonbon, #846 – 5" covered	$47.00 – 55.00		
Bonbon, #1800 – 3-ft. cupped Sheffield	$20.00 – 22.00	$27.00 – 29.00	$24.00 – 28.00
Bonbon, #1800 – 7" covered, flat	$32.00 – 35.00	$68.00 – 75.00	$43.00 – 48.00
Bonbon, #1800 – 7" 3-ft. flared	$20.00 – 22.00	$25.00 – 28.00	$24.00 – 27.00
Bonbon, #1800 – 7½" 3-ft. shallow	$20.00 – 22.00	$25.00 – 28.00	$24.00 – 27.00
Bonbon, #1800 triang. Sheffield	$20.00 – 22.00	$25.00 – 28.00	$24.00 – 27.00
Bowl, #231 – 11" crimped	$32.00 – 36.00		
Bowl, #846, 8½" flared; cupped, ftd.	$27.00 – 30.00		
Bowl, #950 cloverleaf	$32.00 – 35.00		
Bowl, #950 – 11"oval	$32.00 – 35.00		
Bowl, #950 – 11" tulip	$32.00 – 35.00		
Bowl, #1522 – 8"	$27.00 – 32.00		
Bowl, #1562 – 1 – 13½" oval	$32.00 – 35.00		
Bowl, #1562 – 2 – 13" oval	$53.00 – 57.00		
Bowl, #1663 – 10½" tulip	$57.00 – 60.00		
Bowl, #1800 – 11½" flared Sheffield	$32.00 – 35.00	$53.00 – 58.00	$44.00 – 48.00
Bowl, #1800 – 11" crimped Sheffield	$32.00 – 35.00	$53.00 – 58.00	$44.00 – 48.00
Bowl, #1800 – 12" rolled rim Sheffield	$32.00 – 35.00		
Bowl, #1800 – 12" square Sheffield	$32.00 – 35.00	$53.00 – 58.00	$44.00 – 48.00
Cake plate, #231 – 11¾"	$43.00 – 46.00		
Candlestick, #950 – 5½" cornucopia	$27.00 – 29.00		
Candlestick, #1800 Sheffield, ea.	$12.00 – 14.00		$16.00 – 18.00
Cigarette box, #1800 Sheffield	$53.00 – 57.00		
Ice pail, #1616 – 6" Diamond Optic	$63.00 – 75.00		
Pitcher, #1352 ice tea	$158.00 – 175.00		
Plate, #1800 – 8" 3-toed Sheffield	$20.00 – 22.00	$25.00 – 27.00	$22.00 – 26.00
Plate, #1800 – 8" Sheffield	$10.00 – 12.00	$17.00 – 19.00	$14.00 – 16.00
Plate, #1800 – 14" Sheffield	$27.00 – 30.00	$48.00 – 52.00	$43.00 – 46.00
Tumbler, #1352 – 5½"	$13.00 – 15.00		
Vase, #184 – 8" flared	$30.00 – 32.00		
Vase, #184 – 10" flared	$32.00 – 35.00		
Vase, #184 – 12" flared	$34.00 – 38.00		
Vase, #857 – 8" fan	$38.00 – 43.00		
Vase, #1800 – 6½" flared; regular; tulip; cupped Sheffield	$22.00 – 26.00	$45.00 – 50.00	$38.00 – 47.00
Vase, #1800 – 8" flared Sheffield	$26.00 – 28.00	$45.00 – 55.00	$38.00 – 47.00
Vase, #1800 – 8" square Sheffield	$26.00 – 28.00	$45.00 – 55.00	$38.00 – 47.00
Vase, #1800 – 10" Sheffield	$32.00 – 35.00	$55.00 – 60.00	$48.00 – 53.00

#1800-8" Square Vase (Sheffield Pattern)

#1352 Iced Tea Pitcher

#1352 Iced Tea Tumbler

#857-8" Vase

#1800-3 Toed Cupped Bon-bon (Sheffield Pattern)

#950 Cornucopia

#1663-10 1/2" Tulip Bowl

#1800 Flat Candy (Sheffield Pattern)

#1800 -8 1/4" 3-Ftd. Plate (Sheffield Pattern)

#950 Oval Bowl

#1800 Candlestick (Sheffield Pattern)

#1800 Salad Bowl (Sheffield Pattern)

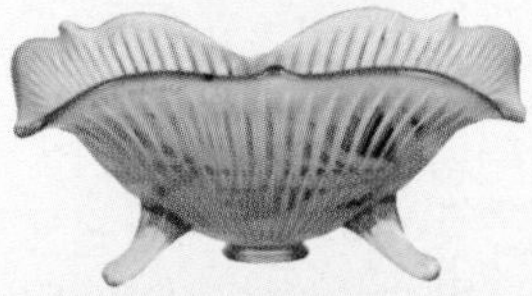

#1800 Triangular Bon-bon (Sheffield Pattern)

Photo Below: **Silvertone Etch Reprint Composite-Circa 1937** *Courtesy Of:* **The Fenton Art Glass Museum**

#950-11" Clover Bowl

#1522-8" Bowl

#1562-13" Oval Bowl

#184-12" Vase

#184-8" Vase

#231-11" Crimped Bowl

#1616 Ice Pail

SNOW FERN

This intricate satin etching, made by Fenton in 1937, on shape #249 has been dubbed Snow Fern. The pattern consists of the #249 – 6 candlestick and various shapes of the #249 3-footed bowl.

Item	Value
Bowl, #249 – E-10¾" rolled rim	$58.00 – 65.00
Bowl, #249 – E-10½" shallow	$63.00 – 68.00
Bowl, #249 – E-11½" shallow flared	$68.00 – 72.00
Bowl, #249 – E-10" flared	$58.00 – 65.00
Bowl, #249 – E-7½" cupped	$33.00 – 36.00
Bowl, #249 – E-9½" cupped flared	$38.00 – 42.00
Candlestick, #249 – E-6"	$22.00 – 26.00

Catalog Reprint Circa 1937 Courtesy Of: The Fenton Art Glass Museum

TWIN IVY

The Twin Ivy etching was created and used on various bowls and vases for a short time in 1939. The appropriately named pattern features a decoration of two ivy leaves with a satin background. This is one of the more elusive etched satin patterns.

Item	Value
Basket, #1616 – 6½" Diamond Optic	$158.00 – 210.00
Bowl, #231 – 11" crimped	$105.00 – 115.00
Bowl, #950 – 11" clover leaf	$105.00 – 130.00
Bowl, #1522 – 9" flared	$95.00 – 100.00
Bowl, #1562 – 13" oval	$105.00 – 125.00
Cake plate, #231 – 11¾"	$90.00 – 100.00
Rose bowl, #894	$90.00 – 100.00
Vase, #182 – 10" flared	$105.00 – 110.00
Vase, #183 – 6½"	$90.00 – 100.00
Vase, #894 – 10" triangle; square; flared; tulip; or regular	$105.00 – 130.00
Vase, #895 – 10" flared	$105.00 – 130.00

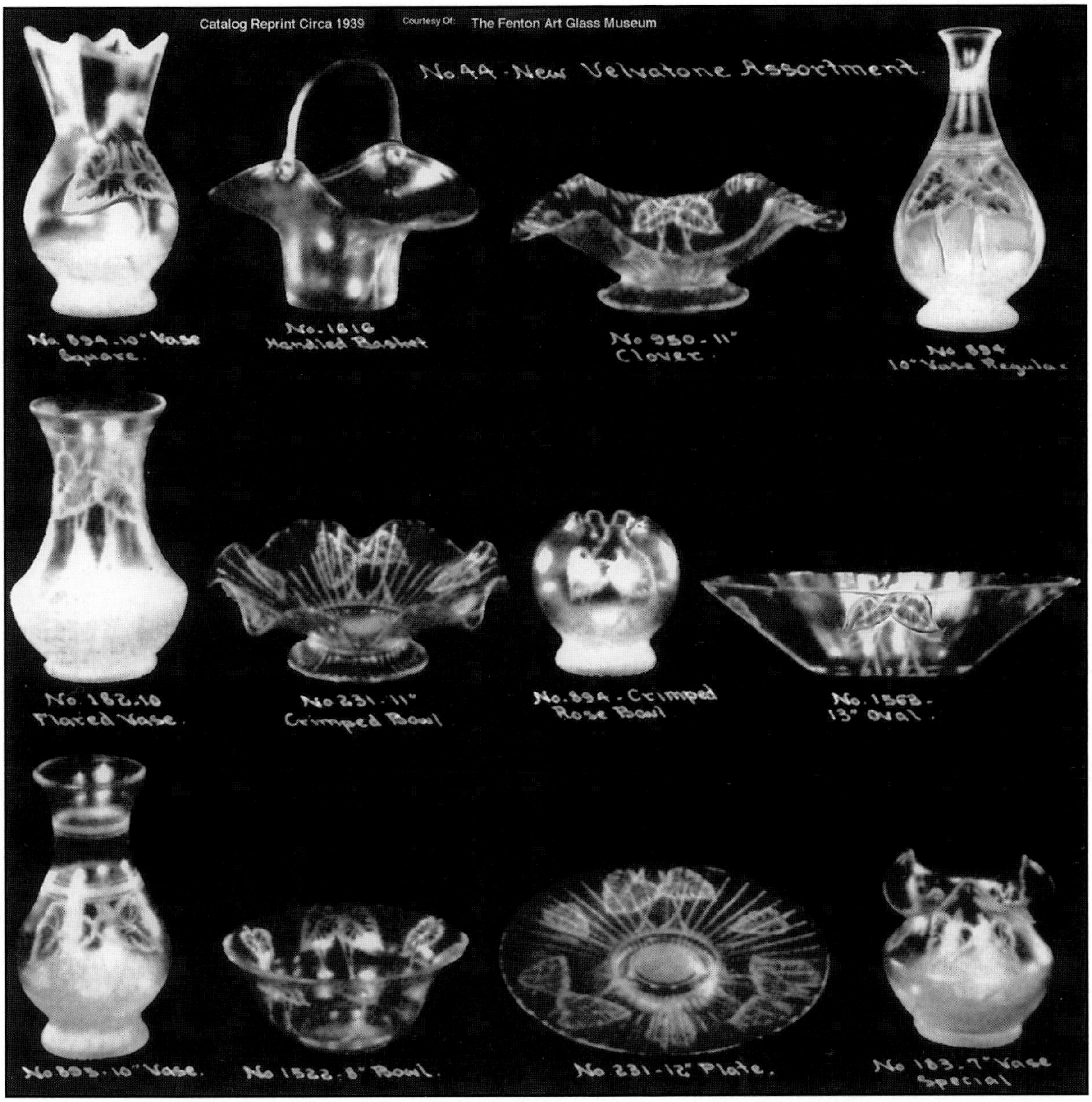

WISTARIA

Wistaria is an acid etched pattern that was made from 1937 to 1938. The variety of interesting items that were produced in this pattern has piqued collector interest. Notice the punch bowl in the photo. The etched guest set, ginger jar, and bonbon with the flower bud finial are especially hard to find.

Item	Value	Item	Value
Basket, #1684 w/wicker handle	$70.00 – 85.00	Jug, #1354 – 10½"	$155.00 – 185.00
Bonbon, #844, 1 lb. w/flower finial	$150.00 – 200.00	Jug, #1355	$180.00 – 190.00
Bowl, #349 – 11" flared	$38.00 – 42.00	Plate, #301 – 6"	$10.00 – 13.00
Bowl, #847 – 6" crimped	$38.00 – 42.00	Plate, #757 – 7¼" salad	$15.00 – 18.00
Bowl, #857 – 11" flared	$50.00 – 55.00	Plate, #1000 – 12"	$35.00 – 45.00
Bowl, #950 – 11" tulip; oval	$50.00 – 55.00	Punch bowl, 12½"	$160.00 – 175.00
Bowl, #1000 – 11" club	$50.00 – 55.00	Punch cup, #604	$12.00 – 15.00
Bowl, #100 – 11" flared	$50.00 – 55.00	Sugar, #349	$27.00 – 35.00
Bowl, #1562 – 2 – 13" oval	$55.00 – 65.00	Tumbler, #1352 – 5¼" ice tea	$20.00 – 24.00
Bowl, #1663 – 10½" tulip	$50.00 – 55.00	Tumbler, #1355 ice tea	$15.00 – 20.00
Cake plate, #249 – 10½"	$50.00 – 55.00	Vase, #183 – 8"	$43.00 – 48.00
Candlestick, #349	$55.00 – 65.00	Vase, #184 – 10"	$50.00 – 55.00
Candlestick, #1000 club, flared	$35.00 – 45.00	Vase, #184 – 12"	$65.00 – 70.00
Creamer, #349	$27.00 – 36.00	Vase, #349 – 8" fan	$43.00 – 47.00
Ginger jar and lid, #893	$155.00 – 180.00	Vase, #621 – 8" flared, cupped or square top	$50.00 – 55.00
Guest set, #200 handled	$235.00 – 285.00		
Ice pail, #1616 – 6½"	$80.00 – 85.00	Vase, #857 – 8" fan	$50.00 – 55.00
Jug, #1352	$195.00 – 225.00		

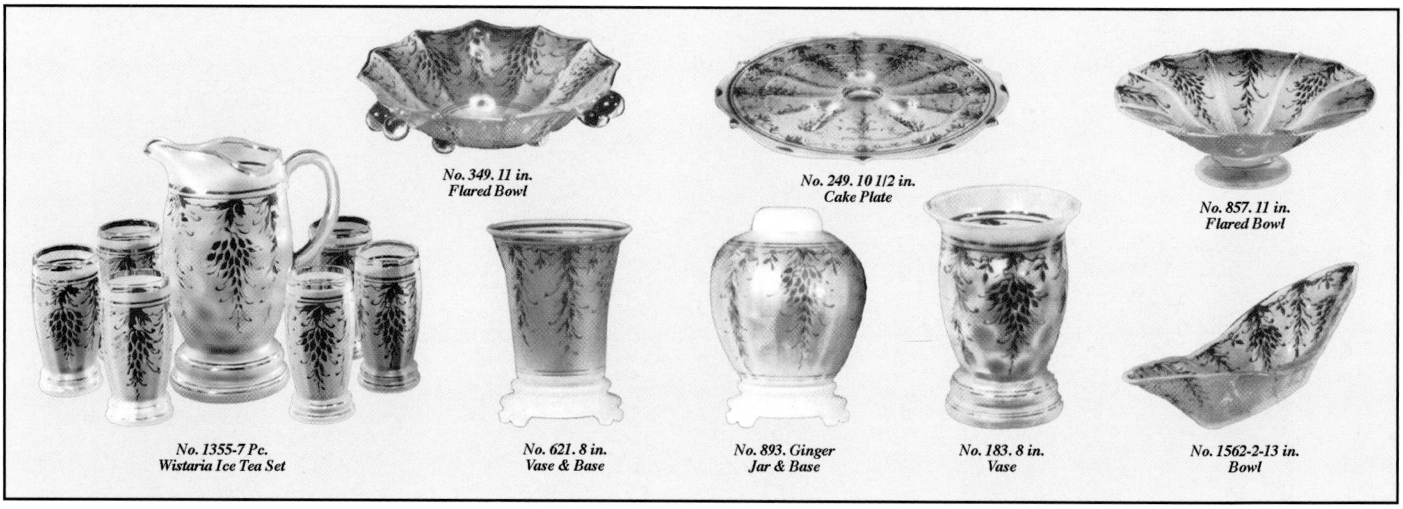

No. 349. 11 in. Flared Bowl

No. 249. 10 1/2 in. Cake Plate

No. 857. 11 in. Flared Bowl

No. 1355-7 Pc. Wistaria Ice Tea Set

No. 621. 8 in. Vase & Base

No. 893. Ginger Jar & Base

No. 183. 8 in. Vase

No. 1562-2-13 in. Bowl

#349-8" Fan Vase

#184-12" Vase

#1354-10 1/2" Pitcher

#1616-6" Ice Pail

#200 Guest Set

Punch Cup

12 1/2" Punch Bowl

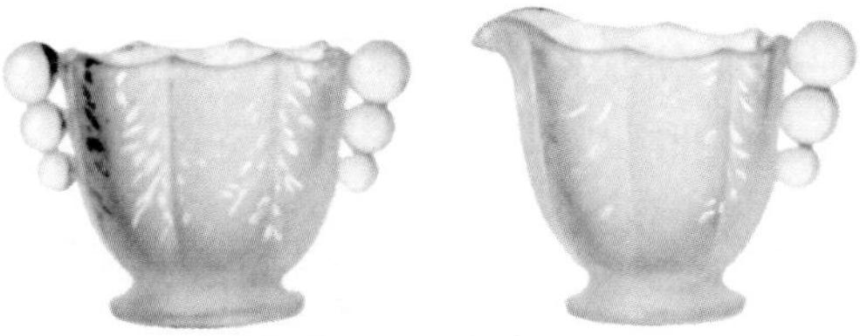

#349 Sugar and Creamer

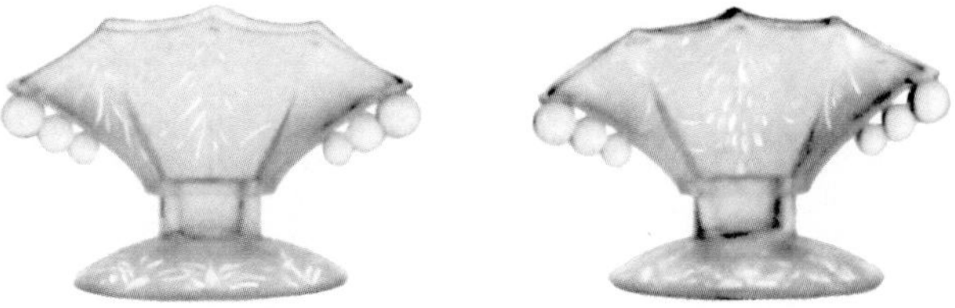

#349 Candlesticks

#857-8" Fan Vase

#1684-9" Handled Basket

#844 Covered Bon-bon

#757-7 1/4" Salad Plate

ETCHED #1621 SHAPES

Fenton used this Dolphin handled shape for a number of cuttings. In 1936, an acid etching was used to decorate some pieces in crystal and royal blue.

Item	Crystal	Royal Blue
Bonbon, #1621 – E-5½" crimped	$16.00 – 18.00	$25.00 – 30.00
Bonbon, #1621 – E-5½" oval	$16.00 – 18.00	$25.00 – 30.00
Bonbon, #1621 – E-5½" regular	$16.00 – 18.00	$25.00 – 30.00
Bonbon, #1621 – E-5½" square	$16.00 – 18.00	$25.00 – 30.00
Bowl, #1621 – E-9" flared	$45.00 – 50.00	$55.00 – 65.00
Bowl, #1621 – E-9½" crimped	$45.00 – 50.00	$60.00 – 70.00
Bowl, #1621 – E-9½" oval	$45.00 – 50.00	$60.00 – 70.00
Bowl, #1621 – E-9½" regular	$45.00 – 50.00	$60.00 – 70.00
Bowl, #1621 – E-9½" square	$45.00 – 50.00	$60.00 – 70.00
Bowl, #1621 – E-10" deep oval	$50.00 – 55.00	$70.00 – 75.00
Candlestick, #1621 – E crimped	$25.00 – 28.00	$35.00 – 38.00
Candlestick, #1621 – E oval	$25.00 – 28.00	$35.00 – 38.00
Candlestick, #1621 – E regular	$25.00 – 28.00	$35.00 – 38.00

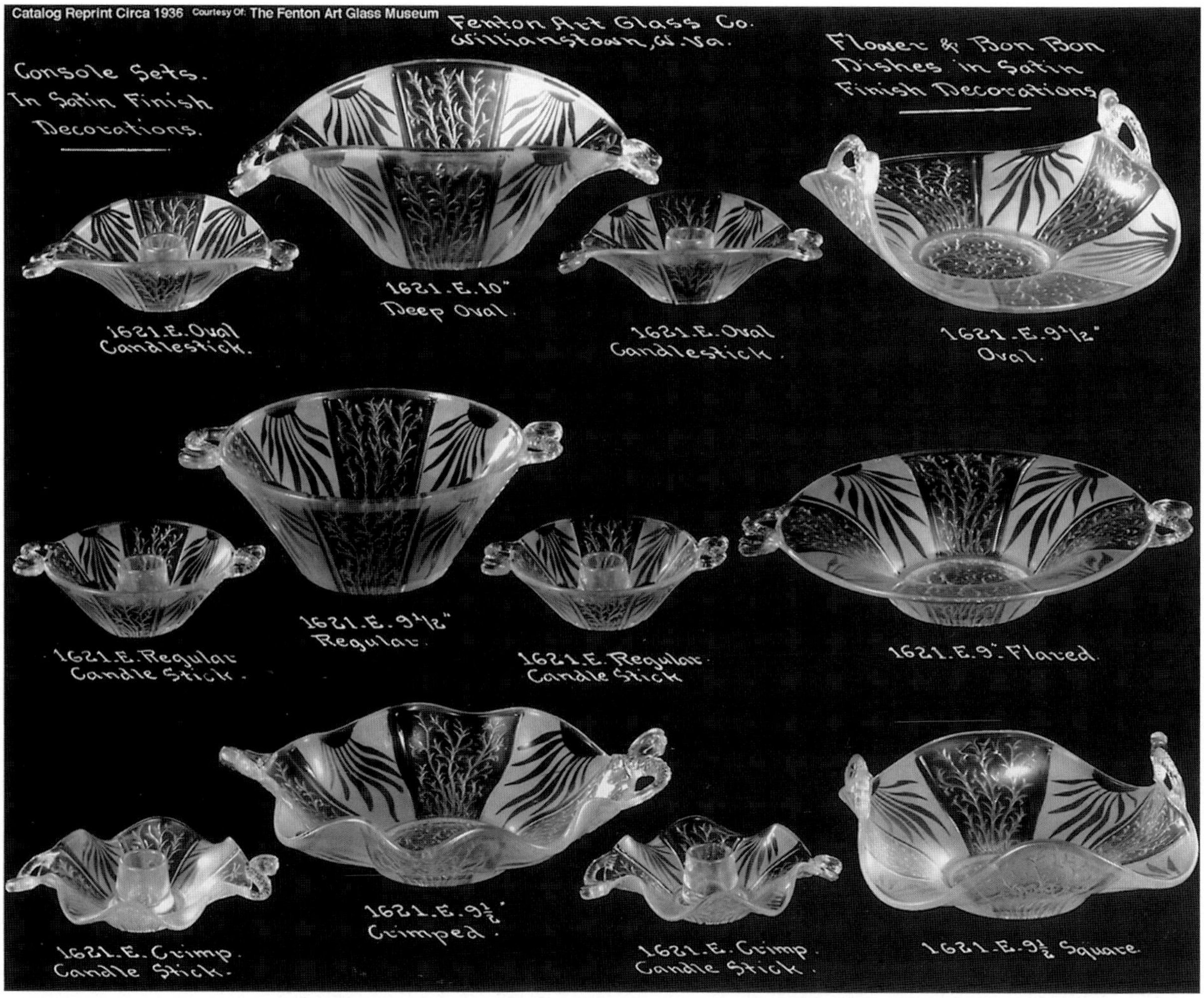

Catalog Reprint Circa 1936 Courtesy Of: The Fenton Art Glass Museum

As the leading producer of handmade glassware, Fenton has produced numerous items that are highly collectible today. Many of these items are listed and priced elsewhere in this book. However, some items are important enough in both Fenton's history and the collector market that they deserve to be assembled and featured in their own special section.

Among the categories assembled in this section are tall candlesticks, lamps, vanity sets, guest sets, animal novelties, and the September Morn nymph.

NO. 449 – 8½" AND NO. 349 – 10" CANDLESTICKS WITH OVAL CUT DECORATION

Early records indicate the No. 349 – 10" and No. 249 – 6" candlesticks were introduced in 1921. The No. 449 – 8½" candlestick is in the inventory records as early as 1922. Cut candlesticks were listed in the records in 1923.

Left to right

Row 1:	**No. 349 – 10" Oval Cut Candlesticks**	**Value**
	A. Florentine Green	$130.00 – 150.00
	B. Golden Iridescent	$110.00 – 120.00
	C. Celeste Blue plain	$90.00 – 95.00
	D. Ebony	$135.00 – 145.00
	E. Topaz plain	$110.00 – 120.00
Row 2:	**No. 449 – 8½" Oval Cut Candlesticks**	**Value**
	A. Ruby Iridescent	$250.00 – 300.00
	B. Persian Pearl	$85.00 – 90.00
	C. Celeste Blue Iridescent	$88.00 – 95.00
	D. Topaz Iridescent	$85.00 – 90.00
	E. Celeste Blue plain	$88.00 – 96.00

All candlesticks are priced each

No. 349-10" & No. 449-8 1/2" Candlesticks w/Cutting

NO. 449 – 8½" AND NO. 349 – 10" CANDLESTICKS

This style candlestick, the long column with the hexagonal base, has been featured in the Fenton line for many years. As a matter of fact, the style is still being made today. The candlesticks were introduced in the early 1920s and will be found in many of the Fenton colors — iridescent, clear, and opaque. Some of the candles are decorated with gold or hand-painted designs.

Left to right

Row 1:	**No. 449 – 8½" Candlesticks**	**Value**
	A. Topaz Iridescent	$125.00 – 135.00
	B. Celeste Blue Iridescent	$95.00 – 100.00
	C. Florentine Green	$95.00 – 100.00
	D. Persian Pearl	$95.00 – 100.00
	E. Ebony w/hand-painted decoration	$95.00 – 100.00
	F. Ruby Iridescent	$150.00 – 175.00
Row 2:	**No. 349 – 10" Candlesticks**	**Value**
	A. Pekin Blue	$110.00 – 115.00
	B. Chinese Yellow	$100.00 – 110.00
	C. Ruby Iridescent	$200.00 – 250.00
	D. Topaz Iridescent	$125.00 – 140.00
Row 3:	**No. 349 – 10" Candlesticks**	**Value**
	A. Ebony w/Gold decoration	$125.00 – 140.00
	B. Florentine Green	$125.00 – 140.00
	C. Persian Pearl	$100.00 – 110.00
	D. Celeste Blue Iridescent	$125.00 – 140.00
	E. Ebony	$115.00 – 125.00

All candlesticks are priced each.

According to the inventory record from 1924, these candlesticks may be found in the following additional colors:

No. 349 – 10"	**No. 449 – 8½"**
Persian Pearl	Ruby
Wisteria	Chinese Yellow
Ruby	Wisteria
Celeste Blue	Florentine Green
Topaz	Ebony
Turquoise	Jade Green
Jade Green	Celeste Blue
Venetian Red	Grecian Gold
Orange	Topaz
Royal Blue	Royal Blue
	Turquoise

No. 449-8 1/2" & No. 349-10" Candlesticks

NO. 749 – 12", NO. 649 – 10", AND NO. 549 – 8½" CANDLESTICKS

The first records of the No. 649 – 10" and No. 749 – 12" candles are in 1924. Most collectors are having a very difficult time finding the larger candlesticks. Two-color combination candlesticks were also listed in the 1924 records.

Left to right:

	Candlestick	Value
Row 1:	**Candlestick**	**Value**
	A. Jade No. 749 – 12"	$180.00 – 190.00
	B. Celeste Blue Iridescent No. 649 – 10"	$110.00 – 130.00
	C. Ebony No. 649 – 10"	$110.00 – 120.00
	D. Persian Pearl No. 649 – 10"	$100.00 – 110.00
	E. Orange or Bright Mandarin Red No. 549 – 8½"	$90.00 – 100.00
	F. Chinese Yellow No. 549 – 8½" w/hand-painted design	$100.00 – 110.00
Row 2:	**No. 549 – 8½" Candlestick**	
	A. Mandarin Red	$100.00 – 110.00
	B. Pekin Blue	$80.00 – 85.00
	C. Florentine Green	$75.00 – 85.00
	D. Celeste Blue Iridescent	$90.00 – 95.00
	E. Persian Pearl	$80.00 – 85.00
	F. Flame	$120.00 – 130.00
Row 3:	**Candlestick**	
	A. Florentine Green/Ebony base No. 649 – 10"	$115.00 – 125.00
	B. Moonstone/Ebony base No. 649 – 10"	$115.00 – 125.00
	C. Mustard/Royal Blue base No. 649 – 10"	$140.00 – 155.00
	D. Topaz Iridescent/Ebony base No. 649 – 10"	$160.00 – 175.00
	E. Chinese Yellow/Ebony base No. 649 – 10"	$100.00 – 110.00
	F. Celeste Blue Iridescent/Ebony base No. 549 – 8½"	$120.00 – 130.00
Row 4:	**No. 549 – 8½" Candlestick**	
	A. Flame/Royal Blue base	$120.00 – 140.00
	B. Florentine Green/Ebony base	$80.00 – 85.00
	C. Grecian Gold/Ebony base	$85.00 – 95.00
	D. Moonstone/Ebony base	$100.00 – 110.00
	E. Jade Green/Moonstone base	$105.00 – 130.00
	F. Grecian Gold/Persian Pearl base	$100.00 – 110.00

All candlesticks are priced each.

The following is a listing of the colors in the Fenton inventory records from 1922 through 1928 when these candles disappeared from the records.

No. 549 – 8½" Candlestick
Celeste Blue & Persian Pearl
Plain Wisteria & Crystal
Plain Green & Ebony
Plain Wisteria & Ebony
Golden & Persian Pearl
Venetian Red
Ebony & Crystal
Plain Blue & Ebony
Golden & Ebony
Chocolate
Grecian Gold
Venetian Red & Royal Blue
Venetian Red & Ebony
Orange
Chinese Yellow & Blue
Ruby & Crystal
Plain Wisteria & Ebony
White & Ebony
Royal Blue
Plain Topaz
Ruby
Chinese Yellow

No. 649 – 10" Candlestick
Venetian Red
Chinese Yellow
Iridescent Wisteria
Orange
Grecian Gold
Plain Wisteria
Topaz Iridescent
Royal Blue

No. 749 – 12" Candlestick
Ruby
Jade Green
Celeste Blue
Florentine Green

No. 749-12", No. 649-10" & No. 549-8 1/2" Candlesticks

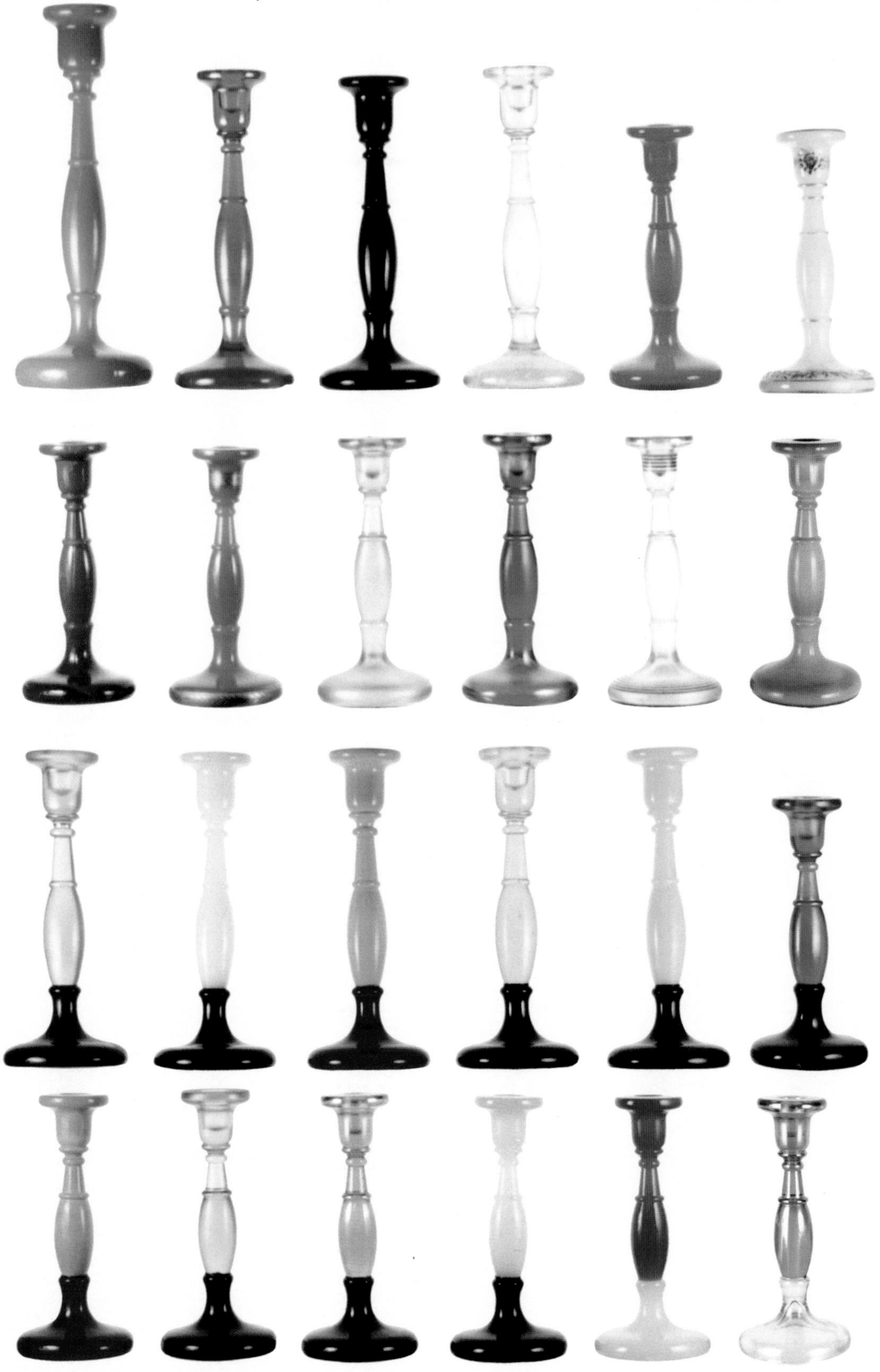

COLOGNES AND VANITY SETS

Colognes, vanity sets, and bath items were produced in iridescent, opaque, and transparent colors beginning in the early 1920s. Some colognes and puff boxes were commonly sold in either three- or four-piece sets. The larger sets included a tray. The #55 colognes are sometimes found with a flower bud stopper. These are then referred to as #55½ colognes. Both the colognes and puff boxes in many of the opaque colors are often found with different colored lids and stoppers. See the photos of the various opaque colors for examples.

Iridescent Colors Item	Celeste Blue	Florentine Green	Grecian Gold	Topaz	Velva Rose	Wisteria
Bathroom set, #16 – 17 – 54	$250.00 – 300.00	$200.00 – 250.00	$140.00 – 160.00			
*Cologne, #53	$150.00 – 170.00			$120.00 – 140.00	$120.00 – 140.00	
**Cologne, #55	$195.00 – 220.00	$140.00 – 160.00	$110.00 – 125.00	$150.00 – 170.00	$130.00 – 150.00	$165.00 – 185.00
***Cologne, #55½		$225.00 – 270.00	$220.00 – 250.00	$220.00 – 250.00	$220.00 – 270.00	$250.00 – 300.00
Cologne, #56	$225.00 – 250.00	$135.00 – 160.00	$115.00 – 130.00	$130.00 – 150.00		$140.00 – 160.00
Cologne, #59	$245.00 – 270.00			$120.00 – 140.00	$150.00 – 170.00	
Jar, #60 bath (smelling) salts	$200.00 – 250.00	$160.00 – 190.00	$110.00 – 130.00	$175.00 – 200.00		$160.00 – 180.00
Puff box, 4¾"			$65.00 – 75.00			
Puff box, #53	$75.00 – 95.00			$60.00 – 70.00	$50.00 – 60.00	
Puff box, #54	$75.00 – 95.00				$45.00 – 55.00	
Puff box, #57	$100.00 – 130.00	$70.00 – 80.00	$35.00 – 45.00	$70.00 – 80.00	$50.00 – 60.00	
Puff box, #743	$120.00 – 140.00	$80.00 – 90.00	$50.00 – 60.00	$80.00 – 90.00		$65.00 – 75.00
Puff box, #744		$150.00 – 200.00		$150.00 – 200.00	$220.00 – 250.00	$200.00 – 250.00
Tray, #53 vanity set	$50.00 – 60.00			$35.00 – 45.00	$30.00 – 35.00	

**Tangerine*, $190.00 – 210.00
***Tangerine*, $210.00 – 225.00
****Tangerine*, $250.00+

Opaque Colors Item	Black	Jade Green	Lilac	Moonstone	Pekin Blue
Bathroom set, #16 – 17 – 54	$200.00 – 275.00	$175.00 – 200.00	$200.00 – 250.00	$185.00 – 200.00	$220.00 – 260.00
Cologne, #53 – 5"	$110.00 – 150.00	$140.00 – 155.00	$200.00 – 225.00	$110.00 – 130.00	$200.00 – 225.00
Cologne, #55		$200.00 – 225.00			
Cologne, #59		$200.00 – 225.00			
Jar, #60 bath salts		$175.00 – 200.00			
Puff box, 4¾"			$55.00 – 65.00		
Puff box, #53	$30.00 – 35.00	$30.00 – 35.00	$55.00 – 65.00	$35.00 – 45.00	$60.00 – 65.00
Puff box, #57	$50.00 – 55.00	$48.00 – 55.00		$45.00 – 55.00	
Puff box, #743	$58.00 – 62.00	$55.00 – 60.00			
Tray, #53 vanity	$45.00 – 58.00	$30.00 – 35.00	$40.00 – 45.00	$40.00 – 45.00	$50.00 – 55.00

Transparent Colors Item	Amber	Aqua	Cameo Opalescent	Celeste Blue	Green	Orchid
Cologne, #53 – 4"					$125.00 – 150.00	
Cologne, #53 – 5"			$110.00 – 125.00		$90.00 – 100.00	$110.00 – 125.00
Cologne, #54	$40.00 – 45.00					
Cologne, #59				$55.00 – 65.00		
Cologne, #1502		$100.00 – 125.00			$120.00 – 145.00	
Puff box, #53			$60.00 – 65.00		$22.00 – 32.00	$45.00 – 55.00
Puff box, #54	$20.00 – 25.00					
Puff box, #1502		$50.00 – 60.00			$30.00 – 35.00	
Tray, #53 vanity			$45.00 – 50.00		$25.00 – 30.00	$35.00 – 40.00
Tray, #1502 vanity		$35.00 – 40.00			$25.00 – 30.00	

COLOGNES AND VANITY SETS

The #60 jar is identified in the inventory records as a smelling salts jar. It was listed in jade green and iridescent colors in 1925 and 1926. See "Elizabeth" in the Patterns chapter for prices of the Elizabeth vanity set. The Daisy & Button vanity sets are priced on page 240.

Item	Rose	Ruby	Wisteria
Cologne, #53	$90.00 – 100.00		
Cologne, #55		$125.00 – 150.00	
Cologne, #56		$150.00 – 190.00	$170.00 – 190.00
Cologne, #1502	$120.00 – 145.00	$150.00 – 180.00	
Puff box, #53	$27.00 – 32.00		
Puff box, #57		$60.00 – 65.00	
Puff box, #743		$75.00 – 100.00	
Puff box, #1502	$30.00 – 35.00	$75.00 – 100.00	
Tray, #53 vanity	$25.00 – 30.00		
Tray, #1502 vanity	$25.00 – 30.00	$27.00 – 32.00	

#1900 Daisy & Button Vanity Set
Royal Blue/Crystal

#55 1/2 Cologne
Topaz Iridescent

#55 Cologne
Wisteria Iridescent

#744 Puff Box
Wisteria Iridescent

#60 Bath Salts Jar
Wisteria Iridescent

#16-17-54 Bathroom Set
Moonstone/Pekin Blue

3" Diameter Puff Box
Topaz Iridescent

#57 Puff Box
Celeste Blue Iridescent

#743 Puff Box
Celeste Blue Iridescent

#1639 "Elizabeth" Vanity Set
Jade/Moonstone

#59 Cologne
Topaz Iridescent

#53 Vanity Set
Cameo Opalescent

#53 Vanity Set
Jade Green/Black

#53 Puff Box
Topaz Iridescent

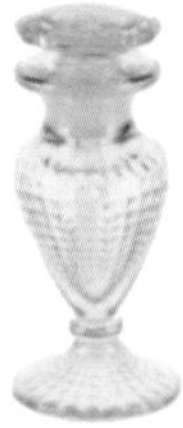

#53 Cologne
Green

#53 Vanity Set
Moonstone/Black

#53 Vanity Set
Pekin Blue/Moonstone

#1639 "Elizabeth" Footed Puff Box
Pekin Blue/Moonstone

#53 Cologne
Lilac

#53 Vanity Set
Velva Rose

#54 Vanity Set
Persian Pearl with Handpainted Decoration

#54 Puff Box
Celeste Blue Iridescent

#1502 Cologne
Green

#1502 Vanity Set
Ruby

#56 Cologne
Grecian Gold

4 3/4" Puff Box
Florentine Green

#56 Cologne
Celeste Blue Iridescent

#56 Cologne
Wisteria Iridescent

#56 Cologne
Ruby

#59 Cologne
Jade Green

#59 Cologne
Celeste Blue Iridescent

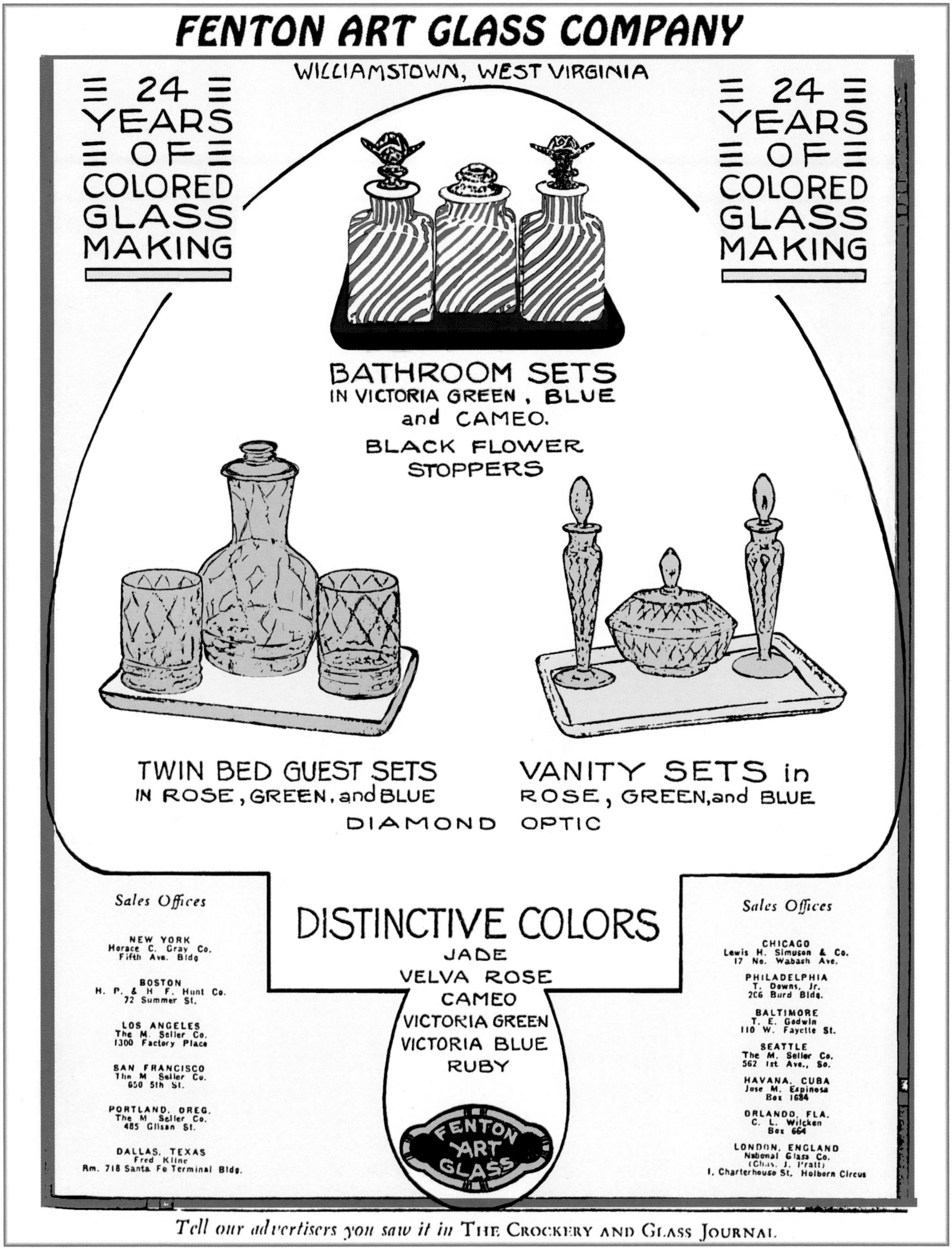
FENTON ART GLASS COMPANY
WILLIAMSTOWN, WEST VIRGINIA
24 YEARS OF COLORED GLASS MAKING
24 YEARS OF COLORED GLASS MAKING
BATHROOM SETS
IN VICTORIA GREEN, BLUE and CAMEO.
BLACK FLOWER STOPPERS
TWIN BED GUEST SETS
IN ROSE, GREEN, and BLUE
VANITY SETS in
ROSE, GREEN, and BLUE
DIAMOND OPTIC
Sales Offices
NEW YORK
Horace C. Gray Co.
Fifth Ave. Bldg
BOSTON
H. P. & H. F. Hunt Co.
72 Summer St.
LOS ANGELES
The M. Seller Co.
1300 Factory Place
SAN FRANCISCO
The M. Seller Co.
650 5th St.
PORTLAND, OREG.
The M. Seller Co.
485 Glisan St.
DALLAS, TEXAS
Fred Kline
Rm. 718 Santa Fe Terminal Bldg.
DISTINCTIVE COLORS
JADE
VELVA ROSE
CAMEO
VICTORIA GREEN
VICTORIA BLUE
RUBY
FENTON ART GLASS
Sales Offices
CHICAGO
Lewis H. Simuson & Co.
17 No. Wabash Ave.
PHILADELPHIA
T. Downs, Jr.
206 Burd Bldg.
BALTIMORE
T. E. Godwin
110 W. Fayette St.
SEATTLE
The M. Seller Co.
562 1st Ave., So.
HAVANA, CUBA
Jose M. Espinosa
Box 1684
ORLANDO, FLA.
C. L. Wilcken
Box 664
LONDON, ENGLAND
National Glass Co.
(Chas. J. Pratt)
1, Charterhouse St. Holborn Circus
Tell our advertisers you saw it in THE CROCKERY AND GLASS JOURNAL

FENTON "MOONSTONE" GLASSWARE
W - 105
W - 106
W - 107
W - 108
Talcum
Soap
W - 100
W - 101
Witch Hazel
W - 113
W - 111
W - 112
Water
Witch Hazel
W - 102
W - 102
No. 122
SANITARY PAPER SOAP HOLDER
Shampoo
Water
Witch Hazel
Shampoo
W - 102
W - 103
W - 103
W - 103
Stand Bottles Decorated — Black or Red Lettering as required
MANUFACTURED AND DECORATED BY
THE FENTON ART GLASS COMPANY Williamstown, W. Va.
DIRECT FACTORY REPRESENTATIVE
JOHN K. HOUSTON 11 West 42nd. Street, New York

Lamp Assortment Circa 1931-1932 Reprint
Courtesy Of:
The Fenton Art Glass Museum
No. G-120 Dec. 2
No. B-20
FENTON Art Glass Company PRESENTS
No. B-30
No. G-135 Dec. 4
a group of its new and original designs in glass lamps emphasizing Early American motifs.
THESE lamps come in a wide range of colors, ornamentations, treatment, sizes and shapes. Equipped either with glass chimneys or parchment shades, they are completely harmonized units.
THE growing interest in glass lamps for ornamentation and utility to meet the prevailing period modes—the revival of things Colonial and Federal-make glass lamps in strong demand. Now is the time to feature them prominently in sales events.
VALUES are extraordinarily attractive. Throughout the range is popular priced.
FENTON lamps are now nationally sold through the salesforce of William R. Noe & Sons, New York, and are permanently displayed by that firm at 1 Park Avenue, New York, and space 319, American Furniture Mart, Chicago.
ON the facing page will be found complete details of the colors and decorative treatment of the eleven numbers illustrated.
Write today for circulars, price lists and complete information about the entire Fenton lamp lines.
THE FENTON ART GLASS COMPANY
WILLIAMSTOWN, W. VA.
No. G-70 Dec. 7
No. G-80 Dec. 5
No. G-70 Dec. 8
No. G-80 Dec. 4
NEW YORK DISPLAY WITH WM. R. NOE & SONS 1 PARK AVE.
CHICAGO DISPLAY WITH WM. R. NOE & SONS SPACE 319 AMER. FURN. MART
No. G70 Dec. 9
No. B-10
No. G-80 Dec. 2

LAMPS

Fenton made lamps and produced lamp parts that were sold to be assembled into lamps by other companies. The following pages are reprinted from a 1931 Fenton catalog. The catalog is an excellent representation of the numerous Fenton lamps that were produced during this period.

Left to right, page 313

		Value
Row 1:		
	A. No. 20 – C-3 Black	$50.00 – 55.00
	B. No. 20 – C-2 Lilac	$110.00 – 125.00
	C. No. 30 – C-4 Amber	$37.00 – 45.00
	D. No. 30 – C-7 Lilac and Moonstone	$70.00 – 75.00
Row 2:		
	A. No. 20 – C-7 Lilac and Moonstone	$70.00 – 75.00
	B. No. 20 – C-11 Amber and Jade Green	$37.00 – 47.00
	C. No. 30 – C-5 Ruby	$70.00 – 75.00
	D. No. 30 – C-1 Jade Green	$47.00 – 57.00
Row 3:		
	A. No. 20 – C-8 Jade and Moonstone	$42.00 – 52.00
	B. No. 20 – C-6 Rose	$42.00 – 52.00
	C. No. 30 – C-12 Moonstone and Black	$47.00 – 57.00
	D. No. 30 C-11 Amber and Jade Green	$37.00 – 47.00

Photo below	**Rose**	**Crystal**	**Green**
Hobnail Lamp	$42.00 – 47.00	$22.00 – 27.00	$42.00 – 47.00

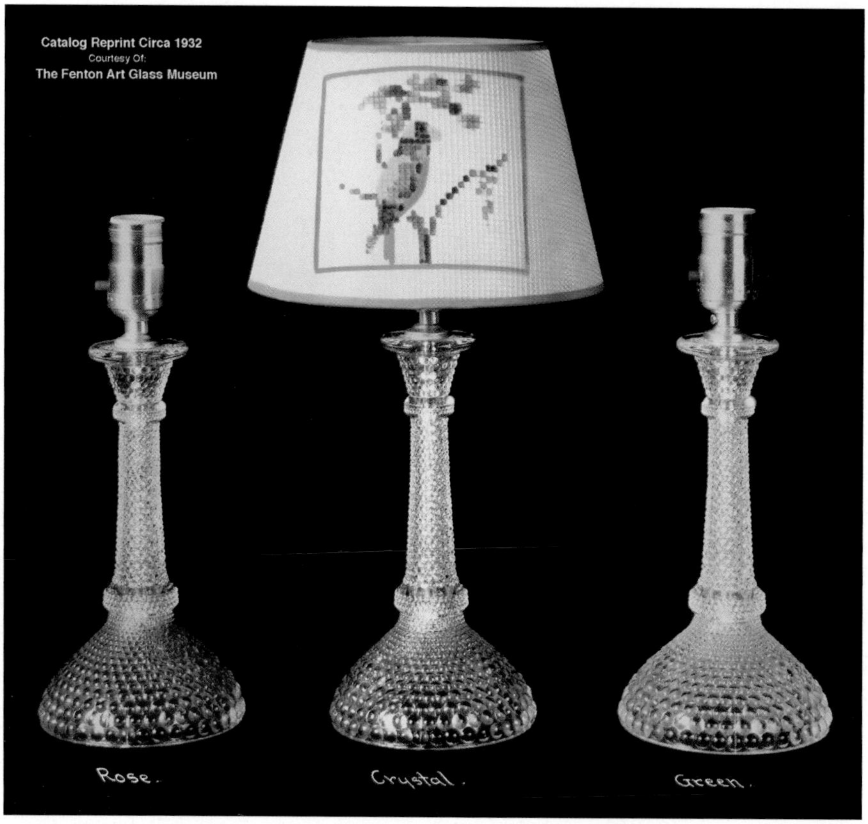

20-C3
HEIGHT 9½''
20-C2
HEIGHT 9½''
30-C4
HEIGHT 10''
30-C7
HEIGHT 10''
20-C7.
HEIGHT 9½''
20-C11
HEIGHT 9½''
30-C5
HEIGHT 10''
30-C1
HEIGHT 10''
20-C8
HEIGHT 9½''
20-C6
HEIGHT 9½''
30-C12
HEIGHT 10''
30-C11
HEIGHT 10''

The ginger jar and various styles of vases were sometimes used in combination with other parts to form lamps. These lamps were sometimes cut with decorations. An example is the jade green lamp in the lower left of the photo below.

Left to right, page 315

		Value
Row 1:		
	A. No. 50 – C17 Jade Green and Black	$180.00 – 190.00
	B. No, 50 – C-19 Lilac and Black	$250.00 – 275.00
	C. No. 50 – C-18 Jade Green and Moonstone	$200.00 – 225.00
Row 2:		
	A. No. 60 – C-20 Spiral Optic French Opalescent and Black	$140.00 – 160.00
	B. No. 60 – C-22 Jade Green and Black	$150.00 – 175.00
	C. No. 60 – C-23 Rib Optic French Opalescent and Black	$140.00 – 160.00
Row 3:		
	A. No. 60 – C-1 Jade Green and Moonstone	$225.00 – 250.00
	B. No. 60 – C-21 Lilac and Black	$300.00 – 325.00
	C. No. 60 – C-15 Jade Green and Black	$150.00 – 175.00
Photo below		
	A. Jade Green w/cut decoration	$350.00 – 400.00
	B. Jade Green hand painted	$150.00 – 175.00
	C. Black w/Crystal Satin decorated glass shade	$125.00 – 145.00

Fenton Art Glass Lamps

Lamp Assortment Circa 1931-1932 Courtesy Of: **The Fenton Art Glass Museum**

NO. 50-C 17
HEIGHT 13½''
SQ. BASE 6''

NO. 50-C 19
HEIGHT 13½''
SQ. BASE 6''

NO. 50-C 18
HEIGHT 13½''
SQ. BASE 6''

NO. 60-C 20
HEIGHT 12''
BASE 7½'' DIA.

NO. 60-C 22
HEIGHT 12''
BASE 7½'' DIA.

NO. 60-C 23
HEIGHT 12''
BASE 7½'' DIA.

NO. 60-C 1
HEIGHT 12''
BASE 7½'' DIA.

NO. 60-C 21
HEIGHT 12''
BASE 7½'' DIA.

NO. 60-C 15
HEIGHT 12''
BASE 7½'' DIA.

The photo on page 317 features Fenton's G-70 series lamps. This is the series of lamps that are usually confused with a similar lamp made by the Jefferson Glass Company. The Fenton lamp base has slight ridges that divide the top surface into sections. Many of the Fenton lamps are decorated with hand-painted designs. This lamp also may be found in the Rib Optic and Coin Spot patterns.

G-70 Lamps
Left to right

Row 1:	Value
A. Jade Green/hand painted	$225.00 – 255.00
B. Custard/hand painted	$220.00 – 240.00
C. Jade Green/hand painted	$240.00 – 265.00
Row 2:	
A. Jade Green/etched decoration	$210.00 – 230.00
B. Amber/cut decoration	$190.00 – 220.00
C. Jade Green/embossed	$200.00 – 220.00
Row 3:	
A. Rib Optic French Opalescent	$225.00 – 250.00
B. Rib Optic Blue Opalescent	$245.00 – 285.00
C. Coin Spot French Opalescent	$200.00 – 225.00

Photo below

Row 1:	Value
A. No. 40 – C-14 Lilac/Black	$100.00 – 125.00
B. No. 40 – C-16 Amber/Black	$45.00 – 55.00
C. No. 40 – C-15 Jade/Black	$55.00 – 66.00
Row 2:	
A. No. 10 – C-3 Black	$35.00 – 45.00
B. No. 10 – C-1 Jade Green	$35.00 – 45.00
C. No. 10 – C-13 Amber/Moonstone	$30.00 – 40.00
Row 3:	
A. No. 10 – C-9 Jade/Moonstone	$35.00 – 45.00
B. No. 10 – C-10 Rose/Black	$35.00 – 42.00
C. No. 10 – C-2 Moonstone	$30.00 – 35.00

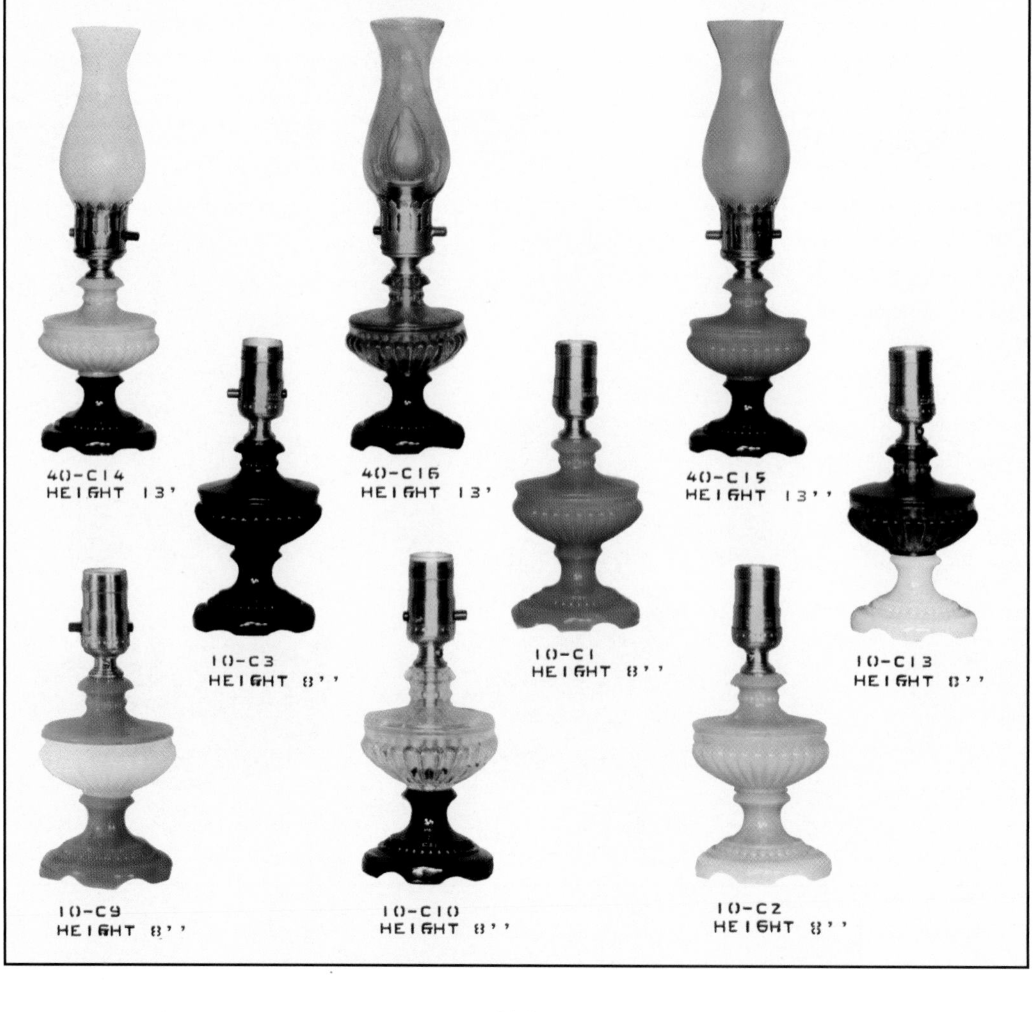

40-C14
HEIGHT 13'
40-C16
HEIGHT 13'
40-C15
HEIGHT 13''
10-C3
HEIGHT 8''
10-C1
HEIGHT 8''
10-C13
HEIGHT 8''
10-C9
HEIGHT 8''
10-C10
HEIGHT 8''
10-C2
HEIGHT 8''

Lamp Assortment Catalog Reprint Circa 1931-1932 Courtesy Of: **The Fenton Art Glass Museum**

G 70 LAMPS
HEIGHT 10½''

Lamp Assortment Circa 1931-1932 Reprint
Courtesy Of:
The Fenton Art Glass Museum

DEC. ROSE
GREEN.

DEC. ROSE
YELLOW.

RANGER.

G 70. DEC. 9.

G 70. DEC. 3.

PEACOCK.

G 70. DEC. 4.

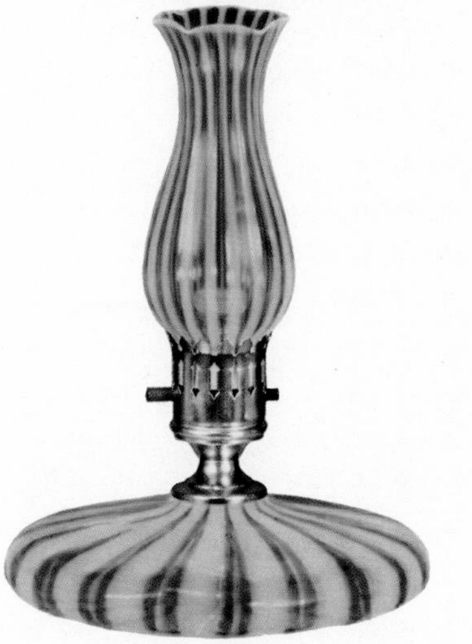

G 70. DEC. 4.

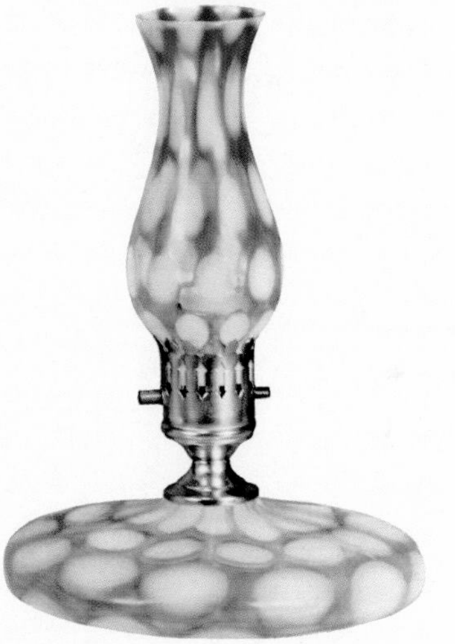

G 70. DEC. 2.

NIGHT SETS & GUEST SETS

Guest sets, or night sets as some people prefer to call them, were made in both handled and non-handled versions by Fenton. These items were kept at the bedside and served a useful purpose at night during the era before many people had running water nearby.

The guest sets featured in the top two rows of the photo are Fenton's #200 handled guest set. These were made during the mid 1920s in iridescent colors and cameo opalescent. In the late 1930s this set was made in crystal satin with the Wisteria etching. Most of these sets are relatively hard to find and command a respectable price. This is especially true of the sets in Victoria topaz iridescent with the Curtain Optic or Rib Optic patterns.

The #401 night set appears in the inventory records as early as 1921. It is listed in iridescent blue, topaz, green, and gold. Many of the golden iridescent sets were sold with cut decorations. In 1925 these sets were made in rose and amber. In 1927, these bottles are listed in Victoria green and Victoria blue. Trade journals indicate this may have been an early Fenton name for their green and blue opalescent colors.

The #1502 Diamond Optic night bottle was made from the late 1920s through the early 1930s in aquamarine, transparent green, and rose. This bottle has the "twin rib" design at the base, like the opalescent bottles which lack the Diamond Optic pattern.

Numerous unidentified numbers for night sets appear in the Fenton records. Undoubtedly one of these will be a number for the opalescent "twin rib" bottles in the picture.

Item	Golden Iridescent	Green/Rose Iridescent	Blue Iridescent	Topaz Iridescent
Guest set, #200	$150.00 – 200.00**	$320.00 – 360.00**	$320.00 – 370.00	$350.00 – 400.00**
*Night set, #401	$40.00 – 50.00	$145.00 – 185.00	$140.00 – 165.00	$145.00 – 175.00
Night set, #1502			$190.00 – 225.00	

**Golden iridescent with cut decoration add 20%*
***with blue handle add 10%*

Item	Cameo Opalescent	Blue Opalescent	Cranberry Spiral Optic	Green Opalescent	Curtain Optic/ Rib Optic
Guest set, #200	$290.00 – 350.00	$400.00 – 450.00	$500.00 – 550.00		$600.00 – 650.00
Night set, #401		$130.00 – 150.00		$120.00 – 140.00	
Night set, "twin rib"	$150.00 – 170.00	$155.00 – 185.00		$150.00 – 170.00	

Item	Green/ Aqua	Rose	Jade Green	French Wisteria	Opalescent
Guest set, #200					$225.00 – 275.00
Night set, #401		$50.00 – 65.00		$110.00 – 130.00	
Night set, #1502	$125.00 – 145.00	$75.00 – 85.00	$190.00 – 225.00		
Night set, #1502 w/ stopper and tray	$200.00 – 250.00	$180.00 – 225.00			

#200 Handled Guest Set
Cameo Opalescent

#200 Handled Guest Set
Velva Rose

#200 Handled Guest Set
Grecian Gold

#200 Handled Guest Set
Spiral Optic French Opalescent

#200 Handled Guest Set
Tangerine Iridescent

#200 Handled Guest Set
Wistaria Satin

#200 Handled Guest Set
Curtain Optic Topaz Iridescent

#200 Handled Guest Set
Topaz Iridescent

#401 Night Set
Topaz Iridescent

#401 Night Set
Grecian Gold
Floral Cutting

#401 Night Set
Rib Optic
Blue Opalescent

#401 Night Set
Rib Optic
Green Opalescent

Rib Optic Night Set
"Twin Rib" Base
Cameo Opalescent

Rib Optic Night Set
"Twin Rib" Base
Blue Opalescent

Rib Optic Night Set
"Twin Rib" Base
Green Opalescent

#1502 Night Set
Green

#1502 Night Set
Rose

#1502 Night Set
Aquamarine

#1502 Night Set with Stopper Top and Tray
Rose

NO. 1934 DECANTER SET

The No. 1934 decanter set has a floral stopper. This was one of a number of liquor sets with which Fenton welcomed the demise of Prohibition. It was made from 1934 to 1938 and was sold with a floral embossed tray. Known colors include ruby, amber, crystal, royal blue, and French opalescent. Some of the sets may be found decorated with platinum trim.

Royal blue, ruby, and French opalescent are the most collectible colors. Trays have been found in crystal, royal blue, and ruby.

Item	Crystal	Amber	Ruby Royal Blue	French Opalescent
Decanter	$60.00 – 70.00	$85.00 – 100.00	$150.00 – 180.00	$100.00 – 130.00
Goblet, whiskey	$5.00 – 6.00	$8.00 – 10.00	$12.00 – 14.00	$10.00 – 12.00
Tray	$22.00 – 25.00			$75.00 – 100.00

NO. 1935 DECANTER SET (FRANKLIN)

Fenton produced the No. 1935 decanter set from 1934 to 1938. The set has since been named Franklin by Hazel Weatherman. The set consists of a heavy footed whiskey tumbler and a footed decanter with a matching colored stopper. The colors this set may be found in are royal blue, crystal, ruby, green, and rose.

Item	Crystal/Amber	Green/Rose	Royal Blue	Ruby
Decanter	$60.00 – 70.00	$80.00 – 90.00	$125.00 – 150.00	$125.00 – 150.00
Tumbler, whiskey	$7.00 – 9.00	$8.00 – 10.00	$12.00 – 14.00	$12.00 – 14.00

#1645 NYMPH FIGURE (SEPTEMBER MORN)

The #1645 Nymph entered the line in 1928 and remained in production in milk glass through the early 1940s when Fenton's energies focused on producing opalescent glassware. Recently this figure has been made in special colors. The new issues are marked with the Fenton logo.

All the known colors of this figure, with the exception of moonstone, are pictured. The moonstone nymph is pictured with the moonstone color photo on page 209.

The nymph was usually offered for sale with a matching color flower block and bowl. In many cases the bowl was either the #1234 or #848 flared bowl. For an example of the milk glass nymph in another style of bowl, see the Blue Ridge reprint on page 327. Numerous other bowls, such as the ones illustrated, are being used by collectors to display these figures.

Although it was a regular production item, the lilac color nymph is extremely rare. As of this writing, only a few examples have been found.

Color	Value
Amberina	$220.00 – 245.00
Aqua	$250.00 – 300.00
Chinese Yellow	$250.00 – 325.00
Crystal	$85.00 – 95.00
Custard	$170.00 – 200.00
Dark Green	$180.00 – 200.00
Ebony	$220.00 – 245.00
Jade Green	$170.00 – 200.00
Light Green	$180.00 – 200.00
Lilac	$700.00 – 850.00
Mandarin Red	$300.00 – 350.00
Milk Glass	$140.00 – 175.00
Moonstone	$165.00 – 200.00
Pekin Blue	$350.00 – 400.00
Rose	$175.00 – 195.00
Royal Blue	$225.00 – 250.00
Ruby	$225.00 – 250.00

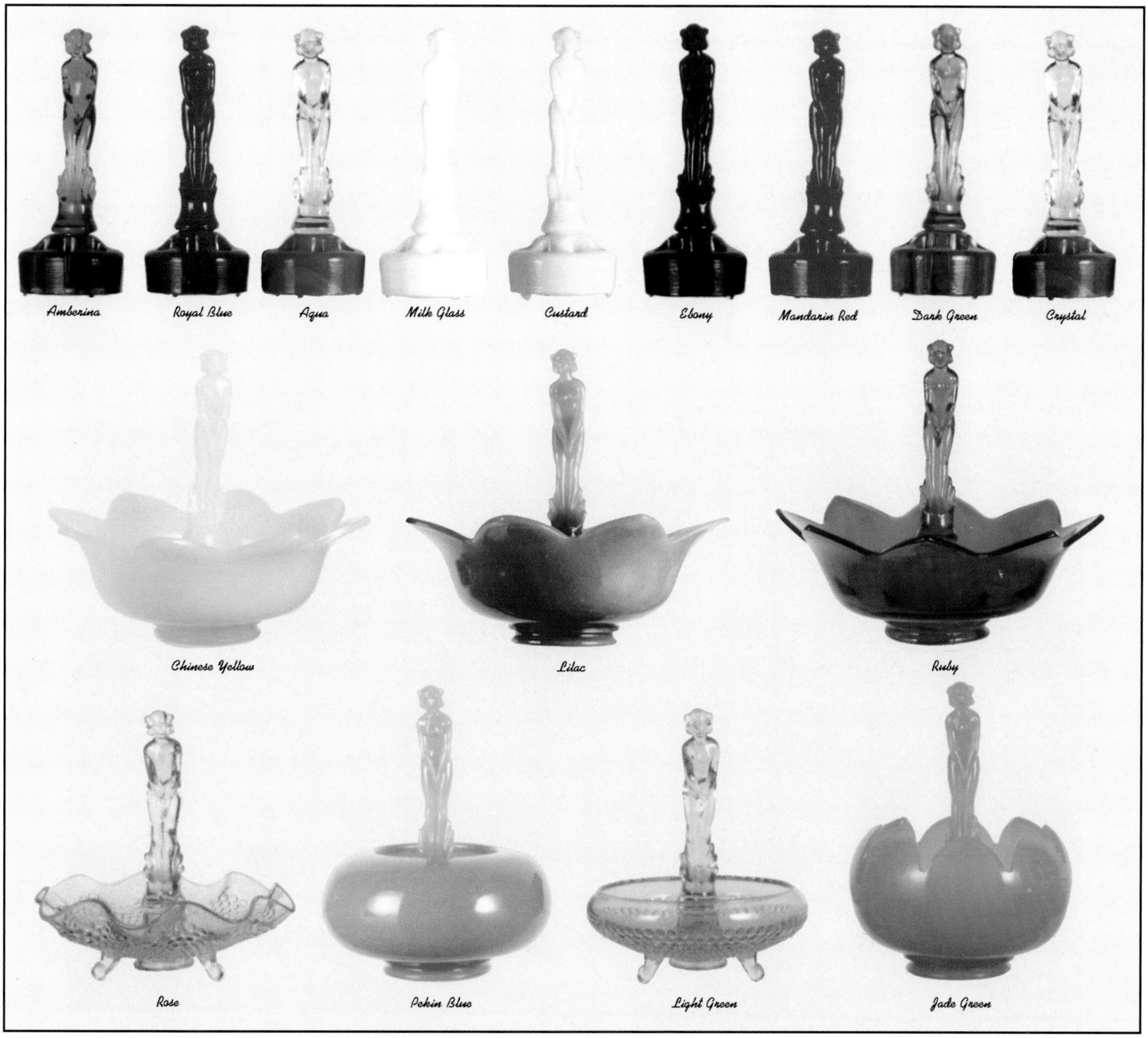
Amberina
Royal Blue
Aqua
Milk Glass
Custard
Ebony
Mandarin Red
Dark Green
Crystal
Chinese Yellow
Lilac
Ruby
Rose
Pekin Blue
Light Green
Jade Green

SWAN NOVELTIES 1938

In 1938, Fenton produced a Swan console set and small novelty bonbons from old Dugan molds. The only confirmed Fenton colors in these items are crystal, crystal satin, and milk glass. Although the blue opalescent candles and large bowl are presumed to have been made by Fenton, there are no records to verify this assumption. Any of the Swan items found in other colors were probably made by Dugan.

Item	Crystal Crystal Satin	Milk Glass
Bonbon, #5 – 5" square or oval	$22.00 – 27.00	$60.00 – 65.00
Bonbon, #5 – 5½" crimped	$22.00 – 27.00	$60.00 – 65.00
Bonbon, #5 – 6" flared	$22.00 – 27.00	$60.00 – 65.00
Bowl, #6 – 11½" console square or tulip	$38.00 – 45.00	$75.00 – 85.00
Candlestick, #6	$33.00 – 35.00	$60.00 – 65.00
Swan, #4	$20.00 – 22.00	

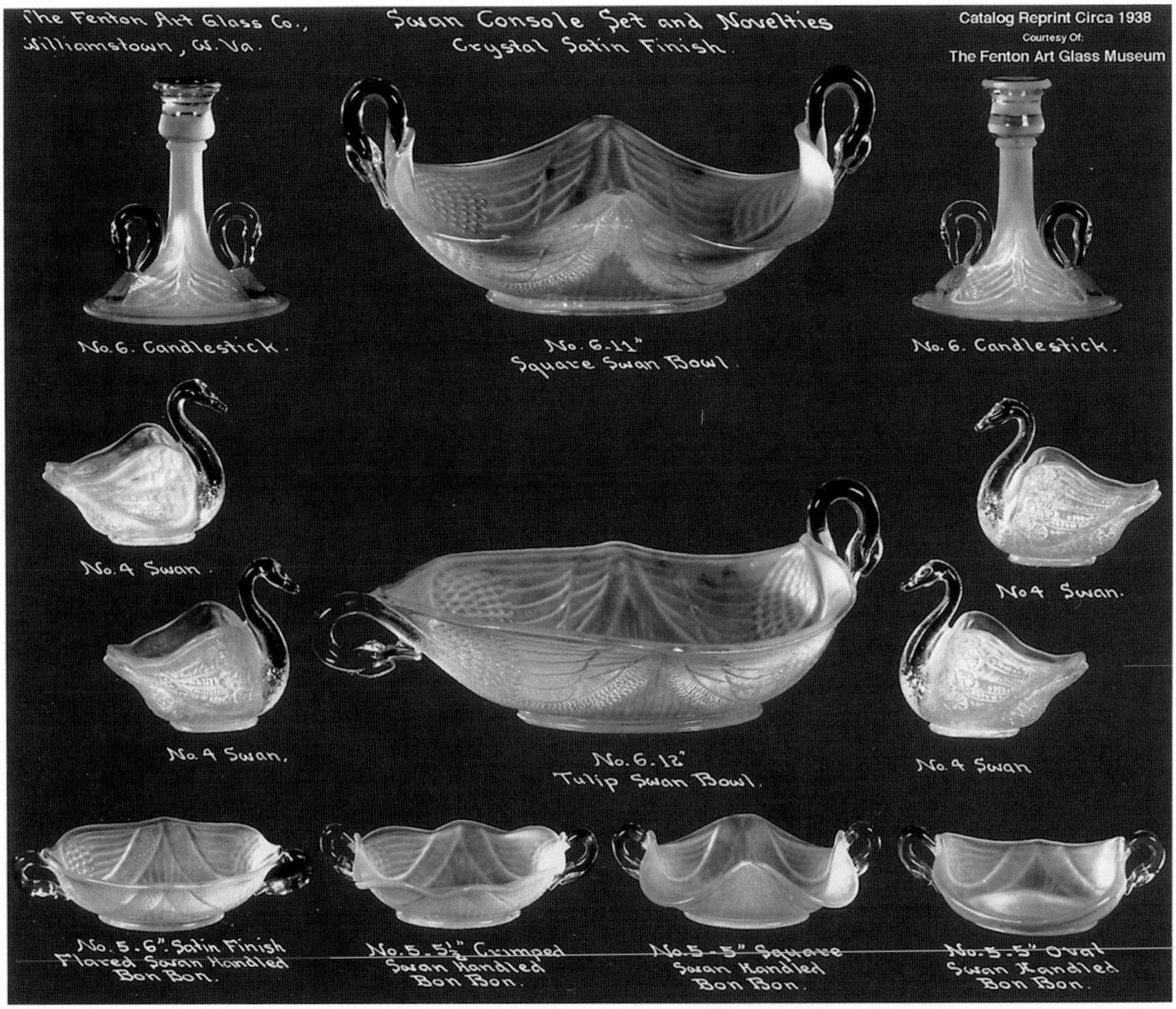

OPALESCENT GLASSWARE

Although Fenton had been producing opalescent glassware intermittently since the early 1900s, a significant change in production occurred in the late 1930s. Fenton began to aggressively produce and market patterns of opalescent glassware. Beginning in 1938 with the appearance of significant amounts of Spiral Optic in French opalescent, Blue Ridge, cranberry opalescent, green opalescent, and Stiegel blue, non-opalescent glassware production began to decline. This was followed by opalescent Hobnail colors in 1939. The demand for these new lines probably allowed Fenton very little capacity to produce other types of glassware.

The reprints on the following pages, from a 1939 catalog, are examples of Fenton's new lines. A detailed examination of the production of patterns from 1939 and later are the topic of our *Fenton Art Glass Patterns, 1939 – 1980.*

Item	Blue Opalescent	French Opalescent	Green Opalescent
Bathroom set, #16 – 17 – 54, 4-piece set	$450.00 – 500.00	$250.00 – 300.00	$450.00 – 500.00
Bonbon, #1092 – 5"	$32.00 – 40.00	$28.00 – 32.00	$32.00 – 36.00
Bowl, #920 – 9" cupped Grape & Cable		$125.00 – 150.00	
Bowl, #920 – 10" crimped Grape & Cable		$125.00 – 150.00	
Bowl, #920 – 11" flared Grape & Cable		$65.00 – 75.00	
Bowl, #950 – 11" oval			
Bowl, #970 – 8"			
Bowl, #1093 – 6" deep crimp Basket Weave	$32.00 – 40.00	$30.00 – 35.00	$32.00 – 36.00
Bowl, #1093 – 8" shallow Basket Weave		$25.00 – 30.00	$27.00 – 32.00
Bowl, #1093 – 9" shallow cup Basket Weave		$25.00 – 30.00	$27.00 – 32.00
Bowl, #1663 – 11" flared		$45.00 – 55.00	$42.00 – 46.00
Candle, #1091 Basket Weave			$42.00 – 46.00
Candle, #6000		$45.00 – 55.00	
Candelabra, #2318		$80.00 – 90.00	
Comport, #1533 – 6" w/Dolphins	$105.00 – 125.00		
Creamer, #3 Rib Optic	$100.00 – 125.00		
Guest set, #200 Spiral Optic	$450.00 – 500.00	$225.00 – 275.00	
Ivy ball, #706 Rib Optic			$100.00 – 125.00
Jug, #222 Rib Optic	$225.00 – 250.00		$225.00 – 250.00
Jug, #1352 Dot Optic	$225.00 – 250.00	$200.00 – 225.00	$225.00 – 250.00
Jug, #1352 Rib Optic	$250.00 – 280.00		$250.00 – 280.00
Night set, #401 Rib Optic	$130.00 – 150.00		$120.00 – 140.00
Sugar, #3 Rib Optic	$100.00 – 125.00		
Tumbler, #1352 Dot Optic ice tea	$25.00 – 35.00	$20.00 – 25.00	$25.00 – 35.00
Tumbler, #1352 Rib Optic ice tea	$22.00 – 28.00	$20.00 – 22.00	$25.00 – 30.00
Tumbler, #1352 Spiral Optic ice tea	$25.00 – 35.00	$20.00 – 25.00	$25.00 – 35.00
Vase, #183 – 6" special Spiral Optic	$65.00 – 75.00	$35.00 – 45.00	$75.00 – 85.00
Vase, #183 – 10" flared, Spiral Optic	$85.00 – 125.00	$45.00 – 50.00	
Vase, #183 – 10" square Spiral Optic	$85.00 – 125.00	$45.00 – 50.00	
Vase, #184 – 10"		$45.00 – 50.00	
Vase, #184 – 12"		$55.00 – 60.00	
Vase, #222 – 10" Rib Optic			$95.00 – 110.00
Vase, #791 – 10" Peacock		$235.00 – 255.00	
Vase, #894 – 10" flared Spiral Optic	$200.00 – 225.00	$75.00 – 90.00	
Vase, #894 – 10" tulip Spiral Optic	$200.00 – 225.00	$75.00 – 90.00	
Vase, #901 – 9" Dancing Ladies		$400.00 – 550.00	
Vase, #992		$35.00 – 45.00	

Item	Topaz Opalescent
Bowl, #100-6" flared	$35.00 – 45.00
Vase, #901 – 9" Dancing Ladies	$600.00 – 750.00
Vase, #1561 – 10" Apple Tree	$250.00 – 300.00

#1352-9" Dot Optic Jug

#222 Rib Optic Jug

#222-10" Rib Optic Vase

#1561-10" Apple Tree Vase

#200 Spiral Optic Guest Set

#920 Grape & Cable Bowl

#1352-5 1/4"
Ice Tea Tumbler

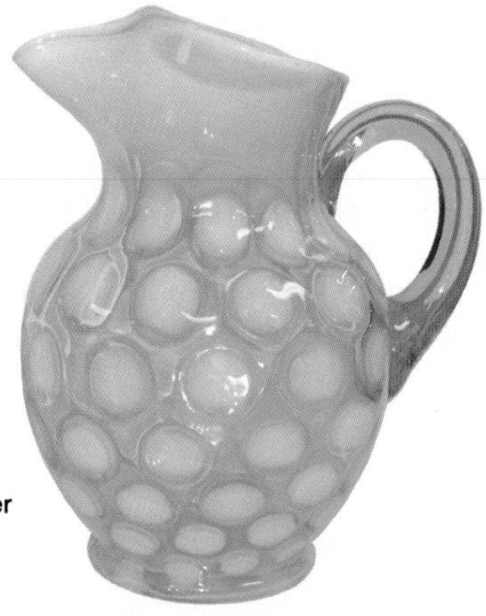
#1352-9" Dot Optic Jug

#1093-7 1/2" Basketweave w/Open Edge Bowl

#16 Spiral Optic
Bathroom Bottle
w/Flower Stopper

#1533-6" Crimped
Comport

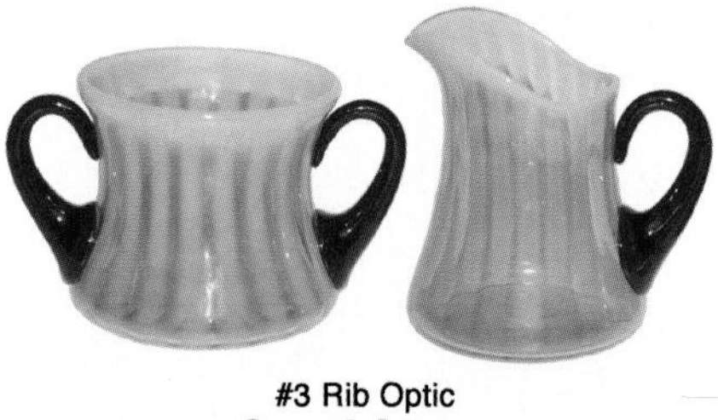
#3 Rib Optic
Sugar & Creamer

#17 Rib Optic
Bathroom Bottle

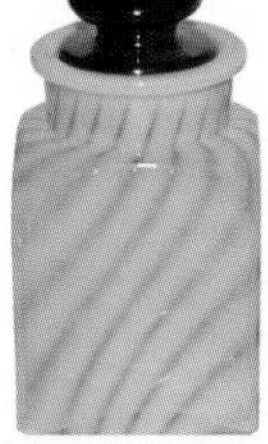
#17 Spiral Optic
Bathroom Bottle

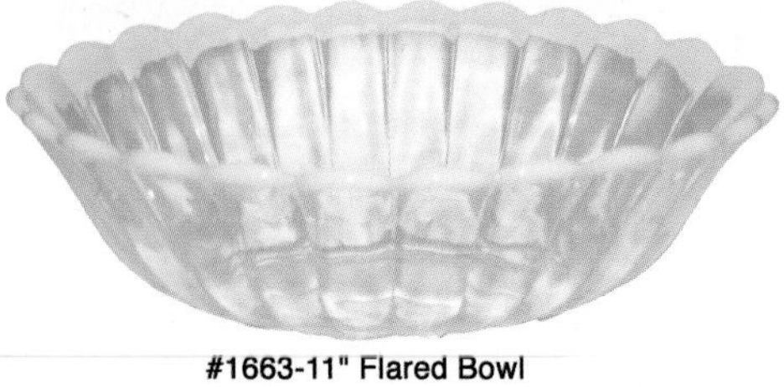
#1663-11" Flared Bowl

#401 Rib Optic Night Set

#950-11" Oval Bowl

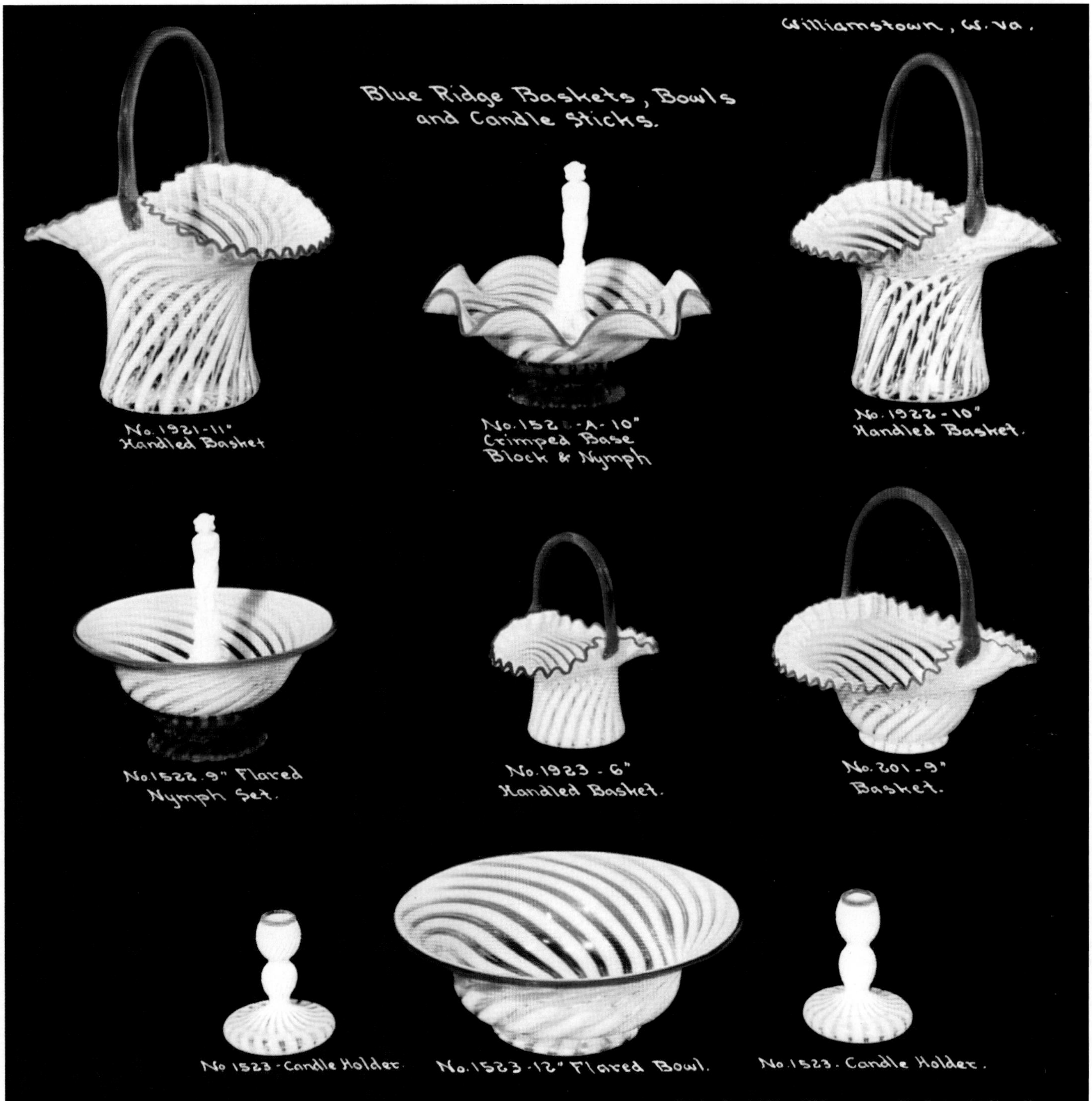
Williamstown, W. Va.
Blue Ridge Baskets, Bowls and Candle Sticks.
No. 1921-11" Handled Basket
No. 152-A-10" Crimped Base Block & Nymph
No. 1922-10" Handled Basket.
No. 1522. 9" Flared Nymph Set.
No. 1923 - 6" Handled Basket.
No. 201 - 9" Basket.
No 1523 - Candle Holder.
No. 1523 - 12" Flared Bowl.
No. 1523. Candle Holder.

Catalog Reprint Circa 1939 Courtesy Of: The Fenton Art Glass Museum

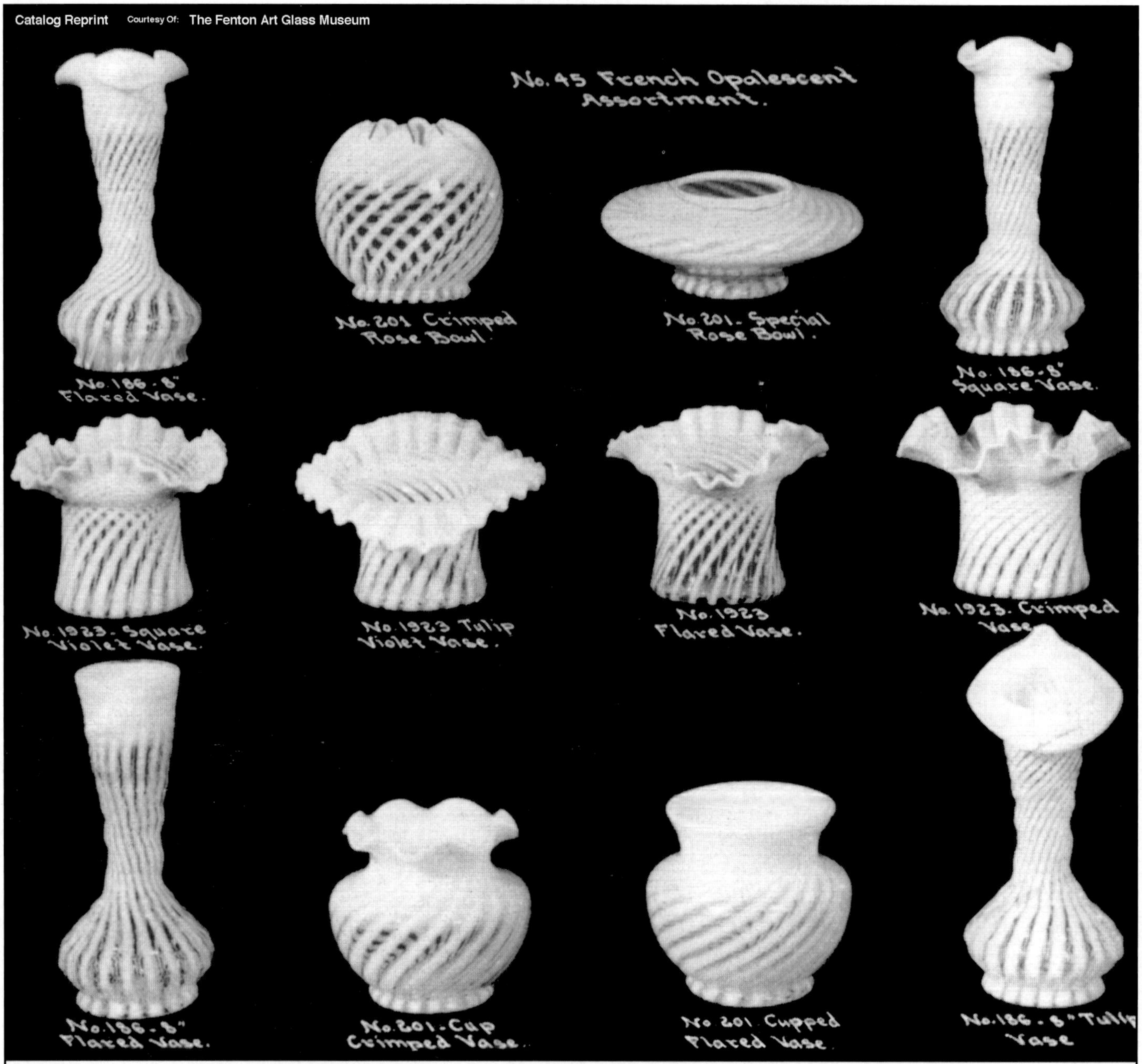

No. 45 French Opalescent Assortment

THE ABOVE ASSORTMENT ALSO MADE AS FOLLOWS:

No. 46 Blue Ridge
No. 47 Cranberry Red
No. 48 Stiegel Blue
No. 49 Peach Blow
No. 50 Opalescent Green
No. 51 Small Cranberry Red Asst.
No. 52 Small Peach Blow Asst.

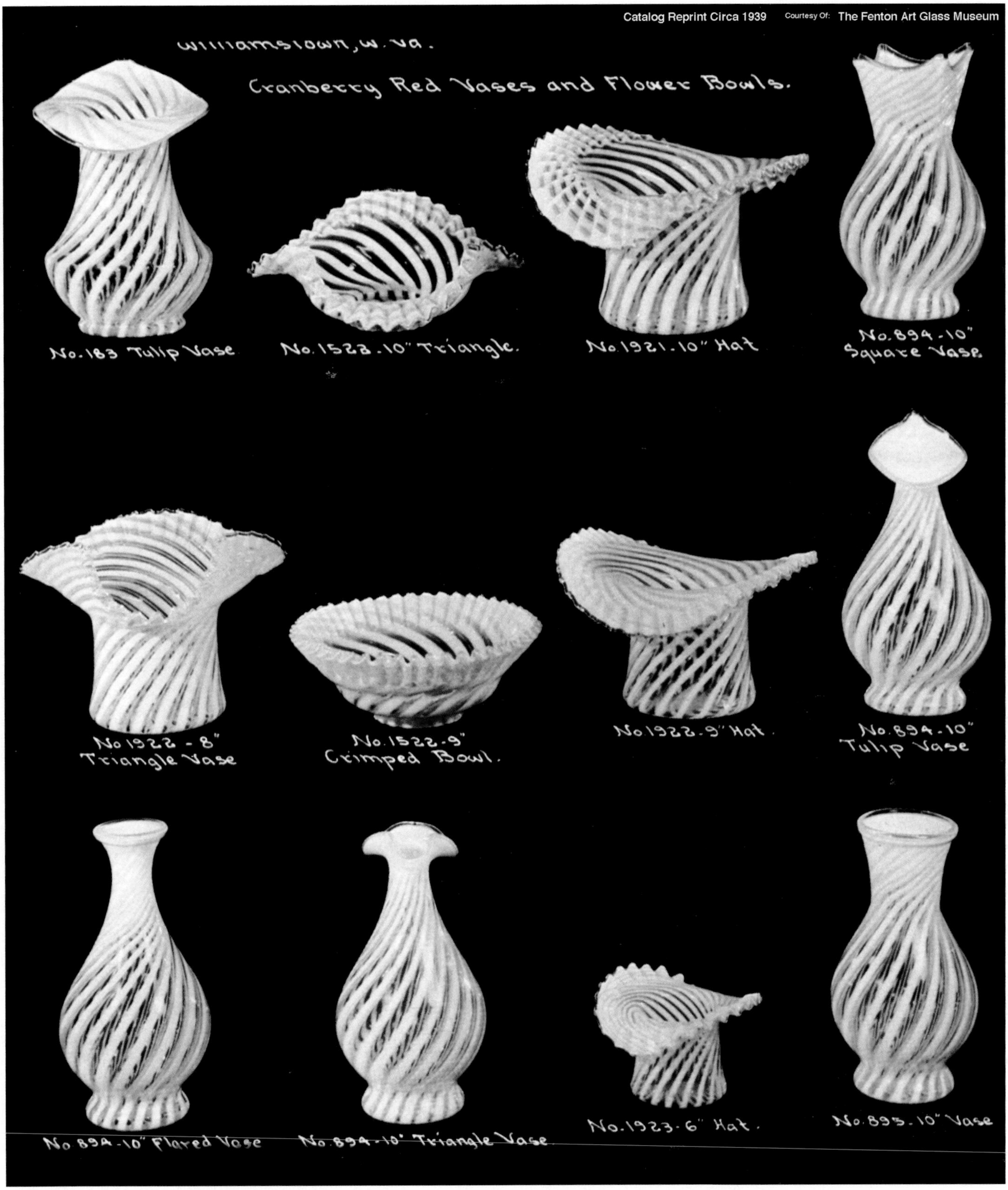
Catalog Reprint Circa 1939
Courtesy Of: The Fenton Art Glass Museum
Williamstown, W. Va.
Cranberry Red Vases and Flower Bowls.
No. 183 Tulip Vase
No. 1522. 10" Triangle.
No. 1921. 10" Hat
No. 894. 10" Square Vase.
No 1922 - 8" Triangle Vase
No. 1522. 9" Crimped Bowl.
No 1922. 9" Hat.
No. 894. 10" Tulip Vase
No 894. 10" Flared Vase
No. 894. 10" Triangle Vase
No. 1923. 6" Hat.
No. 893. 10" Vase

Karnak red with Hanging Vines #3015 handled basket, $1,100.00 – 1,200.00.

Tulip crimped #103 footed comport, celeste blue, $75.00 – 90.00.

Rib Optic covered #220, 9¼" pitcher, celeste blue with royal blue handle, $320.00 – 360.00.

Jade and lilac lamp base, $300.00 – 350.00.

Jade flared 2-cup pitcher, \$200.00 – 220.00.

Green opalescent #220 Rib Optic covered jug with royal blue handle, \$300.00 – 350.00.

Rectangular #308 cigarette box in Mandarin red, \$175.00 – 200.00.

Crystal Stag and Holly 7½" cupped bowl, \$60.00 – 70.00.

Crystal frosted #1561 Apple Tree vase with ormolu mounting, \$85.00 – 95.00.

Gold elephant decanter set, price undetermined.

Rose Ming #846, 6" covered bonbon, $80.00 – 85.00.

Rose Ming #1260, 2-piece reamer set, $310.00 – 350.00.

Milk glass #893 ginger jar with handpainted floral decoration, $250.00 – 300.00.

Crystal silverstone etch #1800, 12" rolled rim bowl, $32.00 – 35.00.

BIBLIOGRAPHY

Edwards, Bill. *Standard Encyclopedia of Carnival Glass 4th Edition.* Collector Books, Paducah, Kentucky, 1994.

Freeman, Larry. *Iridescent Glass.* Century House, Watkins Glen, New York, 1964.

Hand, Sherman. *The Collector's Encyclopedia of Carnival Glass.* Collector Books, Paducah, Kentucky, 1978.

Heacock, William. *Fenton Glass, The First Twenty-five Years.* O-Val Advertising Corp., Marietta, Ohio, 1978.

Heacock, William. *Fenton Glass, The Second Twenty-five Years.* O-Val Advertising Corp., Marietta, Ohio, 1980.

Lee, Ruth Webb. *Early American Pressed Glass.* Lee Publications, Wellesley Hills, Massachusetts, 1960.

Moore, Donald E. *The Shape of Things in Carnival Glass.* Donald E. Moore, Alameda, California, 1975.

Presnick, Rose M. *Carnival Glass and Iridescent Glass Price Guide.* Miskell Printing and Litho, Wadsworth, Ohio, 1962.

Presnick, Rose M. *Carnival Glass and Iridescent Glass Price Guide, Book II.* Miskell Printing and Litho, Wadsworth, Ohio, 1964.

Presnick, Rose M. *Carnival Glass and Iridescent Glass Price Guide, Book III.* Banner Printing Company, Wadsworth, Ohio, 1964.

Presnick, Rose M. *Carnival Glass and Iridescent Glass Price Guide, Book IV.* Advertype, Inc., Cleveland, Ohio, 1964.

Umbraco, Kitty and Russell. *Iridescent Stretch Glass.* Cambura and Avery Publishers, Berkeley, California, 1972.

Weatherman, Hazel Marie. *Colored Glassware of the Depression 2.* Weatherman Glassbooks, Ozark, Missouri, 1974.

Wiggins, Berry. *Stretch In Color.* Green Publishers, Orange, Virginia, 1971.

COLLECTOR BOOKS

Informing Today's Collector

For over two decades we have been keeping collectors informed on trends and values in all fields of antiques and collectibles.

DOLLS, FIGURES & TEDDY BEARS

4631 **Barbie Doll** Boom, 1986–1995, Augustyniak $18.95
2079 **Barbie Doll** Fashion, Volume I, Eames $24.95
4846 **Barbie Doll** Fashion, Volume II, Eames $24.95
3957 **Barbie** Exclusives, Rana $18.95
4632 **Barbie** Exclusives, Book II, Rana $18.95
6022 The **Barbie Doll** Years, 5th Ed., Olds $19.95
3810 **Chatty Cathy** Dolls, Lewis $15.95
5352 Collector's Ency. of **Barbie** Doll Exclusives & More, 2nd Ed.,Augustyniak $24.95
2211 Collector's Encyclopedia of **Madame Alexander** Dolls, Smith $24.95
4863 Collector's Encyclopedia of **Vogue Dolls**, Izen/Stover $29.95
5904 Collector's Guide to **Celebrity Dolls**, Spurgeon $24.95
5599 Collector's Guide to **Dolls of the 1960s and 1970s**, Sabulis $24.95
6030 Collector's Guide to **Horsman Dolls**, Jensen $29.95
6025 **Doll Values**, Antique to Modern, 6th Ed., Moyer $12.95
6032 **Madame Alexander** Collector's Dolls Price Guide #27, Crowsey $12.95
6033 **Modern Collectible Dolls**, Volume VI, Moyer $24.95
5689 **Nippon Dolls** & Playthings, Van Patten/Lau $29.95
5365 **Peanuts Collectibles**, Podley/Bang $24.95
6026 **Small Dolls of the 40s & 50s**, Stover $29.95
5253 Story of **Barbie**, 2nd Ed., Westenhouser $24.95
5277 **Talking Toys** of the 20th Century, Lewis $15.95
2084 **Teddy Bears, Annalee's & Steiff** Animals, 3rd Series, Mandel $19.95
5371 **Teddy Bear** Treasury, Yenke $19.95
1808 Wonder of **Barbie**, Manos $9.95
1430 World of **Barbie** Dolls, Manos $9.95
4880 World of **Raggedy Ann** Collectibles, Avery $24.95

TOYS & MARBLES

2333 Antique & Collectible **Marbles**, 3rd Ed., Grist $9.95
4559 Collectible **Action Figures**, 2nd Ed., Manos $17.95
2338 Collector's Encyclopedia of **Disneyana**, Longest, Stern $24.95
5900 Collector's Guide to **Battery Toys**, 2nd Edition, Hultzman $24.95
4566 Collector's Guide to **Tootsietoys**, 2nd Ed., Richter $19.95
5169 Collector's Guide to **TV Toys** & Memorabilia, 2nd Ed., Davis/Morgan $24.95
5360 **Fisher-Price Toys**, Cassity $19.95
5593 Grist's Big Book of **Marbles**, 2nd Ed. $24.95
3970 Grist's Machine-Made & Contemporary **Marbles**, 2nd Ed. $9.95
5267 **Matchbox Toys**, 1947 to 1998, 3rd Ed., Johnson $19.95
5830 **McDonald's** Collectibles, 2nd Edition, Henriques/DuVall $24.95
5673 Modern **Candy Containers** & Novelties, Brush/Miller $19.95
1540 Modern **Toys** 1930–1980, Baker $19.95
5920 **Schroeder's Collectible Toys**, Antique to Modern Price Guide, 8th Ed. $17.95
5908 **Toy Car** Collector's Guide, Johnson $19.95

FURNITURE

3716 American **Oak** Furniture, Book II, McNerney $12.95
1118 Antique **Oak** Furniture, Hill $7.95
3720 Collector's Encyclopedia of **American** Furniture, Vol. III, Swedberg $24.95
5359 Early **American** Furniture, Obbard $12.95
1755 Furniture of the **Depression Era**, Swedberg $19.95
3906 **Heywood-Wakefield** Modern Furniture, Rouland $18.95
1885 **Victorian** Furniture, Our American Heritage, McNerney $9.95
3829 **Victorian** Furniture, Our American Heritage, Book II, McNerney $9.95

JEWELRY, HATPINS, WATCHES & PURSES

4704 Antique & Collectible **Buttons**, Wisniewski $19.95
1748 Antique **Purses**, Revised Second Ed., Holiner $19.95
4850 Collectible **Costume Jewelry**, Simonds $24.95
5675 Collectible **Silver Jewelry**, Rezazadeh $24.95
3722 Collector's Ency. of **Compacts**, Carryalls & Face Powder Boxes, Mueller $24.95
4940 **Costume Jewelry**, A Practical Handbook & Value Guide, Rezazadeh $24.95
5812 Fifty Years of Collectible **Fashion Jewelry**, 1925–1975, Baker $24.95
1424 **Hatpins** & Hatpin Holders, Baker $9.95
5695 **Ladies' Vintage Accessories**, Bruton $24.95
1181 100 Years of Collectible **Jewelry**, 1850–1950, Baker $9.95
4729 **Sewing Tools** & Trinkets, Thompson $24.95
6038 **Sewing Tools** & Trinkets, Volume 2, Thompson $24.95
6039 Signed Beauties of **Costume Jewelry**, Brown $24.95
5620 Unsigned Beauties of **Costume Jewelry**, Brown $24.95
4878 Vintage & Contemporary **Purse Accessories**, Gerson $24.95
5696 Vintage & Vogue Ladies' **Compacts**, 2nd Edition, Gerson $29.95
5923 **Vintage Jewelry** for Investment & Casual Wear, Edeen $24.95

INDIANS, GUNS, KNIVES, TOOLS, PRIMITIVES

1868 Antique **Tools**, Our American Heritage, McNerney $9.95
5616 Big Book of **Pocket Knives**, Stewart $19.95
4943 Field Guide to Flint **Arrowheads & Knives** of the North American Indian $9.95
2279 **Indian Artifacts** of the Midwest, Book I, Hothem $14.95
3885 **Indian Artifacts** of the Midwest, Book II, Hothem $16.95
4870 **Indian Artifacts** of the Midwest, Book III, Hothem $18.95
5685 **Indian Artifacts** of the Midwest, Book IV, Hothem $19.95
6132 **Modern Guns**, Identification & Values, 14th Ed., Quertermous $14.95
2164 **Primitives**, Our American Heritage, McNerney $9.95
1759 **Primitives**, Our American Heritage, 2nd Series, McNerney $14.95
6031 Standard **Knife** Collector's Guide, 4th Ed., Ritchie & Stewart $14.95
5999 **Wilderness** Survivor's Guide, Hamper $12.95

PAPER COLLECTIBLES & BOOKS

4633 **Big Little Books**, Jacobs $18.95
5902 **Boys' & Girls' Book** Series $19.95
4710 Collector's Guide to **Children's Books**, 1850 to 1950, Volume I, Jones $18.95
5153 Collector's Guide to **Chldren's Books**, 1850 to 1950, Volume II, Jones $19.95
5596 Collector's Guide to **Children's Books**, 1950 to 1975, Volume III, Jones $19.95
1441 Collector's Guide to **Post Cards**, Wood $9.95
2081 Guide to Collecting **Cookbooks**, Allen $14.95
5825 Huxford's **Old Book** Value Guide, 13th Ed. $19.95
2080 Price Guide to **Cookbooks & Recipe Leaflets**, Dickinson $9.95
3973 **Sheet Music** Reference & Price Guide, 2nd Ed., Pafik & Guiheen $19.95
6041 Vintage **Postcards for the Holidays**, Reed $24.95
4733 **Whitman Juvenile Books**, Brown $17.95

GLASSWARE

5602 Anchor Hocking's **Fire-King** & More, 2nd Ed. $24.95
4561 Collectible **Drinking Glasses**, Chase & Kelly $17.95
5823 Collectible **Glass Shoes**, 2nd Edition, Wheatley $24.95
5897 Coll. **Glassware from the 40s, 50s & 60s**, 6th Ed., Florence $19.95
1810 Collector's Encyclopedia of **American Art Glass**, Shuman $29.95
5907 Collector's Encyclopedia of **Depression Glass**, 15th Ed., Florence $19.95
1961 Collector's Encyclopedia of **Fry Glassware**, Fry Glass Society $24.95
1664 Collector's Encyclopedia of **Heisey Glass**, 1925–1938, Bredehoft $24.95
3905 Collector's Encyclopedia of **Milk Glass**, Newbound $24.95
4936 Collector's Guide to **Candy Containers**, Dezso/Poirier $19.95
5820 Collector's Guide to **Glass Banks**, Reynolds $24.95
4564 **Crackle Glass**, Weitman $19.95
4941 **Crackle Glass**, Book II, Weitman $19.95
4714 **Czechoslovakian Glass** and Collectibles, Book II, Barta/Rose $16.95
5528 Early American **Pattern Glass**, Metz $17.95
6125 **Elegant Glassware** of the Depression Era, 10th Ed., Florence $24.95
3981 Evers' Standard **Cut Glass** Value Guide $12.95
5614 Field Guide to **Pattern Glass**, McCain $17.95
5615 Florence's **Glassware Pattern Identification** Guide, Vol. II $19.95
4719 **Fostoria**, Etched, Carved & Cut Designs, Vol. II, Kerr $24.95
3883 **Fostoria Stemware**, The Crystal for America, Long/Seate $24.95

COLLECTOR BOOKS

Informing Today's Collector

5261 **Fostoria Tableware**, 1924 – 1943, Long/Seate ... $24.95
5361 **Fostoria Tableware**, 1944 – 1986, Long/Seate ... $24.95
5604 **Fostoria**, Useful & Ornamental, Long/Seate ... $29.95
5899 **Glass & Ceramic Baskets**, White ... $19.95
4644 **Imperial Carnival Glass**, Burns ... $18.95
5827 **Kitchen Glassware** of the Depression Years, 6th Ed., Florence ... $24.95
5600 Much More Early American **Pattern Glass**, Metz ... $17.95
5915 **Northwood Carnival Glass**, 1908 – 1925, Burns ... $19.95
6136 Pocket Guide to **Depression Glass**, 13th Ed., Florence ... $12.95
6023 Standard Encyclopedia of **Carnival Glass**, 8th Ed., Edwards/Carwile ... $29.95
6024 Standard **Carnival Glass** Price Guide, 13th Ed., Edwards/Carwile ... $9.95
6035 Standard Encyclopedia of **Opalescent Glass**, 4rd Ed., Edwards/Carwile ... $24.95
4732 **Very Rare Glassware** of the Depression Years, 5th Series, Florence ... $24.95
4656 **Westmoreland Glass**, Wilson ... $24.95

POTTERY

4927 **ABC Plates & Mugs**, Lindsay ... $24.95
4929 **American Art Pottery**, Sigafoose ... $24.95
4630 **American Limoges**, Limoges ... $24.95
1312 **Blue & White Stoneware**, McNerney ... $9.95
1959 **Blue Willow**, 2nd Ed., Gaston ... $14.95
4851 Collectible **Cups & Saucers**, Harran ... $18.95
5901 Collecting **Blue Willow**, Harman ... $19.95
1373 Collector's Encyclopedia of **American Dinnerware**, Cunningham ... $24.95
4931 Collector's Encyclopedia of **Bauer Pottery**, Chipman ... $24.95
4658 Collector's Encyclopedia of **Brush-McCoy Pottery**, Huxford ... $24.95
5034 Collector's Encyclopedia of **California Pottery**, 2nd Ed., Chipman ... $24.95
3723 Collector's Encyclopedia of **Cookie Jars**, Book II, Roerig ... $24.95
4939 Collector's Encyclopedia of **Cookie Jars**, Book III, Roerig ... $24.95
5748 Collector's Encyclopedia of **Fiesta**, 9th Ed., Huxford ... $24.95
3961 Collector's Encyclopedia of **Early Noritake**, Alden ... $24.95
3812 Collector's Encyclopedia of **Flow Blue China**, 2nd Ed., Gaston ... $24.95
3431 Collector's Encyclopedia of **Homer Laughlin China**, Jasper ... $24.95
1276 Collector's Encyclopedia of **Hull Pottery**, Roberts ... $19.95
3962 Collector's Encyclopedia of **Lefton China**, DeLozier ... $19.95
4855 Collector's Encyclopedia of **Lefton China**, Book II, DeLozier ... $19.95
5609 Collector's Encyclopedia of **Limoges Porcelain**, 3rd Ed., Gaston ... $29.95
2334 Collector's Encyclopedia of **Majolica Pottery**, Katz-Marks ... $19.95
1358 Collector's Encyclopedia of **McCoy Pottery**, Huxford ... $19.95
5677 Collector's Encyclopedia of **Niloak**, 2nd Edition, Gifford ... $29.95
3837 Collector's Encyclopedia of **Nippon Porcelain**, Van Patten ... $24.95
1665 Collector's Ency. of **Nippon Porcelain**, 3rd Series, Van Patten ... $24.95
5053 Collector's Ency. of **Nippon Porcelain**, 5th Series, Van Patten ... $24.95
5678 Collector's Ency. of **Nippon Porcelain**, 6th Series, Van Patten ... $29.95
1447 Collector's Encyclopedia of **Noritake**, Van Patten ... $19.95
4951 Collector's Encyclopedia of **Old Ivory China**, Hillman ... $24.95
5564 Collector's Encyclopedia of **Pickard China**, Reed ... $29.95
3877 Collector's Encyclopedia of **R.S. Prussia**, 4th Series, Gaston ... $24.95
5679 Collector's Encyclopedia of **Red Wing Art Pottery**, Dollen ... $24.95
5618 Collector's Encyclopedia of **Rosemeade Pottery**, Dommel ... $24.95
5841 Collector's Encyclopedia of **Roseville Pottery**, Revised, Huxford/Nickel ... $24.95
5842 Collector's Encyclopedia of **Roseville Pottery**, 2nd Series, Huxford/Nickel $24.95
5917 Collector's Encyclopedia of **Russel Wright**, 3rd Editon, Kerr ... $29.95
4713 Collector's Encyclopedia of **Salt Glaze Stoneware**, Taylor/Lowrance ... $24.95
5370 Collector's Encyclopedia of **Stangl Dinnerware**, Runge ... $24.95
5921 Collector's Encyclopedia of **Stangl Artware**, Lamps, and Birds, RUnge ... $29.95
3314 Collector's Encyclopedia of **Van Briggle Art Pottery**, Sasicki ... $24.95
4563 Collector's Encyclopedia of **Wall Pockets**, Newbound ... $19.95
2111 Collector's Encyclopedia of **Weller Pottery**, Huxford ... $29.95
5680 Collector's Guide to **Feather Edge Ware**, McAllister ... $19.95
3876 Collector's Guide to **Lu-Ray Pastels**, Meehan ... $18.95
3814 Collector's Guide to **Made in Japan Ceramics**, White ... $18.95
4646 Collector's Guide to **Made in Japan Ceramics**, Book II, White ... $18.95
2339 Collector's Guide to **Shawnee Pottery**, Vanderbilt ... $19.95
1425 **Cookie Jars**, Westfall ... $9.95
3440 **Cookie Jars**, Book II, Westfall ... $19.95
5909 **Dresden Porcelain** Studios, Harran ... $29.95
5918 Florence's Big Book of **Salt & Pepper Shakers** ... $24.95
2379 Lehner's Ency. of **U.S. Marks** on Pottery, Porcelain & China ... $24.95
4722 **McCoy Pottery**, Collector's Reference & Value Guide, Hanson/Nissen ... $19.95
5913 **McCoy Pottery**, Volume III, Hanson & Nissen ... $24.95
5691 **Post86 Fiesta**, Identification & Value Guide, Racheter ... $19.95
1670 **Red Wing Collectibles**, DePasquale ... $9.95
1440 **Red Wing Stoneware**, DePasquale ... $9.95
6037 **Rookwood Pottery**, Nicholson & Thomas ... $24.95
1632 **Salt & Pepper Shakers**, Guarnaccia ... $9.95
5091 **Salt & Pepper Shakers** II, Guarnaccia ... $18.95
3443 **Salt & Pepper Shakers** IV, Guarnaccia ... $18.95
3738 **Shawnee Pottery**, Mangus ... $24.95
4629 Turn of the Century **American Dinnerware**, 1880s–1920s, Jasper ... $24.95
3327 **Watt Pottery** – Identification & Value Guide, Morris ... $19.95
5924 **Zanesville Stoneware** Company, Rans, Ralston & Russell ... $24.95

OTHER COLLECTIBLES

5916 Advertising **Paperweights**, Holiner & Kammerman ... $24.95
5838 Advertising **Thermometers**, Merritt ... $16.95
5898 Antique & Contemporary **Advertising Memorabilia**, Summers ... $24.95
5814 Antique **Brass & Copper** Collectibles, Gaston ... $24.95
1880 Antique **Iron**, McNerney ... $9.95
3872 Antique **Tins**, Dodge ... $24.95
4845 Antique **Typewriters & Office Collectibles**, Rehr ... $19.95
5607 Antiquing and Collecting on the **Internet**, Parry ... $12.95
1128 **Bottle** Pricing Guide, 3rd Ed., Cleveland ... $7.95
3718 Collectible **Aluminum**, Grist ... $16.95
4560 Collectible **Cats**, An Identification & Value Guide, Book II, Fyke ... $19.95
5060 Collectible **Souvenir Spoons**, Bednersh ... $19.95
5676 Collectible **Souvenir Spoons**, Book II, Bednersh ... $29.95
5666 Collector's Encyclopedia of **Granite Ware**, Book 2, Greguire ... $29.95
5836 Collector's Guide to **Antique Radios**, 5th Ed., Bunis ... $19.95
3966 Collector's Guide to **Inkwells**, Identification & Values, Badders ... $18.95
4947 Collector's Guide to **Inkwells**, Book II, Badders ... $19.95
5681 Collector's Guide to **Lunchboxes**, White ... $19.95
5621 Collector's Guide to **Online Auctions**, Hix ... $12.95
4652 Collector's Guide to **Transistor Radios**, 2nd Ed., Bunis ... $16.95
4864 Collector's Guide to **Wallace Nutting Pictures**, Ivankovich ... $18.95
1629 **Doorstops**, Identification & Values, Bertoia ... $9.95
5683 **Fishing Lure** Collectibles, 2nd Ed., Murphy/Edmisten ... $29.95
5911 **Flea Market Trader**, 13th Ed., Huxford ... $9.95
4945 **G-Men and FBI Toys** and Collectibles, Whitworth ... $18.95
6029 **Garage Sale & Flea Market Annual**, 10th Ed. ... $19.95
3819 **General Store** Collectibles, Wilson ... $24.95
5912 The **Heddon** Legacy, A Century of Classic **Lures**, Roberts & Pavey ... $29.95
2216 **Kitchen Antiques**, 1790–1940, McNerney ... $14.95
5991 **Lighting Devices** & Accessories of the 17th – 19th Centuries, Hamper ... $9.95
5686 **Lighting Fixtures** of the Depression Era, Book I, Thomas ... $24.95
4950 The **Lone Ranger**, Collector's Reference & Value Guide, Felbinger ... $18.95
6028 Modern **Fishing Lure** Collectibles, Lewis ... $24.95
2026 **Railroad** Collectibles, 4th Ed., Baker ... $14.95
5619 **Roy Rogers and Dale Evans** Toys & Memorabilia, Coyle ... $24.95
5919 **Schroeder's Antiques Price Guide**, 20th Ed., Huxford ... $14.95
5007 **Silverplated Flatware**, Revised 4th Edition, Hagan ... $18.95
6040 **Star Wars** Super Collector's Wish Book, Carlton ... $29.95
6139 Summers' Guide to **Coca-Cola**, 4th Ed. ... $24.95
5905 Summers' Pocket Guide to **Coca-Cola**, 3rd Ed. ... $12.95
3892 **Toy & Miniature Sewing Machines**, Thomas ... $18.95
4876 **Toy & Miniature Sewing Machines**, Book II, Thomas ... $24.95
3977 Value Guide to **Gas Station Memorabilia**, Summers & Priddy ... $24.95
4877 Vintage **Bar Ware**, Visakay ... $24.95
5925 The Vintage Era of **Golf Club Collectibles**, John ... $29.95
6010 The Vintage Era of **Golf Club Collectibles** Collector's Log, John ... $9.95
6036 Vintage **Quilts**, Aug, Newman & Roy ... $24.95
4935 The W.F. Cody **Buffalo Bill** Collector's Guide with Values ... $24.95

This is only a partial listing of the books on antiques that are available from Collector Books. All books are well illustrated and contain current values. Most of these books are available from your local bookseller, antique dealer, or public library. If you are unable to locate certain titles in your area, you may order by mail from COLLECTOR BOOKS, P.O. Box 3009, Paducah, KY 42002-3009. Customers with Visa, Discover or MasterCard may phone in orders from 7:00–5:00 CST, Monday–Friday, Toll Free 1-800-626-5420, or online at www.collectorbooks.com. Add $3.00 for postage for the first book ordered and 50¢ for each additional book. Include item number, title, and price when ordering. Allow 14 to 21 days for delivery.

Schroeder's ANTIQUES Price Guide

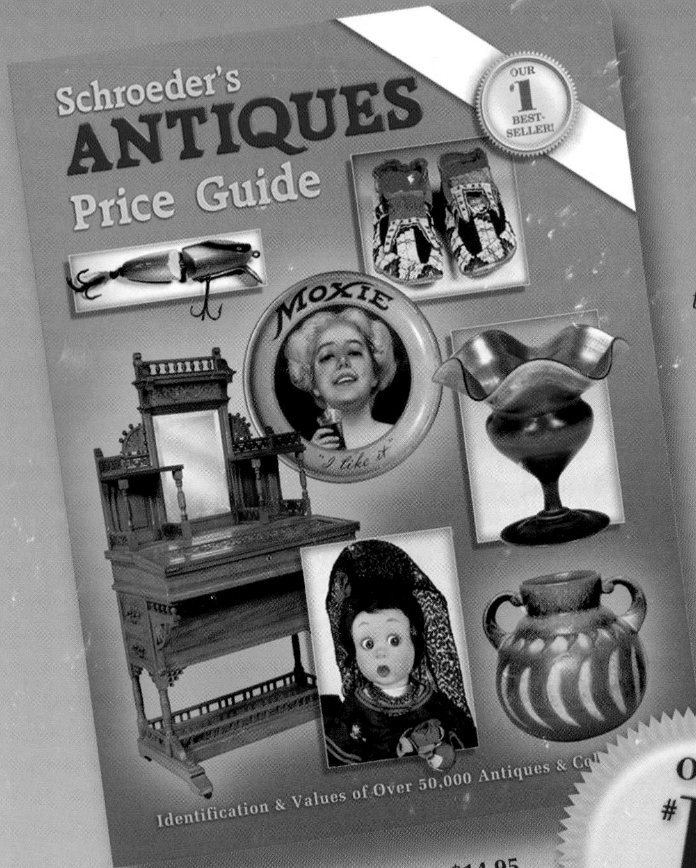

8½" x 11" • 608 pages • $14.95

OUR #1 BEST-SELLER!

...is the #1 bestselling antiques & collectibles value guide on the market today, and here's why...

- *More than 450 advisors, well-known dealers, and top-notch collectors work together with our editors to bring you accurate information regarding pricing and identification.*
- *More than 50,000 items in over 600 categories are listed along with hundreds of sharp original photos that illustrate not only the rare and unusual, but the common, popular collectibles as well.*
- *Each large close-up shot shows important details clearly. Every subject is represented with histories and background information, a feature not found in any of our competitors' publications.*
- *Our editors keep abreast of newly developing trends, often adding several new categories a year as the need arises.*

Without doubt, you'll find

Schroeder's Antiques Price Guide

the only one to buy for reliable information and values.

If it merits the interest of today's collector, you'll find it in *Schroeder's*. And you can feel confident that the information we publish is up-to-date and accurate. Our advisors thoroughly check each category to spot inconsistencies, listings that may not be entirely reflective of market dealings, and lines too vague to be of merit. Only the best of the lot remains for publication.

COLLECTOR BOOKS
P.O. Box 3009
Paducah, KY 42002–3009
www.collectorbooks.com